Praise for Blake Bailey's

Farther & Wilder

"Bailey has made an author come alive in a way that is truly novelistic, has made him submit to becoming a character in a story. . . . A kind of miracle, one that we can all be grateful for." —*The Wall Street Journal*

"The novelist Charles Jackson may not be as well known as the subjects of Blake Bailey's previous biographies . . . but he is no less fascinating. In *Farther & Wilder* . . . Mr. Bailey portrays his life with the same dogged attention to detail, literary panache, and brilliant storytelling that he brought to those other subjects. . . . Mr. Bailey's triumph is in fleshing out both Jackson's literary legacy and the man himself."

—*The New York Observer*

"Impressive. . . . Reminds us not only how biography can be good, but also why the genre matters—how it can excavate importance from histories that might otherwise be forgotten. . . . Bailey's achievement is staggering." —*Los Angeles Review of Books*

"A fascinating anatomy of failure." —*Minneapolis Star Tribune*

"[A] rich, probing biography. . . . Shrewdly analyzes Jackson's sometimes crippling, sometimes fertile contradictions. . . . [A] compelling portrait of a conflicted writer whose genius emerges in dubious battle with his demons." —*Publishers Weekly*

"[A] case for the resurrection of this deeply prescient and problematic novelist, who broke open taboos about alcoholics and homosexuals well before it was cool and championed F. Scott Fitzgerald when he was in the process of being remaindered. . . . [An] eloquent, poignant portrait of the artist as outsider and misfit."

—*Kirkus Reviews* (starred review)

BLAKE BAILEY

Farther & Wilder

Blake Bailey is the author of *A Tragic Honesty: The Life and Work of Richard Yates*, a finalist for the National Book Critics Circle Award, and *Cheever: A Life*, winner of the National Book Critics Circle Award and the Francis Parkman Prize, and a finalist for the Pulitzer and James Tait Black Memorial Prizes. He edited a two-volume edition of Cheever's work for the Library of America, and in 2010 received an Award in Literature from the American Academy of Arts and Letters. He lives in Virginia with his wife and daughter.

www.blakebaileyonline.com

ALSO BY BLAKE BAILEY

Cheever: A Life

A Tragic Honesty: The Life and Work of Richard Yates

Farther & Wilder

Farther & Wilder

The Lost Weekends and Literary Dreams of

CHARLES JACKSON

Blake Bailey

VINTAGE BOOKS
A Division of Random House LLC
New York

FIRST VINTAGE BOOKS EDITION, DECEMBER 2013

The Library of Congress has cataloged the Knopf edition as follows:
Bailey, Blake.
Farther and Wilder : the lost weekends and literary dreams of
Charles Jackson / by Blake Bailey.—1st American ed.
p. cm.
1. Jackson, Charles, 1903–1968. 2. Authors, American—Biography. I. Title.
ps3519.a323z54 2013
813'.52—dc23
[B] 2012036685

Vintage ISBN: 978-0-307-47552-7

Author photo © Mary Brinkmeyer
Book design by Maggie Hinders

www.vintagebooks.com

For Michael Ruhlman

For though the artist may all his life remain closer, not to say truer, to his childhood than the man trained for practical life—although one may say that he, unlike the latter, abides in the dreamy, purely human and playful childlike state—yet his path out of his simple, unaffected beginnings to the undivined later stages of his course is endlessly farther, wilder, more shattering to watch than that of the ordinary citizen. With the latter, too, the fact that he was once a child is not nearly so full of tears.   —THOMAS MANN, *Doctor Faustus*

It was like an affront; I felt a terrible sense of injustice over the way the world uses its artists—and how unimportant the artist has always been considered by society, how troublesome, and how he is popularly deserving of nothing but neglect, and indifference.

> —CHARLES JACKSON (on reading that Mussorgsky, who died young, was "slovenly and drunken and a drug addict")

But there are thousands of Charlie Jackson's stories about his ups and downs with life, and at some point somebody will do rather a good biography of Jackson in my opinion, because he was a very interesting man: he was sweet, he was intelligent, he was kind. I can't stand drunks—that's a terrible thing to have to say as a publisher, because I know a lot—but he was a sweet drunk.

> —ROGER STRAUS, Columbia University Oral History

So free we seem, so fettered fast we are!

> —ROBERT BROWNING, "Andrea del Sarto"

Contents

Farther & Wilder

Prologue

The Problem Child

The Lost Weekend—a novel about five disastrous days in the life of alcoholic Don Birnam—was an improbable success when it was published in 1944. Rejecting the novel, Simon & Schuster had assured its author that it wouldn't sell in the midst of a world war ("Nobody cares about the individual"); within five years, *The Lost Weekend* sold almost half a million copies in various editions and was translated into fourteen languages, syndicated by King Features as a comic strip, and added to the prestigious Modern Library. Its critical reception was no less impressive: "Charles Jackson has made the most compelling gift to the literature of addiction since De Quincey," Philip Wylie wrote in *The New York Times*. "His character is a masterpiece of psychological precision. His narrative method . . . transmutes medical case history into art." The trailer for the classic movie summarized the matter nicely: "Famous critics called it . . . 'Powerful . . .' 'Terrifying . . . ' 'Unforgettable . . . ' 'Superb . . . ' 'Brilliant . . . ' AND NOW PARAMOUNT DARES TO OPEN . . . THE STRANGE AND SAVAGE PAGES OF . . . *The Lost Weekend*." Cut to the book's title page, amid ominous music.

Director Billy Wilder had bought the novel at a kiosk in Chicago, and by the time his train arrived in Los Angeles he'd read it twice and quite definitely decided to make a movie based on the book, despite its then-controversial subject: an alcoholic, as opposed to a comic drunkard or lush. "Not only did I know it was going to make a good picture," said Wilder, "I also knew that the guy who was going to play the drunk was going to get the Academy Award." Hollywood's A-list actors didn't agree, and after the part had been turned down by everyone from Cary Grant to Robert Montgomery, it was given to the Welshman Ray Milland, who refused to heed an all but universal warning that he was committing "career suicide." The day after *The Lost Weekend* won Oscars for Best Picture, Actor, Director, and Screenplay, writers at Paramount Studios celebrated by dangling bottles out their windows, a tribute to Don Birnam's preferred method of concealing his liquor.

Milland, a near teetotaler, had been coached in the ways of drunkenness by the novel's author—a balding, impeccably groomed middle-aged man whose weird combination of wistfulness and zest put the actor in mind of "a bright, erratic problem child." At the time Jackson was working at MGM on a screenwriting assignment, and was bemused to find himself the most popular man in Hollywood. Everyone, it seemed, had read his book and experienced an almost seismic shock of recognition: Robert Benchley told Jackson that he'd found the novel so disturbing that, for twenty minutes or so, he'd been unable to take another drink. Surely such a vivid, inward-looking account had to be based on personal experience, and thus (in the words of journalist Lincoln Barnett) "Jackson was eyed somewhat in the manner of a returned war hero . . . of a man who had been through hellfire and emerged bloodshot but unbowed." Jackson himself bridled at the assumption. Sober since 1936, he had no intention of going down in history as the author of a single, thinly veiled autobiography about a crypto-homosexual drunk with writerly pretensions. "One third of the history is based on what I have experienced myself," he told the movie columnist Louella Parsons and others, "about one third on the experiences of a very good friend whose drinking career I followed very closely, and the other third is pure invention."

Ten years, four books, and twenty-two hospitalizations later, Jackson was ready to come clean: he was indeed Don Birnam, and only two episodes in *The Lost Weekend* were purely fictional (to wit: he never pawned his girlfriend's leopard coat to get liquor money, nor did he stand up the hostess of his favorite bar because of an alcoholic blackout). To be sure, he could afford to be candid by then; very few people had any idea who Jackson was, and even those happy few tended to muddle the matter. "I have become so used to having people say 'We loved your movie' instead of 'We read your book,' " said Jackson, "that now I merely say 'Thanks.' "

The Lost Weekend, after all, is something of an anomaly: a great novel that also resulted in a great (or near-great) movie—somewhat to the author's woe, as there are far more moviegoers than readers of serious fiction; the upshot, oddly enough, is that the movie has all but supplanted the novel as a cultural artifact, even as the novel's impact endures among the literary and medical cognoscenti. Don Birnam remains the definitive portrait of an alcoholic in American literature—a tragicomic combination of Hamlet and Mr. Toad, according to *Time*, whose publisher reprinted the novel in 1963 as part of its paperback "Reading Program" of contemporary classics. A special introduction was written by Selden D. Bacon, the director of the Rutgers Center of Alcohol Studies, who observed not only that *The Lost Weekend* was an impressive work of art, but also that it had "exerted a profound influence on the field with which it deals. Its very title has become a synonym for the condition it describes." The editors of *Time* seemed especially pleased to mention that Jackson himself was now chairman of the Alcoholics Anonymous chapter in New Brunswick, New Jersey, a solemn proselytizer for the Twelve Steps—a man, in short, who had learned the hard way that an alcoholic ("a natural addict") could not be helped by medicine, psychiatry, or religion: "If he does not find escape or evasion in drink," the editors remarked, echoing Jackson, "he will turn to some other form of addiction."

Jackson, at last, had become the sort of respectable burgher he'd always, albeit paradoxically, resembled. In her 1973 profile, "The Fan," Dorothea Straus—wife of Jackson's publisher, Roger—remembered the bow ties and natty pastel shirts Charlie had affected, the little clipped mustache beneath a long elegant nose ("like a sandpiper's beak"): "His prim appearance contradicted what I knew of him: the drinking, homosexual encounters, and attraction to 'rough trade.' Rather, he looked the warm family man he was also, and the small-town citizen of upstate Newark, New York, where he grew up and which, in some sense, he never left." Certainly Jackson preferred the role of provincial family man (a married father of two daughters) to that of a raffish homosexual, but, truth be known, he was becoming more than a little bored with the sober life. Back in 1948, when his third novel (*The Outer Edges*) was published, Jackson had claimed to be writing his masterpiece: "a massive Don Birnam saga" that would encompass at least three Proustian volumes and ultimately describe how Birnam defeated his many demons. But the novel hadn't materialized, nor had any other, and by the early sixties Jackson considered himself washed up. "Malcolm Lowry as novelist was fortunate in his death," he ruefully noted in the *Times Book Review* of another alcoholic, one-masterpiece writer. "Once dead, he no longer had to cope with the impossible struggle, but could become, instead, a legend . . . [one of] the growing glamorous company of Artists Who Died Young. . . . One can't help wondering what would have happened to their careers if they had been put to the cruel test, the *realistic* test, of survival."

Jackson's self-doubt had been certified in 1962, when Roger Straus informed him—during one of their many affable lunches—that Farrar, Straus and Cudahy was dropping him from its list. Straus simply didn't believe that Charlie had it in him to write novels anymore, and the publisher couldn't afford another decade of doling out advances and personal loans. Jackson could hardly argue. His last book (*Earthly Creatures*, a story collection) had been published in 1953—oddly enough, the same year Jackson had joined AA and become one of its most ardent crusaders. Since then he'd (usually) enjoyed a kind of "vegetable health," as he wrote in an unpublished confession, "The Sleeping Brain": "Oh, I was well, all right . . . and was outwardly proud, and very voluble on the subject, of having won my private battle with alcohol and barbiturates." But once his friend and publisher had lowered the boom, he couldn't help reflecting that in the decade *before* 1953—a time of ghastly collapses and domestic tumult—he'd managed to write five books.

Jackson's creative rebirth came about in a curious, if not wholly unexpected, manner. A recurrence of tuberculosis had resulted in the removal of his right lung, and while recuperating at Will Rogers Memorial Hospital in Saranac Lake, New York, Jackson was given drugs that not only reduced his pain but restored his ability to write. Rather heroically—or heedlessly, depending on how you look at it—the decrepit Jackson left his devoted wife, Rhoda, and resumed the "impossible struggle" to realize the promise of his vaunted first novel; a return to addiction was, in the end, a price he was more than willing to pay. By 1967 he was back on the *Times* best-seller list with a novel about a nymphomaniac, *A Second-Hand Life*, and was eager to resume work on his long-awaited "Birnam saga," *What Happened*, the first volume of which was titled *Farther and Wilder*. According to his editor at Macmillan, Robert Markel, at least three hundred pages of this magnum opus had been completed when, in 1968, Jackson took a fatal overdose of Seconal at the Hotel Chelsea, where he'd been living with a Czechoslovakian factory worker named Stanley Zednik.

Chapter One

Et in Arcadia Ego

On November 12, 1916, when Charles Jackson was thirteen, his sixteen-year-old sister, Thelma, and four-year-old brother, Richard, were killed during a Sunday drive with friends, when an express train hit their Overland automobile at a pump-station crossing. Next morning *The New York Times* reported that the two young people in the front seat, Harold Scarth and Gladys Clark, were likely to survive, but that Gladys's brother Malbie had "probably" suffered fatal injuries. Indeed, the boy's back had been broken and he'd died "in terrible agony" a few hours after the collision.

One learned of Malbie's fate in the much fuller account given five days later in the *Union-Gazette*, one of two weekly newspapers in the victims' hometown of Newark, a small village (pop. 6,200) in the township of Arcadia, thirty miles east of Rochester and fifty miles west of Syracuse. "THREE KILLED IN FATAL AUTOMOBILE ACCIDENT," read the redundant headline spanning four front-page columns: "Newark Party of Young People Struck by Sunday Empire State Express—Village in Sadness Over the Calamity—Accident at East Palmyra—The Funerals." Particular attention was paid to Thelma Jackson, who was not only "one of the most beautiful young ladies in the village," but "winsome" and "sunny," too—so much so that her mother had often worried about her parlous attractiveness to men, especially older men such as their next-door neighbor on Prospect Street, a notorious reprobate named Barney. Ever since Thelma was twelve (as Charlie would later recall in semi-fictional form*), the man had made a habit of undressing in front of his window, with the lights on, for the benefit of the pretty girl whose bedroom was opposite his. But Thelma was nothing if not spirited, and when Barney began (on warm summer nights) to wander across the lawn in his BVDs, peeping into windows, Thelma dumped a pail of water on his head from her upstairs window.

The four-year-old Richard (also described as "winsome" by the *Union-Gazette*) was devoted to his older sister, and had begun to cry when her friends arrived that Sunday afternoon to take her on a drive to nearby Palmyra. Thelma had a date with Harold, the driver, and Richard would have been a fifth wheel; nevertheless, a few minutes after leaving, Thelma insisted her friends turn the car around to retrieve her little brother. As the *Union-Gazette* characterized that fateful decision: "In their life, they had spent hours in play and enjoyment and it seemed almost as if Heaven had decreed that in their death they should not be divided."

Harold let Gladys drive on the way home, though she was relatively inexperienced. A freight train was standing to the right at East Palmyra Pump Station, obscuring the approach of the Empire State Express, and when Gladys pulled onto the tracks the car was struck in the rear. All five passengers were thrown clear and lay scattered about while the train went roaring past. Harold, uninjured save for a few scratches, "proved to be a hero and master of the situation," as the *Union-Gazette* reported: "He first picked up Miss Gladys Clark who was not seriously injured, but who was screaming frantically, 'Where is Jim,' Jim being a pet family name for Malbie Clark, her brother." Harold found the others some forty feet away on the Ganargua River bridge: Richard was dead, but Thelma—who'd sat on the near side of the backseat and borne the brunt of the impact—was still breathing, her face bruised on one side; when Harold lifted her, though, he saw she was "terribly mutilated," her lower trunk crushed.

Meanwhile her brother Charlie was at the library, where he spent most

---

* That is, in his hybrid essay/story "The Sunnier Side," about which more below. His neighbor Barney's reputation for lechery is corroborated by a 1949 letter to Jackson from an old hometown acquaintance.

weekend afternoons while other boys his age were playing baseball near the paper mill or sitting quietly on front porches in their Sunday best. The handsome Rew Memorial Library was cause for considerable civic pride, containing almost twelve thousand volumes and presided over by a trained librarian, the formidable Miss Merriman; ladies gathered downstairs for weekly meetings of the Shakespeare Club, the Coterie Club, and the Browning Club, while Nellie Reamer sat at a corner table, day after day, transcribing every word of the King James Bible. As for Charlie, he especially loved the exotic souvenirs lined up around the top of the bookshelves on the main floor—the fruits of founder Henry C. Rew's travels all over the world: a grass skirt, an Orinoco witch doctor's mask, a three-foot totem pole, and (Charlie's favorite) an alabaster model of the Leaning Tower of Pisa. Near the exit was a large globe that boys would spin on their way out, pointing their fingers tensely near the surface and telling themselves, "Where the globe stops, the spot where my finger is pointing at—that's where I'm going to die." At least once, Charlie had discovered ("to his horror") that he would die in his own home state.

The boy was reading his favorite book—*The Red Feathers* (1907), by Theodore Goodrich Roberts, about Indians in Newfoundland—when Miss Merriman told him she'd gotten a telephone call and that Charlie needed to go home right away. Rather ominously, she added that he could keep *The Red Feathers* for good. Turning onto Prospect Street he was hailed by a neighbor, Win Burgess, an affable man who wrote a gag column for the Newark *Courier* (sample item: "A minister's son was run down and killed by an automobile in Brooklyn, the other day. You can get most anything on a minister's son"). Burgess had tears in his eyes, and the front hall of his house was crowded with weeping neighbors. Sitting at the kitchen table, alone, was Charlie's older brother, Herb, sobbing so loudly that Charlie felt embarrassed for him. Burgess explained that Richard and Thelma had been hurt in an accident—nobody knew how badly ("the car was completely smashed, they tell me")—and their mother had gone to Palmyra; Charlie and his brothers, Herb and Fred, would be staying at the Burgesses' for the time being.

The Jackson family had already been under a strain, since the father had taken a job as paymaster at the T. A. Gillespie Shell Loading Plant in New Jersey, and was now living almost full time in Manhattan. The village buzzed with rumors of divorce, an awful disgrace among nice people. "No, no, there's nothing *wrong*—" Win Burgess was saying over the telephone, while urging Charlie's father to catch a train back to

Newark. The latter was not, apparently, deceived. "Mr. Jackson in New York," read a subheading in the *Union-Gazette*, which proceeded to relate a strange encounter at Grand Central Terminal between Fred Jackson and the conductor of the Empire State Express: "The conductor began to talk, not knowing Mr. Jackson, and said he had been having a dreadful experience all the way down, as his train had struck at East Palmyra an automobile containing a number of young people, two of whom had been killed outright and the third of whom would probably die. Mr. Jackson informed him that the two that he had killed were his own children and the conductor fairly quailed." On meeting his family in Newark, Fred Jackson promptly declared that he would sue the New York Central for "a good ten thousand at least," then began to cry in a way that struck Charlie as "somehow cheap, or at least false."

This was a retrospective judgment. In later years, Jackson would dismiss his father as a "trivial, vain man" who had no business raising children in the first place. Charlie remembered how his father ("nostrils distended") would unfailingly pinch the bottoms of Thelma's friends, or otherwise contrive to grope them, until she stopped bringing them home altogether. When he took the job in New Jersey, and his absences became longer and longer, the vulturous Mrs. Van Benschoten would coax Charlie into her house with a cookie and cross-question him: *Why is Mr. Jackson away from home so much? Is he coming home for Thanksgiving? Is he coming for Christmas?* Such neighbors were also careful to let the boy know, with a word here and there, that they were hardly alone in suspecting his father of scandalous behavior. But Charlie and his father were a pair: not only did they look the same (in Fred's childhood photos, he might have passed for his middle son's twin), but even in later years Charlie would concede, dismally, that his father and he were fundamentally alike. "You even blow your nose like your father!" his mother had accused him, sobbing, during an argument (though her mixed feelings were such that she enjoyed Ronald Colman movies, because the actor reminded her of both Charlie *and* her errant husband).

The fact was, Fred Jackson had shown a particular interest in the child he most resembled, avidly reading the boy's poetry and giving him the cardboards from his laundered shirts to draw pictures on. "Papa was proud" of his poems and pictures, the son remembered, and "showed them to the neighbors, complimented me, and himself sent them off to the Children's Page of the *New York Sunday World*. . . . He used to buy fifteen or twenty copies of the *Sunday World* when one of my poems appeared in it, cut them out, sent them to relatives . . ." Once his father had gone, however, Charlie lost interest in writing and drawing for a while, and whatever praise he later got was never enough, since the person he most wanted to please had long ceased to pay attention. Perhaps the blackest day of his childhood—among many black days—was the day his mother received a letter from Fred definitely announcing he wasn't coming home anymore. In *The Lost Weekend*, Don Birnam remembers how he "had run upstairs then and flung himself down on the bed and cried his eyes out": "How could your admiring father do that to you, go away and leave you forever, did he really not care for you any more, was it possible? And though he sobbed and sobbed on the bed in shame and anguish, he realized too the awful importance of that letter, and he glanced up into the mirror of the bureau to see what a moment of crisis looked like."

THAT GHASTLY YEAR—the year of his siblings' death and his father's desertion—Charlie had missed eighty days of school, though he was eager to return and be noticed as a tragic hero of sorts. He'd practiced the role with more long looks in the mirror, and besides, he'd gotten used to a certain amount of attention as a little boy who often seemed almost a prodigy, or at any rate eager to please. "At school Jackson stood invariably at the head of his class," a journalist later wrote, reflecting Jackson's own wistfulness on the subject. After all, his beloved second-grade teacher, Miss Anna Dalton, had been moved to write a letter on the occasion of his eighth birthday, congratulating Mrs. Jackson for having such a "perfect child," or almost: on his report card that year he got straight A's except for a single B in writing, oddly enough.

Since then his grades had steadily declined, perhaps because Miss Dalton was no longer his immediate audience. Instead he ran home (avoiding baseball) and wrote those stories and poems for his father—until, at last, he mostly occupied his solitude with reading about Indians and concocting elaborate fantasies that he would someday, perhaps, commit to paper. The year he turned eleven was consumed by an incipient romance titled "The Story of Strongheart, an Indian Brave," which he talked (versus *wrote*) about incessantly; almost every day he'd regale his exasperated mother with another Strongheart yarn, then rush upstairs and write in big, ornate letters on a fresh page of his notebook: "THE STORY OF STRONGHEART, AN INDIAN BRAVE, By Charles Jackson, Aged

Eleven (11)." He was so obsessed with the subject that a neighbor, Mrs. Coykendall, warned him that he might turn into an Indian if he kept going on like that. "I am already," Charlie lied. "My uncle is an Indian." This became a signature episode of his childhood. From then on, whenever he told a story that seemed the least bit fanciful, his family was apt to remark, "Oh, that's just another one of your Indian uncles." (En route to Hollywood aboard the Super Chief in 1944, he spotted an ersatz Indian hawking souvenirs in the club car. "He pretended not to recognize his nephew," Charlie wrote his brother Fred, "but I knew he knew.") As he later summarized this epoch, "These, then, were the things which occupied me, not only . . . after school, but all day long too in the classroom: a never-ending daydream that made me deficient in my studies, a stranger to my classmates, a nuisance to my mother, and forever restless and dissatisfied with myself."

Things took a turn for the better when Charlie, age twelve, discovered Shakespeare, which would lead, in time, to a voracious idolatry of Whitman, Melville, James, Mann, the great Russians, of Mozart and Beethoven and Mussorgsky, of Courbet and Monet and Goya—a cultivation that was all the richer for being self-imposed. "I'm just a fan," said Jackson, happily admitting his lack of formal education. "But a fan to my fingertips!" Still, his greatest love would forever be Shakespeare, whose likeness was featured on his bookplate ("EX LIBRIS / C. R. JACKSON"), the better for friends to notice the startling resemblance between Charlie and Bard, what with the noble forehead, long nose, and little mustache. "Can you do this sort of thing at the drop of any reasonably sized hat, Mr. Jackson?" said an astonished Clifton Fadiman—host of the popular radio show *Information, Please!*—when his guest had demonstrated, yet again, an all but infallible knack for completing any Shakespeare quotation given a key word or two. It became a kind of compulsion, in life as in art. Don Birnam (named for the "Great Birnam Wood" in *Macbeth*) drowns in the Bard's poetry almost as much as in drink, musing that any novel he ever managed to write would be "so packed with Shakespeare that it [would look] as if he worked with a concordance in his lap . . ."

But this was a charming mania in a child, at least to the ladies of the Newark Shakespeare Club, who made a point of taking Charlie along to lectures given by an expert at the annual Chautauqua—a weeklong event that Jackson would (for the most part) remember fondly, as it brought the great world of culture to an otherwise benighted place: concerts, a Broadway show, a Shakespearean comedy by the Ben Greet Players, and lectures by world-renowned luminaries such as William Jennings Bryan, Thomas Mott Osborne, and (as Jackson put it) "whoever it was who was the author of a famous lecture called 'Acres of Diamonds' (the diamonds were to be found in our own backyard, of course, if we'd only look)." The young Charlie would have no part of the insipid Children's Program, even if he hadn't been taken up by the Shakespeare Club, whose president (Mrs. Coykendall again) hustled him up to the dais when the lecturer had finished and announced that *here* was a child "who reads Shakespeare like other boys read Tom Swift!" "Indeed," said the man, and asked Charlie to name his favorite play. "*Tempest*," said the latter without thinking, and the expert looked pleased: "Now you're talking, young man!" As an adult, Jackson was relieved (if a bit puzzled) to learn that there was, in fact, a real consensus as to the supremacy of *The Tempest*—but on the whole the memory rankled. "I shudder to think what a horrible child I must have been," he wrote the novelist Mary McCarthy, recounting his Chautauqua triumph thirty years later.

And yet how wonderful, really, that a person of rarefied taste and talent should come from such a backwater, and make his mark on the world. Perhaps it was a triumph of heredity over environment; certainly Jackson himself placed a premium on genetic inheritance, at one point railing against Lytton Strachey for "ruin[ing] the art of biography" with "the fatuous doctrine that details of a man's ancestry ought not to be mentioned . . . as if we could fully understand a person without knowing something of those which begot him."* What Jackson knew of his own ancestry, however, was not categorically promising. Reflecting on a photograph he'd seen of his father's family—gathered around the stoop of their little stone house in Lydney, England, circa 1882—he'd noted that they resembled "a band of gypsies," the children melancholy and slightly soiled ("the little boy who was [my] father looked out from the picture with the grave large eyes that had been the admiration of ladies when [I myself] was a child"). Charlie's grandfather, George Frederick Jackson, had been a shiftless man who came to America to accept a genteel sinecure as coal inspector for the New York Central, settling his family around North Salem in Westchester County. George's two brothers, Herbert and Charles, had also moved to New York and become

---

* This from a journal notebook (marked "JAXON" on its marbled cover) that Jackson kept mostly during the early 1930s, when he was drinking heavily and writing little. The penmanship is shaky in places, and sometimes sprawlingly indecipherable.

sexton-undertakers at Episcopal churches in Manhattan: the Church of the Ascension and Church of the Incarnation respectively. But such humble stations may have been a matter of predilection rather than class. George Jackson's maternal uncle was Lord Roberts, an earl, no less, and field marshal during the Boer War. A strain of good breeding was also manifest in the perfect manners of Charlie's paternal grandmother, Eliza; notwithstanding her appearance on that Lydney stoop and the fact that she drank a small glass of whiskey with every meal, the woman dressed beautifully and, while she didn't quite approve of her eldest son—Charlie's raffish father—she nevertheless seemed to believe that he'd married beneath him.

In the late 1960s, Charlie's sister-in-law Cecilia (a decorous woman known always as Bob, who was married to the eldest Jackson boy, Herb) prepared a genealogy of the family for her grandchildren; one bit of research provided by Charlie's younger brother, Fred, was their maternal great-grandparents' wedding certificate, which revealed that Herbert and Mary Jane Nicholes Williams were married in the County of Devon, England, on May 15, 1852—that is, rather abruptly before their son, Herbert Junior, was born. "Must have been a shotgun wedding," Fred opined in his accompanying letter. "*Don't* call attention to it!" As if Bob needed to be told! Earlier she'd learned from another relative that Herbert Junior's wedding to Charlotte Storrier had also been hastily arranged: "Your Grandfather Herbert Williams [Jr.] was like his father," the relative (signed "B. W. F.") wrote Bob. "Your own Grandma [Charlotte] was 'with child' all the time—check those birth dates [i.e., of her many children]—and she was pregnate [*sic*] when she died with advanced TB." That last child would have been the poor woman's fifth in less than nine years; along with fecundity, Herbert Junior and his father had a trade, boilermaker, in common; the son practiced in the village of Depew, near Buffalo. Charlie remembered his grandfather as "a big sweaty man even when he was dressed up"; after the death of his wife, Herbert entrusted the care of his children to his five spinster sisters, who lived with their bachelor brother at 414 Courtland Avenue in Syracuse. For the benefit of Bob's genealogy, Fred described the unmarried siblings as "very religious, frugal people" whose crowded house was "conservatively furnished with all *very good* things" (Fred was an antiques dealer). Charlie was less charitable in the unfinished novella he later wrote about the "414" ménage: "Next to the mahogany music cabinet was the little square gilt chair that Must Not Be Sat In," he reminisced, while describing the sisters themselves as pious harridans and the bachelor brother as an "ageless, artless dolt . . . a Launcelot Gobbo who was an honest man's son." These siblings would someday take a dim view of Charlie and Fred's mother, Sarah, because of her divorce, protesting that no shadow of scandal had previously befallen the family. As Bob remarked in her genealogy, "Charles had said there never was a scandal because they never really lived"—to which Bob demurred (with an almost audible sniff) to the effect that she herself found these people "wonderful": "They lived simply, and enjoyed the simple pleasures of life. . . . They obviously found contentment in their lives, and what more can anyone ask of life." When the residents of 414 died, they left everything to their niece Charlotte, Sarah's youngest sister, a "prissy and penurious" woman who wore a rimless pince-nez and was (according to her nephew Charlie) unlike Sarah in every way.

As a girl Sarah Williams had returned to her father's house after he remarried a stern German widow named Mohr, whom Sarah came to despise. What made matters worse was the woman's cruelty toward Sarah's youngest brother, Herbert, who proved to be slightly retarded. Far from being treated with special patience, the boy was harried by his stepmother and ignored (at best) by his father, who seemed humiliated by his namesake's ineptitude.* Sarah was only fourteen when she ran away to Buffalo, finding occasional work as a nursemaid; four years later, desperate for a home of her own, she coaxed the handsome Frederick George Jackson into marrying her, even though he was already engaged to a girl in Albany. Fred's parents were displeased by his change of heart, all the more so when their new daughter-in-law disgraced herself (as she liked to tell it) by sliding down the banister chez Jackson. "That American Girl!" sighed her mother-in-law, though of course Sarah was almost as English as she.

The couple lingered in Depew for a few years and lost no time growing a family: on January 20, 1899, almost nine months exactly after the wedding, a son, Herbert, was born; Thelma followed on July 12, 1900, and another girl, Winifred, was born on October 31, 1901, but died a few

---

* Herbert was banished as a teenager and became a hobo, occasionally turning up in Newark at his sister Sarah's house (one of Jackson's earliest stories, "A Night Visitor," is about one such episode). According to Charles Jackson's great-nephew Michael Kraham, the family would usually feed and bathe Herb, then coax him back to the train station with a pack of cigarettes. "Readymades!" he'd say, delighting at the bribe.

months later of diphtheria.* By the time Charles was born, on April 6, 1903, the family was living in Summit, New Jersey, and soon after Fred's arrival, in 1906, they moved to Newark, where the father had been hired by the Gillespie Company as paymaster for construction on the local section of the Erie Canal. By 1910 the restless man had taken a new job as office manager at the Emmons & Company nursery, and the family had settled at last into a little Queen Anne cottage at 238 Prospect, in the nicer part of town.

AROUND THE TIME of Charles Reginald Jackson's death, in 1968,† a Newark Chamber of Commerce leaflet identified him as the "most famous person" to have ever been born in the village, though of course he was born in New Jersey and none of his books was available at the Rew Library to which he'd been so devoted. Still, Jackson would have been touched by the tribute, since his love for the place was as profound as it was tortured. The township of Arcadia was aptly named: quietly nestled in the Finger Lakes region south of Lake Ontario, it was a lovely place to be a romantic little boy obsessed with Indian lore, and Newark itself was a village out of Norman Rockwell. On summer nights the children would gather around the pagoda-roofed bandstand in the park for concerts by the Fire Department Band, scurrying off between numbers to buy ice-cream cones and popcorn from Mr. Espenmiller's two-wheeled cart, or a soda from the pearl-handled spigots of the Kandy Kitchen on Main Street. The one traffic light blinked officiously at the intersection of Main and Union, and opposite the park was a Victorian mansion where (as Jackson remembered) "the glow of many cigars mov[ed] up and down as the Elks [sat] in their rocking chairs on the porch." The public life of the village bustled along three downtown blocks (one of Main, two of Union) near the barge canal, where one shopped at the haberdasher, the meat market, the dry-goods and drug store, and was entertained by silent-movie serials (*The Perils of Pauline*, *The Million Dollar Mystery*) at the Crescent Theatre, or else big local productions (*The Elks Minstrels*

---

* Charlie gave her name to Winifred Grainger, the good-hearted nymphomaniac heroine of his last novel, *A Second-Hand Life*.

† Charlie was named after a paternal great-uncle (one of the two sexton-undertakers) and his uncle Reginald Miles Jackson. His early (and mostly unpublished) fiction was written under the name "C. R. Jackson," and for a while he toyed with "Charles R. Jackson" before dropping the middle initial altogether.

& Frolic) at the Opera House, which also featured occasional road shows such as *Uncle Tom's Cabin*, though these were not attended by "the better class."

"Don't tell *me* there are no social distinctions or caste system in America!" Jackson wrote a half-century later to his agent and editor. Newark, he claimed, "was more socially conscious of who was who and what their place should be than any member of the Almanac[h] de Gotha." Physically and otherwise the town was divided by the canal, to the north of which was the poorer section, largely populated by Italians who had helped build the canal a few years before.* Non-Italians on the south side could join a small country club for $125 a year—later a haven for sturdy burghers such as Charlie's brother Herb, but generally shunned by what passed for the smart set. The latter lived in a few stately homes along Grant Street, East Avenue, and Maple Avenue, only a few blocks from the Jackson house on modest Prospect Street. His family was "the very middle of the middle class," Charlie said, "but through a kind of innate 'taste' or a leaning toward matters of learning and culture, [they tended] rather toward the more cultivated element than otherwise."

Perhaps the most cultivated family of all, and certainly one of the richest, was the R. A. S. Bloomers on the corner of East Avenue and Grant; somewhat due to his endearing precocity and nice manners, Charlie became almost a de facto member of the household. In those days Newark was a prosperous village, and the biggest of its half-dozen or so factories was the paper mill owned by the Bloomer Brothers box company, manufacturer of cardboard ice-cream pails and the like.† For the rest of his life (often to his detriment) Charlie would indulge a love of opulence, which arguably began in the richly appointed interiors of the Bloomer house. The father, Robert Anson Sherman ("Uncle Sherm" to Charlie), had studied engineering in Germany, and until the war, at least, made a point of emulating the Kaiser: he wore a Germanic mustache, trimmed and waxed, smoked a big Bavarian pipe, and drank beer made in his own cellar; also in the German style, he was strict with his children,

---

* Many of whom seem to have moved on after the canal was put through. At any rate, a pamphlet about Newark that appears to date from the 1930s or '40s (found among Jackson's papers) proudly announces, "Newark has no foreign language quarters, her population being loyally American; and eighty-six percent of the inhabitants of Wayne County are native born, and white."

† Later known as the Fold-Pak corporation, whose little take-out cartons are familiar to lovers of Chinese food.

insisting that they retire every day at four o'clock to their respective study rooms for an hour of reading ("I nearly always managed to be in on this," Jackson recalled), and formally shaking hands with each of them at bedtime. One of Charlie's fondest memories was the summer he and Jack Burgess (his neighbor Win's nephew) were invited to spend three luxurious weeks with the Bloomers at Sodus Point, on Lake Ontario, twenty miles north of Newark. The Bloomer compound (Neosho) was located on a long isthmus called Charles Point, where the children spent their mornings swimming in the bay, until a servant took them in the family boat (*Wawanesa*) to the point for ice cream. Not long after that idyllic summer, the last Bloomer boy went away to prep school, and for years Charlie was mortified by the memory of how he'd asked their mother ("Aunt Kate") to "sell" him the books that he and her children had enjoyed so much during reading hours past (*The Black Arrow, The Mysterious Island*, et al.). She gave him the books for free—as he'd hoped—and evidently didn't hold the request against him. "He was a dear little boy, Rhoda," the woman wrote Jackson's wife in 1940, when their first daughter, Sarah, was born. Mrs. Bloomer remembered Charlie's touching piety in her Sunday school class, and urged his wife to teach Sarah the Lord's Prayer "with a hope that World Christianity will come to keep for her a better way of life than that which prevails now in Europe."

He was a dear little boy . . . part of Jackson wanted nothing better than to be pious, well-mannered, and beloved by proper people like the Bloomers. He would forever be squeamish about using profanity, and bemused that he could ever have become an alcoholic, given that nice people in Newark didn't drink. Don Birnam remembers the fortitude it had taken, as a fourteen-year-old Boy Scout, to enter a downtown saloon where nice people didn't go—but *he* went, because he was distributing posters for the Liberty Loan and it was the patriotic, the nice thing to do (and because other scouts "would marvel at his courage and tell all the others"). "Tonio! spiritual brother!" Don reflects, invoking Mann's artist-hero Tonio Kröger, whose "deepest and secretest love belongs to the blond and blue-eyed, the fair and living, the happy, lovely, and commonplace." How Jackson longed to be one of them, always desperate for the approval of those who were most likely to snub him—boys who were good at sports, or even, years later, a prim young secretary who came to his gorgeous mansion in New Hampshire to take dictation, radiating disapproval the while. "Mr. Jackson," she asked, after an awkward lull, "how did you happen to become a *writer*?" Eager to win the girl over,

Jackson explained that he'd never wanted to be anything else; why, as a little boy, he used to go straight home after school and write stories while the other boys played baseball. "You must have been whacky!" sneered the girl, as Jackson sadly recalled: "She was so right. Judgments I've had to take all my life: along with the collapses, it is one of the prices we have to pay."

And what did all the happy, lovely, commonplace people of Newark make of Charles Jackson? "He was always viewed as kind of flaky," said Tom Bloomer (R.A.S.'s grandson), who explained that such a "conservative community" was apt to look down on (in effect) a sissy who wanted to write. Most of the Bloomers were broadminded enough to overlook Charlie's peculiarities, but Tom's mother was a Hallagan, a staunch Methodist family who was far more representative of the Newark middle class.* These people, said Tom Bloomer, "would just look at Charlie *aghast.*" Which did not, however, deter him from seeking their love—on the contrary: "This afternoon I went up to your house and your Mother gave me your address," he wrote young Walter Hallagan during the war, when the latter was serving in France; after a wooing, newsy letter full of bluff good humor, the fifteen-year-old Charlie signed himself, "Your friend, Charles R. Jackson / B.V.D., P.D.Q. + R.S.V.P." ("The tragedy of homosexuals," he would later say, "is that we love straight men.")

When Jackson returned to Newark over the years, he was always happy to grant interviews to the local newspaper, in the course of which he'd reaffirm how very attached he felt to the place that had raised him. He said this because it was true, and because he never quite despaired of winning the village over; even at the height of his fame, few things thrilled him more than fan letters from home, to which he always replied with the most abject humility. At the same time he was also delighted by outrage, and was careful to remind his old friends and neighbors (via those interviews) that "he constantly creates with this local area in mind."

But of course they knew that already. Almost twenty-five years after Jackson's death, a local high school student named Kerry Boeye thought to write a scholarship essay about Jackson, and was startled to find that the local library didn't even have a copy of *The Lost Weekend*! The town historian gravely explained: Jackson's work, he said, had many roman à clef elements about various Newarkians—some of them still alive as

---

* The Hallagans lived across the street from the Jacksons, at 241 Prospect—a house that was fittingly occupied, as of 1935, by Charlie's philistine brother Herb.

of 1992—and hence Boeye was well advised not to "pursue identifications" too avidly. For the most part Boeye did as he was told, and also
took a properly deploring tone in the essay that followed (he wanted the
scholarship, after all), explaining why Jackson would forever be a prophet
without honor in his own land: "I am sure people still took exception
to being called adulterers, perverts, or something equally sordid." But
whatever glee Jackson felt about his own notoriety was usually dissembled with a Chaplinesque poker face: He was a writer, he'd say with a
shrug, and a writer uses the material he's been given; and really (as one of
his heroes, Sherwood Anderson, would attest), what's better than being
raised in a small town? "In a small town it's practically impossible not to
know practically everything about practically everybody else. . . ."

In 1950, when Jackson published his first story collection, *The Sunnier Side: Twelve Arcadian Tales*, the Newark *Courier* warned its readers
that Jackson (the newspaper's former editor) had written about people
who were easily identified by anyone who'd lived in Newark from 1907
to 1923, particularly the three women featured in the title story, a curious mixture of essay and fiction. The piece had been inspired by a fan
letter Jackson had received from one Luceine Heniore, who'd known
the author as a boy and had written to congratulate him on a story he'd
recently published in *Good Housekeeping* (about that idyllic summer at
the Bloomer compound on Charles Point): "It is a real pleasure," she
wrote, a little chidingly, "to run across such a clean and delightful short
story—no sex, no murder and no personality problem [i.e., like Jackson's usual fiction] . . . " By way of rebuttal Jackson wrote "The Sunnier Side," which considered the fates of three popular girls ("the great
triumvirate") from Arcadia: Eudora Detterson, Faith Goldsmith, and
Harriet "Fig" Newton, who obviously—despite Jackson's use of "ficti-
tious names" and "mixed up" facts, as the *Courier* noted—were based
on Bernice Coyne, Edith Warren, and Eula Burgess (Win's daughter).
Suffice it to say, their lives had gone badly despite auspicious beginnings
("I did, indeed, thank my lucky stars that you didn't know *me* better,"
Miss Heniore subsequently wrote Jackson). Edith Warren, for example,
had been valedictorian at Newark High and graduated Phi Beta Kappa
from Smith, before coming home to marry her high school sweetheart,
Frank, a wealthy businessman who was the first president of the Newark
Rotary Club, second president of the Chamber of Commerce, and so
on. The Warrens became known as "the first family of Newark." Later,
alas, rumors of Frank's philandering resulted in Edith's abrupt resigna-

tion from her various clubs, and finally on the morning of March 28, 1928, three shots were fired inside the Warren house, which was then engulfed in flames: Frank and Edith, burned beyond recognition, had been shot dead; ditto their thirteen-year-old son. Police determined that the murderer must have been one of the family members, though it was impossible to say which. In any event, Jackson's point in writing about the Warren case was that even the most golden people of Arcadia led far from perfect lives.

THE FUNERAL OF THELMA AND RICHARD was one of the largest ever held in the village, and certainly one of the saddest. The casket was entirely open to reveal Thelma lying slightly on her side, little Richard's head resting on her right arm, one of his hands clasping hers. Mourners were greeted at the door by the father and his two younger sons, Charlie and Fred, before they proceeded one by one past the coffin for a final look. The *Union-Gazette* closed its long, somber account on a lyrical note: "It seems as if the very flower of our young boyhood, of our young womanhood and of our childhood had suddenly been plucked from our village in order that they might, if possible, adorn the very throne of heaven."

In the story he would eventually write about his sister's death, "Rachel's Summer," Jackson described an obtuse form of condolence on the part of a neighbor, Mrs. Kirtle*: "Think how good it was of God," the woman says to the grieving mother, "to keep Rachel home with you all summer. You must comfort yourself with that." The mother's response is snappish, given that her daughter had not been kept there by God—as the shrewish Mrs. Kirtle well knows—but rather for a reason that made her last summer on earth a miserable ordeal. "God in His infinite wisdom," Mrs. Kirtle and the villagers murmur, since it's rumored that Rachel was pregnant, and had died before the disgrace became obvious. Rachel, for her part, had protested her innocence, pointing out to her mother that she'd recently refrained from swimming with friends because she was menstruating. Still, to prevent the rumor from thriving in her absence (she usually spent summers at her grandmother's farm in the Catskills), her mother had kept Rachel home that summer and she'd died before she could absolve herself. A spirited, pretty girl who always refused to act

---

* A character based on the ubiquitous Mrs. Coykendall, as Jackson was happy to explain in letters to former friends and family in Newark.

shocked when boys whistled at her, Rachel is an ideal scapegoat for all the other maidens of Arcadia who might bring shame upon their families. "Thus, periodically," Jackson wrote, "as if by some mystic council, a girl was chosen for the sacrifice, and the pressure of parental anxiety was relieved in the neighborhood for another season or two. What could have been more natural than to choose Rachel, the gayest, the most promising, the loveliest of them all?"

In its most essential aspect, the story was true: Charles Jackson's niece Sally remembers the *eureka* moment when she found letters, as a teenager, alluding to the rumor that Thelma had been pregnant when she died. "I'm *not* Thelma," she said to her father, Herb, who'd always been bizarrely repressive toward his oldest daughter; as Sally recalled, the man looked stricken and turned away. "He couldn't trust me," she said, "and I think it broke his heart that he couldn't trust his sister." As for Thelma's mother, though she tried all her life to dismiss the rumor, she couldn't help seeking reassurance, again and again, that it wasn't true. "For that's what Arcadia can do to you," the narrator of "Rachel's Summer" concludes: "make you doubt when you know otherwise. . . . To me the tragic thing was that, knowing, Mother still had to ask. The damage of more than thirty years was complete."

PHOTOGRAPHS OF FRED JACKSON, with his youngest son, Richard— evidently three or four at the time—suggest that the man had continued to come home until the boy's death, but as Bob Jackson noted in her genealogy, Fred "never got over the children's accident" and might have decided at that point to make a clean break. By then his wife had learned the truth about Fred's other life in New York, having received a letter from the man's landlady to the effect that he was living in sin with a sixteen-year-old Irish girl named Kathleen ("Kitty"), who'd already borne him a child: another Fred, no less. "But Fred dear, certainly you must understand by now that we can't go on like this," Don Birnam's mother remonstrates with her husband after their children's funeral, in *Farther and Wilder*. She even offers to bring up the other child as her own (though naturally the entire village will know the truth), but the man says he can't bear to come home anymore now that little Richard is dead: "It would be too much."

In fact the matter remained unresolved for some time. The following two summers (1917 and 1918) Fred Jackson arranged for his oldest son,

Herb, to work at the munitions plant in South Amboy where Fred was paymaster. "Herbert and his father had great times together," Bob Jackson wrote, "and he never guessed that anything was amiss between his father and a young Irish girl." The job enabled Herb to pay his tuition at the University of Rochester, and that second summer the whole family spent a month in Perth Amboy (where Fred putatively lived at the Officers' Club), then stayed on in New York until early September. Less than a month later—on Fred's day off, as it happened—the T. A. Gillespie Shell Loading Plant, the largest munitions factory in the world, exploded, killing almost a hundred people and resulting in the evacuation of three cities. "Dad was there all the time," Charlie wrote a friend, "carrying dead and injured away, but he was not hurt. During that time mother was nearly frantic."

Be that as it may, the marriage presently ended for good: Sarah Jackson was persuaded by her rector at St. Mark's Episcopal Church that she should get a divorce—"the mistake of her life," she always thought—and Herb dropped out of college and found work at the Bloomer Brothers paper mill. For a couple of years, at least, the father continued to write his youngest surviving son,* but Herb bitterly resented the stigma of heading a fatherless family, and would have nothing more to do with the man. As for Charlie, he preserved his father's address ("2318 Loring Place, Bronx NY") in a memo book he kept as an adult, and wrote in *Farther and Wilder* of a final visit that the twenty-six-year-old Don makes to his father's apartment: the latter, abashed, cautions Don not to let his and Kitty's children know that he is their half brother, then repeatedly calls him "Sonny" in their presence. Don leaves the meeting feeling "depressed" yet oddly "shriven," too, quite certain he and his father will never meet again. On July 31, 1952, however, Jackson was driving with his daughters when it occurred to him that it was his father's seventy-fifth birthday; he mentioned as much to the girls, who asked if he'd sent a card or present. "Well, you see, I never knew my father very well," he explained, whereupon his nine-year-old daughter, Kate, shot back, "You certainly knew him long enough for his wife to be your

---

* The one in Newark, that is. A letter dated December 9, 1920, survives among the younger Fred Jackson's papers at Dartmouth, and suggests that his father was perhaps a more interesting, kindly man than Charles was willing to admit. "Note that you are still taking Dancing lessons," he wrote with evident approval to his (manifestly even then?) gay son. "You must be quite a dancer by now." The letter is signed, "With love from / Father."

mother" (a "truly Shakespearian" line, Jackson reflected). Less than a
month later he learned of his father's death in Washington, D.C., and
went down for the funeral. "I wouldn't have dreamed that it would have
affected me at all," he wrote his brother Fred afterward. "But the sight
of Pop stirred up childhood memories long since forgotten—and I'm the
sentimental sloppy type, as you know."

GIVEN THAT CHARLES JACKSON blamed his mother for both his alcoholism and his homosexuality, the two were bound to have a somewhat
difficult relationship. When Charlie was a boy, though, they were quite
close—perhaps *too* close, as the prevailing wisdom had it. Richard Peabody, whose teachings helped Jackson get sober in 1936, characterized
alcoholism as "a disease of emotional immaturity" caused by overprotective parents (especially mothers), a theory Jackson himself wholeheart-
edly endorsed. As he spelled it out in a 1946 *Cosmopolitan* article, "It is my
belief that alcoholism is largely the fault of parents who overindulge or
overprotect their children to the point where they (the children, grown
older but still childish) cannot face reality and seek 'escape' in drink."

And who—by these rather dubious lights—was a more textbook case
than he? After his father's departure, his mother became "a creature
of sighs and bewilderment," quite unlike the banister-riding hoyden of
twenty years before; her great solace was her two little boys, Charlie and
Fred, on whom she lavished an all but suffocating affection. (In psycho-
analytical terms, Herb escaped their fate by dint of the fatherly attention
he'd received in his formative years; then, too, it probably helped just
being Herb—a man who was hard to dote on, even for so susceptible
a mother.) In *The Lost Weekend*, Don Birnam is forever casting back to
childhood—a time when he was loved and promising and (relatively)
happy, despite his untimely loss of a proper male role model—all too
aware, meanwhile, of his own case of arrested development: "He could
never get used to the fact that he was a grown up, in years at least, living
in an adult world. When the barber said, 'Razor all right, Sir?' he had to
think a minute. What was it men said when asked about the razor? And
when he said it ('Razor's fine, fine' or whatever it was) he felt a fraud."
And so, too, with homosexuality, considered almost a concomitant of
alcoholism in the Freudian ethos of the time; both had a similar etiology,
after all. To dramatize the matter, Jackson later conceived an autobiographical play, *The Loving Offenders*, that would serve as "an Ibsenesque

study, with more than an occasional nod to Freud and the merest genu-flection to Krafft-Ebing," as he wrote his friend Howard Lindsay (of the famous Lindsay and Crouse playwriting team). The cast would consist of a middle-aged mother, abandoned by her husband, who therefore "has shifted all her emotional weight on her two younger sons," Ralph and David, whereas the oldest boy, George, has escaped her fatal influence and is soon to be married. Ralph, however, causes a scandal by attending the wedding in the company of a special "friend"—a charming, slightly older doctor—and, as the play ends, the youngest brother, David, is heard to remark wistfully that he too hopes to have such a friend when he grows up. "The point of the play," Jackson explained to the doubt-ful Lindsay, "is that too much mother-love, the smothering kind, makes for homosexuality—if anything does (and I'm aware that nobody really knows)."

What he suspected, though, was that something of the sort had trans-pired in his own case, and even more so in Fred's. The latter not only pursued dancing in his early teens, but—at the tender age of eleven, dur-ing the war—avidly took up knitting sweaters and mufflers for soldiers via the Red Cross, mortifying his family by taking yarn and needles along to the movies! Charlie himself would always be a lot more furtive. "Do you remember the Presbyterian Church carriage sheds on Vary's Lane," a fellow Newarkian, J. R. Elliott, wrote Jackson in 1950. "On week days and nights, these same sheds were the scene of events that would make even a Kinsey researcher blush." Jackson remembered those sheds, all right, as Elliott would have known if he'd read *The Lost Week-end*, in which a young Don "has fun" with a schoolmate, Melvin, "in the carriage-sheds back of the Presbyterian Church." For Melvin this is only so much boyish horseplay, given that he fantasizes about little Gertrude Hort; Don, however, finds himself bewilderingly fixated on the image of Melvin washing his father's back in the bathtub. Such scenes—so obvi-ously personal—were almost the death of Charlie's poor mother when she first read the novel in manuscript: "Also something about Homo Sexual," she wrote, "why mention that? God knows I have had enough of that and half crazy people to last one a life time. And this one's and that one's remarks that I have to pretend not to hear."

Such remarks had first reached her ears, perhaps, a few months after Thelma and Richard's funeral, at which (according to the *Union-Gazette*) a local tenor named Herbert Quance had caused "many eyes" to fill with tears when he sang "Asleep in Jesus" and "The Beautiful Isle of Somewhere"; likewise, at the Birnam childrens' funeral in *Farther and Wilder*, the latter song is performed by Raoul de la Vergne—called Ray Verne by the townspeople—a character who originally appeared in Jackson's first published short story in 1939, "Palm Sunday," about an unnamed narrator who remembers being molested by Verne as a fourteen-year-old boy.* Bert Quance was thirty-five in 1917, a handsome if rather dumpy man who often came to dinner at the Jackson house, during which he'd sing popular standards ("Pale Hands I Love," "Woman Is Fickle") while Sarah Jackson accompanied him on the piano. As a boy, Quance had been considered a prodigy as both an organist and a tenor; locals expected him to star at the Metropolitan Opera someday, but Quance seemed content to go on living with his mother, Esther, and playing piano at the picture show, or being "imported" to play Ralph Rackstraw in the Newark High production of *H.M.S. Pinafore*—this in addition to his usual duties as organist at St. Mark's. ("To succeed you've got to get out and around," he'd later sigh, age fifty-five, in a newspaper profile about his promising salad days.)

In "Palm Sunday," the adult narrator realizes that he was one of many boys molested by the organist, and moreover that the village was quite aware of the situation but loath to speak about it; indeed, the man's reputation as a musician was more or less unblemished by his tacit notoriety, and his talents were forever in demand.† " 'Pretend it isn't so,' " Jackson once wrote, "which was always Arcadia's attitude when trouble was brewing. . . . Which I suppose is a fairly adequate substitute for what Arcadia really thinks it is: tolerance." In "Palm Sunday," nobody objects when Ray Verne asks the fourteen-year-old narrator to privately rehearse a song, "The Palms," that the boy will perform as a solo during the Offertory at his Episcopal church. ("Herbert Quance will sing 'The Palms' at both services in St. Mark's church Sunday," reads an item from the *Union-Gazette*.) As they practice alone in the chancel, Verne puts his left

---

* Lest there be any doubt about the real-life model for Ray Verne, Jackson made a vast alphabetical list of practically every person he'd ever known and assigned a fictional name to each—this, no doubt, for the purpose of writing his massive autobiographical saga, *What Happened*. Under the Q's one finds: "Bert Quance—RAOUL de la VERGNE (RAY VERNE)."

† "I never heard the term [pedophile] used back then," said Bert Quance's great-nephew, Harold, when asked about Bert's reputation in Newark. "He was just a 'three-dollar bill.' " Harold's wife, Elsie, said that other Quance cousins have attested to Bert's notoriety, but agreed that such matters were "always hushed up."

arm around the boy's stomach and continues playing with one hand, then suddenly turns the boy around and undoes his belt buckle. Reflecting on the incident with perfect candor—with, indeed, an emotional precision that must have seemed shocking when the story was first published, but anticipates much of what is currently believed about sexual trauma—the narrator admits that he wasn't particularly horrified at the time: "I was too scared and excited to do anything about it and anyway it was all over in a minute. My chief reaction was confusion and a consequent resentment, but not against Mr. Verne. It was directed chiefly against myself, was very intense for a little while, and then was easily forgotten." One more sexual encounter follows, the next day, when Verne coaxes the boy into the steeple of the Methodist church; at one point the organist pauses "in the middle of everything" to remark with a chuckle, "You're almost as good as your brother."

According to Jackson's notes, one section of *Farther and Wilder* was to be titled "Ray Verne," and the character also makes cameo appearances in a later story as well as in the novel *A Second-Hand Life*, where he's portrayed as a sodden degenerate living out his last days in a seedy hotel on the wrong side of Arcadia.* "Palm Sunday," for its part, ends on a heartening note: "Isn't it funny how far away all that seems," says the narrator's grown brother, "how unimportant." But the torments of Jackson's adulthood (not to mention his preoccupation with "Ray Verne" as a fictional subject) would suggest lingering ramifications, to put it mildly. Though childhood sexual abuse isn't always experienced as traumatic at the time (especially when perpetrated, nonviolently, by someone the child likes and trusts), its victims are far more likely to suffer the kind of persistent anxiety that made it so hard for Jackson to resist alcohol and drugs, never mind the underlying sexual guilt that stayed with him to the end; part of him, after all, would always long to be loved by Newark's better sort. But there was also Charles Jackson the writer, a rather fearless man who knew that his only hope lay in telling the truth, and hence his struggle to purge the ghost of "Ray Verne": "I had been writing all my life," he wrote a friend in 1951, "till one night something happened: I had the urge to tell the story of PALM SUNDAY; I knew it couldn't be sold or published, so I just forgot about all that, and about everything

---

* Quance spent much of his lonely old age ("Nobody invited him anywhere," said his great-nephew) at the Windsor Hotel in downtown Newark, and died at a Masonic Home in nearby Utica on June 26, 1957, age seventy-five.

else I knew about writing, and just simply told it in the simplest way possible, putting nothing in that wasn't true of people—that is, leaving out the 'telling little touch' and all those devices of professional short story writing. As a result, the story seems to me now to be full of telling little touches—the kind that ring true."

Chapter Two

Simple Simon

Charles Jackson remembered his old high school as a three-story, red-brick "firetrap" in the center of town. The principal was a handsome, athletic man in his mid-thirties, Isaac "Ike" Chapell, who flirted openly with upper-class girls and was generally admired by the boys for doing so. The life of the school revolved mostly around the basketball team: Friday night games were attended by practically every (nice) family in Newark, who afterward stuck around en masse for dances that lasted until eleven, where a musical trio (piano, violin, drums) played such hits as "Hindustan" and "Dardanella."

Jackson did not flourish, academically or otherwise. "You are just the way I was," he later wrote his daughter Kate: "you get good marks in the subjects in which you are interested, and lousy marks in the subjects in which you are not. Don't worry about that. I am utterly confident that you will thrive in the field which you eventually choose for yourself." Certainly he'd found a niche and managed to thrive after a fashion, though in fact his marks—at least by the time he was in high school—were lousy in *every* subject except English, which interested him just enough to rate the occasional B (but no better, and often worse). During his freshman year he tried to make a splash by entering the Wayne County prize speaking contest, though on the face of it he seemed an unlikely public speaker, what with his high, piping voice, which seemed a perfect match for his diminutive frame. According to the *Union-Gazette*, a preliminary contest was held at the gymnasium to select one boy and one girl from Newark High, a cut Jackson made by virtue of being the only boy who'd entered. What followed was a "dreadful fiasco," which he would later describe in three different genres of writing: a short story ("The Last Time") and television scenario (*The Prize Speaking Contest*), both featuring Don Birnam, and a novella (*Home for Good*) about a world-famous author from Arcadia named Mercer Maitland. The details of all three accounts are virtually identical: the protagonist loses the boys' cup to the contestant from Sodus, but the girl from Arcadia wins, whereupon an assembly is held in her honor; after she says a few words, the principal invites to the dais "that other person" who also brought "honor and credit" to the school—meaning the teacher who coached the two contestants—but the protagonist abruptly stands and begins to give a mawkish little thank-you speech. "He got no further, or, if he did, it was not heard," Jackson wrote in "The Last Time." "A roar went up from the assembly. Shrieks and screams of laughter, wave after wave of laughter, deafening, crushing, passed over the room. The windows shook with the sound; the glass panes rattled as if there had been an earthquake." ("Do you know what?" a teacher comforts the traumatized boy in *Home for Good*. "I'll bet you that someday you'll write about this.")

To make matters considerably worse, Herb Jackson seemed eager to distance himself from his sissy little brother, and took to calling him Isabelle at school and circulating his poetry ("to general hilarity") among fellow seniors. More and more, Charlie withdrew. At home he fixed up the attic as his own private study, where began a lifelong tendency to surround himself with portraits of his personal gods—soon to include, in those days, Edgar Allan Poe (whom he hoped to resemble when he grew up), Sherwood Anderson, Eugene O'Neill, and Charlie Chaplin. Weekends, too, were spent alone as a matter of cherished preference, either at the library or on hikes to an old maple sugar camp (Sugar Bush) outside of town, during which he'd pretend to be Father Marquette or one of General Custer's reconnoitering scouts. Among his family he felt almost a stranger, consoling himself with a fantasy of being a foundling, a prince ("someday the secret would be revealed, he was content to wait"), or at any rate a very great poet, scornful of the "clods" in his midst. "When I'd finish a poem," he later told Harvey Breit of *The New*

York Times, "I'd look into the mirror to see if I looked different, if my face had changed"—this à la young Don in *The Lost Weekend*: "Surely there would be some sign, some mark, some tiny line or change denoting a new maturity, perhaps?" If so, his family stubbornly refused to notice. One day, while the rest of them went on a motoring trip, Charlie stayed home and worked on a long narrative poem; when his mother returned, he excitedly demanded she sit down and listen. Rather to his surprise, she sat quietly through the whole thing, staring at his shoes with a rapt expression. "Charles Jackson," she said, once he finished, "first thing tomorrow morning take those shoes downtown and get them resoled."

Jackson's alienation might have been dire indeed, if not for the timely arrival of a soulmate, Marion Fleck, whose family moved to Newark from Taunton, Massachusetts. The girl went by the name Betty, though Charlie liked to call her Bettina or Teens, and in his fiction she usually appears as Bettina Chapin. Jackson wrote an account of their first meeting for *Farther and Wilder**: the Chapin family has just arrived in Arcadia, and while their furniture is being carted into the house, Bettina stands on her lawn with a group of curious youngsters and volubly holds forth about how she used to love horseback riding in Massachusetts ("We had our own stables and everything") while Don silently studies her, observing that her prettiness ("a perfect complexion, and fine, gray-blue, intelligent eyes") is somewhat diminished by her tall girl's tendency to hunch her shoulders and plod about with her head down. Suddenly a person approaches on horseback, and—overhearing the whole equestrian spiel—offers Bettina the use of her mount. "Why, I wouldn't *dream* of taking your horse," says the latter, flushing with embarrassment. "Besides, I couldn't without my—my proper riding habit and all." The little crowd shares a scornful smile, whereas Don "recognize[s] a kindred spirit." ("She was a natural actress," Marion's son-in-law, Gene Farley, attests. Even as an elderly woman, she used to entertain herself on trains by pretending to be a psychiatrist while chatting up strangers.)

Marion likewise felt deeply estranged from her family. Writing to Jackson on the subject of parents and children, she quoted Arnold: "A God, a God their severance ruled!" Her father, an electrician, was annoyed by his daughter's love of poetry and overall artiness, while her

---

* Cannibalized almost word for word into *A Second-Hand Life*, where he changed the two characters' names from Bettina Chapin and Don Birnam to Carol Wilson and Harry Harrison. One of the unwritten sections of *Farther and Wilder* was to be titled "Bettina."

mother expressed a wifely solidarity by avoiding such subjects altogether for the 104 dull years of her life. Both openly preferred Marion's little sister, Helen, who grew up to be a perfect wife and mother. Among people her own age, too, Marion was shunned as intellectual ("anathema to social life in Arcadia"). Naturally she and Charlie became inseparable. "She was the companion of his every thought and almost his every act," Jackson wrote of the friendship, "far closer to him than his mother or brothers . . . the real pleasure of any occasion—book, hike, movie, a day in the city—consisted in talking it over with Bettina before and after, but especially after. . . . Only when considered in its relation to Bettina did anything have any meaning." At school they passed notes at every opportunity,* and afterward would sometimes walk around town until late at night, sitting at last in the deserted bandstand and talking about the lovely, non-Arcadian future. Best of all were hikes, now shared, to Sugar Bush Hill, where they'd sit among the "sad-eyed sheep" and read poetry aloud to each other—the inspiration for an elegiac poem, "World Without End," that Marion would someday write:

> *It was a time both beautiful and sad*
> *(The young need sorrow as they need to breathe)*
> *When we first heard the trumpets of our world*
> *On that far hilltop where we went to read.*
> *I loved it best those gray chill Autumn days*
> *The sun was absent. Then the jeweled words*
> *of Keats and Shelley, Wordsworth, Swinburne, Blake,*
> *like radiant motes from some imagined sun,*
> *Made iridescent the pale quiet air. . . .*
> *When it was time to leave, reluctantly*
> *We turned our faces townward, shivering*
> *And tired now, for light and warmth were left*
> *Behind. Oh, we well knew what was awaiting us;*

---

* Some of which Jackson saved his entire life. Sample exchange from a note found at Dartmouth:
  [HE:] "Would you like to be a boy?"
  [SHE:] "Gee, you bet I would. If I were a boy this school wouldn't have to be so darned unexciting."
In his most notable Bettina story, "A Red-Letter Day," Jackson writes of the time a favorite English teacher intercepted one of Don and Bettina's notes, finally returning it with a lot of blue-penciled marginalia: "unity," "repetitive," etc.

> *Reproachful eyes, recriminations shrill,*
> *The sad bewilderment of those who loved*
> *But never understood us. . . .*
> *Like dim wraiths, we moved*
> *Through our slow separate hours, only alive,*
> *When, books beneath our arms, we started forth*
> *To keep our tryst with beauty and with truth.**

Beauty and Truth were bywords, as both considered themselves Platonists and their attachment chaste—though on double dates they "conscientiously petted" for the sake of appearance. In "A Red-Letter Day," Don is startled when a mutual friend remarks that Bettina is, in fact, madly in love with him. The next day he mentions as much in one of his notes to her: "I told [the friend] it was time she grew up," he writes. "Anyway it's too silly to talk about it."

DURING HIS SOPHOMORE YEAR, Jackson was hired to work after school and on Saturdays at the Newark *Courier.* For ten dollars a week he typed up obituaries and wedding announcements from notes taken over the phone, and also confected long, flattering pieces about local events such as bake sales held by the Eastern Star—always careful to list as many names as possible, along with their respective titles (Worthy Matron, Star Point)—and front-page items about new businesses in town, the better to pique public interest and attract larger advertisements from the merchants in question. Jackson also had his own column, "School Notes," in which he reported on "interesting additions" to the community gymnasium ("A couple of large mattresses for tumbling"), or that Miss Elizabeth Loomis had now "returned to her duties as teacher in the East Newark school" after a two-week absence due to her mother's death.

Jackson loved the job, not least because it gave him a haven of perfect privacy—a "second home," even—especially at night or on Sundays when he had the office to himself. Alone, he could put aside the puff pieces, jocular filler, and often curious personals,† and (while looking

---

* Toward the end of Marion's life, in the late 1980s, her family collected her poetry into a bound volume, *Mismatched Beads on a Broken String.*

† Witness this (not altogether atypical) item from the nearby Clyde *Times* on November 16, 1916, found directly beneath an account of the deaths of Thelma and Richard Jackson: "My wife having left my bed and board without just cause or

busy in the storefront window on Main Street) work on his own poetry, some of which was even published in the *Courier* if it struck a properly whimsical or solemn note—or both, as in the case of "Elegy Written in Newark Churchyard," whose parodic opening quatrain reads:

> *The six-ten trolley speaks the close of day,*
> *The factories disgorge their multitude,*
> *The merchant homeward plods his weary way,*
> *And leaves me in a contemplative mood.*

From there the poem becomes a maudlin lament about the loss of religious faith in an age of Progress (quite unlike what Jackson would write in his last notorious piece for the *Courier*), and beseeches the reader to return to the church and "gain true spirit happiness at last." Such sentiments were perhaps influenced by the newspaper's owner and publisher, Allyn T. Gilbert, who took pains to discourage Charlie's poetry as "high-brow"; otherwise the man was properly grateful for the boy's willingness to write almost every word of the newspaper, while a woman named Hester Herbert handled the books, read proof, and ran down advertisements. "I was always very fond of Allyn," Jackson wrote a fellow Newarkian after Gilbert's death in 1947, "[though we] had our serious differences at the *Courier*. . . ." Apart from the question of poetry, Jackson was disconcerted by the man's constant off-color raillery (Gilbert was apt to notice, for instance, the figure of Justice's "big buzooms" on a poster decrying "hun atrocities" in Belgium), so at odds with his piety at other times, and never mind the rumor that he was conducting a shabby affair with Miss Herbert—one reason, among many, that Charlie's mother didn't like the boy hanging around the *Courier* office, especially after hours.

Before long, however, he'd do everything but sleep there. On June 7, 1921, the commencement exercises for Jackson's class at Newark High were held at the Park Presbyterian Church, where the Honorable Charles G. Gordon of Pennsylvania exhorted graduates "to keep themselves clean, honest, honorable, true, square, conscientious, but, above all, honest," and the renowned local tenor Herbert Quance sang "Pale Hands I Love" to the usual ovation. After that, Jackson became a full-time *Courier* employee, appearing on the masthead as "Local Editor," which meant

---

provocation. I hereby caution all persons not to harbor or trust her on my account. WILLIAM UPHAM."

that he now washed windows and swept out the office in addition to his previous duties. "A Progressive Newspaper in a Progressive Town" was the *Courier*'s slogan, without any apparent levity, and for a while Jackson seemed to relish his newfound civic importance: he declared the Firemen's Picnic a "Howling Success" on the front page; he warned citizens against jaywalking downtown; he endorsed the new "Crook Picture" at the movie theater (commending its happy ending: "The girl, reformed, wins the hand of the district attorney"); and, in general, he ensured a certain social transparency with frequent bulletins on the everyday doings of his friends and neighbors (and family: "Frederick Jackson has been visiting Richard Comstock on Crescent Beach, Sodus Bay").

Meanwhile his friend Marion reminded him of their common resolve to escape Arcadia and realize their dreams in the wider world. Jackson's first unpublished novel, *Simple Simon*—initially written as a three-act play with the same title—as well as a radio script and various Don and Bettina stories (published and not) all concern the central dilemma of an idealistic girl trying to chide a gifted young man out of his small-town complacency.* "You don't want to stay here and be a big fish in a little pond," she says, again and again; "fish don't *grow* in a little pond!" The young man—all but seduced by an insidious sense of self-importance as editor of the local newspaper—concedes her point, and sees too that the "secret of [her] attraction" for him is that she makes him believe in himself.

By the fall of 1922, Jackson had raised enough money to send himself to Syracuse University, whereas Marion had finished her first year at the University of Rochester. In "A Red-Letter Day," Don and Bettina celebrate their imminent liberation with a long, festive day in Rochester (an hour's trolley ride from Arcadia), where they see a movie and a play, eat a good lunch and dinner, and linger at a bookstore on Spring Street, where the proprietor—a funny old man with a goatee and pince-nez—takes a shine to the couple, giving Bettina a tinted print of Botticelli's *Primavera* and Don a copper medallion with Beethoven's profile. Hating the "dull thought of home," the two prolong their adventure with drinks at a speakeasy and thus miss the last trolley back, spending the night at Bettina's brother's house in East Rochester. Don is about to retire,

---

* Freddie and Janet, protagonists of *Simple Simon* the play, are renamed Taddem and Bettina in the novel. A compressed version of the story is told yet again in Jackson's first original radio script for CBS, *A Letter from Home* (1939), in which the characters are named Frederick and Bettina.

when Bettina calls him into her room and asks him to hold her; stiffly Don obliges, though he's suddenly "overcome with a feeling of oppression that amounted almost to a smothering sensation": "He was never to know, later or ever, how long they lay together like that, she under the blankets, he outside, yet clasped together. But it was a stranger he held, and he was a stranger lying there, no one known to her at all."* Desperate to get away, Don rushes out to fetch a cigarette, and when he returns the door is locked against him. The next morning a miserable silence prevails between the two, until finally they get off the trolley in Arcadia and begin walking up Main Street, whereupon Bettina puts Don at ease somewhat by remarking that she wishes he were her son ("I'd love to bring you up"). But apparently her most memorable valediction—precisely recycled in everything from *Simple Simon* to *The Lost Weekend* to *A Second-Hand Life*—was this: "I honestly think you're going to amount to something rather wonderful . . . even though I'm not sure of my own place in the picture."

THE NINETEEN-YEAR-OLD Charles Jackson who arrived at Syracuse University on September 20, 1922, had come a long way from the touchy loner of five years before. His precocious success at the *Courier*—combined with Marion's almost unconditional esteem—had given him a lighthearted confidence "with just a shade of swaggering," as he later put it. At Syracuse he registered for six courses in the College of Business Administration, including economics, stenography, and journalism (probably his intended major). Not that he was particularly interested in academics: "It was the '*experience*' of the thing that he wanted," he wrote in *Native Moment*, an unpublished novel (completed in 1935) about that disastrous year; "but what experience he expected to get out of it, he could not have said."

Right away he found success on the monthly literary magazine, *The Phoenix*, where he was asked to join the editorial staff after contributing work in various genres. His growth as a poet may be measured by a willingness to mock his own derivations. "Where have I been today?" asks the eponymous "Wind" of Jackson's first submission. "Through forests vast and deep / Down canyons bottomless; / Climbed precipices steep . . . "

---

* This scene was also cannibalized into *A Second-Hand Life*—a crucial episode, when Harry Harrison gets his most decisive inkling of eunuch-hood.

His fondness for Thomas Gray was more openly acknowledged in a subsequent poem, "The Rubaiyat of Why-I-Am," to say nothing of Shakespeare, Milton, Byron, and Shelley, who, the narrator admits, have long ago written what he himself would like to write:

> *But just because another got there first,*
> *And wrote the lines I've not as yet rehearsed,*
> *I must, though I am equally as great,*
> *Resign myself to Destiny, accursed.*

Other work for the magazine included an homage to Fitzgerald (Scott, not Edward), "The Beautiful and Slammed," described on the contributors' page as "a change in the regular Phoenix diet." A "racy narration" about an amorous couple in a canoe, Freddie and a flapper named Pete ("the vogue for masculine nick-names had caused her to discard her too uncolorful 'Mary' "), its two pages of banter end suddenly, and racily, when the canoe gives a "violent roll" that results in "the inevitable": "But it wasn't the canoe tipping over." Finally, too, Jackson styled himself as an archly pedantic theater critic, once more alluding to the *Rubáiyát* in his review of the Syracuse dramatic season, "A Book of Curses Underneath the Bough": "If there is anything that makes our blood literally boil," he began, "it is to hear someone say, 'One ought to go to the theatre to be amused; there is enough sadness and trouble in life without having to see it reproduced on the stage.' . . . To believe in the theatre as a place merely to be amused is like trying to 'kid' yourself that the world is a Pollyanna paradise, and that we are all little glad-children."

Perhaps his greatest coup that first semester—so he thought at the time—was pledging Psi Upsilon, the fourth-oldest fraternity on campus, whose distinguished national alumni included Cornelius Vanderbilt and two United States presidents (Arthur and Taft). The fraternity had seemed to augur well from the start: the first night of rush, Jackson had entered the Psi U house and noticed that a young man playing the piano was none other than Wilkie Smith, whom he'd known as a little boy in Newark, just before the Jackson family moved into Wilkie's house at 238 Prospect! "And here he is," Charlie wrote Marion, "a member of the same fraternity to which I am pledged! Can you beat it?!!?!!?!!?!!" Pledging had helped repair his relations with Marion, too, since he'd noticed how others in the house tended to display conspicuous photos of their sweethearts ("It had never occurred to him before to ask for [Bettina's] picture," he wrote in *Native Moment*, "but now he wanted it very much"), and besides he needed a date to the Psi U formal in early December. "Gee, I'm thrilled to tears!" Marion wrote her best friend, Betty Colclough, on getting the news. "I'm paralyzed now for fear something will happen so I can't go (or else Charlie will change his mind)." Certainly he'd seemed rather cool to her those first weeks at Syracuse: when Marion, in a letter, had "casually mentioned" that his old friend Jack Burgess had taken her to see *Oliver Twist*, Charlie had replied with a kind of debonair relief, pointing out that their "love"—"get that!" Marion indignantly glossed for Colclough's benefit—seemed headed for "the same glorious finale . . . as Anthony and his Southern Girl* (and several other Literary Characters whom I [Marion] don't remember just now)." But fate seemed to be working in Marion's favor. In that same letter asking her to the Psi U formal, Charlie had mentioned a bizarre coincidence whereby his best friend in the pledge class, Johnny Brust, had showed him photos one night of "the two Betties, [Brust's] little mountain maids"—that is, Marion and Betty Colclough, who had worked with Brust at the same resort hotel that summer! "Picture if you can the scene that followed my telling him that 'Betty' was the 'Marion' I had been raving to him about for so long," Jackson wrote. "It was a debauch of risibility."

Truth be known, Charlie's eye had wandered well away from Marion, and now "continually rested, with keen enjoyment" on a handsome older pledge named Parton Keyes.† As Jackson wrote in *The Lost Weekend*, "All the woeful errors of childhood and adolescence came to their crashing climax . . . in the passionate hero-worship of an upperclassman during his very first month at college, a worship that led, like a fatal infatuation, to scandal and public disgrace. . . ." Were it not for Keyes, Charlie might have been a model pledge: he was always careful to doff his freshman cap in the presence of a member, to appear at dinner with his pledge pin in his lapel, and even to resist the temptation of befriending a Negro in his English class ("he thought of his fraternity and decided it would not do"). But apparently Keyes exerted a heady pull: his fictional counterpart, Tracey Burke, is portrayed in *Native Moment* as a dashing ne'er-do-well who has pledged "Kappa U" every autumn for the past five years, until

---

* Presumably Anthony Patch from *The Beautiful and Damned*, clearly on Jackson's mind at the time. Anthony's affair with a Southern girl, Dorothy, is sordid, and leads to his nervous collapse.
† The young man's real name, according to Jackson's vast index for *What Happened*. The character is called Tracey Burke in both *Native Moment* and *The Lost Weekend*.

he's invariably expelled by the dean for failing to pay tuition or attend class. Still, the twenty-six-year-old is allowed to linger around the fraternity because of his roguish charm: "He borrowed money without embarrassment, and the smile with which he said 'Thanks' was a tacit, even humorous, acknowledgment that he had no intention of paying it back."

In *The Lost Weekend*, the "fraternity nightmare" is based on a misunderstanding—little more than a matter of "hero-worship"—but the Tracey Burke of *Native Moment* is subtly vicious, contriving to exploit protagonist Phil Williams's essential innocence and susceptibility. At one point he tells Phil about his brothel-hopping in France, and lets drop, "Then there's a couple of houses with guys in 'em, but Toulon's more the place for that." When Phil seems puzzled, Burke laughs and says, "Well, you'll learn." The lesson in question takes place the night of the fraternity formal, after Phil has left his date, Bettina, at a sorority house in the company of a hometown girlfriend.* Returning to the Kappa U house, Phil finds Tracey asleep in his (Phil's) bed, reeking of liquor; careful not to wake him, Phil squeezes under the blankets and is, to put it mildly, surprised when Tracey begins "pressing against him with slow rude pressure," while whispering an awful command into his ear:

> [Phil] lay rigid in that embrace, faint with excitement, but his fright weakened him, he trembled, he closed his eyes. A sweet terror plunged down through his breast again and again, a terror and yearning that left him helpless. He could not think; he knew only one thing: at this moment he loved Tracey Burke (the affectionate rude-pressing arm smothered the violent beating of his heart) and he would do what was demanded of him . . . no one existed for him in the wide world but Tracey here in the night, he could not help himself now. . . .
>
> The arm about him tightened and relaxed, tightened and relaxed, the whispered words came again. The arm tightened, another reached under his head, it encircled his shoulders and held him tight. Then it pressed down, urging him, persuading him, slowly, with firm insistent strength, beneath the blankets. . . .

---

* According to Jackson's letter, Marion was to spend the night of the formal at the Gamma Phi Beta house, as guest of one Mildred Sucker, no less.

Phil gets his first hint of the ordeal ahead when Tracey rolls away from him afterward—"as if from a total stranger"—and goes back to sleep without so much as a good night. Racked with remorse and foreboding, he tries to mollify Tracey with a desperate letter ("I beg you to forgive it, and forget it, as I have tried to forgive it"), but soon learns that committing his deed to paper is a very bad idea. "Have you always conducted yourself like a gentleman in this house?" a member of the Senior Council demands, shortly after Phil returns for the spring semester. Sickeningly it dawns on him that Tracey has nothing to lose by admitting the incident—indeed, is probably "amused by his conquest": "Phil had been the active one, the one who had done what had been done and committed the unspeakable act which was more damnable in the eyes of the fraternity than any other in the whole catalogue of crime—the loathsome, the despicable act, the thing that grown-up men, even boys, simply did not do, or think of, joke about, or even mention." For a while Phil tries to play dumb—given that he'd made Tracey return his apologetic letter almost immediately, he figures it's a matter of his word (that of a model pledge) against the disreputable Burke's—but the third-degree sessions in the Senior Study only become more brutal and insistent. In *Farther and Wilder*, Don remembers being "on trial before the Senior Council in the Kappa U house," during which he's threatened with imprisonment and worse: "Do you know what we used to do with guys like you in the Navy when we caught them doing what you've done?" one interrogator snarls. "We used to take them to the stern of the ship during the middle of the night and throw them over, and nobody ever saw or heard of them again!" Finally, in *Native Moment*, Phil disintegrates under the pressure—despising himself not only for the "crime" he's committed, but also for the "shameless lies" he's forced to tell in his own defense, in one case claiming as an (ineffectual) alibi that he'd slept with Bettina the night of the formal. And meanwhile, worst of all, is "the obsession that there was something wrong with him, he was incomplete, abnormal, an outcast, and had no place among other people."*

---

* In his JAXON notebook, Charlie wrote a scene in which Phil discovers the following passage in *Moby Dick*, which causes him to weep with "a kind of mutual and brotherly misery": "But were the coming narrative to reveal, in any instance, the complete abasement of poor Starbuck's fortitude, scarce might I have the heart to write it; for it is a thing most sorrowful—nay, shocking—to expose the fall of valor in the soul. . . . That immaculate manliness we feel within ourselves, so far within us that it remains intact though all the outer character seem gone, bleeds with keen-

At any rate Phil breaks down and confesses, whereupon it's revealed to him that Tracey had shown his letter, while it was briefly in his possession, to Phil's most rabid accuser (Jackson later told his editor at Macmillan, Robert Markel, that the letter had been read aloud to the entire fraternity). He is then kicked out of Kappa U, effective immediately, with the one consolation that the reason for his departure will remain a secret: "We don't want a scandal going the rounds of the campus about Kappa U any more than you do."* All but dead of humiliation, Phil decides to lie low until June in the rooming house where he'd lived the previous semester, explaining to his family that he needs a quiet place to study ("He knew they would not believe it; but he knew, too, that they would not question").

Jackson was deeply scarred by the experience, whatever its particulars. One more dread, of many, was that he would someday meet a former member of Psi U who knew the ghastly facts. In *The Lost Weekend*, Don finds himself chatting with a total stranger who claims to have been in the same pledge class—impossible, Don thinks, until it transpires that the man hadn't actually joined until May ("They kicked a guy out just before Easter Week and made a place for me"): "Out of the past, across miles and years, the accusing finger of the Senior Council pointed at him over the bar." In *The Common Sense of Drinking*—later a kind of Bible for Jackson—Richard Peabody noted how alcoholics are haunted by a sense of inferiority caused by "shocks, humiliations, accidents, failures . . . and the doing of some act which, even if unknown to the outside world, degrades the individual in his own eyes." For Jackson such shocks would mass into an almost inescapable cloud of guilt, all the more horrible for being hard, ultimately, to define.

THERE WAS SOME COMFORT in returning to a town where the worst was already known about him, more or less. Folks in Newark murmured that

---

est anguish at the undraped spectacle of a valor-ruined man." The title of Jackson's second published novel, *The Fall of Valor*—about a middle-aged professor's infatuation with a handsome Marine—was taken from this passage.

* A final twist of the knife—also suggested in *Farther and Wilder*—is Phil's being forced to confess to his best friend, Johnny, that the accusations are true. The latter, based on Johnny Brust, is named Johnny Carr in *Native Moment*, whereas Don Birnam in *The Lost Weekend* drunkenly phones Johnny *Barker* one night, years later, to ask whether he believed the whole fraternity rumor: "Write me about it sometime," says Barker ("bored and sleepy").

Charlie had been "busted out of Syracuse," but for the most part they kept their speculation to themselves, and Allyn Gilbert was just happy to have such a hardworking editor back on the *Courier* masthead. Jackson embraced the relative security of small-town life with what seemed a kind of chastened zeal. One of the most anticipated events of the year was the *Elks' Minstrels & Frolic*, and Jackson not only hyped it in the newspaper (it "is to the local theatregoer what the Ziegfield [*sic*] Follies is to the Manhattan fan"), but played an unusual role in that autumn's production: "From the standpoint of talent and humor," the *Courier* reported, "Charles Jackson as 'The Rose of Washington Square,' certainly draws honorable, if not first, mention. In a most difficult female impersonation, this young star . . . brought down the house in his almost professional interpretation of the part of a blaze Greenwich Village queen." That Jackson himself almost certainly wrote this glowing notice leaves one musing over whatever level of irony (if any) was intended: what curious form of celebrity had he come to covet in that quiet hamlet?

His friend Marion, anyway, was not amused, and in fact seemed to view her friend's downfall as something akin to tragedy. In *The Lost Weekend*, Don cannot think of his old friend Dorothy (the Marion character) except with shame—not simply because he'd "allowed her to love him as he had not loved her . . . but because he had allowed her to believe in him." Certainly Marion's disillusionment is borne out by a poem she wrote that year (1923), "La Voyage de la Jeunesse," in which "Philemon" sails in quest of the "nameless thing his heart desired," and returns, utterly defeated, "to the home of his youth":

> *He stood no more with his face to the breeze,*
> *Forever behind him were uncharted seas.*
> *His ship came a-limping with tattered black sails,*
> *Her once polished body scarred by mad gales.*
> *Alas, there's nothing worth wanting!*
> > *Wept Philemon.*

"She is never to escape this attachment," Jackson prophesied as early as the late 1920s, when he wrote of their friendship in *Simple Simon*; "her whole life is to be dominated by this spiritual (if not romantic) union." If indeed she never escaped, it wasn't for lack of trying. She later told her daughter that she'd decided against marrying Jackson because he was homosexual, though it's doubtful he ever asked her; meanwhile, around the time of his ignominious return from Syracuse, she'd already met her future husband in Rochester. "Bumpy" was the son and namesake of the city's most celebrated woodcarver, Thillman Fabry, whose work included the grand staircase at the George Eastman House and decorative wall elements in the Eastman School of Music. Young Bumpy had little talent in that direction, though he obediently quit school in eighth grade to work in his father's business. As for Marion, she worshiped the artistic father and found warm acceptance from his wife and nine children—a family where she actually seemed to belong—though she had misgivings, still, about giving up her soulmate, whatever his proclivities otherwise. Another poem she wrote that year, "Medieval Argument," describes a dream in which a battle is waged between "mind and soul":

> . . . *My soul did weep*
> *That parting from my first love I must bear.*
> *My mind rejoiced to see that this affair*
> *Was nearly ended, bidding my soul peep*
> *Into the future and panacea find*
> *For present woe. . . .*
> *When I awoke and still I sadly sighed,*
> *Since dreams wear motley and consciousness is blind*
> *And ten to one that roseate future lied!*

Perhaps, though by all accounts she made the best of it. Three years after she married Bumpy, her father-in-law died and his business failed amid the Depression and Bumpy's incompetence. For a few years the couple made ends meet by selling flowers (since they lived opposite a cemetery) and redwood lawn ornaments that Bumpy would cut—late at night, after a long day pumping gas—and Marion would paint as flamingos, fairies, and the like. At last Bumpy was able to buy his own service station, where he employed their oldest son, Chap, as a mechanic. To the end, sporadically, Marion and Charlie stayed in touch. When she received his wedding announcement in 1938, she wrote a little wistfully that she pictured the couple "as leading a very gay and glamorous life," what with Charlie's work at CBS and Rhoda's at *Fortune*. A year later she listened to Jackson's radio play *A Letter from Home*, about a rich hack of a screenwriter who repines over his lost Bettina, the hometown girl who believed in his talent, whereas his levelheaded wife is only too tolerant of his lucrative mediocrity. ("I like [the wife] so much better than Bettina," Marion wrote the author; "she has her feet planted firmly on the ground.") Also, when Jackson became famous as the author of *The Lost Weekend*, Marion generously acknowledged the publicity photo he'd mailed her (sans comment): "It's a wonderful picture. You look so—well, integrated is the best I can do. There is no trace of the old diffidence." Sheepishly Jackson replied that he didn't deserve such a nice letter, and tried to compensate for past neglect, perhaps, by pointing out "how beautifully you write, dear Teena, and what a lovely mind you have . . ."

In any event, whatever the ups and downs of marriage to Bumpy, Marion did her best to live a cultured, examined life. In middle age she took up painting, and was soon exhibiting her work (portraits of grandchildren, black protesters in Selma) at various local venues. For forty years she met with the Women's Reading Group of Rochester, consuming almost a book a day until, at age eighty-two, a stroke made reading impossible. At night sometimes, sitting in her own living room, she'd plaintively announce that she wanted to go home. "We're here," her gathered family would say. "Look, your paintings are on the wall!" But Marion would insist, until finally they'd have to put her in the car and drive her around the block a few times. One of her last poems (pre-stroke) was titled "Solitary Confinement," about her failure to grasp "the dreadful facts of life" when young:

> *. . . I did*
> *not know that a pattern forms before we are*
> *aware of it, and that what we think we make*
> *becomes a rigid prison making us. In*
> *ignorance and innocence I built my own*
> *confines, and by the time I was old enough to*
> *know what I had done, there was no longer*
> *time to undo it.*

•

AFTER THE MARCH 13, 1924, issue, Charles Jackson's name disappeared from the *Courier* masthead for a couple of months. In the meantime, owner Allyn Gilbert announced that the paper was passing into "abler hands" while he pursued a "new ambition" (unspecified) in St. Petersburg, Florida. The new owner, A. Eugene Bolles, had recently moved his family to Newark from Montclair, New Jersey; for the past seven years he'd worked for Doubleday, Page & Company, as publisher of *World's Work* and other magazines, and now sought a quieter life. With nineteen employees of the Newark and Palmyra *Courier*, Bolles attended a farewell party for Mr. and Mrs. Gilbert at the Gardenier Hotel, where Charlie read a Lewis Carroll pastiche he'd composed for the occasion:

> *. . . The time has come, the walrus said,*
> *To talk of many things;*
> *Of Florida, St. Petersburg,*
> *And cabbages and kings . . .*

Two weeks after Bolles took over, Jackson returned as Local Editor, while at the same time (not incidentally?) dating Bolles's daughter, Cecilia, who was about as different from Marion Fleck as it was possible to be. Young Freddie of *Simple Simon* (the play) is about to give up his job as Local Editor and seek his fortune in Chicago, but is cajoled into staying by the genial and rather sinister publisher, Gordon, whose penetration of human nature is put to "perverted" uses ("He appreciates Freddie's superiority of intelligence, but is careful to keep this knowledge from him, while at the same time taking advantage of it"). Whether Charlie was likewise planning to leave town that spring—as he presently would in any case—is hard to say; ditto the part that Bolles's daughter played in the bargain. In *Home for Good*, Mercer Maitland defers his brilliant career as a novelist by remaining editor of the Arcadia *Blade* and making a miserable ten-year marriage with the publisher's daughter, Ann "Bobbie" Holt, described as "a wife and *hausfrau* in the making, and a mother natural-born . . . no means the ideal mate for Mercer Maitland." As for Cecilia "Bob" Bolles, she'd soon prove a more nearly ideal mate for Charlie's brother Herb—an onerous job, to be sure, but one she'd manage to juggle with those of serial motherhood, "Miss Goody" columnist for her father's paper (recipes and such), as well as, eventually, Arcadia's town historian.

As for Jackson, it's possible that his momentous discovery ("From [age] twenty on, or thereabout") of the great Russian novelists was what saved him, in part, from a life of dreadful Babbittry; he would suggest as much, forty years later, in his "Homage to Mother Russia," *Rufus "Bud" Boyd*, a novel conceived in Pushkin sonnets:

> *. . . Then, when I first was introduced to*
> *Stavrogin, Rodion, Berg, Pierre,**
> *A strange new world I was not used to*
> *(And yet I was!—I had been there!)*
> *Opened, and all at once reduced to*
> *Embarrassing mediocrity*
> *My other books, my former reading;*
> *I found new selves in each succeeding*
> *Novel or tale:—identity!*
> *And, thanks to [Constance] Garnett's heavy labors,*
> *I knew the people in each tome*
> *Far better than I knew my neighbors,*
> *And found, in Czarist Russia, home.*

That symbolic homecoming coincided (in 1924) with his first grown-up attempt to write a short story, "The Silk Bandanas," whose connection to his later work was largely thematic: that is, it has to do with the ambivalent alienation of the Tonio-like artist from the common herd—two types (artist and herd) embodied here by a couple of college friends who like to go slumming in a "rummy chop-suey restaurant," the Tuxedo, while waggishly wearing silk bandanas around their necks. One friend is a shallow wisenheimer based on Johnny Brust,[†] whereas the other is a doting portrait of the author as an exquisitely sensitive young man:

> Poetically beautiful, he had the forehead of a thinker, the eyes of a dreamer, and the nose and mouth of a sensualist; and his highly-coloured olive complexion and shining black, rather long hair, completed the picture of sensitive, almost tragic, good-looks. . . . For the most part he seemed continually wrapt [*sic*] in dreams, but when he did relapse into play, his face shone with a child-like radiance and animation that was positively heart-breaking in its innocence.

This naïf becomes smitten with a languid slattern named Marjie, who ultimately absconds with his bandana to devastating (and obscurely meta-

---

* Characters from *The Possessed* (Stavrogin), *Crime and Punishment* (Rodion), and *War and Peace* (Berg, Pierre).
[†] One gathers from Jackson's 1922 letter to Marion—and even more so from various scenes in *Native Moment*—that he and Brust enjoyed "bum[ming] around" in dive bars, very like the friends in "The Silk Bandanas."

phorical) effect. "Horrific (and lousy)" Jackson declared the story a few years later, though he kept a copy among his papers as a kind of memento or bogey perhaps (and then, too, he simply hated disposing of his own work).

Once "The Silk Bandanas" was out of his system—a first attempt to describe, in acceptable form, the betrayal of his innocence at Syracuse—Jackson entered what he would someday call his "youthful Chekhov period." Among other stories, all unpublished, he wrote about an old married couple who run an unsuccessful hotel in the mountains and remain strangers to each other ("A Manuscript from the Country"); he wrote about hungry peasant children who give their last crumbs of bread to some lovely swans lighting briefly on a village lake ("The Swan Lake"); he wrote about a father and son, Russian immigrants from Illinois, who are visiting family in St. Petersburg when the war breaks out ("Troika"). The narrator's epiphany in "Troika" might suffice as a kind of blanket moral for these gray tales: "For the first time I realized how alone in life I was, and my being with my father only intensified my loneliness, because he was alone too." By far the most successful effort from this phase of his long apprenticeship, "A Pair of Shoes," pays little or no homage to Chekhov or Mother Russia, though it does give a foreglimpse of what Jackson would be writing in another decade or so. Set in a small Indiana town a mile south of Lake Michigan ("a quiescent sea of molten glass in the intense midsummer heat"), the story is about the rape of a fifteen-year-old girl by a gang of a railroad workers. The girl's boyfriend comes from the beach looking for her, and hears her screaming; then, after the rapists depart, he spies her lying naked and unconscious in a boxcar. Later, the boy himself emerges from the boxcar—where (implicitly) he's raped her too—and trips over the girl's discarded shoe: "He recoiled as if stung. . . . Then, after peering about to make sure that he was alone, he picked up the shoe by its little strap and flung it far away over the prairie, in the dark." The idea of human depravity, then and later, served to steer Jackson away from the banal and derivative. The problem, of course, was that such stories were mostly unsalable.

BY THE TIME he'd come to inhabit the "strange new world" of Russian literature, Jackson had spent more than five years writing hundreds of items like these: "Charles Bloomer is back from a fishing trip to the Adirondacks with a fine catch of fish and several new fish stories"; "Miss Frances

Gaffney of Rochester, who has been in Newark the past few days visiting Miss Lucienne Bechard, the French teacher, returned to Rochester, Monday afternoon. . . ." And so on. Eugene Bolles tried to sweeten the deal by giving Jackson his own column, "Callow Comments," where he could indulge his creativity over the coy byline "A Calla Ham," though Jackson's inaugural effort on May 15, 1924, hinted broadly at his real identity: "Behold the return of the native!" he announced, noting that he'd recently succumbed to "the comic urge for higher learning," but since then had "passed through all the wild stages of adolescence . . . and now emerges into the sober philosophy of the fading youth who has finally reached the twenty-first milestone, only to find all wars fought, all gods dead, all horses collared"—this a mocking nod to Fitzgerald, yet again, whose cynicism he now professed to find "obnoxious." It was a point of view that Calla Ham, jolliest of philistines, would sustain nicely over the months to come. "The Leather Tanners' Convention advocates walking as a health-builder," the "colyumnist" typically quipped. "Yes, there's nothing like walking to put you on your feet again!"

No wonder Calla Ham's alter ego was bitter. "Myself: the relic of early fame," Freddie laments toward the end of *Simple Simon*, denouncing himself as "one of these 'only' persons": "I'm local editor of The Arcadia *Courier*, and I'm only twenty! . . . I wrote poems when I was 'only ten'—I wrote a novel when I was 'only sixteen'—Well, what good did it ever do me?" Fiercely he swears to leave town the very next day—right after his final performance as "Simple Simon" in the *Elks' Minstrels & Frolic*—though one is left with the definite impression that Freddie will remain in Arcadia to his dying day. As for Jackson: by the end of 1924 he'd had enough of Calla Ham, nor would he be reprising his Elks role as "The Rose of Washington Square." Along with the great Russian novels, he'd recently discovered *The Mysterious Stranger*, by Mark Twain, and now saw fit to share this "little-known book" with readers of "Callow Comments" (getting "into serious trouble thereby," as he later wrote Dorothea Straus): Twain "reveals himself as a person under no illusions or delusions whatever," wrote Calla Ham, "but who regards this whole thing, life . . . as plain and simple and laughable as it is intolerable and cruel and bitter." By way of illustration, Jackson—in a startling volte-face from his previous disavowal of Fitzgeraldian cynicism—approvingly quoted a passage in which Twain's title character (Satan) delivers a bracing peroration in favor of atheism: "Strange, indeed, that you should not have suspected that your universe and its contents were only dreams, visions, fiction! Strange because they are so frankly and hysterically insane—like all dreams: a God . . . who mouths justice and invented hell—mouths mercy and invented hell—mouths Golden Rules, and forgiveness multiplied seventy times seven, and invented hell; who mouths morals to other people and has none himself . . . "

So ended Jackson's career as local editor of the Newark *Courier*. A month later he'd leave for Chicago, where he could "live and work in the same atmosphere" as idols such as Sherwood Anderson, Theodore Dreiser, Carl Sandburg, and Edgar Lee Masters—an atmosphere more free than Arcadia's, let alone the town's microcosm at 238 Prospect, where the head of the house, Herb, took a dimmer-than-ever view of his little brother, who spent his *Courier* wages on highbrow stuff like books and plays in Rochester, while Herb was stuck with the family bills! The tension would linger after Charlie's departure, though Herb gained an ally when he married Bob in 1927—this at a time when both younger brothers were gadding about (*very* disreputably, Bob thought) in New York and, later, Switzerland. "Charlie and Fred would blow in now and then," said Herb's daughter Sally, "and grandmother [Sarah] would just lay out the red carpet. The Prodigal Sons." Meanwhile, five days a week for the next thirty-five years, Herb would support his growing brood as assistant superintendent at the box factory. As for Bob, she kept her little resentments to herself, for the most part, though she did find sly ways of getting her own back. "Hey! What do you think of this letter!!" Charlie wrote Fred in 1940, forwarding Bob's latest. "There's a surprise toward the end," he added, referring to a note "written" by Bob's one-year-old son, Duncan, thus: "Thank you so much for my he-man suit. You know I have never worn a dress. Believe me I'm no pansy."

Chapter Three

Some Secret Sorrow

The most thrilling sound for Jackson, growing up, was the shriek of train whistles in the night, and finally on January 9, 1925, he boarded a train himself and permanently (more or less) left behind that hated, beloved village where "everybody knew him and had always known him." Within three months he was able to report that his many friends in Chicago had just given him a "perfectly wonderful" birthday, and moreover he'd gotten a job at Kroch's—one of the largest bookstores in the world—working in the art department.* Nothing if not personable (and vulnerable withal), Charlie was taken under the Kroch family's wing: before long he was calling Adolph, the owner, Papa ("he's a crotchety old bastard but an interesting and genuinely cultivated man"), and he would always feel tender toward Adolph's sister-in-law, Lieschen, who

---

* In a 1940 letter to a prospective employer, Jackson claimed to have been "in charge of the French department" at Kroch's, though his wife, Rhoda, later specified the art book department ("the initial source of his great knowledge of painting . . . every experience added to his education"). Rhoda, I think, is right—not only because she's the more reliable of the two, but also because Jackson's French was spotty at best, and the salesclerks at Kroch's were supposed to be experts in their particular departments.

became like a mother to him ("I truly love her"). His outward life, at least, was pleasantly regular: he enjoyed his job, and had time and energy left over to work on his fiction (along with occasional freelancing for *The Chicagoan*,* a new magazine modeled after *The New Yorker*); Saturdays he got exercise by playing tennis in Highland Park, and afterward would eat lunch at the Murrain Hotel on the lake.

Nights seemed mostly a matter of making up for lost time—"sampling such Bohemian diversions as he could uncover," as one journalist wrote. His old Newark friend Jack Burgess put a finer point on it, sixty-five years later, by observing that Charlie had fallen in with a group of "fairies" in Chicago; given that Burgess was able to identify (correctly) his steadiest companion, one assumes that Jackson was a little less inclined to dissemble, at least during these relatively liberated years of his life. Wasn't that, after all, the main point of escaping to Chicago in the first place? Later, as a family man trying to remain sober and solvent, Jackson would often complain about his inability to "get outside of [him]self"—suggesting (on one level) the entombing self-consciousness of a man who'd grown up a "sissy" in the small-town America of that era. "He cultivated a technique of personality, and it worked," Jackson wrote of Harry Harrison in *A Second-Hand Life*. "To all outward appearances it worked; and what else was needed beyond outward appearances? . . . but he knew—only he knew—that he was a prisoner." As a connoisseur of *Winesburg, Ohio*, Jackson also knew that such a prisoner was apt to become warped, a "grotesque," over time. In his early twenties, he wrote a revealing free-verse piece titled "Devil's Dialogue,"† in which a young man is mortified by the knowing smile of "a perfect stranger":

> " . . . *The possible idea I could be*
> *So shallow a mere stranger passing by*
> *Could see in me the thing I most conceal!*
> *—Why it should be, I'd give the world to know!*

---

* Or so he claimed in that same 1940 letter mentioned in the previous footnote. The most complete archive of *The Chicagoan* is at the University of Chicago's Regenstein Library, though it's missing a few early issues. Jackson's byline was not found among the available holdings.
† Written under a pen name, C. J. Storrier, and found among his papers. Storrier was his maternal grandmother's maiden name, and his brother Fred's middle name; Jackson often used it in his early fiction, typically to name characters based on himself and members of his family.

> *. . . Good Lord, I do my damnedest all the time,*
> *And play the part so fully that I almost*
> *Forget entirely my other self . . . "*
> *"I understand [the stranger replies],*
> *Although I think you overdo the matter:*
> *Such strict repression isn't necessary."*
>   *"It isn't, huh?—that's all you know about it!—*
> *Try living in a small town for a while!"*
> *"I know; but did you ever stop and think*
> *What's bound to happen if you will persist*
> *In such subdued restraint, barring all else?*
> *Nature is nature: you can't change its course."*
> *"Why no, but you can stifle it."*
>   *"Granted!—*
> *But in the stifling, what else goes with it!—*
> *All force, all power, all personality,*
> *All spirit, fire, ambition—worse, all love!*
> *And what is left?—a dull automaton! . . .*
> *That's what you will become, unless you change,*
> *Unless you heed your natural desires.—*
> *You're still young yet, and so far this repression*
> *Has had no serious damaging results;*
> *But give it time—a few years more!—and see*
> *The wreck of youth that you will have become:*
> *At twenty-five a human mechanism,*
> *Devoid of that ecstatic soul the gods*
> *Bestow alone upon their favorite children. . . .*
> *I cannot bear to see you made a slave,*
> *Afraid to know or recognize yourself,*
> *Living in fear, your own dread Frankenstein!"*

To some extent Jackson would never be free of that fear, though part of him took considerable pains to heed the advice (often invoked) that Henry James allegedly gave the young Rupert Brooke: "Don't be afraid to be happy." And then, of course, "nature is nature" whether one fears it or not. As Jackson candidly explained to his daughter's philosophy professor in 1964, "The slogan to solicit subscriptions [to *Life*] always said 'Obey that impulse'—which is the story of my life, ought to be put on my tombstone ('He obeyed that impulse') and though at times it's got me into a hell of a lot of trouble, much of it unprintable, it has at other times brought me a great deal of satisfaction and yes, even reward."

A story Jackson wrote the year after he left Chicago, "Some Secret Sorrow," suggests that he managed to find abundant trouble and satisfaction both while in the city, and also gives one a sense of the hazards faced by that generation of gay men, wherever they happened to be. "This strange, beautiful, sordid city," the narrator, Sid, muses of Chicago. "Had I known of some of the things I was to come up against here . . . I should never have had the courage to come. The strength to combat life consisted, apparently, in not knowing what was going to happen."* The story is mostly composed of a long confession ("I'm continually cutting my own throat by telling too much") given by Don,† an artist who senses a kinship with Sid. As a boy, Don was sexually exploited by an older man and his friends, and thereafter went from one disastrous liaison to the next, until at last he "learned to stay more and more by [him]self and became reconciled to the fact that [he] was different from other people, and let it go at that." Recently, though, he tried to pick up a man in Grant Park, and was almost beaten by an angry mob that gathered when the man began loudly denouncing him. Sid, for his part, reflects that Don seems oddly "a stranger" now that he's told his story, and later ignores Don's pathetic attempts to stay in touch. One senses the author divided himself pretty much equally between the two men—gave his desperate need for connection to Don, his wariness to Sid, and something of his self-loathing to both.

But what of the beautiful, satisfying aspects of being in Chicago? *Obey that impulse:* not for nothing was Jackson forever trying out, as a title, some version of Whitman's "Native Moments"—a poem that celebrates "life coarse and rank": "I am for those who believe in loose delights—I share the midnight orgies of young men." Dorothea Straus wrote of her friend's taste for "rough trade," and in his 1953 meditation, "An Afternoon with Boris," Jackson conceded that his acquaintances would be "aghast" if they knew something of his "compulsive excursions" into "the low and the lawless . . . even literally the unclean." But then, he was his father's son—never mind the priapic Williams side of the family—and

---

* The sentence provides a piquant context for Jackson's favorite title, *What Happened*, which is first mentioned in his notes (circa the early 1930s) as a possible title for his never-written "Chicago novel."
† No last name, and in most respects the character's personal history does *not* suggest Don Birnam.

such "excursions" provided, besides, a needed respite ("a revival or cleansing of the spirit") from writerly cerebration. In the opening section of *Farther and Wilder*, set in the summer of 1947, Don Birnam thanks God he is "finally old enough to know that life's problems [do] not consist of *specialités* like alcoholism, syphilis, drugs, promiscuity, and indiscriminate sexual drives toward male and female alike"; but meanwhile (around 1948 and '49) the author himself was undergoing tests at Mary Hitchcock Hospital in New Hampshire for genital herpes and syphilis, the latter first contracted in the early 1930s (if one believes a discarded passage from *The Lost Weekend*), when he endured eleven days in a fever cabinet in hope of a cure.

Amid Chicago's "Bohemian diversions," then, it was probably a relief to find a kindly older man to spend the better part of one's time with. Dr. Thorvald Lyngholm, a Danish osteopath, was thirty-six when Jackson met him on September 19, 1925 (a red-letter day duly noted in Jackson's journal), and would remain at least on the periphery of his life for almost twenty years.* In *Farther and Wilder*, Don Birnam names "Thorvald" as one of the few people he's (almost) been able to love—this apart from the "selfless, pure, undemanding" love he bears his children—and Don of "Some Secret Sorrow" waxes nostalgic about the one time his feelings were requited by another man: "It was as though a veil had been stripped from my eyes and I could now see the whole truth about everything, and beauty where before had been, to me, only existence." The most sustained tribute to Lyngholm in Jackson's work is his appearance as an osteopath named Dan Linquist in an unfinished novella written in 1928, *Three Flowers*, inspired by the author's maternal great-aunts at 414 Courtland Avenue in Syracuse.† Dr. Linquist treats these oafish spinsters—terrified by their teenage niece's pregnancy—with sweet forbearance, and his own "wholesome good-looks" are lovingly evoked: "In repose, his face seemed always as if he were thinking deeply and at the same time scenting the air. When he laughed or smiled, his serious mouth became miraculously boyish and charming, and little lines, of mirth rather than age, appeared below his eyes. . . . his good Scan-

---

* Jack Burgess, for one, remembered meeting Dr. Lyngholm for the first time a few years later in New York, at the Russian Bear Restaurant.

† In Jackson's name index for *What Happened* (probably compiled in the late 1940s), Thor Lyngholm's fictional name is also given as "Linquist," though Jackson changed the first name from Dan to Bue. *Farther and Wilder* includes a number of real names (e.g., "Thorvald") that doubtless would have been changed in revision.

dinavian head was partly bald, but the hair that remained at the sides and top was fine and silky, of a light sand color." In Jackson's play *The Loving Offenders*—also unfinished (indeed hardly begun)—one of the characters was to be a thirty-five-year-old "doctor friend" who causes a scandal by accompanying the twenty-two-year-old Ralph to his older brother's wedding.* As for the actual Thor: five years later, in 1930, a friend in New York wrote as follows to Jackson's tuberculosis sanatorium in Europe: "[Thor] feels very sad and deserted in your absence. If only he could acquire his vast wealth now I am sure he would fly over to you in a moment." Thor was trying to supplement his (evidently meager) income as an osteopath by pitching, to libraries, a process for preserving newspapers in cellophane. "So I am not very sanguine at Thor being financially improved within a short time," Charlie's friend concluded.

ONE NIGHT THAT FALL (1925), while dining at Henrici's in the Loop, Jackson spotted his favorite actress (other than Garbo), Pauline Lord, then appearing in *They Knew What They Wanted*. Jackson "crashed her table" and Lord agreed to let him backstage at her next performance, where she gave him "the thrill of [his] life" by autographing his copy of *Anna Christie*, whose titular heroine was her greatest role. (In *The Lost Weekend*, Don Birnam pays punning homage—"lord, what an artist"—to "the greatest woman in the theatre of our time.") A year later Jackson learned that Lord's play *Sandalwood* was about to close in New York, and abruptly quit his job at Kroch's and moved east in time to catch the last Saturday performance. Soon he was hired at the Doubleday store in Grand Central, and became, at night, "wrapt up in . . . the Bohemian life of Waverly Place and Sheridan Square."

He also resumed a curious friendship that had begun three years before, when (in retreat from the Syracuse disaster) he'd taken a summer job as desk clerk at a posh hotel in Eastport, Maine. As he would later tell it in his "memoir in the form of a novel"—alternately titled *The Royalist* and *Uncle Mr. Kember*—he was reading one day on a pier at the yacht club when he noticed a distinguished older man reclining in the stern of

---

* One suspects that some such "scandal" actually occurred at Herb and Bob's wedding in 1927; one way or the other, the family in Newark certainly knew of Thor's existence. Herb's oldest son and namesake—born the following year, 1928, and always known as Hup—referred to Thor by name in a letter he wrote shortly after his uncle Charlie's death in 1968.

his sailboat, also reading. "I say, young man," the latter called, in a suave mid-Atlantic accent, "it seems you're reading a Modern Library book, too." As it happened ("a coincidence in a million") they were both reading *The Odyssey*; the older man, delighted, took down the boy's name and address and subsequently mailed him the enormous Medici Society edition of *The Odyssey*, with twenty gorgeous plates by the English painter William Russell Flint. "This comes to you over the wine-dark sea," an enclosed card was inscribed, "from Telemachus of many counsels."

This generous personage was a fifty-nine-year-old bachelor named Bronson Winthrop, a man of impressive wealth and pedigree who would prove the most important elder figure in Charlie's all but fatherless life. Such a man, indeed, was far more in line with what Charlie would have liked in a forebear: "I'm afraid I don't know the Vanderbilts," Winthrop once remarked with a casual whiff of disdain, given that he (tacitly) considered them nouveau riche. He himself was descended from John Winthrop, governor of the Massachusetts Bay Colony, though he'd inherited most of his property from his mother's side of the family, the Manhattan Stuyvesants. Winthrop's upbringing was almost breathtakingly cosmopolitan: born in Paris, he was educated at Eton and Trinity College, Cambridge, after which he took a two-year Grand Tour to Peking and points beyond. In 1891 he returned to the States and got his law degree at Columbia, joining the illustrious firm of Elihu Root; when the latter left to become Secretary of State in 1905, Winthrop and his best friend, Henry Stimson (Secretary of War in the Taft and FDR cabinets), became nominal heads of the firm. Except for some time off in 1898—when he traveled (with his lifelong valet, William) to Manila as an infantry captain in the Spanish-American War—Winthrop would, for the rest of his life, devotedly ride the train each morning to his office on Liberty Street in Lower Manhattan.

Stimson referred to his friend and law partner as the Exquisite: Winthrop entertained lavishly and often ("the silver of four generations on his table"), though he liked solitude, too, or so his considerable erudition would suggest. Some of this came from his father, Egerton, also a lawyer, whose enormous portrait by Sargent hung over the son's drawing-room fireplace. A great friend of Edith Wharton,* Egerton is best remembered

---

* Jackson once asked Bronson Winthrop what Mrs. Wharton was like, recording their exchange in his notes: " 'Very interesting, I suppose, though I'm afraid a little odd.' 'How "odd"?' 'Well, in my day, ladies didn't write novels'—much as we would say, 'In my day ladies didn't become garage mechanics.' "

as the model for snobbish Sillerton Jackson (an expert on "the scandals and mysteries that had smouldered under the unruffled surface of New York society") in *The Age of Innocence*, though Wharton's memoir, *A Backward Glance*, gives a more balanced view of the man. Egerton, she wrote, was "easily entangled in worldly trifles" to be sure, but he was also a great reader and art collector, as well as a wise confidant in personal matters: "Sternly exacting toward himself, he was humorously indulgent toward others"—a statement that rather precisely describes his son's attitude, insofar as it was manifest in his relations with Charles Jackson.

Charlie had been in New York for a month or two when he retrieved Winthrop's card from *The Odyssey* and gave him a call at his office. The older man promptly asked him to lunch at the Downtown Club, where the two sat talking about literature. Winthrop seemed "shocked" by the youth's all but total ignorance of Latin and Greek, and even German and French, while Jackson explained that he had no formal education beyond high school. He did allow, however, that he knew something of Shakespeare, and the two began trying to stump each other ("Tell me, young man, the name of the play in which the following line appears . . . ")*—a game they would resume over many postprandial coffees in Winthrop's townhouse on East 72nd Street, or the mansion at his 450-acre estate on Long Island, Muttontown Meadows, where four men were employed each summer just to clear the riding paths and keep the park free of poison ivy. Charlie's time in the Bloomer house on East Avenue in Newark could hardly have prepared him for the sheer luxurious eclecticism on display chez Winthrop: the Sèvres decorated porcelain and bronze-doré boudoir clocks, the Louis XV inlaid tulipwood serpentine-front commodes, the Chippendale carved mahogany and parcel-gilded gesso wall mirrors, the Fukien porcelain statuettes of Kuan Yin, the watercolors by Rowlandson, Rackham, Cruikshank, Leech, and the world's largest collection of original Tenniel illustrations from *Alice in Wonderland* and *Through the Looking-Glass*. A lot of statuary, too—nude youths mostly (Achilles and Patroclus, frolicking satyrs and *putti*)—as well as a gallery of Winthrop's various protégés over the years.

---

* Winthrop's knowledge of the Bard was exhaustive, though Jackson remembered stumping him with the question "Was Lady Macbeth a mother?" When the man seemed flummoxed, Jackson pointed out that Lady Macbeth says, "I have given suck, and know. How tender 'tis to love the babe that milks me . . . " Winthrop slapped his thigh and started to repeat the quote—stopping short of the word "suck," which apparently embarrassed him.

Jackson realized that his own generation was apt to look "with raised eyebrows" on Winthrop's indulgence toward certain young men, though he insisted that the man's "key" trait was his innocence. Indeed, the only thing Winthrop was importunate about—vis-à-vis Charlie, at least—was his beloved Plato: "All through the Twenty's Mr. Winthrop was at me to read Plato," Jackson wrote his daughter Kate (middle name: Winthrop) in 1964, "it was something I *had* to read otherwise I would be all but imbalanced, and he even bought me a small set in the Jowett translation—in vain. I didn't or couldn't connect; I was not a thinker in those days, I was a feeler, rather, and thus got into a lot of emotional scrapes. . . . I see now why Mr. Winthrop pressed me so long to read Plato . . . [he was] trying to help me." Nor was Winthrop only interested in conveying, say, how an older man's passion for a promising youth might be transmuted into a higher spiritual force, but also how a wise man faces death, à la Socrates in *The Apology* ("It is pretty grand in its simplicity," he wrote Charlie). Jackson, for his part, urged Winthrop to read comparatively racy stuff such as Compton Mackenzie's *Vestal Fire*, about a bearded pederast (Count Bob) who moons over his fetching young secretary, Carlo. "It is a curious book isn't it," Winthrop calmly responded. "As you say the world has changed." And meanwhile, too, Charlie introduced his new mentor to Dr. Lyngholm, who endeavored to cure the man's cold with an osteopathic maneuver that "fairly throttled [him]": "my cold disappeared," Winthrop wrote, "but whether it was the black magic or a cough mixture which a milder practitioner gave me I cannot tell."

CHARLIE HAD BEEN in New York for just over a year when his little brother arrived to study painting at the Art Students League, and the two took an apartment together. Fred Jackson was a lovable young man—sweet, ebullient, possessed of a "truly magical charm," as Charlie put it—such that even folks in Newark were somewhat willing to overlook what they considered his dubious qualities; as for his fellow art students and employees at Brentano's (where he worked the evening shift), they adored him, all the more given that he was not only personable but comely. Fred's artistic talent was slight and rather beside the point; like his brother he'd left Newark to *live*, and in that capacity he would always shine. Around this time Charlie and Fred became known among friends as Pou (louse) and Boom, respectively; the latter nickname (a *nom d'amour*, perhaps, whose provenance remains mysterious) would stick for the rest of Fred's life. Night after night the two cultivated "very artistic bars" in the Village, and for that year's Art Students League Ball ("a dusk to dawn affair at the old Webster Hall of fond memory") Boom came attired in nothing but a jockstrap covered with tiny brass bells. Nor was such costume particularly outré in that milieu. Their best friend was a roisterous Stanford graduate with the stately name Haughton College Bickerton ("Bick"), whose home in Sausalito would become a refuge for both brothers (especially Boom, who visited almost yearly). "There's nobody in the entire US I'd rather see, no, not even C. Chaplin & G. Garbo together, than Bick," Charlie wrote Boom from Hollywood in 1949, mentioning a couple of roadside signs he was eager to describe for their old friend: "VISIT THE RATTLESNAKE GARDEN PANSY BEDS"; "MOHAWK CABINS: Lunches, Sandwiches, Hot & Cold Water, Truck Drivers."

Charlie's life was more strenuous than ever, now that his indefatigable brother was in town. The previous summer he'd worked at a hotel in the Berkshires, where, after a long day of tennis, he developed a sharp pain under his right shoulder that began to worsen the following winter; also he was coughing a lot and felt exhausted all the time. Still, he pushed himself harder than ever: he put in long hours at a Womrath branch bookstore on Broadway, while at night (whatever his other diversions) he steadily worked at his writing. His "Chekhov phase"—or at least that part of it involving Russian (or Russian-like) scenes and characters—was coming to an end; now that he no longer lived in Arcadia, he felt a great compulsion to evoke the place in all its galling beauty and sordid, small-minded humanity.

Three Flowers transplants his spinster great-aunts from Syracuse to the smallest house on Grant Street in Arcadia, where each Sunday they make a dutiful round of their neighbors to discuss the relative coldness of the winter, the prospects for a good corn crop, and "just who really was paying off the mortgage for that widow-woman near Boulder Hill." Relegated to a cot in the maid's room is their teenage niece, Evelyn, a spiteful reminder of their dead sister (Evelyn's mother), whom they never forgave for leaving home to marry a worthless man. One night Evelyn is stricken by a mysterious illness, and it falls to the kindly Dr. Linquist to explain to the sisters that the girl has been binding her stomach to conceal a pregnancy, and will probably give birth to a stillborn child ("and oddly enough it was this fact, of all that he had advanced, which seemed to cheer the sisters"). The novella peters out around page 30, when the sisters take the doctor into their confidence with "passionate outpourings" about their empty, ignorant lives—at which point Jackson switches from dialogue to indirect description, except for the oldest sister's one-line lament, "Life might of been different for us if—if—if things had been different." Whatever implausible "outpourings" preceded this pathetic tautology remain a mystery to the reader, and apparently to Jackson, too, who stalled at essentially the same point in the story when he tried to rewrite it as a three-act play.

He also resorted to both genres for his Arcadian bildungsroman, *Simple Simon*, though the novel (unlike the play) survives only as a couple of promising fragments and a few notes in his journal.* Whereas the play focuses almost entirely on the protagonist's rut as the local editor of the Arcadia *Courier*, the novel covers the same character's earlier years as a sensitive adolescent with no interest in sports or girls†—a time when his only friends were Bettina and the odd discontented matron ("childless married women whose husbands are good providers and who have nothing to do"). One of these is Mrs. Crandall, whose "high sarcastic sense of humor" is endearing at first, but proves mostly a matter of idle, self-indulgent bitterness: "In small towns there are always a few people whose quasi-rebellious spirits find an outlet in ridiculing their village and bemoaning the fact that fate has placed them among such a mess of morons." While Arcadia is hardly ideal for such would-be intellectuals, Jackson nicely suggests how Mrs. Crandall becomes her own worst enemy (among many). Wasting the better part of her wit on cursing the darkness—especially her well-meaning boob of a husband (a model Arcadian, naturally)—she suffers the inevitable nervous breakdown, which gives her gleeful neighbors an excuse to spread the rumor she's taking dope. Finally, "recovered," she's reduced to a misanthropic shell ("Ligeia in cap and bells"). As for *Simple Simon* the play, it soon becomes bogged down in dithering conversations about whether or not Freddie will test himself in the wider world, and there is little of the novel's more nuanced satire. Freddie, in effect, is a preening ninny who lets himself be flattered by rubes on the one hand, and browbeaten by the insufferably

---

* "So far as I remember," Rhoda Jackson wrote after her husband's death, "the MSS of SIMPLE SIMON [the novel] was lost, years before. (That loss may have caused his later habit of taking three of four carbons of everything he wrote.)" Again, a couple of fragments did survive—perhaps twenty-five pages in all—that are almost certainly from this novel, or so Jackson's notes suggest.

† Though, as mentioned earlier, the character is named Taddem in the novel and Freddie in the play.

high-minded Janet (the Bettina character) on the other. "If Love is a city, then you and I are only living in the suburbs," the latter declaims at one point. "I once hoped that we could move into the heart of it together."

In the midst of these labors, Jackson began spitting up blood in the morning—though he was loath to mention it, lest he be returned to Newark. On April 27, 1928, however, he hemorrhaged while attending the theater ("rais[ing] three mouthfuls of blood," his doctor carefully noted), and was taken to Bellevue. Within a couple of weeks, his tubercular right lung had been collapsed via pneumothorax—an injection of air between the ribs, the common (if questionable) treatment in those preantibiotic days—and he was left with nothing to do but lie there and wait.

At last, in July, he was sent to Devitt's Camp, a sixty-acre sanatorium in western Pennsylvania ("in the heart of the White Deer Mountains") started by an idealistic physician named William Devitt, a great believer in fresh air, fresh food, sunbaths, and virtuous living very much in general. It was a spartan life: the 128 patients lived two to a cabin—unheated except for a small potbellied stove—and slept on open-air porches in all weathers. Naturally Jackson considered writing a novel about the experience, to be titled *The Dark Confinement*, which hardly suggests the more larkish side of things. "Remember the night the three of us killed a couple quarts of wine," a fellow patient wrote Jackson many years later. "And the bare footprint in the dried puddle of wine on the floor next morning?" Such a telltale spoor would have provoked bitter reproof from Dr. Devitt, though perhaps he was apt to be lenient in Jackson's case, seeing as how the poor young man had abruptly become bald in just that one year.

Meanwhile he'd given his brother Fred a letter of introduction to Mr. Winthrop, thinking the two might hit it off despite an ostensible lack of common interests, as they did ("and thereby hangs a tale," Charlie would write, "a tale, indeed, that was to influence our lives for almost the next eighteen years"). During their first lunch together, Winthrop asked the delightful Boom whether he was enjoying his studies at the League, and the youth replied that while life on the whole was certainly agreeable, he'd recently decided he'd rather do something along the lines of design or decoration, ideally under the tutelage of the great (but expensive) Winold Reiss. Mr. Winthrop thought it might be arranged. A few weeks later, alas, Boom was visiting Charlie—for whose benefit he vivaciously demonstrated Angna Enters's "Field Day" dance, which he'd seen the night before—when he suddenly hemorrhaged. ("I didn't tell her this last part," Charlie later reported, having eventually met Miss Enters in Hollywood.) Soon the two brothers were sharing a large room in the basement of the Devitt's Camp hospital, as their condition was deemed rather grave: "sick as we were," Charlie noted, "the two of us had the time of our lives."

WHILE AT DEVITT'S, Boom was visited by a coworker at Brentano's, Rhoda Booth, a recent graduate of Connecticut College who—ten turbulent years later—would become Mrs. Charles Jackson. Rhoda was a Scot from Barre, Vermont. Her parents, John and Isabella, were born and raised in Aberdeen, and both spoke with thick Scottish burrs; John, a stonecutter and chairman of the Barre school board, doted on his older daughter and saw to it that she got an excellent education. In 1930, after two years at Brentano's, Rhoda would join the staff of Henry Luce's new magazine, *Fortune*, where she worked for such famous writers as Archibald MacLeish ("She was an ideal researcher") and James Gould Cozzens, a good friend whose wife, Bernice Baumgarten, would become Charlie's longtime literary agent.

Rhoda, in short, was "a remarkably interesting woman," as her future husband would be the first to acknowledge—though how these two should come to be married was a puzzle, to put it mildly. As Dorothea Straus observed, they seemed "totally unrelated": Rhoda "was as monosyllabic and repressed as [Charlie] was voluble and dramatic. She was tall and straight, with wide features, a fair complexion, and smiling blue [hazel] eyes that expressed endurance rather than merriment." She would have *much* to endure, and would endure it with a kind of workmanlike stoicism. This, after all, was her style: where her husband was a dandy who favored bow ties and tailored suits, Rhoda wore clothes for comfort ("their children often spoke of a gray-and-white number she was fond of as her 'Puritan' dress") and refused to touch up her colorless hair with even a slight auburn rinse. Their friend Max Wylie considered her "the finest woman [he] ever knew": calm, scrupulous, eminently sensible and literal-minded—a compendium of things Charlie was not, and thus either the perfect or worst imaginable mate (or something of both). "Had there ever been such a thing [as intimacy] between them, even at the beginning?" Don wonders of his wife, Helen, in *Farther and Wilder*. "Not, at least, as he understood the word and had experienced the feeling himself, with so many others." Time and again, for the next forty years, an exalted Charlie would endeavor to share with Rhoda one of his many passions—Schubert's "Trout" Quintet, say, or a passage from Mann—and presently find her snoring or glancing furtively at box scores (she was crazy about baseball), and it would occur to him, again, but with renewed bemusement every time, that "neither one of them, actually, was the kind of person the other even liked."

Be that as it may, Charlie's budding friendship with the taciturn but attractive young woman was only one aspect of his relative good fortune. Now that Boom was also at Devitt's, Mr. Winthrop had begun showering the two with "fantastic gifts": bed jackets and bathrobes and lap rugs of luxurious camel's hair, cashmere sweaters and bed socks, two electric heaters, a portable Victrola, calf-bound editions of Shakespeare and Jowett's *Dialogues of Plato*, and charge accounts at Brentano's and the Liberty Music Shop. One weekend Mr. Winthrop came down to see how the boys were getting along, and was "shocked" by what struck him as an almost ghastly squalor: "Why, it's monstrous! Monstrous!" he muttered, though Boom and Charlie did their best to assure him that they were all but perfectly content. Mr. Winthrop would have none of it, insisting they find a more suitable place immediately.

To be sure, while Boom had much improved, Charlie's condition continued to deteriorate: over the last few months his weight had dropped from 142 to 125, he was running a constant fever that hovered around 102, and fluid had to be drained from his pleura every day. Thus the brothers returned to Newark on July 1, 1929, and Charlie began seeing a doctor in Rochester, John J. Lloyd, who decided to permanently collapse the patient's right lung by severing his phrenic nerve. Awaiting the operation at Rochester General, Charlie wrote a poem suggesting a bleak prognosis:

> *Come for him in the night,*
> *And take him from his bed . . .*
> *The snow is as white as white . . .*
> *The blood is as red as red . . .*
>
> *Heap the dirt over his head,*
> *Pack the earth firm and tight . . .*
> *The snow is as white as white . . .*

And so on, for five lugubrious quatrains. Happily the operation seemed to go well enough, and though he'd been told to expect at least a year of bed rest, Charlie rallied and was up and about in less than two weeks.

One of the nice things about sanatorium life was that Jackson had all the time in the world to read: the Bible ("I kept a notebook on it just as literature"), more Russian novels, and all seven volumes of Proust's *In Search of Lost Time*. The last became a lifelong favorite, though his most important discovery that summer was Thomas Mann, whose *Death in Venice* he'd skimmed at Kroch's four years earlier and deemed "highbrow" in a bad way, because of the stilted translation and lack of dialogue. But now, as he convalesced from his phrenectomy—and waited for a place to open up at a sanatorium in New Mexico—Jackson was persuaded to read *The Magic Mountain* because it was all about his illness: "It is true I learned a good deal about tuberculosis," he later wrote, "but I learned a great deal more about art, about politics, about science, about psychology, about Europe, and about myself." Longing to breathe the same rarefied air as Hans Castorp—and perhaps find a humanistic mentor such as Settembrini, to say nothing of the various Dionysians and ideologues that compose the rest of the cast—Charlie decided that he and Boom simply *had* to go to one of the elegant sanatoria in Davos, Switzerland. ("What!" their German doctor, Hans Staub, would exclaim shortly after their arrival. "You read *Der Zauberberg* and *then* come to Davos? Don't you know that that terrible book—so *krankhaft*, so *morbide*—keeps hundreds and thousands of people *away* from Davos every year? . . . Crazy Americans!")

Mr. Winthrop only wanted what was best for them, and readily agreed to foot the bill. Newark, meanwhile, was in an uproar. Poor Herb was besieged with questions about Charlie and Fred's mysterious benefactor, whom Bob delicately characterized as "a kind friend" for public consumption. Among family she was a good deal more acerbic, darkly insinuating that an old reprobate had "taken a shine" to her disreputable brothers-in-law.

Chapter Four

Magic Mountain

Before sailing aboard the *Rochambeau* on October 10, 1929, the brothers were met at their hotel by Mr. Winthrop, who solemnly presented them each with a letter of credit for 2,000 dollars, as well as 500 dollars in travelers' checks ("for emergencies or spending money till you get to the bank in Davos"). It was a festive nine-day crossing: Charlie and Fred shared a big double cabin, and joked with their fellow passengers that the old boat—creaking and groaning in the warm but windy weather—would crack up on this, its final voyage. From Le Havre they took a train to Paris, stopping overnight at the Palais d'Orsai and going to a "wonderful" nightclub where the orchestra played American tunes such as "St. Louis Blues"; then on to Zurich, where the next morning Charlie stepped out on his balcony at the Hotel Baur au Lac and watched the Jungfrau shimmer awesomely into view as the mist lifted over the lake. Wayne County seemed a rather dreary pastoral in comparison. At Landquart they ascended five thousand feet into the Grisons aboard a narrow-gauge train, excitedly running from one side of their first-class compartment to the other as peak after peak materialized beside them. When at last they disembarked in Davos-Platz, the snow was falling slow and thick through the twilit air; hardly any wind ever blew at the bottom of that mountainous bowl where the health resort was situated.

For the next few days they saw the sights, such as they were—the largest skating rink in Europe (its waiters gliding about with cocktails aloft on little trays), the nude Spengler in the Public Gardens—and arranged for lodging and medical care. They chose the best suite at the second-best hotel, Kurgarten-Carlton, where for fifty Swiss francs a day or about ten dollars ("Of course we were being had, like the Americans we were") they got two top-floor rooms, a bath, and a spacious balcony with two *liegerstuhls* and fur sleeping bags for their afternoon "cure" naps; the rate also included a stern, loving maid named Lena and three meals a day. After unpacking and arranging their effects, they toured a half-dozen sanatoria before settling on the Schweizerhof, a modern white building in the center of town with a big garden and sun terraces overhung with protective blue glass. Afterward they were having tea in the Kurgarten lounge when an Englishman struck up a conversation, inquiring what a couple of Yanks were doing there in the midst of the stock market crash ("I'm told that financiers are popping out of Wall Street windows like so many champagne corks"). The brothers hadn't heard a thing about it, and the impression it made now was muted at best; suddenly their new life seemed stranger than ever: "Davos was a world to itself, an isolated world, a world apart . . . "

They worried the winter would be a dull one—apart from the obligatory afternoon nap, what to do but write letters and read? They were soon disabused. At four o'clock the town came alive: "Sleighs flew back and forth in the street with bells jangling," Jackson wrote, "carrying passengers, very likely, to assignations; skiers appeared by the dozens; the rinks filled up and the bands played . . . the sidewalk cafés were crowded till sundown and the bars filled up. . . . It was as though the raison d'être of Davos was not disease at all but rather winter-sports and the gay hotel life." Seventeen-year-old Sonja Henie, fresh from winning her first gold medal at the 1928 Olympics, practiced daily at the Davos rink, and one day taught Charlie how to do the "spread eagle" (arms extended, heels apart and pointing toward each other); thus the two were photographed by the rink's roving photographer.*

For patients, however, the main diversions of Davos were dancing,

---

* Jackson's daughter Sarah remembered being mortified, as a girl, when her father ostentatiously demonstrated his prowess for the yokels of Orford, New Hampshire—an episode he recounted in *Farther and Wilder*: "On an impulse he indulged in one of his pet tricks . . . the so-called spread eagle. Jean [the Sarah character] turned red as a beet and averted her face, while he sailed by."

drinking, and sex, or some combination of the three, seeing as how life was short but one's leisure in the meantime was long. Indeed, as Jackson noted, doctors made a point of recommending a certain amount of sexual exertion, since it kept the patient's mind off morbid thoughts and was simply good physical medicine besides: "In tuberculosis one's body burns faster; all one does during the cure is to lie around and store up energy, which must be expended somehow—and, after all, what else is there to do in Davos? . . . what happened here did not matter to the outside world and even, in a sense, had not happened at all." In *The Lost Weekend*, Don reminisces about his Davos affair with a Norwegian woman, Anna, a character based on a fellow resident of the Kurgarten, Marion "Tom" Holzapfel; with her sister, Dorothy, she invited Charlie and Boom to a concert their first week in town, after which the four became almost inseparable. "You and Dorothy were (if I may put it in such a high-flown fashion) one of the finest 'chapters' of my life," Charlie wrote Tom in 1945, referring to her rather substantial role in his first novel. In *Farther and Wilder*, too, he would remember the quiet excitement of the Davos cocktail hour, as the four sat in the Kurhaus sipping gin-vermouths and making plans: "Beyond the wide windows, the stark snowy slopes and mountains were fading from their evening pink to dusk; *coucheurs* drove their closed, box-like sleighs up and down the main street, the little candles already lighted within . . . " Such plans included a certain amount of hell-raising in St. Moritz, where Charlie and Tom were "always being arrested," as he recalled, and no wonder: their escapades included stealing a sleigh, going down the bob run after dark, and refusing to pay an enormous taxi fare incurred during a night of drunken meanderings. Also, Don Birnam remembers (in *The Lost Weekend*) "the nightmare time at five in the morning" when he exploded a helium balloon with his cigarette and almost burned down the Suvretta hotel, the flame igniting some streamers and "touch[ing] off the whole room with a sudden hellish roar till the place was all one instant flame—which immediately, miraculously, went out (sparing not only him, that time, but the several hundred . . . who slept in the rooms above)."

Tom was a boon companion, then, but whether she was Charlie's main love interest is problematic. As he later pointed out, the "characteristic assumption" around Davos ("but never with a moral judgment, never a raised eyebrow") was that he and Boom were something more than brothers. One day they went to get their picture taken at a studio, and Charlie noticed the photographer's wry little smile as he posed them in double profile: bald Charlie and the boyishly gorgeous Boom. "Somehow you haven't been able to make us look like brothers in any way," Charlie complained afterward, poring over proofs. The man was taken aback; obviously he'd assumed the two were *amants*, the younger kept by the elder. And what was the truth of it? A love poem Charlie wrote around this time might have been merely playful:

TO MY VALENTINE
(P. S.—There couldn't be 2)

I don't send my heart, I don't want to, much;
For my poor heart has been knocked rather goofy
By phthisis [i.e., tuberculosis] and pneumo and needles and such,
Injected by Doctors Staub, Lloyd and Lafloofie. . . .

But I still have my pencil, if not my brains,
And looking below I see there's still room
To indite in few syllables all that remains
To be said on the subject today:
                                        J'adore Boom.

Davos, again, was another world, and these were unusual circumstances. As for whatever abided between the two in later years: at least one person, who knew them both very well, remembered a kind of allusive, ribald "fencing" that "created an awkward thing in the room," but was never quite definitive one way or the other.

Another reason Charlie might have clung all the more closely to his brother was that, despite surface merriment, he never quite felt at home. In due course—and somewhat at the time—he would consider writing a great novel about the Davos years ("Europe in decay") from the perspective of an American provincial who felt "like a child at a party [he] hadn't been invited to." Sitting in the Kurgarten dining room, he'd survey the cast of this future opus: the Dutch prime minister's son, jauntily sipping white wine while seated, then walking with a painful limp because of his missing ribs; the promiscuous, absinthe-drinking princess from Berlin; and best of all, to Charlie, a family of strapping blond aristocrats on the far side of the room, "voluble and festive" like the Rostovs in *War and Peace*. These were the Mumms: the father, Peter, was grandson of the Champagne magnate G. H. Mumm, but had lost most of his fortune in the Great War, while the improvident mother, Olga, was daughter of

Karl de Struve, Russian ambassador to the United States. Olga would "discover" Charlie during his second season in Davos ("doubtless she had learned that I was an American, and that, of course, meant money"), and was soon regaling him with some of the best dirty stories he'd ever heard, or with memories of the real-life models for Proust's masterpiece. Charlie also befriended her children, bobsledding with the brothers, Brat and Kiki, down the four-mile run from the Schatzalp, or having his portrait painted by Elena, who charged him a hundred francs for the privilege (scribbling the price shyly on a scrap of paper before leaving the room). But Charlie was closest to the youngest, little Olga ("Olili"), with whom he had a standing Ping-Pong date in the Kurgarten rec room each day at five. Out of admiration for the Empress of Russia (whose emblem it was), Olili had inked a little swastika on the handle of her racket, and was shocked when somebody left it outside her door, broken in two, with a note: "We don't want any of this around here." Nobody knew what it was all about. "Isn't it dreadful to think of us all being so ignorantly gay and carefree in Davos?" Charlie later wrote Tom Holzapfel. "Who could have foreseen at that time how horribly Europe would change in ten short years, and what would happen to so many of the people we were so fond of there." By then (1945) Charlie had run into Elena Mumm Thornton in New York, where she worked as an editor at *Town & Country*; the rest of her family, she grimly reported, had become "ardent supporters of Hitler": Olili was a leader in the Mädchen branch of the Hitler Youth, while both brothers had been killed in battle, fighting for the Nazis.*

BY APRIL the season was over in Davos, and Jackson was feeling better (oddly enough). Dr. Staub advised him to take a long vacation in Italy—to soak up the sun and enjoy himself. Getting off the train in Rome, he promptly bought a heavy bronze statuette of Romulus and Remus that he would keep the rest of his life,† then proceeded down the coast to Capri, where he spent the better part of three months at the

---

* So Elena might have thought in the spring of 1945—or so Jackson wrote, at any rate—whereas Brat was actually in a POW camp in France not far from where American soldiers were ransacking the Mumm Champagne estate in Rheims. He survived the war and would soon have a testy relationship with Elena's second husband, the critic Edmund Wilson. As for Olili, she went on to manage the racing stables of Whitney heiress Dorothy Paget.
† He gave it to Don Birnam's girlfriend in *The Lost Weekend*. Don considers using it to brain the maid, Holy Love, who stands between him and a locked liquor cabinet.

Hotel Quisisana. Perhaps the highlight of these travels was a stop in Paris, where he visited his favorite new Davos friend, the Baroness von Reutter—or, as she insisted he call her, Cousin Edith. The heiress of a wealthy Chicago family that had fallen on hard times, Edith lived modestly in Paris at the Oxford & Cambridge Hotel with her husband, Hans, a penurious Austrian baron. Still, the two managed to spend a couple of months each season in Davos, where she endeared herself to Jackson with her flair for misusing words like *gemütlich* and *soignée*, with her fond memories of dancing in New York to "Walt Whitman's Orchestra," and above all with her love of practical jokes (sending a mound of birdshot disguised as caviar to the Countess von Gerlach's table). Fifteen years later—while attending the premiere of *Since You Went Away* in the company of Gregory Peck and Leland Hayward—Jackson would run into the former Patricia Monteagle (by then Mrs. Richard Smart); the two "fell on each other's necks," he wrote, as they remembered the marvelous time they'd had that long-ago summer, dancing at Armenonville in the Bois de Boulogne with Cousins Edith and Hans.

Jackson's girlfriend Tom was also in Paris, where they'd agreed to meet for a final five-day fling before sailing back to the States together aboard the *Bremen*. As he later claimed, it was during that raucous crossing that he began to realize he had a drinking problem. Each morning he and Tom would walk around the deck with their fellow revelers, desperately hungover, and Jackson was always a little startled—and contemptuous—when the others would object to having a morning pick-me-up: "I can't *look* at another drink!" they'd groan, in effect, while Jackson himself was dying for one. Later he'd discover that Richard Peabody actually *defined* drunkards as people who want a drink the next morning: "They say it makes them feel as if they were coming back to life, as if they were no longer going crazy, and so forth." But why the compulsion to be always drunk in the first place (especially in social situations)? Why the question of "going crazy"? While dancing with Anna at Armenonville, Don Birnam's heart sinks when she suddenly turns serious and announces she has a question to ask once they're alone: " 'Why do you only come to bed with me when you are drunk?' He roared with delight. He knew damned well she had reason to ask; but in his relief that it had been no worse he was able to laugh as if it were terribly funny and he almost shouted 'Because I'm *always* drunk!' "

Certainly aboard the *Bremen* that seems to have been the case. The rest of his life he would particularly remember one night (and there would be many like it) when he broke away from Tom, staggering, and clambered up on a slippery railing, threatening to jump into the boiling wake; wisely, perhaps, the woman walked away, and Jackson was left teetering there until a sudden gust of wind filled his camel's-hair coat and flung him back to the deck ("It was just one of those moments," he wrote Tom, "and God, for no known reason, steps in and protects the drunk from himself"). Waiting on the pier in New York—a vision of safe harbor—was Rhoda, to whom Jackson introduced his Norwegian friend, and later, by chance, the three met again at the theater. By then Tom had gotten the picture, though apparently felt no hard feelings: "You are like a plant of slow growth," she wrote him, "but the flower will be beautiful."

BEFORE RETURNING to Davos on October 1, 1930, Jackson was told by Dr. Lloyd in Rochester that his condition was "excellent" except for some slight rales, or rattles, on his right side after coughing. Mr. Winthrop, however, thought his young friend looked "desperately overtired" when he left him on the deck of the *Lafayette*, and urged him to be "sensible just once" and take care of himself. Jackson did not follow the advice. Comforting himself with drink on the ship—none too festively this time—he fell asleep while smoking and awoke to find the eiderdown smoldering away on top of him; he flung it into the shower just before the gaping hole burned through to his chest. "Tired and ill" by the time he got to Davos, he found the place almost deserted that early in the season. Even Boom was gone, as Dr. Staub had given him belated leave to take an Italian tour, and perhaps return to the States for a month or two if he felt up to it.

But Boom would remain in Europe a long time. The next month he suffered a relapse in Venice, and was barely alive when he and Charlie were reunited at the Schweizerhof. Hemorrhaging now from his "good" lung, Boom was forced to lie with an ice pack on his chest in all but total silence, not even allowed to laugh, lest he waste precious breath; the next step, if matters worsened, was the dreaded thoracoplasty—the surgical removal of ribs to collapse a severely diseased lung. "It is most distressing," Winthrop wrote Charlie, "and rather a sad homecoming for you. . . . Of course Fred is a bit apt to make light of things, especially in his own care; so do please give me the right dope—the low down as my tough friends say." Boom was, for a fact, managing rather miraculously to make light of things—"it was his nature," as Charlie would write, "and

I believe that is how or why he recovered." Before long all the nobs of Davos were paying court to the charming invalid—the Duchess of Alba, the Countess von Gerlach, the wealthy Trads from Tehran—listening to his Victrola and admiring the cheerful Dufy prints on the walls of his lovely room overlooking the gardens and ski slopes beyond.

As Mr. Winthrop pointed out, it was Charlie who needed cheering up more than Fred, and indeed the former seemed to be going through an existential crisis of sorts, albeit in good company: Ralph Monroe Eaton was a Harvard philosophy professor who, following a nervous breakdown, had taken a sabbatical to be psychoanalyzed by Jung in Zurich; he and Jackson had met in Italy the previous spring (Eaton had introduced Charlie, in Rome, to George Santayana, Eaton's former teacher), and that second season they shuttled between Davos and Zurich as often as possible. Eaton was a fascinating figure: then in his late thirties, he was a great friend and protégé of the philosopher Alfred North Whitehead, and had himself published one book, *Symbolism and Truth*, and was in the process of completing another, *General Logic*, that would remain in print for almost thirty years. Jackson described him as "rugged, athletic, look[ing] like those early photos of Hemingway (the ski cap and black-mustache ones)," but he was evidently fragile on the inside: recently divorced (his estranged wife had taken their child and moved to California), he'd gotten involved in a chaotic affair with a charismatic Harvard psychologist, Christiana Morgan—"the veiled woman in Jung's circle," as her biographer put it—who was then helping her sometime lover, Henry A. Murray, develop the Thematic Apperception Test. Morgan was witness to Eaton's unraveling: gentle at first, he grew more and more erratic as his drinking worsened, insisting on absolute fidelity and threatening suicide when Morgan refused. Finally he tried to get himself run over on a turnpike near the Parker River on Plum Island, whereupon Morgan and Murray persuaded him to see Jung in Zurich.

By the time Jackson knew him, Eaton seemed more or less on an even keel, and they had wonderful times together. One day the two were drinking in Davos—shortly after they'd attended a production of *Madama Butterfly* in Zurich—and Eaton put his brandy aside, sat down at a piano, and proceeded to play the opera's score from start to finish: "A thrilling afternoon," wrote Jackson, who hadn't even known Eaton could play. When in Zurich, they made a point of being at the Dolder Grand Hotel, above the city, every Saturday evening at seven when all the church bells would ring until they "blended into one prodigious note."

The effect was all the more enchanting, perhaps, given that the friends were rarely if ever sober.* Once again, but at the Dolder this time, Jackson passed out with a cigarette in his mouth and woke up to find his bed in flames. As for his friend: "Alcohol had a place in Eaton's difficulties," Henry Murray's biographer noted; "so did an uncertain sexual identity."

Whatever his problems otherwise, Eaton was above all a mentor to Charlie—his own Settembrini—and perhaps inevitably he, like Winthrop, tried to interest the young man in Plato, to little avail ("there was a barrier of ignorance, or maybe self-interest, that intruded and kept me ever from [Plato's] meaning and beauty"), while Jackson, for his part, appears to have helped the man feel a little happier for a time. While correcting proofs for *General Logic*, Eaton wrote Charlie a desolate letter complaining of the "fatigue" he felt toward his work nowadays; the "passion for coldness" required for such "quibbles and intricacies of thought" was, he'd decided, "a horrible atmosphere to live in":

My life as a pedagogue is ended. I have been in confinement like you; confinement to order, convention, precision—not daring to live or feel in unconventional and irrational forms, except furtively. I think everything is produced out of the irrational, growth, creation, is irrational. If I could only have a year to write—to say what I think, and to feel, to carve out a new and beautiful book, not for money but for the thing itself. It would be worth making any sacrifice for. The alternative is the conventional pedagogue's life I have been leading; I dread going back to that—because I begin to feel free of it; and you have helped to give me that freedom.

Perhaps with Eaton's predicament in mind—and wishing to find a better atmosphere for his own calling, from which he'd strayed too long—Jackson was contemplating a year in Russia, and wondered if Mr. Winthrop would be willing to stake him. "I should think that life in Russia in 1931 would be hard indeed," the latter replied with patient understatement; nevertheless he'd discussed the matter with their mutual

---

* A curious souvenir among Jackson's papers is an astoundingly large bar tab from the Dolder—a *very* selective accounting of which includes the following: "4 Whisky . . . 4 Gin Vermouth . . . 5 Manhattan . . . 2 Kümmel . . . 5 Brandy Soda . . . 5 Gin Vermouth . . . 3 Manhattan . . . 5 Manhattan"—and so on, for some four pages. The grand total was 578 francs, or well over a hundred 1931 dollars.

friend Thor,* and both agreed a Russian sojourn might be a good thing *if* Charlie used the interval for "earnest hard work and study." As for the oats he insisted on sowing in the meantime, well, Winthrop was loath to reproach him ("It is best to get them out of your system"), though he begged him not to "do anything foolish or extravagant" since these were hard times and, besides, Charlie had to consider his health.

Jackson responded by going on his most colossal bender yet, burning through the rest of his money with a two-month, hundred-dollar-a-day trip to Juan-les-Pins on the Riviera. In later years the thought of that place—with its plush nightclubs and beaches and dazzling cerulean sea—would make him smile; at the time he was probably more ambivalent. Don Birnam casts back to the "agonizing mornings at the bank" in Juan-les-Pins when, palsied with hangover, he'd sit outside breathing deeply of the salty air while trying to steady his hand enough to sign a letter of credit under the teller's impassive gaze. "I am afraid that what you have often told me is true," Winthrop wrote him afterward, with an unwonted note of asperity, "that when you get some money you do not spend it wisely. So I have arranged with Thor to send him a remittance, and he will do what is right. Until you get some work to do, I don't want you to be adrift for I don't know what you'd do—so Thor has promised to do what is necessary to give you board and lodging. I hate to write all this. I do wish you would pull yourself together. You really must try my dear Charlie." Duly chastened, Jackson dropped all thought of Russia (hardly an option, in any event, given the new arrangement with Thor), informing Mr. Winthrop that he'd decided to come straight home and get on with his writing, whereby he hoped to win back some of his benefactor's good opinion. The kindly man was mollified: "Everything has been worth while my dear Charlie if only you are well and strong again and able to make good as I always knew and now know you will. But don't talk nonsense about my faith in you being shaken."

JACKSON RETURNED to New York in May, taking a room at the Hotel Earle on Washington Square. For a while he tried hard to stick to his

---

* In the typescript of *The Royalist*, Jackson reproduces several of Winthrop's letters almost verbatim—with, however, one consistent alteration: every time "Thor" is mentioned in the originals, Jackson substitutes "Rhoda" or some equivalent. Thus, in the letter referenced above, Winthrop writes: "Before he left to go back to Boston I talked it all over with Thor," whereas the same line in *The Royalist* reads, "I took the liberty of telephoning your girl . . . "

promise to write steadily and stay somewhat sober: he was approaching thirty, after all, and was still unpublished at a time when most of his friends, in the midst of the Depression, at least had jobs of some sort. Rhoda would later remember that he'd worked "feverishly" that first year back from Europe; whatever his relative gifts, Jackson had realized by then that writing did not come easily to him, and yet he couldn't imagine doing anything else. At the time he was cultivating a kind of brutal cynicism, hoping to title his first story collection *Without or With*, from Byron: "Without, or with, offense to friends or foes, / I sketch your world exactly as it goes." One of his more ambitious efforts was a long story titled "Death on the Rocks," a somber meditation on the centrality of passion. Martha and Lydia are old friends who share a summer cabin near Seneca Falls (about twenty miles southeast of Arcadia), and as the story opens they await the arrival of Martha's husband, Smith, and his friend Pete. Lydia has lost the love of her life, Roger, three years before, and since then has dissembled her despair with a façade of vivid eccentricity; Martha, meanwhile, concedes that she has little in common with Smith except for a sexual attraction so powerful that she wonders whether she could live without it. After many pages of ruminative dialogue in this vein, the men arrive and the four spend a night of heavy drinking and more talking; indeed, nothing much happens until the last ten pages (of forty-four), when Smith falls to his death while climbing rocks beneath a waterfall, whereupon the author waxes lyrical: "Smith lay below, fresh and beautiful as the body of Hector favored by the gods even in his high doom of death. . . . Gone from her now, he poured forth his blood in a libation to death." On the last page Martha stands at the brink of a ravine, pondering suicide, while her friend Lydia realizes it's a moot point: "Though [Martha] might go on in physical life, she would be dead as [Lydia] was dead."

"A Summer Passion" treats the same theme with a good deal more sentimentality, suggesting that Jackson realized his morbidity was doing him no favors in the fiction market. Philip McKenna is a doting older brother to his seven-year-old sister, Mary, "an ideal playmate" who assures him that he is "the onliest person in the world that I will ever ever love." However, after a "grand romp" of a summer with the girl, Philip is about to marry the sophisticated Christabel and begin work as an English instructor in distant Albany. Little Mary despises her brother's fiancée, who treats the girl with gauche condescension ("It's very pretty," she says of Mary's dress, "but isn't it a little too old for you?") and is a rival besides, and Philip is forced to choose between the two. Naturally he chooses passion, with all its "danger and adoration and treachery," assuring himself that his little sister, without his love, will yet remain "uninjured, whole." Thus he bids farewell to the sleeping child ("God bless you, Mary dear") and leaves to take up his life, while the reader is left wondering why sexual love and sibling love should be considered mutually exclusive.

Perhaps the author figured a change of venue would help, and anyway both Thor and Ralph Eaton were now living in Boston, where Jackson moved that winter and took a job as a feeder in a jigsaw factory.* Eaton had recently returned from Zurich, and was planning to teach one more year at Harvard and then practice psychoanalysis in New York. Jackson had found his friend in "wonderful shape"; however, in her biography of Christiana Morgan, Claire Douglas paints a far more lurid picture:

> Just when Eaton needed a tight rein on his growing hysteria, Jung, perceiving the richness of Eaton's unconscious, carried him off into archetypal realms that, alas, further unbalanced the young man. Eaton started to become delusional. He didn't remain in Zurich long enough for Jung to rectify his mistake, but panicked and fled. Jung wrote forebodingly to [Henry] Murray: "He seems to be promising. If only America doesn't swallow him up and grind him to dust."

If America did, in fact, swallow Eaton up in some way, Jackson saw only vague hints of it; during their final meeting Eaton struck him as being in "perfect health."† But in Christiana Morgan's view, the man was so incoherent with drink and mania that she feared for his safety and her own. On April 12, 1932, Eaton became dizzy while teaching a class at Radcliffe, and dismissed his students. At the insistence of Morgan and Henry Murray, he spent the night in a hospital but slipped away the next morning; Murray rounded up some colleagues and went looking for him, and finally they found his body in some woods near West Concord, where

---

* Whether Winthrop had cut him off for the time being or else stipulated gainful employment of whatever sort ("I don't want you to be adrift") is unknown; possibly Jackson hoped such work would leave his mind free for creative flights à la Spinoza's lens-grinding.
† This from Charlie's 1945 letter to Tom Holzapfel, wherein he claimed to have spent an afternoon with Eaton the very day before his death—unlikely, as Eaton's final days were apparently chaotic. Suffice it to say, in any case, that Jackson had seen him shortly before his death and found little amiss.

Eaton had cut his throat. Two days later he was eulogized in the *Harvard Crimson:* "It is our misfortune that frequently, in a world so lonely as ours can be, it is not possible for the questing mind of the teacher to draw peaceful satisfaction from the art of teaching."

Jackson's own ideas about Eaton's death had only a little to do with pedagogic disenchantment or, for that matter, oppressive archetypes and the like. "This seems to me—this kind of thing, that is, seems to me the real American tragedy," he wrote Boom in 1953, after one of Boom's acquaintances had killed himself (and three weeks before Charlie himself would threaten suicide): "the man of fine mind and decent tastes whose deepest basic instincts cause him to go against the social grain whether he likes it or not. . . . It is the story of Ralph Eaton all over again, and thousands and thousands of other far-better-than-average men." After a fashion, then, perhaps America *had* swallowed Eaton up, rather as Jung had feared. What is certain is that he yearned for a more passionate life—"to express all that you see in me," he wrote Charlie, and referred to Whitman's longing to leave behind the "charts and diagrams" of the "learn'd astronomer" and simply gaze at the stars amid "the mystical moist night-air," a sentiment echoed in a poem Eaton had written shortly before his death, which Charlie transcribed in his journal:

> *From the hot hell of life, gazing at the cold eternal stars—*
> *To speak what there is to speak—*
> *Of love, tender, springing green in the soul and turning to desolate*
> *   withered grass;*
> *Of effort given in vain, work ending in death;*
> *Of the passage of all things into nothingness—and the prayers of saints*
> *   and religious men;*
> *Of philosophical systems, buttresses of man's hopes against the unknown;*
> *Of the mystery of the universe, revealed on a summer's day when the sea*
> *   is blue and the sands are white;*
> *The universe—the earth—taking me to its bosom, caressing me,*
> *   holding me,*
> *Because I shall die and descend into it again;*
> *I—a part of the earth, a blessed animal, loving like an animal, dying*
> *   like an animal.*

Chapter Five

A Disease of the Night

Along with his other sorrows, Jackson had begun to accept (or recognize) the possibility that he might not make it as a writer, and this was simply crushing. Charlie "liked the whole *idea* of being a writer," said Roger Straus, his friend and publisher, who knew better than most the extent to which Jackson had pinned his hopes, his entire identity almost, on literary fame. It had sustained him ever since his lonely childhood in Newark, and the thought of his old friends and neighbors deriding him now as a failure (and worse) was haunting to say the least—and yet: wasn't some such reckoning more common than not? As Don Birnam reflects, "He was only one of several million persons of his generation who had grown up and, somewhere around thirty, made the upsetting discovery that life wasn't going to pan out the way you'd always expected it would; and why this realization should have thrown him and not them—or not too many of them—was something he couldn't fathom."

While he was drinking, though, he could go on dreaming, and besides it was almost as habitual (and necessary) as breathing by then. After the first drink of the morning there was little question of getting any serious work done anyway, so why not stay drunk and contemplate the masterpieces he would write later? Morbidly self-conscious at the best of times (solipsistic when drunk), Jackson thought his own antics might ultimately seem funny or interesting—that is, until he tried recording them in his journal for future use. "Confirmed drunk—(myself)—," he wrote, "after pouring many drinks, drinking them, and then seeing his glass empty: 'My Gawd! Have I got to pour another?!!' " So much for wit; elsewhere in the same pages is a bemused, not to say apathetic, diary of a few days circa late 1932* under the heading "IN A GLASS" (the title he'd eventually give to Don's never-written novel in *The Lost Weekend*): "Up early and T. arrived at ten and phoned Al for 2 pints of gin, one of which we consumed right off. At noon we started on the second. B. Woodman arrived at 4 with pt. of alcohol. Later B. and I out to his wops [*sic*] for another pt., then to the Broken Dish for drinks. Then to A. R.'s more drinks. Crazy night. Too much drinking." There was also the time he let a cabbie keep his coat in exchange for a $4.55 fare, or sat reading two hundred pages of *The Moon and Sixpence* in a stupor and was "struck by the extraordinary number of times [Maugham] used 'I do not know why' in the narrative." "In a Glass" soon peters out, and no wonder.

Aside from the occasional calamity, the outward reality of a drunk's life is nothing if not tedious—and besides, one drinks to *escape* reality, and in that regard Jackson lived a rich and varied life: he was a virtuoso pianist, a brilliant literature professor, a Shakespearean actor of unrivaled subtlety, and yes, a great novelist, *except* when his "sober ego" would pounce—as it always did—and punish him for his ridiculous self-deceptions. Don Birnam curses his "mocking habit" of "expos[ing] his own fancies just as they reached their climax . . . It made him a kind of dual personality, at once superior and inferior to himself"—or, as the cofounder of Alcoholics Anonymous, Bill Wilson, described himself, he was "an egomaniac with an inferiority complex." While drunk and grandiose, the alcoholic engages in behavior that causes bottomless chagrin later, such as when Don, sober, suddenly remembers trying to charm (that is, borrow money from) the neighborhood laundress with a bravura display of her native tongue: "Talking German to Mrs. Wertheim—aaah! . . . One more person to shun in the street, one more shop to go by with face averted, one more *bête noire* added to the neighborhood collection of persons he must not see again." Thus the vicious circle of alcoholism, as petty (and not-so-petty) embarrassments accumulate into a mass of amorphous shame that can only be escaped with more alcohol.

---

* "Calvin Coolidge died today," he obliquely dates (January 5, 1933) one entry.

Eventually one begins to hide from the world's judgments, nurse one's dreams in private, drown the sober ego all the more. Become, in short, a loner. Alcoholics "are self-important," Jackson would write with splendid objectivity in 1954, "introspective (or maybe just self-infatuated) to the point where they have come to inhabit an insular world of their own; and, as such, they are unable to subscribe to or believe in anything outside of themselves or greater than themselves." This process was especially insidious in the case of Jackson, who from earliest childhood had been in the habit of consoling himself, when rebuffed by the world, with reminders of his own superiority ("Clods!"), meanwhile lying low or else playing the role of a regular guy, in public, which required constant metacognitive vigilance. And now, alcoholic, he found himself all but trapped in an insular, self-consoling world ("I can't get outside of myself"), unable to bear the company of others, except when drunk, in which case others were less inclined to bear *him.* And given that alcoholics invariably find ways to exonerate themselves, they tend to blame others for failed relations, until at last they're left superbly alone: in remote bars, in locked hotel rooms, residing withal in daydreams and memories ("the only paradise from which we are never thrown out").

Apart from reading, Jackson's favorite way of enjoying his abundant solitude was listening to music—his only real hobby, as he was fond of saying. He'd discovered this passion as a boy, listening to Caruso on his mother's Red Seal records, and later availing himself of the vaster library chez Bloomer. As a solvent adult, Jackson would line his walls with an enormous record collection, including all of Mozart and Beethoven in particular; he could scarcely believe these two had been "earthbound mortals" like himself, and of course he longed to be the ultimate medium of their genius—hence Don Birnam's "favorite daydream": "He came out on the stage of Carnegie Hall, smiled, bowed, sat down at the piano, and awaited the assignment." Dressed in comfortable street clothes rather than the usual white tie and boiled shirt, the debonair Birnam has agreed to be challenged by a panel of music critics, who have racked their brains to produce a list of pieces that Don must play on the spot from memory before a packed audience. "Köchel *Verzeichnis* 331," he calmly emends, when a critic asks him to play Mozart's Sonata Number 12, in F Major. "A dream indeed," the tipsy Don concludes. "Comic, to be sure; ridiculous, childish; but—most musical, most melancholy . . . "

A somewhat less comic fantasy had to do with Jackson's favorite contemporary author, whose nine books he'd had expensively bound in morocco and would keep among his dwindling effects unto that last spartan apartment at the Hotel Chelsea. "He took down *The Great Gatsby* and ran his finger over the fine green binding," he wrote of Don's riveting lecture before a room of rapt, phantom students.

> "There's no such thing," he said aloud, "as a flawless novel. But if there is, this is it." He nodded. The class looked and listened in complete attention, and one or two made notes. . . . "People will be going back to Fitzgerald one day as they now go back to Henry James. . . . Apart from his other gifts, Scott Fitzgerald has the one thing that a novelist needs: a truly seeing eye. . . . The fellow is still under forty. The great novels will yet come from his pen. And when they do, we shall have as true a picture of the temper and spirit of our time as any age of literature can boast in the past."

The Lost Weekend is set in 1936, and Fitzgerald had been dead for almost two years when Jackson began writing it in 1942. Thus, on one hand, Jackson retrospectively invoked the author as a cautionary figure, whereas in 1936 he'd actively worried about his hero's well-known alcoholism and wondered whether his latest novel, *Tender Is the Night*, would also prove to be his last. Indeed, to Jackson's self-referential mind, the book seemed to mirror both Fitzgerald's deterioration and his own, and to some extent *The Lost Weekend* was conceived in homage to that flawed, brilliant novel in particular. When *Tender* was published, in 1934, Jackson stayed up all night reading it ("It's fatal to open the book at any page, any paragraph; for I must sit down then and there and read the rest of it right through"), and afterward managed to run the author to ground, by telephone, in the little town of Tuxedo: "Why don't you write me a letter about it?" said a weary Fitzgerald. "I think you're a little tight now." In 1964 Jackson mentioned that phone call in a letter he wrote his family from Will Rogers Hospital in Saranac Lake, where he'd bumped into a former Princeton classmate of Fitzgerald; the man had mentioned (among other things) that Fitzgerald had once been beaten by police in Rome, just like the drunken Dick Diver in *Tender Is the Night*, which left Jackson admiring his favorite author all the more for making "beautiful and heart-breaking" art out of such material: "I do not for a second, of course, mean to 'excuse' Fitzgerald for any of this mess," he added for his family's benefit: "I only mean that *he* knew it was awful too, knew how much more awful than anybody else, and made a most moving scene out of his own agony, as writers worth their salt always do."

Fitzgerald's work was almost entirely out of print when *The Lost Week-*

end was published in 1944—even *Gatsby* seemed well on its way to being forgotten—and Jackson had meant to be "deliberately prophetic" in calling attention to a writer he considered the foremost chronicler of "the temper and spirit of our time."* More than twenty years later he finally received credit, in writing, for having played a key role in the so-called Fitzgerald Revival: "Indeed, no author has been more outspoken or more generous than Jackson in his admiration of Fitzgerald's work," wrote Henry Dan Piper in *F. Scott Fitzgerald: A Critical Portrait* (1965), which Rhoda gave Charlie for Christmas that year. Meanwhile a number of Fitzgerald's old friends and admirers had also taken notice of Don Birnam's discerning idolatry, and made a point of getting in touch with his creator. While in Hollywood in 1944, Jackson got a call from a thirty-year-old novelist and Navy lieutenant, Budd Schulberg, who was drinking with his father (B.P., former head of Paramount Studios) at Romanoff's, and wondered if Jackson would join them. Both father and son had "gone crazy about" *The Lost Weekend*, and now Budd regaled its author with the tale of his chaotic collaboration with Fitzgerald on the movie *Winter Carnival* (1939). (Five years later, Schulberg spent a weekend at Jackson's house in Orford—seventeen miles north of Dartmouth College, Schulberg's alma mater, where *Winter Carnival* was filmed—and showed him his work in progress, *The Disenchanted*, about an alcoholic novelist based on Fitzgerald. Jackson found the manuscript "truly wonderful," and insisted that Schulberg *not* delete his hero's dying line—"Take it from me, baby, in America nothing fails like success"—a sentiment that had begun to resonate with Jackson.) That same summer in Hollywood (1944), Jackson was also summoned by the English gossip columnist Sheilah Graham, a total stranger who (as only a handful of people knew at the time) had been Fitzgerald's mistress in his final years: "Well, we met—" Jackson wrote a friend afterward, "a three hour lunch at the Beverly Wilshire—and she poured it all out, poor girl: what he was like in bed, how big, how many times, and you'd be surprised."†

---

* In 1934, the Modern Library published an edition of *Gatsby* that was already out of print by the time Fitzgerald died on December 21, 1940, while his other books had all but vanished. "How much will you sell the plates of 'This Side of Paradise' for?" Fitzgerald wrote of his once-famous first novel, eight days before his death, in a letter to Max Perkins. "I think it has a chance for a new life." In 1941, Fitzgerald's unfinished novel, *The Last Tycoon*, was published in an omnibus edition edited by Edmund Wilson, who included *Gatsby* and a selection of Fitzgerald's short stories. The book was widely and respectfully reviewed, but sold poorly.
† Graham wrote a more circumspect version of this encounter in her memoir, *The*

When Henry Dan Piper wrote of Jackson's outspoken generosity in Fitzgerald's behalf, he wasn't only referring to *The Lost Weekend*; for the rest of his life, Jackson would never miss a chance to promote the man's reputation in whatever way he could. In 1945, he hectored his friend Bennett Cerf to publish a selection of Fitzgerald's short stories (offering himself as editor), as well as to reinstate *Gatsby* in the Modern Library. Also, when Arthur Mizener's pioneering biography *The Far Side of Paradise* was published, in 1951, Jackson appeared at Columbia with Mizener and Lionel Trilling to discuss Fitzgerald's essential place in American literature. Along with worshiping the work itself, Jackson could hardly have related more keenly to what Trilling characterized as Fitzgerald's "exemplary role": He "lacked prudence, as his heroes did, lacked that blind instinct for self-protection which the writer needs in double measure. But that is all he lacked—and it is the generous fault, even the heroic fault." Above all there was Trilling's observation that Fitzgerald had "put himself . . . in the line of greatness [and] judged himself in a large way." That was true of Jackson, too, for better and (decidedly) for worse.

JACKSON SPENT the summer of 1933 in Provincetown, on Cape Cod, and then remained for a number of "nightmare weeks" into the fall; as he later wrote Harry Kemp—the town's most notable vagabond poet, with whom he'd tippled that bygone summer—the whole ordeal was described "on pages 204-5-6" of *The Lost Weekend*: the first time Don Birnam seriously considers suicide. The episode had begun as a lavish holiday, and was doubtless another instance whereby he'd exhausted Mr. Winthrop's patience, or at least whatever resources had been available to him. As he wrote of Birnam, "He had carried on wastefully, wantonly, with all kinds of people, for weeks, throwing money away, drinking up more money in a weekend than the Portuguese [fishermen] made in seven days of hard work." The local fishermen would exact a terrible revenge, and they seem to have been provoked by something more than simple prodigality on Jackson's part. At any rate, he awoke one morning in September to find himself penniless and deserted—the town all but shuttered for the season—and perhaps too sheepish or exhausted to beg Mr. Winthrop, or anyone else, for further help. With no money for food or even drink,

---

Rest of the Story (1964): "[Jackson and I] talked of Scott, but it was a strain for us both."

he sank into the blackest depression of his life, hardly able to leave the little shack he'd rented (but could no longer pay for) "at the tip end of Whoopee Wharf," where every night he was systematically terrorized by the "drunk and predatory" Portuguese:

> Out of an absolutely silent night . . . they would come thundering along the wharf at two in the morning shouting his name, demand-ing money, demanding to be let in, yelling for booty, clothing, drink, his very person. They would pound on the flimsy walls and curse him with laughter, calling him names he didn't dare listen to or think of the meaning of. He would lie breathless in the dark, knowing only too well what they would do to him if they got him (he covered his ears as they shouted insanely: "Donnie boy! Come out and get your breakfast!") He was the more terrified because he knew he had brought this on himself, it was a kind of grotesque retribution, he and he alone was solely responsible for their wrath.

Whatever Jackson had done to warrant such abuse, such "hatred and contempt," apparently left him so ashamed and hopeless one morning that he wrote "three notes, exactly alike," and began to draw "hair-like lines of red" across his wrists with a Bavarian hunting knife. As would often happen, though, he decided to give himself a bit more time—maybe things would look up in a day or two, as they generally did. On Sep-tember 18, his friend Thor (who'd been visiting family that summer in Copenhagen) arrived in Boston aboard the *Minnequa*, and four days later Boom returned from France aboard the *Deutschland*. Quite likely both had been summoned (given their almost simultaneous arrival) by a dis-tressed Mr. Winthrop.*

At whoever's behest Charlie lived for several months afterward at Apple Ridge Farm in Saugerties, between Poughkeepsie and Albany on the Hudson, where he used to spend childhood summers with Grand-mother Jackson. A child again in certain respects, he was vigilantly watched by the farm's caretakers, Basil and Thorborg Ellison.[†] "Remem-

---

* "Isn't it too bad Mr. Kember [the Winthrop character] couldn't have lived to have seen all this," says Don Birnam's mother in *Farther and Wilder*, "—this beautiful house I mean, Don, and the way you live now. After all, the way he picked you out of the gutter and all . . . "

[†] Thorborg Ellison (née Brundin in 1886) was a storied bohemian: educated at Bar-nard, the tall Swede was a staunch turn-of-the-century feminist who advocated total

ber the episode of the key to the applejack closet?" he wrote Thorborg in 1943, a few weeks after his novel had been accepted for publication. "If you don't, buy *The Lost Weekend* and read all about it!" Probably Thorborg didn't need to be reminded. The closet in question had been in the bedroom she shared with her husband, and contained several kegs of apple brandy; naturally the door was locked at all times and the keys kept on the caretakers' persons. Each morning, however, while the Ellisons were elsewhere, Jackson would tiptoe into their bedroom and try the door, and once or twice he'd found it unlocked and managed to siphon off several pints and hide them around his room. After an Easter visit with Boom in New York, he returned to the farm and noticed a new tension between the couple: Thorborg had lost her key, and Jackson soon discovered it in the pocket of his camel's-hair bed jacket, which the woman had evidently worn in his absence. Oddly enough, he couldn't bring himself to use it—to take "such an easy advantage"—though he persevered along more challenging lines, once propping a ladder against the little closet window. On the morning of his final departure in June, Jackson presented the astonished couple with the missing key and told them of his curious scruples.

Perhaps encouraged by such episodes—and given that Charlie's intervals of sobriety did seem to be lengthening somewhat—Boom agreed to share an apartment at 311 East 55th Street, and was even willing to let Charlie, as the older brother, have the only bedroom.* In every other respect Boom was now his brother's keeper, dispensing a modest allowance (fifty cents a day for cigarettes; the rest as needed) out of the Winthrop money. For a while Charlie was simply grateful to have a roof over his head, and determined to prove himself worthy of greater trust; pres-

---

sexual freedom; in her twenties she became friend, mentor, sister-in-law, and possibly lover of Agnes Smedley, a journalist whose support of Red China and five-year tenancy at the Yaddo artist colony led, in 1949, to an infamous Communist witch hunt incited by the manic poet Robert Lowell. Charles Jackson seems to have tried in vain to endear himself to the formidable Smedley. As he later wrote Thorborg, "Agnes may hate my guts and despise the kind of punk she feels me to be and I'll still say this to my dying day. . . . 'Agnes Smedley is a gr-r-r-eat woman!' "

* Anyone who wonders what this apartment looked like should watch the movie *The Lost Weekend*, for which Billy Wilder asked Jackson to draw a floor plan from memory. The subsequent set design, said Jackson, "was absolute perfection in every detail": "My god if they didn't actually select one of the very same pictures with which I had decorated my 55th Street flat more than ten years ago: the drawing of Brahms playing the piano."

ently, though, he rebelled against the arrangement ("Driblets handed out to him as if he were a child") with an addict's petulance and cunning. "Send me some money at once," he demanded of Boom while visiting mutual friends in New Jersey. "I have not one cent, and can't imagine how you could leave me in such a position." In another note—Boom was about to join him on vacation—Charlie casually mentioned that he'd just redeemed his typewriter from a pawnshop on Third Avenue, just north of 57th, but couldn't also carry the gramophone, which he directed his brother to retrieve (pawn ticket enclosed) on his way out of town. By then Charlie was spending more and more time at a neighborhood bar,* pawning his typewriter as often as possible, along with the posher items of his European wardrobe. And yes, one desperate day—just like Don in the novel (a scene "written directly out of my own experience")—he staggered all the way up to 120th Street, typewriter in hand, fruitlessly searching for an open pawnshop on Yom Kippur.

But for three summers, at least, beginning in 1935, the brothers left New York for the comparative idyll of Brattleboro, Vermont, where Charlie endeavored to meet his responsibilities as stage manager and publicity man for a new summer theater started by an art dealer, writer, and would-be actor named John Becker. Becker was friends with the playwright Paul Osborn, who had a vacation home nearby, and that first summer the company gave a production of his *Oliver, Oliver,* which had flopped on Broadway (eleven performances) the previous season[†]; during the second summer (1936), they staged the debut of Osborn's *Tomorrow's Monday,* attracting a respectful notice from *The New York Times,* which applauded a "thoroughly competent cast" including Charles Lindbergh's sister-in-law Constance Morrow, who performed under the name Constance Reeve. Her sister Margot would later describe the Brattleboro group as close-knit and mostly temperate, given their quite earnest ambition to establish a reputable summer theater; she further recalled that Charlie discharged his duties with only the odd lapse (invited back three years in a row, after all) and that he and Boom were well liked among

---

* Legend has it that Jackson was a great patron of P. J. Clarke's on 55th and Third (the model for the bar in the movie), though in fact, as he wrote a friend, "my favorite joint (and the one described in *The Lost Weekend*) was Gus's, between 55th and 56th on Second."

[†] Osborn is best known for his 1939 comedy, *Morning's at Seven,* which was successfully revived on Broadway in 1980 and 2002. He also wrote the screen adaptations for *South Pacific, East of Eden,* and other movies, and was one of Charlie's neighbors in Newtown, Connecticut, during the 1950s.

an eminently likable group. The plays were staged in a converted coach house on the Jacob Estey estate, where the theater company lived in servants' quarters on the top floors of a Victorian mansion—a ménage that included the eighteen-year-old newlyweds Mel and Franny Ferrer, who became lifelong friends of the Jackson brothers. Mel went on to relative fame as an actor and husband of Audrey Hepburn; as for Franny—his first and third wife, a great beauty in her own right—she in time would be nothing less than the (platonic) love of Boom's life.

Charlie and Boom had probably become involved in the summer theater through their friendship with Becker, then the center of an arty social circle that seems to have been largely composed of gay and bisexual men.* Indeed, Becker was remarkably versatile in every respect: his gallery in New York was among the first to bring Picasso's work to the United States, and meanwhile he also took an abiding interest in certain social causes. From a well-to-do family in Chicago, he returned to his hometown after graduating from Harvard in the early 1920s and found hardscrabble employment at the Institute for Juvenile Research and the Illinois State Penitentiary. But his most concerted efforts would always be on behalf of African Americans; he later served on the Council Against Intolerance in America, for which he wrote *The Negro in American Life* (1944), and the following year he co-authored one of the first children's books featuring a black heroine, *Melindy's Medal*. As for his various artistic interests, they had a way of ending badly—his gallery had failed by the time he started the summer theater, which he seemed to hope would serve somewhat as a vehicle for his own talents, but it was not to be: "I began as leading man in *Oliver Oliver* and I have been demoted with honors," he wrote a friend. "My ambition is to have a non-speaking 'walk-on' but no such luck yet." His writing career, ultimately, would fare little better.

A few months prior to that first season in Brattleboro, Becker had put Jackson in touch with an old Harvard classmate, Paul Spofford,† who'd received his medical degree from the University of Vienna, where he'd

---

* "I thought they were all gay," said Margot Morrow Wilkie of the Brattleboro men, citing Becker, director Paul Stephenson, and the Jackson brothers (perhaps forgetting Mel Ferrer's vaunted heterosexuality). In 1934, Charlie wrote this provocative couplet "To Johnnie Becker": "Public Enemy No. 69 / Will you be my Valentine?" Be that as it may, both men eventually married, and when I asked Haidee Becker Kenedy about her father's orientation, she replied that he likely had "homosexual leanings during his youth," but was always "evasive" on the subject.
† Not his real name, which I changed at the request of his son.

studied under some of Freud's disciples and heard a number of the great man's lectures firsthand. Alas, his only enduring fame would prove ignominious (if happily anonymous)—that is, as "the foolish psychiatrist" in *The Lost Weekend*. Back in 1935, however, Jackson had enlisted Spofford to help him return to moderate drinking via psychoanalysis. The doctor agreed it was possible, and Mr. Winthrop was evidently willing to pay his rather exorbitant fee.

But Spofford wasn't a psychiatrist at all, foolish or otherwise; he was, in fact, licensed in New York as a general practitioner. His son remembers that Spofford liked to discuss psychiatric case histories, and indeed his second wife (whom he'd met in Vienna) was herself a psychiatrist; moreover he took an interest in the drinking problems of artistic people he'd met through Becker and another mutual friend from Harvard, the poet and dance critic Edwin Denby. The latter referred Willem de Kooning to Spofford, who was happy to help the great abstract expressionist recover from a string of benders in the mid-1930s, for which de Kooning (not yet famous) paid him with a few paintings.* Spofford's son doesn't recall his father ever presuming to practice actual psychoanalysis, and suggested that his treatment of de Kooning, for instance, was strictly physical: "He was a big believer in exercise and healthy diet," said the son, "which was ironic, because he smoked cigarettes pretty heavily all his life." Nevertheless it does appear to be the case that Spofford pursued a lucrative sideline in psychoanalysis; after all, Freud's ideas were only just gaining currency in the States, and perhaps Spofford figured he was better qualified than most to apply them, having heard the man speak with his own ears. Louise Rosskam remembered that her husband, Edwin, a writer and noted photographer, had also sought help from Spofford—*qua* psychiatrist—who advised the man to conquer his depression by getting on with his writing.

He gave the same advice to Jackson, more or less, who later mentioned their sessions in a piece he wrote for *Life* magazine:

> At considerable expense I went, in my early thirties, to a psychiatrist. After many weeks and much outlay of money he told me that my problem was psychological merely; that I was frustrated, hadn't "realized" myself, and that as soon as I began to make some headway as a writer and to achieve the recognition that I seemed to crave,

---

* Spofford gave one of these to Denby (his best friend and his son's namesake), who later sold it and used the proceeds to buy a house.

my alcoholic difficulties would clear up and I would be able to drink again like a normal drinker. This made sense to me, probably because I wanted it to.

Spofford was hardly alone in thinking alcoholics could become "normal" drinkers. Though it has since been established that alcoholism is a virtually incurable condition that can only be "arrested" by way of total abstinence, it was widely believed among Freudians in the 1930s (at the Menninger Clinic, for example) that one could relearn moderate drinking if one's neurotic conflicts were resolved. And besides, for a while anyway, Charlie enjoyed his morning sessions with Spofford. He'd always liked making new friends—a new audience, that is, for the fascinating story of his life, though it also followed that certain friendships tended to pall once the story was told ("He could almost gauge the length of such a relationship by how much or how little he had revealed of his past"). And then—as he would complain in a letter he wrote for a subsequent (non-Freudian) therapist—Jackson became contemptuous of the glib way Spofford attached "fancy psycho-analytical labels" to highly specific complaints, with little of the deeper human insight that the patient himself brought to the study of Charles Jackson. Nor did he really believe, at bottom, that he'd ever be able to drink normally, and thus "began to doubt the superiority of [Spofford's] judgment, began to hold out on him and fool him."

Once he discovered that Jackson was, indeed, drinking quite a lot again, Spofford tried various novel approaches toward containing the problem. In *The Lost Weekend*, "the foolish psychiatrist" gives Don an envelope of sodium amytal tablets to help calm his nerves and wean him off alcohol, whereupon Don takes the whole packet at once and (as he'd halfway intended) almost kills himself. Finally—the better to shame his patient into cooperation, perhaps—the psychiatrist writes up, for Don's signature, a little document that reads in part:

> I hereby acknowledge that I am a pretty good guy when I am sober but that when I am tight I am not responsible for what I do or say. . . . In order therefore not to become a nuisance when I am tight I should like to make the following agreement.
>
> If I feel the urge to drink, and am able to control this urge enough to go home and in the presence of my brother or doctor drink 6 bottles of beer, I agree that I shall then remain in my house two days. If . . . I am not able to control myself in this manner and I

feel myself forced to drink whiskey or more than two beers without consulting my doctor, I agree that I must spend seven days the first time this experience happens, 8 days the second time, nine days the 3rd time, etc. in my house. . . . except for two hours from 10:45 to 12:45 during which time I shall visit my doctor and get fresh air. . . .

I wish this agreement to hold until I and my doctor decide it should be dissolved.

Jackson refused to sign the agreement ("Childish he was, but not that childish—nor so foolish as the foolish psychiatrist"), which survives among his papers word for word as it appears in *The Lost Weekend.** Two and a half years later, sober and gainfully employed, Jackson considered returning the paper to Spofford with a twitting little note: "Dear [Paul]— Look what I found 'among my souvenirs.' . . . Anyway I'm proud of myself that I refused to sign it, because I knew, even then, that it would never do any good." Instead he terminated therapy on the spot.

Then and now, psychoanalysts (manqué and otherwise) have rarely gotten good results with alcoholics. Though it may be correct to assume that compulsive drinking is symptomatic of an underlying neurosis, the symptom meanwhile evolves into a separate and no less pressing problem—chemical dependency—which in turn may be exacerbated by the analyst's efforts to address the neurosis. Saint-Exupéry's tippler in *The Little Prince*—who drinks because he is ashamed, and is ashamed because he drinks—is a nice illustration of the conundrum, one that Jackson struggled with in life and art. "He knew what no one else knew, no one he had ever met yet," Jackson wrote in a discarded passage from *The Lost Weekend*: "His 'disease' [i.e., alcoholism] was not disease, or at least not the principal thing from which he suffered." This was meant to reflect the Freudian notion of an underlying neurosis, though perhaps it pointed too directly at what Freud himself considered almost a constant among alcoholics: repressed homosexuality. According to Freud, male homosexuals drink because of their failed relations with women, and because it provides an excuse to seek the company of men. Don Birnam, for his part, implicitly blames his drinking on the more fearful "disease" of homosexuality, though at other times it's precisely the other way

---

* With one difference: in the novel, the agreement is dated "April 13th 1936"—roughly six months before the lost weekend in question—whereas the actual agreement is dated April 13th *1935*.

around: "What Bim"—the male nurse at Bellevue—"did not see was that the alcoholic is not himself, able to choose his own path, and therefore the kinship he seemed to reveal"—i.e., their common homosexuality—"was incidental, accidental, transitory at best." Thus Don is homosexual because he drinks, and drinks because he is homosexual.

While it wouldn't do for Jackson to mention as much for the benefit of *Life* readers in 1954, homosexuality—along with his frustration as a writer—was most assuredly ventilated in his sessions with Spofford, who likely counseled acceptance. Freud himself (though a later generation of disciples would take a decidedly different line) was almost nothing but tolerant on the subject, once writing to the distraught mother of a gay son: "Homosexuality is assuredly no advantage but it is nothing to be ashamed of, no vice, no degradation, it cannot be classified as an illness; we consider it to be a variation of the sexual function." Radiantly enlightened for the times, Freud was doubtful that homosexuality was something that could (or need) be "cured," though he wrote the mother that he might be able to "bring [her son] harmony, peace of mind, full efficiency" if indeed the young man was unhappy—that is, Freud would try to help him come to terms with his nature. As for Dr. Spofford, he was often fiercely indignant about the way homosexuals were treated in twentieth-century America, as he had every reason to be. His lifelong friend Edwin Denby had left Harvard his sophomore year because of homophobic harassment, and Spofford agreed to leave with him; together the friends took a steamer to England, and later—after an interval of "study" in Greenwich Village—Denby decided to accompany Spofford to Vienna. Still haunted by the ostracism he'd suffered at Harvard, and afraid he had no future in mainstream society, Denby was suicidal by the time he finally knocked on Freud's door and was referred to a colleague, Dr. Paul Federn, whose patient he became for many years. One assumes the relationship was fruitful. Returning to the States, Denby began writing a column for *Modern Music* magazine, and a few years later Virgil Thomson recruited him for the New York *Herald-Tribune*, where he became one of the most influential dance critics of his time, as well as an estimable poet.

He also became more openly gay, as Spofford's son remembers, though one can only speculate about Spofford himself: in the penultimate draft of *The Lost Weekend*, Jackson deleted a reference to the foolish psychiatrist's "homosexual lover," and was all the more vexed, therefore, when John Becker accused him of being "ungenerous" in his portrayal of Spofford. Jackson's reply may well be the most uncharitable letter he ever wrote, suggesting perhaps that he was still feeling ill-used by these two (or at least Becker) nine years later:

> By my lack of generosity, I suppose you mean the way I handled "the foolish psychiatrist." It was absolutely in keeping with the character of Don Birnam in the state he was in, to treat the psychiatrist in just that way and no other, and to call him "foolish"—which, to the knowing reader, is a commentary more on the protagonist than on the doctor. If you think it was ungenerous, you should have seen the original version, from which I later deleted many many facts (and I mean *facts*) because they might possibly hurt [Paul Spofford], though of course the general reader would never know who the character was based on. . . .
>
> Or, if you want to feel that you are right and think that I am "generous" and "ungenerous" to my friends as characters, wait until you read the next book. Perhaps someone will then rise in defense of you as you do now in defense of [Paul], because of my portrayal of an ineffectual, aging dilettante whose motives in desiring to help the colored race it would not need a psychiatrist to define. Still, this will hardly apply to you, because by the time the book comes out you will probably be trying to run an art gallery, or summer theater, or write somebody else's children's book, or study criminology, or learn to be an actor . . . —You see? You say I'm ungenerous, so I will be.

Nor did he leave it at that. Five years later, in "The Sunnier Side"—his long meditation on the parlous relationship between life and art—Jackson mentioned an aggrieved reader of *The Lost Weekend* who protested his characterization of "the foolish psychiatrist" as follows: " '*I am literally appalled at your cavalier treatment of Dr. Becker* [*sic*] . . .' "

Dr. Spofford's son was nine years old when *The Lost Weekend* was released as a movie, and he remembers his father mentioning the man who'd written the novel it was based on. Whether he was rueful is hard to say, though his son feels certain that Spofford would have agreed, later, that as a thirty-four-year-old "psychiatrist" who'd just completed his residency, he'd been foolish indeed on the subject of alcoholics; in any case he learned the hard way that they're unlikely to revert to moderate drinking. Spofford himself "became a heavy alcoholic for many years," his son pointed out, until finally he got sober with the help of Alcoholics

Anonymous. He died in 1983, within a few months of his friend Denby's suicide.

AROUND THE TIME he broke with Spofford, in April 1935, Jackson resumed writing fiction after an almost two-year lull. He had reached a point of desperation whereby he was willing to write about a seminal trauma—the "fraternity nightmare" at Syracuse—despite the taboo nature of the subject. In a 1943 letter to his agent, Bernice Baumgarten, he remarked of a subplot in the soon-to-be-completed *Lost Weekend*, "I could write a book in itself about the fraternity"—eliding the fact that he'd already written such a book. If *Native Moment* had found a publisher (and it seems to have come rather close), it would have been a work of pioneering frankness in American fiction.

Primavera, the original title of *Native Moment*, suggests the Arcadian ambience of "State University," where carefree freshmen gad about the streets in pajamas to celebrate football victories, where they rise to the chimes of the Fine Arts tower, evoked with arch lyricism reminiscent of Fitzgerald's *This Side of Paradise*: the chimes "served the double purpose of summoning the student to his eight o'clock class and smiting his impressionable breast with a sonorous reminder of the dignity and prestige . . . of his Alma Mater." Into this pastoral comes Phil Williams, an *ingénu* who can't bring himself to grasp why the company of the "handsome but rather dissipated" Tracey Burke makes him so happy: "It was something like being on a hill at home, in his childhood—something, but not quite like it. . . . On the hill at home, all had been plain and clear." Groping for ways to express his adoration, Phil treats the older boy with a kind of doting, maidenly servitude, loaning him all the money he can spare (and some he can't), and each night stealing downstairs in the fraternity house to cover him, passed out on the couch, with his own sheepskin jacket. "There lies Tracey, like a beautiful warrior in vinous sleep," he writes Bettina, "with, more often than not, a bottle of gin beside him." That even Bettina should find this a bit much ("you sound like a mother") suggests the breadth of Phil's confusion before his own nature, as he wrestles with the difference between that "hill at home" and whatever compels him to tell Tracey, bemusedly, "I'm very fond of you"—the same phrase that, ten years later, would cause another beloved object, Cliff Hauman, to pummel the hapless John Grandin with a pair of fire tongs in *The Fall of Valor*.

But Hauman is a relatively innocent cretin, horrified by his own latent homosexuality, whereas Tracey Burke—well, Jackson was unsure *what* to make of him. "He's not our kind and doesn't belong here," Johnny Carr warns Phil. "He's corrupt and he corrupts." Certainly his eventual seduction and betrayal of Phil would bear this out, but then a certain ambivalence is suggested in a passage elsewhere that seems almost to celebrate, or at least exonerate, Burke as a "man of appetites": he "was the complete male of whom Phil was always to stand in awe . . . untouched by worry or woe, cruel only in being true to himself, and chiefly concerned—and rightly—with his body, his belly, and his bed." *And rightly:* such an idea was likely derived from Santayana's *The Last Puritan*, which Jackson discovered in early 1936 while revising *Native Moment*. In a letter to Boom, he enthused that the novel's author was "the most civilised man" he knew ("so wise, so witty, so good-humoured about life, and so right"), and that Boom was apt to "fall in love with" one character in particular—the sexually ambiguous Jim Darnley (expelled from the Navy for "immorality" with sailors): "He is Tracey Burke without viciousness, a healthy animal, the paragon of what man is intended no doubt to be, unruffled, untroubled by the problems of the age. . . ." Darnley and Tracey Burke (who, it seems, was rendered a bit less vicious in revision) were creatures that Jackson could only contemplate, wistfully, through the bars of his own cage; whatever his abstract hopes to the contrary, and whatever his actual behavior, he would remain stubbornly troubled by the problems of his age.

Such anyway was the divided mind that could admire *The Last Puritan* on the one hand, and yet go on longing for acceptance from "the blond and blue-eyed, the fair and living, the happy, lovely, and commonplace," as Mann would have it. That Phil Williams might be exiled forever from that happy fraternity—both Kappa U and the blue-eyed world at large—is so dreadful a prospect that he searches the mirror for some sign of his own sexual corruption, a little surprised to find his face "as young and clear as ever—the tilted quizzical eyebrow, the clear eyes and forehead, the adolescent mouth—absurdly young." And how does such a vulnerable youth find his way in the world? The novel's last pages—composed mostly of a long and rather ponderous colloquy between Phil and his revered English teacher, Ralph Monroe (named in honor of Jackson's dead mentor Ralph Monroe Eaton)—remind one that Jackson was even then casting about for reasons not to drink himself to death. "Things *are* as bad as you think they are," says Dr. Monroe, "or you wouldn't be thinking it. But man grows richer by his fate, they say, even if it kills him, and still greater when he endures it." Along with a mulish refusal to give up, then ("You'll get used to it"), the way one endures would seem to be twofold: "The only thing that matters," Monroe continues (laying a hesitant hand on Phil's knee), "is to look about, to see whom it is you love, and to love *him* [my italics] . . . " Jackson would be long overdue in following that advice in earnest, though another course is suggested by a scene in *The Lost Weekend*—when Don flees the Kappa U house for the last time and finds himself standing, dazedly, in front of a bookshop with Fitzgerald's new (as of 1922) *Tales of the Jazz Age* in the window; the book is open to the story "May Day," the first two pages of which are so wonderful that Don, reading them, all but forgets his recent disgrace.*

Hence the consolations of art that would stand Jackson in good stead almost to the end, though his own writing would prove a mixed blessing at best. As Dr. Monroe remarks to Phil, with uncanny prescience, "Your writing is going to be damned interesting—twenty years from now, say . . . " Almost twenty years exactly after his time at Syracuse, Jackson began writing *The Lost Weekend*; meanwhile he tried bearing in mind that he was "a plant of slow growth," as when the Curtis Brown agency rejected (on December 23, 1936) the latest product of his long apprenticeship: "[*Native Moment*] has received more than the usual attention in this office but we regret to say that we do not feel sufficiently confident of the commercial possibilities to be able to undertake to offer it in the market for you."

CURTIS BROWN'S careful attention took a long time, and their eventual decision was almost certainly a foregone conclusion. Jackson's behavior for much of 1936, at any rate, was hardly that of a man with great expectations, literary or otherwise. Later he would remember the eerie sensation of waking up—after weeks of free-fall drinking—in a strange hotel,

---

* The typescript of *Native Moment* ends with that long conversation between Phil and Dr. Monroe, but Jackson's notes suggest that he'd once had a far more dramatic ending in mind: "Night scene, Professor and stadium" is followed by "Scene XIV—Return dejection, suicide letter, walk downtown at night, *book in window* [my italics], sees Johnnie [*sic*], is run over." Thus a piquant irony: the suicidal Phil sees the "book in window"—*Tales of the Jazz Age*, no doubt, as in *The Lost Weekend* (and real life?)—and is duly cheered up, only to be distracted by Johnny and killed by a passing car.

where he would try to act nonchalant as he rang for a bellhop to bring him the morning paper so he could see what city he was in and what day it was ("if not the week and the month"). In 1942, while researching *The Lost Weekend*, he asked a doctor at Bellevue if he could tour the alcoholic ward, candidly admitting that he'd been there "twice as a patient, but I remember nothing of it." Actually he remembered at least two things; as he wrote in his unpublished confession, "The Sleeping Brain," he'd overheard a doctor explaining to a visitor that delirium tremens was "a disease of the night," and hence Don Birnam's reflection: "God what an expression. Beautiful as a line of verse, something to remember and put down sometime—remember in quite a different way and for quite a different reason than he meant to remember *paraldehyde*. . . ." The latter item—a foul-tasting but highly effective sedative that was then the staple drug for alcoholics in withdrawal—had struck Jackson as the "discovery of [his] life," and would someday become known to his daughters as "Papa's medicine," the ingestion of which was signaled by a curious odor ("like butter rum Life Savers") that hung in the air when they'd go to his room to kiss him good night.

The Lost Weekend is set in October 1936, and the bender it describes suggests that Don Birnam is very nearly at the end of his rope—and so with Jackson, who finally stopped drinking in November of that year. One rumor, which lingered for years after the novel was published, was that Jackson had been frightened into sobriety by the murder of his friend Nancy Titterton—that he'd been drunk at the time and could remember nothing when the police questioned him as a suspect: the worst possible consummation, this, of the drunkard's constant "terror," as Don Birnam puts it, "of some dreadful deed committed for which, though you were called to account, you could never bear witness." For what it's worth, Jackson dismissed the Titterton story as apocryphal: yes, he'd been questioned by police, and had responded with "perfect lucidity"—besides, the murder had occurred on April 10, 1936, some seven months before he'd gotten sober. And yet the episode deserves at least summary elaboration here.

"Did you know that Nancy was with us when we went to the boat to see Thor-and-bride sail?"* Jackson wrote his mother, ten days after the murder. "It was a very pleasant day we had with her and I'm glad for I

---

* Thor Lyngholm and his fiancée, Alice—twenty-two years his senior—were on their way to Bermuda, a development that will be discussed in the next chapter.

shall never forget it, nor how charming she looked and was. Funny, after they moved out of Hell's Kitchen (10th Ave) last fall and took the apartment in Beeckman [*sic*] Place, Nancy said, 'Now at last I can feel safe, living in a decent neighborhood.' " Nancy Titterton was, like Jackson, a thirty-three-year-old aspiring novelist; she and her husband, Lewis, who headed the literary rights department at NBC, were part of Charlie and Boom's arty cocktail set. On April 10, an upholsterer named Theodore Kruger and his young assistant, Johnny Fiorenza, went to the Tittertons' apartment at 22 Beekman Place to return a couch they'd repaired the day before; the door was ajar, water was running inside, and when they entered they found Nancy's naked body facedown in the bathtub. Beneath the body was a length of venetian-blind cord that was eventually traced to Kruger's shop, whereupon Fiorenza confessed to the crime: while picking up the couch the day before, he said, he'd formed the impression that Nancy was attracted to him, so he'd returned early the next morning, alone, and ended up raping and strangling her. In the meantime the case had become one of the biggest murder investigations in New York history. Lewis Titterton had pointed out that his wife was almost morbidly shy, unlikely to admit a total stranger, so the couple's acquaintances were all exhaustively interviewed; Lewis himself was the main suspect, but police were also considering the possibility that a secret lover had done it. After Fiorenza confessed, Charlie wrote his mother that he was relieved Lewis had been spared "some hideous unknown scandal," while wondering how Nancy "of all people" should suffer such a fate: "I know of no one among my friends more retiring, more prim, demure, more lacking in obvious sex-appeal, than Nancy was. Except that the week before the murder she'd had her hair bobbed, and it did make a big difference in her appearance."

Eight years later, while in Hollywood for the first time, Jackson was surprised to find that the most common reason given for his sobriety was his alleged role in the Titterton case—and the following year (1945), sure enough, an item appeared in Irving Hoffman's *Hollywood Reporter* column: back in his days as an "incurable inebriate," Hoffman wrote, Jackson had been questioned by police about "the murder of a model" in his East 55th Street apartment house; it had been "proven that someone in the building was guilty," but while the other tenants had alibis, Jackson ("just recuperating from a three-day drunk") remembered nothing and was therefore taken to jail. Six days later, the real murderer was apprehended: "Jackson was dismissed and has never taken a sip of the stuff since that time." Jackson, who wanted to sue, pointed out that Hoffman had conflated the details of the Titterton case with the murder of a model named Veronica Gedeon, but in any event he'd had "nothing to do" with either crime. Soon a contrite Hoffman issued a retraction: his story had been "absolutely untrue in every aspect."

Not quite *every* aspect: as it happened, the Titterton case had caused Jackson a certain amount of vexation and even trauma. Once the crime had been solved, Lewis Titterton sent him a sheepish note: "I have found it hard to write to you after the turmoil into which the police through the necessity of their work cast your and Frederick's lives." The fact was, Charlie *had* been a suspect of sorts, however fleetingly, because of the affectionate way Nancy had inscribed a book she'd given him at that last luncheon in the Lyngholms' honor ("She was very fond of you," said Lewis, deploring the coincidence, "and the gift was her way of showing it"); Boom and Rhoda had also been questioned, perhaps by way of exculpating Charlie. His drinking, however, seems to have had little to do with it, though the rumor would prove a hardy part of his alcoholic legend. "It was the week of the Gideon [*sic*] murder case," Leonard Lyons wrote in his syndicated column a few days after Charlie's death, "and Jackson couldn't remember where he'd been at the time of the murder . . . " Afterward Jackson had gone on the wagon, said Lyons, who waggishly added, "[he] fell off only once. He came to on the rim of the Grand Canyon." The next day Lyons corrected himself: he'd meant, of course, the *Titterton* case.

Charlie may or may not have been drunk on the day of Nancy's murder, but certainly he drank a lot afterward. For the rest of April and much of May, he left New York and took a room at the Grove Lawn Inn in Clayton, New Jersey, an area where he and Boom had friends. Until then, Rhoda's support and encouragement had rarely wavered, but finally she began to lose hope: "For years Charlie was here," she wrote Boom in late April, "and when Charlie was here I didn't need anyone else. And when he was away, still there was Charlie and I didn't think anything about not going out or seeing anyone or meeting new people. And it's just hung on, although Charlie hasn't." In fact, their relationship had been strained in recent years, even at the best of times. In *The Lost Weekend*, Don broods about his weekend dinners "chez Helen": "so charming and cosy and *intime*—so God damned *intime* that you weren't even left alone long enough to sneak a drink out of the hall-closet where she kept the liquor (and kept it is right)." Scarcely able to go to the bathroom without being furtively watched ("to see if it was the bathroom door you had opened and not the door to the closet next to it"), Don makes excuses to leave as early as possible, the better to bolt around the corner for a drink. As for Charlie's behavior when drunk, it would be hard to say whom he hurt more; in the novel, the sodden Don insists on reading his favorite writers to Helen, aloud, and then exclaims, "Isn't it *wunderbar*?"—which afterward leads to the usual awful chagrin ("for having mutilated the beautiful passage, . . . for having pretended to accept Helen's pretense [of enjoyment], and for having used the word *wunderbar*"). For Rhoda's twenty-seventh birthday, in 1934, Charlie wrote a little poem that nicely reflected their dynamic:

> *I would sing you a clever song,*
> *With many a fine word;*
> *And it would be the best song*
> *You ever heard. . . .*
>
> *But my song will go unstated*
> *I will never write it, never;*
> *Because you're irritated*
> *When I have been so clever.*

For "clever" one should perhaps read "drunk," and also bear in mind that the clever Charlie liked to attribute Rhoda's irritation to her absolute lack of imagination.

Rhoda had come by her stoicism honestly, in every respect: loyal, patient, and considerate by nature, she was descended from a line of women who'd perforce learned that drinking was a "sickness," as Rhoda's mother, Isabella, liked to remind her vis-à-vis Charlie. Isabella's father had drunk away the family money ("they lost everything in Scotland and came here because of it"), and Rhoda also remembered the way her two cousins would come stay with them whenever Uncle Tommy was "off" again. So she understood all too well that Jackson couldn't help himself, and besides she loved him and really had no choice in the matter. Charlie, in turn, was alternately rueful for letting himself be infantilized by her kindness, and apt to take advantage of it whenever it suited his purpose. As he would often point out as a sober man, alcoholics tend to relish their "nuisance-value" ("in a perverse and childish way, they often enjoy being something of a problem")—or, as Richard Peabody put it, "prevented by his habit from living a constructive life, [the alcoholic] is unconsciously anxious to make a stir in the world, even though this stir is of a purely destructive nature. Anything is better than oblivion. In fact, he often considers himself a heroic villain or martyr."

By 1936, however, it appears that shame had gotten the upper hand, and Charlie knew better than to impose on Rhoda when he was drunk. It was simply too galling, later, to remember the uncomplaining way she'd nursed him, all the while refusing his mawkish proposals of marriage even though (as they both knew) she would have liked nothing better—if, that is, he could ever stop drinking, a possibility that seemed increasingly remote. "Boom, think of it," she wrote that April, "I'm getting to be twenty nine years old. And I'm nowhere at all. Miss Wells in our office got married, to everyone's surprise. . . . And it just makes me realize what a dead end I've let myself into. I never see people, and I never meet new ones. . . . Maybe I should join a lonely-hearts or something." Meanwhile she encouraged Boom to get Charlie into a dry-out sanatorium ("He'll do nothing himself, won't even try"), which at least might lead to some menial job "to keep the cure in place": "Charlie is pitiful," she concluded, "and when I think of what fun he used to be it makes me sad."

Boom, for his part, was getting fed up with Charlie, and never mind the wreck he was making of Rhoda's life. As Don's brother Wick chides him in *The Lost Weekend*, "It's all right for you to ruin your life, that's up to you . . . but you have no right to ruin someone else's." To underline the point, Boom was about to give up their apartment, and besides, he was simply too frail to get the most out of Manhattan anymore. Since returning from Europe, he'd been spending more and more time in South New Jersey, where he'd fallen in love with a thirty-five-year-old doctor (an osteopath like Thor) named Jim Gates. The lanky, pipe-smoking Gates kept an office in Bridgeton, but also spent part of the week in nearby Malaga—little more than a crossroads by a lake, where he was popular among locals for his kindness and quiet, rather naughty sense of humor. Still, for the sake of appearances (and other good reasons), he and Boom thought it best to live apart, and just recently a charming old house on Malaga's main highway had become available when its owner, an elderly schoolteacher, had died. The place was perfect for Boom's purposes: two blocks away from Jim's house on Defiance Road, and almost equidistant (about forty miles in either direction) from Philadelphia and Atlantic City, where Boom could indulge his still considerable appetite for cosmopolitan diversion. Also, there was room in the front of the house for the antique shop he wanted to open, and a barn out back where he could hang wool for the braided rugs he had started making. Within a few months Boom would move there permanently, and Charlie would be bereft of a caretaker.

For now Charlie lay low in Clayton, about five miles from Malaga, and affected to be serenely unaware that others were considering drastic measures. In his letters, he wrote of possibly visiting the Lyngholms in Bermuda, or just biding his time until June, when he would leave for another summer in Brattleboro. In the meantime he whiled away his days watching movies in Philadelphia ("Gary Cooper [in *Mr. Deeds Goes to Town*] has never been more charming, and I do like Jean Arthur so much"), getting "terrible" headaches from reading in the sun, and (between the lines) drinking. Later he'd tell of how he almost drowned in Malaga Lake—nearly swept over the dam, drunk, into the churning waters below.

The six months between Jackson's stay in Clayton and his abrupt sobriety are all but lost to posterity. He did not, it seems, go to a sanatorium; rather he spent another few weeks at the farm in Saugerties, then resumed his duties as stage manager in Brattleboro. Again, the ghastly bender in *The Lost Weekend* takes place in October 1936, and something of that sort might have happened to Charlie, proving climactic. Suffice it to say, Jackson hit bottom: "I didn't want to live this way, but I was helpless," he'd later tell AA gatherings all over the country. "I hated it as much as everyone around me. I knew I was sick and couldn't get help anywhere." On the night of November 11—Armistice Day ("I don't know why I chose that date")—he and Boom were drinking highballs at the Taft Hotel in New York. "That's the last drink I'll ever take," Charlie decided, then said goodbye to his brother for many months. The next day he moved to a shabby rooming house on the Upper West Side and resolved to stay there, alone, until he was sober for good. "I didn't tell anybody what I was going to do. I knew better than to say I was through drinking—I'd said this many times. I knew I had to say it to *myself*, and I did."

Chapter Six

Sweet River

In the 1930s, most doctors believed that alcoholics ("dipsomaniacs") were hopeless cases. Maybe a handful had the willpower to quit on their own, and as for the rest—"once a drunkard, always a drunkard." Jackson, however, thought he might get the help he needed from "an exceptionally intuitive man" who could understand how the alcoholic felt inside—from a man, better still, who was himself an alcoholic—and so on November 12, 1936, he met with an intuitive alcoholic named William Wynne Wister.

Bill or "Bud" Wister was an eccentric, gesticulating redhead who practiced (unlicensed) as a "psychotherapist in alcoholism," and would later boast that he'd cured 294 out of 300 patients—including the author of *The Lost Weekend*. Born into an affluent family in Chestnut Hill, Philadelphia (one of the "Philadelphia Main Line Wisters," as he liked to say, and nephew of the great Western novelist Owen Wister), Bud would always assert that his plush upbringing was primarily to blame for his disastrous twenty-year drinking career. After graduating from The Hill School in nearby Pottstown and serving in the Royal Canadian Air Force during the Great War, he became a consummate Jazz Age wastrel: racing to speakeasies in his Stutz Blackhawk four-seater, a tipsy flapper at his side, he could always count on his wealthy parents (an overprotective mother in particular) to get him out of jams. Even the private sanatoria they chose for him only pandered to his habit: since doctors figured their patients were hopeless anyway, they fed them one drink an hour to keep them happy, while their families went on shelling out $150 a week.

Wister hit bottom in the fall of 1934, when he woke up in yet another seedy, anonymous, sickishly spinning hotel room, "one hundred per cent licked." Wondering where else to turn, he remembered a book he'd skimmed several months before (planted at his bedside by the overprotective mother): *The Common Sense of Drinking*, by Richard Peabody, who, according to the New York directory, was then living on Gramercy Park South. A lay therapist, Peabody would have anticipated the depth of Wister's misery—as he'd written in his book, "No action may result until some particularly depressing series of events has brought vividly home to [the alcoholic] the futility of trying to continue drinking and the apparent impossibility of giving it up unaided." Such ideas—and some of the catchier phrases with which he conveyed them—would later be appropriated by Bill Wilson for his "Big Book," *Alcoholics Anonymous*, whose famous admonition in favor of total abstinence ("Half measures availed us nothing") was first expressed by Peabody as "*Halfway measures are of no avail*," as was "*Once a drunkard, always a drunkard.*" (Peabody was fond of italics: "A fairly exhaustive inquiry has elicited *no exceptions* to this rule," he said of the second phrase.)

Wister figured that Peabody had also been a drinker, but their affinity went further. Peabody, too, was from an illustrious family, a graduate of Groton School (where his uncle, Dr. Endicott Peabody, was headmaster) and Harvard; moreover he'd served in the Great War as an infantry captain, which left him with a keen sense of how alcoholism was, to some extent, a byproduct of the zeitgeist. "In the twentieth century," his book begins, "with its high-pressure demands on nervous systems which have not yet become adapted to big business, mass production, telephones, automobile, high economic standards—in fact, bigger, faster, and noisier living conditions—alcohol has come to play an ever-increasing part as a narcotic, rather than a mere social stimulant." Above all, there was the sheer nihilism of those who'd survived the war's mechanized carnage, and who thus found it hard to cope with the noisy vacuous boredom of the peacetime world. Apart from drinking, Peabody had but a single passion after the war—chasing fire engines—to which end he'd installed a special alarm in his house, and would hastily don helmet, hip boots, and rubber coat whenever the call came. Finally, after the usual alcoholic mishaps, Peabody had gotten sober with the help of the so-called Emmanuel Movement (though he went on with his fire hobby), whose more practical methods he eventually refined into a program all his own—*minus* the emphasis on fellowship and spirituality that would later become the bases of Alcoholics Anonymous.

Peabody prided himself on a purely "scientific" approach ("common sense and sound psychological principles"): "He never mentioned the moral aspects of drinking," Wister observed. "He spoke objectively, as though he were discussing the proper treatment for a broken leg." The first thing Peabody explained to his new patient was that he could never drink again; also, the patient had to get sober for his *own* benefit—nobody else was to blame if things went awry. Given the alcoholic's long habit of petty deceptions, *honesty* in all things was now key, and hence Peabody (and later AA) would instruct patients to make amends toward people they'd hurt, and notify creditors that they planned to repay them. Perhaps the most essential aspect of the Peabody Method, especially in the early stages of treatment, was keeping a routine: each night, before retiring, the patient was to make a careful schedule accounting for every fugitive minute, if possible, of the following day—shaving, dressing, eating breakfast, looking for a job, reading *improving* books, and making allowance for a bit of chaste, well-earned diversion in the evening. Such a routine, said Peabody, accomplished "three very important results: (a) The individual is continuously occupied; (b) he is conscious that he is doing something *concrete* about his problem (in contrast to mere intellectualizing); (c) he trains himself constantly in minor ways to obey his own commands." The last was crucial to Peabody's notion of "thought control": restoring reason to its throne, as it were, and putting one's emotional self in its place. The latter, of course, wanted to keep drinking—to remember the music and fellowship of the tavern, to feel petulant about old grievances, to succumb to childish nostalgia for a more romantic life. One must learn to detect the siren song of the emotional self in all its insidious variations, and quash it as a matter of reflex.

In April 1936, Peabody declared that Wister no longer needed his services; indeed, he'd been so successful a patient, said Peabody, that he might consider taking up psychotherapy himself—ever vigilant withal, lest he deceive himself about being "irrevocably cured." Three weeks later the forty-three-year-old Peabody died of a "heart attack," according to *The New York Times* (he "attended all large fires in the city and was well known to many Fire Department officials"), and Wister was desolate: "A truly great man had left the scene." He called Peabody's widow, who told him that Dick had been feeling run-down lately; he'd been resting at their house in Vermont when a bad cold developed into pneumonia and he died suddenly in his sleep. So Wister reported in a "biographical novel," *The Glass Crutch* (1945)—though a friend and colleague of Peabody, Samuel Crocker, claimed that the man had actually died drunk. As Bill Wilson wrote in his copy of *The Common Sense of Drinking*, "Dr. Peabody was as far as it is known the first authority to state, 'once an alcoholic, always an alcoholic [*sic*],' and he proved it by returning to drinking and by dying of alcoholism—proving to us that the condition is incurable."

Whatever the case, Wister picked up a fallen standard, renting a studio near his master's on Gramercy Park and arranging to see patients who'd been "cleared up physically" and referred by doctors. Jackson was among the first,* and felt immediately at ease with the practical, no-nonsense nature of the Peabody Method. Unlike "the foolish psychiatrist," Wister never asked him to make promises he couldn't keep, never reproached or patronized him, and therefore gave him no reason to be anything other than absolutely honest: "We regard each other as two average normal individuals with sufficient intelligence to regulate our lives in orderly and profitable fashion without benefit of Freud," Jackson wrote in a progress report (prescribed by Peabody) after the first month:

Constantly cropping up now (as they have been for years) are my misdemeanors of the past: times when I made a fool of myself, the night I did this-or-that, the week I disappeared, the grief I caused So-and-so, the damage I did when, etc. etc. etc.—nightmare experiences, all of them, especially when heightened by the light of sober reality. But since I have given up drinking I can look back upon all these unflinchingly now, with the knowledge that I was truly *not responsible* then. As opposed to this, however, is the *real* responsibility I have lately acquired, a sound responsibility based on sobriety and my true self.

---

* It's unknown how Jackson first heard about Wister, though one may safely assume that Mr. Winthrop was paying for his treatment. Wister charged between two and ten dollars per daily visit, depending on a patient's ability to pay—either way, a lot of money in 1936.

Another thing Jackson liked about the program was its "sustaining power," the way it gave him something to think about between sessions—a good thing, because he had a lot of time to think, the more positively the better. For a while Jackson hardly stirred from his dingy little room except to see Wister; the rest of his (carefully scheduled) free time was mostly given over to reading Shakespeare.* Despite the upbeat tone of his progress report, Jackson's first months of sobriety were grim: withdrawal had left him enervated and suicidally depressed, and it didn't help that his days were passed in almost total, shabby solitude. He tried taking a mindless job at an electrical equipment plant (inspired by his time at the jigsaw factory, perhaps), but the eleven-hour workdays were more than his shattered nerves could stand.

At any rate he made it. Eight months after saying goodbye at the Taft Hotel, Charlie announced to Boom, Rhoda, and others that he was through drinking forever. Wister agreed: "I consider that you are cured," he wrote, warning however that Charlie should be careful about his tendency to procrastinate ("It would be dangerous for *you*"), and urging him to "develope [*sic*] the habit of giving out . . . get your mind off yourself"—even suggesting that he support an orphan ("Perhaps you have one of your own tucked away in NY or Syracuse," Wister quipped). He concluded as Peabody had taught: "*Don't ever forget <u>one</u> drink could wipe away all you possess so respect it*—perhaps fear it as I do."

Wister was right to fear it. A few years later he moved to Los Angeles in the hope of attracting a wide clientele of film-business alcoholics, until a "big slug psychiatrist" threatened to expose him for practicing without a license. Next he took an engineering job (though he wasn't an engineer) at Douglas Aircraft, and had a disastrous relapse once he'd been fired—at one point smashing off the neck of a whiskey bottle because his hands were too palsied to unscrew the cap. Returning sober (if not quite chastened) to New York, Wister took a job in advertising and married a long-suffering girlfriend—his second wife—who, he vowed, would be "neither nurse nor servant" but "an equal partner." And though he'd sworn off psychotherapy, he continued to regard himself as a leading

---

* Quite possibly Peabody would have warned him away from such potentially defeatist literature. In *The Common Sense of Drinking*, he specifically recommends reading about the lives of successful men: "Napoleon, Lincoln, Lee, Washington, Pasteur, and Disraeli cannot fail to act as an inspiration to a man who is endeavoring to get rid of an undesirable habit. Conversely, literature which deals with the charms of hedonism . . . should be carefully avoided until the patient is definitely cured."

authority on alcoholism. Jackson, for one, found him a little tiresome on the subject: "Oh well, I guess I've outgrown Bill Wister," he wrote a mutual friend in 1943, "and maybe a good thing too. But of course, if I should say such a thing out loud, Bill would be bound to get the idea that I was cocky, over-confident, and in a 'dangerous state.' "

The two fell out for good over a controversy involving their respective novels. Rather unfairly, Jackson accused Wister of undervaluing *The Lost Weekend* when he first read it: "[It] was simply beyond your comprehension," he wrote, adding that Wister's eventual appreciation was prompted by the good reviews. In fact, Wister had found an early portion of the manuscript "splendid"—though he (like many readers) hoped that Birnam would reform in the end—and finally provided a clumsy but glowing blurb: "Mr. Jackson's unusual ability to vividly portray the gamut of emotions and subsequent behavior so characteristic of the alcohol addict—makes the work a masterpiece." But soon Jackson heard a rumor that Wister had been working on his own book, with a chapter on Jackson, no less. Ironically it was none other than Roger Straus—later Charlie's best friend—who played midwife to this curious project, approaching an editor at *Collier's*, Jim Bishop, to write Wister's story.* "The smiler turned out to be strange," Bishop remembered of his quasi-affable subject. "He seemed convinced that I was a stenographer, taking down his recollections word by word." Detecting the man's "inner irritation," Bishop asked why he was so determined to write such a painful book in the first place. "That's easy," said Wister, explaining that one of his old patients was also writing a potentially groundbreaking work about alcoholism—but happily the man was a procrastinator: "Charlie Jackson is very slow. Besides, he's writing a novel. . . . We're writing the facts."

Jackson beat him to the punch by more than a year, whereupon someone at Doubleday (Wister's publisher) saw an opportunity to capitalize on *The Lost Weekend*, informing the columnists Walter Winchell and Dorothy Kilgallen that a book titled *The Glass Crutch* was forthcoming from "the man who cured Charles Jackson." Wister (who "had a habit," said Bishop, "of bandaging his wounds in venomous letters to friends") heard that Jackson was considering a lawsuit, and hence let him know,

---

* *The Glass Crutch: The Biographical Novel of William Wynne Wister* was published as the work of Jim Bishop, who ultimately overcame its stigma by writing popular historical narratives such as *The Day Lincoln Was Shot* (1955) and *The Day Christ Died* (1957).

among other things, and in somewhat opprobrious terms, that Jackson wasn't mentioned even *once* in *The Glass Crutch*. But actually Charlie had no intention of suing, and had even offered to blurb the book for old times' sake. "I thought your letter one of the most outrageous I have ever received," he replied.

> You ought to be ashamed of it. I do not know what you are talking about when you talk of me "suing." . . . What I do object to more strongly, however, is the ridiculous statement in your letter: "If you are going to pretend you have never been an alcoholic, you are headed for trouble later." In the first place, I do not think you are a very good one to talk of "trouble later"; and in the second place, you are not showing very much sense in saying I am pretending I have never been an alcoholic. If I had pretended any such thing, would I have been fool enough to write such a book as *The Lost Weekend*? Really, Bill, use your head.

As it happened, *The Glass Crutch* would indeed be associated with Jackson in the public mind, though not in the way Wister might have liked. In a gleefully vicious notice for the *Times Book Review*, Wolcott Gibbs blamed Jackson ("who wrote that excellent book called 'The Lost Weekend' ") for having obliquely inspired—that is, by inaugurating the genre—a ghastly "tract" such as *The Glass Crutch*, which Gibbs described as the story of a reformed drunk who went on to become "a lay witch-doctor . . . and one of the great bores of our time." Nor could Charlie himself resist a bit of ambivalent schadenfreude: "By the way," he wrote a friend, "did you happen to read that unconsciously screamingly-funny life of William Wynne Wister of the Philadelphia Main-Line Wisters? I was embarrassed for him throughout: [Bishop] couldn't have played a dirtier trick on poor Bill if he had tried, though god knows he thought he was doing an honest job of hero-worship."

It was the beginning of a last, brisk decline for the man who cured Charles Jackson. Fed up with his pompous bickering, Wister's wife and friends left him in toto, and finally he lost his job too. "Alone and lonely," as Bishop later described him—without, that is, the kind of support system that AA was meant to provide—Wister began drinking again. One day in January 1947, a maid let herself into his Tudor City apartment and found him standing in the living room, unsteadily, strings of blood dangling from his open mouth. Once again he'd smashed off the neck of a whiskey bottle, but this time he'd swallowed some of the broken glass. He bled to death within a few hours (or rather died "after a brief illness," according to the *Times*).

"AND THEN BEGAN [in 1937] quite a wonderful period for me," Jackson would preface this part of his AA talk. With sobriety came a newfound confidence, "paradoxically" fortified (so he noted at the time) by a world that remembered his past all too well: "the skepticism I meet on all sides urges me to prove myself twice over." The first order of business was finding work—no easy feat, given that he hadn't held a nonmenial job in almost ten years. For the benefit of prospective employers, Jackson attributed the gap to his long spell of tuberculosis, doubling the time he'd spent in sanatoria—that is, claiming two years at Devitt's and four at the Schweizerhof, and thus accounting for all but four years of leisure. Beyond that, he affected a kind of nervous swagger that was found endearing by at least one man: Max Wylie, a script editor at CBS, and one of Jackson's best friends beginning in July 1937, when Jackson walked into his office "trembling like a whippet," as Jackson later put it.* Asked if he'd published anything yet, Jackson replied, "No, but I should have been published by now. I write well, I think." By way of evidence he provided a copy of *Native Moment*, which the broad-minded Wylie read that night with measured enthusiasm: "It was not a good novel," he remembered. "But it had some great pages."

As a trial assignment, Wylie asked Jackson to adapt the tale of Jacob and Esau for the CBS radio series *Living Stories of the Bible*; Jackson delivered the script the next day. "Where have *you* been!" said Wylie. "You're a writer!" Just to make sure, he asked for two more Bible stories, and received them within three days. Clearly Jackson had taken to heart Wister's advice about procrastination, and Wylie hired him as an assistant at $72.50 a week. It was money well spent. Wylie was struck by how "extraordinarily teachable" Jackson proved to be in the new (to him) medium of radio; he mastered it immediately, and was simply an

---

* Wylie, the younger brother of writer Philip Wylie—whose friendship with Jackson would prove less resilient—had written a forgettable novel, *Hindu Heaven* (1933), and would write a couple more. Alas, he became best known, in 1963, as the father of Janice Wylie, one of two victims in the famous "Career Girls" murder case. In 1968, Wylie's wife died of cancer, and his remaining daughter followed five months later (flu). Wylie committed suicide in 1975.

ideal employee besides. "Without any doubt Charles Jackson is the finest writer I have ever had on my staff," Wylie wrote two years later, when Jackson left CBS. "He is poetic, creative, brilliant, perceptive, and terribly conscientious." Wylie's main province was *The Columbia Workshop*, one of the most acclaimed radio programs of its time, for which it became Jackson's job to read, edit, and select almost every script, as well as to write continuity and introductions where needed. Some of the most famous broadcasts of the era were produced for the *Workshop*: Orson Welles adapted *Hamlet* and *Macbeth*, and also performed (with Burgess Meredith and a cast of some two hundred extras) in Archibald MacLeish's *The Fall of the City* (1937), an allegorical verse play about European fascism, aired from the Seventh Regiment Armory in Manhattan.

Though it wasn't part of his regular employment, Jackson also managed to sell seven of his own scripts to the *Workshop*, including a highly regarded adaptation of "The Devil and Daniel Webster" by Stephen Vincent Benét (who also wrote for the program), as well as two originals, *Dress Rehearsal* and *A Letter from Home*. The latter was a thirty-minute reworking of his apprentice play, *Simple Simon*, largely told in flashbacks and vastly improved by compression. In the frame story, a successful screenwriter named after Boom—Fred Storrier—receives a letter from "the girl [he] didn't marry," Bettina, who writes to congratulate him on his latest movie, a prison drama. Fred recites the gist of her letter while railing against his own mediocrity: " 'Young—intelligent—talented— charming!'—Hm!—'I picture you in New York—a gay and glamorous life!' . . . No, my dear Bettina, decidedly no." Chided by a blasé, mercenary wife, Fred casts back to his small-town youth, when he was a promising editor at the *Courier*—and so he might have remained were it not for the selfless Bettina, who, despite her love for him, demanded he get on with his life rather than marry her and languish in Arcadia. ("You wouldn't like me long if we stayed here . . . I'd sit at home and get green-eyed because you couldn't have clothes like—like Archer Brown. . . .") "Oh, it's sad to think of," Fred sighs to his wife. "I hadn't a doubt, not the faintest doubt, that I was going to be the great man in modern literature. . . . [And] now I write movies—at forty thousand a throw." "So would Shakespeare if he were living now," his wife sensibly concludes.

Along with Jackson's other accomplishments, Wylie noted his "extraordinary ability for recognizing talent." He made a point of reading the slush pile, welcomed visitors who wanted to pitch ideas, and thus personally discovered a number of writers who went on to considerable careers—including Norman Corwin, whose fame rests all but entirely on radio work. Corwin's reputation was established with his play *They Fly Through the Air with the Greatest of Ease* (1939)—about Mussolini's brutal bombing campaign against helpless Ethiopians—which was published as a book (his first of many) and dedicated to Jackson. "He had inspired that work," said Corwin. "Charlie was a great encouragement to me, who was then a novice in all things requiring sophistication on the part of a radio writer." In fact, Jackson often behaved as if he'd sooner help other writers than himself, though the flip side of such manic generosity was, as Corwin learned, a furious refusal to forgive slights. "Do I know Norman Corwin indeed!" he wrote a friend in 1945, pointing out that he'd been the dedicatee of Corwin's first book. "But something happened which is too long to go into now, and though we keep up a semblance of mutual admiration, I haven't much respect for him." What happened—as Corwin sadly remembered some seventy years later—was that he had buckled to a superior at CBS and cut Jackson's credit from a script: "I objected, but not strongly enough . . . and I never met or spoke to Charlie again. It was a dismal ending to a glorious friendship."

A more enduring friendship was with Nila Mack, a former vaudeville actress who found fame with her children's radio program *Let's Pretend*. Mack doted on Charlie (whom she regarded as "a rare and superior person," according to the playwright Howard Lindsay), and was perhaps even happier than he when *The Lost Weekend* made him famous: "To this day," she wrote him in 1945, "I still have that almost uncontrollable urge, when I see someone reading the book to kiss them first and then tell all about you." Along with warmhearted, morbidly sensitive natures, the two had alcoholism in common, which naturally led to a few snappish moments. When Jackson suffered a very public relapse in 1951, Mack ("three-sheets to the wind") gave him a "long tragic scolding" over the phone: "I took the whole thing very nicely for about fifteen minutes," he wrote Dorothea Straus, "because she *was* concerned . . . and said she was right, et cetera, and finally I got tired of it, and simply said, 'Okay, Nila, you've played that scene very well, but long enough—now go on back and have another drink.' "

CHARLIE'S SUCCESS at CBS helped convince Rhoda that his sobriety was permanent, and on March 4, 1938, they were married in Brooklyn by the former rector of St. Mark's Episcopal Church in Newark, Rush Sloane.

After a honeymoon in Boston, the couple took an apartment in the Village at 156 Waverly Place. "In the early years we . . . read the same things, heard music together, went to the theatre, shared much—oh, much," Charlie wrote his daughter Sarah in 1964, when he and Rhoda were sharing little more than living space. For a long time, though, he was extravagantly proud of his wife's character and competence ("she is one of FORTUNE magazine's ablest women"), and eager to show his devotion. Once, in 1942, he was emboldened to write directly to FDR—both he and Rhoda were avid New Dealers, despite coming from Republican families—and implore the man (unsuccessfully) to autograph a portrait as a Christmas gift to his wife. "A mother's prayers have been answered," Father Sloane remarked at the wedding, and certainly Charlie would have agreed that Rhoda deserved most of the credit for his relative well-being. At the same time he could be a trifle mordant when considering the matter privately: Yes, she was the "perfect-wife," all right, for the same reasons that made her nigh insufferable. As he wrote in *Farther and Wilder*, " 'No imagination,' [Don] sometimes said [of Helen], to justify his impatience or frustration—knowing as he said it, that his own susceptible, restless, hyperactive imagination was his curse fully as much as his blessing, the source of such recurrent impulses and enthusiasms, turmoils, gifts, explosive pressures, rewards and actual woe in any given year as would not come her way in a lifetime." As for Rhoda, she would only become *more* reserved, *more* literal-minded, by way of a corrective to her husband's "impulses and enthusiasms," which she learned to dread; as she wrote Boom, with weary insight, in 1947, "it's the same excitement that comes with addiction."

And what about her husband's sexual nature? Rhoda knew all about it, and seems to have accepted it as yet another facet of his protean personality: "If you should write the story of your life just as it was," she once told him, "nobody would believe it. You've been too many different people." Charlie, for his part, wanted children and a normal social life—wanted (it bears repeating) "to belong"; as Don puts it in *The Lost Weekend*, homosexuality "was a blind alley, not shameful but useless, futile, vain, offering no attractions whatever, no hope, nowhere a chance to build." Cruising, after all, became unseemly (and less fruitful) in middle age, and then there was the decorous, sublimated, crushingly lonely dotage that men such as Winthrop were given to endure. On the other hand, it went without saying that married life could go badly awry when one partner was gay. Tchaikovsky, for one, was married for all of two weeks before he almost succumbed to madness and suicide, and at least one gay friend of the Jackson brothers—a man nicknamed Flew—did, in fact, kill himself as the result of a marriage gone wrong. "The irony of it!" an acquaintance wrote Boom afterward. "Flew told me once that he married as an 'insurance against a lonely old age.' It worked, but not quite the way he had figured." Flew, an English professor in his fifties, had fathered two daughters during a sixteen-year marriage, when his wife suddenly learned the truth and decided (as she wrote at the time) that the situation "was more than [she] could handle." Flew celebrated a final birthday with Boom in Malaga ("I knew on my birthday I would not be seeing you again," he wrote in his subsequent thank-you note), then killed himself a few weeks later.

To be sure, Charlie was hardly averse (especially in later years) to complaining about the aridity of his own marriage, cursing "the perversity of the Fates" for having arranged the union of a man "who needs so badly to be loved" and a woman "who is unable to give it." "MY WIFE IS A GOOD WOMAN," he wrote with a wobbly hand in his journal (quoting Gauguin); "I WISH SHE WERE DEAD." But such moods were passing, and most of the time he realized better than anyone that he'd been almost miraculously fortunate. His gay friends were frankly amazed by Rhoda's forbearance, given that Charlie had assured them that, yes, he told her everything! The writer Ron Sproat—one of Charlie's protégés in the 1950s—was invited to the Jacksons' for dinner, and was struck by how pleasantly the evening proceeded: "Since Charlie was gay, I thought it was kind of—I felt strange about the situation. I thought his wife would think I was Charlie's boy. But if she did, she didn't show it. She was nothing but nice." *Nice* was the tip of a sizable iceberg. As Jackson wrote of the wife of his alter ego Jim Harron in *The Outer Edges*, "She was the balance wheel: without her he was lost. If he tried to go on alone, there was no telling what would happen to him."

His old friend Thor Lyngholm, meanwhile, had married a much older woman with money, and the two divided their seven years together between an estate in Bermuda ("with sixteen tenant houses no less," Charlie noted) and a place in Lynbrook, Long Island. Thor died at age fifty-four on July 1, 1943, the day after Charlie finished *The Lost Weekend*.

IN EARLY 1939, while still at CBS, Jackson resumed writing fiction on weekends, and one day he pursued a donnée that had occurred to him during a recent stay in Malaga. Harry and Grace Peech lived across Harding Highway from Boom, and on Palm Sunday Harry had invited the brothers into his basement to admire a sailboat that his teenage son, Freddy, had built all by himself. While the proud father boasted, Charlie couldn't help reflecting about how different the boy's life was from his own fatherless adolescence; then, from upstairs, he heard a hymn on the radio, "The Palms," and was powerfully reminded of his encounter with Quance, the predatory organist, more than twenty years before. Back in New York he wrote "Palm Sunday" in rapid longhand, then read it over and thought, "My god, you can't *say* that!"—while realizing, too, that it was easily the best thing he'd ever written; besides, if it was true of *him* . . . "He saw himself as an American everyman," Mary McCarthy would write of a character based on Jackson. "He felt that if he could tell the whole truth about himself, he would tell the whole truth about any ordinary American. This, in fact, he conceived to be his duty as a writer."

There was no question of selling the story to the mass-market "slick" magazines, but as it happened Charlie was far more attracted to the purely literary prestige of *Partisan Review*, whose commitment to "Marxism in politics and Modernism in art" might prove the ticket for his indictment of bourgeois hypocrisy in Arcadia, New York. It didn't hurt that a mutual friend had brought the manuscript to the attention of James T. Farrell, of *Studs Lonigan* fame, who personally recommended it to the journal's editors. "We like your story, 'Palm Sunday,' very much," wrote Dwight Macdonald (no less), accepting it for the summer 1939 issue—twenty-five copies of which Jackson purchased (beyond the usual author's allotment) for general distribution among family, friends, and detractors: "You probably think I'm crazy to order so many," he wrote, "but after all, it's Baby's First Story." A month later Macdonald informed him that "Palm Sunday" was perhaps their most acclaimed fiction since Delmore Schwartz's famous debut, "In Dreams Begin Responsibilities." Jackson was ecstatic: not only was he *finally* launched as a serious writer, but he was also getting invited to a lot of Village parties full of bona fide *New York intellectuals* such as Macdonald, Schwartz, and the journal's founding editor, Philip Rahv, who began writing chatty letters to Charlie on all sorts of earnest sociopolitical topics ("Today the whole city is agog with the news of the Nazi-Soviet rapprochement . . . ").

The iron was hot, and Jackson promptly wrote another story about a childhood trauma—"Rachel's Summer," based on the rumor of Thelma's pregnancy that had circulated so grievously around the time of her death—and once again *Partisan Review* snapped it up. When Macdonald proposed to publish it in their winter issue, Jackson argued with admirable chutzpah that his two stories should run in *consecutive* issues: "If PALM SUNDAY by any chance should cause 'talk' or make trouble for the news-dealers . . . it might be a very good thing to follow it up at once with another story by the same writer but this time a pleasant one [!], 'normal,' like RACHEL'S SUMMER, just to show that PR (and its writers) aren't necessarily limited to this sort of thing." The editors agreed: " 'Rachel's Summer,' by C. R. Jackson," appeared in the fall 1939 issue, and was subsequently listed among the "distinctive" stories of the year in Edward O'Brien's *Best Short Stories* volume. Indeed, Jackson would later reflect on his first two published stories with a kind of awe: "If I had it then, why haven't I got it now?" he wondered in 1951, after a spate of inferior work in the genre (though a year later he would produce "The Boy Who Ran Away," his third-favorite story thereafter).

Publishers began to inquire whether Jackson was working on a novel. He was and he wasn't. Certainly he had a very precise idea of the novel he wanted to write, and also he thought he had the confidence, now, to bring it off: a story about an alcoholic written "from the inside," a riposte to those who thought such a person was "a deliberate troublemaker . . . having a good time." At the moment, though, Jackson simply couldn't afford the luxury of novel-writing: Rhoda and he were trying to have a child, and soon they'd be taking a bigger apartment. For the time being, then, in a burst of inspiration—only a few days after finishing "Rachel's Summer"—he wrote an outline for his novel on a single sheet of yellow tablet paper that he would later frame and proudly show journalists: "Used it all," he'd declare. "The whole book is right there." This is true (give or take the odd detail)—all the more impressively so when one considers he wouldn't begin the actual writing for another three years. For the outline Jackson listed the five days of *The Long Weekend* (his working title) in the left margin, next to which the highlights of each day were scribbled in cramped, hurried cursive: "Carnegie Hall recital . . . sees movie—goes in—finds prison picture . . . Bellevue 'He awoke in a world of white' . . . nearly kills maid with Romulus and Remus as she brushed out fireplace . . . " That done, Jackson wrote a single paragraph of finished prose marking the start of Don's binge ("When the drink was set before him, he felt better"), which would appear almost word for word on page 11 of the published book. "I knew," he said, "I could pick it up anytime thereafter."

The better to accomplish the work that would buy time for a novel, Charlie and Rhoda moved to a larger place on Eighth Street, between Fifth and University, where they converted the dining room into Charlie's "brown study" (as he would forever call such sanctuaries). There he could keep office hours at a peaceful remove from (increasing) domestic distractions. The little brownstone near Washington Square was almost perfect: their apartment was a second-floor walk-up over a tailor shop ("Is he a good tailor?" Mr. Winthrop inquired); Charlie tastefully appointed the living room with a baby grand piano (he briefly took lessons, but never came close to fulfilling Don Birnam's Carnegie Hall fantasy), lined the walls with books and his enormous record collection, and hung a few of his own amateur paintings. There were two fireplaces and a small balcony—all for a hundred dollars a month.

Economy and a room of his own were crucial: the previous October (1939) Jackson had been laid off because of budget cutbacks at CBS, and since then he'd been scrambling for freelance work. Much of this was provided by his previous employer, which promptly hired him to write thirteen weekly programs titled *What's Art to Me?* ("rather on the dull side"), and gave him sporadic work on shows such as *You Decide* and *A Friend in Deed*. Also, in January, Jackson was employed by the Census Bureau at $19.80 per diem to write propaganda broadcasts urging citizens to cooperate with the 1940 census; the work required him to spend weekdays in Washington, and he was glad when the assignment ended in March—or rather, it was good to be home, though naturally money was tighter than ever, especially since his pregnant wife had taken leave from her job at *Fortune*. At a loss, Charlie decided to borrow a thousand dollars from Mr. Winthrop, though he worried this would strain their newly disinterested friendship. He even consulted Wister, who advised him (per Peabody) to approach the man "in a purely impersonal and strictly business-like way." Hence Jackson drafted an almost painfully formal letter, listing, at length, his various debts and plans for the future, and concluding with: "I would welcome the opportunity and the test of being able to repay you, for once, as promised, and hope this letter will serve as that promise." Winthrop gave him the money the next day. Almost two years later, Jackson was able to muster a $500 check, and a few months after that—while dining with Winthrop on February 1, 1943—he announced that he was ready to repay the rest ("a happy moment for me"). Winthrop told him to forget it, and a few days later returned his initial check, uncashed, with a note Charlie would cherish after the man's death.*

A few months prior to that crucial loan, Winthrop had sent roses and a crib in honor of Sarah Blann Jackson, born on Mother's Day (May 12), 1940. Charlie had anticipated the baby's arrival with mixed emotions: what with the turmoil in Europe, he felt a "growing reluctance to bring a child into such a world," and also worried about his unsettled finances and (worst of all, perhaps) the possibility of her inheriting "certain traits." That Sunday, while Rhoda endured a long labor, Charlie was an all but speechless wreck: he and Nila Mack passed the time at Schrafft's, unable to eat, until finally they "drove through lights" to the hospital. "When first I saw her small, awakened face," he wrote in "A Sestina for Sarah" (published exactly one year later in F.P.A.'s column, *The Conning Tower*, in the *New York Post*),

> . . . O, then my anxious prayer turned thankful grace,
> And straightway I was happy as today!
> Clear was her cry, pink was her little face,
> Clear as the morn, pink as the month of May!
> At once her heart assumed its rightful place
> Within my own—as my fond heart gave way.

The girl would be the love of his life. He spent rapturous hours sitting beside her crib, pondering her tiny foot in the palm of his hand ("It was as perfect as a seashell, but warm, with a little animal life of its own"). Everything about her was "indescribably charming to him"—all the more potently because she was unlike him in every conceivable way save physical (they shared the almond eyes and dark skin of the Jacksons). "Sarah is a square," he'd say, lovingly evoking her Rhoda-like levelheadedness, the prim way she pursed her lips ("like a baby anus") when studying a hand of cards, her winsome tendency to transpose consonants so that "cemetery," say, became "temecery." Dubbing her "the dimsal girl" (after his favorite of her neologisms, used to describe a dark, cheerless day), he would hide behind the window curtain and watch her "like a

---

* Winthrop's note does not survive among Jackson's papers, though one may assume he cherished it in view of the following: after Winthrop died, his law firm wrote Jackson a letter noting the unpaid $1,000 loan on their books. Jackson replied to Winthrop's secretary ("Miss Nelson") telling the story of the loan, and enclosing (a) the uncashed $500 check that Winthrop had returned to him, and (b) Winthrop's note, which Jackson asked Miss Nelson to send back to him for sentimental reasons.

love-sick fool" when she left for school each morning—so he remembered in a 1966 poem he wrote for his granddaughter, Sarah's firstborn:

> *And I thought then (and told my wife):*
> *No child was ever better armed*
> *To face this less than perfect life*
> *Than she was, calm and unalarmed.*

•

JACKSON APPEARS to have written no fiction in 1941, as he struggled to make ends meet with occasional employment. That year he began teaching two courses on radio writing at NYU, which he mostly enjoyed ("[I] was sorry when the final session came") despite having to read as many as sixty scripts for his lecture class. Characteristically he took pains to promote the work of his better students, pressing five scripts on an old *Columbia Workshop* colleague and writing a cogent little pitch for each: "Herman Land is a discovery—depend on it," he remarked of a student who'd written about a strife-ridden Jewish family in Brooklyn, while another script—an adaptation of Fitzgerald's "Babylon Revisited"—gave him the chance to plug not only his student but also "one of the most misunderstood writers of our generation," whose nascent revival, eight months after his death, made the script "perfect Workshop material."

Jackson himself wanted to write a daytime serial, which would give him a steady paycheck and a static cast of characters to work with—preferably an "amusing family situation," though he was willing to be flexible. With one writer he proposed to collaborate on something called *Women in Defense* ("Incidentally, doesn't that strike you as a ribald title?"), which would cater to the growing number of women working in munitions plants; he also tried to interest an executive at New York's WOR in letting him produce his own showcase series comparable to the *Columbia Workshop*. But nothing seemed to click, and once war was declared, in December, Jackson went back to writing propaganda (to be aired in Japan) for the government.

His patience was finally rewarded in March 1942—though he was reminded thereby to be careful what you wish for. "In the history of soap opera," James Thurber wrote in 1948, "only a few writers have seriously tried to improve the quality of daytime serials. One of these was Charles Jackson." The latter, to his slight chagrin, found he had an actual knack for spinning out schmaltzy story lines ad infinitum, but was so revolted by his specific assignment that he later endeavored to forget everything about it, even the name of his sponsor (Staley cornstarch). The master-mind of this fifteen-minute-a-day soap, *Sweet River*, was his old friend Max Wylie, who'd taken a job in Chicago with Blackett-Sample-Hummert—as it happened, the country's top producer of radio material: *top*, that is, in terms of quantity rather than quality, as the company managed to churn out soaps on behalf of some twenty sponsors (cereal, floor polish, cosmetics, etc.). Known—indeed notorious—for keeping costs down, B-S-H paid writers roughly half of what was customary. Thus Wylie was offering two hundred dollars a week (forty dollars a script), and mean-while Charlie had eight days to catch a train to Chicago, learn the plot, flesh out the characters, and write a backlog of scripts before *Sweet River* went on the air.

For the next few months he traveled to Chicago every six weeks and swapped ideas with Wylie, who'd based the town of Sweet River on Dela-ware, Ohio, where he and his brothers had been raised by a minister. Wylie—a great admirer of "Rachel's Summer"—thought Jackson was the right man to tease out the following premise: Willa McKay, a school-teacher, is accused of murder but eventually acquitted, albeit not in the minds of her fellow Sweet River residents; despite this cloud, she catches the eye of a local minister, Bob Tomley, a widower raising two young sons. And so it went for many months—a piquant daily puzzle: how to devise fresh complications for (as Thurber put it) a "mild and prolonged love affair with a schoolteacher whose cheek [Tomley] never petted and whose hand he never held, for ministers and schoolteachers in Soapland are permitted only the faintest intimations of affection." The challenge, of course, was to invert the usual rules of good writing (telling details, subtle ellipses) via a kind of engaging prolixity. "I kept two people on a raft in the middle of a lake for five weeks once," Jackson proudly recalled, "just talking to each other!"

He'd begun to reconcile himself to the work when, late that summer, he got a call from Wylie, who'd just quit his job: Charlie had better come quick to Chicago and make a case for staying on as writer for *Sweet River*, since B-S-H was apt to save money now by hiring someone local. For-tunately the new boss, Alan Wallace, regarded the soap as "the bright spot of his life," and promptly raised Jackson's price to fifty dollars a script—on the condition, however, that he keep six weeks ahead on the show, and this without Wylie to help guide the story line. Jackson, as ever, found inspiration "in far away Arcadia"—the hometown, it turned out, of the Reverend Tomley's mother, even then conspiring to prevent a marriage between her son and "this terrible Willa McKay," whom she meets in person (amid "many clashes") during a visit to Sweet River, where she finds a kindred soul in Addie Norris, the gossipy librarian, all of which drives Willa into the arms of Harry Nichols (only temporarily, since Jackson was saving Nichols for Maggie Burgess—"but that's miles and years away yet, and so is the ultimate marriage of Tomley and Willa"). "I'm getting fonder of 'Sweet River' by the minute now that the conflict is honest again and there's a chance for some good writing once more," he wrote Wallace that August, remarking three weeks later to a friend, "I am sick unto death of SWEET RIVER . . . "

Now more than ever, though, he needed the steady employment, which had finally allowed him to get on with his long-deferred novel about an alcoholic. Pushing forty, and keenly aware of how suddenly one's luck can change—witness his friend Max, now looking for work in New York ("and drinking too much on the side")—Jackson was determined to make up for lost time: he gave himself exactly one year to finish the book, beginning on July 1, 1942, and writing every Sunday and all night Thursdays, while teaching at NYU and dictating *Sweet River* to a public stenographer at the Hotel Albert. The novel's long first chapter was written in a single feverish week, as he rushed to fill tablet pages before Rhoda came into his study, whereupon (so he claimed later) he'd stuff the pages into a drawer and affect to ruminate over *Sweet River*. For the chapter's climactic purse-stealing scene he decided he needed ten pages exactly, numbered the pages, and scribbled until he'd reached the bottom of the tenth. Only then—"drunk with excitement"—did he seek his wife's blessing. For the sake of posterity, perhaps, he saved her written response: "I think it's wonderful. As a matter of fact, I found my heart pumping and my breath coming fast as I read it. . . . It's grand—and such a change from all your other writing. I almost think it's your best so far."

So engrossing were his labors that first week that he'd let *Sweet River* slip, until Max (still employed at the time, though not for long) gave him a scolding phone call. "When you know why the scripts are late, you'll be ashamed of yourself," said Jackson, and hung up on him. A week later a package arrived addressed to "<u>MRS.</u> MAX WYLIE," who read the chapter and immediately pressed it on her husband. "We both think that this is not only the finest piece of writing that you ever did," she wrote, echoing Rhoda, "but that it is beautiful writing. . . . I always knew you had it and this is only the beginning." Eager now for validation from practically everyone he knew ("like the spoiled child I am I just had to be paid attention to quick"), Jackson distributed copies of the chapter far and wide, gleefully reporting that he'd received "a good dozen letters, a couple of wires, and many phone calls . . . most all of them enthusiastic, some wildly so." Philip Rahv wanted to publish an abridged version of the chapter in *Partisan Review*, though he cautioned Jackson that Don was perhaps a little *too* narcissistic: "[This] is understood by the author, to be sure, but still some margin of misunderstanding is left." Betty Huling of *The New Republic* agreed, advising Jackson—who was unwilling to cut the piece in any case—not to publish it as a short story, since the reader needed to know more about Don in order to sympathize with him: "The terror is there all right, now, but not the pity."

Jackson tried to press on with the next chapter—more introspective, with precisely the sort of nuanced exposition that might satisfy Rahv and Huling—but was stymied by its somewhat subtler demands; feeling himself sliding into "a horrible depression," he promptly skipped ahead to chapter five—"The Mouse," Don's climactic bout of delirium tremens—and the words began to flow again. He was trembling by the time he finished. "I can see every reviewer in the land," he wrote a friend, "(whoops, here we go again—just like my hero!) quoting that passage in his review, and then spoiling it all with exalted and destructive comment about its pityandterror [*sic: pace* Huling]." In the meantime he'd mailed the first chapter to a psychiatrist at Bellevue, Dr. Stephen Sherman, whose permission he sought to visit the alcoholic ward for the sake of verisimilitude, since he remembered "nothing" of his time there as a patient; in his novel, he explained, the protagonist ("a completely narcissistic character") wakes up there, refuses to submit to a spinal tap, and is given a dose of paraldehyde and sent on his way. Dr. Sherman arranged to meet Jackson at Bellevue the following Saturday, and effusively commended his "extraordinarily revealing study of the real inner life of the alcoholic":

> It should have definite clinical value. It has taught me more about what the alcoholic is really thinking about than most of the material of my patients so far has ever been able to do. I think the character delineation is really very fine, and certain specially interesting aspects—the loneliness, the identification with forlorn genius, the study of the face, the psychic dependency on the brother, the subtle undercurrents of homosexuality, and so on—are all superbly brought out. . . . I trust that you will not fail to finish the other chapters, and that the work will come to the attention of the psychiatric world at large.

Jackson—writing to the novelist James Gould Cozzens (Rhoda's colleague at *Fortune*)—derided the doctor's prose style and bristled at the
idea that his novel should have "clinical [versus artistic] value": "but of
course," he added, "I ate it up too, read it 20 times in succession, and even
took it to bed with me."

He did, however, have at least one staunch detractor: his mother. The
poor woman had been appalled by Charlie's stories in *Partisan Review*
("I don't see anything so wonderful about it, it all happened, all you had
to do is write it down"), but that opening chapter of *The Long Weekend* was almost the death of her. "You said I wouldn't like what you had
written—I didn't," she admitted.

> I am not a psychiatrist nor am I a literary critic, I'm just an ordinary
> person who happens to be your mother. I sat down and read your
> article as soon as it came and I am telling you the truth, I was a
> complete wreck afterward. For I read those things differently from
> outsiders for I know it was you and Frederic[k] and Rhoda. . . . You
> had terrible experiences but they are over and I wish you could forget
> them. And Frederic[k]—what he went through and how he always
> stood by and helped you out of one mess after another, as he stands
> by all of us. The things he, yes and your friends, who stood by you,
> have taken from you. . . .

But the book's confessional aspect was only the beginning. Don Birnam,
considering whether to steal the woman's purse, idly wonders whether
she's sleeping with her boyfriend ("Was he big?"). "What has *that* to do
with it?" Charlie's mother indignantly demanded. "Why write that?" And
here she'd been telling everyone in Newark about the great book Charlie
was working on, but she wouldn't dream of showing them *this*. "This is a
small town, and my *home*, and I want them to say and think only the best
about all of you."

When he wasn't furious over such philistinism, Charlie would (essentially) shrug: "In the long run, of course, nothing matters but the story,"
he wrote Mary McCarthy,* "which is what I'm always telling my poor
mother."

---

* Jackson did not meet McCarthy until 1945, though he was a great admirer of *The
Company She Keeps* (1942), and had paid subtle homage in *The Lost Weekend* by mono-
gramming the filched purse "M. Mc."

Chapter Seven

The Lost Weekend

Jackson's headlong progress on his novel was derailed in April, when a second daughter, Kate Winthrop, was born three days before his fortieth birthday. For weeks he was scarcely able to think about the book, and finally rented a friend's apartment during daytime hours. This daughter, indeed, was something different from the calm paragon that had preceded her. "Only yesterday, it seems you were in your playpen," Jackson wrote her in 1957, "raising hell there, too. Sarah was content with her playpen for at least six months, as I recall—but not you!" As the infant ran amok, Jackson met his self-imposed deadline with some difficulty, finishing a draft on June 30, 1943.

By his own estimation, *The Long Weekend* was "probably the most talked-about unpublished novel in New York." Simon & Schuster had been keeping tabs on Jackson ever since his *Partisan Review* debut, though he worried the publisher might be "a little too high pressure" for his purpose; meanwhile Max Wylie had alerted his own publisher, Farrar & Rinehart, and the previous November Jackson had mailed them his first chapter along with a copy of Dr. Sherman's letter attesting to its clinical validity. The publisher replied that several editors had found the book "tremendously interesting": "The only doubt in our minds is whether or not there is enough variety in a long drunk to sustain the reader's interest through a novel. We are anxious to see more of the book and hope you will send it along as soon as it is completed." When the book was ready, Jackson was almost frantically eager to gratify all the mounting curiosity; handing the typescript to his prospective agent, Bernice Baumgarten of Brandt & Brandt, the voluble author began to give a blow-by-blow, but was abruptly cut off: "No, don't tell me anything about it, I just want to read it." This brand of candor, bordering on the austere, had won Baumgarten the trust of such illustrious clients as John Dos Passos, Mary McCarthy, E. E. Cummings, and many others, including her then-celebrated husband, Cozzens. As for Jackson—her temperamental opposite—he had only to wait a single day for her verdict ("a fine job").

By then he entertained the hope of becoming the legendary editor Max Perkins's next great find ("Scribners, too, wouldn't mind at all the passages about their Scott Fitzgerald"), but Baumgarten thought it best to oblige Simon & Schuster, which promptly rejected the novel as too morbidly insular in a time of world war. Publisher John Farrar, however, was almost beside himself with enthusiasm, and would always take pride in the fact that he'd insisted on the book's greatness in the face of some initial timidity. "I finished the manuscript on the train coming down from the country last night," his partner, Stanley Rinehart, wrote Baumgarten on August 2, "got off at 125th Street in a non-alcoholic daze and walked right through the edge of the Harlem riot at midnight without knowing anything about it." And yet Rinehart was a bit squeamish about publishing, especially given the downbeat ending, which Jackson would not hear of altering a whit; on the other hand, Dr. Sherman's letter had given Rinehart an idea to present the novel as a kind of case history "in the field between fiction and non-fiction." At any rate, by the time Jackson visited the firm two days later, Farrar and Rinehart and their various colleagues had conquered their misgivings en masse. "*Every*-body came in to meet me," Charlie wrote Rhoda afterward, "and each one exclaimed over his favorite chapter or passage. . . . Stan expects it to sell for years, to offend many, to infuriate M. D.'s et cetera, but he said they (F&R) couldn't help themselves: it's the most extraordinary piece of writing he has seen (he said) in many years."

One problem was the book's title, *The Long Weekend*: though Jackson was attached to it ("the only logical title"), he'd recently discovered at least two other books with the same title. Max Wylie suggested *Time-Out*, which the author considered "trivial"; for the sake of gravitas he was attracted to his beloved Shakespeare, asking Rinehart's opinion of *This Confusion* (from the novel's *Hamlet* epigraph) and *All Is the Fear* (from *Macbeth*: "All is the fear and nothing is the love, / As little is the wisdom, where the flight / So runs against all reason"). He also liked the more denotative *A Weekend in the City*—since the novel begins, after all, with a proposed weekend in the country—but worried that it sounded like "a short-story and one by Charles Brackett* or some other 'light' writer." In the end he left it up to the publisher, who added a phrase to the language by changing only two letters of the working title.

Later in August, Jackson did a last thorough revision, adding twenty-four pages to the typescript: namely, a scene at the end of Chapter Two where Don, to his horror, meets the man who took his place in Kappa U (Jackson thought the "fraternity nightmare" needed some slight amplification "without throwing the book out of balance"), and also several new pages in the Bellevue section establishing that the nurse George (as he was then known)† "really had some cause" for implying that Don was homosexual. Indeed, as Jackson told Rinehart, *most* of the additional twenty-four pages "are further developments of the same, and will start controversy all over the place."

"I AM DOING SO WELL that it's almost shameful," Jackson wrote a friend that fall. "The daytime serial that I have been writing for the past 20 months begins going out over WJZ on October 4th, which means even more money. On top of that Farrar & Rinehart has bought my novel The Lost Weekend which is going to curl the hair of the entire country." What would prove the most exciting (in a good way) year of Jackson's life had begun with a long family vacation in Nantucket that summer, during which he'd revised his novel, kept up with *Sweet River*, and met a handsome Marine captain recently wounded at Guadalcanal, Vince Kramer, who would reappear as Cliff Hauman in *The Fall of Valor*. Also, while relaxing at the actress Patricia Collinge's house, Jackson had pleasantly caught the attention of Bette Davis ("Who's that sweet little man on the

---

* The future producer and screenwriter (with Billy Wilder) of *The Lost Weekend*, and Charlie's lifelong friend thereafter. Brackett's varied career included writing popular novels and short fiction for "slicks" such as *Saturday Evening Post* and *Collier's*.
† Jackson changed the nurse's name to Bim in puckish tribute to Bronson Winthrop's godson and namesake, Bronson Winthrop "Bim" Chanler, the son of their mutual friend Stuyvesant Chanler.

couch?"), with whom he'd be reunited in Hollywood. The MGM contract that would make this possible was still months in the future, but
something of the sort was already in the air ("on account of the reputation the book will shortly earn me") when Jackson demanded a raise of
ten dollars per script from Blackett-Sample-Hummert; given that *Sweet
River* was soon to be picked up by the Blue Network and aired over 172
outlets (up from the original 12), the agency decided to grant the raise
retroactively—effective March 1943—which meant an additional lump
sum of $1,050, and Jackson planned to *double* his price once the show
went network in November, by which time he would have written five
hundred scripts ("and I think it *still* stinks," he wrote Boom).

Farrar & Rinehart went on debating whether to present *The Lost
Weekend* as a kind of fictionalized case history, and therefore asked the
obliging Dr. Sherman to expand his letter into a foreword that would
serve to contextualize, perhaps, certain of the novel's more troubling
points. For his part, Jackson lucidly argued that a "clinical apology"
would "scare the average reader, and the superior reader doesn't need it":
"Psychiatrists could write their foolish heads off 'explaining' HAMLET,
CRIME AND PUNISHMENT, REMEMBRANCE OF THINGS
PAST, etcetera, but these works will stand long after 'modern psychology' has been superseded by a new science even more modern." A few
days later, however, Dr. Sherman faithfully submitted his piece, which
after a fashion was sensitive to all sides of the issue: "I can think of few
documents which have more impressed me with the truth that fidelity
to clinical fact is art," he wrote. "The author of this extraordinary tract
on the secret passageways of the alcoholic mentality has taken clinical
experience and raised it to the level of high poetry." Dr. Sherman further assured the reader that the dread subject of homosexuality—crucial,
alas, to any intelligent treatment of alcoholism—was presented with "the
greatest delicacy." The word "tract" was perhaps sufficient to steel Jackson's opposition to the foreword; in any event he allowed that Sherman
might be quoted in advertising, but again cautioned against "launch[ing]
the book on a flood of merely clinical approval." Stanley Rinehart agreed
not to include the piece in the book (grudgingly: he thought it a "humdinger"), though he promptly attached it to advance copies of the novel
that went to med-school faculties all over the country. Responses were
diverse, and seemed largely to depend on whether a given reader perceived
alcoholism as a scientific or moral issue. As Rinehart had anticipated,
some of the letters he received would prove nothing less than marketing

gold. Dr. Morris Fishbein, editor of *The Journal of the American Medical Association*, claimed that the book captured "the very soul of the dipso-maniac" ("I found myself at the end . . . full of sympathy and a desire to help"), while another specialist, Dr. Herbert L. Nossen, called it "expert and wonderful—the work of a courageous man." Dr. Haven Emerson of Columbia, however, deplored the "continuous subtle pleading for a social and individual indulgence towards all such periodic drunkards," though he considered the book "a masterpiece as a case history."

Fiction writers were mostly enthusiastic, but here again it was a highly personal matter. Sinclair Lewis, who knew whereof he spoke, found the novel brilliant on every level—"the only unflinching story of an alcoholic that I have ever read . . . as terrifying yet as absorbing as the real thing"—and subsequently made a point of mentioning Jackson as one of the few American writers who showed promise of greatness. William Seabrook, on the other hand, seemed almost to despise Jackson. Nowadays forgotten, Seabrook was then well known as the author of *Asylum* (1935), the record of his voluntary incarceration at a mental hospital in Westchester County; the book depicted alcoholism as a disease deserving of one's compassion, but in this regard Seabrook had found *The Lost Weekend* decidedly wanting. "Here's my honest reaction to The Lost Weekend by Charles Jackson which I read word by word to the end with increasing pain and anguish," he wrote Rinehart.

I hate the goddam book almost as much as I hate my own inflamed conscience. "There go I but for the grace of God" and all that stuff, in that horrible, hopeless, cumulative nightmare this guy's devil-guided pen (or portable) has envoked [*sic*].

I've suffered as a drunk but not like that and hope to Christ I never will. It's the only book that ever scared me. It should be soberly read by every white-collar souse in America. If it doesn't scare the liver, lights and daylights out of him as it did me, it means the poor bastard has softening of the brain and is already sunk. . . .

The Lost Weekend is a lousy-cheerful title for such a deadly book. A truer title would be the Spanish proverb, "There Is No Cure for Drunkenness But Death." If Charles Jackson wrote this book cold-sober without ever having gone through those hideous horrors himself, I hope as a once-celebrated drunkard, hope to god and pray, that he'll make you-know-what-kind-of-a-pot of money out of it, spend it all on lousy Cuban rum, drink himself into delirium tremens, die of acute alcoholism in Bellevue or the gutter and be buried face-downward in a drunkard's grave so that the more he scratches the deeper to hell he'll go.

One reason for the man's oddly peevish tone was that he did, in fact, suspect that Jackson was "a sober, self-righteous bright-boy who can take it or leave it alone," and thus his book contained, in Seabrook's highly subjective view, "not a grain of pity ponderable enough to balance the left hind leg of a louse."* As it happened, Seabrook was then in the midst of a final alcoholic relapse; twenty months later he'd kill himself with an overdose of sleeping pills, though friends claimed it wasn't a matter of deliberate suicide so much as "another drastic attempt to accomplish what he had tried, vainly, all his life to do—to get away from himself." Jackson, needless to say, would have understood only too well.

Another writer to whom *The Lost Weekend* came as a blow was Malcolm Lowry, who at the time had spent almost a decade working on his own alcoholic masterpiece, *Under the Volcano*. "After reading the book," he wrote his English publisher, Jonathan Cape, "it became extremely hard for the time being to go on writing and having faith in mine." Still, for all his vagaries, Lowry tended to be a good sport about things; weathering thoughts of suicide, he resolved to get over his "unworthy professional jealousy" and even wrote Jackson a congratulatory note to the effect that he'd "beaten him to it" (and never mind the damage done to Lowry's *Lunar Caustic*—about a drunk in Bellevue!—which he'd envisaged as the second part of a trilogy that was to include *Under the Volcano*). Nor was Lowry entirely misguided in his despair: "The mescal-inspired phantasmagoria, or heebie-jeebies, to which Geoffrey [Firmin, in *Under the Volcano*] has succumbed," noted a reader for Cape (whose ambivalence would necessitate a prolix apologia on Lowry's part), "is impressive but I think too long, wayward and elaborate. On account of [which] the book inevitably recalls . . . The Lost Weekend."

The only response to which Jackson took adamant exception was that of Edna Ferber, whom he'd fondly remembered waiting on while a clerk at Kroch's in 1925. Indeed, he might have mentioned this to Rinehart, whose request for a blurb was met with startling vehemence, as Ferber saw

---

* Jackson didn't think much of Seabrook either, irrespective of the latter's weird vitriol. "Willie Tells All [in *Asylum*], all right—and tells you nothing," he'd written in 1942. "He gives you only the external spectacle."

fit to condemn "the Hitlerian treatment of the Jew in this book": "There they are," she wrote, "lumped together on page 146—homosexuals, drunks, Negroes, Jews. Well, I resent it and here is my written resentment, however futile. These are frightful times for the Jews of the world. In the name of the millions of murdered men, women and children I wish to record my objection to this added drop of poison."* Jackson detested bigotry in every form, particularly anti-Semitism; writing in 1945 to a German publisher who (he worried) might have objected to passages in *The Lost Weekend* about a Jewish pawnbroker, Jackson claimed he would have rather destroyed his book than give offense of that kind. As for Ferber, at the very least she was "irresponsible," or so he determined to make unforgettably clear to her: "I resent and protest [your letter] bitterly," he wrote, "because of my own passionate and active concern over the tragic plight of the Jew in these times." The point of the passage under attack, he continued, was "purely psychological . . . no more anti-Semitic than the not dissimilar passage in Proust (the son of a Jew) who first pointed out the curious anomaly of the uncertain position held in society by the homosexual and the Jew"; Jackson had added the Negro ("so quick on the trigger . . . ") as another example of "persons suffering from a consciousness of being different from (or above, or below) the social norm, and alternately proud and sensitive on the point." He doubted, however, that his friend Richard Wright (of *Native Son* fame) would have accused him of bigotry as a result.

And indeed, I cannot help but feel that such a reaction as yours, Miss Ferber, is witch-hunting and (if we must use the word) "Hitlerian" book-burning in reverse. If things have come to such a pass that the word "Jew" cannot be set down in print without someone crying "Race-prejudice!", then alas, the Jew is already lost. . . .

I have carefully read over your letter and mine, and you might be interested to know that the net effect of both of them has been to make me race-conscious and uncomfortable as I have never been before . . . and every time I have here set down the word "Jew" in my letter, I have had the astonished and awful feeling (for the first time

---

* The passage in question occurs after Don's return from Bellevue; still bitter about Bim's animadversions, he muses, "Nobody was quicker with the word 'queen' . . . than the queen himself—like the Jew who cringes under the term 'kike' but uses it twice as much as anybody else; like the Negro so quick on the trigger with the word 'nigger' . . . "

in my life) that it was a term of opprobrium and abuse, rather than the ancient and dignified name of a noble and intelligent people.

A year later Ferber remarked in *Time* magazine that, among current writers, she was "most interested in Charles Jackson for *The Lost Weekend*." Jackson replied: "I have seen many small allusions to *The Lost Weekend* during the past year, but no single one of them (nor, I think, all of them combined) has given me anywhere near the same joy . . . I salute you humbly but from the depths of my heart."

JACKSON'S CONFIDENCE began to surge as publication approached—especially since he'd received the endorsement of his good friend and "severest critic," Elling Aannestad, an editor at Norton whose only (faint) claim to fame was having coaxed the classicist Edith Hamilton to publish her first book, *The Greek Way* (1930).* Pitilessly candid, Aannestad had been one of the few readers of *The Long Weekend*'s first chapter to withhold any hint of praise: he'd been bored, he said, by the surfeit of internal monologue, and moreover cautioned Jackson about his "simple style" ("sometimes it approaches what you wish most to avoid—affectation"). Having read the finished manuscript, though, Aannestad found it "a triumphant"—if still flawed—"piece of work": "I don't see why anyone should ever need to deal fictionally with alcoholism again; you've done it. . . . I'm hoping, Charlie, that you can withstand fame, because I think you're in for it." One key to keeping his head, the man advised, was not to take the more lavish praise too seriously; critics, after all, were likely to think the novel "better and more important than it is." As if promptly to prove his point, a seasoned literary editor for the *Cleveland Plain Dealer*, Ted Robinson, beat other reviewers to the punch by sending his early appraisal directly to the author (for whom it became his "most prized single letter"): *The Lost Weekend*, said Robinson, was "one of the most brilliant performances in modern fiction . . . among the permanent masterpieces of the literary art . . . the book of the year . . ." And so on.

Another reason for high hopes was the ingenious campaign devised by Farrar & Rinehart's publicity manager, Helen Murphy, who would receive an award that year for her efforts. "Five days out of a man's

---

* In 1947, Hamilton dedicated *Witness to the Truth: Christ and His Interpreters* thus: "To ELLING AANNESTAD / 'A friend should bear his friend's infirmities.' "

life—one of the strangest, most remarkable narratives ever written," read the cryptic advertisements that began appearing in early January 1944, accompanied by an illustration of five fluttering calendar pages. Title, author, and subject were omitted, and the word "narrative" was chosen to obscure whether the work in question was fact or fiction. A second series of ads gave a synopsis of the plot as it would appear on the dust jacket: "The minute his brother Wick closed the door behind him Don Birnam felt positively lightheaded, joyous . . . five whole days ahead of him with no one watching him"; another coy paragraph mentioned Don's "insatiable appetite for experience" and "passion for Scott Fitzgerald," until—at last—the beguiled reader was informed that Don was "in the grip of alcohol." Meanwhile advance copies were sent not only to literary and medical worthies, but to entertainers and politicians such as Wendell Willkie; curiosity was so aroused that the first printing was raised from ten thousand to twenty thousand—ten times higher than usual for a first novel. And finally, on January 25, 1944 (four days before publication), Farrar & Rinehart planned to give an elegant party in Jackson's honor at the Burberry Room on East 52nd: "Gobs of celebs will be there from the stage, screen, press, radio and publishing world," Charlie reported to Boom, "and my knees go weak at the thought." Boom shared the letter with their mother, who (somewhat mollified by all the fuss) wrote Charlie, "Isn't it wonderful it is the party instead of what used to make [your knees] shake that way in the book. And it will *never* be like that again thank God—happy, happy days!"

To some extent the fix was in, since the most important critic—for *The New York Times Book Review*—was Philip Wylie, older brother of Charlie's best friend, Max, and himself an editor at Farrar & Rinehart! For almost every conceivable reason, in fact, Jackson could safely anticipate "that special Wylie excitement," as he put it: the latter's most recent book, *Generation of Vipers* (1942), had introduced the concept of "Momism" into the cultural discourse—a term of abuse for the emasculating, infantilizing role of the American matriarch, a theme very dear to Jackson's heart; even more promisingly, Wylie was also an alcoholic who'd "cured" himself by means of "expert advice" and (self-taught) psychotherapy. Little wonder, then, that he loved *The Lost Weekend*: not only was it "the most compelling gift to the literature of addiction since De Quincey," but a potential "tool" for psychiatrists and a veritable "textbook for such organizations as Alcoholics Anonymous" (which both Wylie and Jackson eschewed). Also, quite aside from the author's clinical insights, Wylie sincerely believed in his literary greatness. "To a writer I never heard of," his review concluded, "and one I expect to hear about the rest of my life, my hat is off."

Other major reviews were almost as enthusiastic. The *Times*'s daily critic John Chamberlain called the novel "wild, phantasmagoric, a story of tumultuous pace and nervous, broken rhythms." Nor was Chamberlain (a fastidious man) daunted by the subject matter—because of it, indeed, he considered *The Lost Weekend* "the most moral book in a decade," and was only partly in jest when he recommended it to the Women's Christian Temperance Union as the "best bet" for their cause "since Billy Sunday reformed and hit the sawdust trail." At the very least, most reviewers agreed that Jackson had taken a singularly unpromising premise—the adventures of a solitary, narcissistic drunk—and turned it into a narrative "by turns horrifying and curiously moving" (New York *Herald Tribune*) that kept readers "riveted to their chairs until the end" (*Saturday Review*). Even *Time* magazine—rarely nice in those days to first novels of a controversial savor—was willing to concede that Don Birnam ("a clever coward who is drinking himself to death") was a memorable creation: "If [he] were more purely comic he would be Mr. Toad; if he were more purely tragic he would be Hamlet."

"The irrational newspaper reviews of extravagant praise truly meant nothing to me after the first day," Jackson suavely assured his friend Aannestad; "what I did take seriously and pay attention to was the sober long criticism of Edmund Wilson, [Robert Gorham] Davis in the Partisan Review and a very few others." These critics were more in accord with Aannestad's tempered view of the novel, and for a fact Jackson had taken them *very* seriously; Wilson's *New Yorker* review had caused him (as he later told Lincoln Barnett) to take "to his bed for the rest of the day." Commending the book as "a tour-de-force of some merit," Wilson enumerated those features, bad and good, that made for a promising apprentice effort but little more: the prose was workmanlike, the flashbacks rather arbitrary, the protagonist "dreary in the extreme," and yet Jackson did manage to create "a creepy psychological atmosphere" that kept one turning pages, more or less. No doubt Wilson meant to be encouraging, wistfully so, when he summed up: "The book, in fact, has so much that is good that it ought to have been three times as good and a really satisfactory piece of fiction." Jackson, to be sure, was chastened, but also flattered that a critic of Wilson's caliber would take such trouble on his behalf; Davis's treatment in *Partisan Review*, however, was *most* embittering, especially given the way Jackson had supported the journal with cash donations since his debut in 1939. Still, he couldn't have been terribly surprised: Davis, after all, was a typical contributor, inclined to fault the novel for its apathy toward "politics or ideas": "the impairment of the self from within [as in Don's case] parallels (but with how much less emotion and drama and meaning!) the threat of impairment of the self from without in the real world of the concentration camps." Philip Rahv had alerted Jackson to leftist objections when he also noted a failure to connect Don's malaise to that of the larger world ("the book conveys a sense of isolation"), in the course of which he made a remark that would have fateful implications, perhaps, for Jackson's next novel: "I noted an insufficient separation of the author from his hero, with the result that the narcissism seems to be distributed fairly equally between the two of them."

But on one level, of course, Jackson had never intended to separate himself from his hero. On the contrary: by looking inside himself and describing precisely what he saw, no matter how bizarre or compromising, he hoped to give a credible sense of what an alcoholic was going through. The fragments of personal experience (small-town childhood, father's desertion, homosexual tendencies) were not meant to amount to some ideal case history, though certainly they happened to be pertinent ("He saw himself as an American everyman"). "Jackson's purpose is to describe, not to explain," the critic Granville Hicks wrote in his reader's report. "The result, it seems to me, is as extraordinary a study of psychosis as I have ever read." As an intricate portrait of one individual's suffering, then, the novel is a brilliant success, and those who insist on sociopolitical resonance should look elsewhere—most notably to *Under the Volcano*, in which the implications of alcoholism are personal, political, metaphysical, and more, the result of Lowry's awful decade-plus ordeal of adding filigree to each ingenious layer of meaning. Jackson was far less ambitious, though arguably more successful (or at any rate readable) in achieving his aims.

And ultimately Rahv is wrong to confuse Don's narcissism with that of his creator, who transcends narcissism by exposing it so thoroughly. Whereas it is Don's curse to see his own self-deceptions objectively, before he can quite enjoy them, Jackson the novelist removes himself once further—that is, by objectifying both the deluded and the self-knowing Don. The first is the artist-hero of Don's never-to-be-written masterpiece, *In a Glass*—the brooding, dissolute apotheosis of the boy who, twenty years before, had stared into his bathroom mirror in hope that poetry writing had wrought some change, some outward sign of his cherished superiority ("Clods!"), now preserved only by alcohol: "Suppose the clear vision in the bathroom mirror could fade (as in some trick movie) and be replaced by this image over the bar. Suppose that lad— Suppose time could be all mixed up so that the child of twenty years ago could look into the bathroom mirror and see himself reflected at thirty-three, as he saw himself now. What would he think, that boy?" As Don excitedly considers the possibilities—gloating over the clever multivalence of his title, *In a Glass* (the whiskey glass, the mirrors past and present)—for a moment he becomes not only the hero but the author, too, of this "classic of form and content," a kindred of Poe and Keats and Chatterton at whom his boy-self would have "nodded in happy recognition."

But of course the book doesn't exist, could *never* exist, and Don catches himself yet again—smiling tipsily, fatuously, into a barroom mirror: "Faithless muse!" he reflects (melodramatically in spite of himself). This, again, is the Don who is both tragic clown and audience ("staring back at the performer in silent contempt and ridicule"), while hovering above is the triumphant novelist—Jackson—and hence the implicit irony of Don's self-loathing diatribe:

> "In a Glass"—who would ever want to read a novel about a punk and a drunk! Everybody knew a couple or a dozen; they were not to be taken seriously; nuisances and troublemakers, nothing more; like queers and fairies, people were belly-sick of them; whatever ailed them, that was *their* funeral; who cared?—life presented a thousand things more important to be written about than misfits and failures. . . . Like all his attempts at fiction it would be as personal as a letter—painful to those who knew him, of no interest to those who didn't . . . so narcissistic that its final effect would be that of the mirrored room which gives back the same image times without count, or the old Post Toastie box of his boyhood with the fascinating picture of a woman and child holding a Post Toastie box with a picture of a woman and child holding a Post Toastie box with a picture of a woman and child holding . . .

And yet Jackson—producer of that evocative Post Toastie box—has written just such a novel as *In a Glass*, and here we are reading it.

And what of Jackson's vaunted clinical insights? "I have never once resorted to the glib jargon of modern psychology," he boasted to Bennett Cerf, emphasizing again that Don is an individual presented with all his quirks intact—not a type, not a composite—and so we see *something* of ourselves in him, and can generalize based on that. This is what Don does: "Why were drunks, almost always, persons of talent, personality, lovable qualities, gifts, brains, assets of all kinds (else why would anyone care?): why were so many brilliant men alcoholics? And from there, the next [question] was: Why did you drink?" Naturally Don can give any number of answers—and does—while understanding, too, that answers don't matter "in the face of one fact: you drank and it was killing you. Why? Because alcohol was something you couldn't handle, it had you licked." This is the "bottom" (noted by Peabody and AA) to which the alcoholic must descend before seeking help—and yet Don keeps drinking. Again, one thinks of Saint-Exupéry's tippler, who drinks because he is ashamed and is ashamed because he drinks—an insidious cycle of remorse that can either save or destroy the alcoholic: that is, either shame him into stopping once and for all, or goad him into further escape and final destruction. Not for nothing is *Macbeth* invoked again and again in the novel, the original title of which (pre-*Long Weekend*) was *Present Fears*, taken from Act 1, Scene 3: "Present fears / Are less than horrible imaginings . . . " Thus Don constantly weighs his remorse over past misdeeds ("fraternity nightmare . . . Juan-les-Pins . . . the unaccountable things you did . . . the drinking the drinking the drinking"), with his fear of what lies ahead—the "horrible imaginings" of a future that is, after all, only logical in light of the past:

> Obviously there was the will in him to destroy himself; part of him was bent on self-destruction—he'd be the last to deny it. But obviously, too, part was not, part held back and expressed its disapproval in remorse and shame. . . . But the foolish psychiatrist knew so much less about it than the poet, the poet who said to another doctor, *Canst thou not minister to a mind diseased. . . . Raze out the written troubles of the brain?*, the poet who answered, *Therein the patient must minister to himself* *. . . .

Only Don can save himself, and yet (as poor William Seabrook and other fellow sufferers are apt to foresee) he almost certainly won't.

---

* The italicized lines are from *Macbeth*, Act 5, Scene 3, lines 40–46.

Already he's passed the threshold where cumulative remorse becomes unbearable—where even in dreams he's harried toward suicide by masses of blond-haired fraternity boys chanting "Get Birnam! Get Birnam!" And meanwhile he drinks to escape and ends up committing further misdeeds, piles remorse on remorse, until almost everything reminds him of his own loathsomeness. Even his comforting knack for quoting Shakespeare is fraught with pitfalls, as Iago's speech (*"Who steals my purse—"*) brings him smack into his antics of the night before (*M. Mc.'s* purse)—the ramifications of which are so ghastly that only more oblivion can quell his panic: "In spite of his trying to rationalize the whole episode of last night and his fear today, a sinking sensation plunged down through his breast again and again, his body began to get hot all over, his palms sweated: it was shame."

Dr. Sherman's discarded foreword had it right: "fidelity to clinical fact is art," at least in the case of *The Lost Weekend*. In the early chapters there is a kind of black, picaresque comedy to Don's misadventures, grading subtly into tragedy until the climactic horror of Don's delirium—which serves, superbly, both to recall the comedy and to foretell Don's ultimate self-destruction, as his wheeling, drunken bat-self murders (and seems gruesomely to copulate with) the passive mouse: "The more it squeezed, the wider and higher rose the wings, like tiny filthy umbrellas, grey-wet with slime. Under the single spread of wings the two furry forms lay cuddled together as under a cosy canopy, indistinguishable one from the other, except that now the mouse began to bleed. Tiny drops of bright blood spurted down the wall; and from the bed he heard the faint miles-distant shrieks of dying." This, then, is the consummation of Don's narcissism—subject and object merging in death—though at the novel's end we leave him alive if not very well ("Why did they make such a fuss?"), preparing for another binge.

Is there hope for Don? What did Jackson think? On the one hand he considered writing a sequel about Don's ultimate deliverance; on the other he seemed expressly to forbid any such possibility. In Don's fraternity dream, an ecstatic Wick reaches him before the vengeful blond multitude, pressing a tin of pills into his hand, which Don ("Unable to bear the sight of Wick's relief, so soon to break into grief as passionate as his joy") slams into his mouth and awakes, sobbing: "He knew the dream was a good dream, it told him where help lay and would always lie, but that too was no comfort. . . . He wanted now to die, he would never be able to shake the stifling depression the dream had left with him, it would hang darkly over him as long as he remained alive." And so the nightmare lingered—at whatever remove—though Jackson never forgot where help lay.

THE SPECTACULAR SUCCESS of *The Lost Weekend* (and never mind, for now, the movie) would hang over its author's head for the rest of his life. It appeared on best-seller lists all over the country, and by the end of 1944 had sold more than 70,000 copies (an impressive figure for a literary novel, but not quite impressive enough for Jackson, who could rarely resist adding ten or twenty thousand when reporting sales to friends). In Jackson's lifetime the novel sold over 100,000 in hardback, over half a million in paperback, and almost 200,000 in a special Armed Services edition during the war; also, sales of the novel's fourteen translations (Jackson was particularly proud of its global appeal) came to approximately 150,000 copies. "Oh, I'm not as broke as I sound, though I'm always in debt," Jackson remarked the year before his death. "*The Lost Weekend* is in 24 [*sic*] languages and sells regularly. There are two editions in this country right now. It's always taken care of me: $24 from Greece here, $16 from Finland there.* It adds up."

Even more important than sales, to Jackson, were intimations of his permanent place in the literary firmament. That first year of publication he was careful to alert friends and family to any sign of a growing reputation: there was a big spread in *Look* magazine on "Five First Novelists" ("I lead off and am No. 1"), an even more promising piece in *Saturday Review* about "Outstanding Novelists" generally ("a fine photograph of me"), and naturally Jackson was thrilled to be on the *Times* critic Orville Prescott's list of the six best novels of 1944, as well as *Time*'s "Fiction surprise"—singular—"of the year." But his fondest dream was to see his work included in the Modern Library ("the nearest American equivalent to immortality"), and with this in mind he cultivated the friendship of Random House publisher Bennett Cerf, until in 1948 his dream came true—briefly: "Cerf and I know each other very well," Jackson noted in 1964, "and used to dine back and forth when he was trying to woo me away from Rinehart (I'm sure he's not sorry now that I couldn't be 'won'), we no longer really like each other. . . ." Which is to say, when

---

* There was no edition of *The Lost Weekend* in either Greece or Finland, according to a 1967 letter from Brandt & Brandt listing the various translations.

Jackson did change publishers in 1949—to Farrar & Straus, *not* Random House—Cerf retaliated by yanking *The Lost Weekend* from the Modern Library in favor of *Little Women* (Charlie "is pretty well disturbed," observed his new publisher, Roger Straus).

This was a bad augury, though at the time Jackson felt certain he'd eventually do better than *The Lost Weekend*, whose relative meagerness he sought to emphasize by labeling it "a story"—not a novel—on the jacket of the first edition: "It was a character study, merely," he explained, pointing out that a full-blown novel is about "the gradual development of character" in a complex situation, as opposed to the single epiphany of a short story, whatever its actual length. Ten years later, however—after any number of setbacks, personal and professional—Jackson reread *The Lost Weekend* and was "thunderstruck":

> It was absolutely honest, syllable for syllable . . . it was a writer really
> on the beam, telling nothing but universal truth, and again and again
> I could hardly believe my eyes (it made me know how much I had for-
> gotten of myself). There are details and insights in that book that I
> have never been up to since; and to me the most revealing thing of all
> was that *The Lost Weekend* was the only book, out of five books, that
> I wrote sober, without stimulus or sedative.

That last insight was indeed the crucial one, which would occur to him again and again—without, alas, much practical result. After all, give or take the odd naysayer, the world had proclaimed *The Lost Weekend* a masterpiece or very near, and Jackson (when sober) could hardly stand writing sentences that didn't bear out that original promise. How he longed for the days when he was "writing in the dark," when nobody expected a thing from him! How sick he became of always, *always* being credited as "the author of THE LOST WEEKEND," as if his other books didn't exist! But then, too, it was his only real prestige; convalescing on the lawn of Will Rogers Hospital, in 1963, Jackson distracted himself with the *Times* crossword puzzle when he noticed 23 Down: "Charles Jackson novel." No question which one they meant. "And do you know what?" he wrote his family. "Not a single telegram came in during the day, or since."

Things had changed, all right. Back in 1944, Jackson had rightly anticipated a big response from his hometown, at least, which he'd identified (over Boom's objection) on the book jacket. "The important thing is your work, not the opinion of your friends and family—they get over it in time anyway," he'd calmly informed a *PM* reporter shortly after publication, citing the enduring value of *Look Homeward, Angel* despite the outrage that Wolfe's novel had caused in Asheville. Jackson took a somewhat different line, however, when interviewed a month later by the Newark *Courier-Gazette*, confessing that he'd been "greatly concerned" about the reception of *The Lost Weekend* in his hometown, and was therefore "highly pleased" by the general enthusiasm. This was true. Letters from friends and family were mostly glowing, usually pointing out that the correspondent had never lost faith in Charlie ("of all the old gang who had their pet day dreams, you are the only one to fulfill your ambitions"), who in turn was so touched that he not only responded to each and every letter (marking them "ANSWERED") but also took it upon himself to provide autographed copies to Newarkians who'd enclosed checks ($2.50) for that purpose. Meanwhile he was anxious to see whether R. A. S. Bloomer—a pillar of the community—would be able to persuade Mrs. Van Duser and Miss Munson to accept a copy (autographed) for the public library. At first the man was not sanguine: Miss Munson "looked the book over here and there for about 10 minutes and simply shook her head," he wrote Charlie in December. Once the book was actually published, though, and the subject of so much "clamor throughout the nation's literary circles" (*Courier-Gazette*), a compromise was reached whereby *The Lost Weekend* was handed out at the discretion of Mrs. Van Duser, who wrote warmly to the author, "We are very flattered that a former patron—one of our own home boys—is now numbered among literary celebrities. I always thought you had it in you, Charles."

As for his brother Herb and sister-in-law Bob—well, they tried to seem gracious. Bob wrote that most of their neighbors had found the subject pretty "terrible," but they couldn't put the book down and of course the *writing* was lovely ("That's what appealed to me—also the hero was such a gentleman in such amazing circumstances like the fall downstairs!"). Still, Bob was constrained to admit that the basic effect was one of "heartache," and Herb somewhat agreed: "Certainly you—or Don—went through some terrible times and knowing you are on the wagon now—and so happy with your family—and very successful—makes it stand out." For the most part, though, Herb was proud to be "known as the brother of the leading author." He'd cut out the novel's full-page ad from *The New York Times* and tacked it up in the barn where he entertained cronies; maybe Charlie could visit and do a book signing there? This was extravagant coming from Herb—and never to be repeated—but Charlie had expected roses, and nothing but, and was especially disgruntled with Bob: "She seemed pleased to be telling me only how terrible people thought the book was," he wrote Boom; "and though she may mean 'terrible' in the sense that Uncle Winnie uses it, still we feel she might have done better."

"Oh that *terrible* book," said Mr. Winthrop, who previously had been "horror-hushed" by "Palm Sunday," though he'd kept his copy of *Partisan Review*—Charlie's first published story, after all—on the library table ever after. But when he persisted in calling *The Lost Weekend* "terrible," Jackson protested: "It's not 'terrible,' it's good!" "Well," said Winthrop, "*Macbeth* is a terrible play, isn't it?" In fact the man was thrilled, all the more because he knew the terrible real-life story: "You've staged such a wonderful come back and it makes me very happy," he'd written after reading the typescript, signing himself with "much love." When it was officially accepted by Farrar & Rinehart, Winthrop took the author to dinner at the St. Regis, and later gave him a lavish party ("the happiest evening of my life," Jackson remembered) on publication day.

By then poor Winthrop was failing, which broke Charlie's heart in more ways than one. During the last few years, in particular, the two had become very close—according to Jackson's fictionalized "memoir," he was one of "two or three persons at most to whom [Winthrop] chose to talk, at length and in detail, of his youth and his past." This, of course, was bound to touch on the most vital of their mutual interests, which also related to Winthrop's "dread of losing his faculties." Indeed, the most painful aspect of his decline, for Jackson, was the spectacle of this distinguished, punctilious man descending, Aschenbach-like, into senile displays of lechery—as when he ogled a youth one day at the Plaza, to the disdainful amusement of other diners. As Jackson wrote in *Uncle Mr. Kember*, "I wanted to get up and say boldly, 'Look here, you! Do you know who this man is? . . . He's the finest, the kindest, the most decent man I've ever known, that's who!' " Happily the end was swiftly approaching, and soon Winthrop was asking Charlie to take one of his belongings as a memento; the latter figured he'd taken enough already, and chose only a silver-plated, bayonet-shaped letter opener that he kept the rest of his life. "Not for anything would I part with it," he wrote—"not for my car, my books and pictures, nor even, I sometimes think, my fine house in New Hampshire."

He was in Hollywood when Winthrop died on July 14, 1944, at age eighty. "Oh dear," he wrote Rhoda, "I hate to think it's finished and that he's gone. . . . I loved him very much, as you know, and I'm so glad we named our Katie for him." Along with the letter opener, he always kept a small gold-framed photograph of Winthrop on his writing desk (between Garbo and his children)—a reminder of the man who'd never lost faith in him, and who'd lived just long enough to see his faith rewarded. Curiously, his death on Bastille Day had coincided with a far happier occasion ("oddly significant, no?"): the final episode of *Sweet River*, whose audience had drifted away once Jackson quit the show in March, his future secured by a famous novel and the inevitable (in those days) Hollywood contract. Winthrop's departure notwithstanding, it seemed as if Charlie's life could hardly be sweeter: "This was something I'd always looked forward to, I'd always wanted, it was what I thought I'd been living for," he would one day tell Alcoholics Anonymous. "I didn't dream what it was going to mean to me in the way of disaster. For unstable characters, like myself, success can be as difficult and dangerous as failure."

Chapter Eight

The MGM Lion

Jackson had said that he wanted to raise awareness about alcoholism, though he would always be ambivalent about this aspect of his fame—which, to put it mildly, tended to overshadow his literary achievement. Walter Winchell hailed *The Lost Weekend* as "the *Uncle Tom's Cabin*" of alcoholism, and for his part Jackson professed to be unsurprised by the book's popularity—there were, after all, a *lot* of alcoholics in the world, whether or not people saw fit to talk about them: "Almost everybody has somebody in their family who's a drunk but who's worth worrying about," he said. In the past, however, such people had been pariahs merely—bums, losers, jokes—and nobody wanted to identify with *that*, no matter how much they drank. "Since the publication of Charles Jackson's somber novel about an alcoholic," *Life* reported in 1946, "an unprecedented amount of attention has been paid to the drinking of alcohol and the problems arising therefrom." As a direct result—so the magazine applauded—the "complicated disease of alcoholic addiction" was now widely regarded as a medical rather than a moral issue.

Jackson's life, meanwhile, was "turned completely upside down": rarely averse to publicity, he didn't mind so much the constant requests for interviews and public appearances, but the letters and late-night phone calls from drunk and disturbed people, who desperately wanted to know his "secret," were another matter. That he *was* Don Birnam, to them, simply went without saying: "Now, that day you carried the typewriter up Third Avenue—" a person would begin, and Jackson became more and more belligerent in his objections. "It was Don Birnam!" he'd retort—so many times that he almost believed it, backing away from earlier, more candid statements in the press ("I used to drink like a lot of other people and now I don't drink at all like a lot of other people") in favor of his elegant "one third" formula (i.e., Don was one third himself, one third an alcoholic friend, one third "pure invention"), and finally flat denial: "I wish," he remarked to one reporter in late 1945, "that you'd say too how *sick* I am of being asked if *The Lost Weekend* is autobiographical. It isn't."

No matter. His readers kept calling, and especially writing ("I have yet to receive a fan letter from a reader who is not primarily a crack-pot," Jackson observed to his sister-in-law)—often in a palsied hand that expressed, touchingly, an almost childlike faith that the novelist was ready to help, whether by sending his book "C. O. D." or offering a saving and highly personalized piece of advice. In most cases ("ANSWERED") their faith was not misplaced: "I do not see how you can go on letting him make such a monkey of you, if I may put it so crudely," Jackson sternly admonished one woman ("I'm one of the 'Helens' . . . "). "[Jones] only thinks to telephone you when he is drunk, and then, I am sure, does it partly out of a compulsion to make himself important. . . . For your own sake, you should pull yourself out of this and forget it." At the same time Jackson couldn't resist showing some of the choicer epistolary specimens to his publisher, who hit on the idea of quoting them in a full-page ad for the *Times Book Review* on the first anniversary of publication. There was, for instance, a letter from Mrs. G. F. Lyle, whose husband had read *The Lost Weekend* and recognized himself "in black and white as the scoundrel" he was: He "said that if every woman and man, young or old could have a copy of your book, that it would do more for humanity than all the sermons in the world." Jackson's "reluctance" over the printing of such testimonials was duly noted in the *Times* (his "great sense of responsibility for people's confidences"), and hence his relief when Mrs. Lyle, at least, wrote to say she hadn't minded: "It was a dirty trick to play on you, I felt," he wrote back. "Now your new letter makes everything all right." To a friend, however, he admitted that the *Times* ad had left him "shrieking with laughter": "If there is anybody on the Atlantic seaboard with whom people's confidences are *not* safe, it's ME!"

The novel's efficacy as a temperance tract was belied by an exclusive interview Jackson gave to *The Beverage Times* ("The Weekly Trade Newspaper of the Beer, Wine and Liquor Industries"), in which he permanently alienated organizations such as the WCTU by declaring himself staunchly opposed to prohibition in any form. Pointing out that Don Birnam had gotten his start during the Prohibition Era, Jackson said he would never have published his book if he thought it might be used as "dry" propaganda: "Others shouldn't be deprived of the privilege of drinking alcoholic beverages simply because a few neurotics can't handle such drinks. I think drinking is one of the real social pleasures for those who can handle it. It is a pleasure and a social asset." That said, Jackson was wary of becoming a spokesman for any side of the argument. A few months later, Stanley Barr of Allied Liquor Industries made a special trip to New Hampshire (where Jackson had since moved) in hopes of persuading him to address their convention at the Waldorf and repeat his opposition to prohibition. "I'm a novelist, not a public speaker," Jackson replied, wryly offering to make such a statement in exchange for two thousand dollars or two Darrel Austin paintings worth the same amount. "You're asking $1,995 too much," said Barr, who would later mount a campaign to prevent the movie release of *The Lost Weekend*.

Jackson's relationship with Alcoholics Anonymous was problematic. By the time he learned of the organization, in 1940, he'd been sober for almost four years and had little reason to expect a relapse; privately he believed that AA was for "simple souls" and "weaklings" who needed mutual comfort and a lot of "mystical blah-blah." The American Medical Association agreed, more or less, dismissing *Alcoholics Anonymous* (the book) as "a curious combination of organizing propaganda and religious exhortation" that had "no scientific merit or interest." But doctors themselves, again, had little idea what to do about drunkards, continuing to treat (with a singular lack of success) underlying causes, while scarcely conceiving of alcoholism as a primary, independent disease. It was on this pragmatic level—find a remedy first, *then* worry (if at all) about etiology—that AA and Jackson were at least somewhat in accord: "To hell with causes," says Don Birnam, who realizes he's reached the point where "one drink was too many and a hundred not enough"—this a conscious homage to AA, as Jackson conceded.* Little surprise then that the organization assumed he'd be an ally. "Every member should read" *The*

---

* The famous AA slogan is usually quoted as "One drink is too many and a *thousand* not enough."

Lost Weekend, wrote an old acquaintance, Carlton Hoste (later president of the Newark Rotary Club), who identified himself to Jackson as the only AA member in their hometown. Stanley Rinehart, meanwhile, had pressed the novel on founder Bill Wilson, who approved providing free copies to new recruits.

This seemed to mitigate Jackson's reservations somewhat, though he remained skeptical. AA's emphasis on the spiritual was bad enough, but he also believed that it failed to offer "any real substitute" for drinking: whereas he had his writing and various other inner resources, AA could only provide (apart from the bogus spirituality) a kind of banal fellowship; the average Joe, thought Jackson, was likely to relapse once he figured "he was more interesting as a 'problem' than he ever was as a useful citizen." At any rate he simply couldn't abide the "Rotarianism" of such gatherings. "I am a writer first of all, and a non-drinker second," he wrote the Hartford AA chapter, whose invitation to speak he'd reluctantly accepted at his publisher's behest. "I am not interested in reform of any kind, so please don't look for me to give an inspirational talk or any kind of harangue on the evils of drink." Once he arrived, though, and was greeted by no fewer than six hundred receptive people, Jackson couldn't help trying to ingratiate himself. AA, he said, just might prove a good thing for Don Birnam—a solitary drinker who needs fellowship from people who don't consider addiction a stigma, and who can help him overcome the shame of his past while making him see, too, that he must never drink again . . . all the reasons, in short, why *any* drinker might benefit from such a program, and why Jackson himself would someday become one of its foremost advocates. As for Rotarianism: "Just a word now about Charles Jackson, the man," reported a writer for the *AA Grapevine*. "I expected to meet someone a little on the aloof side—someone above the usual level, where of course Jackson has a right to be. But Charlie won't let you look up to him. When he's talking to you or listening to you he makes you feel that you *matter* to him. Friendly, modest, sincere, unspoiled. That's Charlie Jackson." Scratch a superbly aloof artist and find a small-town boy who wants nothing better than to be well liked by "the happy, lovely, and commonplace." "Strike me dead if this sounds corny," Jackson wrote Dorothy Parker (pointedly) after his Hartford appearance, "but I don't think I ever met a happier bunch of people in my life."

And still he protested that he was a *writer*, by God, not an authority on alcoholism ("I'm awfully tired of all this identification with drinking!"), and still he accepted invitations to speak publicly on the issue. And it rankled, to say the least, when others seemed as doubtful as he about his credentials—when, for example, a prominent scientist, Dr. Anton J. Carlson, all but refused to acknowledge him during a panel discussion on behalf of the Washingtonian Hospital in Boston. "Dr. Gorrell and—and that fellow there," Carlson said, repeatedly, in a "casual and careless fashion" meant to "belittle" Jackson, or so he indignantly wrote the man afterward. Why, the many letters he'd received about his novel—Jackson would have Carlson know—had been "in almost every case" from "distinguished men in your profession as well as men of letters" (no mention of crackpots) who felt indebted to the author for teaching them something new about human nature:

> If the book is good enough to be the only work of fiction on the Required Reading list of the Yale Clinic, to cite only one example, then I think it is good enough for you; and I further think that as a scientist, you should acquaint yourself with what it has to say. . . . the intuitive artist—the artist who knows more than he knows, is of inestimable value to the progress of mankind, no less than the scientist.

Very true, no doubt, though one has to wonder whether Jackson's public engagement with the subject was entirely disinterested. Rather it seemed compounded of roughly one third earnest desire to be of use, one third longing for the limelight, and one third need of cash. When he saw the hit Broadway play *Harvey* (about the amiable tippler Elwood P. Dowd and his eponymous rabbit friend), Jackson claimed to be shocked, *shocked* by the audience's unseemly mirth when, say, Dowd retrieves a hidden bottle of whiskey from behind a book in his sister's living room.* "I wanted to stand up," Jackson subsequently wrote for *Cosmopolitan*, "turn around and cry out: 'What in God's name are you laughing at—what the hell's funny about it?' " Alcoholism, after all, was *no laughing matter*, and Jackson was quite willing to say so even at the risk of seeming (as he grimly admitted) "a stuffed shirt"—at any rate he was willing to say so for a price: "I'm god damned sick of the subject of alcoholism," he wrote his agent, not for the first time. "I'm a writer first of all, et cetera, but if

---

* One can only imagine Jackson's indignation (and/or delight) over the movie *Educating Rita* (1983), in which a boozy professor played by Michael Caine conceals his whiskey, aptly enough, behind a copy of *The Lost Weekend*.

I can get $1500 out of a good strong provocative or even controversial piece on the alcoholic in our society . . . why not?"

He could be especially humorless on the subject of his own alcoholism. One morning in April 1944 he got a call from one Mr. Horton, the proprietor of a nearby bookshop on Washington Square and "a bloody bore," Jackson thought, who was forever bending his ear about AA whenever he'd stop by to check on sales of *The Lost Weekend*. One day Horton phoned him at home: "I read in the paper today that you're going to Hollywood," the man said, and Jackson allowed it was true. "Well, I wish you'd do yourself a favor—" Horton continued, and began to give him the address and telephone number of the AA chapter in Beverly Hills. "You S.O.B.!" Jackson exploded. "If you don't think I know what I'm doing by now, after *eight years* of sobriety on my own, then you don't know very much! Go and talk to those people who need it! That's the trouble with you holy rollers!" Then he hung up on him.

Nine years later, detoxing at the Saul Clinic, Jackson remembered his abuse of poor Mr. Horton. "And I thought, 'My gosh. All that man was doing was trying to be kind . . . ' " If Jackson had been truly secure in his sobriety, he realized, he wouldn't have lost his temper like that. "It was a sign of danger ahead that I didn't even know."

MGM HAD OFFERED Jackson a screenwriting job a month before his novel was published—Brandt & Brandt had sent them a copy—and prior to his interview at the New York office he fretted over the baneful influence of Hollywood on him, a serious writer ("Will I have the courage to say No?"). "One best seller did it," Hedda Hopper announced on March 22, when Jackson happened to be visiting Newark, where word of his movie contract was received with far greater awe than a mere novel could ever command, and gave Jackson another chance to wear his eminence lightly (he was "modest in spite of his mushrooming literary success," the *Courier-Gazette* noted). He was careful to point out that this was only a temporary detour: four months in Hollywood that summer, then five during each of the following two winters, and meanwhile his thousand-dollar weekly salary would serve to finance another novel.

Still, he was filled with misgiving when he parted with Rhoda, the kids, and Boom before boarding the Twentieth Century Limited on April 15; he'd even gotten emotional saying goodbye to Herb on the phone, but when little Sarah ran back to kiss him on the platform, he could scarcely drag himself onto the train. Soon, though, excitement got the better of him. In Chicago he changed trains to the Super Chief, which made the Century "look like the Newark & Marion": "Shower baths, barber shop, super-de-luxe club cars, bars, diners decorated with indian designs, wonderful food . . . " At the Kansas City station he couldn't resist revealing his identity to the bookstore owner, who breathlessly informed him that *Bette Davis herself* had bought a copy of *The Lost Weekend* en route to Hollywood the other day. "I hope she connects the author with 'that sweet little man on the couch' [in Nantucket]," wrote Jackson, who intended to drop her a note just as soon as he arrived. Later, as his journey continued, the gorgeous Western scenery put him in a subdued, philosophical mood: "It seems hard to believe, doesn't it," he wrote Boom, "that movie-people pass untouched through this incredible landscape which is the very *utter* in the eternal verities, and then pass on to the make-believe and sham of Hollywood."

In that dubious milieu Jackson was thrilled to learn that he was something of a legend, and that the title of his book had become "part of the language": at the Ruban Bleu, Imogene Coca was doing a popular drunk sketch she called her "Lost-Weekend number," and many, many actual drunks were anxious to glimpse the author of the most-talked-about book in town. "You know, I think you're a great writer," the novelist Laura Hobson blurted, informing Jackson that everyone on the MGM lot had "talked of nothing else" the week before he arrived, though some were a little reluctant to meet him. "I wish they really would be reluctant," he wrote Rhoda, "because I know they're always disappointed; that is, they have some preconceived idea about you and expect you to be 'interesting' or intense or drunk or something different from just a normal average guy like anybody else." But Jackson's mild-mannered demeanor was perhaps the most exotic part of all, and never mind his artless affability. His fame, wrote Mary McCarthy, seemed foremost a means of making friends with strangers ("as though the friendship already existed on the ideal plane, in the mind of God, and had only to be cemented in the real world by the manly handclasp"). Everyone was disarmed: this dipso novelist—the model for Don Birnam!—was, quite simply, the nicest guy they'd ever met. As for Jackson, he was naturally pleased that he never had to dine alone, but more than a little bewildered: "Why I am wanted by these people I truly don't know; I offer nothing and merely am amiable."

What they hoped he offered—apart from amiability—was, of course, "the secret": "I just stopped drinking," Jackson would shrug, whereupon people would pry even more. He was flattered when big stars such as Spencer Tracy "hounded [him] for days on end," but others made him nervous. *Citizen Kane* screenwriter Herman Mankiewicz had reputedly attempted suicide after reading *The Lost Weekend* (his doctor suffered a dislocated shoulder while tussling with him), and Jackson was relieved when he managed to get out of lunching alone with the man in Malibu. Algonquin wit Robert Benchley—whose career had devolved into odd, demoralizing cameos for movies such as *National Barn Dance*—"hung onto [Jackson] for dear life," and later wired his friend Dorothy Parker that the novelist known as "the MGM lion" ("literary lion," Charlie glossed for Rhoda) was returning to New York. "I've got to meet the man who saved my life," she would greet him. "Well, it's all fun," he'd written from Hollywood that first month, "though it truly goes in one ear and out the other . . . " Sometimes, though, he could hardly restrain his ecstatic incredulity: "This fantastic town! My fantastic life! . . . the other night when I got in there was a note that Vincent Price had called; I don't know him yet . . . "

The provincial lad with stars in his eyes was pleased to realize that (in those days anyway) a top-tier writer was considered something of an "aristocrat" in Hollywood. Sitting in the MGM commissary with his fellow wordsmiths and new best friends—Whitfield Cook, Robert Nathan, and Donald Ogden Stewart—Jackson was stunned when Clark Gable sat down opposite him *just like that* and began chewing the fat ("I still can't get over it . . . it is something that's happening to somebody else, not me"). Nor was commissary talk the sort of bland gossip one heard on the stoop in Newark, but rather shimmering effortless repartee—"real brilliance," which Jackson was at pains to report to the folks back home with curatorial precision: "They tell the story about the Hollywood writer who got tired of it all and committed suicide by jumping into his Capeheart while it was changing records, for instance."

Jackson felt esteemed in every way. His minder at MGM was a fatherly Russian producer named Voldemar Vetluguin, who counseled Charlie to be choosy about his assignments and would-be collaborators. "Arsur is hard to work with," the man gravely advised, when Jackson wondered whether he should team up with the producer Arthur Hornblow. Jackson was touched by "Vet's" concern, but also dismayed to find that such a brilliant, kindly man lived all alone in an enormous house and commenced getting drunk every night, without fail, at 5:30 on the nose.

He did, however, steer Charlie to a plum assignment within a single week: a big ensemble picture tentatively titled *A Day to Forget*—about the one day in the lives of various characters that they would most like to relive—featuring all the big stars at MGM (Garland, Tracy, Hedy Lamarr, et al.), with Van Johnson in the lead. The producer was Carey Wilson, screenwriter for the original *Ben-Hur* and *Mutiny on the Bounty*, and Jackson envisaged the key credits as follows: "Story by Harry Ruskin and Charles Jackson / Screenplay by Charles Jackson." Indeed, the episodic narrative offered an intriguing technical challenge—namely, how to weave together so many disparate plots without seeming to start the movie over again every few minutes—and Jackson was eager for the chance to prove his "virtuosity" and become known as a "name writer and sound craftsman." "Already ballyhooed as an all-star drama to spotlight virtually every major player on Leo's lot," *Box Office* trumpeted a month later, "*Nor All Your Tears* [as it was now called] is a story of human conflicts laid against the background of an American coastal city . . . "

The coastal city in question was San Francisco, to which Jackson was sent for three days in late May to "absorb some of the atmosphere"—both *haut* and *bas*, it would seem: put up at the elegant Mark Hopkins Hotel at the crest of Nob Hill, Jackson was taken under the wing of professional hostess Elsa Maxwell, no less, who "paved [his] way with social engagements that are too-too," he reported, including lunch with the mayor at the Pacific-Union Club and entrée into houses of "some of the old families." Nights, however, were spent in the company of his roguish old friend Haughton C. Bickerton, who lived with his mother in Sausalito. "You must remember bad Bick, don't you?" he wrote Whitfield Cook ("Angel") a few months later, which suggests that Cook had come along for the trip. By then Cook had begun to feel like "an old old friend" to Charlie: "We have many many laughs to the minute . . . and we almost always lunch together." Cook's seventy-year career as a screenwriter, novelist, and composer is now best remembered, if at all, for his contribution to Hitchcock's *Strangers on a Train* (1951), for which he's generally credited as having underlined the sexual tension between Farley Granger and Robert Walker. Later, as a sixty-year-old widower, Cook became attached to the gay Australian writer Sumner Lock Elliott; the two lived apart until Elliott's stroke in 1985, when Cook moved in and became the man's caretaker for the last six years of his life.

Around this time Charlie received a "sharp letter" from his mother—"reminding me" (as he indignantly related to Rhoda) "that I

have a good wife and two perfectly good children, and I mustn't do anything to . . . 'bring shame upon them.' Imagine!" Indeed, this seemed
unduly harsh, given that almost every single day Charlie wrote long,
newsy letters to his wife (urging her to keep them "as a kind of diary" in
case he needed to look stuff up later), and twice a week they spoke on the
telephone—though, truth be known, these chats tended to be "less than
satisfactory" ("we never know what to say . . . and besides we're probably
too conscious of the fleeting expensive minutes"). "Lately I have longed
for you physically—which may surprise you," Charlie wrote shortly after
that trip to the Bay Area. "I could have sex if I wanted it, but funny thing
is it doesn't enter my head: what I want is love, someone to hold and love
and be with long hours through the night, even if it's only lying side by
side . . . " Certainly he wanted his family around him—in fact, he was
considering buying a house in Hollywood so they could spend winters
there, and meanwhile he wanted Rhoda to leave the kids with her family
and join him for a few weeks that summer, while he was still "a so-called
'celeb' ": it "will never be the same after this year," he accurately predicted. Rhoda protested that she would feel "terribly ill at ease" in such
a place, and Charlie replied that he'd felt the same way until he realized
everyone felt that way, even the "Big Names": "it's the 20th Century neurosis, and keener or more acute here than anywhere, because everyone is
really so insecure and this is such an unreal world." This failed to reassure Rhoda, who decided to stay put in the East.

THAT SPRING, director Billy Wilder had discovered *The Lost Weekend*—
piqued by the title—while traveling between coasts. Back in Los Angeles
he chatted with various doctors and AA people, all of whom vouched
for the novel's verisimilitude and agreed that an adaptation would be a
pioneering work: that is, a movie that didn't milk the subject for laughs.
Paramount's production head Buddy De Sylva was skeptical about the
commercial end, and almost assuredly would have vetoed the idea if it had
come from anyone but Wilder—who, with his writing partner Charles
Brackett, enjoyed an almost unrivaled "prestige and independence" in
the industry, according to a 1944 *Life* profile. After eight years together,
Brackett and Wilder ("the happiest couple in Hollywood") had never
misfired, producing a string of quirky classics including *Ball of Fire*, *The
Major and the Minor*, and *Ninotchka* (one of Jackson's favorites, needless
to say: "Garbo laughs!"). They were an odd pair: Brackett, a Harvard
Law School graduate, was vice-president of the bank his family owned

in Saratoga—"a courtly, somewhat rumpled, affable gentleman," as *Life*
put it, whereas Wilder was a foul-mouthed Austrio-Hungarian Jew with
a bleak view of humanity that (said Brackett) stood their partnership in
good stead.

The agent Leland Hayward had arranged for Jackson to meet the two
at Romanoff's in early May—"a triumph, nothing less," Charlie wrote
Boom: "Wilder and Brackett were wonderful, crazy about the book, anxious to do the picture, and that's what we talked about." He was especially
smitten by Brackett ("the nicest man I have met here"), who in turn was
even more fascinated by *The Lost Weekend* than Wilder: "It had," he said,
"more sense of horror than any horror story I have ever read—lingering
like a theme in music." A few days later, Wilder "dragged [Jackson] away"
from a party to attend a screening of his latest movie, *Double Indemnity*, after which he stood up and announced, "Next picture coming up:
The Lost Weekend!" Jackson could hardly demur, since he'd found *Double
Indemnity* "truly wonderful" and considered himself "the luckiest guy
in the world"—but wait: yet another genius, Alfred Hitchcock, had also
read *The Lost Weekend* and wanted to buy it, or so he told the author (who
was dining with Whit Cook) one night at LaRue's. Toward the end of
May, not a day passed that Jackson's name didn't appear in one of the big
columns: "Yesterday I read that four major movie companies are all hot
about the book," he wrote Philip Wylie. Without a doubt, he announced,
The Lost Weekend would sell by the end of the month, "and certainly for
not less than $75,000."

Two years later—sadder but (perhaps) wiser—Jackson wrote his agent:
"I feel, and will always feel . . . that The Lost Weekend was handled very
badly indeed." Jackson had been in San Francisco on May 29, when his
agent Carl Brandt called to relay Paramount's decidedly lowball offer:
$35,000. Other studios, Brandt explained, were only willing to option
at that point, so there was no competitive bidding; in any event Paramount wanted an answer within two hours. "I'm no businessman," said
Charlie. "What should I do?" "I cannot take the responsibility of deciding for you," Brandt replied. Frantic, Jackson tried to reach his newest
best friend, Brackett—who had urged him, in confidence, to ask Paramount for the moon, since he and Wilder were determined to make the
movie "come hell or high water"—but Brackett was away from his desk.
Charlie waited, then waited a little more, then caved. "I wish this did
me some good financially," he'd later sigh, whenever someone reminded
him of *The Lost Weekend*'s astounding box-office success. "Me, I sold it
outright for $35,000." At the time Louella Parsons speculated in print

that he'd doubtless gotten "a pretty penny—up in six figures" for such a hot property.

Still, it was a long way from writing *Sweet River* scripts at forty bucks a pop, and Jackson consoled himself that Wilder and Brackett would, after all, do a "brilliant job." Tacked on their door at Paramount was a sign: "DO NOT DISTURB: MEN WORKING ON NEXT YEAR'S ACADEMY AWARD"—a bit of desperate bluster, many thought, given what seemed an almost unfilmable novel about a single major character who hardly spoke except inside his head. "If they bring it off," a colleague remarked, "I bet they'll try next to make a musical out of *Finnegans Wake*." In fact, as Brackett later claimed, it turned out to be "the easiest script we wrote, thanks to the superb novel," and Wilder agreed: the more you took the book apart, he said, the better it seemed. Also, they were glad to consult with the author, to whom they'd promised not to make drastic changes without his approval—as, for example, when they toyed with the idea of turning Helen into an ex-alcoholic whom Don meets in a psychiatrist's office: "Simply won't permit such a thing," said Jackson, winning the point. But mostly he was nothing but pleased: the script's opening was "brilliant," and the new "Boy-Meets-Girl" sequence (Don and Helen are given each other's coats by mistake while leaving *La Traviata*) was "original & effective." And meanwhile the columns buzzed with rumors about who would play the controversial lead. Wilder and Brackett wanted Cary Grant, Alan Ladd, or Ray Milland, in that order, while Jackson had hoped for Robert Montgomery (the two had hit it off at a party chez Brackett), who, he thought, had the "charm" and "knowledge of 'psychopathia' " to do justice to such a difficult role.* As for the long-suffering Helen, an actress named Andrea Leeds ("remember her? the lovely girl in STAGE DOOR who committed suicide?") was then the top candidate, and Jackson moreover observed that a live bat ("Actually") was being trained for the climactic hallucination.

THAT FIRST MONTH in Hollywood, Jackson had gotten a call from the MGM publicity department, asking about his marital status: "Lovely,"

---

* Montgomery was still in the Navy at the time, or he might have gotten the part. Ten years later he played Don in a *Lost Weekend* adaptation for his own live television show, *Robert Montgomery Presents*—a performance applauded by *Time* for its "artistry" and "careful delineation." Wilder had also considered José Ferrer, but Buddy De Sylva put his foot down: audiences would reject the character, said De Sylva, if he wasn't handsome enough.

he replied, and thereupon learned that he was being linked in the press with Phyllis Thaxter, a starlet who'd accompanied him to a party once and called him "sir" all night. "Romance, hell," he wrote dismissively to Rhoda, but a couple of weeks later the idea began to seem less absurd—since, as he liked to confess to whosoever would listen, he'd fallen "like a ton of bricks" for "a scared shy little girl" of twenty-one (even younger than Thaxter): Judy Garland. They met at a dinner party on June 2, after which he lost no time writing his wife that, yes, "I all but fell in love with Judy—strictly as an artist, I mean":

> She reminds me of one of those lovely little appealing calves, or fauns [*sic*]—and they say she cries at night because she isn't beautiful. But she is so much more beautiful, really, than any Hollywood actress of her class, with the kind of beauty that comes from within, and an honesty and simplicity about her that are almost pathetic. She has worked so hard all her life that she has never had a chance for herself or any private life at all: that's why she's so insecure. . . . One of the troubles is people her own age don't appreciate her: older men love her.

Older bisexual men particularly loved her—not just for the vulnerable, fawn-like quality noted above, but also for her androgynous looks ("like the girl and boy next door," said theater critic Margo Jefferson) and a well-known tendency, fragility withal, for seducing such men (and other women).

Probably, though, her seduction of Jackson was on a higher plane, from afar, as when he watched her rehearse a big number for *Ziegfeld Follies:* between performances, he noticed, she seemed "all but lifeless," looking like a sleepy child waiting for a bus, but when she got her cue to speak or sing, "she was transformed"—a personality sprang forth and filled the studio, sucked up the very air. Jackson felt as though "he was seeing nothing less than a demonstration of the workings of art itself," and the disparity between bigger-than-life persona and "terribly mixed up" girl moved him profoundly. "Dear Judy," he began a poem for her twenty-second birthday (June 10), inscribed on the flyleaf of *The Lost Weekend*:

> *. . . Once, within a wood,*
> *The willows parted and there stood,*

Soft-eyed and innocent, a fawn;
One moment later it was gone. . . .

Never did I expect to see
Again such simple purity
So be it, too: susceptible man
Must bear such moments as he can. . . .

A few days later he shyly asked his "new love" (as he frankly described her in a note to Alma Pritchard at Brandt & Brandt) whether she'd accompany him to the "preem" of *The White Cliffs of Dover* on June 19, and was startled by her ready acceptance. Vetluguin, ever the mentor, explained that "no man in his right mind" would take Judy Garland to a premiere: "You'll be mobbed," he said. "You're taking your life in your hands." But Charlie figured it was "all part of the Hollywood experience," and was determined to see it through. In his subsequent letter to Rhoda (souvenir police pass enclosed), he described the atmosphere at Grauman's Theatre that night as being akin to a "Nazi demonstration," complete with a "battery of search-lights" and rabid, howling fans packed into bleachers along the street:

As the car pulled in to the curb the crowd screamed "There's Judy!" over and over again. . . . Your heart would have been touched (as mine was) if you could have seen how Judy turned to the crowd and gave a tiny little wave, acknowledging the applause, though all the while, her hand on my arm was trembling and shaking against me. We were stopped, then, every few feet, and photographed; and Judy kept saying "For God's sake, Charlie, smile!" Each time the flash went off, Judy's face was turned toward mine, looking up at me in a charming smile, as though I were The Only Man In The World. . . . My legs knocked together, but I wouldn't have missed it for the world: a real experience.

Rhoda was understandably bemused by her husband's effusive tone (never mind the photos and rumors that had begun to appear in the press), and he hastened to assure her that she needn't feel "the slightest twinge of jealousy"; writing to Alma at Brandt & Brandt, meanwhile, he mentioned that he was taking tea with his idol Thomas Mann the following Saturday, though his "real passion" was for Judy: "Alas, how are the mighty fallen, when I go from Mann idolatry to Garland worship. But that's Hollywood."

Which is not to say that his Mann idolatry was inconsiderable: ever since *The Magic Mountain* had changed his life, Jackson had read almost every word of Mann's work that had been translated into English; the only greater writer, in Jackson's eyes, was Tolstoy. When he learned, then, that his hero would be a fellow guest at the home of producer Edwin Knopf (brother of Mann's American publisher, Alfred), he was stricken by a bad case of "stage-fright" exacerbated by sobriety ("such a handicap, at moments like that"). Happily he was soon seated beside Mrs. Mann, and in the course of an easy chat about Davos and the like, he mentioned his admiration for her husband: "Then you must talk with him yourself after dinner," she said, and arranged for the two to be left alone, more or less. At first Mann seemed to take it in stride that Jackson knew his work (essays too) like a rabbi knows the Talmud, but presently he flattered Jackson—and stunned guests within earshot—by inquiring about *The Lost Weekend*. "Oh, but that's very well!" he exclaimed, when Charlie told him how it was selling. As Mary McCarthy wrote in her roman à clef about Jackson—wherein he appears as Herbert Harper, author of the confessional novel *A Short One If You Don't Mind**—his meeting with Mann became something of a legend among writers whose own books "the great *dichte*" had never deigned to notice:

> So when Herbert Harper approached the great man at a Hollywood party, the meeting was watched with a good deal of sardonic anticipation: the irresistible force was meeting the immovable object. To the astonishment of everyone, a conversation began and continued all evening, and the phrase, "A Short Vun" was heard, by those nearby, to drop frequently from Herr Danz's [Mann's] lips.

When they subsequently took tea at Mann's house in Pacific Palisades, Mann presented Jackson with an inscribed copy of his new novel, *Joseph the Provider*—in exchange for the "fine gift" of *The Lost Weekend*—and a mutual admiration society was born. Mann compared Jackson's novel to Knut Hamsun's *Hunger*, while *Joseph the Provider* became one of Char-

---

* Alternately titled *The Lost Week* or *The Caged Lion*, this unfinished novel will be discussed in due course. Suffice it to say that McCarthy had asked Jackson's permission (eagerly granted) to use him as the model for Herbert Harper. Thomas Mann appears as Heinrich Danz.

lie's indispensable masterpieces ("I know of no book," he wrote Dorothea Straus, "that leaves one with a greater sense of fulfillment than this one"). For a few years the two kept up a correspondence that, as McCarthy put it, "echoed benevolently Goethe's conversations with Eckermann." The following spring, Jackson wrote Mann of a visit he'd received in New Hampshire from G. B. Fischer, Mann's German publisher, whom Charlie had spirited upstairs to see his portrait of Dr. Mann, framed in red lacquer and proudly displayed (along with Garbo, Spencer Tracy, Beethoven, et al.) in his study. Fischer had solicited an essay from Jackson for a special issue of *Die Neue Rundschau* in honor of Mann's seventieth birthday: titled "Strictly Personal," Jackson's contribution (the only one printed in English) was a charming, eminently readable history of the author's unrestrained adulation, going back to his choice of sanatoria in 1929 and proceeding to the present day. "I was really delighted with this little piece of prose which, though informal, touches the heart in a truly poetical manner," Mann wrote. His last letter, in 1948, acknowledged Jackson's "generous and gratifying impulse" to phone Mann one Sunday night and express his indignation over certain unsatisfactory reviews of *Doctor Faustus.* Probably, by then, it was not an entirely sober impulse on Charlie's part; in any event Dr. Mann pleaded a "very bad" connection, though he clearly appreciated the thought.

Back in Hollywood that summer, Jackson's social life had crystallized around two households: the Bracketts and the Gershwins. Every Sunday the former gave daytime dinner parties whose attendance by "the most entertainingly articulate writers . . . and assorted geniuses of the craft" inspired *Life* to liken them to "Madame de Staël's salons in 18th century Paris"—an ambience due in part to Brackett's witty wife, Elizabeth, who was sometimes, alas, absent from public view. The fact was, she'd struggled with severe alcoholism for years, as had their twenty-four-year-old daughter, Alexandra ("Zan"), and hence at least one reason Charles Brackett had been eager to adapt *The Lost Weekend* and re-create, as he remarked, "the strange and sometimes beautiful things" that transpire in an alcoholic's mind. "It's genuinely tragic," Charlie wrote Rhoda, "because Elizabeth is almost one of the most loved women I ever knew."*

From the Bracketts', Charlie would hitch a ride with playwrights John

---

* Elizabeth Brackett died four years later (whereupon the widower married her sister, Lillian), and their daughter Alexandra died in 1968 after falling down a flight of stairs.

Van Druten or Marc Connelly and spend the rest of the day—often past midnight—at Lee and Ira Gershwin's house. His "nicest day in Holly-wood" was spent thus: lunching and playing charades at the Bracketts', then lazing around the Gershwins' pool (the swarthy Jackson fancied a tan) with twelve others; later they feasted al fresco on "tremendous steaks (they shot all their coupons for a month, they said) . . . and the most wonderful ice cream with chocolate sauce I ever ate" before heading inside, as the evening turned cool, and sitting for hours around a cozy fire. The Gershwins, said Charlie, were "nice people, who really love you: Ira sat around like a fat old woman in the most preposterous shorts, all day and evening, looking something like a toad, but a nice toad, and Lee is just like a happy affectionate little girl . . ." As tokens of their friend-ship, they gave Charlie rare photographs of George and Ira, as well as an original pastel drawing by George. Almost twenty years later Jackson would reflect, a little sadly, that "out of all the people [he] used to see so much of [in Hollywood]"—and there had been many—his only lasting friendships had proved to be with the Gershwins and Charles Brackett.

THOUGH HE was having a "wonderful time," Jackson was eager to get back to his own work. After all, he never would have taken the MGM job in the first place if he'd known that *The Lost Weekend* would sell to the movies, and besides he was longing to write a sequel about Don's recovery (and the world was expecting as much) titled *The Working Out.* Or rather, sometimes he was "hot and bothered" about the sequel, and sometimes about an entirely different novel that had recently begun to germinate—to be titled, he thought, either *My Two Troubles* or *Who Can Wonder?* "Damn it to hell," he wrote Rhoda in mid-May (even before the Paramount sale), "why can't I get myself fired at once! . . . Darling, it's such a magnificent rich idea I feel all trembly at the thought that it was 'given' to me to do: that I am to be the instrument through which such a story will reach people." What he wanted, ideally, was to get out of the second term of his MGM contract—requiring him to return in November—so he could have an uninterrupted fifteen months to work on his fiction, an ambitious program that was to include *The Work-ing Out*, a story collection, and *My Two Troubles.* As for the other poor hacks at MGM, well, he simply pitied them: his friend Bob Nathan, for instance, had just signed a contract that would pay him $700,000 over the next five years, and was therefore "the unhappiest man alive": he "knows it's his death warrant," Jackson wrote, "knows he will never write another book."*

Meanwhile he'd more than acquitted himself as a screenwriter, arriving at the studio every morning at six o'clock ("the other writers say they'll report me to the Screen Writers Guild as a scab and saboteur"), the better to oblige Carey Wilson's demands for draft after draft—theirs, indeed, was a "hair-raising" relationship: "he doesn't know what he wants until he gets it, and then he doesn't want it . . ." Still, Charlie felt certain that old "Vet" would be in his corner when push came to shove, and to this stalwart man he appealed once he'd proven his mettle. As he recounted their meeting to Carl Brandt:

> I proposed that my fall option be suspended for one year, as I needed more time to write my second book. Vet acquiesced with such alacrity that my breath was taken away, practically; and even suggested that I go off payroll right now. I said, "But what is to become of my assignment with Carey Wilson?" And he replied, to my astonishment, that I had been taken off the assignment three weeks previous, and another writer put on—put behind me, as the expression is, out here.

Actually as many as *five* writers had been "put behind" him, including (but not limited to) Harry Ruskin, Michael Arlen, James M. Cain, I.A.R. Wylie, and his friend John Van Druten, each working separately on his own sequence of *The Common Sin* (as it was now called), which in any case was never produced. "I have been taken in and how by Vetluguin"—Jackson noted afterward with no little rue—"who is the smoothest bird this side of a[n] Archipenko sculpture." On the brighter side, he and MGM had mutually decided to dissolve their contract, though he'd get paid for the full sixteen weeks of his first term. And when he next encountered the wily Vetluguin—later that November, in the office of Brandt & Brandt—the man seemed hardly to recognize him ("I think he remembered that I was a writer, maybe, and that my name was Johnson").

For his last three weeks in Hollywood, anyway, he was free to enjoy the fruits of his abundant popularity, as his friends all but fought for the

---

* The glibly prolific Nathan—best known for *The Bishop's Wife* (1928) and *Portrait of Jennie* (1940)—would produce no fewer than twenty-one more utterly forgotten novels (and almost as many plays, children's books, and poetry collections) before his death, in 1985, at the ripe age of ninety-one.

chance to entertain him one last time. Judy Garland and the Gershwins were giving him big parties, while Kate Hepburn and "Spence" wanted to see him both en masse and privately. Finally, with a week to go, the exhausted Charlie wanted nothing more than to go home to his family and his own bed: "Darling, I go all funny at the thought," he wrote Rhoda on August 7. "It means more to me than anything that has happened in 4 months: you are mine, you are what I want in life and—what is more—what I have. Truly I am the luckiest guy in the world to have so much." Before the homecoming proper, though, he suggested they give a smallish cocktail party at the New Weston Hotel in New York (this for some Hollywood friends on the East Coast, as well as friends of friends such as Dorothy Parker, Celeste Holm, Sally Benson . . .). He was to arrive on August 14—or rather *we*, since "our Whit Cook" also happened to be heading to New York, and the two had booked a double-bedroom compartment aboard the Chief and the Century.

Chapter Nine

Six Chimney Farm

Seventeen miles north of Hanover, New Hampshire, along the Connecticut River, is "the most beautiful town in America," according to Washington Irving: Orford. On the east side of its single street, atop a natural twenty-five-foot-high ridge, are seven houses that have been called the finest examples of Federal architecture in the country. The northernmost (and arguably best) of these caught Jackson's eye as he was driving from Brattleboro in 1935: If he could only have such a house, he thought, it would be the "absolute peak of fulfillment and happiness"—though of course that was an impossible dream for an alcoholic without prospects. Later, though, as a married and sober man, Jackson would insist on stopping the car in Orford each summer en route to Rhoda's family in Barre, Vermont: "When I'm rich," he would vow, "it will be mine!"

Six Chimney Farm—"one of the most beautiful houses in New England," said a 1927 issue of *House Beautiful*—was built between 1825 and 1829 by a manufacturer of beaver hats, William Howard, on ninety-seven acres of property that included a separate five-room farmhouse and a working dairy farm. The main house was designed by Asher Benjamin, an eminent Boston architect influenced by Bulfinch—though Jackson would always prefer to believe that Bulfinch himself had done it ("He also did the Capitol at Washington!" he excitedly informed Boom), and he dated it at various times to as early as 1788 and rarely later than 1807. More accurately Jackson pointed out that the five-thousand-square-foot house had been completely restored in 1916 by Judge William Dana, who installed modern appliances and plumbing, and added open porches on either side. Each of the five bedrooms had its own fireplace, as did the living room and gorgeous dining room, which featured a built-in Hepplewhite china cupboard and lovely, antique wallpaper of North American scenery (Niagara Falls, West Point, Boston Harbor) first printed in Alsace by Jean Zuber et Cie, and also found in the Diplomatic Reception Room at the White House.

What would seem an outlandish extravagance—even for a man with so fanciful a view of personal finance—was, objectively at least, a bargain: for thirty thousand dollars he got the two houses, the land, and Judge Dana's collection of Sheraton furniture. As of 1944 the owner was John Owsley, a former head football coach at Yale who lived most of the year in New Haven; by all accounts a colorful man, he'd evidently wearied of the aesthetic charms of Orford, which (apart from its proximity to Dartmouth) was bereft of cultural diversions. As for Charlie and Rhoda, they'd both grown up in small country towns and thought at the time—for whatever reason—that they wanted their children to do the same. A little surprising is the fact that Jackson had decided to buy the place pre-Hollywood, purely on the basis of his earning potential as a radio writer and first-time novelist: "The possibility of our buying your house hinges on the success of a new book of mine," he wrote Owsley on October 30, 1943. "I am not financially dependent on the success of my books, but I would have to be assured of a good sale on my new book in order to raise the cash required for a down payment . . ." He got the good sale, of course, and put down ten thousand dollars; then came the Paramount deal, on the strength of which he jubilantly reported to Nila Mack that the house was now "paid for twice over." Not so, and the math would become even more creative once taxes, maintenance, and certain appurtenances entered the picture.

Rhoda and Boom had worked hard that summer to prepare the place for its master, and on arrival he was enchanted, especially, by his own upstairs bedroom—separate, that is, from Rhoda's ("but won't it be wonderful to visit each other back and forth across our little private hall?"), since he planned to use it as a "study-and-retreat-and-bedroom in one." The high-ceilinged room, as he first found it, was Colonial simplicity itself: the mahogany furniture included a carved four-poster, secretary, highboy, and stately desk placed at a window with a view of Main Street and the verdant hills of Vermont across the river. When Charlie was finished decorating, however, the room bore his own vivacious stamp: his old fondness for all things Indian was reflected in the kachina dolls (bought in Arizona when the Super Chief passed through) arranged here and there, as well as a conspicuous war bonnet on top of the secretary; thirteen Revolutionary flags were hung along the ceiling border, while the patriotic pièce de résistance was splashed over his bed—an eleven-by-seven-foot, thirty-eight-star American flag made out of homespun serge ("the colors more beautiful than you can imagine"). The rest of the wall space—almost every square inch—was covered by signed portraits of Charlie's Hollywood pals and other personal gods. On the floor was a polar-bear rug. "Rhoda does admit the room at least has 'personality,' " he wrote a friend, "but she shakes her head sadly while saying it." Perhaps to compensate for the quirkiness of his own sanctuary ("I call it the Museum, or the Lodge Room"), the rest of the house was more or less conservatively adorned with paintings by Frederick Papsdorf, Darrell Austin, Camille Bombois, and Raoul Dufy, most of them raided from the Klaus Perls Gallery in New York.

The upkeep was considerable, and Charlie employed a married couple and their daughter, the Jobins, to take care of the cooking, cleaning, babysitting, gardening, snow-shoveling, and so on. He also wanted to hire Rhoda's younger sister, Katharine ("Kay" or "Kitty"), as an occasional secretary—because he needed one, somewhat, but mainly because he was fond of her and sympathized with her predicament: Katharine's "ne'er-do-well husband" (as Charlie called him, not without cause), Fred Brock, was currently in the Army; before the war he'd gone looking for gold in South America and dabbled in farming, while his formidable mother in Montpelier doled out a prudent allowance. Now that he was gone, Katharine and their five-year-old son had been living in Barre with her parents, and Charlie wanted to bring them to Orford. This would be pleasant for him, too, since he and Katharine had a rapport—so much so, indeed, that a rumor (among others) persisted in Orford that the two were *involved*. This, for any number of reasons, was unlikely, though Charlie did have a keen appreciation for Katharine's finer qualities—her sense of humor, for one; a certain well-concealed worldliness—and had playfully flirted with her from the beginning of his courtship with Rhoda. "To Kittuh, written in the poet's Heart's Blood," he'd addressed some verse to her on Valentine's Day, 1934:

Sad is my lot, it is you who make it;
Sorry my plight and frequent my tear;
Heavy my heart, because you can't take it,
Though I've offered it often enough, my dear. . . .

Mostly he was at pains to mitigate her shyness, her almost morbid insistence (not unlike her sister's) on plainness both in appearance and manner, which included an "exasperating" tendency to pass the back of her hand under her nose, as if in want of a handkerchief.

He proved his affection further in 1945, when Fred Brock resumed his life as an unemployed civilian; "at whatever rental or cost they could afford," Charlie let the family move into his farmhouse and till the vast acreage between his own garden and the graveyard almost half a mile away. Such generosity, to be sure, did not result in any discernible increase of friendliness on Fred's part—on the contrary, the man was more aloof than ever, seeming to regard fiction-writing as a dubious livelihood at best, at least when compared with his own honest toil. Charlie, meanwhile, bristled at the "almost ostentatious laziness" of his brother-in-law, a handsome man who liked to loiter in the bathroom combing his hair. What made matters worse was Charlie's guilty animus toward the Brocks' five-year-old, an irksome "escapist" (thought Charlie), whose vagaries were largely due to the "disinterest of his ne'er-do-well father."

With those two exceptions, however, Charlie was devoted to his in-laws—more so, in fact, than to his own family. He thought his melodramatic, self-pitying mother could learn a thing or two from Rhoda's parents, John and Isabella, a kindly couple who called each other Mr. and Mrs. Booth and never complained about their poverty (they lived on a modest pension, supplemented by occasional checks from Charlie) or anything else for that matter. Charlie liked having them around: John seldom imposed his company, preferring to tend a strawberry patch on the Ridge or paint the lovely countryside, while his wife was so retiring that Charlie teasingly dubbed her the Sword-Swallower (from an old joke: after ten years of marriage, a husband learns that his wife had been a sword-swallower in the circus before they met; "Why didn't you ever *tell* me?" he demands, and she replies, "Because you never asked"). Her tact was another trait he wished his own mother would emulate: "I read your manuscript and just can't get over the extent of your vocabulary," Mrs. Booth had congratulated him on *The Lost Weekend.* "I am no one to criticise, because I don't know enough to, so you will just have to be satisfied with my saying that it ought to bring you a nice pot of money." His main nickname for this endearing creature was Queenie—since her name was Isabella—and so he called her each night after dinner, when the two would retire to the library for a few games of rummy 500, the woman's only passion apart from her grandchildren.

Charlie loved the whole idea of being a paterfamilias, and could hardly get over the fact that he'd gone from being a feckless, drunken misfit to the author of a celebrated best-seller and now the proprietor of Six Chimney Farm. "Boom, you can't realize how much I love this house and living here," he wrote shortly after moving in. "The night we got home Rhoda and I just walked from room to room and admired, as I do often." And meantime he dreamed of the day when all the Booths and Jacksons—even (or especially) Herb and Bob and their brood—would gather under his roof and admire the splendor of it all. Such a reunion (never realized in real life) formed the long "Preview" section of his Birnam epic, *What Happened*—the main point being that, for all his travails, everything had worked out in the end for Don: "He would be host to the gathering, they should come to him and be his guests, and he would not only take care of them all but be able to take care of them all—did it not mean, in effect, that he would be head of the family?" A related point was, of course, that reality never quite measures up, and that such a gathering would invariably prove more of a headache than anything else.

THE TOWN ITSELF soon began to pall. There was nothing to do but admire the countryside: one had to cross the bridge into Fairlee, Vermont, to buy a newspaper, and most of the natives (retired farmers and the like) didn't read much anyway—except for "That Dreadful Book" ("probably the one book they have read in ten years") by their new neighbor, Mr. Jackson. "My, you're a lot nicer than I thought you'd be," a member of the local ladies' club remarked to Rhoda, whose husband was notorious before he'd even arrived. Not only was the word out that his book was *true*, more or less, but also that the author worked in Hollywood ('nuff said!), and, besides, Orford was just determined not to be impressed by his relative wealth and highbrow ways. "I know you write," said one of the townsfolk, "but what do you *really* do?"

If Jackson had expected to find solidarity or stimulation among his fellow Ridge dwellers—that is, the prosperous residents of the other six Federal-style houses in the group—he was to be sorely disappointed.

Two houses to the south were the Warrens, who seemed especially wary of the new arrival. "Why do you suppose Mr. Jackson ever wrote a book like that?" Edward "Ned" Warren asked one of Charlie's friends—more in sorrow than anger, it seemed. Warren (Dartmouth 'o1) did not keep liquor in his house, and for the most part spent his autumn years clipping coupons and newspaper articles of interest, including several reviews of *The Lost Weekend* (pressed between the pages of a laconic but persistent diary), once he'd learned who was moving into the old Dana place. Aware of Warren's reservations where he was concerned, Jackson was startled to learn that the man had actually donated copies of his novel to three local libraries (Orford, Orfordville, and Fairlee), and indeed Warren seemed well-meaning after a fashion. Every morning he'd stroll across the bridge and back, then walk along Main Street greeting passersby and giving nickels to the nine or ten children of the town, before heading home for the noon stock report on the radio while he plied his scissors. "Ned loved everybody," said his granddaughter, "but he lived in his own little world." In that world you took an avid interest in your neighbors' affairs, whether or not your relations were especially friendly: "Mr. Jackson to Hanover," Warren noted in his diary, two weeks after Jackson had moved in. "Attended movie in the evening called Going My Way." And four days later: "Invited Mr. Jackson to go with us this AM but he said next time." So it went for the next few years.

Even the more enlightened citizens were a little nervous around Charlie, who, early on, had scandalously availed himself of the local beauty parlor to get a manicure, an item that was combined uncomfortably with a rumor that his second novel was about a very taboo subject indeed. For his part Jackson was fond of at least one person on the Ridge, Isabel Doan Dyer (not so much her second husband, Lyman), whose thirty-year-old son, Daniel Doan, was himself an aspiring writer who did his best to give their acclaimed neighbor the benefit of a doubt. One day Jackson announced that he'd been up all night working on his novel and needed some fresh air and exercise, so the two went for a hike in the woods. Coming to a little pond along Jacobs Brook, Jackson suddenly proposed they go for a swim; Doan ("defensive before this impulsiveness") said the water was too cold, and Jackson tried it with his hand and agreed the idea was foolish. As Doan later admitted, he was worried about more than the water:

I was aware of the areas of human behavior about which he wrote, but I was withdrawn and provincial, a disapproving spectator. I knew him to be a former alcoholic himself, assumed he had experienced the homosexual tendencies about which he was writing, and I felt something strange and fearful from the inconsistencies of humanity, and an emotion that represented for me a new sort of awareness that no human being was as simple as I had been led to believe.

As for the other Ridge dwellers: what might have seemed a kind of charming paternalism, or Yankee insularity, was—so Jackson concluded—at bottom bigotry and snobbism. "Mrs. Jackson cleans ice back of house so children could skate," Warren observed in his diary, with his usual inscrutable literality, though in fact he might have been annoyed or at least perplexed. According to Robert Richmond—a recipient of Warren's nickels who'd grown up on the other side of Main Street and bootstrapped his way into Dartmouth—"Uncle Ned," as he liked to be called, had argued in favor of closing Orford High School and thereby lowering property taxes ("Those kids aren't worth educating"). So it might have rankled when the Jacksons not only arranged for skating on the Ridge, but also cleared the hill behind their house and invited the high school principal to give skiing lessons there to local children, no matter how humble their stations, the better "to encourage [Sarah and Kate] to play with all and sundry."

By then Jackson had noticed the "horror" on his neighbors' faces when he wore a Roosevelt button around town during the fall campaign ("Mr. Roosevelt's speech last night very poor," Warren opined in his diary), and was therefore all the more sensitive when the president died the following spring. "I've never seen Rhoda so broken up," he wrote. "My head has hurt and throat ached for days." On the day in question, however—April 12, 1945—Jackson was greeted on Main Street with: "Have you heard the good news?" So provoked, he made a point of knocking on the Warrens' door, a visit they never forgot. "He was in a dark suit with a black necktie and a black band on his arm," said Julia Fifield, Ned Warren's stepdaughter. "And he looked at mother and said [reproachful voice]: 'Mrs. Warren, our president has died. Why aren't you in mourning?' " Mrs. Gertrude Warren, a lifelong Republican needless to say, was rather at a loss ("I don't think there was any further conversation")—though perhaps it reflects credit on both parties that (according to Ned's diary) the Warrens and Jacksons subsequently took turns hosting each other for dinner, on May 6 and 20 respectively.

But there was a knottier problem that was unlikely to be solved by mutual hospitality. "Anti-Semitism is something awful here," Jackson reported, telling of how their real-estate agent had refused to sell Six Chimney Farm to previous buyers who'd offered cash, because (as the man jovially explained) "they didn't have the right names." As for Uncle Ned, he casually used the word "nigger" and would remark with sober consternation that a "white girl" had married a Jew. Jackson, for his children's sake ("we do not want to make it difficult for them"), was mostly holding his tongue for now—however: "I refuse to take some of the things that have been said by 'careless people' in our own living room. If there is anything in modern life that more enrages me than this irrational anti-Semitism, I do not know what it is."

JACKSON FELT TERRIBLE PRESSURE to surpass or at least equal the achievement of his first novel; as he'd often stated for the record, he was an author of large ambition (not an expert on alcoholism!) who had no intention of resting on the laurels of a single book. "You've got to write not one, not two, not three—you've got to do it over and over," he told *PM*. At first he'd wanted to follow *The Lost Weekend* with "the Big Book"—*What Happened*—of which the former had been "merely a chapter, so to speak"; but the world, he knew, was clamoring for a proper sequel that would explain, specifically, "how you [*sic*] got out of it," as his old doctor in Rochester, John Lloyd, put it: "It may fall into the hands of someone whom it would help." Harshly criticized for the unhappy ending of *The Lost Weekend*, Jackson had protested that it was not the novelist's job "to solve psychiatric problems" but only to "state the case," and anyway how was Don supposed to "cure" himself in five days? The sequel, then, would have to be a far more ambitious book—a gradual "working-out" of Don's addiction "in a more leisurely and novelistic style"—though not quite itself a *novel*, not yet, as Jackson held that genre to the sky-high standard of the great Russians. *What Happened*—now *that* would be a novel, but first he decided to write this troublesome sequel, *The Working Out*.

The more he thought about it, though, the more it seemed that the sequel could wait a while, too. Lest he be branded a confessional author who only writes about alcoholism, he wanted to try a totally different subject—something to do with Vince Kramer, that wounded Marine he'd met in Nantucket: "It will be a story about the reaction of the public to soldiers in wartime," he wrote Rhoda from Hollywood, "how the proximity of death heightens one's consciousness of youth." Casting about for an epigraph, he asked her to retrieve his old JAXON note-book and find a poem he'd transcribed there by "one Karl Somebody Ulrichs"—meaning Karl Heinrich Ulrichs, a gay German writer, as translated by J. A. Symonds, a gay English writer. Rhoda dutifully sup-plied the poem, albeit with a cocked eyebrow perhaps:

> *Dearer to me is the lad village-born with sinewy members*
> *Than the pale face of a fine town-bred effeminate youngling;*
> *Yea, or a sailor on board: but dear to me down to the heart's depth,*
> *Dearest of all are the young, steel-thewed, magnificent soldiers . . .*
> *Who with clashing spurs and martial tread when they meet me,*
> *Know not how goodly they are, the sight of them how overwhelming.*

"Well, the Ulrichs poem didn't turn out to be much, did it?" wrote Char-lie, a tad abashed. "Of all the duds! It's the kind of thing that makes me creep, now." He thought maybe he'd find what he needed in Whitman, but then he remembered something from Housman that seemed nearer his purpose and gave him a title besides:

> *The stars have not dealt me the worst they could do:*
> *My pleasures are plenty, my troubles are two.*
> *But oh, my two troubles they reave me of rest,*
> *The brains in my head and the heart in my breast.*
>
> *Oh grant me the ease that is granted so free,*
> *The birthright of multitudes, give it to me,*
> *That relish their victuals and rest on their bed*
> *With flint in the bosom and guts in the head.*

Warming to the idea—even becoming rather feverish ("Damn it to hell, why can't I get myself fired at once!")—Jackson excitedly described *My Two Troubles* to his agent, Bernice Baumgarten, and his admiring friend Philip Wylie. Both were guardedly discouraging. Baumgarten warned him that "there is nothing so important for an author's repu-tation as his second novel" (as if Jackson didn't know!), and it was her impression that *My Two Troubles* would be a risky successor to *The Lost Weekend*: "I'd rather see a collection of short stories . . . or perhaps, and why not, nothing at all until you are ready with the second Don Birnam." As for Wylie, he considered it an even greater imperative for Jackson to complete "the two parts of [his] famous novel about Don Birnam" before anything else, unless he felt certain that *My Two Troubles* would be a masterpiece. Which, incidentally, Jackson did ("I feel confident that the book will come to be recognized instantly as an American classic"), but *The Working Out* would have to be even better than *that*—all the more reason to wait—until finally *The Lost Weekend* was made to seem "a kind of half-hearted finger-exercise done with the left hand. Which it is."

"I am very sorry but I never discuss a book in progress," Jackson stiffly replied to a book reviewer in Amarillo who'd wanted to know what he was working on. Toward nosy reviewers in the provinces he was apt to be reticent, perhaps, but a number of friends and colleagues would be barraged with work-in-progress talk during the two years Jackson spent on his vexatious second novel. The process got under way in earnest on May 24, 1944, when—by way of proving to Wylie, Baumgarten, et al., "how completely thought-out" *My Two Troubles* was—Jackson dictated a twenty-six-page, single-spaced "outline" to his secretary at MGM, "Miss Ross" (whose reaction one is pleased to imagine):

> The story will be heavy with lazy summer atmosphere, a holiday mood, a sensual halcyon time-out feeling, idleness, the sun, luxury (in the Shakespearean sense), all as a kind of contrast to the keyed-up tenseness of the war and of people living with the war in their hearts. All the value and beauty of the story will be in the telling, never really in the events of the story; *the telling is all.* It will be a great opportunity for a kind of poetry in fiction about the troubled heart of man today . . . his prescience of death; his consciousness of youth all about him leaving—to what; his anxiety and concern because the ideal of today is brutality and destruction; though please believe me, none of this will be defeatist: far from it. . . . The nearest I can describe it briefly is to say that MY TWO TROUBLES will be an idyll, but tough.

"An idyll, but tough"—fair enough—and gradually Jackson worked his way around to the story itself, the first half of which, at least, was quite similar to that of the finished novel: a fortyish professor, here named David Williams, was to find himself oddly (because he's "very happily married") attracted to a Marine named Cliff—a hulking youth "rather like a big puppy," who "might be a complete bore and headache but for the fact that he is so good natured and natural." Jackson proposed that

their relationship would be (thematically speaking) a matter of contrast-
ing ideals: the professor represents the "life of the mind," passé in the
midst of world war, whereas Cliff (romping about the surf) is the man of
action, "the thing required in 1944." After exploring the dialectic at some
length, Jackson arrived ("or jeepers, I'll never get this outline finished")
at the moment of truth: "What under the sun does Williams really want
anyway?"—*that* is the question, especially when Cliff visits his apartment,
post-Nantucket, prior to getting fitted for a new uniform and returning to
war. While the two sit there, chatting, something ineffably ghastly hangs
in the air . . . but Williams restrains himself, and the "crisis is passed."
Afterward they walk to the tailor together, so at ease now that Cliff feels
free to put his arm ("puppyishly") around the professor's shoulders. Thus
Williams conquers his weird spell of homosexuality—or hero worship,
or what you will—by dint of willpower alone (rather the way Don would
bring his addiction to heel in *The Working Out*).

This long apologia was addressed primarily to Wylie, and copied to
Baumgarten, Stanley Rinehart, and Jackson's young editor, Ted Amussen. All endeavored to let him down gently. Writing his Birnam sequel,
Wylie reiterated, "is your first responsibility not just towards alcoholics
and not just toward literature, but towards me. This is because I represent
both in my own fashion" ("them's my sentiments also," chimed the amiable Amussen). Meanwhile Rhoda had also read the outline, and found it
"too similar" to *Death in Venice*—not at *all* what the author had intended.
Casting a cold eye on his handiwork, he wrote Rinehart (copying the
others as usual) that whereas Mann's novella was about "decadence and
death," *My Two Troubles* would be, ideally, a "not unpleasant story of
normal homosexuality, the kind that is a part of all men: sublimated,
understood, a natural affinity of man with man, needing no physical
expression"; however, the story as it now stood, he realized, was "neither
one thing nor the other; and it most certainly must not fall in between."
Here Baumgarten took her turn: such uncertainty only confirmed what
she'd already suspected—"There are a great many things to be worked
out before you have a book"—but, that said, if he *really* felt strongly about
it, "don't be swayed by outside opinions, write it." For a while he vac-
illated, at one point alerting Louella Parsons that he was going ahead
with his new Birnam novel after all (which she promptly announced
to the world as *It Worked Out*); finally, though, in September—during
an interview with the *Times* at his "newly acquired Bulfinch-designed
New Hampshire home"—he declared that he'd definitely postponed

the sequel in favor of *My Two Troubles.* "I am a little tired of writing true-confessions," he explained to a friend.

Indeed, he did *not* want to be identified with homosexuality, but at the same time he deplored those authors who lean, coyly, "on the Greek ideal" in order to sublimate motives that are ("if examined properly") "fleshly." Fortunately a solution seemed to present itself that summer in Hollywood, when Jackson dined with Dr. Sam Hirshfeld ("Vet's doctor and Zannuck's [*sic*] & Mayer's & Selznick's"), to whom he'd also sent a copy of that twenty-six-page outline. "We talked solid from 7 pm to 1 am, and I learned more stuff!" he wrote Rhoda.

> Sam believes [the novel] has the possibilities of becoming one of the most important single stories of the times, with a real contribution to our understanding, and he told me what the story was about and what it was not. He is wildly enthusiastic about it; wants me to keep it the story of a war-shock in a civilian, with the three stages (or rather four) which are the normal course of all war-shock: fright, panic, disorientation, and resolution.

Thenceforth Jackson took care to describe his book as an "account of a war neurosis in a civilian, and only incidentally the story of a Professor's infatuation for a Marine." Elaborating for the benefit of Dr. Anton J. Carlson (his fellow alcoholism pundit), Jackson wrote that "the domination of the uniform over our lives, war-fever, the deaths of so many young men, deranged the liberal but emotional man, sending him off into an unconscious homosexuality or, in some cases, worse." It was the "worse" part that worried Farrar & Rinehart, and Jackson knew he'd have to bring all his intuitive artistry to bear in "trying to steer a safe and sane course" around the pitfalls of such a nuanced theme. Assaying some "POSSIBLE COPY FOR CATALOGUE OR JACKET BLURB," Jackson described his book as "a major contribution to the literature and psychology of war," and barely hinted at anything untoward: "In this, his second novel, Charles Jackson has again demonstrated, with consummate skill, his masterly understanding of the 'irregularities' that can beset the civilized man, here the sensitive adult in war time.... the magnificence of the writing is indisputable." And now that he'd settled the question in a seemly manner (for the time being), Jackson didn't mind so much discussing his work in progress with appealing strangers—such as one Fritz Requardt, to whom he admitted that his hero's " 'war neurosis' ... settles itself upon

a wounded Marine . . . and takes the form of an infatuation. All most difficult, as you can see.

"So you are a shipyard worker. . . ."

TOWARD THE END of his time at MGM, Jackson had affected to be thoroughly jaded on the subject of Hollywood—"a delusion and a snore,"
he remarked to Robert Nathan, while assuring Rhoda that ("to [his]
eternal credit") he could "take celebrities or leave them alone." Amid
the vast silence of New Hampshire, though, he confessed to "a kind of
home-sickness for the place," and was almost giddy about sharing his tri-
umphs with old friends such as Marion Fabry: "Remember how we used
to read him many years ago?" he wrote of Robert Nathan, now one of his
greatest pals, not to mention Judy Garland, "whom I really loved (and in
fact fell in love with), and Greer Garson who is a hell-raiser and not at all
the Noble Woman MGM would have you think . . ." The list, of course,
went on, and meanwhile Jackson couldn't help wondering whether all
these golden people—whose benevolent faces beamed all around him in
his bedroom—missed him back. According to Gregory Peck, they did:
"You have left a good many friends, not to say fans, behind you in Hollywood," the actor wrote. "Mrs. Peck and I would like to be included on
that list." Whereupon Jackson made room for another photograph ("I
like to show off to my New Hampshire neighbors that I am just-like-that
with the Hollywood great"), asking Peck to sign himself "To Charlie,
with mad love." The breakfast table had become a place of solemn quiet,
as Jackson pored over *Hollywood Reporter* and the like ("I subscribe to
'em all"), looking for his name and often finding it. As for his social life,
it was now almost entirely conducted in the privacy of his room, late at
night, in epistolary form.

His main preoccupation was still Judy Garland. He claimed to be
nettled by certain indiscreet photos of him and Judy together—in the
October *Screenland*, for instance—and when one of these appeared over
the caption "Judy's new beau," even the meek Queenie let her displeasure
show: "What will people think? Poor Rhoda . . ." But Charlie did little to
allay speculation. One of his first errands in New Hampshire was to take
a "stunning picture" of Garland to a framer in Hanover; in its absence,
so he wrote Nathan, he couldn't relate her inscription because it was too
long to remember verbatim. Soon, however, he began to suspect that he'd
"kidded himself": "Like the adorer I was (or perhaps celebrity-chaser, to

call it by its right name), I sent her what I thought was a charming present for Christmas, but she [has] not even acknowledged it." The present was one of Boom's specialties, a stylized cut-paper lamb, prettily matted and framed, at the bottom of which he'd written, "For Judy, who is one. With love from Charlie." Bitterly the months passed, until one day in April the local Western Union agent phoned, astonished, to read aloud a telegram from *Judy Garland:* "CHARLIE DEAR, DUE TO CHANGES OF ADDRESS YOUR SWEET CHRISTMAS PRESENT REACHED ME ONLY TWO DAYS AGO. PERHAPS THE LOST LAMB WILL LEND ITSELF TO AN IDEA FOR A NEW BOOK. . . ." Jackson put the receiver down ("all tingly in the legs and swimmy in the head") and promptly wrote Garland an abject apology for any impudent "complaints" he may have made in regard to what he'd rashly suspected was her neglect. Two months later she married Vincente Minnelli, the bisexual director of her latest hit musical, *Meet Me in St. Louis* (wherein, thought Charlie, "The sins of MGM were never so clearly revealed"). Meeting the couple a week later, Jackson bestowed a magnanimous but measured blessing, admitting afterward his "faint qualms" about the union: "But when I saw you together in New York, saw your interest in each other, *felt* what was going on across the table from me,—well, I don't know how else to say it, but I was very happy about the whole thing."

Despite Orford's disdain for the fleshpots of Hollywood, a flutter nonetheless passed through the village when Jackson got letters (and the odd telegram) from big stars and any number of lesser lights. The high school principal knocked on his door one day and asked if Mr. [Spencer] Tracy might be persuaded to address the students during his stay at Six Chimney Farm. Jackson blamed such "violent rumors"—of visits from this star and that—on a gossipy local postmistress, though he'd been less than diligent about keeping things under wraps. "Wait till Orford hears of our guests Christmas week!" he enthused to Fabry. "For Katie Hepburn and Spencer Tracey [*sic*] are to spend a week with us beginning Friday December 29th." This had been in the works a while, ever since the three friends had parted the previous August with such desperate reluctance—"almost an anxiety to see me," as Charlie had reported to Rhoda: "[Tracy] has developed a dog-like devotion to me (why, I will never know) and now says he's going to come east this winter and shovel snow and saw wood for us—and funnily enough he wants to. Can we let him? Would you mind? What will we ever do with him?" Charlie, in turn, had stoked the embers by visiting Hepburn's family in Hart-ford ("How nice, how very nice, I thought them") during his November trip to address the local AA, and later endeavored to be gracious when Hepburn ("too busy a gal") had to cancel her and Spence's trip to New Hampshire.

He and Robert Benchley wrote sporadic letters, mostly conferring about their mutual friend Dorothy Parker and her own struggles with alcohol. "I don't know who I am to be wishing salvation for others," Benchley wrote Jackson,

> but I can't feel sorry for myself quite yet as I feel so *well*. I don't *look* right, I realize that, and I am more and more liable to horse's-assery after several drinks, especially Martinis, but I still have a fatuous confidence in my ability to recoup in short order, thanks to a sturdy constitution inherited from my teetotaler mother and my alcoholic father, neither of whom worried much about health (one died at 86 and one at 77). This is the kind of remark that usually preceeds [*sic*] by a week or so a complete breakdown on the part of the boaster, with his friends saying: "only a week ago he was saying how well he felt."

Grasping the fact that his mystique among such people was largely due to his role as Alcoholism Guru, Jackson played the card whenever possible. Dorothy Parker, he wrote Benchley, had been avoiding his calls since their meetings at the New Weston in August, and he gravely feared that she'd "gone 'off' again and so is dodging [him]." That was mid-October; two weeks later he wrote Fabry that Parker had visited Six Chimney Farm and the two had enjoyed "wonderful talk all day and almost all night." There was, in fact, no visit,* though not for lack of trying on Charlie's part: as he apprised Benchley, he would run Parker to ground whenever he went to New York ("She still keeps on the wagon, [but] I do feel her constant keyed-up state is not 'normal' "), and afterward write her emotional letters ("I'm going to need you in my life"), which she rarely answered. As for Benchley, he made a daily point of appearing on the set of *The Lost*

---

* Like many writers—not to mention addicts—Charlie was hardly averse to stretching the truth now and then, especially for the benefit of awed fellow Newarkians such as Fabry (herself something of a fabulist, one may recall). Partly this was due to an insatiable need for admiration and love—but also, perhaps, it was a generous impulse: a way of sharing glamour with old friends whose own lives were relatively humdrum.

Weekend at Paramount—"Nat's Bar," to be exact,* where he'd ask the actor Howard Da Silva (Nat) to pour him a shot of bourbon for fifty cents. On November 21, 1945, five days after the movie's premiere, he died of complications from cirrhosis.

ONE WAY of keeping in touch with show-business friends—and also bringing in "badly needed cash"—was to write screen treatments for them to star in. Within the schedule he had set himself of completing *My Two Troubles* by November of 1944 and *The Working Out* by the following April (May at the latest), Jackson also planned to dash off a three-part *Collier's* serial that he could later adapt as a Hepburn and Tracy vehicle titled *Little Mother*, about a radio actress who neglects her real-life responsibilities as a wife and mother while acting bumptiously "noble" on others' behalf à la her soap-opera role. "Sweet Kate, bonnie Kate (and I believe He goes on: 'The prettiest Kate in Christendom'),"† Charlie wrote Hepburn, chatting about one thing and another until ("incidentally") he pitched his "simply wonderful idea": "The acting possibilities in it for you would be tremendous, and it would take the most subtle understanding and fine balance between comedy and pathos . . . " But nothing came of it, either as a *Collier's* serial or as a Tracy and Hepburn vehicle.

More ambitious was his proposed "free, modernized, American adaptation" of Chekhov's *The Seagull*, which in one swoop would reunite him with a number of MGM stars. Jackson envisaged the cast as follows: Judy Garland as Nina, Walter Pidgeon as Trigorin, Robert Walker (or Peter Lawford) as Treplev, Jessica Tandy as Masha, and her husband, Hume Cronyn, as Medvedenko. His greatest coup, however, would be to recruit *Garbo herself* as Arkadina—to which end he made a special trip to New York in early November, his way paved by the agent Leland Hayward. "You ask about Garbo," he wrote Baumgarten afterward. "But god, don't speak of it." The meeting, alas, had been botched. Jackson had waited for days to be summoned, and finally took an afternoon to see his agent and get a little fresh air. Back at his hotel he found, to his horror, a message: Garbo had phoned (twice)!—or rather "Miss Harriet Brown" at

---

* An almost exact replica of P. J. Clarke's on East 55th in New York. Wilder had tried shooting in the actual Clarke's, but there was too much noise from the Third Avenue El.
† From *The Taming of the Shrew*, Act 2, Scene 1, lines 180–81.

the Ritz Towers had phoned. She had given up an entire hour of her day to meet with Jackson, but now refused to do so unless they were joined by Hayward, who was then on his way back to Hollywood aboard the Century. "There's no getting around it, she's a very difficult woman," Jackson grumbled, "and makes things not only fantastically difficult for everybody else but for herself as well. Why in Christ's name can't she relax? Nobody's going to tear her limb from limb these days. . . . After all, the gal hasn't had a picture in nearly three years."* In due course Jackson recast Ina Claire (or Greer Garson) as Arkadina, while remaining an unabashed Garbo worshiper, maybe even more so in light of her beguiling elusiveness.

The following summer he took a couple days off from the protracted ordeal of writing his second novel to dictate a seventeen-page treatment of *The Seagull*, intending to render it more accessible to Philistia by emphasizing the "truly dramatic action" that happens offstage or between the acts in Chekhov. That, anyway, was the idea, though what Jackson managed to get on paper ("somewhat hastily," he confessed) followed the original almost point by point. The names were Americanized (Irina Arkadina became "Irene Carradine," etc.) and the setting moved to "a big old-fashioned country-house in Vermont or New Hampshire," but the Treplev character ("Charles") still shoots a seagull and offers it to Nina with the dire prediction that he too shall kill himself. He doesn't, though, and therein lies the crucial difference: "Now I know," says the failed actress, Nina, at the end of Jackson's version, "what matters is not fame, not glory, nor money . . . what matters is how to endure, to work, and have faith." Whereupon Treplev/Charles—rather than kill himself—agrees: "You've found your way. So have I, Nina, but it's lonely, our way being separate. We'll go that way together . . ." Thus the girl's previous apathy toward the fussy, neurotic Treplev/Charles sparks into ardor, and the two live happily ever after. "I know you will simply fall in love with this wonderful story I have made out of that static action-less play," Jackson gushed in his cover letter to Hayward, who gamely passed the thing along to MGM. When the studio rejected it, Jackson abruptly dropped the idea, since after all the point had been to cast his old MGM friends.

Another friend from Hollywood was Sally Benson, author of the

---

* Her most recent had been *Two-Faced Woman* (1941), which turned out to be her last movie.

stories that had inspired *Meet Me in St. Louis*, and an ecstatic admirer of *The Lost Weekend*. Benson—no stranger to addiction or mental illness generally—had ordered twenty copies of the novel for friends, and insisted it "belong[ed] to her" as a screenwriter. Shortly after the Paramount sale, Jackson had lunched with Brackett and Wilder to bat ideas around, and Benson had tagged along to the greater benefit of all: "I've never been in on such a brilliant and fascinating discussion," Charlie wrote Rhoda: "a picture was formed and molded and planned right under your eyes." How pleasant, then, that Benson should follow through with an actual visit to Six Chimney Farm in the fall, proving such an ideal guest ("Such wonderful company . . . such character and spirit") that Charlie asked her back for the holidays, and Benson eagerly accepted.

In the meantime she'd agreed to take one of Jackson's stories to *The New Yorker*, where she herself had published almost a hundred pieces between 1929 and 1941. "The New Yorker has just bought five [*sic*] short stories of mine," Jackson boasted to Fabry, after Benson had persuaded the magazine to take *one*, "A Dream of Horace," for $304. Jackson's four-page story was slight in every way, but then, too, it was precisely the kind of frothy "casual" that editor Harold Ross preferred. The protagonist, Joe Callush, describes to Bobbie, his wife, a dream in which a neighbor they barely know, Horace Goodsell, has died; while waxing sentimental ("[he] thought lovingly of Horace"), Callush learns that the man has, in fact, suffered a fatal heart attack in the night. Crestfallen—*not* because Horace is dead, but because this fascinating coincidence has occurred on Sunday, when he's away from the office—Callush proceeds to phone everyone he knows and tell them the story.

The sketch was important to Jackson for a number of reasons: its humor ("a scream, truly hilarious," he wrote Fabry) would help mitigate his reputation as a "morbid" writer, and besides he badly wanted to appear in *The New Yorker* in whatever form; also, he'd laced the piece with a number of in-jokes, using actual Newark names (e.g., Bobbie the wife) and mentioning his beloved Judy Garland at one point. But when Jackson received galleys from the magazine, he was horrified. As the editor William Maxwell breezily informed him, "I think Sally [Benson] told you over the phone that she had gone over 'A Dream of Horace' with a pair of scissors. Anyway, she did, and [Harold] Ross likes it fine . . ." *A pair of scissors* indeed!—the story was nearly unrecognizable: his allusive names had been changed (Callush became Miller; Bobbie became Barbie), and a lot of whimsical descriptive business added ("She picked up a strip of bacon with her fingers and ate it")—the latter to satisfy Ross's yen for particularity, perhaps. Worst of all—most gallingly random and silly—was the new title: "Dreams Are Funny"! Jackson, under the circumstances, expressed his pique quite temperately (" 'Dreams Are Funny' sounds to me like a parody of a New Yorker story") and offered to return the check, but was somewhat mollified when Maxwell took him to lunch in New York and agreed to change the title—to "Funny Dream." When the piece ran in the March 17, 1945, issue, Jackson asked Maxwell to mail him a few copies ("I want to send one to Judy"), but added a dour postscript: "I still don't like the story."

The aftermath would manifest itself over the course of many years. First of all, Benson was confronted with her presumption when she returned to New Hampshire for the holidays—a showdown for which, apparently, her guns were loaded: "I won't begin to tell you about my evening with her the other night," Jackson wrote Ted Amussen on January 2. "I aged ten years in those three hours. And God protect me hereafter from writers: they're a lousy class of people." Later that summer he made a point of crossing her name off the invitation list for a big *Lost Weekend* screening party, and moreover vowed never to submit a story to *The New Yorker* again. There matters might have rested, were it not for Jackson's extravagant admiration for *The Folded Leaf*, Maxwell's novel about a homoerotic friendship, which Jackson applauded in *Chicago Sun Book Week* on April 15, 1945: "Katherine Anne Porter, it seems to me, is the one American writer who has no reason to envy William Maxwell his gifts; and offhand the only novel I can think of that is at all comparable to *The Folded Leaf* is *The Apple of the Eye*, also a story of adolescence [and also homoerotic], written by Glenway Wescott twenty years ago." Maxwell loved the review, not least because it made his family in Illinois take him seriously for once, as opposed to being embarrassed by what they'd always assumed were mere memoirs: "Their main reaction to 'The Folded Leaf,' " he wrote Jackson, "before your review, was surprise that I knew such vile language, and had been unhappy in my youth. Now, thanks to you, I am a credit to the family. Sometimes the world's opinion, operating on middle class minds, is almost terrifying to watch."

But if Jackson thought his review ("I was frankly log-rolling," he wrote a friend; "but it's a good book, isn't it?") would ensure future sales to *The New Yorker*, he would be disappointed again and again—seventeen times in a row, to be exact, during a single interval from 1951 to 1952. Rejecting, for example, a long story ("The Outlander") about a Jackson-like protagonist in Bermuda, Maxwell invoked Ross's prohibition against stories about writers ("nobody cares about them except another writer"), whereas Jackson's portrait of a loose woman, "Janie," was unsuitable ("Mr. Ross feels") for a magazine that might be read by a minor. Nothing if not tactful—indeed legendary in that respect—Maxwell usually concluded his letters with the wistful hope that Jackson would reappear in *The New Yorker* someday. By the summer of 1951, though, Jackson was fed up ("to hell with The New Yorker from now on"), and sternly corrected his friend Dorothea when she ventured to praise the magazine's fiction: *New Yorker* stories, he wrote, "are artful, full of evasions and half-truths, and almost always stop where they really should begin." However, a few months later, Jackson wrote what he considered a masterpiece, "The Boy Who Ran Away," and abruptly recanted his boycott of the magazine: "it's one story for a change that Maxwell would *love*," he promised Baumgarten. "(In fact it *is* Maxwell.)" But no: once again Maxwell replied—with his usual dolorous tact—that the story was a little too patly "clinical," and so on. "I could punch him in the nose," said Jackson. "My God! He has seen countless stories and has rejected every one except a punk tale I wrote way back in 1945 and that Sally Benson rewrote for them under the sickening title of FUNNY DREAM. . . ."

Chapter Ten

Will and Error

By the time Ray Milland was offered the part of Don Birnam, he'd been a contract player at Paramount for a decade—generally considered a competent light comedian for supporting roles, the main exception being his star turn opposite Ginger Rogers in Brackett and Wilder's *The Major and the Minor* (1942). Wilder knew how desperate the actor was to be tested, even at the expense of forfeiting a glamorous image, and gave him a copy of Jackson's novel. "I took it to bed with me that night," Milland recalled, "but after a dozen pages I fell asleep." Waking in the wee hours, he forged ahead, though he found the subject repellent: he himself "could not abide" drunks, and hardly ever took a drink himself. At age thirty-nine, though, it was now or never, and Milland threw himself into preparing for the role: before production began, in October 1944, he cultivated a seedy gauntness by subsisting on dry toast, coffee, grapefruit juice, and boiled eggs; he also insisted on spending a night, incognito, in the alcoholic ward at Bellevue. Dozing off in his hospital pajamas, Milland was jarred awake by a door banging open nearby, as two attendants wrestled a violent, wailing patient into a bed that the patient thought was on fire. The others protested the disturbance "in the foulest language imaginable": "Suddenly the room was bedlam. I knew I was looking into the deepest pit." But anyway it was a change.

The first sequence to be shot was Don's awful slog along the pawn-shops of Third Avenue,* which Wilder had decided to shoot on location rather than try to re-create that particular jumble of scenery—including the El and its jagged shadows—on a Paramount soundstage. Lest a crowd of pedestrians interfere, cameras were concealed inside delivery trucks and empty storefronts, and for sixteen mornings a disheveled, unshaven Milland waited in a cab for his cue to shamble along for another block or two while the cameras furtively rolled. (Once, he was recognized by a motorist who happened to know someone at Paramount: "I just want to tell you," the man reported, "that I saw your friend Ray Milland dead drunk on Third Avenue. If I were you I'd try to get hold of him and straighten him out.") For the first ten days of shooting, Jackson was put up at the Sherry-Netherland and invited to do a walk-on as a Third Avenue passerby—indeed, he'd "figure[d] rather prominently" in the scene, or so he wrote Robert Nathan ("the Hitchcock signature, so to speak"). Milland, stumbling along with his typewriter, had seemed startled at Jackson's approach: "Hello, Charlie," he muttered. For that reason, perhaps, the footage wasn't used; at any rate Jackson doesn't appear in the finished movie.

A few weeks later, Brackett sent him the bulk of their screenplay, and Jackson was ecstatic: "FOR COMMENT SEE CELIA'S SPEECH AS YOU LIKE IT LINE 194 ACT THREE SCENE TWO," he wired back, indicating the following passage: "O wonderful, wonderful, and most wonderful wonderful! and yet again wonderful, and after that, out of all hoping!" Jackson was especially impressed by the seamless way one scene flowed into the next, the tension always rising, and he even conceded that the characterizations—"except Don's"—were "far better than they were in the book." More than ever he felt cooped up at Six Chimney Farm; how desperately he wanted to be part of such an exciting project!

They hadn't, however, shown him the last pages yet, and naturally he was curious to see what they would make of his unhappy ending. "To please the Hays office," Louella Parsons had predicted, "Wilder and Brackett will probably have to reform their hero." Given Jackson's plans for writing an upbeat *Seagull*, he couldn't have expected perfect fidelity to his novel, and meanwhile Brackett and Wilder kept telling him they simply hadn't written the ending yet—they were "trusting to luck" that

---

* *Second* Avenue in the novel—a mistake, Jackson admitted, since most of the pawn-shops were on Third.

inspiration would strike "when they got to it." Finally (a week after shooting was wrapped up over Christmas), they sent Jackson the final pages. "Talk about neat, pat, cheap endings," he wrote a friend; "but also talk about betrayal." As written, the movie now ended with Helen's talking Don out of suicide by getting him to believe in himself as a writer again; thus, as Wick returns to the apartment ("Quiet, Wick, we are working. Just fix us some breakfast"), Don is pounding away at his much-pawned typewriter, his long-deferred novel in the works at last! "Now, naturally I resent this conclusion because of the personal complications," Jackson remonstrated with Brackett and Wilder. "It implies that Don Birnam was Charles Jackson (implies hell, says so, in practically so many words) and this is the way I 'worked it out.'" But worst of all was the fact "that a very distinguished movie" was now rendered—in one vulgar stroke—utterly "make believe" and ordinary. So Jackson declared in his first, relatively measured letter; when an inscrutable silence ensued, he wrote again six days later:

> Since the night I first read your final scene, I have been getting madder by the minute . . . you are basing your movie far less on the book than you are on what you happen to know about my private life. I should have suspected something like this all along. The tip-off should have been when I first learned you were making Helen an employee of Time Magazine.* The final scene, as you sent it to me, with the hero working out his problem by writing a book (the implication being, of course, that the novel is the very movie we are seeing and the book we have read) is an out-and-out Judas kiss. Can you think how difficult it will be for me, for instance, to sit in the local movie house and see that film on the screen among my neighbors?

And still the two screenwriters laid low, evidently more concerned about the Hays Office censors than Jackson's reputation among his neighbors. "I am beginning to loathe and detest all that Hollywood represents," he wrote Nathan. "The moral of all this is that, once Hollywood gets your best friends, you can't trust 'em: Hollywood comes first every time; you don't count a-tall!"

Two months later, though, in March—after a preview in San Francisco that seemed to go well in every respect but one—Brackett phoned:

---

* That is, paralleling Rhoda's employment at another Luce publication, *Fortune*.

"Charlie, I've got a fine present for you: we're throwing out that ending. . . . Any ideas?" Jackson was invited to Hollywood for a week or two, expenses paid, but decided he couldn't be interrupted in the midst of his maddening novel; still, he was "flattered enormously that they, so expert and so professional, should have had to come to [him] for help," and promised to think it over. Almost three weeks passed before inspiration struck, whereupon he wired Brackett that he'd just written a four-and-a-half-page final scene that was "wonderful." Certainly it was more ambiguous: as in the finished movie, Helen urges Don to distinguish between "Don the drunk and Don the writer"; one may be "dead already," but the other ("The one I love. The one Wick loves") is worth saving. "Promises [to stop drinking] are easy," says Don. "Words, words, words . . . I'd feel like a heel promising you—" "Promise yourself!" says Helen. At last she seems to prevail by force of reason alone (no festive novel-writing follows): Don surrenders his gun, and Helen leaves to take it back to the pawnshop and recover her leopard coat. Left alone with a "nearly full whiskey bottle," Don ("After visible struggle") drops it out the window. And hence the final shot, which Jackson was especially proud of ("it lifts the whole story out of the personal . . . and passes it over to us"):

> He looks a couple of inches to the left of the camera; and finally, as his face clears entirely and becomes confident and calm (but with complete reserve: nothing corny here), we see him looking directly into the camera—directly at us. It is an indication he is facing the world . . . and it puts it up to us to believe in him. He is looking at us, clear-eyed, calm, the slight breeze blowing his hair, as—FADE OUT . . .

Three months later, Jackson received the final version—slightly different from Brackett and Wilder's earlier attempt, but still suggesting that Don will cure himself by writing a novel titled *The Bottle*.* By then

---

* In the finished movie, at least, Don doesn't go straight from a suicidal hangover to actual novel-writing, nor does Wick turn up to cook breakfast. Don's final lines (spoken over a panoramic shot of New York) are an effective part of what is usually considered a masterpiece of screenwriting: "And out there in that great big concrete jungle, I wonder how many others there are like me. Poor bedeviled guys, on fire with thirst. Such comical figures to the rest of the world, as they stagger blindly towards another binge, another bender, another spree . . . "

Jackson was resigned, more or less, though he would "derive a small (but very small) satisfaction" from an advance review in *Variety*, which mildly faulted the ending of what was otherwise hailed as an "outstanding achievement."

JACKSON'S SECOND NOVEL was proving quite a bit more problematic than he'd expected. His first few months of work had gone swimmingly—particularly the long opening section about the inner life of his hero, John Grandin, as the character was now more evocatively called. Jackson was also enthusiastic about his new title, *The Middle Mist*, from Rupert Brooke: " . . . there are wanderers in the middle mist / Who cry for shadows, clutch, and cannot tell / Whether they love at all, or, loving, whom . . ." His enthusiasm waned, however, when Marion Fabry informed him that a recent novel about lesbians ("merely coincidence?") had the same title; Jackson decided he couldn't afford that kind of "lavender taint." Indeed, he liked the name Grandin not only for its connotation of grandeur, but also because it seemed "masculine"—even more so when he dropped the "John" and just wrote "Grandin" ("You'd be surprised what a difference it makes"). He expected to send a finished manuscript to Farrar & Rinehart by December 15, 1944—only a little past his original deadline—and was quite convinced he had a masterpiece on his hands: "I read it over and think, 'my god, I've simply got to write that guy a fan letter, American literature owes a debt of gratitude to an author like that who et cetera.' "

Within a month his confidence had evaporated. It occurred to him that the middle part of the novel ("when the story begins to be 'dramatized' ") wasn't nearly as good as the first; writing conventional, cause-and-effect, nonintrospective narrative was proving damnably difficult. "The story kills me to write it," he confessed to Philip Rahv: "I've never done anything that takes so much out of me; and during the past month it's gotten me down so that I've become neurotic as hell, nervous, depressed, and even at times have thought the only solution is suicide." What made matters worse (and the middle section even more insoluble) was that, truth be known, he had little idea where he was going; his original ending now struck him as both uneventful and inexplicable, but on the other hand he couldn't just kill off his hero, say, as Mann did in *Death in Venice*: "Ashenback [*sic*] simply dies (almost arbitrarily) just as the story begins to demand that he 'do something about it,' " Jackson pointed out. "But my John Grandin has to work out his dilemma, to our satisfaction and his, and he's got to be either the better or the worse for the experience." Jackson still preferred that he be the *better* for it, but worried that the reader would be fed up with the whole infatuation by the time Grandin resolved it one way or the other.

Enter Jackson's twenty-nine-year-old editor, Ted Amussen, who revered the author of *The Lost Weekend* and was willing to endure almost any inconvenience on his behalf. Jackson had been "sunk" after finishing a draft in late January, so Amussen made a special trip to Six Chimney Farm and spent the weekend reviewing "every single syllable" of the manuscript, pointing out "sticky passages" and explaining exactly how the last four sections (of ten) needed to be reworked. Afterward Jackson felt "restore[d]," if all the more "heartbroken" that Amussen would soon be leaving for the Navy. As he admitted to Stanley Rinehart (who, he thought, undervalued Amussen because of his relative inexperience and touching stammer), Jackson was following the young editor's advice so closely that the novel "will be little short of a collaboration: the credit should read, in all honesty, 'By Charles Jackson and Theodore Amussen.' "

Meanwhile he couldn't resist canvassing the views of various other friends and colleagues, though he deplored his "inability as a writer to stand on [his] own legs"; but then, it was quite in his nature to assume that others were every bit as interested in his problems (especially creative) as he was. In any case he sent copies of the manuscript to Baumgarten ("If you have any ideas, I need them bad"), Rinehart, Boom, Rahv, and his "severest critic," Elling Aannestad, who did not disappoint in terms of severity. As Jackson dolefully reported to his agent, "Elling was simply unable to discuss the story at all because, he said, he found it dull, banal, untrue, and I don't know what all." Reeling from the critique, Jackson had proceeded to an appointment at Schrafft's with Rahv, who (as he promptly informed Aannestad) seemed "mightily impressed." True, the man had a few qualms, but these were minor points of technique: in describing a day at the beach, for instance, Jackson "must learn to skip"—that is, he needn't inform the reader "how they got there and they got back, with whom, how long, et cetera." Also, Grandin was perhaps a bit *too* grand, as in flat, nondescript; he would be more sympathetic, Rahv thought, if the author "put more of [him]self" into the character. That said, the story had plenty of potential, and Cliff the Marine was nothing less than a triumph ("one of the most interesting characters [Rahv had] ever read in his life").

But mere potential wasn't good enough, and so in February—after Farrar & Rinehart had announced a May publication date, allotted paper for a first printing of fifty thousand, and taken orders from bookstores all over the country—Jackson withdrew the manuscript. For the next two months or so, he told friends, he would be pruning "all the passages that do the readers' thinking and feeling for him, . . . all the explanation, over-elaboration, emotion, rhapsodies, et cetera." He worried, too, that he wasn't doing justice to the whole "war neurosis" angle: if Grandin was entirely beguiled by "the uniform"—as he *should* be (versus, that is, being "homosexual to start with")—then it was wrong for him to be smitten with Cliff right away, instead of "slowly and gradually," only after he's learned of the youth's ordeal in the South Pacific. But really, the more Jackson thought about it, the more he wondered whether he had the "intellectual equipment" to bring off such a Jamesian novel of ideas—never mind the most ticklish turn of the screw: namely that Cliff proved, in the present version, something other than the naïf he pretended to be; rather it transpired that he ("out of vanity") had led poor Grandin on to some extent. "[Anyone] who dares to write anything less than heroically about a Marine today is sticking his neck out," Jackson wrote, fretful after viewing footage of Iwo Jima in Hanover.

The better to shift the emphasis somewhat, he decided to amplify the conflict between Mr. and Mrs. Grandin, so the husband's infatuation with Cliff would seem to result as much from "the 'fatigue' of marriage that sets in in the Forties" as it did from "war neurosis" or the wiles of an insecure young Marine. "I need a rest badly," he wrote Boom in May; "and the book is so damned good now, and so right, that I almost don't care when I finish it." The hopeful mood lasted another two or three weeks, until—as he approached the novel's end once more—Jackson began to lose confidence, and finally could hardly work at all.

IN THE EARLY DAYS Jackson wrote all his serious fiction in longhand, revising carefully before typing up a clean copy for still further revision. The older he got, though, the more he was convinced that *what* a writer said was far more important than *how*: "The books of Dreiser and [James T.] Farrell were clumsy and terribly written," he noted, "but the authors had something to say and it makes the books last." Since Hollywood, anyway, he'd simply been too busy to fuss overmuch with mere prose style; by dictating his work he could get the words on paper and go over them later if necessary. In Orford then—what with novel-writing, screen treatments, freelance pieces, and a florid correspondence with "agents, publishers, Metro, etc."—he often required a secretary three hours a day, five days a week, and would eventually become so facile at thinking on his feet that he'd hardly bother to revise at all: "He pretty much knew what he wanted to say," said Pat Hammond, a secretary who helped with Jackson's prolific story output in the early 1950s. "I remember making very few changes."

Which is not to say he was getting lazy—far from it: he was "working harder and harder," as he wrote friends in late 1944, a time when he rarely bothered to leave his room except to take meals in his pajamas and dressing gown. Rhoda, often lonely and bored in Orford, nevertheless guarded her husband's privacy with the utmost vigilance: "Papa is working," she'd shush the children, who hardly needed to be reminded. As the months went by, and his second novel waxed more and more recalcitrant, Jackson's industry began to seem pathological—working as he did from the crack of dawn until two or three in the morning sometimes, bolting the odd meal at his desk. "I don't sleep at all," he wrote the Cronyns: "I take pills instead; and pills too instead of meals; as for the other functions, well.—"

Strangely enough, his pills of choice tended to be barbiturates, especially Seconal ("reds"), which for some reason had a tonic effect—so noted by a bemused attendant at Mary Hitchcock Hospital in Hanover: "This drug [Seconal], taken to promote sleep, actually seems to have a stimulating influence" on Jackson. Or rather, his body became stimulated while his brain was "[put] to sleep," as a "very didactic doctor" once lectured Jackson, who nodded with pleasant recognition. As he would later write in "The Sleeping Brain":

> Fully conscious, alert, "healthy," critical, even super-critical because afraid, one is stumped, blocked, paralyzed as a writer. But with the assistance of the often damaging medicines of which the didactic doctor warned [me], inhibitions go, fear and anxieties go, confidence returns, the unconscious is released and takes over, and intuitions you didn't even know you knew, well upward without check of a mind on guard. So, at least, it has been for me; so it has been for many others. What is not produced out of the unconscious is not worth writing.

To be sure, Jackson was nothing if not insecure as a writer: he never quite got over the idea that he was only Charlie Jackson, after all—a misfit from the sticks—who somehow, miraculously, had won the overwhelming esteem of the world. How to do it again? How to do it now that a "man-eating public or publisher was looking over [his] shoulder"? Now that he was proprietor of Six Chimney Farm, with an extended family to support? His wife, for one, understood the pressure all too well, but deplored his means of coping with it and shrewdly assessed the results. As she wrote Boom, "He can't deny that he has done his best writing, most of it, in a period of sobriety—i.e., Lost Weekend, Palm Sunday, Rachel's Summer. He doesn't see that pills change his sense of values and that his writing, under pills, hasn't the same fundamental honesty."

And what about the effect on his health? It wasn't simply a matter of barbiturate abuse, but various collateral issues as well: that is, while taking pills and skipping sleep, the once-tubercular Jackson was also smoking four packs of cigarettes a day and getting "no physical exercise," according to his doctor's notes at Mary Hitchcock, which soon became his "favorite little hospital" and no wonder. Beginning with his first weeklong visit in March 1945—because of "overwork," he wrote Herb ("because of intermittent dependence, in last year, on Seconal," wrote his doctor)—he was treated with ideal leniency. "I prescribed my own treatment," Jackson recalled in 1959, for the benefit of AA: "put paraldehyde on my chart, and sober[ed] up the easy way." The man who presided over what added up to twenty-some hospitalizations was Dr. Sven Gundersen, an eminent respiratory specialist who was also consulted in the care of such personages as Robert Frost. "On a scale of one to ten"—the man was eulogized after a long and useful life—"his gentleness and moral conscience were ten-plus." Jackson would not have disagreed, and the two became fast friends. Aside from Gundersen's (very) gentle admonitions with respect to Charlie's health, the two shared a love of music and literature: Gundersen was a fine amateur violinist, and occasionally the first audience for Charlie's stories, some of them very long, another role to which he brought his vaunted patience and tact.

It was no coincidence that Jackson's first hospitalization in Hanover followed hard on the discovery that he was facing dire financial difficulties. "I don't complain, ever, about income taxes," he'd told *PM* in early 1944, while noting that January was a bad time for a best-seller to be published, since most of the royalties accrue in a single calendar year; still, as an ardent New Dealer, Jackson was proud to support the president's social programs. The fiscal year of 1944, however, would prove too much of a good thing: on total earnings of $47,700, Jackson owed a total of $23,000 in federal income tax; by the end of the year he'd managed to pay only $7,000, and was left with less than $3,000 in the bank. Bitterly he realized that almost his entire second payment from Paramount ($17,500)—due in January 1945—would have to be turned over to the government, rather than applied (as he'd hoped) to the mortgage on Six Chimney Farm, which, he quipped, would now have to be burned down for insurance.

"I haven't a nickle [*sic*] coming in and won't have till next summer, and I'm distraught as it is, wondering what under the sun I'm going to do about the December 15th tax," he lamented to Brackett in November 1944, while inquiring (in the same letter) whether Wilder would be willing to sell him a Bombois painting for a thousand dollars. "Charlie was a very high liver," Roger Straus reminisced. "Whether he was drunk or sober he was a high liver, and he liked certain things that cost a lot of money." Paintings, antiques, rare books, bespoke clothing, jewelry . . . Jackson loved all things fine and beautiful, and rarely bothered to ask the price when some such item caught his eye, like a gold cigarette case at Tiffany's (six hundred dollars) he fancied in passing. But stern times called for stern measures, and after that winter ("the coal bill has been truly frightful") he resolved to sell a beloved grandfather clock and Sheraton sofa, while returning two paintings to Klaus Perls, whom he owed almost three thousand dollars. "Poor Rhoda"—he wrote the artist William L'Engle, whose painting of baseball players he coveted—"dies a thousand deaths when I receive a communication from Perls; and if she knew that at this very moment I was writing you about those god damned baseball players, she would dash up to the attic and hang herself in despair." A month later Rhoda informed him that they had exactly twenty-seven dollars in the bank, and Charlie presented their predicament to Baumgarten—"God knows *I'm* not doing it (I never even leave my room, not even to buy a soda)"—asking her advice on how to cover their quarterly income tax as well as an imminent trip to New York. Meanwhile he trusted in the success of *The Lost Weekend* (movie) to get his novel selling again.

JACKSON ACCEPTED an invitation to spend a week in early July 1945 at the Nathans' charming house (the Parsonage) in Truro on Cape Cod. "If I had any guts or character I would have said no, I have to stick to my knitting here," he wrote the Minnellis; "but dammit I *want* a week on the Cape, I need to get away for a complete rest and spell of relaxation (whether or not such a thing can be found in the Nathan menage remains to be seen) and it is two years since Rhoda and I had a holiday together." Besides, Robert Nathan really had become a dear, dear friend: prior to meeting Jackson in person he'd written an ecstatic blurb for *The Lost Weekend* ("superb . . . wonderfully sustained"), and so in Hollywood he took special pains to make the author feel at home; in fact, nobody had been kinder, as Jackson was the first to admit, though he couldn't help noticing that Nathan was "a little on the gloomy side" (especially after Jackson's social success began to outstrip his own), and as for Nathan's writing: "I love Bob dearly, but he is without doubt one of the worst writers the world has ever produced."

Jackson's fame was such that *tout* Truro was in a fabulous dither over his visit. Nathan had been boasting about his celebrated guest for weeks, at one point letting slip to a fellow resident, Mary McCarthy, that he and his wife were throwing two parties in Jackson's honor—one "for the really interesting people" (locals such as John Dos Passos, Waldo Frank, and Susan Glaspell), and a more democratic gathering "for the rest." McCarthy observed that she herself had been invited to the latter, wryly describing the whole imbroglio in a letter to her soon-to-be third husband, Bowden Broadwater:

> Mr. Jackson does not like to meet more than seven or eight people at a time (he masochistically counts the drinks, I suppose, and higher multiplication or simple accumulation of envy unsettles him). So they are having two parties for him. Mrs. Nathan, through lack of information, invited me to the inferior, non-intellectual one, and now Mr. Nathan is scrambling and desperately trying to repair the mistake and has finally floundered into asking me to both, but I will accept Mrs. Nathan's category.

As it happened, Jackson found the trip to be "quite a whirl," and certainly enjoyed being fawned over by so many writers and painters who were positively eager to discuss the niceties of his second novel, perhaps because it took their minds off their own careers. Indeed, thought Jackson, Truro was "a kind of lotus-land where people talk all day about what they're going to do and are jealous of each other"—or, as McCarthy would put it in the abortive novel she was about to undertake, "The salient feature of this community of writers and artists was that most of the writers did not write and most of the painters did not paint."

That, of course, had never been Robert Nathan's problem; on the contrary, the man wrote incessantly, though Jackson found that his output did little to improve his mood. "Bob will only be happiest when he is lying in his coffin," Jackson wrote Brackett on returning to Orford, "preferably with a sourpuss undertaker standing by reading aloud from an inane book called THE BISHOP'S WIFE or THE WOODCUTTER'S HOUSE or THE ENCHANTED VOYAGE"—all by Nathan—"or any one of those anemic fantasies (take your choice)." Nathan had made the mistake of showing Jackson his latest, *Bridgit*, about an angel who helps a down-at-the-heels pianist write a great symphony, thereby freeing him from a degrading gig in a honky-tonk while helping to care, too, for his tubercular wife. In its present form *Bridgit* was a screenplay for MGM, though Nathan (who "can never let bad enough alone") also planned to publish a book version.* During his final morning in Truro, Jackson spent three "pretty grim" hours unfurling his frank opinion of *Bridgit*, while pointing out that he himself was about to begin a third draft of his novel and would gladly continue his toil rather than let inferior work see the light of day. "I seem, to myself, a very old man compared to you," the demoralized Nathan wrote him afterward; "old in effort, old in sadness, and in disappointments. To write a book three times over—to be so sure of it, and of yourself—it's all beyond me now, though I might have, once. Good luck to you. We loved having you both." The friendship did not long survive Jackson's visit.

Happily a more promising attachment had been formed with Mary McCarthy, who'd recently left her second husband, Edmund Wilson, and rented a cottage in Truro for the summer. Jackson was a little terrified of McCarthy, what with her daunting intellectualism; he was well aware that she and the whole *Partisan Review* crowd had come to regard him, at best, as the lucky author of a middlebrow, non-engagé novel, whatever friendly feelings they reserved for him otherwise. And yet he couldn't help admiring McCarthy's own fiction (despite its lack of "a warm human something") and sensed that she, too, aspired to a more general readership among "business men and Scarsdale matrons who had never heard of Kafka"—as she herself put it in her roman à clef about

---

* *Bridgit: A Story for the Screen* was published that year by Knopf, and appears to have vanished with barely a ripple. When I searched for the book on Worldcat.org ("the World's Largest Library Catalogue") I found a single copy at Yale. *Bridgit* the movie was never produced.

that week in Truro, wherein she analyzed Jackson's hope for their friendship: "For Herbert Harper [Jackson] this woman whom he had never seen figured as a potential sister, wise and kind, a High Church nun full of sweet severity, a worldly recluse from the world. He expected from her indulgence, guidance, plain song on the victrola, and high-minded conversation, clarity and mild reproof." All of which he got in spades, to his almost giddy delight: the "high point of the week" were his talks with McCarthy, he wrote friends, though she made him "feel like a babe mentally." At one point, Jackson—negotiating the shoals of a conversation with both her and the art critic Clement Greenberg—ventured to suggest that Jean Stafford was a good writer: "Mary and Clem all but tore me to shreds," he said, with a kind of chastened awe, more or less convinced that, in retrospect, he'd erred in his opinion of Stafford.

Amid the euphoria of new friendship, Jackson stopped in Boston on his way home and ordered a couple of books he thought McCarthy might like (*Shakespeare's Comedy*; *Tolstoy and His Wife*), writing her a note on Ritz-Carlton letterhead: "I liked you so much." McCarthy, in turn, was also giving a lot of thought to her new friend, whose visit had caused a "sensation" and seemed to lend itself to the subject of a "witty novelette": "A satire, it was to be," she remembered at a distance of almost thirty-five years, "on the literary life and the thirst for fame, just as dangerous to self-respect as the thirst for alcohol." The "Chaplinesque hero" would be none other than Charles Jackson, whose permission she decorously sought in advance: "You and your visit here would provide a marvelous focus for a study of literary types and literary errors. . . . The whole thing is full of Aristotelian unity, but if you have qualms, I will abandon it." McCarthy had parsed her customer well, though, and was already hard at work on *The Lost Week*, convinced it would "make [her] fortune." Meanwhile her endearingly self-involved subject was little other than thrilled; true, the woman "wouldn't leave [him] a shred," but what an opportunity to see himself as one of the most astute (and caustic) satirist-critics of her time saw him! "My life is in your hands," he promptly replied, assuring her that he'd only be hurt if the story "turns out to be lousy," and expressing but a single caveat: "Please let my sex-life alone."

In the present case, however, McCarthy wasn't interested in people's sex lives; this was a story entirely occupied with the literary aspect of things, and her most immediate challenge was coming up with fictional names for a large cast of real-life writers: James Theobald (Nathan),

William De Los Rios (Dos Passos), David MacGregor (Dwight Macdonald), and Frani Farrar (herself). Jackson endeavored to be helpful by
suggesting that she refer to *The Lost Weekend*, in her book, by its original title, *Present Fears*. But McCarthy had that part covered, and as her
story opens we find the dapper, mustachioed Herbert Harper—author of
A Short One If You Don't Mind—waiting with his stoical wife at the Not-
tingham (that is, Truro) bus stop for their host to come collect them.
He is, as usual, pondering the fate of his second novel, which he has just
withdrawn from his publisher (again)—in an agony of doubt whether
he can repeat the success of his confessional first novel. A prescient but
rather pitiless narrator thinks not:

> . . . for such successes can never be duplicated. The mood of
> self-revelation comes but once to an author; it cannot be revived
> but only counterfeited. In fear and trembling, he lays his whole soul
> on the table, risking universal condemnation, for the sake of some
> higher forgiveness—"Love me," he cries, "as I am." It is this sense of
> risk, this mixture of temerity and terror, that authenticates his story;
> but once he has won the gamble, been accepted, admired, forgiven,
> his confessions, if he persists in them, will become spurious, since
> he is sure in advance of absolution. Moreover, his private life is no
> longer private; it is a museum through which he himself has shown
> visitors, and if he continues to live in it, it is only as a custodian or
> janitor. . . . If he is to go on with his career, it must be on a differ-
> ent basis; he himself must disappear from his work, or appear in it
> disjointed, as it were, one part of him being given to one character,
> one to another, one part to the style, so that the work of art is an
> assemblage of disjuncta [*sic*] membra poetae. Yet often, as in Herbert
> Harper's case, he has given himself away with such rashness that he
> has very little left of himself with which to equip his characters; the
> autobiographical novelist is notoriously improvident. Furthermore,
> in the autobiographical novelist, the interest in the world, either of
> reality or of forms, is much weaker than the interest in the self. Once
> he is deprived of his main topic, he has very little left to say and very
> little interest in saying. He will observe this slackening of excitement
> and attribute it to a diminution of creative powers, while in reality
> he has become a creator, an artist, by sheer accident—the need for
> self-revelation has precipitated him into a career for which he has not
> the metier.

Harper is "half-articulately conscious" of his dilemma, and while he wants desperately to succeed, he's loath to do so by way of shoddy work. An essentially honest man, he's more than willing to discuss the matter openly (indeed exhaustively) with friends old and new, though he also enjoys—via "a voluminous correspondence"—touching on the cheerier aspects of his fame:

> To the superficial, this preoccupation with himself . . . this rever-sal of the principles of Dale Carnegie, might seem a poor basis for friendship. In reality, it was not. His colleagues received his letters with a certain amount of astonishment, but they were not chilled by them. How could they be? They were the letters a man writes to his mother. . . . Our mothers, our sisters, and our uncles are never convinced by our successes—that is why they demand of us the cor-roboration of facts and figures, why our letters home are naively full of the celebrities we have met, the cars we have bought, the restau-rants we have lunched at, and why these letters, no matter how care-fully documented, have a faint air of fraudulence, the contagion of disbelief having spread from the recipient to the sender. It makes no difference how many trophies we send home, how many med-als, Japanese coins, press clippings, publicity photographs, menus, autographs, cheques—it is all in vain. Our relations know better, we are transparent to them; at the bottom of the fishbowl of our achieve-ments they see us sitting, very small, the ordinary, nugatory person whom they have always known. . . . [Harper's] profound disbelief in his success took the sting out of the subject for his colleagues. It was impossible to envy a man who envied himself.

One wonders what Jackson would have made of these observations, but alas, his intense curiosity was never to be gratified. "Dear Minx," he wrote McCarthy a month later. "Have you finished it? Are you happy with the result? Where will it be published? When am I to see it? Don't you know I can't wait? Etcetera." But the witty novelette had already been put aside. Working in the dreary town of Yarmouth, Nova Scotia, McCarthy had typed away at a brisk pace for a few days, until she began to notice the story becoming "very very John Marquand"; her vivisec-tion of Harper appeared in the lively early pages, but she found her will weakening as she moved on to the literati of "lotus-land" per se ("they *will* name their station wagon 'Hemlock Grange' "), and the manuscript expired after fifty pages or so. She packed it into her suitcase, departed Nova Scotia, and entombed it among her papers without a further look.

THAT SUMMER, as Jackson staggered to the end of another draft of his novel (which Farrar & Rinehart were now announcing for November), he vowed not to "touch so much as a comma of it" once the damn thing was done again. But the truth remained: it *still* wasn't right. To account for Grandin's ultimate triumph over instinct (and to emphasize that the instinct in question was not exactly homosexual in nature, but rather a morbid infatuation with "the uniform"), Jackson had written an ending whereby the coquettish Cliff tries on Grandin's tweed topcoat when the latter is out of the room, then hastily wriggles out of same—undersized and absurd-looking on him—before Grandin can see him at such a disadvantage . . . but too late: Grandin returns to the room, and the scales fall from his eyes. The dashing Marine, when out of uniform, is just a dopey overstuffed lug that the judicious professor can take or leave alone.* But the ending was unsound, even nonsensical, and the main reason was right there in the text: "Does the war cause the deterioration," the author had written at one point, "or does it merely bring to the surface a disorder long dormant, long pressing, long dangerous?—We are what we are, under any conditions, and moments of crisis or strain make acute or intensify the conflicts in men's natures present from the beginning." In other words, it was finally time to put aside the whole "war neurosis" theme and admit that he was writing a novel about a middle-aged man who discovers he has homosexual tendencies.

Nudging him toward this epiphany was Donald Ogden Stewart,[†] another good friend from Hollywood who'd met with Jackson that summer in Boston, where the two had put their heads together for some six hours at the Fox Club. Why, Stewart wondered, would a seemingly naïve young Marine exploit the professor's interest in him? And why, afterward, would Grandin be so blithely inclined to go back to his wife as if nothing had ever happened? What, really, was the *meaning* of that

---

* Jackson, an avid reader of Colette, quite possibly derived this device from her famous story "The Kepi," in which an aging woman impulsively dons her young lover's kepi (a soldier's hat) in bed. All at once she looks ridiculous, and old, and he abruptly loses interest.

† Now best remembered as the screenwriter for *The Philadelphia Story* and as model for Bill Gorton in Hemingway's *The Sun Also Rises*.

story? Jackson found he "was not able to answer" such questions, where-upon Stewart steered him gently toward the light. "So help me God I finally know what my story is about and what it should tell," Jackson excitedly wrote in a nine-page letter-*cum*-outline to Amussen, Baumgarten, Wylie, and various others:

> It is primarily a story of marriage. . . . The story of a hitherto happily married man and normal man, a useful citizen in society, a gentle-man and a *good* man, suddenly discovering at the age of forty-some that he has strong homosexual leanings, is a very big story indeed. I don't mean to sound pompous about it, but the story has implications as big as the Greek dramas, in which the fine hero has a strain or flaw or sin which must be brought to the surface, faced, and accounted for, for good or bad.

Stewart thought the story could still have a happy ending, but Jackson was now carried away by the idea of Grandin as a tragic hero à la the Greeks, and of course such heroes had "to pay the very utmost for the flaw or stain that was beyond their control." A tragic hero also had to be *big* ("big enough for Spencer to play in," he coaxingly wrote Hepburn a few days later), and thus Grandin would be all the nobler in this latest version of his novel, soon to be retitled *Will and Error*, which (he wrote Boom) would have "as bloody a finish as you ever read in your life." Many years later, reckoning the wrong turnings in his career, Jackson would claim that he'd ended his second novel in a hackneyed way—that is, by "punish-ing" his hero for the "sin" of homosexuality—"because Farrar & Rinehart wouldn't accept my more intelligent, much more honest version—and to get it published at all, I had to accept the compromise . . ." But in fact Farrar & Rinehart were happy to settle for his penultimate version (in which Grandin decides the Marine is merely ridiculous), and urged him to publish already and get on with another book.

Baumgarten, too, was getting more and more exasperated with Char-lie's dithering, and scolded him for constantly pressing his work on others ("She thinks that I only get confused by submitting my work to several different and often contradictory opinions"); that said, she agreed with Farrar & Rinehart that his latest draft was an improvement, and yes, the outline of further changes looked fine, too. Perhaps such encouragement was wholly sincere, but to say otherwise, of course, was to risk further bombardment. As for Amussen, he was especially enthusiastic—"100%"

in favor: "I don't think it would turn your head or frighten you if I told you quite simply that it could be a classic." Exultant, Jackson promptly related the young man's endorsement to others, and boldly predicted that his second novel would be "so far superior to The Lost Weekend that no one will be able to see that the two different writers of those two different books are, or were, one and the same man." Which would prove at least half true.

Critiques from Amussen et al. had been waiting for Jackson when he returned from Truro on July 10, though he was a little surprised not to find a letter from Philip Wylie among them. "I am, as you know, not just one of your greatest and most sympathetic admirers, but also, Cookie, one of your most articulate," Wylie had once written Jackson, who still treasured his career-making rave of *The Lost Weekend* in the *Times* ("the most compelling gift to the literature of addiction since De Quincey"). Still, the man was a little on the mercurial side, and Jackson might have worried that he'd overshot the mark by assuring Wylie, a year earlier, that *My Two Troubles* would be "an American classic." Meanwhile, too, he'd had the temerity to dismiss Wylie's fourteenth novel, *Night Unto Night*, as virtually unreadable, frankly admitting to the author that he'd abandoned it on page 115: Wylie's "penchant for using difficult words," he wrote, made the "fantastically-involved style" of the late-manner Henry James, say, seem like "simplicity itself." Wylie, in reply, had affected serene magnanimity. True, he rebuked Jackson for objecting to his "two-dollar words" ("Nuts to you and your fine Anglo-Saxon ding-bats"), offering a precise inversion of Jackson's own aesthetic formula: "I have always taken the view that *what* [my italics] the true artist is considering is of zero importance, but *how* [ditto] he expresses it is . . . the guarantor of his success." For this reason, wrote Wylie, it had been "a kind of hooey" on his part to discourage Jackson from writing *My Two Troubles* instead of his Birnam sequel, since *whatever* Jackson saw fit to write would be estimable: "In other words," he concluded, "a state of fascination in your work and progress now exists in me. And I want you to stop being concerned with my soul, so that your two troubles won't become three troubles." Humbled, Jackson had offered this latest draft of his second novel (plus that nine-page outline) in a spirit of abject gratitude, calling Wylie his "literary conscience" while continuing to believe, more or less privately, that *Night Unto Night* was terrible.

Wylie's letter arrived, at last, a week after Truro, and its tone of exquisite archness must have caused Jackson's brow to furrow. "Dear Charlie, old kid," he began, breezily commending "every syllable" of the revisions proposed in Jackson's outline, especially his plan to flesh out the wife, Ethel Grandin, and dispense with the whole "war neurosis" business: "Bravo, I say." From there, however, the letter took a darkly insinuating turn:

> Your story as it stands has a quality of inference that is as if too subtle, too brilliant. John's character—for instance. To use language deliberately contrived to suggest his mediocrity of emotional estate is dazzling in a way. In theory. The iteration on every page of what might be called mannered cliche—(romantic schoolgirl, aristocratic nostrils, etc, etc) . . .
>
> Yet—too ingenious. . . . For, any slightest similar error of the author will inevitably cause the reader to believe that John's errors [are] not carefully deliberate, but a lapsis mentis of the writer. . . .
>
> By this same token, your superlatively caustic manhandling of language—your phrase awkwardness—your use of borderline bilge-like phrase . . . is too devious a method of composition for even high-intelligence readership, I fear. Even such readers will hardly realize and appreciate what you have done. "He wrote the Lost Weekend," they will say—"now—why does that tremendous prose take on this sudden, tripey complexion?" . . .

In other words: since it went without saying that the author of *The Lost Weekend* could not unwittingly write so badly, why then it *had* to be some Modernist point of craft—masterly in a way, but perhaps a bit much? That, anyway, was Wylie's modest opinion. As for Charlie's question about whether the ending should be happy or tragic ("in the classical sense")—well, the latter idea *was* a little puzzling: "To me, the problem is not one susceptible of tragical conclusions. . . . [Homosexuality] is no sin, no matter for any but morbid atonement, and no intrinsic crime—such as, say, self-murder, which was Don Birnam's crime."

"The Wylie letter still baffles me," Jackson wrote Amussen almost a month later. "In fact it's beginning to make me mad. . . . Maybe, as you say, the guy is just plain crazy, and doesn't see what I see in it; but if the veiled insults are intended, then to hell with Phil Wylie forever after." And the more he thought about it, the more he became convinced that Wylie *was* elaborately twitting him, and this was an outrage on any number of levels. As he wrote Wylie's employer, Stanley Rinehart: "Why didn't he have enough guts and/or sense to come right out and say he thought my story stank, as I did about NIGHT UNTO NIGHT? . . . I have no respect for him whatever—certainly not for his intelligence or integrity."

But then, he had no way of knowing just how earnestly Wylie had grappled with his own bewilderment. The high irony of his letter was, in fact, a style he attained only after attempting two previous letters (at least) that took as gutsy an approach as Jackson could possibly have wished for.* The first, dated July 12, begged Jackson to set his novel ("a mess") aside: "You don't have to produce a book a year, or every five years, or every ten." As for what exactly was wrong with it . . . where to begin? The writing was no good, for one thing, and in this letter, too, Wylie tried in all seriousness to give his friend the benefit of a doubt: "You have endeavored to set a style of English prose commensurate with the mental process of your protagonist," he wrote, as if it *had* to be a deliberate effect on Jackson's part, as if that were the only conceivable reason for such offenses against "grammar, rhetoric, usage, good sentence structure, and general literary taste." Gaining steam, Wylie began to forget his manners and grow belligerent in spite of himself, as if he were reciting an indictment against a hero who'd grievously betrayed the commonweal. Far from being "a great, tragic figure," he wrote, Grandin was "a dull little man with the big-head" (whose wife, incidentally, was "a jerk")—and speaking of "tragic" figures, the proposed ending was simply laughable: "A punishment for the sin, as you put it several times. Now, nobody with sense enough to read your books is going to think homosexuality of any sort is a sin—especially a sin of that magnitude. . . . [Grandin's] crime is infantilism, no crime; his real sin is extravagant egoism." And whereas *The Lost Weekend* had rendered Don's pathology from the *inside*, so that any reader could identify with it, what was even a sophisticated reader supposed to make of Grandin's weird homoerotic fetishes ("Caps, uniforms, bathrobes, bottles of suntan oil")? Presented with pokerfaced objectivity, as if one should merely accept such phenomena as typical, they gave the reader "the feeling that he is catching onto more of Charlie Jackson than Charlie Jackson has caught onto himself . . ." And finally—lest the author seek refuge in the good opinion of other, less exacting admirers—Wylie skewered the usual suspects one by

---

* Wylie made a point of preserving these unmailed letters among his papers at Princeton—the better for posterity to judge, perhaps.

one: Donald Ogden Stewart was "feeble," the author of "hack movies"; Baumgarten was "a very bad judge of writing"; Amussen was "juvenile." And so on.

The next day (July 13), Wylie tried again. It occurred to him that Charlie might view a harsh critique as retribution for their little set-to over *Night Unto Night*, which Wylie would "hate intensely": "I am so keen about your writing when it's on the beam that I did something for you I never did before and perhaps may never do again: I asked the Times to let me rave about it." But reminding himself of Jackson's superlative first novel only got his blood up all over again, until his second letter degenerated into an almost precise replica of his first. On July 16, finally, he managed that waggishly detached third letter—"the gist of which was," as Jackson wrote a friend (six months later, and still furious): "what a stroke of genius on your part, how super-subtle, etc., to make the characters so dull in themselves that their problem becomes all the more interesting because they don't matter." At length he consoled himself that Wylie was probably insane, and many years later he couldn't entirely conceal his glee when he bumped into the man ("much in need") at an AA meeting in Manhattan.

SHORTLY AFTER PRODUCTION BEGAN on *The Lost Weekend*, the redoubtable Stanley Barr of Allied Liquor Industries fired a warning shot across Paramount's bows: all too familiar with the novel's invidious portrait of a drinker, Barr expressed his "very serious concern" that Prohibitionists would use the film version to persuade the public that Don Birnam is typical of anyone who sips an occasional cocktail, or of "the working man who has a glass of beer with friends at his neighborhood tavern." Brackett tried to defuse the controversy with an interview in the *New York World-Telegram*, pointing out that Don Birnam was hardly a typical drinker: "We are making the movies' first attempt to understand a drunkard, a chronic alcoholic, and interpret what goes on in his mind. This has been done with an opium smoker, so why not a drinker?"

But was the public ready for an unfunny drunk? The movie's first sneak preview, in Santa Barbara, resoundingly suggested otherwise. To Wilder and Brackett's horror, the audience burst into laughter from the get-go, when Wick discovers the bottle his brother has dangled out the window—and things went downhill from there. By the end of the movie the theater was almost empty, and the few who remained scribbled words like "disgusting" and "boring" on their preview cards. Afterward, sitting in a car with a subdued Brackett and the studio head, Henry Ginsberg, Wilder announced that he was leaving for Washington in the morning: There was nothing he could do about *The Lost Weekend*, and meanwhile he'd been offered a chance to go to Berlin and help de-Nazify the German film industry; Brackett would have to deal with this mess alone. (Jackson, for his part, had been told by a friend that the preview was boffo: "She was so thrilled her letter was almost incoherent," he wrote Brackett. "Only fault she had to find was the ending . . . ") Word of the debacle spread, and the liquor industry tried to make hay by offering five million dollars for the movie's negative through a dummy corporation. "If they would have given *me* the five million," said Wilder, "*I* would have burned the negative."

The tide turned in the nick of time. The composer, Miklós Rózsa, was certain the movie's temporary score—upbeat Gershwinesque jazz—was to blame for the disastrous reaction in Santa Barbara, and his eerie theremin-dominated music made it clear that the story wasn't supposed to be funny. Nobody laughed at a second preview in San Francisco; indeed, as *The Hollywood Reporter* observed, everyone in the theater stayed put well past midnight and were "positively limp" by the end. Realizing the movie was likely headed for success, the liquor industry tried a radically different tack: producers of premium-brand whiskey reminded the public that Birnam only drank cheap stuff, and the House of Seagram went so far as to run an advertisement promoting the movie: "Paramount has succeeded in burning into the hearts and minds of all who see this vivid screen story our own long-held and oft-published belief that . . . *some men should not drink*, which might well have been the name of this great picture instead of *The Lost Weekend*."

It galled Jackson that practically every single one of his Hollywood friends had already seen the movie, while he was stuck in boring Orford: "I can't sleep nights, I want to see it so bad," he complained that summer. He would have to wait until September 11, however, when Paramount was giving a private screening in New York for Jackson's publisher and a list of friends, pundits, and creditors that Jackson had devised with particular care: Klaus Perls, Philip Rahv, Bennett Cerf, Tracy and Hepburn, Edmund Wilson, Harold Ross, and Edna Ferber ("ah, there!" he noted of the last), among many others. "I believe it's the only movie adaptation of a novel which actually pleases the novelist," he remarked afterward, ranking *The Lost Weekend* fourth on his personal list of favorite movies, behind *The Informer*, *All Quiet on the Western Front*, and *The Gold Rush*. There were all sorts of little touches he wished he'd thought of himself (especially the bottle's shadow behind the light fixture), and no matter how many times he saw the movie, tears sprang to his eyes anew whenever Don died for a drink during *La Traviata*, or screamed in horror at the bat hallucination. Not that Jackson considered the movie perfect: during his eleventh viewing he noticed that certain actors in the opera audience (notably the girl whose purse Don steals) reappear in other parts of the movie, and he would always cringe at the ham actors who played Helen's parents ("they are something which Vincent Minilli [*sic*] might have dreamed up and often does"). For the most part, though—and despite the ending, which he would always despise—his cup ran over: "To my dying day," he wrote Ginsberg, "I shall be enormously grateful to Paramount for handling my novel with such respect and for making such a big thing of it."

To his dying day, too, he would resent Ray Milland for what he perceived to be base ingratitude on the actor's part. During filming, Milland hadn't hesitated to pick his brain about the fine points of alcoholic behavior, but later, when Jackson accosted him "for a good two hours" to gush about his performance—Don's escape from Bellevue, say ("a dancer couldn't have done it more beautiful")—Milland did little more than nod: "I was disappointed in him," Jackson grimly noted. But as Milland would write in his memoir, *Wide-Eyed in Babylon* (1974), he'd never taken himself very seriously as an actor, and often felt embarrassed unto speechlessness by all the lavish praise. Worse was the widespread perception that he'd based his portrayal on real-life alcoholism, which made him the butt of drunk jokes for the rest of his life ("Ray Milland's been here," said Bob Hope—a common offender—on finding a bottle in *My Favorite Brunette*). Eager to distance himself from such an undeserved image, he refused to reprise his Don Birnam role for a 1951 radio production that would have paid Jackson five hundred dollars—money he desperately needed by then, as perhaps it goes without saying.

Back in the fall of 1945, though, there was still some question as to whether the movie would ever see the light of day. British censors were especially appalled, threatening to ban *The Lost Weekend* unless Paramount agreed to a "drastically altered" version: such scenes as Don's delirium tremens were cut, and moreover a monitory, idiotic subtitle was imposed: *Diary of a Dipsomaniac*. Sensing a chance to generate worldwide publicity, the studio decided to give the movie a premiere in London, whose critics (according to *The Hollywood Reporter*) went on "a praise binge for *The Lost Weekend*": "Even with the paper shortage, it's gotten more comment than any picture since *Gone with the Wind*." At home, too, censor boards in Ohio and other states provoked even further buzz by insisting on cuts, particularly zeroing in on a speech that Brackett and Wilder had written to forestall solidarity with the temperance movement: "Good old Prohibition days," says Bim, the sinister male nurse at Bellevue. "That's what started half these guys off. Whoopee!"*

By the time the movie opened at New York's Rivoli Theatre on December 1, executives at Paramount (who at one point had been "resigned to box-office receipts on a par with a collection plate in a Wesleyan chapel," as Milland put it) went out of their way to milk the controversy as much as possible: "THE AMAZING NOVEL YOU WHISPERED ABOUT," blared the ads, "ROCKS THE SCREEN WITH ITS DARING! / The shock best-seller that 'no one would dare to film,' " etc. Most reviewers responded by commending the "courage" of what was, as Bosley Crowther wrote in the *Times*, one of "the best and most disturbing character studies ever put on the screen. . . . truly a chef d'oeuvre of motion-picture art." One of the very few mixed reviews was James Agee's in the *Nation*; he began by saying the movie had left him "pretty consistently gratified and excited," but seemed to change his mind as he went along: "Thinking it over, though, there are curious and disappointing things about the picture. Good as he is, Milland is too robust for the best interests of his role . . . neither he nor the director happens to know very much about the particular kind of provincially born, genteelly bred failed artist Milland is supposed to be playing." Agee (who incidentally had worked with Rhoda at *Fortune*, and had also been on Charlie's invitation list for the Farrar & Rinehart screening) ended his review on a wry, somewhat conciliatory note: "I understand that the liquor interesh: innerish: intereshtsh are rather worried about thish film. Thash tough."

The consensus, however, was reflected in a full-page ad that ran after the movie's release: "THE MOST WIDELY ACCLAIMED MOTION PICTURE ENTERTAINMENT IN THE HISTORY OF THE INDUSTRY"—and some even agreed with Howard Barnes of the New York *Herald-Tribune*, who ventured to suggest that Brackett and Wilder had "taken an absorb-

---

* Bim knew whereof he spoke. According to a 1936 study by Norman H. Jolliffe, admissions to the Bellevue alcoholic ward rose precipitously under Prohibition— from 2,091 in 1920 to 9,542 in 1933, the year of repeal.

ing book . . . and made it into a far more absorbing film." Before long, indeed, Jackson began to feel slighted in any number of ways. Though Brackett had assured him that he'd be credited as "Charles Jackson," the title card for the finished movie read: "From the Novel by Charles *R.* Jackson"—an initial that never appeared on any of his books, though he was glad to be mentioned in whatever form, seeing as how Paramount liked to give "credit to their smallest bit-player in preference to the author of the novel," or so he irritably observed. By the time the movie almost swept the Oscars in March 1946, Jackson was hardly surprised to learn that his name hadn't been mentioned *once* during the ceremony—"but," wrote Brackett, who certainly would have plugged Charlie if given the chance, "for the reason of your omission, the rules of Academy Presentations are to be changed to include a brief speech by the winner in future, if that's any comfort."*

Scant comfort, and over time the movie became such a classic that even literate people tended to forget that it had been based on an acclaimed best-seller of the same name. Sometimes, too, well-meaning types would remark to Jackson that they'd especially loved the part of his story where Don spies the hidden liquor bottle in the light fixture—which, of course, isn't in the book. On the other hand: this "chef d'oeuvre of motion picture art" *was* based on his novel, and they couldn't take that away from him. In later years he'd often drag his friend Dorothea Straus to see the movie, "quiver[ing] with pleasure" in the dark: "There was Charles Jackson the awed fan," she remembered, "admiring Charles Jackson the celebrity and his inimitable success."

---

* Brackett (and Wilder) had won for Best Screenplay, a category whose winners were not invited to give an acceptance speech in those days.

Chapter Eleven

The Fall of Valor

One awful night, Jackson sat with his friend Elling Aannestad and weathered a lot of well-reasoned abuse about his second novel—but that wasn't even the worst of it. When, to cheer himself up a bit, Jackson would mention, say, a recent dinner at "21" with one of his celebrated pals, the captious Aannestad would sit back and smile behind his hand, regarding Charlie as if he were an oddly risible specimen of bug. How Charlie hated such sour grapes! As he wrote the man afterward, "I remember your telling me before The Lost Weekend was published . . . 'I hope you can stand success, Charlie, because I think you're in for it.' Well, I can—but you won't let me. You have this preconceived idea that I am dizzy with a little 'celebrity' . . . "

Whether such an idea was entirely preconceived is at least somewhat debatable. In many ways Charlie was, and would forever be, the kindest and most approachable of men, while at the same time he clung like grim death to his fraying cloak of fame. During that first summer in Hollywood, of course, he'd been mostly bemused by his own popularity, and appalled by such cautionary figures as Bernie Schoenfeld, a fellow MGM writer who would walk around Chasen's doling out tips to waiters so they'd remember him next time. "Well that sort of thing—well, you know," Charlie sadly wrote Rhoda, who two years later would complain to Boom about her husband's "perverted sense of values": "The insatiate lust for fame, for recognition. The tipping of five dollars right and left so the head waiter will say 'Goodbye Mr. Jackson' when he goes out. All the rest of that." The dividends, however, could be sweet: at "21" he was invariably seated in the VIP room (second floor, front), and sometimes he even rated a mention in Leonard Lyons's column, as when Toots Shor accosted him one night: "You're the guy who knocks drinking," the colorful saloonkeeper cracked. "I don't knock your racket, so why do you knock mine?"

With many a witty, sweet-talking letter, Jackson had wooed the rich and famous, convincing himself that he liked them as human beings, too, and vice versa. One of his favorites was the lovely young tobacco heiress, Leonora "Bubbles" Schinasi, who'd recently married (chez Bennett Cerf) the producer Arthur Hornblow. "Though I never did see much of you in Hollywood," Charlie wrote her, "I sort of bank on seeing Leonora when I'm in New York." He also banked on seeing her mother, Ruby, whom he characterized as "chic beyond Vogue's wildest dreams, and a swell guy besides." Ruby, he drolly suggested, was perhaps the very woman who (as Elizabeth Brackett had predicted while reading his palm) would leave him a fortune—and later, after their friendship had soured, he wrote a story about it, "Money"*: Patton Hillyard, "in desperate need of a thousand dollars," naturally tries borrowing it from Mrs. Mercereau ("She was not only rich, but they were friends"). Sensing her distaste with the subject, however, he never quite gets around to asking, and finally he's left watching "the splendid massed pigeon feathers of her gorgeous hat" in the rear window of a taxi as she leaves his life forever.

Perhaps Jackson's finest hour as a celebrity per se was neither as a writer nor as a society figure, but rather as a contestant on the popular radio show *Information, Please!* Among friends and family it had long been commonplace to say that Charlie would *kill* on the show, what with the wealth of trivia at his fingertips—as he reminded Nila Mack (in the course of correcting her impression that *The Jungle* had been written by Sinclair Lewis): "I've many times seen you raise your eyebrows when I innocent-like happened to name not only the understudy of the actress who had a walk-on as parlor-maid in Act 3 of THE LION

---

* "My story MONEY did not sell to The New Yorker—God knows why," he wrote Boom. "The lady was modeled on Ruby Schinasi."

AND THE MOUSE but also . . . the glove-sizes and maiden-names of the ushers' mothers; but I guess you've lost faith in me." *Information, Please!* was moderated by the critic Clifton Fadiman, and featured a regular panel of experts including, at one time or another, Oscar Levant, Franklin P. Adams, and John Kieran, as well as celebrity guests such as Boris Karloff and Orson Welles. The night of Charlie's debut in the latter role—January 7, 1946—he was, by his own admission, "a bundle of nerves" ("When I resisted the temptation to reach for a tall one," he quipped, "I knew I was cured for good!"), but soon he began to "spout quotes by the yard," as he wrote Katharine Hepburn. On questions relating to Shakespeare, of course—and there were plenty—he was all but untouchable: " 'The counterfeit presentment of two brothers,' " he rattled off in a high-pitched, pedantic voice, when asked to provide line, scene, and speaker based on a one-word prompt ("Counterfeit"). "The closet scene. Hamlet is comparing his father's picture with that of his uncle." But he could be versatile, too, as when Fadiman asked what opera included a scene wherein the set depicted a cross section of a temple with a dungeon beneath. "*Aida* . . . the death of Radames . . . Verdi." And so it went ("I was wow").

The best part was that all of *Newark* was listening—far more impressed by Charlie as a radio savant than as a writer of whatever sort. "I feel all puffed up this morning just to say I know Charlie Jackson," a neighbor ("Irene") wired his mother on January 8, whereas his prissy aunt Charlotte sent her own telegram to the NBC studios "care of Radio City." "I got sixty eight letters," Charlie informed his brother Herb, whose own letter (reporting the respectful critiques of R. A. S. Bloomer and other worthies) had "overjoyed" him most of all: "The reactions of the home folks honestly mean more to me than the congratulatory wires from my Hollywood and New York friends or from personages in the business, who send these things as a matter of course without really giving a sh--, well, a damn." Orford, too, was listening, or at least Charlie's neighbor, Mr. Warren, who noted in his diary, "Mr. Jackson was good it was much Shakespeare." Indeed, it occurred to Charlie that radio was a faster—and *much* easier—route to fame than mere fiction-writing ("authors being somewhat less than dirt"), and he cultivated the medium as often as possible. He claimed to despise one show, however, as a matter of principal—*The Author Meets the Critics*—since he believed a writer "should never be called on to speak for his book," and besides he felt as though he'd emerged "the worse for wear" after defending *The Lost*

Weekend vis-à-vis psychoanalyst Gregory Zilboorg ("that charlatan"). But his next appearance on the show was apparently more pleasurable, as he would return a *third* time on account of the same book (a record), and later he expressly requested at least two appearances for his second novel: once on publication, then a month or two later, "after the talk has got started."

LIBERATED FROM his elaborate "war neurosis" theme, Jackson was glee-fully convinced that he'd nailed his novel at last. With almost lunatic aplomb he cast about for superlatives, predicting that *Will and Error**
would be "one of the most distinguished books of 1946"—nay, that it would lend "more prestige to Rinehart & Co. [as the firm was now called] than any other single book you have ever published," and ultimately be considered "the best novel published in America in many years." "To hell with *The Lost Weekend*," he wrote, again and again (as if sparring with a phantom Philip Wylie): it was a trifle, a "sketch" merely, whereas *Will and Error* was downright "Greek in it's [*sic*] bigness." Gratified by his client's renewed confidence, Carl Brandt agreed that the book would probably be "a triumph," whereupon Jackson chided the man's timidity: "Brother, you don't know the half of it. 600,000 book buyers will buy that book the moment it's banned in Boston, which of course will be publication date."

With this windfall in mind—along with the fact that his first novel was (or so *Publishers Weekly* reported) selling 1,500 copies a week because of the movie publicity—Jackson no longer felt obliged to economize. In the fall of 1945, he paid five hundred dollars for a long-coveted "Keane" painting† from Klaus Perls, and meant to buy more—a *lot* more: "If you think I'm worth any dough," he blithely wrote the dealer, "that is if you don't mind my owing you twenty or thirty thousand instead of 3 (or is it 4?), will you send me the yellow Vedovelli with the childess [*sic*] blaz-ing sun? . . . What is the best figure you can give me for the two Jean

---

* Jackson liked the title, at the time, because it seemed pithily reminiscent of "WAR AND PEACE, CRIME AND PUNISHMENT, etc." Awkwardly, though, he wasn't quite sure what the title *meant* in the context of the original quote—to wit, from *Love's Labour's Lost*, Act 5, Scene 3, lines 470–71: "Now, to our perjury to add more terror, / We are again forsworn, in will and error." At one point he asked Mary McCarthy for her interpretation ("in plain English").
† Which he sometimes spelled "Keene" or "Kane," making it difficult to positively identify the artist in question.

Yves? I want them." "Stan, I need money like the devil," he wrote his publisher one week later. Though Rinehart & Company had just loaned him five thousand dollars to pay his income tax, Jackson wanted another fifteen thousand dollars for reasons he explained with winsome candor: he still owed John Owsley fifteen thousand dollars for Six Chimney Farm, and wanted to pay off at least ten thousand dollars of it; as for the five-thousand-dollar balance, well, it was "to 'play with,' so to speak." That same day—January 27, 1946—he wrote Boom as follows: "What a truly good soul you are. Thank you so very much for offering to cash one of your bonds so I could pay Bea" (a secretary and friend) "you do have a real appreciation of the fact that, though I seem to be getting all kinds of kudos these days, I'm actually making no cash at all."

But apparently Rinehart & Company didn't come through, and the following month Jackson arranged for a fifteen-thousand-dollar mortgage on the house, which he was able to reduce to ten thousand dollars (putting aside five thousand dollars for income tax) when Paramount paid him a bonus of ten thousand dollars "in view of [his] unusually fine and extensive cooperation in the promotion, exploitation and technical consultation in behalf of *The Lost Weekend*." Alas, this wasn't enough to satisfy his debt to Perls, and Jackson endeavored to make amends: "If you are still interested in the large Keane painting and want to buy it," he wrote Billy Wilder, "would you be able to do it now, by sending your check for $1,000 directly to Klause [*sic*] for me. This is $250.00 less than I had originally wanted for it [and $500 *more* than he'd paid for it], but that's because I love you."

To be sure, Jackson was going through some complicated emotional weather, given his constant all-nighters working on his novel, to say nothing of the international acclaim for *The Lost Weekend* (movie) and renewed scrutiny of the book on which it was based—the grinding, incessant pressure to equal that success or at least not disgrace himself. And then, even at the best of times, Jackson's "fluctuations between elation and despair [were] violent," as Lincoln Barnett would point out in his long profile of the author. At any rate, once he'd completed his third overhaul of what would finally be titled *The Fall of Valor*, Jackson was so exhausted and bewildered that he didn't know whether the book was good or bad and didn't much care: "All I want to do now is to forget it," he wrote Boom. Indeed, much of his recent euphoria (and strange behavior generally) had been chemically induced, and once the novel was off his hands, even Jackson had to admit he was badly addicted to Seconal again. On March 3, 1946—two days after mailing his manuscript to Rinehart & Company—he gave himself over to Dr. Gundersen's care.

Recently, too, he'd consulted with the eminent German psychiatrist Fredric Wertham, who at the time was about to begin a crusade against comic books that would result in his controversial study *Seduction of the Innocent* (1954), followed by a congressional inquiry that would lead to the infamous Comics Code with which Wertham was forever identified. The man was, in fact, a rather progressive and erudite scholar whose argument against comics was more nuanced than most care to remember. Whether or not one agreed that Batman and Robin's domestic arrangement was pederastic in nature (and likely to be emulated as such by young readers), Wertham's concerns about the violence, racism, misogyny, and overall crudity of the genre, as it then existed, were hardly without merit. Be that as it may, Jackson was mostly attracted to the psychiatrist because of his efforts to found the Lafargue Mental Hygiene Clinic in Harlem, where black patients could receive (at a fee of twenty-five cents for those able to pay) the kind of help that would give them, as Wertham put it, "the will to survive in a hostile world."

Wertham was appalled by Jackson's deterioration when the two had met in New York around the time of that first *Information, Please!* broadcast, and insisted he hospitalize himself as soon as he finished his novel. "I take a rather serious view of Mr. Jackson's condition," Wertham subsequently wrote Gundersen. "I think it is necessary to break him of his addiction. . . . It is fortunate that he is willing to do so. I explained to him that such a long addiction must inevitably have some physical results and that these should be fully straightened out in a hospital." Wertham prescribed a withdrawal period of "at least a month—preferable [*sic*] even longer," though Jackson's time at Mary Hitchcock would, as it happened, last only two weeks and be interrupted at least twice. "Patient admitted in a greatly fatigued and nervous state," Gundersen had noted that first day, when Jackson began his usual treatment of paraldehyde in cracked ice. Though he'd readily admitted to others that he was "practically in a state of collapse" ("Mr. Jackson in Mary Hitchcock for a rest," Mr. Warren scribbled in his diary), he blamed his debility entirely on overwork and urged his friends to be discreet: "You know how people are if the author of The Lost Weekend gets sick," he wrote Brackett and Wilder, "what they say, I mean." And he had good reason to worry about gossip, since *The Lost Weekend* was opening in Hanover one week after he'd entered the local hospital ("Nobody ever perpetrated worse timing in their life"), and he knew his fellow Orfordians would come to the movie in force. Attending with the Gundersens, Jackson would later claim that his neighbors had pointedly avoided him in the lobby afterward, though at least one of them was quite impressed: "Lost Weekend crowded," Mr. Warren recorded that night. "Well and fine. Powerful show."

After Ray Milland won the Oscar on March 7 ("I'm surprised they just handed it to him," quipped Bob Hope, the emcee; "I thought they'd hide it in a chandelier!"), he agreed to appear jointly with Jackson as guests on *Information, Please!* for the Monday, March 18, broadcast. This time things didn't go so well for the weary novelist-*cum*-Shakespeare maven. "Anybody else in these United States could have wired and said he was too ill to come," Jackson wrote with perhaps understandable self-pity, "but not me: *I* can't afford to be sick or even let it be known that I've been in the hospital." Jackson, "unstrung," came to New York with Gundersen's blessing and did his best, though he seemed flustered and even a little frightened at times—as when Fadiman asked panelists to give a Shakespearean hero's *first* line in a play when prompted with the same character's *final* line:

FADIMAN: "The rest is silence."
JACKSON [After a long pause]: Oh dear—I'm sorry I took this . . . it's, uh, "And flights of angels . . . "
FADIMAN: But isn't that the *end* of the quote?
JACKSON: Oh, the first speech? [Stammers a little; John Kieran says, "It's Horatio."] No, it's Hamlet speaking. His first speech is, um, to his mother . . . very sarcastic line . . . I can't remember it. . . .
FADIMAN: It begins with "A little"; will that help you?
JACKSON: "A little less than kin, and more than kind."
FADIMAN: "A little *more* than kin, and *less* than kind."

That, alas, was pretty much Jackson's best moment, after which he mostly kept silent. Milland, meanwhile, was red hot, as if *he* were the more bookish of the two, almost running an entire category about literary works with a hunting theme ("The Most Dangerous Game," *Rogue Male*, etc.), while the demoralized Charlie even saw fit to pass on an easy one about a favorite novel of his, *The Ambassadors*. ("Mr. Jackson on radio," wrote Mr. Warren. "Not as good as last time.")

The next day he visited Dr. Wertham, who now advised a convales-

TOP, LEFT: Charles Jackson in the bloom of his adorable boyhood. One of his teachers called him a "perfect child." *(Courtesy of Jackson family collection)*

TOP, RIGHT: The Jackson family shortly before their arrival in Newark, New York, in 1907. From left to right: Herb, Thelma, Charlie, Fred (the baby), Sarah, and Fred (father). *(Courtesy of Jackson family collection)*

BOTTOM: The Jackson family—minus the errant father—on their lawn in Newark, circa 1916, shortly before a series of tragic disasters befell them. Standing from left: Thelma, Sarah, Richard, Herb. Kneeling in front: Charlie and Fred. *(Courtesy of Jackson family collection)*

LEFT: Fred Jackson and his youngest son, Richard, whom he doted on. Fred's visits with his family in Newark become more and more infrequent, as he'd secretly had a child (another Fred!) with a sixteen-year-old Irish girl in New York. After the four-year-old Richard was killed, Fred abandoned his first family altogether. *(Courtesy of Kraham family collection)*

ABOVE: Charles Jackson's older sister, Thelma, with their youngest brother, Richard. Thelma insisted that her friends include little Richard for a Sunday drive, and the siblings were both killed when a train smashed into the car. As the *Newark Union-Gazette* characterized that fateful decision: "In their life, they had spent hours in play and enjoyment and it seemed almost as if Heaven had decreed that in their death they should not be divided." *(Courtesy of Kraham family collection)*

ABOVE: The young Charlie loved to go on long hikes (either alone or with Bettina) and dream of his glorious destiny in the wider world. *(Dartmouth/Rauner)*

LEFT: Marion "Bettina" Fleck, the great companion of Charlie's youth. The two considered themselves soul mates, though their friendship was more platonic in Charlie's mind than in Bettina's. *(Courtesy of Fabry family collection)*

LEFT: Charlie's mother, Sarah ("Sal"). Charmingly high-spirited in her youth, Sarah became "a creature of sighs and bewilderment" after her husband abandoned the family, and lavished a suffocating affection on her youngest surviving boys, Charlie and Fred. Charlie would later subscribe to a then-popular theory that both homosexuality and alcoholism ("a disease of emotional immaturity") were caused by overprotective mothers, and resented Sarah for that and other reasons. *(Courtesy of Jackson family collection)*

Taylor Mitchell Goreth Shults Conklin Jackson Jacobson
Partridge Allardice Goldrick Gibson Speirs

Editorial Staff

Margaret Goreth '24	Miriam Jacobson '24
Everett Partridge '24	Demetria Taylor '24
Lester Maxon '25	Cecilia Martin '26
Miriam Conklin '24	Wilma Wright '26
Charles Jackson '26	

ABOVE: Charlie spent a single year (1922–23) at Syracuse University, where he joined the editorial staff of the monthly literary magazine, *The Phoenix*. He also pledged a fraternity, Psi Upsilon, that hounded him out of Syracuse after Jackson's scandalous behavior with an older pledge—an episode that inspired Don Birnam's "fraternity disaster" in *The Lost Weekend*. *(Syracuse University Library)*

ABOVE: Dr. Thorvald Lyngholm, a Danish osteopath whom Charlie met when he was twenty-two and Lyngholm was thirty-six. The latter was lovingly evoked (as osteopath Dan Linquist) in one of Charlie's unpublished stories: "In repose, his face seemed always as if he were thinking deeply and at the same time scenting the air. When he laughed or smiled, his serious mouth became miraculously boyish and charming, and little lines, of mirth rather than age, appeared below his eyes. . . . His good Scandinavian head was partly bald, but the hair that remained at the sides and top was fine and silky, of a light sand color." *(Wilmette Public Library)*

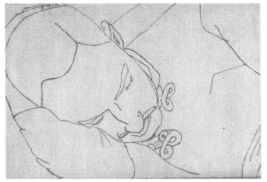

ABOVE: Charlie's brother Fred ("Boom") attended the Art Students League in New York before contracting tuberculosis. He drew this portrait of his sleeping brother while both were patients at Devitt's Camp, a tuberculosis sanatorium in Pennsylvania. *(Courtesy of Jackson family collection)*

ABOVE: Rhoda Booth, who became lifelong friends with Fred/"Boom" when they both worked at Brentano's in New York. Soon Rhoda was hired at *Fortune* magazine, where she researched articles for writers such as Archibald MacLeish and James Gould Cozzens. A Vermont Scot, she was the temperamental opposite of her volatile future husband, Charles Jackson, who often accused her of having no imagination but realized he couldn't survive without her. *(Courtesy of Jackson family collection)*

ABOVE: Bronson Winthrop, wealthy Wall Street lawyer and blueblood, a descendant of John Winthrop on his father's side and the Manhattan Stuyvesants on his mother's. Called the Exquisite by his best friend and law partner, Henry Stimson (Secretary of War in the Taft and FDR cabinets), Winthrop was a vastly cultured man whose father, Egerton, had been one of Edith Wharton's best friends. A lifelong bachelor, Bronson took a shine to the Jackson brothers, subsidizing their treatment in Davos, Switzerland, where Charlie longed to go after reading Mann's *Magic Mountain*. *(Dartmouth/Rauner)*

ABOVE: Charlie, always a dandy, used his Winthrop money to buy himself an expensive European wardrobe, pieces of which he often pawned during his drinking years. *(Courtesy of Jackson family collection)*

RIGHT: The Jackson brothers on a sleigh ride in Davos. Many assumed the two were *amants* rather than brothers—the boyish Boom "kept" by the bald Charlie. *(Courtesy of Jackson family collection)*

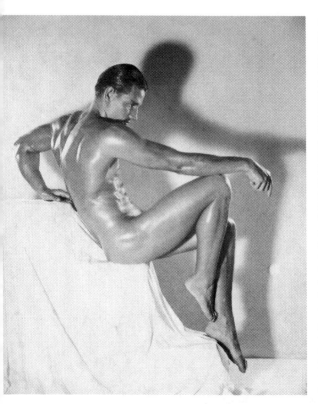

LEFT: A nude Boom, photographed in Paris by the famous gay photographer George Platt Lynes. Boom was also photographed by Man Ray, and became a favorite of the European haut monde. "He had not been the least bit impressed by his social success in Paris, London, St. Moritz, Davos, Berlin, the Riviera, Rome, Capri," wrote Charlie; "he simply took it all for granted in the most disarming, artless way that only added to the charm he had been so unself-conscious of." *(Dartmouth/Hood Museum)*

BELOW: Charlie and an unidentified reveler, during his Don Birnam years in the 1930s. *(Courtesy of Jackson family collection)*

RIGHT: Charlie's bookplate, which reflected his passionate love of (and resemblance to) the Bard. His all but infallible knack for quoting Shakespeare made him a big hit on the radio show *Information, Please!* *(Courtesy of Jackson family collection)*

RIGHT, TOP: Charlie and his older daughter, Sarah, whom he dubbed "the dimsal girl" because of her charming tendency to transpose consonants. Sarah had her father's almond eyes and dark skin, but was unlike him in every other way—and therefore the love of his life. He later wrote that he used to hide behind the curtain and watch her leave for school "like a love-sick fool." *(Courtesy of Jackson family collection)*

RIGHT, BOTTOM: Kate, though she resembled her mother physically, was volatile and precocious like her father. He once offered to drown her ("for your own sake") if she turned out to be a genius. *(Courtesy of Jackson family collection)*

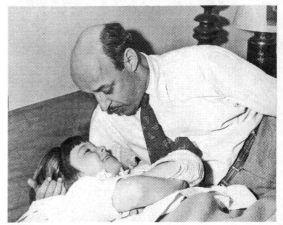

ABOVE: Six Chimney Farm in Orford, New Hampshire—"one of the most beautiful houses in New England," according to a 1927 issue of *House Beautiful*. Charlie thought that owning such a house would prove the "absolute peak of fulfillment and happiness," but he was wrong. *(Courtesy of Jackson family collection)*

LEFT: Rhoda, Charlie, and Kate at the entrance of Six Chimney Farm in happier days. *(Courtesy of Jackson family collection)*

RIGHT: Jackson became friends with *The Lost Weekend*'s director and producer, Billy Wilder (left) and Charles Brackett (right), though their friendship was strained by (among other things) the sentimental, uncomfortably personal ending of Wilder and Brackett's screenplay: "The final scene," Jackson wrote them, "as you sent it to me, with the hero working out his problem by writing a book (the implication being, of course, that the novel is the very movie we are seeing and the book we have read) is an out-and-out Judas kiss." *(Courtesy of Jackson family collection)*

ABOVE: *The Lost Weekend* was an enormous critical and commercial success, winning Oscars for Best Picture, Actor, Director, and Screenplay. *(Courtesy of Jackson family collection)*

LEFT: After his great social success in Hollywood, Charlie covered the walls of his bedroom with autographed portraits of his celebrity friends. "I like to show off to my New Hampshire neighbors that I am just-like-that with the Hollywood great," he wrote Gregory Peck. *(Courtesy of Jackson family collection)*

RIGHT: Charlie with Boom and Rhoda at the Stork Club. Rhoda took a dim view of her celebrity husband's "perverted sense of values": "The insatiate lust for fame, for recognition," she wrote Boom. "The tipping of five dollars right and left so the head waiter will say 'Goodbye Mr. Jackson' when he goes out. All the rest of that." *(Courtesy of Jackson family collection)*

LEFT: After Jackson became disenchanted with the small-town bigotry of Orford—outraging his neighbors by writing about the subject for Leonard Lyons's nationally syndicated column—he lived most of one year (1946–47) in Sniffen Court, a mews of carriage houses on East Thirty-Sixth in Manhattan. One of the boons of city life was the availability of like-minded companions. From left to right: Ted Amussen, Boom, Midy McLane, Charlie, Ann Amussen, the poet Phyllis McGinley Hayden and her husband, Charles (both seated at piano), Tar McLane (the family obstetrician), and Rhoda. *(Courtesy of Jackson family collection)*

LEFT: Boom and his mother, Sarah, who lived with him in Malaga for the last seventeen years of her life. Boom was a devoted caretaker, though Sarah's self-pitying complaints got on his nerves (and drove Charlie up the wall). *(Courtesy of Jackson family collection)*

ABOVE: Boom and Jim Gates were popular among their neighbors in South Jersey. Here they saunter along the boardwalk in Atlantic City with a lifelong Malaga friend, Barbara Peech. *(Courtesy of Pepa Ferrer Devan)*

RIGHT: Roger and Dorothea Straus with their son, Roger III, on the porch of their home in Purchase, New York, in the early 1950s. Roger had become Jackson's publisher a few years before, and Charlie remained smitten with the couple (and mostly vice versa) amid the many ups and downs that would follow: "There's only one thing to do about it," Charlie wrote Dorothea, shortly after their first meeting in 1949: "we all just have to manage, somehow, to get ourselves shipwrecked on a desert island together." *(Courtesy of Laura Straus)*

LEFT: Dorothea, whom Charlie bombarded with ebullient letters addressed to "Madame Straus," in homage to Proust's great confidant, Madame Émile Straus, *salonnière* and widow of Bizet. Dorothea shared Charlie's passionate love of certain writers, though she viewed both Jackson and the world at large with a rather cold eye: "Charlie's violent swings did not disturb me," she later wrote, "nor did I feel pity for him." *(Courtesy of Laura Straus)*

BELOW: Charlie and Roger Straus (on the right) remained friends even after Roger dropped the author from Farrar, Straus and Cudahy's list in 1962—"a dreadful black hour and black day in my life," as Charlie wrote in his unpublished confession, "The Sleeping Brain." Here they appear at a cocktail party in honor of Jackson's last novel, *A Second-Hand Life*, which made the *New York Times* best-seller list in 1967. *(Dartmouth/Rauner)*

ABOVE: Rhoda and Charlie with their daughter Sarah and her stockbroker husband, Alexander "Sandy" Piper III, after the young couple's wedding, on Christmas Day, 1963. Charlie could hardly stand his son-in-law, though for Sarah's sake he tried to ingratiate himself. *(Courtesy of Jackson family collection)*

ABOVE: Charlie and Kate at Sarah Lawrence, where Kate was elected president of her senior class. Charlie "discovered" his younger daughter during her college years, and (for better and worse) she became the closest confidant of his final years. *(Courtesy of Jackson family collection)*

RIGHT: Charlie at his desk in New Brunswick, New Jersey, surrounded by his "household gods": Beethoven, Mozart, Shakespeare, Fitzgerald, Chaplin, et al. The picture was taken for a 1964 *Star-Ledger* profile that tactlessly adverted to Charlie's "slightly prissy manner." "You should have seen *her*!" Jackson wrote of his interviewer. "A dyke, yet. All butch and a yard wide." *(Courtesy of Jackson family collection)*

ABOVE: Boom in his backyard with one of his gorgeous hand-braided rugs. To the end, he enjoyed showing off his legs. *(Courtesy of Jackson family collection)*

RIGHT: Stanley Zednik, Charlie's final companion. "To [Stanley]," wrote Dorothea Straus, "Charles Jackson was a dazzling celebrity and he the faithful servitor." *(Courtesy of Marta Kadrliak-Zednik)*

LEFT: Charlie in Room 405 of the Hotel Chelsea, where he moved after separating from Rhoda in 1965. He kept his room "neat as a pin," one journalist observed, "his books standing in serried ranks on the shelves, his paintings hung at precisely the right level, and not a speck of dust visible anywhere." *(Dartmouth/Rauner)*

RIGHT: Charlie adjusting his necktie in the Chelsea lobby beneath a nude painted by one of his fellow residents. *(Dartmouth/Rauner)*

LEFT: During his Chelsea years, Charlie ate almost every meal at the Riss Diner, around the corner on Eighth Avenue, where he was a great favorite among proprietors and patrons alike: "Hello, Charlie!" they always greeted him, as did the newsie on Twenty-Third Street where Charlie bought his daily *Times*. *(Dartmouth/Rauner)*

cence of at least two months in the country, away from work and family, after which it would be time to address the psychological aspects of his addiction. "I have briefly spoken to Mrs. Jackson over the telephone about this," Wertham wrote Gundersen on March 20. "What I am concerned about is that if he should start this addiction again, the next time his withdrawal symptoms may become even more pronounced and possibly more serious than they were this time." Jackson agreed to a *one*-month vacation with the Gershwins in Beverly Hills, but only after he'd spent another week in Orford poring over the edited typescript of his novel. On March 28, he returned to New York to catch the Century, and promptly collapsed in his hotel. His brother was summoned from South Jersey to get his affairs in order—a job that took Boom at least two days ("Who packed the bags, did the running around, stayed overnight with Charlie, did all the dirty jobs," Rhoda gratefully wrote)—finally escorting him to Staten Island, at Wertham's behest, where he was kept "incommunicado" at a local hospital.

But Charlie was nothing if not resilient, and within ten days Wertham was letting him venture into Manhattan, alone, for lunches with Rinehart and Amussen; the doctor even began to think he was well enough to go home by the end of April or earlier. For the patient's family this was a mixed blessing, at best. "The dreadful thing is that I have no feeling of missing Charlie at all," Rhoda wrote Boom on April 10.

Nor have the kids. He has been such an irritant and problem for so long it seems much more like home with him away. And I don't even feel like writing him. . . .

If I go on feeling this way, I shall write Wertham about it. If he's building Charlie up to a resumption of what he (Wertham) thinks existed before, it isn't fair. Because I can't face the same Charlie we've had for the last year or so, even without any pill problem. . . .

Charlie phoned tonight and it only depressed me more. If only he hadn't picked today when I was feeling so hopeless about us! For while he sounded fine and top-of-the-world so I really needn't have worried, it only made me think "God damn it, can he only think of himself always." If only he'd say once that he was sorry for what he put the kids and me through, maybe I'd feel better. And what he'd put everyone else through. But it's only his concern—*he* suffered, *he'll* never put himself through it again. . . . And he's loving the treatment—he's the lead horse again; everyone has to think about him.

•

WELCOME OR NOT, Jackson was back in Orford a few days later, eager to get on with his work. Wertham, too, felt "optimistic about the whole situation," though he and the patient agreed that another winter in Orford was (as Jackson put it) "out, impossible, verboten . . ." The sleepy hamlet, off-season, was hardly congenial for a recovering drug addict with gregarious tendencies, but there were other problems as well. Perhaps the last straw was a rumor that the black novelist Richard Wright—a mutual friend of Jackson and Wertham—had moved his family to France after being refused a house in the area. Jackson was furious; as he wrote Wertham, he'd have relished the chance to entertain the Wrights in his own home, or, better still, at the Hanover Inn for the benefit of his benighted neighbors. But then, he had to admit that Wright was "better off" in France: "He would be most unhappy in this community; God knows we have suffered because of local attitudes, and been regarded as 'peculiar' as well—think what Dick would have been up against, especially with a white wife and child, and even more especially because he is well-to-do and not in the economic class that people around here believe negroes should be in." Jackson had been (mostly) biting his tongue in Orford, until one night at Six Chimney Farm with the Warrens and poet Phyllis McGinley, an old friend, who was visiting with her husband, Charles Hayden. The main topic, it seems, was either the welfare state or domestic labor ("Had grand discussion on social help," Warren wrote; "Mr. and Mrs. Hayden Catholics"), and Jackson, after hearing his neighbor blandly drop the epithet "nigger" for the umpteenth time, finally protested: "This is neither Munich nor the Deep South, and the word is 'Negro.' " "Oh really?" said Mr. Warren, who was from Boston. "Well, I say nigger."

Nor was Jackson's quirky liberalism the only problem. He was, after all, the author of "That Dreadful Book," and given the movie's notoriety he was regarded with ever more dire suspicion. A minister in Fairlee, Vermont, directly across the river, inveighed from the pulpit against both movie and Jackson, to whom he wrote a personal letter: "I pray that God Almighty will lead you back to the ways of clean living." Such a stern remonstrance was not only due to Jackson's writing a best-seller that *reputedly* (the minister hadn't sullied his mind by reading it) celebrated "debauchery," but also to his peculiar personal habits—which, to this day, are still bruited about Orford. "He was up very, very late, and according to what *he* said he was doing, he was writing," said Mr. Warren's stepdaughter, Julia Fifield.

> And you know Orford was a very, very caring town, and there was a lady who lived right opposite his house—Mrs. Prescott by name, she was a widow. About four o'clock [a.m.] she got up and found the Jackson house well-lighted, and she called up and asked if there was trouble and if there was anything anybody could do. Mr. Jackson took a terrible—he was incensed by that call! And very shortly after that, he announced that he was going to take his family back to New York and he was going to have an apartment where he could go out and take his milk bottles in his pajamas if he wanted to and nobody would care!

This is true. As *Life* magazine reported a few months later, Jackson "moved back to the city with his family chiefly because he likes the anonymity of city life and hates the small town's 'prying, malicious gossip.'" Jackson also remarked on the radio that such gossip, in his case, mostly revolved around "what time [his] light went out last night," until he'd gotten the distinct impression they were "waiting up or watching" ("I think there was a lot of speculation that he didn't go to bed because he was too well loaded," Mrs. Fifield pointed out).

Before leaving Orford (though he planned to keep the house for summer use), Jackson couldn't resist a parting shot, a cannonade, in the form of a guest column for the nationally syndicated Leonard Lyons, who'd invited friends to fill in while he traveled in Europe. "NOTED AUTHOR DELIVERS SOME CAUSTIC COMMENTS ON HIS WEALTHY NEIGHBORS," read the August 1, 1946, headline in the *Manchester Union Leader*. "I had always heard that New England was the epitome of the American spirit, and believed," Jackson wrote for Lyons. "Brother, it's a myth." The beauty of his house and the town itself, he continued, had been spoiled for him by the iteration of words such as "Jew" and "nigger" and the kind of talk generally that "would be regarded as reactionary" in Franco's Spain or Peron's Argentina. "So, Leonard," he concluded, after giving various examples of this, "we are moving back to New York—if we can find an apartment."*

---

* That fall the Jacksons moved to Sniffen Court, a historical mews of ten carriage houses on East 36th in the Murray Hill area of Manhattan. The children were

The next day the *Union Leader* sent a reporter, John Pillsbury, to Orford, to investigate what threatened to become a "New England-wide controversy." The main targets of Jackson's column had been his wealthy neighbors on the Ridge, most of whom professed startled resentment (thinking it odd indeed that Jackson "should come here from New York and Hollywood to pose in New Hampshire as the 'Puritan in Babylon' "), whereas other, humbler townsfolk were simply "confused": "Mr. Jackson is well-liked here," Pillsbury wrote: "He and his wife and two young daughters are well-known and accepted as kindly and friendly people." The better to refute the notion that New England, and Orford in particular, had failed to live up to the "American Spirit," residents proposed holding a forum and inviting Jackson to speak.

It soon became apparent, however, that the novelist's disgruntlement was mainly directed at a single man: Mr. Edward W. Warren, his neighbor to the south. While perhaps not the most racially sensitive person in town, Warren was nonetheless regarded as a pillar of the community—chairman of the local Red Cross! Known for handing out nickels to poor children! Asked for his reaction, Warren was ever the gentleman, noting only that Jackson's column had impugned graduates of Harvard, Princeton, and Yale ("Cultivated [these Ivy Leaguers] may be," Jackson had written; "but they have no real culture whatever"), and therefore Warren himself felt "proud again" to be a Dartmouth man. In his diary, however—perhaps the one instance of this over a shelf of volumes containing naught but the most measured, prosaic observations—Warren's benignity wavered a little: "Orford all excited about Mr. Jackson's article in Manchester Union," he wrote. "He is a very foolish man."

One can only imagine Warren's chagrin as the tide turned somewhat against him. "Orford needs a jolting," applauded one resident, and meanwhile Warren's old campus newspaper, *The Dartmouth*, sent a reporter upriver to "test the validity of Mr. Jackson's allegations," finding that the local citizenry was, in fact, for the most part, politically "reactionary": "They hated Roosevelt and did not regret his death . . . [and] they definitely consider the Negroes and Jews inferior races." One of the Ridge dwellers (unidentified) confided to the newspaper that Mr. Jackson was

enrolled at the Dalton School, where, as Jackson was pleased to observe, the student body was forty percent Jewish and ten percent black: "After a week or two," he said, "[my daughters] did not even notice the difference. They have come to take it for granted, which is as it should be."

considered "maladjusted," a charge Jackson was glad to address: "I am maladjusted in the sense that I don't fit into their type of environment which is represented by bigotry and intolerance. I consider this type of maladjustment a compliment." As for Ned Warren, he would write fewer and fewer diary entries about his cranky neighbor—whose animus had probably left him more bewildered than anything—on whom he yet kept a weather eye ("Jacksons lighted up tonight"), and even listed *The Fall of Valor* among books he'd read that autumn, perhaps with a sense of appalled vindication.

JACKSON WAS UNDERSTANDABLY nervous as publication approached. Though he wanted his new novel to take readers' minds off alcoholism where he was concerned, he wasn't altogether sure he preferred being associated with homosexuality ("and so help me," he wrote Mary McCarthy, "but the third novel is about syphilis"). Still, he hoped reviewers would choose to describe it as a "novel of marriage"—which would hardly explain why it was expected to "cause as much tongue-wagging as *Lost Weekend*," or so Bennett Cerf speculated in his *Saturday Review* column: "It is the story of an unsuccessful marriage—with homosexuality the real root of the trouble." Given such a provocative root, Cerf thought Jackson's work would once again be discussed by psychiatrists as much as literary critics, and among the former was Fredric Wertham, who'd offered to review the book for *The New Republic*. "Empty ninety percent of this year's novels from your shelf to make room for *The Fall of Valor!*" he feverishly proclaimed. "The other ten percent may remain to serve as acolytes to this slim volume"; so compelling was the book, said Wertham, that he found himself turning pages "so quickly as to constitute a form of brisk finger exercise." Jackson, though flattered, begged his friend to tone it down a little, lest their personal (never mind clinical) relationship become known or at least surmised. Some of the more breathless hyperbole was therefore excised from the published review, wherein Wertham contented himself with comparing Jackson favorably to Thomas Mann: "There is a healthier and fresher breeze in Nantucket than in Venice."

Little wonder the author had great expectations. "I'm afraid this letter is going to sound pretty egotistic," he wrote Boom a month before publication; "it'll be all about ME." Enclosed was a typescript of Wertham's over-the-top first draft (tentatively titled "Tragedy of Deviation from the Norm"), as well as the July 27 issue of *Publishers Weekly*, which featured *The Fall of Valor* on its cover. And that wasn't nearly the half of it: "Other big news is that LIFE is doing a 10,000 word story about me (one of their 'Profiles'), with pictures, about the 2nd week of October, just in time to cash in on the nationwide reviews. . . . The photo of me standing against the garden wall, looking very Nobel Prize and tragic, has been selected tentatively (now hold your breath) for the cover of the magazine."* Meanwhile letters from advance readers were ecstatic ("Boom, they would bring tears to your eyes"), including a lapidary endorsement from Charlie's idol, Thomas Mann, who envisaged "another sensational hit" for his friend:

> It is a courageous, ruthlessly probing book, uncovering without a trace of speculative frivolity the difficulties, embarrassments and fears of marital and sexual life in general, and far from denying the knowledge we have attained of the so-called perversions and aberrations in this sphere, namely above all the homosexual component, a phenomenon which, as Goethe says, is *in* nature, although it seems to be directed against nature. . . .

With some of its more labyrinthine clauses trimmed, Mann's letter would be a mainstay of Rinehart's promotional campaign ("A letter from THOMAS MANN to Charles Jackson," a full-page ad was headed)— a useful rebuke to critics who insisted on wielding *Death in Venice* as a cudgel against what was (usually) considered its lesser American counterpart.

Another full-page ad, two months after publication, quoted critics both for and against the book, while suggesting that those in the latter camp were motivated, lamentably, by an aversion to homosexuality per se: "For Charles Jackson has put his finger on truth; and because there are many things in marriage that cannot be explained on a 'normal' and

---

* Who knows whether a cover story was actually contemplated, but in any case the photograph never appeared in *Life*, though it did end up on the jacket of *The Sunnier Side* four years later. Jackson's next appearance in *Life* would be in the March 17, 1947, issue—a (non-cover) story titled "City vs. Country," in which his rejection of Orford in favor of Manhattan was explored vis-à-vis critic Granville Hicks's preference for Grafton, NY (pop. 850). Illuminating the boons of metropolitan life were photographs of the Jacksons "swap[ping] literary gossip" with the Donald Ogden Stewarts at "21," as well as paying a backstage visit to a bemused-looking Patricia Neal.

superficial plane, this truth comes frighteningly close to the experience of everyone." Whether a bad marriage or homosexuality or both were being touted as so "frighteningly" universal is hard to say, but with only a few exceptions ("Subject, and especially bluntness of presentation, limit library use," warned *Library Journal*), most critics made a point of arguing the book's merits on aesthetic rather than moral grounds. Charles Poore's early review in the daily *Times* found the novel too "contrived" to succeed as "a study in abnormal psychology": Grandin's fate is a foregone conclusion, said Poore, citing the fire tongs that are planted so portentously in the opening pages (a residual point of craft from Jackson's radio days that Wertham, for one, found ingenious: "His sense of theatre is displayed in the beautifuly [*sic*] tying together of the incidents of the fire-tongs at both the beginning and the end of the story").* Also, it may as well be noted that at least two other major reviews, along with Wertham's, were written by friends of the author—Clifton Fadiman's in the *Herald Tribune* ("Mr. Jackson tells his story swiftly, clearly, humanely") and A. C. Spectorsky's in the *Chicago Sun* ("one of the best books I've ever read, [and] one of the least sensational").† Also of interest was Harrison Smith's glowing but squeamish piece in the *Saturday Review*, piquantly titled "The Seed of Evil": in its treatment of such an "ugly theme," Smith wrote, the novel represented "a milestone in our literary progress, and we can only hope that few writers less gifted than Mr. Jackson will dare to approach it."

One may recall Jackson's dismissive attitude (for Aannestad's benefit) toward all the "extravagant praise" for *The Lost Weekend*, though he did attend to the "sober long criticism" of Edmund Wilson in *The New Yorker* and Robert Gorham Davis in *Partisan Review*; indeed, despite Wilson's mixed review, Jackson had written the man a letter commending him as "the most informative and also the most entertaining [critic] to be found anywhere today." It's unlikely this sweetened Wilson's judgment toward *The Fall of Valor*, though he evidently took pains to be sympathetic insofar as he could. Calling it "less effective" than *The Lost Weekend*, he yet

---

* As mentioned earlier, Cliff Hauman ultimately uses the tongs to pummel Grandin over the head when the latter makes his fatal pass at the Marine.

† Two years before, Spectorsky and his fiancée had gotten married in Orford as guests of the Jacksons—raising a few eyebrows (or so Jackson seemed to hope) since the Spectorskys were Jewish. Spectorsky went on to become literary editor of *Playboy*, the cultural profile (and circulation) of which he is rightly credited with elevating.

conceded the challenge of writing about homosexuality in a way that would not prove "hopelessly repulsive" to the general reader—which might explain, Wilson thought, the novel's implausible protagonist, who has somehow "arrived at the age of forty-four with no inkling of his sexual proclivities." And Wilson did find the book worthy in one respect: Jackson "has made homosexuality middle-class and thereby removed it from the privileged level on which Gide and Proust had set it." As for Robert Gorham Davis, he had a much larger forum this time—*The New York Times Book Review*—for which he took an even dimmer view of *The Fall of Valor* than its predecessor. John Grandin, he wrote, was "a dreadful ninny," what with his rhapsodic comparisons of the loutish Cliff to Achilles, Lancelot, and so forth; such a "boyish outlook" was unlikely to shed light on a theme that had already been "treated by experts" (Gide, Proust, et al.): "Such an expert, in the precise sense of the word, Mr. Jackson quite obviously is not—happily for himself, and unhappily for 'The Fall of Valor.' "

That Davis could, with such calm assurance, conclude that Jackson himself was no "expert" would attest, it seems, to Jackson's success in conceiving his hero along purely objective lines—or, depending on how you look at it, in rendering Grandin so naïvely high-minded that he scarcely relates to the human race, much less to his creator (though certainly there are more than a few traces of Jackson in the character). Like Aschenbach at the outset of *Death in Venice*, Grandin is portrayed as having strenuously cultivated the Apollonian throughout his adult life, cloistering himself in his study night after night (to his wife's dismay) in order to finish his magnum opus, suggestively titled *The Tragic Ideal*. Such austerity is partly due to an intrinsic nobility of soul, but also Grandin buries himself in work to elude a mysterious dread—a sense that he is somehow guilty and will shortly lose everything: "But what he would lose, or why, was the mystery." One clue is the "stern disapproval" he "surprise[s] in himself" while watching—obliquely, from the shadows of his empty classroom—the young men playing tennis outside his window, their arms and legs thrusting about "like pistons or driving rods." And why ("of all the volumes in his library") should he choose *Housman* for his journey to Nantucket? The worldly reader cocks a knowing brow, but Grandin remains in the dark.

He's also a great fan of Whitman, naturally, and Ethel Grandin is reminded of "Drum-Taps" (one of her husband's favorite poems) when she finds a photograph of a sleeping Marine under his desk blotter. The poignancy of this comely young man, his doom foreshadowed in deathly sleep, harks back to Jackson's "war neurosis" theme—an obsession with "the uniform" that in early versions of the novel was supposed to derange Grandin into *temporary* homosexuality, but here becomes a kind of safe, sentimental exercise, since Grandin can gaze upon a dead or sleeping soldier with relative impunity. Thus, amid the enervating luxury of Nantucket, Grandin lapses into maudlin reveries of Cliff Hauman "in battle dress, gaitered, helmeted, strapped about with cartridge belts, a tommy gun grasped in his outstretched hand, lying (as he here lay) on a beach, but sprawled face down, with the first small waves of the incoming tide washing gently around him . . ." Wishing he could die instead, Grandin regresses into the hero worship of childhood, when he looked up to older, more athletic schoolmates—this the kind of "boyish outlook" that so exasperated Robert Gorham Davis, but was, after all, in accord with certain Freudian notions about the infantile nature of homosexual attraction (which also explains Grandin's frisson whenever Cliff calls him Johnnie).

Grandin romanticizes the loutish Marine, though this is never played for laughs—there are no laughs in this book—but rather reflects the older man's need to find something ennobling in his obsession. Prepared to believe that Cliff's "innocent language" is the result of a "mind so clean it could almost seem inane," Grandin is bitterly disappointed to overhear a bit of coarse, cruel banter between Cliff and their friend Bill Howard: "I want you to lay off that pretty boy over there, the fag," Cliff says of the effeminate Arne Eklund. "*You* can't have him—he's mine!" As it happens, Cliff is afflicted by the same tortured latency as Grandin, though his motives for ventilating the matter (so far as he understands it) are unclear. What abides in the finished novel is a blurred composite of the earlier, more guileful Cliff who toys with Grandin out of vague, egotistic perversity, and the childlike Cliff who seems to flirt almost unwittingly, perhaps in hope that Grandin will provide fatherly insight into their mutual predicament. In any event he titillates Grandin with tales of threesomes with his buddy Walt ("He loved it and so did I, but it was never any good, I don't care how hot she was, unless Walt was there too"), and confides about an all-too-helpful English professor, Scott, whose advances he once had to spurn (though he adds seductively, for Grandin's benefit, "Of course I was a lot younger then").

But when the question comes to a point (so to speak), both men respond in extreme ways: Cliff will assault the valor-ruined Grandin at the end of the book (gratuitously, given his mild rebuff of the earlier professor—"Uh-uh, Scotty, none of that!"—but in keeping with the *de rigueur* "tragic" ending), and even the decorous Grandin "pull[s] violently away" when Cliff tries innocently (in quotes?) to put suntan oil on his back. Later, Grandin's discovery of that same suntan-oil bottle on the dark, foggy beach will lead to an erection ("he felt a slow rude pressure growing in his loins") and thus a ghastly epiphany, as he finds himself imagining Cliff's "broad fingers" on his back. Weighing the implications, Grandin remembers a fellow who was once "caught screwing a pig," and formulates a triangular hierarchy of human sexuality, at the apex of which is a monogamous heterosexual such as Bill Howard ("the world's favored"):

> It was only a question of degree, upward from the professor who screwed the pig . . . to the teacher or philanthropist or minister or banker beaten up by a sailor in a water-front dive . . . to the brilliant dancer or artist whose neurosis was the very foundation of his art, to the scoutmaster or headmaster in a boys' school whose sublimated passion for boys in knee pants fitted him so completely for his tasks, to John Grandin himself, and to the well-adjusted happy Bill Howard, and from there, downward, it was only a matter of degree again, to the husband who must be at his wife day and night . . . to the so-called sex maniac whose lust for girl children culminated in murder and mutilation. All were pitiable, helpless, or tragic—except Bill Howard, who was just lucky.

"Tragedy of Deviation from the Norm" indeed: that homosexuality might itself be considered "normal" was hardly an idea whose time had come for Jackson or his generation at large. And lest the moderately deviated Grandin seem too repugnant, readers are given a flaming caricature, Arne Eklund—"a well-known decorator" whose 4-F status is dissembled by his being "sole support" for a doting mother—whom everyone can safely hate. "Isn't it tragic?" says Eklund, leering over a photograph of a dead Navy flier. "So young, and so attractive." Grandin—indignant at this parody of his own fetishizing—wants "savagely" to denounce the "yellow-haired" queen: "Look here, Eklund," he forbears to exclaim, "if people dislike you and your kind, it's your own damned fault!"

But even a stereotype like Eklund is no more flat a character than Grandin, Cliff, or the rest of the cardboard cast—all serve their mechanical purpose, all are conceived for the sake of a very general reader. Jackson had occasionally persuaded himself that *The Fall of Valor* was an "advance" on his first novel for the same reason that it is, by comparison, such a bewildering failure: whereas Don Birnam is evoked from the inside of his singular, Mr. Toad–like mind—that is, Jackson's mind—*The Fall of Valor* is "objective," and therefore banal. Startled by such a rain of clichés, by the "borderline bilge-like phrase" on page after page, Philip Wylie urged the author to rewrite "subjectively": "In your Lost Weekend style you have the better instrument, I think." But no; Grandin had to be a proper tragic hero, a great man brought low by his "flaw," and such men apparently express lust—unlike Don Birnam ("Was he big?")—in terms of the classical: Cliff's physique "was heroic: Hercules, Hector, a younger Odysseus, seen as they were never seen in the storybooks, and made modern by the startling whiteness of the hips above and below the tan," Grandin muses, grandly, and a few pages later he further eulogizes the youth's "heroic physique, as though he were some giant figure out of mythology come down to show these mortals what a Homeric god looked like." Nor can such a theme be treated lightly, with any leavening humor, though one irresistibly wonders what Wodehouse, for instance, would have made of Grandin's epiphanic tumescence on the beach ("Oh, I say—!").

Many readers were well disposed toward Jackson for wrestling with such a dicey subject, and doing so with his heart decidedly in the right place; still, the more disinterested among them were apt to echo Edward Weeks of *The Atlantic*, who regretfully concluded that *The Fall of Valor* was "a dull story, about dull people, dully written. The theme, and I suspect we shall meet it more frequently, need not be narrowed down to the triangle of an anemic, dry-as-dust professor, his starved and expostulating wife, and a handsome, dumb baboon."

WHATEVER ITS SHORTCOMINGS, *The Fall of Valor* was a bold book that few mainstream novelists would have gotten away with publishing—indeed, the prestige Jackson had earned as author of an acclaimed best-seller about alcoholism was precisely the sort of thing needed to broach this other, far riskier taboo. And yet pitfalls remained. An elderly gentleman in Boston named John Grandin was livid over the coincidence, and Jackson's royalty account was charged $150 to settle attorneys' fees in a threatened lawsuit. And once again there were censorship problems in

England, where publishers remained skittish over the scandal caused by Edmund Wilson's *Memoirs of Hecate County*. Jackson's initial British publisher for *The Fall of Valor* had been Sampson Low, whose editor not only proposed myriad cuts in the text but personally composed a number of "bridge passages" (written in what he deemed "the style and spirit of the book") to bandage the more gaping holes. Jackson, "outraged," changed publishers to Robert Hale, whose more reasonable tweaks addressed, for example, Grandin's morbid arousal on the beach, which became "a slow tumid emotion" that obliges him to roll over on his back.

A rather dire aspect of the controversy, for Jackson, was the book's salability to the movies: given the success of *The Lost Weekend*, his second novel was bound to be a hot property in Hollywood—if, that is, it were about almost any other subject. Agent Leland Hayward quietly tossed up his hands when Jackson told him the gist of it, though he thought maybe a Broadway play was possible. Eventually, though, Jackson tried hard to pitch it to the studios ("I have become awfully hard boiled about dough, now that everybody in the world is making piles of money on Lost Weekend except me"), since, after all, no less than Irving "Swifty" Lazar had assured him, only a little facetiously (and without reading the book in question), that he could get "$150,000 just to have them take a look at it." Sure enough, the summer before publication, word got out that at least three major studios were bidding: "Metro is considering buying *The Fall of Valor* and advertising it thus," quipped one columnist: "GABLE'S BACK AND VAN JOHNSON'S GOT HIM." But it wasn't MGM that would almost buy the book; despite what *The Hollywood Reporter* called the "downright lunacy" of even *considering* such a movie, Jerry Wald of Warner Brothers announced that he'd taken a sixty-day option pending approval by the Production Code of a treatment written by Jackson himself. The "homosexual angle" had been "quietly dropped on the floor," and hence the proposed movie would be "a serious clinical study of the decay of a modern marriage after ten years." Joan Crawford, fresh from her Oscar-winning comeback in *Mildred Pierce*, was quoted as being "crazy" about the story. A few days later, though, Warner Brothers decided to pass without further comment. Jackson, then, would have to be content with book sales alone: almost 75,000 in hardcover and 291,000 in paperback—rather spectacular, if not quite up to his most euphoric dreams.

As for the pioneering cultural impact: in early 1948, Jackson was pleased to note that the English anthropologist Geoffrey Gorer's "fascinating" study, *The American People: A Study in National Character*, commended *The Fall of Valor* as the "only book" that dealt "directly" with a theme most Americans viewed with outright "panic": "It is difficult to exaggerate the prevalence and urgency of this unconscious fear," Gorer wrote. "It was presumably to dramatize this endless insecurity that Charles Jackson in *The Fall of Valor* made his unfortunate protagonist a married man of forty [*sic*] with two children." Nor was Jackson's trailblazing in this respect limited to *The Fall of Valor*, if one considers his candid treatment in "Palm Sunday" and *The Lost Weekend* (to say nothing of *Native Moment*, which, if published, would have been an even bigger bombshell in the 1930s). Mindful of his place in this vanguard—soon to be succeeded by Gore Vidal, Truman Capote, and many others—Jackson would come to regard his second novel as a "great disappointment," mainly because of its "lugubrious" punishment of the erring hero: "the problem of homosexuality"—he wrote his daughter Kate in 1964—"needs only a forthright statement of the facts that may be true or dormant in anybody's life, an intelligent meeting of the minds involved, and an acceptance of the facts and then a fitting of those facts into one's social world as best & intelligently as one can." This was pretty much the way Jackson himself had worked things out (unbeknownst to the letter's recipient), but alas, his second novel would persist only as a cautionary (if compassionate) tale about "the cruel web of homosexuality"—so noted on the cover of a 1955 paperback, which depicts the brawny Cliff ravishing his wife in the surf while Grandin crouches furtively amid the dune grass ("he was a prisoner of his own unnatural yearnings," read the publisher's copy, "and he had to have the Marine even if it meant giving up everything he had stood for, worked for, hoped for. It meant all that—*and more*").

Nevertheless, the book did find an admiring audience among a generation of gay men who were glad to read about their dilemma in whatever terms. In 1972, the novelist Richard Amory wrote that *The Fall of Valor* deserved "a place of utmost honor" in the history of gay fiction: "Jackson captures the national man-worship of the forties with almost heartbreaking clarity. Like Grandin, I too pondered the photographs in LIFE of war-weary combat troops, and remember the one time in 1944, age fifteen, standing in an Arizona cotton field and watching a trainful of swabbies pass by, some of them lounging shirtless on the platforms, and experiencing the first, sweet, painful foreknowledge of my own sexuality." Among this segment of readers, at least, Jackson was not primarily known as the author of *The Lost Weekend*. Meeting Bobby Short at the

Carlyle in the 1960s, Sarah Jackson mentioned her father. "*The Fall of Valor!*" the cabaret singer exclaimed.

IN FEBRUARY 1947, after most of the smoke had cleared, Jackson took a month-long vacation, alone, to Bermuda. He hardly bothered to keep in touch with his family. At one point he gave an informal talk to the AA chapter in St. George's, and also struck up an acquaintance with James Thurber: "If you see a photograph of Charles Jackson and me," Thurber wrote a friend, "the glass on his table contains Coca Cola."

In fact—as Thurber might have been insinuating—Jackson had fallen off the wagon. As he'd later recall in countless AA talks, it began because of the heat: "I longed for some ice-cold beer. It's madness, I thought immediately; I've not touched alcohol for eleven years" (he had, however, resumed taking Seconal); "I'm not going to start now. And the intellectual part of me replied: 'Exactly; after eleven years of complete abstinence a glass of beer can't possibly do you any harm.' " Besides, everything had changed: he was a successful author now; he was fulfilled; he could take it or leave it alone. At any rate he was on a long solitary vacation, with plenty of time to recover if things went awry. "What do you know, I'm drinking again," he freely admitted to Rhoda as they drove back from the airport. He'd only been drinking beer, he told her, and this without any untoward consequences—from now on, then, he'd stick with beer. "Well, Charlie," she (reportedly) said, "I think that's great if you can."

In *The Common Sense of Drinking*, Richard Peabody tells of a man who decided to quit drinking until he'd made a million dollars, whereupon he'd resume drinking "in moderation": "It took him five years—of sobriety—to make the million; then he began his 'moderate' drinking. In two or three years he lost all his money, and in another three he died of alcoholism." For his part Jackson considered writing a novel about a "brilliant actress who finds it easy to reach the pinnacle and just as easy to drink herself out of fame." He himself, by his own later reckoning, would be hospitalized for alcoholism and/or drug addiction some twenty times in the next seven years.

Intermezzo

Boom in Malaga

Frederick "Boom" Jackson would lead a carefree life for the most part—remarkably so for a mid-century gay man from the provinces, and decidedly in contrast to the swooping ups and downs experienced by his more gifted, troubled brother. Both lives, each in its own way, were very interesting. As Charlie wrote in *Farther and Wilder* (as well as various other unpublished reminiscences), his little brother had been wildly popular throughout Europe—the sort of gilded youth who attracts comely people of all classes:

> He had not been the least bit impressed by his social success in Paris, London, St. Moritz, Davos, Berlin, the Riviera, Rome, Capri; he simply took it all for granted in the most disarming, artless way that only added to the charm he had been so unself-conscious of. Perhaps he was not genuinely loved, but he himself seemed to love everybody; he had, in short, a flair for life, all too rare in those blasé times in Europe between the Wars.

While in Davos, Boom had fallen in love with a fellow TB patient named Hamlet (no less), who had planned to pursue a Ph.D. in English at the University of Michigan, but soon died.* Boom appears to have picked up the pieces with relative dispatch. At the height of his youthful beauty he was photographed in Paris by Man Ray and George Platt Lynes—the latter famous for his nude portraits of gorgeous young men, many of whom Lynes slept with. Along with his lovers Monroe Wheeler and Glenway Wescott—a ménage that endured for years on two continents—Lynes was at the center of gay expatriate life in Europe, and for a while Boom was evidently part of their circle. Years later, during a 1947 holiday at Somerset Maugham's villa in Cap Ferrat, Monroe Wheeler wrote nostalgically to Boom: "It is enchanting to be back here on the scene of my misspent youth and find nothing changed; many people I knew then are still here, and the youngsters are more beautiful than ever. . . . I think of you often very tenderly . . . and send my love."

Like his brother, Boom never returned to Europe after his final season in Davos (1933), though for the rest of his life he affected certain cosmopolitan mannerisms—always using his fork with his left hand, and abbreviating his middle name (Storrier) as "St" (a quirk that complicated his life a bit, as he was initially listed as "St. Jackson" in the phone book). Such refinement stood him in good stead as co-proprietor of Scotland Run Antiques in his adopted town of Malaga, New Jersey; the shop occupied the front of a charming old house (bought for him by Mr. Winthrop), and was named after a stream that ran behind the home of his lover, Dr. Jim Gates, two blocks away on Defiance Road. For three years or so, Boom's business partner was another Winthrop protégé named Reggie Bacon, a former Shakespearean actor who was best remembered for playing Rosencrantz opposite his twin brother's Guildenstern. His association with Boom, however, was troubled. Bacon, two years older, fancied himself an expert in antiques, treating Boom as a novice and acting highfalutin in general (he could recite even more Shakespeare than

---

* Hamlet was friends with the doomed Flew, who would later kill himself after celebrating a last birthday with Boom in Malaga (see page 113). Indeed, Hamlet and Flew had been planning to live together once Hamlet returned to the States—that is, until Boom entered the picture: "[Flew will] be dreadfully disappointed," Hamlet wrote Boom, "but I can't help it. I refuse to run away from happiness. And even if Ann Arbor is as full of the brotherhood as Flew's boyfriend says, there will be none to replace you. Ah, Boom, my dearest lover!" Hamlet's fate is recorded in an entry Charlie made in his JAXON notebook, circa 1932, that also noted a ribald quip from Mercutio in *Romeo and Juliet:* " 'I tell you, for the bawdy hand of the dial is now upon the prick of noon.' The above was first quoted to me by R---- Hamlet, in Davos, now dead."

Charlie, and did, to the latter's chagrin)—this despite humble origins on a farm in Gorham, Maine, to which he happily (for Boom) returned after his cottage in Malaga burned down in 1940. Alas, by then he'd gained the upper hand in Mr. Winthrop's affections ("You can be sure Reggie loses no time inviting [Winthrop to Maine] on every possible occasion," Charlie grimly noted), and when the latter died he left $75,000 to Bacon and a measly $3,000 to Boom.

But again, Boom had a flair, and by then Scotland Run was a going concern. The quaint house on Harding Highway, with its two antique carousel horses out front (stylized versions of which appeared on Boom's stationery and place mats), became a popular destination in the area, and soon Boom was supplying many of the better dealers in New York. Arguably, though, he was even more acclaimed for his stunningly intricate hand-braided rugs, custom-designed for well-heeled clients at a considerable fee. A nearby manufacturer of wool coats supplied Boom with scraps of fabric in every color, which he hung in his backyard barn and sold to his rug-making students—matronly women, mostly, who (according to a friend) were "just crazy about Boomer" and would have paid for the charm of his company alone.

Charlie's attitude was contemptuous. As far as he was concerned, Boom was a peddler of kitschy bric-a-brac ("you may expect [as a gift] some cracked object from the shop," he wrote his daughter Sarah, "which is unkind of me but you know Boom's shop"), and toward the end of his life he almost caused a permanent rift when he made a sneering reference to "Boom's rag rugs." By then, however—especially when things were going well in his own affairs—Charlie liked to say that he and Boom had little in common anymore. As he pointed out in *Farther and Wilder*, on the rare occasion that Don Birnam still thought of his little brother, Warwick, he couldn't help picturing him "sitting in a corner of his living room, listening to a soap opera and sewing with elaborate gestures the carefully chosen, tightly-braided strands of a rug together":

And when Don recalled his brother's gay days of study at the Art Students' League and the often promising paintings of his early years, he was puzzled and saddened. Somewhere along the line Warwick had given up (Don never knew why); he must secretly have decided that he did not have real talent after all; he refused to compete with others, as if he was loath to be doomed to mediocrity in an art he loved; and at a comparatively early age—thirty at the most—he had

retired to a small Delaware village that could hardly be called a village at all, to run an antique business, on the assumption, perhaps,
that it was more sensible to be a big fish in a little pond. Life could do
awful things to one; and it was sad to think that, after such a promising start, he had wound up nothing more than a small-town queen.
But, in spite of a certain bitterness, he was happy. And who could say
which of the two had instinctively chosen the righter way? As for
Don, he was anything but happy; and he knew it.

Who indeed could say? One might venture to suggest that Boom's
greatest talent had always been for friendship, and by accepting (quite
cheerfully, it seems) his limitations as an artist he had freed himself to
enjoy life. Boom had friends all over the world that he happily kept in
touch with, and around Malaga he was a beloved figure. "He knew half
of South Jersey," said a neighbor, noting that it was hardly a secret Boom
was gay. One reason he'd come to Malaga in the first place was that Don
Hastings and Dan Crane, a couple he'd met among the theatre crowd in
Brattleboro, had settled a block away on Harding Highway. And then of
course there was his lifelong partner, Dr. Gates, who kept an office in
nearby Bridgeton and came to Malaga on Wednesdays and weekends,
when Boom was apt to have neighbors over for martinis and speak of his
"gentleman caller."

All his neighbors became dear friends. Across the street were the
Peeches: Harry, an insurance underwriter; Grace, his Scottish wife; and
their children, Freddy and Barbara. Grace's broadmindedness was apparent from the beginning, in 1936, when Boom and Charlie had approached
Barbara at Malaga Lake and asked her to have lunch with them; the vivacious twelve-year-old went home to ask her mother's permission, and
Grace sized up the two strange men in their touring car and readily
agreed—insisting, however, that the girl change out of her bathing suit
into a little pink dress with bows on each shoulder, whereupon the brothers realized she was still a child. (At the restaurant, the waitress assumed
that bald Charlie was her father.) From that day on, Charlie and Boom
were good friends with all the Peeches,* and Barbara became especially
close to Boom; she took a job at the DuPont plant after high school and

---

* Grace, a great reader, was perhaps Charlie's favorite among Boom's neighbors. He
and Grace would play cards into the wee hours, chatting and smoking. Grace liked
to wear silver bracelets, and Charlie gave her one with an inscription from *Hamlet:*
"Rich gifts wax poor when givers prove unkind."

spent the rest of her life in the Malaga area. Her one-time babysitter, Bea Smith (who lived three houses away on the lake), also worked at DuPont, and also became one of Boom's most devoted friends, often doing secretarial work for Charlie.

"Boom was Mrs. Tiggy-Winkle," said a friend. "His house was this cozy place with lots of nice things to look at, and he loved to cook for you." Before dinner, Boom would serve his guests martinis with an appetizer of scallions and salt; almost every night of his adult life, he allowed himself two cocktails, rarely more or less; unlike his brother, he didn't feel any particular need to drink heavily. (After seeing *Who's Afraid of Virginia Woolf?*, he wrote his niece Sarah: "But how terrible, the language was *nothing* compared to the viciousness and meanness in it. . . . How can people be so cruel? I think liquor helps, and therefore should be taken moderately.") Any of the hundreds of friends he wrote letters to, and remembered with presents, were welcome to stay at his house whether he was home or not; he told them where to find the key, and they let themselves in at whatever hour and went to sleep in the downstairs bedroom.

Every single day Boom wrote a postcard (at least) to his dearest friend in the world, Franny Ferrer, who lived across the country in Pacific Palisades. Boom had met Franny and her husband Mel when the couple were young actors in Brattleboro, and for the rest of his life he'd spend a few weeks out of every year visiting her family (with detours north to see his old pal Bick)—until, in 1953, Franny divorced Mel for the second time and asked Boom to marry her. He was wonderful with her children, and besides they loved each other and had such a good time. Boom, after some reflection, declined: "It would have been a damn bad idea," said Franny's daughter Pepa, whose first bath was given to her by Boom. "A lot of fun, but I don't think so." And meanwhile he stayed in touch with Mel, too, and became friends with *his* new wife, Audrey Hepburn.* Perhaps this had something to do with Boom's disapproval, in 1956, when Franny married the artist Howard Warshaw; he let his displeasure be known by sending the couple a set of towels monogrammed "F" as a wedding gift. When Warshaw proved a decent husband after all, he and

---

* Barbara Peech's "favorite night ever" was in 1954, when Boom told her to pack a bag and come to New York, where he had orchestra seats for *Ondine*, starring Hepburn and Ferrer, with whom they chatted backstage. Afterward Mel took them to a nightclub where Erroll Garner was playing the piano, and *Marlon Brando* of all people sat down at their table and began chatting, just like that!

Boom became friends, and Boom continued as a kind of surrogate father to Franny's children, writing Pepa every day in college and attending her two weddings.

BOOM AND CHARLIE'S MOTHER, Sarah—called Sal by her sons—was both a blessing and a curse to Boom: a blessing because he doted on her and vice versa; a curse because in old age she'd become indolent, grossly obese, and self-pitying to a degree that annoyed Boom and infuriated Charlie, what with her constant whinging about "sick headaches," gas, and above all the hideous neglect and downright cruelty she'd suffered at the hands of Herb and Charlie. When Thelma and Richard were killed by the train, the New York Central had awarded Sal enough money to pay off the mortgage on 238 Prospect, after which she'd always say that Thelma and Richard had "given [her] a home." By 1943, though, the house was in disrepair and she couldn't afford to maintain it, nor was she ambulatory enough to take proper care of herself, so her children insisted she give the place up. Right around the time she was "forced" out of her house, Charlie published *The Lost Weekend* and bought himself a mansion in New Hampshire!—or so Sal bitterly complained to whoever would listen, pointing out that a *single painting* of Charlie's was worth enough to keep her in Newark! But no! . . . In fact, during the four or five years he was flush, Charlie had paid his mother a seventy-five-dollar monthly allowance, but when he tried to remonstrate about her complaints—which she even voiced to Rhoda and her sister, while a guest in his house—she would "rub her eyes in the most corny hammy fashion (without listening at all)," as Charlie wrote Boom, "pity herself more than usual, and then go upstairs to pack." "I have gotten where I am afraid to talk before people," Sal wrote Boom during that same visit. "One has to take much insult when in a position like mine and dependent on others." As for Charlie's donations toward her upkeep: "I'd like to shove his old check down his throat."

The problem was solved, it seemed, when Sal came to live with Boom in Malaga. Each day had a placid sameness: in the morning she'd make her way slowly, painfully, down the stairs, with Boom's help, then sit in her chair reading a magazine or listening to the radio (later watching TV) while Boom brought her meals and whatever else she needed until bedtime. "I often think that Sal couldn't be pried loose from her sedentary moorings by the H-bomb," Charlie wrote his sister-in-law in 1954, cheered by the fact that his mother was now safely ensconced elsewhere; "and why not, if she is comfortable that way?" Usually, to be sure, she seemed quite comfortable. Not only did she have a tender companion in her dotage—as well as many charming guests who professed to find her delightful—but Boom often made a point of buying her lovely new outfits at the Lane Bryant (for large women) in Philadelphia, and other little gifts that might please her. The only downside for Sal, really, were those long trips her son insisted on taking to California each year, during which she'd pepper him with scolding letters ("I don't know when I have felt so all alone"—though Jim Gates and others were looking after her. "You told me you couldn't afford to go to Orford . . . Well—how could you *afford* to go to California" etc.)—this, even when Boom informed her that he was suffering from one of his lung ailments: "I AM REALLY SICK," he wrote in big red letters across a page of her kvetching, "AND YOU WRITE A COMPLAINING LETTER LIKE THIS TO ME." But of course he didn't mail it.

Nor did he mail a letter to Charlie, in 1956, that began, "It's high time you contributed to Mother's financial support. . . ." By the early 1950s Charlie could hardly pay the grocer, much less provide an allowance to his mother. Recently, though, he'd boasted to Boom about his "fabulous" salary at *Kraft Television Theatre* ("my cup runneth over"), and yet he'd failed to send so much as a Christmas gift to Sal. For that matter, neither had their brother Herb, though Bob sent ten dollars a month and wrote an occasional note. "Jim [Gates] does more for her than you or Herb," Boom indignantly wrote Charlie. "You don't care to remember when I helped you out. I could paper a wall with the checks I've given you—and what have you ever done for me? *Nothing*—even when you've been able to." But perhaps he remembered that Charlie had, in fact, been generous in various ways (inviting Boom to live at Six Chimney Farm, for instance)—and then, things were just complicated in Charlie's case; anyway he declined to mail such an irate letter.* No such compunction applied, however, where Herb was concerned, and for his pains Boom received a scalding rebuttal from Bob, who hadn't forgotten what it was like squeaking by on her husband's piddling salary at the paper mill while Charlie and Boom gadded about Europe—and besides: why should a lonely, aging homosexual complain about the "privilege" of taking care of his mother? "My Gosh, Fred," Bob wrote, "she is the only family you

---

* An incomplete draft of which was found among Boom's papers at Dartmouth.

have [in Malaga] and I should think you would be so darned glad you had someone to think of besides yourself you would be down on your knees thanking the good Lord." At any rate Boom continued to be a dutiful son, mostly at his own expense.

And he was nothing but grieved over his mother's decline at the beginning of 1962. "It's all she can do to get downstairs for her noon soap opera and then she dozes off many times during the day," he wrote his niece Sarah. "She may pull out of it as she has before. I hope so." Within a few weeks, though, she died, under circumstances that must have rankled. Charlie had been visiting while their mother lay on her deathbed, and at one point Boom stepped out to the post office for that day's voluminous mail: the big event of his day, after all. When he returned, the mother he'd so lovingly tended these many years was dead. As Charlie would always tell it, "Well, Boom was off somewhere, but I was here and she died in my arms . . ."*

IN THE END Boom forgave his brother (almost) everything, and the two even seemed to rediscover the pleasure of each other's company—so many wonderful memories in common, from Newark to the Riviera! And nobody was a more devoted admirer of Charlie's work, as the latter knew well: "To my younger brother, Frederick Storrier Jackson," he wrote for an elaborate "Card of Thanks" he'd hoped to include in his last novel, *A Second-Hand Life*, "who has always touchingly believed there is no writer living like you know whom, and whose blind but pure faith, goodness, and generosity of spirit have helped me through years of discouragement, ill-health, and just plain laziness." Finally, not least, Boom was always an attentive uncle to Charlie's daughters—especially Sarah, who moved to Manhattan as a young woman and often accompanied Boom to the theater and such, as well as visiting him in the "safe haven" of Malaga. "I was so lucky to have these two men in my life who just

---

* Charlie's own grief should not be discounted. "Foolish woman or not, she was his mother," he'd written in an autobiographical story, "Parting at Morning" (1953), in which a long-suffering son anticipates his mother's death. "And once the tie had been severed, you were probably alone in the world in a way you had never been before." The day of Sal's death—January 27—Charlie phoned his family and said he'd be coming right home to Connecticut and proceeding to Newark the next day for the funeral. When he arrived that night and found his daughter Kate had gone bowling with a friend from Sarah Lawrence, he was *furious* over what he perceived to be her callousness.

adored me," she said of her sweet-natured father and uncle, though Charlie (by far the more problematic of the two) wasn't altogether approving of his daughter's bond with Boom, grumbling that homosexual men like to be "seen" with attractive young women . . .

More and more, though, Boom was content to be a homebody in Malaga, and why not? He had everything he wanted there, including a man who loved him to the exclusion of all others: "I don't seem to enjoy anyone but you and everyone else tires me so," Jim wrote him during one of his vacations, teasing him on another occasion (when he was in Sausalito with louche Bick) to "have a swell time . . . and let your conscience be your guide." The two shared everything—houses, cars, pets ("Annie," Jim would say to one of his many dachshunds, "show Barbara what girls do in the park," whereupon the dog would roll over on her back)—and during the last decade of Boom's life, they bought a place together in Strathmere, New Jersey, south of Ocean City, since Boom had always loved the beach and enjoyed showing off his legs to the end. "Jim is still out of control periodically," Rhoda wrote in March 1972, nine months after Boom's death, when Jim continued to weep at any reminder of his beloved.

Chapter Twelve

The Outer Edges

On May 13, 1946—after *The Fall of Valor* had been written, edited, and tinkered with for the last time—a weary Jackson wrote the following resolution: "It's about time I stopped dishing Krafft-Ebbing [*sic*] material in novels." At the same time, however, he was afflicted with an idea that was an even *more* sensational foray into aberrant psychology than either of his first two books: a story based on ghastly real-life murders. As he wrote Brackett and Wilder (whose interest he hoped to pique), "When a social crime is committed, all of society is guilty, not just the murderer; and the victim of the murder is not the person killed but the one who does the killing." The book would be a "very fast tour de force like Lost Weekend," and contain some such word as "contagion" or "infection" in the title.

Jackson's inspiration was the Edward Haight case, the details of which had haunted him ever since he'd read newspaper accounts in September 1942. Haight was only sixteen when he stole a station wagon in Stamford, Connecticut, and coaxed two little girls to go for a ride: Margaret Lynch and her sister, Helen, aged seven and nine. Helen was tied up in the trunk while Haight tried raping her little sister, whom he finally strangled when she continued to struggle; then (after stopping for lunch in Bedford, New York) he drove to a secluded area, raped Helen, and ran over her with the car several times before tossing her mangled body into a creek. That Haight's childhood had been grim—he lived in a kind of squatter's shack, the son of a convicted thief—hardly explained his almost flamboyant lack of remorse: during the trial he either smiled or looked bored, twiddling his thumbs and laughing out loud when photographs of his victims were produced; no surprise, then, when he became the youngest person ever to die in Sing Sing's electric chair. Though such cases were exceptional in their brutality, rampant media coverage had stoked public hysteria, until most states adopted draconian laws meant to preempt the crimes of sexual psychopaths, resulting in lengthy prison terms even for minor offenses, often including homosexuality—which might explain, to some extent, Jackson's notion of "contagion" or universal guilt. Also, of course, he was the father of two girls, and so felt Haight's crime all the more keenly.

Fearing he'd managed yet again to hit on a subject that precluded a big movie deal, Jackson reluctantly agreed to write an assuasive seventy-page outline for his agents to shop around to the studios. Bernice Baumgarten, for one, was unimpressed and even a bit puzzled by this document: Jackson's protagonist was a middle-class family man, Jim Harris, who feels morbidly connected to a murderous Haight-like pedophile because he, Harris, is having an extramarital affair. "As the outline stands," Baumgarten wrote, "I am simply not convinced that Jim Harris could sufficiently identify himself with the crime to feel even a remote sense of guilt." For the story to work at all, she thought, Jackson would have to involve Harris more directly with the murder—but really such a book was bound to be "minor," at best, and Baumgarten advised him to put it aside until he'd written something more substantial.

But Jackson needed money *now*, and with Irving Lazar's less discriminating assistance, he managed to sell the outline to MGM for what he always implied was $200,000 outright ("which ain't hay, even by Texas standards") but was actually a partial option of $50,000, with the balance due only if the studio liked the final product. Either way it was a sweet payday for what Jackson figured—mistakenly—would amount to a single summer's worth of work. "The novel is a horrible headache," he wrote on August 26, 1947, complaining that his deal with MGM seemed to inhibit him. "Somebody said that when you write for profit, it ends up being not only bad art but bad business. Still, my story is so good it seems I can hardly fail."

Granted, there were many distractions. Shortly after he'd returned from Hollywood the previous May, he'd driven to New York to spend a few days shmoozing with Lazar (who was slated to serve as "associate producer" of the MGM adaptation), but Jackson's ego was plainly in a delicate state: "It wasn't the same old Lazar," he wrote the Gershwins. "Maybe he's got too many irons in the fire these days to have time for me . . ." He also went to the theater with Mrs. Leonard Lyons, lunched with Ruby Schinasi at "21," and attended cocktail parties with the likes of Bennett Cerf and Dorothy Gish. Meanwhile—though he was always careful to drink Coca-Cola in public (while fortified with Seconal)—rumors began to spread that he'd fallen off the wagon, despite his almost operatic denials: "Nothing could make me take another drink," he insisted. "My house could burn down, my capacities could fail, my wife and children could be killed, and I still would not drink." In his own mind, perhaps, he qualified "drink" as meaning hard liquor, and of course he said nothing about his pill habit, nor did he tell loved ones of his dread that he was obscurely on the brink of disaster. While dictating to a secretary each day from ten to four, he found himself thinking more and more—pacing, checking his watch—about the beer he could start drinking at five, a blessed relief from work that wasn't going at all well.

Most of his anxiety was vented against Rhoda, whose every utterance seemed to irritate him. Either she didn't take his work seriously enough, cheerfully asking what he'd written that day ("in accents that were reminiscent of his 4th Grade teacher asking about his pet hobby," as he put it in *Farther and Wilder*), or, worse, she'd take it very seriously indeed, gravely inquiring about his progress when there were bills to be paid. Her own literary tastes ran closer to Erle Stanley Gardner, but she could be censorious when she thought Charlie was pursuing an idea that wasn't in his (their) better interest. She'd reacted coolly to his murder story, at a time when he was still bristling over her attitude toward *The Fall of Valor* ("a book I know you always deplored and were often snidely 'amused at,' " he wrote her in 1968, three months before his death). And ever since his return from New York, she couldn't help noticing that he was on the verge of collapse—so "jittery" he didn't bother to deny he was taking pills again, though he insisted he was well enough for another long stay in Hollywood beginning July 9th. Rhoda begged him to reconsider, worried "he'd really go to pieces and perhaps even die" if left to his own devices, but her "nagging" seemed only to make him more determined. "He's a terrible addict," she wrote despairingly to Boom.

I don't know how or when something will help him. He has to find something. I realized yesterday really, for the first time, how he managed to stop drinking. He held on to the fact that he was a great writer and he'd show everybody. When he got fame, that thing that sustained him all the time was gone—and he has nothing yet to replace it. Of course I always hoped it would be love—a happy family life, a feeling of full living in a generous sense. Not in present-giving, but in giving of himself without doing it for show and self-gratification. He must lose his utter egoism some way before he can ever find a peace that will relieve him from addiction.

At any rate he ended up going to the hospital rather than to Hollywood, though it was an uphill battle for Rhoda. At the very time he was serenely telling Baumgarten that July was "the great month of the year" in Orford—he was working well mornings and evenings, and knocking off afternoons "just to lie about on the lawn and see the lovely place we live in"—Rhoda was demanding he get help, and finally confiscated his Seconal only to discover he had a stash of some other mysterious pill he'd managed to obtain in New York. One night he washed these down with a lot of beer, accusing her of being "the cause of all his troubles" and announcing that he was leaving her for good, and yes (tearfully) the children, too. A couple days later, though, he was back in Mary Hitchcock. ("On May 28, 1947, you filled a prescription for Mr. Charles Jackson," Dr. Gundersen wrote a drug store in the Barclay Hotel. This "called for some capsules which I assume contained some sort of sedative . . .") By early August he was "in good shape" again, or so Rhoda reported: a bit restless, but sober and able to laugh, if not write.

THINGS BECAME unequivocally better that fall, when the Jacksons moved to a luxurious townhouse at 140 East 65th Street. New York, for Charlie, was conducive to work: he got into a healthier schedule, for one thing, since he wasn't as tempted to stay up all night writing (or trying to); rather he quit around six o'clock and went out with charming, like-minded friends. Penitent about his bad behavior that summer, he was trying to be a better companion to Rhoda, who in turn was tactful when she suspected, from time to time, that he was still taking pills. "Only when his speech thickens can I really tell," she wrote Boom. "But he is working so well, and it's so important for him to, that I try to quell the uneasiness I feel." The important part was that he did seem the old Charlie again, more or less, and Rhoda was determined to be supportive.

Most heartening of all was his decision to seek extensive psycho-analysis. The catalyst had been a last, embarrassing pill jag that August: Rhoda had gone to Maine with her sister and their children, and when she phoned home she "discovered [Charlie] was off again." A doctor had interceded, and for many weeks afterward the despondent Charlie had been "lost"—"play[ing] solitaire for hours on end"—until finally he was forced to admit he could no longer stay sober without professional help.

He chose one of the most eminent psychiatrists in the country, Law-rence S. Kubie, president of the New York Psychoanalytic Society, whose clients included (or would include) Tennessee Williams, William Inge, and the actor Clifton Webb, all of whom were conflicted over their homo-sexuality. Kubie was particularly interested in creative people—though some said it was *celebrity* that interested him foremost ("he was what was called even then a 'star fucker,' " said playwright Arthur Laurents)—and perhaps because of his experience with such people he'd been asked, in 1942, to draft a paragraph titled "Sexual Perversions" that was added to the Army mobilization regulations: "Persons habitually or occasion-ally engaged in homosexual or other perverse sexual practices," Kubie wrote, were "unsuitable for military service." And how did one identify a homosexual? Kubie listed three of the most salient traits: "feminine bodily characteristics," "effeminacy in dress and manner," and "a patu-lous rectum."

Homosexuality, in fact, seemed to fascinate Kubie almost as much as creativity per se, and he'd been a great admirer of *The Fall of Valor*. "I respect the book completely," he wrote the novelist Laura Z. Hobson (*Gentleman's Agreement*, et al.), a former lover who'd probably recom-mended his services to Jackson. Kubie's main qualm with *Valor* had to do with Jackson's handling of Ethel Grandin, whose bitterness on learning of her husband's proclivities had not, Kubie thought, been explicated in properly clinical terms. As he wrote Hobson:

> Blame it rather on the ancient and primitive and universal envy of the phallus. Her anger says, "How dare he, even if only in fantasy or impulse, share with another man that which they both already have, and which he merely loans to me so rarely and so briefly?" This is the inevitable source of her unforgiving hate; because for Grandin to turn to another man would seem to her to prove the truth of what

she had always believed and dreaded anyhow, namely that men are whole and beautiful, and that women (and more particularly herself) are mutilated and repulsive.

But again, Kubie deemed the book basically sound, and couldn't help wondering ("as I do so often") whether it would benefit a "first-rate creative writer" such as Jackson, who surmised so much by intuition alone, to learn "more precise and more technical knowledge of human psychology." Be that as it may, Kubie did find the novel's ending misguided, since he thought Grandin had already gained the "insight" that would "free him emotionally toward Ethel"—in other words, that his homosexuality had effectively been *cured*—when he made that implausible pass at Cliff: "I suspect that something in Jackson made him punish Grandin in this fashion."

On that last point, at least, he was on to something, as he would learn firsthand when Jackson began appearing six days a week at his office near the Metropolitan Museum. Later Jackson would bitterly claim that Kubie had charged him an exorbitant fee ("$40 a throw"), but at the time Kubie allegedly told his friend and eventual publisher, Roger Straus,* that he was treating Jackson for *free*. As Straus remembered in 1978:

> I said, "Larry, how come you are doing it free?" He said, "You know, I don't like to do this because it's just a question of policy, and I like Charlie,"—everybody loved Charlie, he was very popular—"But he is such a prototypical person, he has this terrible problem about his homosexuality, and it makes him juvenile, and in order to sort of keep himself going he goes into pills, he goes into alcohol, and it's just a terrible adolescent thing that he has."

One wonders whether "juvenile" is the right word for a married father of two who feels anxious and even suicidal about an orientation that was perceived by the greater part of society—abetted in no small part by the psychoanalytic establishment—as a sickness and a crime. In 1948, it was none other than Kubie who most notably rose to his colleagues' defense when Alfred Kinsey published *Sexual Behavior in the Human Male*, which

---

* Farrar, Straus and Cudahy published a 1961 reprint of Kubie's *Neurotic Distortion of the Creative Process*. As of 1947, Straus had yet to become Jackson's own publisher and best (male) friend.

found that the psychoanalytic view of homosexuality as "abnormal" was *not* supported by evidence suggesting that it was, in fact, a quite prevalent practice: "A choice of a partner in a sexual relation becomes more significant only because society demands that there be a particular choice in this matter," Kinsey wrote, "and does not so often dictate one's choice of food and of clothing." Kubie—perceived as a relative moderate in such matters—replied that the actual position among most psychoanalysts was that homosexuality could be viewed "as either normal or neurotic or . . . a mixture of both," but that certainly it was Kubie's view that neurosis was more likely to be found among homosexuals than not. *Time* magazine, with no little glee, subsequently announced that Kubie had "unraveled the Kinsey report," and quoted him in somewhat franker terms on the subject: "The implication that because homosexuality is prevalent we must accept is as 'normal,' or as a happy and healthy way of life," said Kubie, "is wholly unwarranted." An understandable position, given that much of Kubie's own practice was devoted to "curing" or at least mitigating homosexuality.

The gist of what Kubie told Jackson, as the latter would recall seven years later, was as follows: "That I had a deep psychological aversion to 'success,' that I suffered from a compulsion to toss it all overboard, and that I had not really wanted it in the first place." This was in keeping with the common neo-Freudian idea of homosexuals as "psychic masochists"—espoused most notoriously by Edmund Bergler, the highly esteemed author of a 1956 manifesto, *Homosexuality: Disease or Way of Life?* (a strictly rhetorical title). According to Bergler and most of his colleagues, the male homosexual remained unconsciously angry at his mother for not giving him enough breast milk, and since he could not punish *her* (and risk even further neglect) he became his own worst enemy—mostly by denying himself the love of women, but also by sabotaging his life in various other ways. Bergler ended his book on a strident but oddly optimistic note, pointing out (in italics) that this loathsome "disease" was, after all, treatable:

> *The only effective way of fighting and counteracting homosexuality would be the wide dissemination of the knowledge that there is nothing glamorous about suffering from the disease known as homosexuality, that the disease can be cured, and that this apparently sexual disorder is invariably coupled with severe unconscious self-damage that will inevitably show up outside the sexual sphere as well, because it embraces the entire personality.*

But stridency, vis-à-vis Jackson at least, wasn't the problem with Kubie. Though he could be quite confrontational when the situation warranted it—the psychoanalyst, he wrote, "must be merciless in forcing a patient to face his neurosis," which might explain why he saw fit to scream at Tennessee Williams in imitation of the playwright's father—toward Jackson he assumed a more conventional "tabula rasa" approach, sitting behind the patient in almost total silence. As Jackson wrote Dorothea Straus in 1951, "I never knew if he were doing a cross-word puzzle while I rambled on, if he had gone to sleep, or even if he had left the room." Soon enough Jackson decided, in effect, that he could listen to himself talk for free, and terminated therapy. Kubie, however, endeavored to stay in touch. In 1953 he expressed an interest in chatting about Charlie with their mutual friend Dorothea ("give Kubie a wide berth," Jackson warned her), and occasionally he commented on Jackson's work: "This is the kind of thing that we psychologists hope literature will do," he wrote of "The Boy Who Ran Away," what with its satisfying implications of homosexual masochism and immaturity.

JACKSON WOULD later consider his third novel, *The Outer Edges*, another relative failure, frankly admitting that he was "over-drugged" when he wrote it. But then, he was serving two masters—Mammon (that is, MGM) and his own artistic conscience—and under the circumstances he was even more blocked than usual. Once he resumed taking drugs, though, the novel proceeded very breezily indeed: after scrapping a number of false starts, he began the final version on October 10, 1947, and finished exactly two months later. All that remained was the vexing question of a catchy title (one "that would suit both the movies and Rinehart"), and among the many he considered were *The Lost Generation*, *Rendezvous with Murder*, *This Is Murder*, *I'll Pray for You, Pray for Me*, *I'll Shed No Tears*, *No Tears to Shed*, and *In Every Man*. Flummoxed, he sent the manuscript to his friend Dorothy Parker, who was known to have a knack for such things. "I've got it!" she announced over the phone: "*Crime and Punishment, Junior.*"

Given his relative haste and method of composition, Jackson worried that his latest novel was somewhat less than first-rate, though his publisher and even Rhoda claimed to like it, as did many of the myriad friends to whom he naturally sent advance copies. Charles Brackett, who'd been less than enthusiastic about *The Fall of Valor* ("I think you listened to too many people"), found *The Outer Edges* "an advance" and noted that its hero, Jim Harron,* was "self-portraiture at its best." Fredric Wertham was also warmly complimentary as ever, applauding the author for showing "greater understanding and insight than did the psychiatrists who handled the [Haight] case." Rinehart & Company was going to considerable lengths to promote the novel, commissioning a profile of Jackson by Lincoln Barnett,† an author and *Life* editor who perhaps had something to do with an article that appeared in the magazine a week before *The Outer Edges* was published: "Authors' Ordeal," about Jackson's appearance (with Cleveland Amory and three others) at an event sponsored by the Richmond Junior League. Jackson, looking polite but rather pained, was featured in an inset column titled "How to Question an Author":

"How does it feel to be famous?" (*Sir, won't you have a drink?*) . . .

"What's your new book about?" (*You really pick some odd subjects—well, I mean alcoholism and homosexuals, you know.*)

"Why did you become a writer?" (*Did you just start writing the story of your own life?*)

This, according to *Life*, was the "most grueling and most embarrassing experience" that an author is forced to endure, and Jackson "was the favorite target of inquisitors at Richmond."

Meanwhile MGM decided to drop its option: "It was an interesting idea, and Jackson has carried it out," their reader commented, adding however that the narrative was too "disjointed" for effective dramatization. Billy Wilder had also been "very much interested," according to the *Times*, and his friendship with Jackson pretty much ended when he decided to pass. That left producer and director Robert Rossen, who bought the rights for the "announced" price of fifty thousand dollars— that is to say, considerably less: since he wanted to pay a sizable fee under the table to blacklisted screenwriter Dalton Trumbo (one of the "Hollywood Ten"), Rossen could only afford five thousand dollars up front for Jackson, with thirty thousand dollars payable once production began.

---

* Emended from the more common *Harris*, perhaps in fear of a veritable horde of Jim Harrises coming out of the woodwork to protest their association with a fictional adulterer.

† Rinehart tried placing this long and quite literate piece, "The Lost Novelist," in various magazines, to no avail; it was finally published as a separate promotional brochure.

The following summer (1949) Columbia announced it was ready to start shooting *The Outer Edges* in November ("I couldn't be happier about it," said Jackson, more strapped for cash than ever), but Rossen apparently decided not to follow *All the King's Men* with a movie about a child murderer.

Hopes for the book, anyway, had been high. An early "Forecast for Buyers" in *Publishers Weekly* was nothing but upbeat, given the "big ad campaign" planned by Rinehart for this "effective and skillful novel," as well as the impressive sales of Jackson's previous efforts—which, as it happened, would decidedly *not* prove the case this time around: within two months, sales of *The Outer Edges* had petered out just shy of the twenty thousand mark. Baumgarten blamed it on a "very bad book year," since after all the novel had been mostly well received, at least at the outset. Nash K. Burger, in the *Times Book Review* of May 27, 1948, called it a "fast-moving, many-sided narrative," and while he thought Jackson hadn't treated his theme "as extensively or profoundly as he might have," the novel "could hardly be improved on" within its limited scope. Three days later, in the daily *Times*, William DuBois gushed without reservation (or nuance) that Jackson had "rung another bull's-eye" that was bound to "hold a wide public spellbound": "[He] belongs among the truly creative writers of his time—among the novelists capable of dissecting our present-day jitter-and-fritter down to its benzedrine-ridden heart." Similarly, in the *Saturday Review*, Lee Rogow applauded the book as "craftsmanlike, tough, exciting . . . a considerable growth in the author's interests, and in his talent."

Sterling North's early demurral in the *New York Post* was, alas, more indicative of things to come: Jackson's "theory that all men are potentially criminals," North wrote, not only helped explain the vast circulation of the " 'yellow' press" as well as "brutal and vicious" comic books, but also "the success of Mr. Jackson's novels." A week later Lewis Gannett essentially agreed in the New York *Herald Tribune*, calling *The Outer Edges* "a tabloid blow-up, in the form of a novel," whereupon the graver weekly magazines tended to follow suit in more elaborate, punitive terms. That a murderer is not dissimilar to the general run of mankind, wrote J. M. Lalley in *The New Yorker*, was a "rather shallow" point of view on Jackson's part, albeit symptomatic "of the new literary puritanism, with its insistence on the total depravity of human nature and its doctrine that grace consists in recognizing the inherent evil in oneself." And doubtless Jackson winced at John Woodburn's judgment, in *The New Republic*, that he had "whipped out a quickie while his publisher breathed down his neck," and never mind a late, perfunctory slur in *Time* ("The Lost Effort") that *The Outer Edges* was a "chapter from Freud-made-easy."

The latter judgments are too harsh. Certainly whole libraries of socio-cultural texts could be devoted to Jackson's main themes, and hence such a brief, impressionistic novel is bound to seem shallow at points. Simply as a piece of craftsmanship, though, *The Outer Edges* is in fact (as per Brackett and others) an "advance" on Jackson's earlier work—certainly not superior in a larger sense to *The Lost Weekend*, but arguably more successful in terms of a tight, conventional narrative, and far more engaging than the dreary *Fall of Valor*. "I find that the faster I write this one, the better," Jackson remarked to Baumgarten, sensing that the intellectual demands of his book were potentially overwhelming, and that he was better off sticking as closely as possible to the basic mechanics of plot.

The primary thematic questions may be boiled down as follows: Why *are* we so fascinated by acts of gruesome perversity, as sensationalized by the modern American media? What is it about humanity, and our society in particular, that makes us so susceptible? As Jackson would have it, there is more than a touch of guilt in our titillation—a sense of vicarious urgency bubbling up from the murky unconscious, and thus the novel's epigraph from Plutarch: "Geographers crowd into the outer edges of their maps the parts of the world which they know nothing about, adding a note, 'What lies beyond is sandy desert full of wild beasts,' or 'blind marsh,' or 'Scythian cold,' or 'frozen sea.'" Such "universal guilt" is shared by the protagonist, Jim Harron, "an ordinary fellow" who makes good money as public relations director for a major airline. Lest Harron seem ordinary to the point of Grandin-like dullness, though, the author touches him up with chiaroscuro borrowed from his own personality: an "irrepressible boyish ebullience" that can change in a moment to petulance, an essential "gayety and kindness" that is matched or surpassed by an "inaccessible, resisting, foreign" darkness. Harron—a doting father and husband, who usually feels only minor qualms about keeping a mistress (though he sometimes suspects "depths of viciousness" in himself)—is tipped into a panic of self-loathing by the widely publicized rape and murder of two little girls, until he finds himself identifying with both the victims' father, Aylmer Smith, and their murderer, Aaron Adams: "Was it possible to suffer bereavement of children he had never known? Was it possible for a man to feel guilty of a crime he did not commit?" Unfortunately for the novel, one is inclined to answer *no*—or rather not as bereaved and guilty as Harron, who ultimately seeks out Aylmer Smith and offers money in restitution for his own far-fetched sense of kinship with the murderer. "If his trip to see the father of the victims has any drama it escaped me as it will thousands," wrote MGM's reader, echoing Baumgarten's perplexity on the same point. Which is to say, heterosexual adultery was a weak objective-correlative for the more criminal (circa 1948) homosexual kind that haunted the author, and even then the connection with homicidal pedophilia was tenuous at best.

But critics were more apt to complain about Jackson's characterization of the murderer, Aaron Adams, whose callous brutality seemed too awful to be true. Mel Heimer, a journalist who'd covered the Haight case, remarked that such criticism made him "shake [his] head sadly, because he was real, just the way Jackson drew him . . ." Adams embodies the banality of evil, years before the phrase was coined. Gratified by all the attention he's getting, the childlike murderer recounts his crime "with intelligence and evident enjoyment":

> "I strangled one of them with a handkerchief and the other one with my belt. I had fun with them for awhile, and then just kept driving around. Jeepers, I must have traveled a couple hundred miles, today. . . ."
>   "Did you do it after they were dead, or before?"
>   "Do what?"
>   "Molest them."
>   "Oh, before. What do you think?"

Just as an alcoholic is in the grip of forces beyond his control, Jackson suggests that a psychopath like Adams is another kind of Everyman, unbridled by such an elusive and perhaps imaginary concept as "free will": "His fate cried out; he had gone as relentlessly and surely to his fulfillment as if others had driven him to it. The moment arrived, and he, not the children, was the unwitting, the unwilling victim." The second part of this formulation is a bit much—it's hard to see how the children are less victims than the murderer—but to a disturbing degree Jackson does succeed in humanizing Adams as "a young primitive, happy to be alive," who indulges his viciousness simply because it's his nature, his "fate," to do so. And such nature does not entertain remorse, but rather longs for ever greater stimulation: "I'd like to have a big four-engine bomber," Adams says at the end, " . . . a great big one . . . and fly high over a big city. . . ."

A longing for excitement is another thing Adams has in common with the rest of humanity ("It was only a question of degree," as Grandin mused in a different but not unrelated context)—indeed, his rampage is explained in part by a desire to re-create the thrill he'd felt one "famous night last winter when his parents' house had been destroyed by fire and his mother burned alive." Among the postwar middle class, meanwhile, is an all but rabid need to be entertained with accounts of sex and violence, the better to compensate for the bleak, repressive boredom of a society where material comfort is the highest good. Jackson is especially mindful of the plight of suburban matrons such as Harron's wife, Ruth, and the Bovaryesque Fan French: Ruth's "deepest interest"—essentially the only one permitted her—is her husband, whereas "his interests were scattered and diverse, absorbed equally in his home and his wife and his child, his work, his hobbies, his outside pleasures, and other people"; as for Fan French's husband—a smugly prosperous oaf—he likes to point out that he'd never hire a chauffeur because driving him to the train station "gave Fan something to do." Desperate not to seem as otiose as she feels, Fan becomes morbidly aware of her housemaids, Hazel and Edith, and wracks her brain for ways to seem occupied when one of them enters a room; otherwise her inner life is dominated by fantasies afforded by a suave radio personality, Curley Kendrick, whose four o'clock program is the high point of her day. To be sure, Fan doesn't ultimately resort to murder by way of transcending the emptiness of her life, but she does end up sleeping with Kendrick, whose real-life loutishness leads to a wan epiphany: "There didn't seem to be anything left but to settle down to the life of another Westchester wife and accept that fact. Try and stay busy when Hazel and Edith were in the room, drive Del to the station and be sure he was on time for his train, wait for the new magazines to come. A hell of a life but that's what it was."

Fan French's story is one of several recurring threads in the novel that have only a slight connection to the main narrative (Fan's car is forced off the road by the murderer at one point). That Jackson found his themes a little too capacious for his own good is suggested by his last-minute idea to include one more discrete vignette (as Chapter Sixty-one, which would have followed Fan's shabby tryst with Kendrick) about a genteel nymphomaniac named Jane Sommeier. This further illustration of boredom and anomie would eventually be turned into a short story ("Janie") and later cannibalized into *A Second-Hand Life*, but was deemed a little too random even for so fragmented a work as *The Outer Edges*. Not that the episodic narrative is always a liability: jumping from scene to scene makes for a lively reading experience, and was probably a nice relief for the author, too, as he declined to fret overmuch about fine points of architecture or character development. But sometimes his facility seems slipshod to a fault: dialogue would never be Jackson's forte, and his promiscuous use of words like "jeepers" and "cripes" ("Why jeepers, what in cripes was he waiting for?") fails to evoke his murderer's psyche in any very nuanced way, and again he resorts to dismal clichés (Harron's mistress sends "hot shivers of excitement up his spine"), all of which serve as reminders that the novel was dictated to a secretary, hastily, with the movies in mind.

For all that, though, *The Outer Edges* showed signs of growing virtuosity. No less a novelist than Angus Wilson, reviewing the British edition for *The Listener*, thought Jackson was the man to write a definitive satire "upon the sad, sophisticated, sex-ridden never-grown-ups that appear to form the business community of the rich American suburbs." At the very least, one had to wonder what Jackson might achieve if he ever buckled down, took his time, and really focused his talent (soberly?) on the right material.

WHEN MGM PASSED on its option, and book sales began to slump, Jackson was forced to take another Hollywood screenwriting job beginning in July 1948. The project began, at least, auspiciously: for two thousand dollars a week he was hired to write a screenplay titled *The Third Secret* for Lewis Milestone, who in 1930 had directed one of Jackson's favorite movies, *All Quiet on the Western Front*. Indeed, theirs was something of a mutual admiration society. Not only had Milestone ("Milly") read Jackson's novels, but he adored "Palm Sunday" and "Rachel's Summer" too—or so it seemed one night in Chasen's, when Jackson observed the volatile Bessarabian "[holding] an audience of about ten spellbound" with detailed accounts of both stories. Jackson had also managed to endear himself during his first Hollywood summer in 1944, when he'd been pressed against a wall by Milestone's wife and regaled for some two hours about one nugatory topic after another; whenever Jackson endeavored to reply, she'd stare at him blankly and resume her spiel. "Only after a long time did I get it," Jackson wrote: "she is stone deaf, must do all the talking because."

That summer Rhoda finally went out to the Coast to see what it was all about, reporting to Baumgarten that her trip had been "fun, if a little wearing." Probably more than a little wearing. A few days after her return, on August 1, Charlie received a bill for three hundred dollars from one Gabriel Segall, a psychiatrist, whose nurse Julie had written a chirpy note addressed to "General Jackson," congratulating him on his "strong and courageous battle": "May I add, General, that your adjuncts are right proud of you and also of any part they may have played in assisting you to reach this victory. Perhaps we are a good team!" The battle in question had been the beginning of what appeared to be a psychotic break on Jackson's part, doubtless exacerbated by pills and alcohol; since a quick recovery was imperative—before, that is, word spread that Charles Jackson was off the rails again—he'd engaged a private hospital room, where he was intensively treated by Dr. Segall and his staff. As he would recount the episode in *Farther and Wilder*, his nurse had sat by the bed "pretending to read a detective story" while the terrified, sweat-drenched patient watched a sinister woman peeking at him from behind a canvas screen—a "vicious vigil" that finally caused him to shoot up in bed, "like a trap unsprung," and complain that he must be "losing [his] mind," because he saw a woman who wasn't there. The nurse assured him that he *wasn't* losing his mind—because, after all, he *knew* she wasn't there.

The fact is, for most of Jackson's adult life—more and more as he got older—he displayed all the classic symptoms of bipolar disorder, or manic depression, as it was then known. "But it was humiliating, dumbfounding, and defeating," he wrote in *Farther and Wilder*, "that these conflicting extremes of well-being and despair, achievement and collapse, could run together side by side in the same life—an ironic and deadly paradox, like fatal poison and healing antidote indiscriminately mixed in the same vessel." In *The Lost Weekend*, too, Don Birnam reflects on his "pattern" of "peaks and depths," while Jackson himself often observed that his favorite contemporary poet was the manic-depressive Robert Lowell: "[His] poems, which I love, *couldn't* be more personal & intimate unless they began, each one, 'Dear Charlie. . . .' " In those days, symptoms of bipolar disorder were usually viewed from a psychodynamic perspective—as being largely the result of unconscious conflicts, in other words, rather than a chemical imbalance that required a more biomedical approach. Once the disease became better understood, after Jackson's death, his family realized he'd almost certainly been bipolar to some degree. This would help explain the "boyish ebullience," the bursts of frantic creativity, coupled with long spells of utter apathy and self-loathing ("Cured, I am frizzled, stale and small," Lowell had written in one of Jackson's favorite poems), to say nothing of the self-medicating substance abuse, wild spending sprees, grandiosity, and occasionally voracious libido.

That summer in Hollywood, Jackson reconciled with his former friend Sally Benson (the writer who, a few years back, had butchered his only *New Yorker* story), when the two spent a long evening confiding their very similar problems: Benson, too, had a long history of drug and alcohol abuse related to an ungovernably erratic temperament. "She is about mid-way between Judy Garland and me (if you know what I mean)," Charlie wrote Rhoda (who did). Garland, too, was given to wild extremes of "euphoria and suffering," as Jackson put it in *Farther and Wilder*, where Garland appears as "Maxine." During his previous trip to Hollywood the year before (May 1947), Jackson had visited the soundstage where Garland was shooting a scene for *The Pirate*—a wrenching experience he recalled in his novel. Garland ("primed with dexedrine") was on the verge of a breakdown, and Louis Mayer had hired a psychiatrist to mind her on the set; "her brown calf's eyes had struck to [Don's] heart," Jackson wrote of Maxine, "but, for his own salvation, he had rigorously rejected her at the same instant." Jackson—trying to stave off hysteria himself—knew only too well what was coming, and sure enough Garland soon succumbed to an uncontrollable screaming fit at the Gershwins'; finally, just before *The Pirate* finished shooting, she slit her wrists when she caught Vincente Minnelli in bed with another man. A year later she was still fragile, and Jackson was neither surprised nor (very) disappointed when she cancelled their only dinner engagement, explaining that her two-year-old, Liza, had measles.*

Jackson liked to say that the only "great originals" ever to come out of Hollywood were Chaplin, Garbo, and Garland, and during that 1948 visit he had much better luck with the first two. He'd met Chaplin the year before, and during a dinner at the Ferrers he was delighted when Chaplin greeted him warmly and chided him for not being in touch, inviting him to a lavish party two weeks later. Thus Jackson was sitting

---

* Many have concluded that Garland was bipolar, including her biographer Gerald Clarke. As for her friendship with Jackson, the two rarely met after 1947. Jackson took his family to the New York premiere of *A Star Is Born* in the fall of 1954, and several years later his daughter Sarah introduced herself to Garland after a concert. "This is the 'dimsal girl'!" the latter announced, remembering Charlie's nickname for Sarah.

near Chaplin's pool, chatting with the actress Constance Collier, when he almost fell over "dead of shock": *Garbo* had just walked by! Jackson couldn't bring himself to approach the beloved apparition, until Chaplin himself insisted he come along and be introduced. "Well, she couldn't have been nicer," he wrote Rhoda. "It's futile to try to tell you how stunning she is—in every way: voice, looks, eyes, speech, manner, charm, and, surprisingly, real humor and wit. She talked to me again and again during the afternoon, and seemed to know that I had long admired her and thus she was specially nice to me, as if giving something of herself." Her pettish refusal to meet him four years before (as "Miss Harriet Brown," *re* his abortive *Seagull*) apparently didn't come up. "Between Chaplin and Garbo, it was Quite A Day," he happily concluded of the two idols whose framed, inscribed portraits ("From Charlie to Charlie" in Chaplin's case) he would avidly flaunt to the end.

Suffice it to say, Lewis Milestone would not appear in this pantheon. For the first few weeks, Jackson's relations with "Milly" were so serene that his only complaint was having "to eat strange foods like shashlik." By the end of August, the honeymoon was almost over. For a long week the two had holed up in Milestone's beach house in Ventura County, bickering over the script; the director, said Jackson, was "all childish stormy ego, which is okay so long as it is yessed, but bad when disagreed with." Still, he felt confident that his finished product was good enough to mollify even Milestone—but he was mistaken. The director, he decided, was "nothing less than a pig—wants much too much, and I told him I would never work for him again (nor would any other writer I could get to and warn) if he paid me ten thousand a week." Milestone had demanded he remain in Hollywood an extra week (at least) to work on revisions, but Jackson arranged to depart in keeping with his original contract, quite certain his script would "be entirely re-written and ruined" whether he stayed or not.

A copy of Jackson's script remains among his papers—a curious artifact. "There is the secret you dare tell only your best friend," reads a portentous "FOREWORD" that was to scroll among the opening credits. "There is the secret you dare tell only yourself. There is the secret you dare not even tell yourself. This story is about the *third* of these secrets." The man with a secret is Frank Ransome, an editor at a sophisticated magazine ("like the old VANITY FAIR") who begins to notice he's being followed by a mysterious person in a white suit and mourning band. This proves to be Harry Layne, an old friend whom Ransome hasn't seen in nine years—ever since he broke off an affair with Layne's wife, Irene, who has recently died. Now alcoholic and distraught, Layne is living in a seedy New York hotel with his traumatized eight-year-old daughter, Frances, whom he torments by threatening to hang himself whenever she cries. The titular "secret" is that Ransome himself is Frances's father, an inkling of which causes a guilty pain in his liver. Layne explains that Irene used to get the same pain, and nurses Ransome with compresses and hot tea until a bizarre climax, when the ailing Ransome wakes up just in time to stop Layne from murdering him with a razor. Two years later (dénouement), Ransome and Frances—now legally father and daughter—encounter Layne with a shrewish new wife at a train station, whereupon the henpecked lunatic ducks into the club car, while Frances and Ransome indulge in a bit of undismayed, Dickensian laughter: The End. The movie, never made, was Jackson's last attempt to write for the big screen.

AFTER HE'D FINISHED *The Fall of Valor*, Jackson had been eager to get started on his Proustian saga, *What Happened*. By then his magnum opus—"which will earn me (I truly know) an international prestige"—had begun "plaguing [him] day and night," but at the time he simply couldn't afford to take a three-year (at least) break from more lucrative, less demanding projects. By 1948, however, Jackson could hardly wait to get on with it, realizing that another hastily written failure like *The Outer Edges* might damage his reputation beyond repair, and besides he felt certain that he was at the height of his powers—indeed, that it was now or never.

But alas, Jackson had a big nut—the mansion in New Hampshire, the townhouse on the Upper East Side, children in private school, a lavish fondness for pretty things—and his financial situation seemed almost immune to improvement. That summer in Hollywood, then, he'd found himself sorely tempted on meeting the great Fanny Brice, who was shopping around for a biographer to tell her story on a more or less fifty-fifty financial basis. "When I meet the guy I'll know him," she said, whereupon Jackson tried to look "keen as all hell" and ask "Just the Right Leading Questions" as to how Brice had gone from a ragamuffin singing for pennies to an internationally acclaimed star. "Anyway," he wooed her afterward, "whether we like it or not, Fanny dear, we're hooked. I won't be able to get you out of my system until I try to explore and capture on paper that personality that is yours and those tremendous gifts that are yours."

Brice's agent, Abe Lastfogel, drew up the papers, and Leonard Lyons announced to the world that the famous comedienne had finally found her "ideal" biographer: "Jackson was about to start his new novel, but found the Brice offer irresistible. It was a package-deal, covering magazine serialization, book publications, movie sale and the screenplay—which would net him more than $200,000." Jackson wrote Brice that she would likely consider it "so much bull-shit" (a rare bit of profanity on his part, the better to seem a fellow rough-diamond type) if he claimed that his "chief interest" in such a project was "the story of Fanny Brice and to hell with the money, but the fact is that this wild-sounding statement isn't far from the truth"; to the Gershwins, however, he admitted that his interest was pretty much equally divided between the two, Brice and money. In fact he was utterly miserable: he'd already interrupted *What Happened* to work on the Milestone script, and now he was proposing himself as a show-business biographer. Hardly the sort of thing Proust would do.

Nevertheless Jackson had resigned himself to another nine months (at least) of very exacting hack work, when Rhoda—at two in the morning, the night before he left for New York to close the Brice deal—came into his room and begged him not to do it. Yes, they were deeply in debt, and nobody knew it better than she; but *What Happened* was the novel Charlie was born to write, and "nothing should come in its way": "We would retrench in every way," he wrote the Gershwins; "she would get rid of all help, run this big house and do the cooking and housecleaning herself . . . so long as I stuck to my novel. She believes in me as a writer and believes I have an important future (and I don't think I've ever had a finer compliment in my life, for, as I say, the real burden of the family and house fell on her)." Within a few days Jackson had cleared the decks: for three years (or more) there would be no lavish trips, no Hollywood jobs, no freelancing (if he could help it)—nothing but work on *What Happened.*

In 1951 Fanny Brice died of a cerebral hemorrhage, and two years later Norman Katkov published a biography, *The Fabulous Fanny,* that Brice's family disliked. Katkov (who in any case hadn't negotiated a cut of the movie sale, as Jackson had) was therefore not involved when a production of *Funny Girl*—based on Brice's life, and produced by her son-in-law, Ray Stark—ran for 1,348 performances on Broadway, launching the career of Barbra Streisand and later becoming the top-grossing movie of 1968. Katkov, meanwhile, had tried his hand at live TV, and one day was pitching a story to some admen at J. Walter Thompson—producer of *Kraft Television Theatre*—when a "short little guy, very gentlemanly, very diffident" entered the room: Charles Jackson, author of *The Lost Weekend*. "I felt really sorry for him," Katkov remembered.

Chapter Thirteen

What Happened

It's hard to overstate Jackson's expectations for *What Happened*. In early 1945 he'd written Baumgarten that he was tempted to "chuck everything"—both *The Fall of Valor* and his *Lost Weekend* sequel, *The Working Out*—in favor of this "Major Work," which he felt certain had "greater possibilities than any other American novel I can think of. Big words, these; but it's true." Three years later he wrote Baumgarten again—in a similar if somewhat more rueful vein—dismissing everything he'd published to that point in view of the awesome possibilities of *What Happened*, which would be the "first *real* novel" he'd ever written: *The Lost Weekend* was "a character sketch merely"; *The Fall of Valor* was a kind of prose play in three acts; *The Outer Edges* was "a series of character sketches collected together under one theme." But if he could pull off this colossal, multivolume masterpiece, his "ultimate wordage" would likely rival that of Tolstoy.

As Jackson never tired of explaining, his novel's title described the foremost function of an author ("If a man could ever set down exactly what happened—about *anything*—he'd be the finest writer in the world"), and also related to certain implications of its proposed epigraph, from the Irish novelist and poet James Stephens: " 'The music of what happens,' said great Fionn, '—that is the finest music in the world.' He loved 'what happened,' and would not evade it by the swerve of a hair." Our hero, then—Don Birnam, or Jackson himself (who flatly described *What Happened* as "True Confessions")—is the kind of fatalistic, "unguarded" fellow who "compulsively let himself in for anything." Such a ravenous appetite for experience is largely due to his protean nature, and hence the novel would trace the progress of "many different characters at different stages of development"—that is, the progress of *one* many-sided character, Don Birnam, whose alcoholism ("how [he] got that way and how he un-got that way") would prove a small part of the whole story, a single facet of the paradoxes that would be reconciled over the course of three or four volumes. Jackson would thus respond to the artistic challenge posed by Rhoda's observation that "nobody would believe" the actual story of his life: "You've been too many different people."*

In a long letter explaining the project to "Stan [Rinehart], Bernice, and Company," Jackson took a cue from his favorite near-contemporary, Fitzgerald, and explicitly put himself "in the line of greatness": like the most important novels of "our generation"—*Ulysses, In Search of Lost Time*, the *Joseph* books of Mann—*What Happened* would open with a lengthy preamble meant to "serve as a kind of musical theme," setting the mood for the story to follow. Proust had an "Overture," Mann had a "Prelude," whereas Jackson's more modern book ("modern in the extreme") would open with a "Preview": a detailed account of one day in Don Birnam's middle years—namely, a summer day in 1947, shortly after Don has returned from Hollywood to his fine New England home.[†] Despite any number of harrowing setbacks in his life, Don is now prosperous and at least ostensibly content; indeed, that day in 1947 will mark an occasion he "has been looking forward to for as long as he can remember": a family reunion that will take place under his own commodious roof, in the course of which all the various events, characters, and themes of *What Happened* will be touched on in passing. Finally, as the

---

* "Who was Charles Jackson?" his best friend Dorothea Straus wrote in 1973. "Less than ever was I able to answer that question. . . . it seemed that several human beings emerged under one name."
[†] Jackson had originally proposed to set the preamble in 1943, shortly after Don first becomes famous as author of *Present Fears*, "a serious but popular play . . . which has had a striking success on Broadway and in the movies." When Jackson finally wrote the bulk of "Preview," however (c. 1953–54), he decided to set it rather in 1947, the better to account for Don's already rather jaded attitude toward his own success.

day winds down—after some two hundred pages of ambivalent (at best) interaction with his wife, children, mother, brothers, nieces, nephews, and others—Don sits holding his beloved older daughter and brooding in front of a fire: "He is happy; indeed he has everything to be happy for; but happiness as he has expected it to be is an illusion." Wondering whether the "meaning of life" (no less) will ever be revealed to him, Don suddenly experiences an epiphany or "visitation" ("as if God suddenly tapped him on the shoulder and said, 'The moment is now' "): "What life means, it means *all* the time, if only you have sense enough to be aware of it."

So ends the preamble, whereupon Book One of the first volume, *Farther and Wilder*, would begin in Don's childhood, with the violent death of his sister and brother, and from there the novel would follow "all the apparently contradictory ramifications of [Don's] growth, up to the very day that we have just seen in PREVIEW, and then on again for some years after that." Jackson concluded this prospectus to "Stan, Bernice, and Company" with a further rationale for that long preamble (the one section he seemed to envisage with almost perfect clarity):

> One of the great advantages of PREVIEW is that, in seeing how the hero "turns out," so to speak, we will read through anything, really anything (and there is going to be some pretty rough stuff), confident that, however tough the going, it comes out all right in the end. Though almost all the early sections seem fatally against even the remotest possibility of such a conclusion, the novel turns out to be, after all, a prodigious "success story," to put it in trite terms. But in the purest sense of the words, it is a novel of affirmation and acceptance of life.

•

AS PART of the "retrenchment" that would give Charlie the security to work on his novel for three years, the Jacksons arranged for a bank loan of $10,700 (this in addition to the $32,500 he'd already earned [and spent] in 1948), and resolved to remain in Orford that winter rather than pay for another posh Manhattan townhouse (especially since they still owed rent for the place on East 65th). The only further income due was $4,000 from Milestone, payable in June 1949 at the latest, or earlier if *The Third Secret* went into production. Rhoda asked Baumgarten to negotiate a

$5,000 advance on *What Happened* to cover their immediate debts ("not long-term debt at all—just accumulated bills, long-standing doctors' bills, coal for the winter etc."), and meanwhile they also tried to sell most of their paintings as well as Charlie's collection of custom-bound first editions, including twenty-four volumes of Melville, twenty-seven of Hardy, the complete New York Edition of Henry James, and so on. Somehow they had to figure out how to live on roughly $1,000 a month—$500 for the mortgage and bank notes, $500 for living expenses—but it wouldn't be easy after "spending so riotously for these years," Charlie admitted. "Wouldn't it be wonderful to think that we've passed the lowest point in our lives and that from now on everything gets better?" Rhoda wrote Boom that September.

But the lowest point lay well in the future. Two months later, in November, Rhoda's father suffered a fatal lung hemorrhage in front of the Greenmount Candy Shoppe in downtown Barre, where he'd gone to follow the Truman-Dewey election returns. He died penniless, having lost his house some years before. Charlie, who "adored" both parents-in-law, naturally paid for the funeral and insisted that the widow, Queenie, come live with them. Within a few months their financial situation was already dire: in May, Charlie borrowed another $1,000 on the condition that he repay it the following month, once the Milestone money came through; but Milestone (traveling in France at the time) claimed he was broke and could only afford $1,500 as a final settlement. "My errors of three and two years ago have certainly caught up with me," Charlie reflected in July, having just reported a bank balance of exactly $46. "What I wouldn't give to be able to go back to 1944 and start over."

Much of his bitterness was directed against his publisher, who, he thought, had made a colossal botch of *The Outer Edges.* Ted Amussen once remarked that his main job as Jackson's editor was "to keep him bucked up" when he lapsed into his periodic funks, and certainly Jackson had come to expect a lot in that regard after the whole *Fall of Valor* ordeal. "I'm quite sore about their silence," he wrote a friend, when nobody at Rinehart got right back to him about his latest title idea (*The Self-Condemned*) for his third novel; he proposed to write them a "stinging note the gist of which will be: 'If it doesn't make any difference to you, okay, I'll move on to somewhere else.' " Less petulant were his objections to a number of unauthorized changes in his text, presented as a fait accompli once the book had gone into production. Jackson enumerated these in a long indignant memo, and was especially incensed over a sentence they'd seen fit to cut toward the end of the book—to wit, when Ruth Harron contemplates losing her husband and being left with only a daughter to care for: "A child is no fulfillment to a mature man or woman." Jackson had been especially pleased with this key psychological point—a "fundamental difference" between Jim and Ruth Harron—and could not forgive its peremptory deletion: "In all my experience (radio writing, movies, books) I have never known or heard of such a thing happening—not, in fact, since school days when your teacher took the liberty of blue-penciling one of your grammar-school compositions."

But it was, of course, the financial side of things that rankled most. Both Charlie and Rhoda believed that the publisher had "just allowed [*The Outer Edges*] to die," though Stanley Rinehart showed facts and figures to Baumgarten that "undoubtedly" proved he'd spent more on promotion than sales warranted, and was even then throwing bad money after good ("There is more advertising to come"). But Jackson was not appeased. As far as he was concerned, Rinehart had never taken proper advantage of the better reviews, and given the relative success—financial *and* critical—of his first two novels, this was nothing less than a matter of "criminal negligence": "The very thought of Rinehart sickens me at this point . . . from the beginning, Rinehart has never had a proper appreciation of what they have in me." It came as no surprise, then, when Baumgarten wrote the publisher on November 19, 1948, asking that Jackson be released from their option on his next novel. Rinehart's response was gracious but pointed. He reminded Baumgarten that she, too, had expressed misgivings about following *The Fall of Valor* with the murder story, and regretted that "Charlie's very considerable financial problems have taken precedence over his freedom as a writer": "I hope you will tell Charlie that our faith in his ability as one of America's foremost creative writers is unshaken, and that we are only too sorry that he should lay on us the sole responsibility for his last book."

Meanwhile Jackson had decided to return to his first publisher, John Farrar, who for his part would always be proud of the fact that he'd "battled for [*The Lost Weekend*] and insisted on its publication"—indeed, the novel had been the next-to-last book he'd added to the Farrar & Rinehart list before leaving in 1944 to do war work in Africa. On his return the following year, Farrar had joined with the young Roger Straus, Jr., to form Farrar, Straus & Company, which would struggle along with a modest list until 1950, when Gaylord Hauser's *Look Younger, Live Longer* ensured the firm's prosperity with its wildly popular advice about the virtues of low toilet seats, yogurt, and blackstrap molasses. What was important to Jackson at the time, however, was that Farrar had almost unparalleled faith in him as a writer. "You have so fine a chance to be one of our American novelists who can sustain and maintain a great talent," the publisher had written him on March 1, 1946. "Whether you go on being a free and amazingly acute writer of fiction, or fall into the welter of what I have found to be the publishing and writing scene, and some of its tendencies, on my return to it, I wouldn't know. Forgive me for this avuncular frankness." But Jackson didn't mind his frankness at all—on the contrary: such a goad to high seriousness was precisely what he wanted after going (as he saw it) somewhat astray in recent years, and never mind "the practically unheard-of royalty rate of 20%" that Farrar was offering by way of compensation for the firm's rather modest advances. Jackson's contract stipulated a story collection to be published in 1950 that would "keep [his] name alive" until *What Happened* began to appear (or so was the hope) in 1952.*

Everything would have been just about perfect, if not for the fact that John Farrar was, alas, a dreadful bore. His visit to Six Chimney Farm, in April 1949, had left Jackson more than a little rattled: "By Saturday noon I thought I'd go nuts (some day I'll write a character sketch of him and call it BUT WHAT I STARTED OUT TO SAY WAS), I found I had nothing to discuss with him at all . . ." Four months later, however—and not a moment too soon—Jackson finally met Farrar's partner, Roger Straus, when they attended the Marlboro College Fiction Writers' Conference that summer. Having spent the previous night chez Farrar in Lyndonville, Vermont, Jackson might have seemed pensive that day, or so he struck Straus's wife on her first-ever glimpse of the "small and plump" man in his "neat buttercup-yellow" Brooks shirt: "In spite of his meticulous grooming, he had the vulnerable, wistful air of a Charlie Chaplin Tramp."

Whatever else the Strauses were, they were not boring, and both had storied pasts. The thirty-two-year-old Roger came from two of the most prominent Jewish families in America: his mother was a Guggenheim, while the Strauses had founded Macy's Department Store and Roger's

---

* Originally Jackson had planned to include in his first story collection a lot of unpublished early material—written before *The Lost Weekend* had made him famous—but the scheme changed somewhat, as we shall see, once he began to write other "Arcadian Tales," beginning with the story "Tenting Tonight" in December 1948.

paternal grandfather, Oscar, had been the country's first Jewish cabinet member (Secretary of Commerce and Labor in Theodore Roosevelt's administration). At age twenty-one Roger had married an intellectual childhood friend, Dorothea Leibmann (whose grandfather had owned the Rheingold brewery), and the two pursued a literary life as a matter of temperament—they were both well-read, charming eccentrics who enjoyed the company of writers. The couple's charm, in fact, was hardly incidental to their success, given that Roger considered himself a gentleman publisher to whom money was, well, secondary; as he liked to say, he'd always wanted to be "a proper, important, medium-sized literary publisher," and in that respect he would succeed brilliantly. "If you're an author and have an editor who's interested in your work," said his son, Roger III, "you think, My God, I've died and gone to Heaven. But to have a *publisher* who's interested in your work—and a publisher who also owns the goddam place—that's an aphrodisiac the like of which authors don't come by very often."

To Charles Jackson it was nothing less than a dream come true: a golden couple, rich and witty and sophisticated, who became (as Dorothea put it) "members ex-officio of his family" and published his work to boot! "I'd be so happy," he wrote Dorothea, a few months after that first meeting in Marlboro, "if now, right this minute, the Strauses could come in, sit down, and I could enjoy with you the kind of feast of good talk that we have had before, though, as I say, I have never yet had enough. There's only one thing to do about it: we all just have to manage, somehow, to get ourselves shipwrecked on a desert island together." Charlie, at his best, was scintillating company—"puckish, penetrating, opinionated, full of insight, and rich in reference," as Max Wylie described him—and the Strauses were his ideal interlocutors, cultured and not a little naughty. Roger, also a dandy (a great wearer of cravats and lilac socks), was legendary for his salty, flirtatious gossip ("Listen, Baby . . . "), and neither of the Strauses was much inclined to look askance at Charlie's excesses. Their townhouse on East 70th became almost a personal pied-à-terre for Jackson, where he could let himself go and to hell with consequences; one of Roger III's earliest memories is the time he walked in on Jackson, vomiting into his toilet. Indeed, for the Strauses' benefit, Charlie was even willing to parade his dark side at home in Orford, a performance foreshadowed on their arrival by an "unshaven, wild-eyed" appearance ("the family man had gone under"), though generally deferred until his children were safely in bed. "He was never loud," Dorothea remembered, "but curiously menacing and willfully self-destructive. The alcoholic and homosexual at these times strutted exhibitionistically before the footlights, the husband, father, and friend having made an exit, seemingly never to reappear." But reappear he/they almost always did—"rested and rosy," in fact, and ready for a picnic or some other wholesome family fun. As for his homosexual persona: with the Strauses, at least, he was quite unabashed about it, even a little shameless. "I'm willing to share a bath with someone," he wrote Roger, when the latter offered him a room at the Lotos Club. "If the other occupant is tall dark and handsome, I'll be big about it and share more than that."

But it was Dorothea who excited his greatest love. Slender, intense, yet oddly dispassionate about people (Charlie's "violent swings did not disturb me, nor did I feel pity for him"), she had a fondness for Edwardian finery—wide-brimmed hats, veils, and the like—that made her husband's foppery seem almost modest in comparison, and her passionate knowledge of Proust, Tolstoy, and Mann was nearly the equal of Jackson's. "Truly, darling Dolly," he wrote her, "if ever anybody in this world brought out the best in me, it is you." Sometimes she was "Dolly," but in letters Charlie was apt to address her as "Madame Straus" (or simply "Madame"), in homage to Proust's great confidante, Madame Émile Straus, *salonnièrre* and widow of Bizet. It was the sort of thing she grasped without elaboration, making her the perfect receptacle for Charlie's unself-conscious (and generally unsober) outpourings about whatever he happened to be reading or rereading ("Levin so often just misses being a boob, don't you think?") and, above all, writing: "I am embarked on a world Masterpiece," he enthused in 1965, when first inspired to write a modern novel entirely in Pushkin sonnets, "humbly grateful for this thing that seems to be passing *through* me, that I am merely the instrument of . . . oh, all this sounds so high-flown but it's true." It was this aspect of Charlie's letters and life—the gulf (*so* vast in his case) between the budding idea and the problematic execution thereof—that Dorothea remembered best: "I do not know what literary rank Charles Jackson will hold in time or whether he will even be remembered," she wrote, five years after his death. "But of this I am certain: the stirrings of his imagination, whatever their results, were kindred to the masters he loved."

And then, of course, again, he was just a splendid companion—a man whose joie de vivre was radiant and transforming. Dorothea remembered one gorgeous spring day she sauntered along Fifth Avenue with Charlie, who was resplendent in a glen plaid suit, straw hat, and bow tie ("like the pinioned wings of a butterfly"). When his well-being was at its utmost, he simply had to buy presents: a rare edition of Tolstoy (lovingly inscribed on the spot) for Dorothea; a heart-shaped paperweight for Roger; an enamel Easter egg for Sarah; a box of paints for Kate; a dress for Rhoda ("who would accuse him, later, with some justice, of insane extravagance"). And finally they sat on the Plaza fountain amid the tulips and lunching office girls. "I did not care that my holiday was unreal too," Dorothea wrote, "triggered by the weather and the scene, intensified by the alert antennae of the sad-comic little Charlie Chaplin man at my side."

AFTER THE RETRENCHMENT PLAN went into effect in the fall of 1948, Jackson lost no time violating his pledge to work exclusively on *What Happened*. Because he needed money—and because of sheer trepidation toward his masterwork—Jackson instead wrote a long story about the Bloomer family, "Tenting Tonight," that he'd been contemplating ever since his last story, "A Dream of Horace," had been published as "Funny Dream" almost four years earlier in *The New Yorker.* The core of "Tenting Tonight" was to be his childhood trip to the Bloomer's summer compound near Sodus Point—but, as he readily admitted, the story was really just "an excuse to describe everything I know about the [Bloomer] family," especially their beautifully appointed (by Newark standards) home on East Avenue: the glass doorknobs, music room, and individual studies for each child, the little delicacies (like powdered sugar) they took for granted. Indeed, he went on at such lavish length that it took almost twenty-five pages to come to the climactic moment, such as it was, when "Clyde Blanchard" (based on Harrison, the Bloomer boy nearest Charlie's age) tries to serve eggs to his fellow campers: "He called for us to be seated when the cataclysm came. . . . the pan turned upside down in his hand and the eggs all spilled with a small sickening *plop* in the sand. Without a word, he gave us one awful look and suddenly burst into tears." Hardly a "cataclysm," and the rest of the trip is summarized in rather perfunctory terms until another droll moment at the end, when little Don Birnam disgraces himself by replying "I will if I'm asked" when Mrs. Blanchard expresses the cordial wish that he come again next year.

Rhoda disliked the story ("she thought it tedious, verbose, very rambling, and 'talked' rather than written"), so Charlie was all the more gratified when Baumgarten declared it "charming": it had "the authentic air of shining wonder that most of us lose at twelve." Moreover she knew exactly where to send it, since an editor at *Good Housekeeping*, Margaret Cousins, had written recently to say that her boss, Herb Mayes, was aware that Jackson would soon be publishing a book of stories and would likely have something to submit. Jackson was naturally delighted when the magazine bought "Tenting Tonight" for $2,500, though sobered when he saw what selling to mass-market "slicks" was apt to entail: without a word of warning, *Good Housekeeping* changed his title to the egregious "Thanks for a Wonderful Time," and not only made drastic cuts in the text but actually *rewrote* certain passages! Baumgarten, however, told him not to worry: "Nobody who reads the magazine is likely ever to read your books. When your books come out you will have your stories exactly as you want them."

With that in mind, Jackson promptly got to work on another long story about the early years of Don Birnam, "Sophistication," which recounts his time as a dreamy fifteen-year-old reporter and factotum for the Newark *Courier* (called the Arcadia *Blade* in this story and others). At the outset Don idolizes his blandly charming boss, Marvin Tyndall (based on Allyn Gilbert, who'd recently died), and ludicrously romanticizes the man's affair with another employee, a coarse mustachioed woman named Arlene Arthur (Gilbert's rumored paramour, Hester Herbert), who dissembles her wantonness with a lot of pious organ-playing at church every Sunday. Don, meanwhile, imagines himself "a kind of other-spirit, an androgynous twin to each," who abets their affair by coming along for "little office dinners" with the couple in public, and composes poetry comparing their "high adulterous love" to that of Lancelot and Guinevere. By far the best scene in the story was, unfortunately, the very scene that all but guaranteed its rejection by the high-paying slicks—when Tyndall stops his car while driving Don home and delivers a little sermon on the sanctity of marriage (*his* marriage in particular):

" . . . But you know something? Not once in all those fourteen years that I've been married to Ruth Whitcomb, not *once*, mind you, have I ever laid eyes on her naked. Or even so much as caught a glimpse of her bare—well, breasts. And that's God's truth so help me." He sank back, as if exhausted; but the lonely intense eyes still looked challengingly into Don's. "Now do you believe me, what I said about marriage? That's what I meant when I said it was holy. . . ."

Both were silent. Don thought that he had never felt so alone in someone else's presence as he now felt sitting side by side with Marvin Tyndall.

Margaret Cousins rejected the story—Jackson had regretfully declined to cut the "questionable" scene—and saw little hope for it elsewhere, though she found "a lot of truth" in it and deplored the "namby pamby" magazine market. As usual Jackson hoped *The New Yorker* might take it, and as usual they passed: not only was the magazine rather puritanical in its own right, at least during the Harold Ross era, but also its editors probably found the story too prolix, as once again Jackson had indulged in longueurs of almost Proustian nicety, as if these stories were part of something far larger (as perhaps they were): Jackson "explores a situation more thoroughly and leisurely than he did in his fast-moving novels," the jacket copy for *The Sunnier Side* would read. "Thus it might be said that while his novels read like short stories, his short stories, paradoxically, read like novels." Jackson himself, at any rate, was philosophical about the unsalability of "Sophistication": The story "has done a good deal for me," he wrote Baumgarten, "—broken down the mysterious dam that was holding so much back and for so long." His view of his adolescent self had hitherto been so cynical that he could hardly evoke the youth sympathetically, but here he thought he'd managed it at last, and from now on the reader would follow *this* Don into "all sorts of trouble."

But months passed and nothing else, or very little, came. Stalled on his novel and stymied, too, about how to write short stories that would satisfy his artistic conscience yet also pay the bills, Jackson had begun to lose hope ("Really it seems as though I ought to come to New York and take a job") when *Good Housekeeping* forwarded a fan letter from Miss Luceine Heniore, an old Newarkian who now lived on the Upper East Side. "Thank you so very much for writing 'Thanks for a wonderful time,' " the letter began. Heniore was roughly ten years older than Jackson ("I am of the era of Ethel Nicholoy, Bernice Coyne and Eula Burgess") but remembered him as a boy and had been following his career with great interest: It was a "real pleasure," therefore, to *finally* read a Charles Jackson story that was so "clean and delightful"—that his own mother could "show [it] with pride to her friends"! At first, no doubt, Jackson read the letter with rue: having been congratulated for leaving out sex, murder, and any mention of a "personality problem," he might have found it ironic that at least two of the women Heniore had mentioned as contemporaries—the most popular girls of their time, part of a threesome known as "the great triumvirate"—had actually led sordid lives involving sex and personality problems in spades.

But then, giddily, he got an idea.

For the next four days, Jackson rose at three in the morning and worked straight through (well stimulated) until ten at night. The result was a genre-defying work that opened with that fan letter from Miss Heniore, or rather "Miss Dorothy Brenner,"* and proceeded with an eighty-page response from Charles Jackson—or "Charles Jackson," a character in his own story, whose older sister Thelma, to take an odd instance, is called by her *Birnam* name, Rachel. In the course of recollecting the great triumvirate's various fates—poverty, violent death, nymphomania, and alcoholism—"Charles Jackson" undertakes to explain to "Miss Brenner" why looking on "the sunnier side" is, for a writer, dull, untruthful, and artistically inept (" '*Fine feelings are the stuff that bad literature is made of*,' writes André Gide"). Thus, repeatedly, he interrupts the narrative to call attention to his own artifice—the extent to which, even now, he's manipulating so-called real life to tell a story in the most diverting and believable (and therefore often morbid) way. Or not. What author in his right mind, for example, would advert to the quasi-idyllic nature of his hometown by dubbing it "Arcadia"? How baldly, fatuously obvious! And yet, when life hands you such material on a plate, so to speak, what to do? Oh, and should he *really* point out that "Fig" Newton married a man who exactly resembled her own doting father? "My God," Jackson remarks, "by that time the reader is practically writing the story for himself. He has read his Freud and knows exactly what's coming next. . . . But the same thing goes for Fig Newton's very name ('Fig' Newton—why I wouldn't dare!) . . . "

So unorthodox, at the time, was this "strange box of mirrors"—as the scholar Louis Paskoff characterized it, comparing it to the metafictional trickery of Borges and Nabokov (who were followed by Barth, Barthelme, and myriad other American "post-realists" in the 1960s)—that the *Times Literary Supplement* of London, reviewing *The Sunnier Side* in

---

* In the story Jackson transcribed this letter almost word for word, tweaking the prose here and there and adding a few lines to emphasize his theme and give the piece its title: "It's nice to know that you can write about the sunnier side of life, life as it is & should be," he added to Miss Heniore's first paragraph, and then to her fourth, "Still it sometimes does seem a pity that a man with your gifts should dwell so much on the morbid & sordid, neglecting the sunnier side aforementioned & the wholesome." Also, of course, he changed the names of "the great triumvirate" to Faith Goldsmith (actually a surrogate for Edith Warren—of the notorious Warren murders in Newark—*not* the Ethel Nicholoy mentioned by Heniore), Eudora Detterson, and Harriet "Fig" Newton respectively, and moved the sender's address from East 73rd to 72nd Street.

1950, actually presumed to chastise the author for making "the elementary mistake of interrupting his narrative in order to lecture the reader on the art of composition and truthfulness to nature." Jackson's publisher, however, "wish[ed] to go on record"—that is, in advertisements and jacket copy—"as claiming that the title story, 'The Sunnier Side,' will rapidly become a classic, unique, unlike anything we have ever read." And so it might have transpired, were it not for the fact that the story (or novella, or essay, or whatever one chooses to call it), for all its innovation and readability, is a little less than first rate. The writing is slapdash in places, and some of the dialogue is painful ("Listen, stupe . . . We're not in Arcadia now. You might as well get used to the idea, Eudora's a nympho and dipso from way back"). Which is to say, once again, that haste and pills had impaired the author's better judgment—and yet, were it *not* for haste and pills, it's doubtful he would have written "The Sunnier Side" (or much else) in the first place.

Be that as it may, Jackson knew at the time that he'd written something special—"a *won*derful short story" that would serve as "a kind of apologia" for his collection, though he and Baumgarten had scant hope of selling it to the slicks; rather it was submitted to *Partisan Review*, which couldn't accommodate an eighty-two-page typescript, and then to *Saturday Review* in hopes that the magazine would devote an entire issue to it, as *The New Yorker* had done with John Hersey's *Hiroshima*. Finally Margaret Cousins was given a look, and Jackson was abidingly "astonished" when she offered five thousand dollars to publish the piece in *Cosmopolitan*, another magazine edited by her and Mayes, and known (at the time) for more serious fiction than *Good Housekeeping*. "['The Sunnier Side'] says so much about a subject that magazine readers need to hear," wrote Cousins, who furthermore gave personal reasons for deciding to run the story in all its ungainly length (deleting only some profanity and a reference to masturbation): in the small west Texas town where she'd grown up, Cousins explained, the three most popular girls had been called the Three Graces—Louisa, Savannah, and Floy—and had seemed destined for the charmed lives they'd always known as girls. "I do not know whether it will surprise you when I tell you that Louisa became Louise Lawson, a New York show girl who was murdered in her tub in one of New York's unsolved crimes," Cousins wrote Jackson.

I believe a book named The Canary Murder Case was written about it. Savannah married a man named Custis who became a fantastic millionaire in oil. He kept a mistress for twenty years and immediately after Savannah died in the agonies of cancer, he married this woman who had destroyed Savannah's home. Floy, who came of a strait-laced household . . . was not allowed to marry the man she fell in love with, because she "would be lowering" herself. She docilely accepted her mother's choice, bore five children in rapid succession, threatened her husband with a butcher knife and was carted off to a madhouse, where she still resides. . . .

You can understand why THE SUNNIER SIDE struck me between the eyes.

Seeing that Cousins was indeed invested, Jackson pressed her to publish his enormous story in the March 1950 issue because, for one, he didn't want to postpone the April publication of his collection, but mainly because Hemingway's *Across the River and into the Trees* was being serialized in *Cosmopolitan* beginning in February. As Charlie excitedly wrote his agent, "They're bound to feature him big in the February issue and not so big in the March—maybe even behind me!" And lo, it came to pass: the cover of the March issue gave top billing to THE SUNNIER SIDE by CHARLES JACKSON, followed (in smaller letters) by Hemingway, Faith Baldwin, and other lesser lights. "It's fun to know that the whole story was written as a reply to my letter (very clever)," wrote a bemused Luceine Heniore on March 26.

THE SUBTITLE OF *The Sunnier Side* was *Twelve Arcadian Tales*, since Jackson's most recent stories gave him enough to discard earlier work (mostly inferior in any case) that wasn't set in Arcadia. Carl Brandt applauded his client's book as "a distinguished job," and thought it could easily be published as a thematically unified novel, but Jackson himself was opposed to the idea—perhaps because he intended to use much the same material for a bona fide novel, *What Happened*, and besides he was particularly fond of only four stories: "Rachel's Summer," "Palm Sunday, "The Sunnier Side," and a comic story titled "The Benighted Savage" about a boy caught masturbating by his father.* That said, he was unequivocally pleased by his new publisher's packaging of the book: the dust jacket was

---

* Another tough sell to the magazines, needless to say, though it finally appeared in the September 1956 *Gent*.

a handsome robin's egg blue with pink pigeons, reminiscent of the dyed pigeons released at Fig Newton's "pink party" in "The Sunnier Side," in further tribute to which the Strauses launched the book with a "pink party" at their townhouse. According to the Hartford *Courant*, the guest of honor appeared wearing a light blue polka-dot tie and pink carnation ("At last report no one saw any big pink elephants on leaving," the reporter slyly quipped).

Reviews for *The Sunnier Side* were so overwhelmingly positive that, a few weeks after publication, *The New York Times Book Review* quantified the matter for its "In and Out of Books" column: "Only five reviewers out of fifty-seven who spoke up on Charles Jackson's 'The Sunnier Side' didn't approve. Fourteen gave ground reluctantly and thirty-eight plumped for it." One of those in the middle category was the *Times*'s daily reviewer Charles Poore, who found the stories "penetratingly written" but so sordid the volume might have been titled "The Seamier Side." However—writing for the Sunday *Times* and *Herald Tribune* respectively—both Alice Morris and Frederic Morton commended Jackson, in effect, for what Morris called his "simple, unpretentious, almost offhand gift for story-telling," and Morton went so far as to make a claim for the author's uniqueness: "It is not possible to squeeze Mr. Jackson's technique into any one school. First and foremost he is a creator of his own world." Other reviewers, prompted in part by the book's jacket copy ("the collection has a unity comparable to WINESBURG, OHIO, of which this is, perhaps, the modern counterpart"), thought Jackson bore quite obvious comparison to Sherwood Anderson, for better and for worse: *The Providence Journal* thought Jackson wrote "more concisely, flexibly, and surely than Anderson did," whereas *The Boston Globe* flatly declared that Jackson ("obvious, slick, commercial") was "no Sherwood Anderson."

Though Jackson was hardly more "concise" than Anderson—at least in his ruminative short fiction—his best work justifies the comparison, and indeed *The Sunnier Side* was conceived in some ways as a deliberate homage. Like *Winesburg, Ohio*, Jackson's book follows the progress of a particular character, keenly self-conscious, who observes, judges, and is victimized by the repressive hypocrisy of small-town America. In both cases, too, there's a kind of tortured ambivalence—nostalgia for the pastoral loveliness of the hero's native land, the place where he was young, and sympathy for its more "grotesque" inhabitants, stunted by a paranoic, insular society. Both books follow the same pattern of initiation, and certain stories and characters are inevitably similar. The young teacher in Anderson's "Hands" can't help caressing his pupils' hair and shoulders in a fluttery, tentative way, until he's run out of town by neighbors who assume the worst (knowing their own impulses all too well); the rough equivalent among Jackson's stories, "Palm Sunday," involves a more predatory teacher, whose less ambiguous violation of the village children results in a different but no less plausible response—that is, his neighbors know and yet pretend not to know, since such matters can't be acknowledged among "nice" people. Meanwhile Don Birnam and *Winesburg*'s George Willard grow increasingly aware of these uncomfortable realities—the penultimate stories in both books (almost surely by design on Jackson's part) are titled "Sophistication"—until they decide to leave their hometowns for good. Aptly, the final story in *The Sunnier Side* is "Rachel's Summer," which ends with the adult Don returning to Arcadia to visit his mother and learning, for the first time, the rumor of Rachel's pregnancy that had compounded the tragedy of her early death and cast a further pall over his mother's life:

> I got up and walked to the window. I didn't trust myself to speak, and I knew I would have to wait quite a while. I looked out the window at the street—this street I had played in, it seemed, all my life—and across the way was the house that always resounded to the thumping of a player piano, and next to it was the O'Connells' house, and next to that was Mrs. Kirtle's neat little home, kept neat and trim and painted for her by the son who now lived in New York, the same as I did. What drew us back to this town, anyway, and why did we ever come home?

Thus Don is, at last, disabused of any lingering nostalgia for the place. We leave him standing at the window gazing at the street where he grew up—the same street and yet so unlike the one in "A Band Concert," the second story in the book (after the prefatory "apologia" of "The Sunnier Side"): on that street, as a child, Don had watched the Dettersons' hired girl, Angela, return to her employer in disgrace, having been seduced (implicitly) by an Italian on the canal bank. "I guess Angela has had her fling," Mr. Detterson sardonically remarks, and the innocent Don, overhearing, imagines "a lovely picture of Angela leaning over the balustrade of a balcony, flushed and happy, tossing flowers to a throng of admirers below."

Such a deft patterning of narrative point of view—from innocence to experience, and in the best stories (such as "Palm Sunday," in which the adult narrator considers his adolescent self) a nuanced mingling of both—enhances the book's unity of effect, as Poe would have it, so that one can safely say *The Sunnier Side* is greater than the sum of its parts. Jackson himself thought so: despite his downright aversion to certain stories ("One or two I actually cannot bear to re-read"), the book itself remained "the one [he was] fondest of," as opposed to his best; as he inscribed one copy to friends, "I put love in it."

A FEW WEEKS before publication of *The Sunnier Side*, the Newark *Courier* alerted its readers that Jackson's book was "definitely" about Newark and seemed intended more as an exposé than a serious work of fiction: "There seems to be little plot to the narrative, in truth it seems to be more of a diary that the author might have kept in his boyhood days." Jackson, naturally, would have demurred (the writer "must essentially draw from life as he sees it, lives it, overhears it, or steals it," he'd noted in the title story, "and the truer the writer, perhaps, the bigger the blackguard"), though certainly he didn't expect his former neighbors to pardon him on aesthetic grounds; indeed, he'd made a point of visiting Newark the previous autumn "while [he still could]," as he wrote the Strauses, "that is, before the book comes out."

Trouble had been brewing ever since the appearance of "Tenting Tonight," though it might have been worse: originally Charlie had changed the name "Bloomer" to "Harrison," before realizing that he'd "unconsciously" used the name of his old playmate Harrison Bloomer, who now owned the box factory where Herb Jackson was assistant superintendent. Charlie was careful, then, to rename the family "Blanchard" in the story, since he "thought it best to 'protect' [his] brother to this extent; though he'll be sore as hell at the story, and so will Harrison and all the Bloomers." He was right, of course, though "sore" was a reductive term for what Herb was; he was also mortified, incredulous, etc. "Look, Charlie," he protested: "I still live here! I *know* these people! They know me!" But it was no good, and for Charlie's part there was no point explaining the Artist's Prerogative and so forth. Besides, in various ways, it had always been thus: in 1930, when Charlie had first returned to Newark from Europe, he wore a Basque beret he'd been wearing abroad for a year, until Herb took him aside and begged him to desist: "For my sake if not your own. Please. What will people think?"

After *The Sunnier Side*, Herb pretty much gave up. "For Christ's sake, here's another one!" he'd cry, whenever his brother's stories appeared, whereupon he'd retire to his backyard barn and lie low, drinking and brooding. Indeed, more and more Herb sought refuge in the barn—for any number of reasons—refusing to travel or even go to parties. "It was his safe place," said his oldest daughter, Sally, who remembered many curious things about their lives in Newark. Since Herb stayed in the barn, his cronies would come to him: every Saturday night they'd gather around a potbellied stove and get drunk, while Herb's wife, Bob, brought them Boston baked beans and sticky buns. Every now and then a friend would totter into the house to use the bathroom, and Sally's older brother would make her hide. Years later she went to a psychiatrist—"I was so afraid of men"—who helped her remember things she'd "blanked out" about her youth: those friends of her father, for instance, who used to drunkenly ask where she was, or a foul-smelling dentist who held her down and groped her breasts when she was thirteen. At the time Bob refused to believe it ("Oh Sal, *not* dear Dr.——"), though at length she grudgingly agreed to accompany the girl to her next appointment. "If your mother ever saw life as it really was," an old family physician once said to Sally, "she'd be destroyed."

Herb, in turn, seemed to err on the side of caution, and to this end he endeavored to know as much as possible about his neighbors ("He was the kind of guy who'd call you up and tell you if your attic light is on," said Gilbert Burgess, the son of Charlie's childhood friend Jack). If Sally mentioned a boy she liked, her father would promptly veto any prospect of dating him, because—*as he happened to know*—the boy's cousin (or whatever) had done this or that. And while Herb made a point of passing out lollipops to the children of the neighborhood, he had little in the way of lollipops for his own family. Sally was a particular target: though she made straight A's in school, played every sport, and took care of her younger siblings (with little help from her father, who spent almost all nonworking hours in the barn), Herb seemed constantly in a rage at her, drunkenly "grounding" her again and again whenever she got "fresh." And Sally—as her mother often assured her—was his *favorite*. Her younger sister, Martha, later told her son that she'd been "scared to death" of her angry, agoraphobic father, and implored him not to make the same mistake with his children.

"I couldn't wait to get out [of Newark]," said Sally. "I hated the fact that everybody knew *every* move I was making. What they didn't hear, they thought they knew, and they'd spread it around anyway." She found escape in marriage, moving to nearby Rochester, which was far enough away to discourage her father ("He'd walk in, look around, and say 'Time to go home' "). More congenial by far were visits to her kindly uncle Boom in Malaga, where she'd made a point of taking her fiancé for a weekend shortly before the marriage, having "wonderful times" and finding little amiss in Boom's friendship with the courtly local doctor. "Do you know your fiancé's gay?" Boom puckishly remarked to Sally at her wedding. "He's so polite!" "Takes one to know one," a family member glossed, and Sally, thoroughly puzzled, mentioned as much to her parents. "Don't listen to them!" they insisted, appalled, meaning *any* of them.

Whatever the truth of the matter—she and her husband got along fine—a day came when Sally's grown-up son, Bill, summoned her to Syracuse and took her for a walk: "I think I'm gay," he announced, and his mother blurted ("without even thinking"), "If you think I'm going to love you any less, you're crazy." Bill became a protocol manager for drug research studies at the Johns Hopkins School of Medicine's AIDS service, as well as an HIV case manager at Beth Israel Hospital in Boston. When his partner was dying of AIDS, he asked his mother to come along for hospital visits ("I learned so much about compassion from my son"), and soon after, when Bill himself was dying, his mother stayed by his bed and finally made the decision to take him off life support.

Still, in some ways, she remained her parents' daughter. A born-again Christian, Sally doesn't keep any of Uncle Charlie's books in her house. "To me, he wrote about the seamier side," she said, unwittingly echoing one of his critics. "I remember thinking [of his characters]: those people never wanted people to know what they were thinking, and I didn't want to know these things either."

Chapter Fourteen

The Outlander

Jackson's talks at the Marlboro College Fiction Writers' Conference had gone so well that the college president, Walter Hendricks, invited him to teach a couple of classes during the 1950–51 academic year. Jackson was firm in his conviction that so-called creative writing couldn't be taught, and besides he thought most college students (especially male) were philistines who considered all talk about art to be "highbrow, therefore balls." But then, too, he needed money as well as a change of scenery, and Hendricks had become a friend. Besides, Jackson liked the whole ethos of Marlboro, a tiny college occupying a couple of clapboard farm buildings atop Potash Hill in a town near Brattleboro. The program had begun a few years back in Biarritz, France, where classes were held in villas for soldiers who didn't have enough points to go home. After the war, then, Hendricks turned his Vermont farm into a college for some of these same returning soldiers, flush from the GI Bill, and two years later Marlboro graduated its first class—a single student, Hugh Mulligan, who went on to get advanced degrees from Harvard and Boston University.

For his first semester Jackson spent Monday through Thursday in Marlboro at the Whetstone Inn, commuting from Orford (about ninety miles one way) in a car he'd borrowed from Dorothea Straus. His two

courses included a seminar for undergraduates on the modern novel and
an adult extension class that he insisted on calling practical—as opposed
to *creative*—writing. "Creative," he explained, connoted "the very opposite" of what he wanted to achieve, namely "to help writers, amateurs
and professional alike, to unlearn the grandiose notion we have all accu-
mulated about the nature of writing"—that it was, in short, a matter of
"inspiration" rather than (as Jackson would have it) "impulse"—"and to
learn, instead, how best to express . . . exactly what they mean and no
more and no less." By way of compromise, the course was listed in the
catalog as "Practical and Creative Writing," since students could submit work (essays, reports, poems, stories) arguably belonging to either
category.

Jackson seemed to bring his greatest enthusiasm to his literature
seminar, for which he composed a vast syllabus listing a kind of long-
term reading program in addition to what was strictly required for the
course; among the hundred-plus books on the first list were a number
of cinderblock opuses of the kind he himself was putatively working
on—*An American Tragedy, Moby-Dick, Buddenbrooks, Of Time and the
River, U.S.A.*—as well as six novels by Evelyn Waugh (whose seamless,
witty economy he wistfully envied), and, more surprisingly, four by
Hemingway, including the latter's recent, relatively inferior novel, *Across
the River and into the Trees* (perhaps because it gave Charlie a pretext for
mentioning that he'd recently appeared alongside same in *Cosmopolitan*).*
In all modesty, too, Jackson included his own four books: "For the
purpose only of pointing out good construction and bad, techniques
concealed or faulty, passages of tour-de-force as opposed to the 'real,'
symbolism obvious or successful, et cetera." His exams for this class were
rather inspired; an essay question, for instance, asked students to choose
one quotation from a list and discuss how it related to (a) at least two of
the books they'd studied, and (b) their own experiences ("Would you
frame it to hang over your writing desk?").† He also wanted to know "the

---

* Jackson's attitude toward Hemingway was complicated. An unpublished
twenty-page memoir of Jackson by a late-life friend, Alex Lindsay, records his reaction to a remark Hemingway allegedly made in a letter to Charles Scribner (which
I've been unable to trace): "In Charles Jackson's first book we learned that he can't
drink; now in his second we learn that he can't fuck, either." According to Lindsay,
Scribner "mischievously" showed this to Jackson, who at first was furious but later
amused. When he learned of Hemingway's suicide in 1961 (so he told Lindsay), he
reread "Up in Michigan" with tears in his eyes.
† One of these quotations, from Sherwood Anderson, suggested an aspect of what

sole and primary purpose of all fiction," warning students *not* to reply that "it is to instruct or uplift": "These reasons couldn't be farther from fiction's true purpose. If you think otherwise, then we've wasted our time."

One of Jackson's students, Bruce Bohrmann, remembered the course as one of the best he ever took, and Jackson himself was moved to admit, at the time, that he was hearing a lot of good things about his classes. "I'm glad you find teaching stimulating," Baumgarten wrote, with a touch of exasperation, "but *please* get back to your novel. It is of first importance and nothing should keep you from it."

JACKSON SEEMED to concede that he was being distracted from a higher calling. His New Year's resolution for 1951, as reported in the *Times Book Review*, was to finish his "new long novel," *What Happened*, and thus he cut back to a single weekly lecture at Marlboro for the second semester, spending all but Friday and Saturday at his desk in Orford. "I'm shooting the works in this one," he remarked to Harvey Breit of the *Times*, describing his novel's subject as the "hazards of success."

While struggling with *What Happened*, Jackson was haunted by the recent suicides of writers Ross Lockridge Jr. and Thomas Heggen, both of whom had become despondent after being unable to repeat the success of their first novels—respectively, *Raintree County* and *Mister Roberts* ("The best novel I've found in years," Jackson had said of the latter, when it was first published in 1946; "I've read it three times already"). Jackson knew all too well the strain imposed on authors of acclaimed first novels, deeply resenting what he characterized as the American "cult of success"—the way, in his case, certain critics insisted on making gleeful comparisons between *The Lost Weekend* and his subsequent work, branding him a failure because he hadn't managed to top himself. "The worst thing that ever happened to me was the success of *The Lost Weekend*," he proclaimed at the Marlboro College Fiction Writers' Conference. "The writer knows his own worth, and to be overevaluated can confuse and destroy him as an artist."

Jackson was hoping to achieve in *What Happened*: "A man keeps thinking of his own life as a loose flowing thing. There are no plot stories in life. . . . Do we not live in a great, loose land, of many States, and yet all these states do make something, a land, a country. A new looseness—human lives flowing past each other—this is a form that our younger writers might be thinking of."

And yet, for all his seeming humility about being "overevaluated," Jackson couldn't resist mentioning *What Happened* at every opportunity, plainly intoxicated by the self-perpetuated rumor that he was working on a masterpiece that would justify—surpass, abolish—the great expectations created by his first novel. " 'The conviction that "such a thing has not been done before" is the indispensable motor of all artists' industry,' " he wrote Baumgarten in early 1949, quoting Mann in connection with his own certainty that he had "never written anything like" *What Happened*, and "neither has anybody else!" Many years later, Jackson would claim that the novel's first hundred pages constituted "the best writing [he had] ever written," but one wonders when exactly he managed to write those pages. After rejecting the Fanny Brice offer in November 1948, Jackson had proceeded to write "Tenting Tonight" and then dabbled with a novella-length piece, "The Visiting Author" or "The Outlander" (more on that in a moment), until February 1949, when Rhoda reported that he was "in a writing lull—that terrible period (for him and for us) of hanging around not knowing what to do with himself. He's stuck a snag and until he irons it out in his mind he'll just have to fiddle around like this." Jackson would later describe this "lull" as a spell of "paralyzing anxiety" toward his novel, during which he distracted himself with long walks around the hill behind his house. Every afternoon he'd sit beside a brook in the woods and brood over his novel, finally returning along a dirt road that descended to the cemetery across an open field from his house—still there, he'd reassure himself ("It had not burned down in my absence"); the precious opening pages of *What Happened* were safe!

By the summer of 1949—having written "The Benighted Savage" and "Sophistication" in the meantime, but not yet "The Sunnier Side"— Jackson was so fed up with his own dithering and financial woes that he thought surely, at last, he'd have to accept defeat and find a job in New York ("My God I'm even incapable of decisions these days"). By early 1950, however, he claimed to be writing what sounded like the opening passage of *What Happened*, informing Boom that he was looking out his window at the "snowy landscape" while trying to describe "the very same scene in terms of early August and full summer," as he does in the initial pages of "Preview" (which wouldn't be finished for another four years). By June, alas, he was stumped again: "Everything I put down on paper reads to me, an hour later, like sheer crap," he wrote Baumgarten, whose frequent offers to read the manuscript were always politely refused. Indeed, Jackson admitted that he himself could hardly bear to read the thing anymore, much less write it, though by the end of that year, 1950, he told a reporter for *The Dartmouth* that he'd written "about 800 pages" and expected the finished novel to be at least twice that long.

But a curious thing, one that bears repeating: as Jackson readily admitted, the long "Arcadian Tales" he'd recently been writing, while also claiming to write *What Happened*, were composed of "the same material" that "[would] turn up in" his novel (albeit "in a different way"), such that he'd even considered titling the "Arcadia" section of *The Sunnier Side*—as it was then conceived, before he decided to drop the non-Arcadian stories—"Notes for a Novel."

In all likelihood, though, he was working on every conceivable thing *but* his novel—save, perhaps, for occasional pages that failed to measure up to the almost Platonic ideal he'd imagined for his masterpiece. Everything else was so much slumming in comparison, even relatively ambitious work like "The Visiting Author." Begun in December 1948, this Jamesian story about "the peculiar fish that a writer is" drew on his experiences in Bermuda, when he'd done a certain amount of socializing with pilots at an Army base in St. George's (so a Visitor's Pass among his papers would suggest). In the story, one of the pilot's wives fancies herself a writer, and presses one of her stories on the Jackson-like protagonist, Benton Hargrave, who in turn seduces her. Later, the woman's husband drunkenly boasts about bombing German civilians, whereupon Hargrave lets him know by innuendo that he's been cuckolded—partly a matter of indignant reprisal, this, but also fodder for a story Hargrave hopes to write, "which" (so reads the final line, à la "The Sunnier Side") "like any story worth the telling, would bear little relation to, and be far more interesting than, the dull original." Whatever "the dull original" consisted of, one wonders how much duller it could have been than "The Outlander" (as the story was ultimately titled), which takes seventy pages to make the feeble point that writers are "freaks" who "will do anything for material," as Jackson explained to Mary McCarthy, adding that he'd originally wanted Hargrave to sleep with both wife *and* husband ("I was talked out of it, like a fool"). The final product, anyway, hardly seems worth the fourteen months of intermittent labor he poured into it, while his wife, agent, and others were clamoring for *What Happened*.

And just as Jackson was finishing "The Outlander" in February 1950, he got started on a short "memoir in the form of a novel" about Bronson Winthrop, alternately titled *Uncle Mr. Kember* or *The Royalist*. Jackson thought he could dash the book off with his left hand, and confidently pitched it to Roger Straus for his fall 1950 list: "The book has everything, humor, pathos, real social comment, and I feel very strongly it would have a wide popular sale on the order of Goodbye, Mr. Chips. . . ." Scribbled in the margin: "Movie and play possibilities—also N.Y. pieces—on account of original characterization." But after an "excellent beginning" of thirty or so pages, Jackson experienced what was becoming a familiar dilemma: "a kind of block or protest against writing it two ways, one way for the story, another way for its later inclusion in the novel." Far from making the fall list, Jackson took almost five months just to recognize this impasse, and would never return to the manuscript except in a speculative way.

The following February, 1951—a month after that optimistic New Year's resolution in the *Times* about finishing his novel, which of course had followed months of intensive teaching at Marlboro—Jackson wrote a sketch about his time in Zurich with Ralph Eaton, "Old Men and Boys," which he hoped would be the first in a long salable series about his Switzerland years. With, again, visions of a smash Broadway play resulting from his efforts ("my fondest dream at the moment, one that will keep me solvent for some time to come"), Jackson managed to write four more stories in five days, including one about the Mumm family, "Ping Pong," which focused on the time Olili's paddle was smashed because of the swastika inked on its handle. Dubbing the whole series *Crazy Americans* ("a title that connotes Europeans' regard of us, and is also a selling title"), Jackson advised Baumgarten to send all five pieces to *The New Yorker,* which was known for its light-comic serials such as Clarence Day's *Life with Father* and Sally Benson's St. Louis vignettes. A long month later, however, William Maxwell rejected the stories with his usual decorous, nicely considered letter:

> In spite of fine moments here and there . . . the overall effect seems to us of something—of a great deal, actually—held back. I think it is simply the emotional content of the experience that is missing. Mr. Jackson's admiration for the monumental achievement of Thomas Mann may have tied his hands, so to speak. Remarkable though The Magic Mountain is, it's only one man's vision. Mr. Jackson's Davos completely recaptured would undoubtedly have its own interest and validity. Whether it would be better as a continuous narrative than as short pieces, he alone, of course, can know.

This time, on reflection, Jackson was inclined to agree, and asked Baumgarten to withdraw the stories for good. Maxwell, after all, had picked up on the fact that Jackson had aimed his prose at a middlebrow market, while reserving his *real* firepower, as ever, for *What Happened*, where of course the Davos material and so much else were ultimately meant to appear.

And so at last—"desperately in debt"—Jackson began slumming in earnest. "The Problem Child," he bleakly confessed, was "strictly from hunger": the story of a middle-aged drinker named Grace Dana, it traced all the author's favorite truisms about alcoholism. "There was something fine and delicate about her," the heroine's boyfriend, Smith Weston, tensely reflects, "an imagination, a vitality, a gift for life, that tragically was all going the wrong direction. . . . On the other hand, he had enough sense to know that she had to stop drinking for herself first, not for him; otherwise it wouldn't hold." The most non-hackneyed part of the story is the end, which—like almost every line of *The Lost Weekend*—is informed by Jackson's weird objectivity toward his own narcissism: Grace considers killing herself with pills, the better to teach Smith a lesson, until she realizes she won't be around to savor his reaction; instead she flushes the pills down the toilet, leaves the empty jar in plain sight, and passes out on the couch to give him a good scare. "No one, of course, has approached his classical treatment of the alcoholic," wrote a surprisingly dour-sounding Maxwell, "and this story, it seems to me, doesn't approach it either." The editors of *Women's Home Companion*, however, were only too happy to take a piece about alcoholism from Charles Jackson, paying $2,500 for "Last Laughter," as the story was retitled when it finally appeared in the June 1952 issue.

JACKSON'S UPS AND DOWNS were taking a toll. On April 14, 1950—the day after publication of *The Sunnier Side*—Earl Wilson included the following item in his syndicated "On Broadway" column: "Charles Jackson, author of 'The Lost Weekend,' whose going on the wagon was famous, now takes a drink or three . . . " This came to the notice of Jackson's prissy aunt Charlotte, who fired off a note to Boom: "That is bad, Frederick . . . If Rhoda was smart—she would not have cocktails herself or serve it. It would be too bad for her and their daughters if he slipped back." Probably word had leaked about Jackson's latest hospitalization, two weeks before, at Mary Hitchcock—a messy business, according to records. On admission he groggily insisted his wife *not* be contacted, and later that night was found lying on the floor after what appeared to be a half-hearted suicide attempt: "He had a bottle of yellow capsules," noted a nurse. "Stated he had taken capsules." The next day, dressed and packed and stoned on pills, Jackson announced he was going home, whereupon Dr. Gundersen was gotten on the phone to talk him back into bed; nine days later he lay there still, in a state of sweat-drenched withdrawal ("diaphoresis").

That autumn Rhoda remarked to Boom that her morale was "persistently low." Charlie's absences during the week, while he taught at Marlboro, only made weekends worse than ever, since he felt all the more constrained to take pills in order to catch up on his writing. In November they decided to sell the house—the Strauses had offered the use of their summer home in Purchase, New York ("they'd do anything for Charlie")—which at least gave Rhoda the hope of a new beginning, without debts, so that Charlie could get on with his work relatively free of anxiety. "Maybe life will be better," she wrote. "Anyhow it can't be worse."

On that point she was decidedly mistaken. More than three years would pass before the house was finally sold, and meanwhile Charlie's behavior remained unpredictable at best. In late January 1951, he went to New York for a weeklong vacation with the Strauses, who, as Dorothea remembered, listened to their guest's "endless talking" about his novel and "watched helplessly" as he went from beer to straight whiskey. Finally, on the day of his departure (he was supposed to be in Marlboro), Jackson was so stupefied that his friends called a doctor—or rather several, since their usual doctor refused to come ("I don't treat drunks"), and others were equally obdurate. The man who finally appeared ("I can't stand alcoholics") carried his bag into the library where Jackson lay on the couch, then emerged "like a startled deer" a moment later: "I've given him something," he said, agreeing to stick around, at a distance, while the Strauses tried to find someone to take Charlie back to Vermont. This proved to be Harl Cook—the raffish stepson of Susan Glaspell, a celebrated writer Jackson had met in Truro five summers ago—who also carried what appeared to be a doctor's bag as he urged Jackson to his feet. "Charlie looked up at him with obvious relief," wrote Dorothea, "and there was an expression in his almond-shaped Tartar eyes that reminded me of a young girl about to be whirled away by an attractive, sophisticated dancing partner, admiration mingling with an awakening attraction." The next morning Cook reported that his bag had contained a bottle of liquor, and once Jackson had taken a nip ("I'm an old hand at managing these types") he'd slept soundly on the train and arrived in Vermont "none the worse for wear."

But no. Alerted by Roger, Rhoda had phoned the Whetstone Inn that evening and discovered that her husband was, in fact, still very drunk; asking the management to keep an eye on him, she drove to Marlboro and eventually found him around midnight in Brattleboro, all but incoherent yet determined to catch the 3:00 a.m. train back to New York. After coffee and food at a diner, Rhoda persuaded him to stay in Marlboro, and the next day she drove him home. "We're in a drying out phase just now," she wrote Boom afterward, "but I'm afraid he isn't really drying out. I think he still has pills somewhere and is keeping himself going with them." But he denied this, and since complete withdrawal was apt to result in a "terrifying depression," Rhoda agreed to dose him with paraldehyde at night; presently, though, she found "a giant jar of pills" and some loose pills too, and soon he was impelled to return (still "ambulatory," according to records) to Mary Hitchcock and the kindly Sven Gundersen, who understood his need to indulge in "periodic bursts" of pill-taking for the sake of his writing—or rather, Charlie *claimed* that the doctor understood it. "Which is what discourages me so," said Rhoda. "I disbelieve Sven's statement, if he made it."

A lull of about seven weeks followed, until the night of March 15, 1951—three days after Maxwell's mass rejection of the Davos stories—when Jackson had a serious car accident while driving to Marlboro. According to the *Brattleboro Reformer*, Jackson was heading south along Route 5 in the vicinity of Westminster when he drifted over the center line and plowed his—that is, the Strauses'—sedan head-on into a car driven by one Ida Monte. The fronts of both cars were demolished, but, miraculously, Monte and her passenger, Arthur Karones, suffered only minor injuries, while Jackson seemed to emerge without a scratch. He was, however, vividly intoxicated, and after a night in jail he pleaded nolo contendere to a charge of driving under the influence, for which the judge suspended his license and fined him $75 plus costs ($8.05). Unfortunately the incident was picked up by the AP wire and got a good deal of publicity: "AUTHOR OF LOST WEEKEND LOSES ONE HIMSELF" read the headline in the *New York Journal American*, while on the other coast Franny Ferrer spotted the news on the front page of the *Herald Express*. Jackson affected bemusement at all the fuss: "Well good God," he wrote Dorothea, "where did they ever think that the author of The Lost Weekend got his material?"

But in truth he was quite chastened, and promptly agreed to resume seeing a psychiatrist, Niels Anthonisen, at the Veterans Hospital in White River Junction. At first Jackson saw the man two times a week, but soon they were getting on so well that he increased it to three (which meant Rhoda had to drive one hundred fifty miles a week for this errand alone). Dr. Anthonisen—"Tony" to Jackson—was a small, fiftyish Norwegian with big ears ("he looks like the Seven Dwarfs rolled into one"), who followed the usual Freudian protocol of saying very little, although (unlike Kubie) he did face his patients and seem attentive enough, his head cocked always to one side. Also he was a cultured man who loved Shakespeare and made a point of reading Charlie's books,* and when he chose to speak, he did so with spirit and candor. Once, he observed that *The Lost Weekend* wasn't quite "terrible enough," and Jackson huffily replied, "I'm not exactly Dostoyevsky!" "That's true, you're not," said the doctor; then: "Well, why *aren't* you?" Another time Charlie was volubly holding forth ("in my usual self-interested fashion"), when he noticed Anthonisen shaking his head. "Mr. Jackson," he said, "I don't think I've ever known anybody else in my life who needs love as badly as you do." As Charlie recalled many years later, "I almost burst into tears; I didn't know it showed that plain; nor did I know it was that true."

ONE OF THE WORST aspects of Jackson's drunk-driving imbroglio was the way certain neighbors seemed deliberately to make pointed remarks around his children. "Jesus, what a cruel community!" he wrote Dorothea. "But it's amazing, and gratifying, how little it has bothered Sarah and Kate—in fact not at all. It's wonderful what they can take—and I do think it is because they know they are so much loved at home. They asked me about it, I told them, they assimilated, and that's all there is to it." His daughters would not have disagreed. After Charlie's death, Dorothea kept in touch with her goddaughter, Kate, and was bemused by how

---

* In 1965 Anthonisen would publish a lively paper in the journal *American Imago*, asserting that Hamlet's ghost "represents Shakespeare's most important contribution to the understanding of 'madness' and the 'supernatural' in his time . . . " Anthonisen notes that Hamlet's first glimpse of the ghost is shared by Horatio and others, but when the ghost reappears in the closet scene, Hamlet alone can see him; thus Gertrude thinks her son is mad, whereas the ghost suggests to Hamlet that the queen herself is going mad: "Shakespeare, with uncanny insight and skill makes use of a well known and typical psychiatric reaction: that of projection."

"unshared" their memories were of "Papa," the different man Kate had known. As a father, that is, Jackson was all but unfailingly wise and kind and doting ("he always knew how to handle things"), careful not to expose his children to the mawkish, grandiose addict, much less the homosexual; indeed, his ability to compartmentalize these personae—under a single roof, yet—was simply astounding. As far as his daughters were concerned, the only real oddness was that he did spend a lot of time in his room, while the life of the house went on around him . . . *quietly:* "Papa's working" or "Papa's sleeping" were constant refrains, along with (after a night when loud music had rumbled behind his door) "Papa doesn't feel well." Then, too, he tended to drink a beer while playing cards with their grandmother, and sometimes there was a curious medicinal odor ("like butter rum Life Savers") when they went in to kiss him good night.

Charlie, in turn, was fascinated by the contrast between his daughters—as he wrote in *Farther and Wilder*, they "were so completely unlike that one could almost believe they were not only not sisters . . . but almost from different races." This, of course, reflected their almost polar-opposite parents, whom they resembled in a curiously inverted way: Sarah was dark and almond-eyed like her father, but loyal, responsible, and literal-minded like her mother; Kate was fair and snub-nosed like her mother, but otherwise resembled her father to a perfectly turbulent tee. "They were like small mirrors of himself," Jackson wrote, "one external, the other internal; and it was this constant twin-mirror that presented a small conflict in him that he had been unable to resolve." It irked him, for one thing, that he could hardly dissemble a preference for Sarah, at least when the girls were children. Her obedience and solemn honesty—so unlike himself as a boy—delighted him. One day, in 1948, Sarah came home from school, upset, because some boys had taunted her at recess, yelling "Your father drinks whis-kee, your father drinks whis-kee!" Charlie, a little abashed, asked what she'd said. "Good old loyal Sarah spoke up vehemently in my defense," he wrote the Gershwins. " 'I told them Papa does not,' she said: 'he never drinks it at all, he doesn't like the taste of it . . . but Mama drinks it all the time.' "

As for Kate, she was "brilliantly interesting" but "a pain in the ass to live with": funny, talkative, precocious, and above all imaginative—an extravagant fabricator, in fact, who stuck to her stories with a kind of bitter determination when, as often happened, her father tried to expose her. This, he knew, was perversity on his part, but he couldn't help it: "The secret inner mirror was all too clear. She could enrage him in the same way and for the same reasons that his own mother enraged him, precisely because he saw his own failings in them both—outrageously caricatured in his mother, perfectly matched in [Kate]." And yet he felt deeply sorry for her, too, in quite the same way he'd pitied himself as a child; for all her maverick high spirits, Kate was morbidly sensitive, and lonely, and Charlie knew she was bound to have a hard life.

Both daughters adored him, and could talk to him with almost perfect ease. "Make Katie stop teasing me about my pubic hair!" the eleven-year-old Sarah demanded, and her father, intrigued (he "didn't know she had any"), mildly drew her out until they were having a matter-of-fact discussion about sex: "I found out what Sarah knew and didn't know, and filled in the gaps," he wrote Dorothea. Together the girls liked to keep him company on his bed—"because it's big and wide (and possibly, Dr. Freud, because it's mine)"—and Charlie bore such lovely moments in mind when, say, he encountered Gore Vidal and Tennessee Williams at the ballet one night, having drinks at intermission and discussing their travels in "Africa, Rome, Barcelona, Paris, et cetera." At length Vidal asked Jackson what *he* did, and the latter purported to reply, "Why, I'm a bourgeois family man the year-round in a small town in New Hampshire." Sensing the pair's condescension, Jackson smugly reflected that a single moment of sweet rapport with his daughters "was worth all their Africas, Romes, Barcelonas, and wherever they might be free to go next." Not long after, however, he explained to a magazine editor that Henry Price—his alter ego in "The Boy Who Ran Away," an anxious father like himself—"unconsciously would like to be rid of his daughters, would really like to be free."

TWO MONTHS AFTER his car wreck, Jackson experienced a sudden renewal of energy that seemed to visit him almost yearly in spring.* Right away he got to work on what would become one of his best stories, "The Break," about a dramatic day in the life of twelve-year-old Don Birnam, who learns that six convicts have escaped from Auburn Prison, only forty miles from Arcadia. The first half of the story is a nostalgic evocation of the hikes Jackson took as a boy, past the asylum for

---

* Up to twenty percent of bipolar patients experience predictable seasonal changes in mood, with mania likely to occur in spring and summer months; psychiatrists often refer to "the manic month of May."

"feeble-minded" women (who used to shout wild obscenities as he passed) and along the train tracks to the old maple sugar camp (Sugar Bush) outside of town. But when he reached the crucial part of his plot—Don encounters one of the escaped convicts in a culvert under the tracks—he was briefly stumped. The problem, he wrote Baumgarten, was that the main episode had no basis in real life: "And I find it increasingly hard to write make-believe. But then I've always found it hard to do that; and in that sense, perhaps I am not a real writer." Aglow with seasonal euphoria, though, Jackson pressed ahead via his sure grasp of the boy he was—a born fabulist whose "chance to be a hero" would likely summon his most resourceful self: swearing "on his honor as a Boy Scout," Don assures the desperate convict that he (Don) can stop a train long enough for the man to hop a freight car to Lake Ontario, but then betrays him to the engineer, Mr. Colvin, who alerts the police. Don feels a fleeting shame, and kindred alienation, when he sees the convict taken away at the station ("his small eyes staring straight ahead in lonely hatred"), but then remembers he's a hero, after all, and begins "to look forward to the papers."

Jackson was thrilled when the story—the only one he'd "ever invented out of whole cloth," and the first in almost two years he wasn't ashamed of—promptly sold to *Collier's* for $2,500. Sensing he was on a roll, he decided now was the time to tackle a novella he'd been considering for nearly a decade, *Home for Good*, about a writer who leaps suicidally from a train as it speeds through his hometown. "I should be giving that energy and even 'material' to The Novel," he wrote the Strauses. "What I should be doing, of course, is a story that doesn't require so much of one*self*—but—this is the story that happened to turn up." He hoped (in vain) to keep it under eighty pages and perhaps sell it to *Cosmopolitan* for $5,000, as he had "The Sunnier Side"; anyway, if it panned out, he promised "plain sailing on *What Happened* for months to come."

The Writer, needless to say, was an intensely romantic figure to Jackson—a role he loved to play, though the actual writing part was problematic—and some of his favorite stories ("Tonio Kröger," James's "The Middle Years") were about writers. *Home for Good*, then, was to be his statement about the peculiar dilemmas of the American writer, though he'd long hesitated because he didn't "feel up to it intellectually." This time, though, he girded himself for the task with even more pills than usual, the better to cope with a breakneck, round-the-clock writing schedule that forced him to get words on paper with the least possible reflection (besides, if it wasn't great, he could always tell himself he was keeping his best in store for *What Happened*). The Arcadian protagonist, Mercer Maitland, was essentially Charles Jackson disguised as Sinclair Lewis*; like the latter, Maitland is a murderously prolific author of caustic yet compassionate satires on American life—a parallel Jackson makes explicit when he writes of the hero's first novel, *Emily Sparks*, as follows: it "did for (or perhaps to, as many people prefer to think) the American school teacher what Sinclair Lewis later did for the American businessman in *Babbitt*." Like Lewis, too, Maitland is an antically boorish drunk (and pill-popper), though it's often unclear whether his creator is quite aware of his boorishness as such.

Perhaps the best way to describe *Home for Good* is as the writerly equivalent of Don Birnam's "favorite daydream" in *The Lost Weekend*, wherein he imagines himself appearing at Carnegie Hall, blithely performing whatever pieces are thrown at him by a panel of experts. Maitland, in short, is the writer (and human being) Jackson would have dearly loved to be. He even goes so far as to mock his own paltry achievement, implicitly, by way of comparison with Maitland, "a man who knew how to write a *true* novel, not merely one of those disguised memoirs, a long-drawn-out short story, or a series of tenuous 'sensitive' episodes from a remembered childhood that had never really ended, such as so often pass for novels nowadays." Somewhere in the subtext, however, was the fact that *What Happened* loomed in the offing, and hence in a lesser way Jackson might redeem himself as Maitland does, late in his career, as critics begin harping on his declining powers, when "suddenly, out of the blackness of defeat, [his novel] *Stay, Illusion!* burst upon a thunderstruck public." But wait!—there's posthumous redemption too: after the four relatively disappointing novels (of twenty-six total) that follow *Stay, Illusion!*, a final masterpiece is discovered: "Brilliantly it laid its finger on one of our deepest American compulsions—the desperation that drives us to succeed far beyond our powers, to keep up with the Joneses, to work harder and harder for more and more money. . . . The novel is called, of course, *To Try Is To Die*." Not only is Maitland the triumphant author of every book Jackson ever considered writing, but also an "intransigent

---

* Rather thinly disguised in most cases: in the typescript, Maitland is initially described as "short" (like Jackson) but the word is struck out and "too tall" (like Lewis) scribbled in its place. "The now-dead protagonist you will have no trouble identifying," Jackson wrote an editor in 1966 (even then hoping to sell the book), "though much of it (indeed most of it) is me more than it is him."

and incorruptible" artist who appears in Stockholm to refuse—in perfect Swedish—the Nobel Prize: "I decline it in the name of my betters, those great men of literature who, again and again and again, have been over-looked or ignored utterly by the Nobel Committee . . ." So the speech proceeds, unsparing, awesomely pompous, encompassing Cather, Chekhov, Dreiser, James, "Tolstoy, my God!"—and so on.

But then, quite apart from the question of Maitland's integrity, the Nobel Prize would only be ashes in his mouth as long as he doesn't enjoy the approbation of little Arcadia, from which he sprang. Even the signal man who finds his battered corpse opposite the local train station, a dingy chalet, can't help remembering him as a "figure of fun"; the only soul in town who ever foresaw his great destiny was a beloved fourth-grade teacher, Lucy Espenmiller, whom he cruelly "betrays"—as the town sees it—by using her as the model for the lonely spinster heroine of *Emily Sparks*. Arcadia does, however, concede Maitland's international renown just enough to invite him to be guest speaker at the annual joint banquet of the Rotary, Elks, Lions, and Kiwanis Clubs, exploding into applause ("to his uttermost astonishment") as he rises to speak. Afterward, Maitland greets his old neighbors with great folksy warmth, lest they mistake him as a celebrity ("which he loathed being, above all things"), or, heaven forbid, "a stuffed shirt": "Why listen here, Alice Shaub! . . . Of course I remember you and of course I remember Rogers' store and good God how could I ever forget it? I peddled papers for Rogers' store . . ." Here was a man, after all, who would forever mourn the loss of his Arcadia High School class pin ("it had cost a hard-earned four-fifty and it was stamped AHS, '12"), wishing that the Juan-les-Pins prostitute who'd stolen it had taken his platinum watch instead. And little wonder he eschews requests from the great libraries of Harvard and Yale ("et cetera") for his vast manuscripts, relinquishing them instead to "little Arcadia Library where he had sat for so many, many hours, so long ago . . . and from which he had lugged home that ten pound [Shakespeare] Concordance."

In one respect, then, *Home for Good* is a rueful billet-doux to the village that had forsaken Charles Jackson (and whose library, indeed, would disdain any trace of his existence). Perhaps he wanted it known in Wayne County that—every time he passed through town aboard the Century a few minutes to midnight—he, like his hero, felt an urge to "dive out into that eternal Arcadian night where [he] belong[ed]." As the unnamed, Nick Carraway–like narrator ("the only friend [Maitland] ever managed to keep") reflects at the end of this 120-page paean to misunderstood genius, Maitland longed, above all, to be "a regular guy": "Like all artists he was a lonely man, and he coveted the commonplace; his deepest love and even admiration went out to what Thomas Mann calls 'the simple, the average, the blue-eyed, and the ordinary.' "

Jackson finished a draft in eight days, and saw that it was good. Rhoda, too, waxed enthusiastic, declaring it a "masterpiece" (a bit of rare hyperbole on her part, surely for the sake of her husband's volatile morale). Exuberantly he wrote his mother that *Home for Good* would be published as a book in February, appearing in the meantime, he hoped, as a two-part serial in *Cosmopolitan;* but the big news ("hold your hats") was that it would be dedicated to *her*—the first time—and what's more it was clean ("there isn't a naughty word in it"). Such were his high spirits that he decided not to be daunted overmuch by the misgivings of his agent Carl Brandt, who gently pointed out that general readers are unlikely to care about the problems of writers, and whereas the novella might find an audience as a book, its prospects for the magazine market were dim. On the same day Jackson wrote that celebratory note to his mother, he angrily reminded Brandt that he was an agent, *not* an editor: "My business is to write what I have to write and your business is to sell it, if you can." As for Baumgarten, who'd also been skeptical ("But it's not a story, Charlie, it's a biography")—well, all such sentiments were just "rubbish": Had they not read "Tonio Kröger"? Cather's *A Lost Lady*? And what about Schulberg's latest, *The Disenchanted*? "If you didn't get it, Carl, that's your funeral, not mine," he concluded. "I think the story is okay. It will never win for me the Nobel Prize, and maybe some day, if I decided to include it in a collection, I will want to re-do it with a lighter touch. . . . In any case, I am sending [Farrar, Straus] today the complete second, and I hope final, draft—final, I hope, because I've got to get back to WHAT HAPPENED."

It was Baumgarten who replied to this, noting that Brandt had already left for Europe and a good thing, too, as Charlie's letter had been uncharacteristically harsh: Carl, she wrote, was very aware of his "pressing financial situation," and therefore felt obliged to do everything in his power "to see that there are as few failures in the magazine market as possible"; *Home for Good* was a hard sell because of subject *and* length, and meanwhile, too, they needed to bring up Charlie's book sales, and both she and Carl thought it "essential" they follow the story collection with "the big book," *not* a novella. Nevertheless—as ever—she would do her best to sell *Home for Good* to the slicks, sending it to Jackson's great fan at *Cosmopolitan*, Maggie Cousins, who read it with "profound inter-est" but decided to pass for a reason that echoed Carl Brandt: "I wish writers would look into the lives of people in other businesses, with the same care and profundity."

Charlie, for his part, would let eight weeks pass before rereading *Home for Good*, which, on (mostly) sober reflection, left him "utterly disgusted" and "depressed": "It has moments and individual passages of interest," he wrote Brandt and Baumgarten, "but the whole thing seems to me now a nothing-at-all, rather frenzied besides, careless, angry, and—which is worst of all—smarty-pantsy." For the time being, then, whatever his har-rowing debts, he would put it aside.

FOR THE REST of that summer (1951) Jackson wrote stories at a desper-ate pace, producing slipshod work that was weirdly, almost wantonly inappropriate for the commercial market. "I wish Mr. Jackson would get back in the popular groove and do something printable," wrote Kath-ryn Bourne of *Cosmopolitan*, returning "Death in Concord," about an art curator named Miles Holden who abandons a "brilliant career" at age forty-four to live in his Bulfinch mansion with a twenty-two-year-old "protégé" and a crabby, homophobic mother who mocks them both. While being interviewed by the narrator—a journalist who hopes to write a "substantial article" for *The Atlantic* or *Harper's*—Holden gets drunker and more indiscreet (while Jackson's thirty-nine-page manu-script becomes more and more riddled with typos, as if the author were keeping up with his hero), regaling his guest with tales of the various scandals that led to his early retirement. Finally it transpires he's being blackmailed by a man he tried to pick up in Boston Common, and in the end Holden hangs himself, spitefully, in his mother's lavender dress! ("It was a clear case of suicide," the narrator muses, "but it was also murder.") "Janie" was another story from that summer—a slightly expanded ver-sion of the vignette about a nymphomaniac Jackson had hoped to include in *The Outer Edges* and would later incorporate into *A Second-Hand Life*: like Winifred Grainger in the latter, Janie Debbins Safford Larkin Driscoll Sommeier (a name reflecting her many marriages) gets plenty of sex with "bell-hops, valets, waiters, elevator operators" and the like, but still can't "get enough different *kinds* of men." "Whee! No!" wrote an editor at *Redbook*, amazedly rejecting it. "Our audience would be shocked clear out of its habit of buying Redbook."

By September the financial pressure was "unbearable": the only money he'd made since spring was eight hundred dollars from the sale of a Darrel Austin painting, "Girl with Black Dog," and now there was all of thirty-seven dollars in the bank. "Sounds corny but it's ghastly true," he reported a month later: "both the children need shoes (they're still wearing sneaks) and we can't write out a check for twenty dollars." Morbidly aware that Rhoda was listening outside his door for the sound of typing, he forced himself to write stories of whatever sort, or at least long, ruminative letters, quitting in the wee hours and reading himself to sleep as the sun came up. "I look like hell and feel like hell but for some reason I survive," he wrote Dorothea. "Is God keeping me for Higher Things?"

His wife wasn't the only one wondering about him, for better or worse. "This is a very small town," observed his neighbor Julia Fifield, "and everybody knows everybody else's business whether you know they know it or not." Charlie, to be sure, knew. Mrs. Richmond, the postmistress, lived opposite his house on Main Street and was, he complained, "the nosiest of women": "I see you revised that story you sent in last week," she'd greet him, handing over an acknowledgment card from Brandt & Brandt, and meanwhile on her wall was a list of locals owing back taxes, which naturally included Jackson, who also owed a notoriously large and longstanding debt to the grocer, Charlie Clifford, among many others.

The nosy postmistress, oddly enough, had all but adopted Sarah Jackson as a younger sister to her three children, Pete, Roberta, and Bob—three, four, and five years older than Sarah respectively. It wasn't that Sarah was actively fleeing her family, but simply that there were few young people in Orford, and besides the Richmonds loved having her and seemed to recognize that she might prefer a happier, more stable home. In any case she spent almost every day with the siblings, riding bikes and playing baseball in summer, taking skiing lessons in winter from the high school principal, Elmer "Spike" Fulton, on the hill behind Six Chimney Farm. Charlie welcomed such gatherings in the abstract, but rarely emerged from his room except (briefly) to watch. And then, for all his egalitarianism, he rather deplored how his children were forced to play with a rougher element than one found, say, at the Dalton School ("no nice children's parties, things like that"), and also, of course, he knew how their parents talked behind his back about his debts and drunkenness, how they pitied his children for having such an errant father, not to mention the bad feeling left over from his Leonard Lyons column. He felt he didn't belong, in short, and often longed to escape, but was held in thrall—producing more and more wretched fiction in a frantic effort to pay bills—by his family, who ultimately didn't understand him either. As he'd later remark to Alcoholics Anonymous, what he "remember[ed] most" about these years was "looking forward to night": "To being alone in my room. When I didn't have to see anybody. And then at night I remember lying awake in my bed and thinking of my New Hampshire neighbors in their little frame houses. . . . But I knew how much I envied them, and I envied them because they had love in their lives and I didn't. And I didn't seem able to have it."

During his last years in Orford, however, Jackson did make a somewhat greater effort to be sociable—more for his family's sake than his own, as he hated being an embarrassment ("*Pa*-pa, why don't you go to a job like other fathers?" Kate would complain, sometimes pretending not to know him in public). In the past he'd compensated for his reclusiveness with a great show of affability on the Fourth of July, wearing a flamingo-colored shirt and working a ring-toss booth on Main Street. Within a month after his car wreck, though, he'd gone so far as to join the Orford bowling team, and occasionally hosted poker nights with some of the local gentry. Among the latter was a wealthy retired lawyer named DeWitt "Dee" Mallary, who once made a point of visiting Charlie after he'd returned from the hospital, yet again, having recovered from an overdose motivated in part (as everyone knew) by despair over his many debts. Mallary announced that he was going to help Charlie straighten out his affairs, and proceeded to jot down facts and figures, asking what he owed and what he might reasonably expect to earn, and so on. When the session was over, Mallary stood up and ceremoniously produced a bill from his wallet to help "tide [Charlie] over": "God help me if it wasn't a $20 bill—(yes) and I was so embarrassed (embarrassed for him that is) that I found myself thanking him profusely, even abjectly," Jackson wrote Dorothea; "whereas all the while, if I'd had any guts, I'd have said: 'For Christ's sake, Dee, what the *hell* good do you think twenty dollars will be?' " But far from shaming this kindly burgher, Charlie lost no time inscribing a copy of *The Sunnier Side* to him: "Dear Dee, Never, as long as I live, will I forget your kindness to me this week. It's nothing for me to be proud of, God knows, but it makes me feel good just to think of it because of your kindness."

Chapter Fifteen

The Boy Who Ran Away

The more Jackson became blocked on *What Happened*, the more he liked expounding on how great it would be—a tendency Baumgarten had warned him about in 1948, after he'd been talking the poor woman's ear off on the subject for almost five years. "I think you should get started on it," she said. "You can keep a book too long, you know—so long that it remains only an idea and will never be a book." Charlie replied that the book was still *forming*, he hated to rush it, though perhaps she was right and he was as ready as he'd ever be . . . and three years later, he was readier still: "What is the sense of writing at all unless you have something new, original, or fresh to say, a real contribution?" he wrote Dorothea on January 2, 1951.

> I long to be at my book—to be engaged, wholeheartedly, with something worthy of my talent. I have a very big book . . . and it is downright criminal for me to be writing—or spending my time trying to bring off—merely saleable stories for lady-readers in the mags. I am simply unable to tell you, in even the remotest degree, how that book consumes my attention and thoughts during almost every single waking moment. I live with it, I eat it, I sleep it, I dream it . . .

Anything but write it, and in the meantime he was haunted by a premonition that he would die soon—"be killed in an accident" (as he nearly was two months later)—"and (God help me) my fear is not at all about what will happen to the children and how will they get along, but that I will have left What Happened unfinished."

And while he ingeniously contrived to avoid work on his novel, his optimism remained perennial as the grass: If only he could sell *this* story—and maybe one or two others—why then finally he could afford to get back to *What Happened*, which, he informed Dorothea that summer, he'd perforce neglected now for some "five months." If anything, indeed, the manuscript had *decreased* in that time: as he wrote Lillian Hellman in May, he'd just discovered that the gorgeous "Preview" section he'd been so proud of ("it was one of the finest pieces of writing I'd ever read, *knew* it was going to be famous, etc.") was, alas, terribly overwritten. "Far from being disappointed," he added, with typical stalwart buoyancy, "I felt nothing but a wonderful feeling of 'health'—I set to and cut the hell out of it, cut all the fancy work, left in nothing but simplicity, so that now (I think—though I may change again next month) it reads like something that hasn't even been written, so to speak."

In August, the Strauses took Charlie and his family to Nantucket for a month, and on his return he allowed himself to reread *Home for Good* and whatever there was of *What Happened*. His response was curiously schizophrenic, resulting in a frenzied letter to Dorothea, in which almost every square millimeter of a margin-less page was crammed with single-spaced typing. The badness of *Home for Good* had been plainly demoralizing; Charlie felt as if he were in a forlorn, losing competition with his earlier self: How was it, he wondered, that he could *ever* have written stories as good as "Rachel's Summer" and "Palm Sunday"? But then—hastening to reassure his admiring friend (and himself)—he gushed over the incomparable greatness of *What Happened*, which was "so full of *interest*, and so provocative (and evocative of life, life every second), that I am dumfounded that I could ever have done it and not at all doubtful that I can do it again." He had, in fact, "nothing but a passion to go on with it," but within a day or two he admitted to Baumgarten and Brandt that he'd reached a state of almost total paralysis: "The awful dilemma I'm in (though I sometimes wonder if I'm using it as an excuse, too) is that I cannot turn out really good, finished, and thoroughly *brought off* short stories because my chief interest lies in the waiting novel, and I cannot write the novel with a free mind because I have to write short stories in order to get from month to month."

As it happened, he was on "the verge of a breakdown," as Rhoda confided to Boom: "We're in a worse mess than ever. I'm trying to get a job. I wanted a divorce (which brought everything to a crisis of course). . . . We're miles in debt—and nothing ahead but bills. I'm afraid right now he's in no shape to do any work—fearfully depressed. I still believe that my life would be easier and better if we were apart. But the thought of not having the kids means death to him." Always mindful of Charlie's welfare, whatever the state of their marriage, she begged Boom to write his brother a nice letter ("He needs love and help so badly"). Presumably Boom obliged, as usual, though Charlie's funk was such that he took almost two months to reply, during which matters had clearly deteriorated: "I sleep not at all, I enjoy myself not at all, I have lost 15 pounds since early summer, but somehow I survive." The novel, needless to say, was going badly, and he was beginning to wonder whether it was "one of these books that can't be written." Finally—a little over a week later, in early November 1951—he was returning from one of his aimless walks when he came to the cemetery and saw that his house and *What Happened* (such as it was) were still there: "God," he found himself thinking, "if they had only burned up, I would be free." As he later wrote in "The Sleeping Brain": "From that moment I knew that the book, or at least my earlier profound absorption in it, my total commitment, my love-affair, were gone for good—unconsciously it was what I wanted all along. I was free; and dead."*

FOR A FEW WEEKS Charlie was in a state of perfectly lucid despair, mourning his lost novel—his very future, all hope of enduring fame. "I know at last that I am not up to it," he wrote Dorothea. "I am a sick man right now . . . I've got to accept it." The next day he emended himself on that point: he was not at all "sick," and therein lay the problem; *because* he was aware of his folly, *because* he was unable to work, he was in perfect health. "It is humiliating, but a fact, that, with me, health does not seem to go with productivity . . . I suppose that's because of the long habit of depending on stimulus for release of work." With Dr. Anthonisen's help, though, he hoped to overcome his block in a sober way.

And so he would—overcome his block—though whether it signaled

---

* In the final typescript, Jackson crossed out the last sentence and wrote: "For the book, so personal and painful, was proving too much for me."

a return to health, so to speak, is hard to say. In any case it appeared to be true that his obsession with *What Happened* had increasingly prevented him from writing first-rate stories, given the inhibitive notion that his vitality and best material should be reserved almost entirely for his masterpiece. Once he let it go, the wheels began turning again. One day in January he was struck by what he immediately grasped was the "best story idea [he'd] ever had," whereupon he spent a long day pacing the floor of his room, patiently, "getting closer and closer," as he wrote Dorothea: "It is astonishing, the more I keep adding to it and inventing, the more it falls absolutely correctly into place—as though the missing accurate pieces were just waiting for me to find them." Within a couple of weeks—taking his time—he'd crafted a long story that was very nearly commensurate with those first ecstatic stirrings. "It's great to be alive again!" he wrote Boom and others.

The title, "The Boy Who Ran Away," refers both to the protagonist, Henry Price, and his sister-in-law Betty's son, Danny, an effeminate boy whom Price despises in spite of himself. A successful but almost pathologically self-absorbed advertising man, Price has fled the city, with his wife and two daughters, to live in a tiny New Hampshire village, the better to ensure a solitude devoted to quirky, somewhat juvenile habits and hobbies. One of these involves collecting models of old-time vehicles, and as the story begins he has just received a "magnificent toy" from his older daughter for Christmas: a beautifully detailed model of a 1909 Stanley Steamer automobile. Price's almost unseemly attachment to such toys—in lieu of socializing with his "awful" neighbors, or, for that matter, paying much attention to his family—is one reason his stoical wife, Janet, is constantly reminding him that he's "acting like a ten-year-old" and, indeed, that their relationship is "scarcely different" from the one between Betty and *her* difficult ten-year-old, Danny. Price bridles at the comparison and yet validates it, again and again, in one case childishly repeating the phrase "Because I want to" when he decides he'd rather stay home than attend their neighbors' New Year's Eve party—the exact phrase Danny uses at a key point earlier in the story. Meanwhile Price longs to escape again—to escape in actual fact, and not simply into the fantasy world of his toys (which includes the very emblem of his escapism, a covered wagon "open at each end so that one could look inside to what was surely the most snug, the coziest tent in the world, and a traveling tent at that").

What Price wants to escape, above all, is himself: the weak, awkward, tormented "sissy" he was—and (despite a plausible veneer) still is—the boy for whom his nephew serves as the mirror image: "[Danny] had cultivated a deliberate heavy stomp as if to give his inadequate body a kind of manliness that he sensed, in his precocious little heart, he did not really possess; when he walked, he held his chin in the air defiantly, his bony shoulders ludicrously high, and swung his arms widely as if marching to a band . . . He lived in a dream world where nobody could get at him." Because Danny's family rents a farmhouse on Price's property, and because his wife and her sister are close, Price cannot escape the boy's presence—as though he were being haunted by the ghost of his own childhood—and the more he identifies with him, the more he hates him: "All his experience and sympathy urged him to help Danny. . . . His instinct, on the other hand, his deepest inner emotions, and his painful memories, made him recoil from the boy in contempt."

Price greedily seizes a pretext for venting his hatred when the boy accidentally breaks his precious Stanley Steamer toy, then tries to run away when Price calls him on the carpet. "Because I wanted to," the boy murmurs, when Price "savagely" demands an explanation. "*I'll* tell you why you ran away," says Price. "Because you're a coward. Isn't that true? You're a coward!" The more shameful his own behavior, the more Price lashes out at others, pettishly sending his children to bed and refusing to take his wife to the New Year's Eve party. Alone at last, he proceeds to get drunk, and drunkenly arrives at a bleak, bleak epiphany:

> A thought struck him like a shock: there is probably nothing in life more unbearable than to hate oneself, to not be able to stand oneself. . . .
>
> He drank.—How does one ever get outside of oneself? How is it possible, when one loathes oneself so much. . . . What does one do about it? Can one become somebody else? Another person? A new man, say? The answer was a dreadful No, No, and again No! . . .
>
> He was his own devil, his own black beast; and no quantity of drink, no staggering sum of money, no amount of parties, no dear friends, no charming children, no adoring but all-too-suffering wife, could ever expunge the beast and the devil and the falsely nice guy that he really was all the time, underneath, inside. . . . He hated himself with an active hatred that was almost too much for a single human body to contain without running amok, and he did not think he could contain that hatred for another hour.

Rather than kill himself, Price becomes all the more resigned to his estrangement from the world, and more certain, too, that he will "never, never, never forgive" the boy who has brought him to such depths.

Having accomplished this scathing, exhaustive self-indictment, Jackson was gleeful, though he knew the sixty-five-page manuscript would be almost impossible to sell in its present form. *Collier's* offered the usual $2,500, but only if Jackson agreed to cut the story almost in half and write a happier ending that involved some kind of reconciliation between Price and his nephew. Jackson refused. He was ready to relinquish the thing to *Partisan Review* for a pittance, when the fiction editor at *Harper's Bazaar*, Alice Morris—who'd admiringly reviewed *The Sunnier Side* for the Sunday *Times*—offered $500 and proposed to cut only ten pages or so ("a grueling task, tempered by love"). Again Jackson refused, arguing point by point against even the most picayune edits—*everything* was there for a reason—and concluding with a heartfelt defense of his best work: "Once in a blue moon a good story is given to you to write, or rather, passes through you, for you are in reality only the grateful instrument . . . and when it does happen, my God, you want to do everything you can to protect that rare moment, which after all was like a gift out of the blue." Unless *Harper's Bazaar* was willing to run the story exactly as written, Charlie would regretfully have to return the check.

The story was accepted for the November 1952 issue, and (Jackson claimed) would be the longest ever printed in the magazine. Given his string of failure in recent years, Charlie's hopes for "The Boy Who Ran Away" were almost desperately high; he begged Carl Brandt to pass along any "talk" he heard about the story, which he predicted, in exalted moments, would become a much-anthologized classic. For now, however, it was just another story in the slicks, quickly forgotten as Charlie had also rather feared ("God knows who reads the Bazaar, for fiction I mean")—though, for what it was worth, his old friend Marion Fabry found it "marvelous," and even Mary McCarthy saw fit to write a note of encouragement tempered with sternness. Beginning with the backhanded compliment that the story had all the "best qualities" of Jackson's *early* work ("an uncomfortable honesty and directness"), McCarthy was obliged to point out that Henry Price's hatred for the boy, and hence himself, was "too crude and patterned": "Nobody is capable of self-hatred of such really heroic proportions; much as we think we dislike ourselves, we are too self-loving, biologically, not to feel a little tendresse for people we think are embryo 'we's.' " Cowed as ever by McCarthy's grinding intellectualism, Charlie decided she was "right on all counts," and thereafter downgraded "The Boy Who Ran Away" as being "a little too agonized—too subjective about my own personal self-distaste."

BUT IN THE MEANTIME, while waiting for "The Boy Who Ran Away" to appear, Jackson had experienced a "tremendous burst of productivity"—this, once again, as spring got under way—dashing off a slew of mostly forgettable stories and planning a short novel titled *Poor Martin Coyle.** The latter was "a kind of American *Madame Bovary*," no less, set in Arcadia ("I have really given it the business," he wrote Boom: "tried to make it as drab and as lower middleclass as possible, with social climbing all over the place") and featuring a well-meaning, henpecked husband based on Sven Gundersen. While invoking Flaubert, Jackson insisted his new novel was unambitious—a "pot-boiler" even, for women readers who adored men like his hero ("the very kind of man they wouldn't put up with in real life for two minutes"). He predicted he could write the whole thing in a single summer.

Among Jackson's papers at Dartmouth, the only remnant of *Poor Martin Coyle* consists of exactly two sentences, written in pencil, as follows: "Martin Coyle had been married long enough to know better; to know, that is, that you simply don't fall in love with your wife all over again, not after 18 years. But he had, or thought he had, which is the same thing." On September 11, 1952, he admitted to Baumgarten that he was now "stuck"—too broke to poke away at a novel (even the unambitious kind), and really too depleted and depressed to write even the most dreary, "emminently [*sic*] saleable" trash, such as a story about Judy Garland he'd been tinkering with, "Rainbows, Bluebirds, Stars," which turned out to be "absolutely bum": "My heart just isn't in these stories; and when I

---

* Of the nine or ten stories Jackson wrote that spring and summer (1952), the best was "Parting at Morning"—a fictionalized rendering of his difficult relationship with his mother—which was sold to *Today's Woman* for $1,500 and published, to the author's chagrin, as "A Mother's Day Story." This, along with an unsold curio titled "The Sleeper Awakened," were the only stories from these months that would be included in his next (and final) collection, *Earthly Creatures*, though two uncollected pieces were also sold to *Esquire* for a relatively negligible sum ($250 each), "The Old War" and "Millstones."

write them with the market in mind, it shows all over the place. You can't fake it, and I shouldn't try. Meanwhile—what to do?"

Things were pretty much at a nadir. For two years the Jacksons had been unable to pay their property tax, while vainly trying to find a buyer for their house, and a tax sale was now slated for the end of the month; local merchants, hitherto solicitous of Rhoda and the girls, seemed on the verge of gathering about their lawn with torches and pitchforks. "Charlie I fear for," Rhoda wrote Boom on September 3, "he's under such depression and tension that Anthonisen even said he should go on a long bender just to save himself. That sounds dreadful I know from his doctor—but I really think he's afraid Charlie will crack under the strain."

First he gathered himself for a final gambit: a long, businesslike letter to Roger Straus, who'd been keeping the family afloat with personal loans. "This is a letter to present our financial problems to you, as clearly as we can, in an effort to discover whether Farrar, Straus & Young can help us out," Jackson wrote, proceeding to list their debts with laudable aplomb, to wit: they owed $14,081 on the house, and had missed their last two mortgage payments; they owed roughly $7,000 for items such as unpaid income tax, coal bills, grocery bills, clothes bills, hospital bills, electric bills, and so forth; Farrar, Straus and Young had loaned Jackson $2,000 (*not* an advance, since *What Happened* was off the table), and Roger's personal loans also came to about $2,000. Along with other odds and ends, Charlie reckoned his total debts at $25,528.51. His tone brightened slightly as he turned to his assets: given that his house was worth about $40,000, furnished, they actually had a net *worth* of almost $15,000, not to mention such potentially lucrative properties as his two unfinished novels, *Uncle Mr. Kember* and *Poor Martin Coyle*, and any number of unsold short stories. Moreover, Roger was, after all, "in the business of publishing authors and [knew] their ups and downs," and Charlie's ups had been considerable: from 1944 to 1947 he'd averaged an income of $42,703 a year, though admittedly he'd made about a tenth of that in 1952, so far, and the general trend had been precipitously downward. What he wanted, at any rate, was a loan of $11,500 from Farrar, Straus and Young on the security of a second mortgage: "It will not increase our indebtedness, it will only consolidate it—and vastly relieve the local pressures on me."

"Two great minds with a single thought," Roger jauntily replied. While regretting that a loan of $11,500 was "beyond our reach," he promised to "brood" a few days and phone that weekend to hash things over. But apparently their discussion was unfruitful, as Charlie took a lethal dose of Seconal (twenty-six tablets) the following Monday, September 15, leaving a farewell note for Rhoda, who rushed him to the hospital, where Dr. Gundersen noted that the patient arrived "groggy" but conscious ("49 year old author here frequently in the past who has various problems that do not require elucidation here"). The next day Charlie was sheepish but not, it seemed, suicidal anymore, and meanwhile his friend Dorothea had sold some of her jewelry to help pay a few of the more pressing local bills. Less than a week later Charlie was home again, tapering off with paraldehyde, and naturally unable to write (albeit sustained somewhat by the prospect of "The Boy Who Ran Away" in the November *Harper's Bazaar*). Already they dreaded the coal bills of winter, and were at a loss what to do for Christmas; Rhoda wrote Phyllis McGinley in Larchmont, wondering if she knew anyone who might be interested in buying a second-hand mink for $1,500, less than half what they'd paid for it in 1947 ("I doubt if, in the last two years, it has been worn more than ten times"). And perhaps something of that sort was arranged, since they seemed to have jolly holidays; indeed, at a New Year's "kids party," Charlie proved such a "cavorting parent" that his twelve-year-old daughter was a little mortified.

His high spirits were, alas, short-lived. Almost two weeks later, while visiting the Strauses in New York, Charlie abruptly disappeared. Alarmed, Dorothea phoned Rhoda, who ("sound[ing] cool, experienced, and resigned") advised her to pack his valise and leave it by the front door: "You shouldn't have the responsibility for him at a time like this." Dorothea did as she was told, discovering a cache of Seconal ("looking as innocent and cheerful as a jar of candies") in one of Charlie's drawers; deciding she had no right to confiscate his things, she packed it under some shirts and went out for the day. The valise was gone when she returned, but the library door, upstairs, was "ominously shut." Inside was Charlie, unconscious on the couch; like the needy, spiteful alcoholic Grace Dana in "The Problem Child," he'd left the now-almost-empty pill jar in plain sight. "It was an 'opera bouffe,' " said Roger in 1976. "He kind of knew he was going to be [saved]." Roger phoned Bellevue after hearing from his frantic wife, and an ambulance was dispatched to take their guest away.

The next day (Wednesday) he checked on Charlie, who was locked up in the Men's Violence Ward but otherwise in decent spirits. Aside from the "indescribable" terror of the place—mitigated somewhat by liberal doses of paraldehyde—his main concern was that word would leak to the media again, and he'd be hearing about his latest disgrace on Walter Winchell's Sunday night broadcast. Certainly the family had been well apprised, and Boom immediately sent money to Rhoda and invited her and the kids to come live with him in Malaga. Rhoda's sister, Katharine, was moved to write Boom a letter of thanks: "More than anything else I think your loyalty has given [Rhoda] the strength to finally take the step which certainly seems, after these past two years, inevitable. I hope with all my heart that she will go through with it. It's a pitiful and tragic thing to have seen Charlie disintegrate as if by his own wish." Rhoda agreed that it was time for a change, though she hated to impose on her kindly brother-in-law, and she couldn't bring herself (yet) to discuss the matter with the girls. As usual, she felt little other than tender concern for her husband: "Please don't say Charlie is a bastard and a wastrel and everything else," she wrote Boom. "He really is sick. His world and our worlds just don't jibe. If he can recover enough to fit into our world, it will be wonderful for him. For really no one suffers more from it than he does." Charlie, for his part, experienced "mixed feelings of relief and chagrin" when—after his release that weekend—he wasn't mentioned in any of the columns.

Rhoda, unassisted, grimly set about putting their house in order. The antique Sheraton furniture was up for sale, and her appeals to some Hollywood friends had brought in $250 from the Gershwins and $500 from Brackett. She closed her husband's checking account, and directed Brandt & Brandt to make all checks payable to her until further notice. Before leaving for New York to see about getting a job with her old employer, Time Inc., she had a frank discussion with Anthonisen, who agreed that her "first concern" should be the welfare of her children and herself; he hoped Charlie wouldn't have to be institutionalized, but "if he becomes a tramp then that must be done." As if to dramatize the prospect, Charlie managed to wangle a paraldehyde prescription in his wife's absence, going on a two-day "binge" with a lot of beer-drinking, too, and meeting her train in a barely controlled stupor. This time Rhoda was seriously vexed. It was "demoralizing," she wrote, to have "to watch him all the time"—watch him, that is, do nothing at all except read and play solitaire. He hadn't been able to work for months, and was beginning to wonder whether he'd ever work again.

In February he became briefly excited about the possibility (Roger's idea) of writing a syndicated column titled "You Know What?" about whatever happened to capture his promiscuous fancy. In a letter to his poet friend McGinley, he claimed to be putting together a package of twenty sample columns to submit to an agency; so far topics included Shakespeare in Everyday Life ("the way we go around quoting the Bard all day long without realizing it"), Name-Dropping, Anti-Semitism, The Curse We Are to Our Children, and others. Rhoda thought it might help sell the idea if McGinley wrote a few light-hearted verses for the column, and Charlie agreed it wouldn't hurt to ask ("Look, dear, when you're on a sinking ship—"). Before the poet could oblige, however—and she *had* promised to try—Charlie had already become discouraged: "This is to release you, dear—and won't you be glad!" he wrote a few days later, glumly vowing to "confine [his] daily chatter to Dorothea" and leave McGinley, a working writer, "free."

On Charlie's fiftieth birthday—April 6, 1953—Roger phoned with another idea: He'd seen a piece in *Look* about a narcotics agent in Houston, Tex Foster, who'd dedicated his life to fighting drugs because his "pa" had been an addict and Tex had suffered as a child, etc. Who better to write his story than Charlie? Roger thought he could do a "quickie" for Ballantine paperbacks, split the proceeds fifty-fifty, then maybe sell it to the movies for big dough! Two days later Tex arrived in Orford to tell his story, but for whatever reason it didn't pan out. Meanwhile Charlie's birthday had been "pleasant" if unexciting, said Rhoda, who cooked a canned ham she'd been "hoarding" for the occasion. "Wouldn't it be awful if I lived to be 100?" Charlie sighed.

THAT YEAR he experienced his usual springtime "re-birth" (as he put it) in early May—the ninth, to be exact: "the Great Day," as he excitedly wrote friends. For years he'd been considering a long story, "The Education of Harry Harrison," about a charming eunuch, and that day it suddenly occurred to him that he had a whole book on his hands—a *wonderful* book! "The novel is called A SECOND-HAND LIFE," he wrote McGinley, "the scene is my old Arcadia in the present and also 30 years ago, the two major characters are a woman of fifty who has a tremendous, almost an abnormal capacity for love, and a man who is unable to feel love at all—their lifelong friendship, and eventual desperate union." The Arcadian nymphomaniac who would serve as a foil to Harry Harrison was loosely based on Virginia "Ginny" Peirson, the disreputable daughter of a Newark bank president; she and Charlie had been childhood friends, and had stayed somewhat in touch over the years.* The character had also been suggested by the titular heroine of "Janie," who reads of a convict's death in the electric chair and elegiacally muses that there will be one less man in the world "to be had, if only once"; Jackson would put a finer point on that passage in *A Second-Hand Life*, as Winifred mourns the loss of "that which hung concealed behind the folds of the mechanic's jumper" rather than of the man per se.

Creative juices fizzing, Jackson quickly produced an outline, character sketches, and the opening scene ("just to 'set' it"), then embarked on a spree of story-writing meant to finance the novel. Rising before five each morning and working until lunch, he managed to write seven stories in just over a week—the first of which, "The Education of Wally West," he promptly sent to Baumgarten with a giddy cover letter: "*Well,* Madam: after eight months—*eight months* of hell—I've written another story again." As ever he hoped to crack *The New Yorker,* but, failing that, he suggested she send it to the munificent Maggie Cousins at *Cosmopolitan* ("I want $28,000, but will settle for $25,000"). Five more stories followed, feverishly, and finally he spent an entire week dumping a farrago of material into a long story originally (and aptly) titled "A Lazy Day on the Water." "It is hard to realize in the present age what an important part the Canal once played in the life of Arcadia," the story begins, "and in the life of all the other towns and small cities strung out through the state from Buffalo to Albany." The narrator remembers how once, as a boy, he'd hitched a ride as far as Lock 27 in Lyons, six miles away, aboard a canal boat with four raffish passengers: an unmarried couple, Captain Andersen and Mrs. Wacha (who scandalize the boy by ducking below deck for their "nap"), and their respective children, Carrie and Joe. Various sights along the way pique the narrator's memory, and so provide a pretext for telling about the time, say, when he saw the Cigarette Fiend at the county fair (thus recycling "The Cigarette Fiend," a story Jackson

---

* In the 1920s, Jackson had written a short apprentice novel about the Peirsons, *Family Portrait*—or perhaps "memoir" is more apt, since he didn't bother to change real-life names, and even included cameo appearances by mutual friends such as Marion Fleck. The Virginia of *Family Portrait* is high-spirited and mischievous, but hardly the ravenous trollop of *A Second-Hand Life*. Indeed, one scene in the earlier novel suggests that Peirson was little more than a flirt, at least while in the first bloom of youth: at age thirteen, during World War I, Virginia borrows her older sister's shirtwaist and skirt, rouges her cheeks, and goes for a nocturnal stroll along the canal, where a soldier tries to kiss her. When she bursts into tears and admits her age, the doughboy gives her a brotherly lecture and sends her home.

had written the day before he began this one), or the time a famous avia-
tor landed in Arcadia, and so on. For fifty pages.

"Do try to do a story that's a little closer to the commercial thing,
won't you please, Charlie?" begged Carl Brandt, who nonetheless ultimately managed to sell "A Lazy Day on the Water" for $500 to *Charm*,
where it would appear in abridged form two years later as "Still Waters,"
illustrated by Ben Shahn. During that whole hectic summer of 1953,
however, Charlie's only sale was "Landscape with Figures"—a racy sketch
about a sinister tramp who ogles a girl lying in a daisy field—which went
to *Esquire* for $250. "I'm really working hard—but alas, it seems entirely
fruitless," he wrote his agents on July 2. "Any news?"—then, scribbled
meekly in the margin: "You know I'm not nagging, don't you? I'm just so
eager to get back to Second-Hand Life, which was going so well."

He was more than discouraged at that point; he was suicidal again,
even somewhat in earnest, perhaps. He'd gotten stumbling drunk in
front of his children—the first time ever—on the Fourth of July. Each
year fireworks were set off from the hill behind Herb Lawrence's house
on the southernmost end of the Ridge; Charlie's daughters were friends
with Herb's step-daughter, Ann, and that year they were horrified when
their father (still dressed in his flamingo-colored shirt) started "career-
ing around" during the festivities. Three days later he took an overdose
of Nembutal, and was comatose and bloodied from a fall when Rhoda
got him to the hospital. Nigh unsinkable as ever, he was released on
July 12 ("Good recovery"), and cautioned to stay on paraldehyde lest he
succumb to delirium tremens.

He got right back to work, though the results were "grim," as he was
the first to admit. The manuscript for "Liebestod" does not survive
among his papers—a rare occurrence—though the gist can be gleaned
from rejection letters (as well as subsequent events). "LIEBESTOD
shook me up rather," wrote an editor for *Women's Home Companion*, "as
I'm one for all night record binges." In a nutshell, the story appears to
have been based on the author's tendency to accompany late-night pill,
booze, and/or paraldehyde sessions with music, in this case ending with
Wagner's "Liebestod" and the hero's suicide. "A music lover reaches his
last note. Very satisfying to me," an *Esquire* editor wrote in an internal memo, only to be overruled by chief editor Arnold Gingrich ("Let's
pass"). And whereas Charlie himself thought the story "*really* seem[ed]"
suited for *The New Yorker* ("Of course I have said this a million times
before"), he was again mistaken.

The same day (July 23) that he sent this lugubrious piece to Baumgarten, he cheerfully mentioned the arrival that afternoon of Roger and Dorothea and their small son, Roger III, for a weekend visit ("we couldn't be happier about it"), and that night his daughter Kate saw (or rather heard) him drunk for the *second* time ever. She was staying in her mother's room because of the guests, when—very late, after a long disastrous evening—Charlie unsteadily entered and began pleading for his "medicine" (paraldehyde); Rhoda refused; the ten-year-old Kate nervously feigned sleep. As for the Strauses, they had just collapsed in bed when the mournful, soaring strains of "Liebestod" began echoing throughout the house, followed by a knock on the door: "I must talk to you," said their host. "I am about to kill myself." Roger vaulted out of bed, but Dorothea stayed put. "For the first time, I had had enough," she later wrote.

> I did not believe in Charlie's suicide attempt. And the appropriate background music, in spite of its intrinsic beauty, or perhaps because of it, sounded as tinny and tawdry as a juke box in a penny arcade. . . . Then there was a knock on the door again, and Charlie stood in my room, swaying and angry. "Why are you the only one not downstairs? Do you want me to kill myself? Is that it?"

For the rest of the night, until the sun came up, they "begged, scolded, reasoned" while Charlie menacingly waved a pill jar whenever he detected a want of zeal ("What was the good of carrying off such a thing [suicide] if its full effect was to be lost on the one person most interested?—himself," Don muses in *The Lost Weekend*). Finally he was coaxed back to bed, sans pills, and the next day—prior to a hasty departure—Dorothea heard faint snoring and peeked inside her friend's room: "He was lying on his back, clad in pink Dr. Denton pajamas, primly buttoned up the front, with feet, like those worn by children downstairs on Christmas morning to see the tree."

Rhoda, at last, had reached the end of her vertiginous tether. "I'm leaving today," she announced, "and I'm taking the children with me. I've left a check for you on your desk, and we're going. We have to go." For the benefit of Alcoholics Anonymous, Charlie would relive the events of that "terrible day" again and again and again: "It was a beautiful morning and I will never forget, as long as I live, the sight of the children carrying out to the car armloads of books, and then they were gone.

And I was relieved." It was horrible, yes, and soon he'd be desperately depressed . . . but he would think about it tomorrow. For now he was free! "I went to my desk and there was a check for $250. Well, this was great: there would be no policemen around in the form of my wife. . . . I could do just as I pleased and have a whale of a time."

That night Charlie drank and drank, listened to music as loud as he liked, and almost went mad with loneliness. For a few days he badgered Rhoda with phone calls ("We promised the children summer camp! You have to bring them back!"), and finally took a taxi to Hanover, boarded a plane to Boston, then to New York, then to Philadelphia, where he took another cab some fifty miles to Malaga. Kate was playing in her uncle's yard with some neighborhood kids when the cab drove up and disgorged its drunken passenger; Kate, embarrassed, skittered off in the opposite direction. Rhoda refused to speak to her husband; she gathered the girls and promptly left the house. It occurred to Charlie that he could make a better case for himself once he was sober again, so he decided to go home and check himself into Hitchcock ("put paraldehyde on my chart, and sober up the easy way"). As Boom was driving him back to the airport, though, a flicker of lucidity asserted itself: "I was not responsible," he remembered. "I might be dead that night." He asked his brother if he knew of a hospital in Philadelphia where he could dry out, and Boom drove him to the house of a doctor in New Castle, Delaware, Tom McGuire, who came out to the curb and peered at Charlie inside the car. "You need a shave," he said. "What I need," said Charlie, "is a drink." McGuire directed him to a bar at the corner, where Charlie ordered a double scotch and a glass of beer; he quickly chugged the scotch, then innocently nursed the beer before heading back to McGuire's house. "You're in luck," the man said. He'd managed to get him the last available bed in the Saul Clinic at St. Luke's in Philadelphia: "It's not the Ritz-Carlton; it's pretty rough, but they'll take care of you." Charlie, with owlish dignity, declared that he wanted a place where he would be amongst "intellectual equals." McGuire laughed: "What are you talking about? *I'm* a better man than you are now." Charlie asked how he figured that. "Because I'm sober and you're drunk."

The Saul Clinic was founded by C. Dudley Saul in 1946, two years after Saul had written a personal letter to Charles Jackson, urging him to write about the rehabilitation of Don Birnam: "I am neither a 'foolish' nor wise psychiatrist. I am thinking solely of the responsibility that is yours and the great good that you can do; as every alcoholic, his friends, and his family await the sequel to 'The Lost Weekend.' " And now, nine years later, here was the author in person, far from rehabilitated and taking a *very* dim view of Dr. Saul's "dirty" clinic, where they refused to give him medication of any kind (he'd carelessly mentioned his pill habit to Dr. McGuire). In the throes of withdrawal that night, as he felt his mind giving way, Charlie was struck by an awful thought: "This is your natural home. This is where you belong." He totted up eighteen hospitalizations in the past six years; that would seem to suggest a pattern.

On the third day he met with the medical director, Martin D. Kissen, a kindly man who believed in the crucial importance of gaining an alcoholic's trust. "Well, Charlie," he said to his celebrated patient, "what are we going to do about it?" Jackson, in an agony of trembling embarrassment, said it was hopeless: He'd been sober for eleven years; he'd written the definitive novel about alcoholism; he'd been psychoanalyzed by "one of the big men in New York" . . . and nothing had worked. "I know everything there is to know about the alcoholic but the answer," he said, "and there isn't any such thing. I'm just through!" Kissen asked if he'd ever tried AA, and Jackson was contemptuous. As he'd later recall in his standard AA talk:

> I said, "Now really, doctor, don't give me that. You're a medical man, a man of science. You know better. . . . They say the Lord's Prayer at their meetings; this I couldn't possibly do. They're always talking about the spiritual; I haven't got an ounce of the spiritual in my makeup."
>
> He said, "You love your children, don't you?"
>
> And I said, "Yes."
>
> He said, "You believe in doing what's right when you can, don't you?"
>
> And I said, "Yes."
>
> And he said, "Isn't that spiritual? It's not material."

Still skeptical—but eager as ever to please—Charlie agreed to attend a meeting the next day at the hospital. Shuffling along in "paper slippers" and a terry-cloth robe, he sat down "with the other bums" and waited, tightly folding his arms to express a seemly intransigence and control his shakes. Then a shock: the first speaker was Dr. Tom McGuire, the very man who'd sent him there. He was a member of AA. Had Charlie gone five hundred miles out of his way to find this man by accident?

What's more, everything he said made perfect sense, and he seemed so happy! Indeed, Charlie felt a "major bond" with everyone there, though he could hardly remember a thing they'd said afterward. "These people *knew* about me . . . these people had been where I had been and had something I didn't have," he said. "And I wanted it."

Chapter Sixteen

A Rain of Snares

Jackson was released a couple of days after his meeting with Dr. Kissen, though he decided to stay in the area and attend AA meetings with his new friend and sponsor, Tom McGuire. He also continued to consult with Kissen, who insisted they include Rhoda, to her considerable gratification. "I've always felt the need for a three-sided conference," she wrote Boom afterward. "Which is a technique where analysis or psychiatry or whatever fails and will continue to fail by the very nature of the science: i.e., psychiatry attempts to fit the person into his environment and adjust to it. And it continues to be a very lonely way." After a week or so Charlie was ready to go home, and for the first time ever he stayed under the speed limit the whole way, and was even willing to stop for a leisurely meal at "Horrid Johnson's" (as his daughters called it) or just to admire the view. At least one AA slogan seemed to have taken hold: "Easy does it."

Word, as usual, traveled fast in Orford. Pat Hammond, a young woman who'd agreed to take dictation from Jackson, wrote in her diary that the job appeared to be scratched: "Charlie's wife left him, he went to pieces—is now in alky ward at a Phila. Hospital." Then, on August 11: "C. Jackson returneth." The locals were all agog, needless to say, even more so given that a sodden Charlie had done a certain amount of stumbling about town in his family's absence, enlisting the sympathy of the new minister, no less, who subsequently made a point of avoiding Rhoda at the post office. "I'm sure he believed whatever Charlie had to say to him," she wrote. "Of course the town has had a field day of rumor and report and guesses and speculation." Unlike the "very young" and "simple" minister, however, most of their neighbors had nothing but scorn for the incorrigible dipso in their midst. ("All town down on him," noted Hammond.)

But now, at least, he knew where to go for support. His sister-in-law gave him the name of an AA member in Montpelier, Fred Laird, and when Charlie phoned for information, the man asked if he wanted to address their chapter; no, said Charlie, he just wanted to attend an open meeting with his wife. In that case, said Laird, would he mind picking up a backslider named Stan Weeden, who ran a store across the river in Fairlee? ("Charlie stopped in to see [Weeden] yesterday," Rhoda recorded, "and found him in a most variable state.") Jackson was thus reminded that AA offered him more than merely a place to go at night—something to do instead of sitting in his room wrestling (or not) with temptation; here, rather, were people to call when he was in trouble, people who made a point of helping each other. During his previous years of putative sobriety, he'd found comfort in the idea that he was unique ("I was the whole cheese!"), but ultimately the prospect of a long, lonely, increasingly problematic future without even the hope of an occasional bender had become intolerable. In AA, though, he was asked only to be sober for 24 hours ("One day at a time"), and when the next day came, there were always others around to remind him, yet again, what lay in store if he resumed drinking.

But then, he'd always admired the *practical* side of AA, and more than ever he wondered why he should go on seeing a psychiatrist. Regaling Dr. Anthonisen with his adventures in Philadelphia, he kept pressing the point: if AA was something that *worked*, well then why spend time and money trying to find out *why* he was an alcoholic? Too late! He *was* an alcoholic, and he'd still be one with or without the answers. Anthonisen laughed, and finally admitted that he himself had been a sponsor for the AA group in Hanover for many years; "flabbergasted," Jackson asked why he'd never mentioned it, and the man replied that he simply didn't think it would work in Charlie's case—most AA members were, after all, pretty dull. Jackson could hardly deny it. The Montpelier group, in particular, had consisted of "the average, the blue-eyed, and the ordinary" in spades ("quarrymen and truck drivers and so on," according to Rhoda), and afterward Charlie couldn't resist telling the Strauses about the speaker who quoted "that great American poet Edgar A. Guest." But of course it was also true that Charlie coveted the love of such people intensely, and with renascent humility was willing to overlook what he'd hitherto considered their "Rotarianism." As he would presently confess for a *Life* article, "In my loneliness and, if you will, desperate need to be accepted again, I saw that the friendliness was well-meant, honest, utterly genuine." Part of Charlie liked nothing better than to rub elbows with "the gang" during a post-meeting coffee klatch, savoring his regular-guy persona all the more because of his certainty that others recognized him as the (lovably humble) author of *The Lost Weekend*. It was a role he could play, conceivably, for the rest of his life. "He really is so different sometimes, that I pinch myself," Rhoda wrote at the end of August. "He really is trying to change his attitude and point of view. And he really, for the first time in years, thinks of me as a person instead of just someone to do the work and take out gripes on."

After a few weeks, he decided to stick with the slightly less proletarian chapter in Barre, where he attended closed (members only) meetings on Tuesday and open meetings, with Rhoda, on Saturday. The seventy-mile round-trip was a chilly, winding drive, but Charlie was "having the time of [his] life" and wouldn't dream of missing a meeting. Such was his zeal that he was soon named chairman, and also asked to give his first talk on the four-month anniversary of his sobriety, November 28. Meanwhile, for Thanksgiving dinner, he and Rhoda invited a Barre alcoholic "with the elegant name of Gerard MacCarthy," whose wife had recently divorced him and gained full custody of their children, refusing to allow the wretch visiting privileges of any kind. Jackson wondered what kept the man going; to him, such a life was hardly worth living. ("Luckily he doesn't think deeply enough to know this, so he just goes on.")

Charlie himself was determined to be a better, more attentive father—by far the most rewarding way of "getting out of [him]self"—and to this end he formed a club called the Big Three that met Mondays at four in the library. With Kate presiding (Sarah was Treasurer and Charlie Secretary), the three discussed whatever was on their minds: books, music, what they wanted to be when they grew up, and Charlie's alcoholism, which he candidly explained was a problem he'd had for most of his adult life that was now being helped via AA. On the last subject he was careful to stress that his daughters needn't be *scared* of alcohol; unless they were alcoholics like him, they'd probably find it an asset. As a sober man, too, it occurred to him that he should pay more attention to his insecure younger daughter, and so proposed a collaboration on a children's book, *Dr. Happenstance*—"by Charles Jackson (age 50), illustrated by Kate Jackson (age 10)"—about an eccentric doctor who lets children indulge their "bad" habits until they get tired of them and revert to more "normal" behavior.* "I can't tell you how much good it is doing [Kate] to be 'working' on something with Papa," he wrote Dorothea. "She is all sweetness and light—so much so, in fact, that I am mistrustful, it is so unlike the usual slam-bang showy-off noisy Kate who has to demand attention every single minute—and why not. With so much talent, it's got to be used *some*how, even if she had to ram it down our throats 24 hours a day." But naturally he understood the girl—his virtual double—all too well, even offering to drown her ("for your own sake") if she turned out to be a genius.

JACKSON'S SECOND STORY COLLECTION, *Earthly Creatures*, was published in September, and he wanted it known that he didn't think very highly of the book; indeed, the only two stories he was "satisfied with" were "The Boy Who Ran Away" and "The Break"—or so he announced in a prefatory "Note to the Reader," which he'd written that awful July and hoped to publish on the front page of the *Times Book Review* ("one of his alcoholic pipe-dreams," as Rhoda later discovered). The other nine stories included "A Sunday Drive," first written in 1939; "Money," a comic sketch about his well-heeled ex-friend Ruby Schinasi; "Old Men and Boys," from his ill-fated sequence of Switzerland stories; and the interminable "Outlander"—all of which he offered to the reader in a spirit of almost abject apology, "fully (perhaps I should say 'bitterly') conscious of the knowledge that they are somewhat less than the ideal in a form I love."

---

* Jackson had planned seven chapters, each devoted to a particular child and "problem" (e.g., reading past bedtime or not taking one's bath). In the partial first chapter that survives ("ROUGHAGE"), a mother named Mrs. Wilkins complains that her son won't eat his spinach, whereupon the doctor gives *her* some pills and asks to see the boy alone. The doctor's chat with Mrs. Wilkins goes on for six typed pages—much revised—and that's all there is of *Dr. Happenstance*.

Critics—mindful, perhaps, of Jackson's recent travails—were mostly generous. By a stroke of very good fortune, *Earthly Creatures* was reviewed at length in the Sunday *Times* by his old Hollywood friend Budd Schulberg, whose glowing remarks seemed all but exclusively concerned with the better stories: "In their compassionate but merciless self-examination," he wrote, "their almost unbearable integrity, their penetrating (unarty) artfulness, they force the reader back upon himself, make him reflect upon his own motivations, his own worth." William Peden, in the *Saturday Review*, commended the author's willingness to address large themes ("man's loneliness, his capacity for self-destruction"), while quietly noting that "his treatment . . . doesn't always measure up to the demands of his subject matter." *The New Yorker*, however, was more unsparing than ever, disposing of *Earthly Creatures* with a few derisive lines in "Briefly Noted" ("The reader sees the point [of each story] well ahead of time and is left tapping his foot, waiting for the moment of revelation").

Still, Jackson's main reasons for publishing such an uneven book—namely, to make money and remind the world of his existence—were more than vindicated. Through a new marketing arrangement between Ballantine and Farrar, Straus and Young, the book was simultaneously published in a hardbound edition for $1.50 and a paperback for 35 cents, and the latter, at least, sold remarkably well (about eighty-five thousand copies). For the most part, too, Charlie was bucked by the moral support he received in the media, including an October mention in Harvey Breit's *Times Book Review* column: "We have never seen Mr. Jackson better," Breit wrote of a recent meeting with the troubled author; "he was trim and severe looking, very calm, precise in his speech, and what we mean is simply that Mr Jackson gave us the sense that he had been working hard and well." Breit's remarks, said Charlie, could hardly have been "between-the-linesier," but of course he appreciated the thought and agreed that he was, for a fact, "in fine shape": He had "a swell book to write," after all—*A Second-Hand Life*—and all he needed to bring it off was time (fourteen years, as it happened) and money.

As part of a healthier work regime, he'd rented a pine-paneled office on Main Street opposite the cemetery, and left his house early every morning so that his wife and children could move about freely without bothering him or vice versa. On August 13, two days after his return from Philadelphia, he'd met with his new amanuensis, Pat Hammond (whose father, the local doctor, had an office in the same building), and got to work on the sort of "salable trash" he hoped would pave the way for *A Second-Hand Life*. "Fascinating to watch his creative mind in action," Hammond noted in her diary that first day, when Jackson dictated the entirety of "Allergy," a winsome bit of fluff about a playwright who develops an allergy to his actress-wife's hair dye (the problem being that she staunchly denies dying her hair). The next day he came up with "The Bard in a Tent," about the time he wowed the ladies of Arcadia by correctly guessing that *The Tempest*—according to at least one Chautauqua lecturer—was Shakespeare's greatest play. "Not bad for a twelve-year-old kid," he half-heartedly ended the piece, seeming to anticipate the response of magazine editors ("Very nice, but after all only a reminiscence").

That pretty much exhausted his enthusiasm for salable trash. Among other, more ambitious projects to which he'd devote himself for the rest of 1953 was "Solitaire," a long story suggested by his own despondent card-playing that previous winter. Jackson had been contemplating this "marvelous, almost Dostoyevskean idea" for months, and the first pages seemed promising. His protagonist, Killoran, is an advertising executive who has lost his job and can't find another, so he distracts himself with endless games of solitaire; finally, goaded by his wife, he deigns to make himself "available" again on the job market. The dreariness of Madison Avenue in the Eisenhower era (soon to consume Jackson himself) is nicely evoked, as when Killoran waits for an interview with Sam, a former "friend":

> From time to time he caught the eye of the immaculate receptionist, who gave him a bright, antiseptic smile. As he was putting out his fourth cigarette in the immense malachite ash tray on the coffee table of glistening straw-blond wood, Sam stepped from the elevator, greeted him effusively, said he'd be with him in two jerks, waggled the tips of his well-manicured fingers at the receptionist, and disappeared down the corridor. Twenty minutes later Killoran was called in.

Unable to stomach such humiliation, he begins to skip appointments and spend aimless days drifting among the seamier bars of the city, where he won't be recognized, but finally returns home, for good, to his solitaire. As the story ends—or rather breaks off (on page 25)—Killoran is going quietly insane, pretending and then somewhat believing that he's playing for a thousand dollars a card—more!—and that his debts will soon be erased. . . . "I think I covered a little too much ground in it," Jackson observed of the story, which he never got around to finishing.

By then, however, he'd been carried away by "An Afternoon with Boris," an elegant if somewhat static meditation on the symbiosis of flesh and spirit. Jackson loved the idea and worked it out for weeks, zestfully, even though he conceded from the start that such a piece would be "much too cerebral for selling." "Boris" described a September visit to the studio of his friend Ilse Bischoff, a wealthy illustrator who lived a life of aesthetic, unmarried ease at her country home in Hartland, Vermont. That day Bischoff was drawing Jackson's portrait while they listened to the entire four-hour recording of Mussorgsky's opera *Boris Godunov*, which Charlie had once seen at La Scala "in [his] callower drunkener youth," loving the spectacle but somewhat missing the point of the music; that day in the studio, though, with few visual distractions to speak of, the music "seemed grander and more beautiful than ever." Meanwhile a piquant tension was provided by an apparent dalliance between Bischoff's coarse young servants, which led Jackson to reflect on his own taste for "the low and the lawless . . . even literally the unclean," and how that replenishes (rather than blunts) one's appetite for loftier diversions. Ravished by Mussorgsky's music, titillated by the servants, Jackson celebrates the sublime mingling of art and eros: "*Life* beckoned him, in short; he felt it burning inside his body as if he had taken some hot, intoxicating drink—poison or stimulant, it didn't matter which."

Jackson was thrilled with "Boris," which he considered nothing less than a milestone in his artistic development—a "new level of writing," as he excitedly wrote Dorothea: "it shows a discipline, craftsmanship, and yes, if you'll forgive the word so used by myself, an intellectuality that I have never yet achieved. . . . Really, when I read it over, it surprises the hell out of me—it just isn't me!" This, he felt certain, would finally silence his critics at *The New Yorker*, most notably William Maxwell—who, alas, swiftly disabused him of any such idea, citing the prejudice of his (now deceased) boss, Harold Ross, against stories about "the psychology of writers." *Partisan Review* and *Harper's Bazaar* would eventually follow suit, until in 1962 the story "almost made it" at *Playboy*, of all places, where Charlie's old friend Augie Spectorsky reluctantly decided that "this extremely well-written tale . . . wasn't quite strong enough plotwise for us at this time." Back in 1953, at any rate, the fiction market was simply drying up, as more and more middle-class readers turned to television for entertainment, while many of the slicks had either reduced or stopped running fiction altogether—an irreversible trend. At the end of that torturous but productive year, Jackson had sold a single story (for all of $250) and yet remained philosophical to an almost heedless degree: "It isn't only that the fiction market grows less and less," he wrote Brackett; "the failure was entirely in me, I think. I didn't do [the stories] quite wholeheartedly . . . and I think the reason was partly financial but even more, because my real love is the novel."

And so to the novel he returned, albeit *not* the novel he'd been raving about these many months. "And—hold everything!—I have gone back to WHAT HAPPENED," he announced that September to the Strauses. Revisiting the opening pages of *Farther and Wilder*, the first volume of his planned masterwork—wherein Don lies abed on the morning of his much-anticipated family reunion—he'd decided to start all over, rewriting in "sensual, almost 'tactile' terms rather than in interior terms of brooding introspection and intellectuality." (This around the time he was effusively congratulating himself for the "intellectuality" of "An Afternoon with Boris.") He refused, from now on, to agonize over the "rightness of every single sentence," as he tended to do in his best work; while reading great, super-prolific authors such as Tolstoy and Mann, it occurred to him again and again that they were simply *writing*, by God, getting *on* with it for heaven's sake, and that's what he would do! As for *A Second-Hand Life*, well, he'd recently reread it and found it "ashes in [his] mouth": "It was loaded with perfect craft; I might even go so far as to say that it was crafty, almost, with the author obviously knowing more than he was telling. . . . No thank you—I hate such skillful craft—such wiseness. [*Farther and Wilder*] reads as if the author actually doesn't know what lies ahead . . . in short it reads like life, *is* life on every page." Thus, by the end of 1953, Charlie had all but entirely reverted to the glorious hyperbole of three years before: *What Happened* would be his masterpiece! "It has dignity, humor, calm, beauty of form . . . love, charity"—et cetera. Indeed, his fondest dream was to publish that first volume as early as the fall of 1954.

Privately, though, he had grave doubts about his whole non-crafty, "life unfolding moment by moment" approach, which occasionally seemed only "careless and rambling." On January 7, 1954, he was moved to type a few pages of diary, as he'd been reading Hart Crane's letters and was struck by the young man's unyielding passion for the mot juste: "I am more and more aware of my total lack of originality," Charlie reflected, "my *un*use of language, and at fifty it seems to be a hopeless proposition to expect any change in this. I can only write the human, meanderingly." Unsatisfied with mere diary writing (like suicide, it was only worthwhile if one could observe its effect on others), Charlie transcribed this doleful confession word for word into a letter to Dorothea. Then, lest she lose faith in his work, he hastened to add that his "prosaic" style in *Farther and Wilder* was mitigated—nay, transformed—by certain deftly placed images hinting at "a higher plane and meaning," a kind of "poetry at times" . . . and so on, until he'd whipped himself back into an ecstasy over what amounted to a revolution of his art and self: "It is easily the finest thing I have yet written—no inward preoccupation with self-important ego, no self-evisceration and personal agony—all of it *outside* of myself—outside!—part of a general, even perhaps universal, experience: life, in short." And this had a lot to do ("well, everything to do") with his sobriety, thanks to AA, or so he humbly added in a different letter written that same day.

WHILE JACKSON plugged away at *Farther and Wilder*, his finances continued to deteriorate. He'd been allowed to keep his advance for *Earthly Creatures*, $4,500 (less commission), but all other proceeds had gone toward his yawning debit balance at Farrar, Straus and Young. Time Inc. hadn't been able to hire Rhoda, and that autumn she accepted a dollar an hour to work on a trial basis for Dartmouth's Tuck School of Business. October had proved a particularly cruel month. First, the Internal Revenue Service had confiscated the Jacksons' bank account ($219.78), then the Motor Vehicles Bureau noticed that Charlie hadn't paid his auto insurance, and revoked his driver's license; they'd "watched [him] like a hawk" since his drunken head-on collision in March 1951, and now, ironically, he was unable to drive himself to AA meetings.

Charlie took it hard. That night—still enthralled by *Boris Godunov*—he consoled himself by reading about poor Mussorgsky, growing incensed when his eyes fell on the following: "His life was not admirable; he was slovenly and drunken and a drug addict. He died in St. Petersburg on his 42nd birthday." "It was like an affront," Charlie wrote Dorothea; "I felt a terrible sense of injustice over the way the world uses its artists—and how unimportant the artist has always been considered by society, how troublesome, and how he is popularly deserving of nothing but neglect, and indifference." If he ever ran dry as a fiction writer, he'd devote himself to a book that would " 'wake up' the world" to the predicament of great, shabbily treated geniuses like Mussorgsky, whose own wealthy patrons might have prevented his early demise . . . but no! They could only spare "discreet" little gifts, lest they hurt a drowning man's pride! Worried, perhaps, that he was overplaying his hand a little, Charlie added, "*Liss*-en: are you following me still in the impersonal detached way in which I'm writing this? You did say that no subject *as* subject should be barred between us, and I trust you on that score." If indeed Dorothea had guessed that she was being twitted, not so obliquely, for her kind but all too occasional sops (as Charlie saw it), she was dead-on. "I dearly love [her]," he wrote in his diary three weeks later, "[but she] knows not what it is to earn a living"; given his ongoing poverty and fading star, he feared they could "no longer meet on equal ground."

That December (1953) he'd gone to New York for three days, returning in triumph with an assignment to write a two-part article on AA for *Life*. "The More Social Disease," as he proposed to call it, would "shake the complacency of the citizenry from coast to coast," appearing (he hoped) on the magazine's cover and perhaps leading to a lucrative new career in journalism. *Life* had offered him $1,250 on receipt of the manuscript, and another $1,250 if they decided to publish, and meanwhile Roger wanted him to expand the piece into a two-hundred-page book for Ballantine, followed perhaps by a juicy post-publication sale to *Reader's Digest*.

More than a month later—five days past deadline—Jackson wrote his *Life* editor, William Jay Gold, that he was down to fourteen dollars cash and needed a bit more in the way of an advance. The work had proved tricky. One problem was AA's policy of anonymity, which prevented his admitting that he was a member; rather he portrayed himself as a curious outsider who'd attended a few open meetings: "In all honesty I cannot say that my interest has been entirely academic, but it is true that I have gone to these meetings largely in the spirit of research. . . ." Part One, "Personal Background," was mostly a recapitulation of what was becoming Jackson's boilerplate AA talk, covering his own history of alcoholism, his long resistance to AA, and finally his conversion at the Saul Clinic. The main problem was Part Two, "Possible Answers," which focused on the policies, procedures, and philosophy of AA—all vastly misunderstood, as Charlie would have it. His *Life* editor found this part a letdown, urging the author to "dramatize" more, while also deploring (via marginal admonishment) such gags as this: "An AA in my community wrote to his sister in California that he had become a member of the organization, and she replied, by postcard, 'I'm so glad to hear that you have joined the A. A. A. and do you wear a uniform?' "* Nonetheless Gold remained hopeful that, with revision, the article might yet prove a boon to humanity—but Charlie had already slung his bolt. "I never did finish it," he admitted eight months later, once his life had taken a radical new direction.

BACK IN OCTOBER, Charlie had written his old Hollywood agent, Leland Hayward, that he was "trying [his] damnedest to stay out of TV," but soon enough he gave in: "For too long, now, I've babied myself with the delusion that I was a respectable novelist, too good to go out and make a living in the commercial field. But I've done it before and can do it again." Indeed he'd done it before, long ago as the briskly efficient author of the popular radio serial *Sweet River*, and quite recently, in 1952, when he'd written an unsold teleplay for *The Aldrich Family*. Now, returning from New York in December, not only did he have that promising *Life* article to write, but also "definite commitments on 3 TV shows" for *Studio One*, as he wrote Bischoff—or rather, "three *not quite so definite*" (my italics) scripts for *Studio One*, as he wrote a different friend the following day—and so he'd be coming back to New York on January 18, after he finished the *Life* piece, to get started with *Studio One* and perhaps run down a few other assignments as well. Needing a cheap place to stay for six weeks, he took a room on East 66th at the Lotos Club, where Roger was a member and would be "footing the bill as usual," or so Charlie claimed, though in truth Roger had soberly advised him that he'd be charged at least $4.20 a day.

Skipping along the path back to solvency, he hoped, Charlie had a rattling good time in New York. He lunched with his old Bermuda pal, James Thurber ("blind as a bat but marvelous as ever"); he attended the National Book Award ceremony at the Commodore Hotel, subsequently lunching with that year's fiction winner, Saul Bellow ("I like him so

---

* A ghastly joke, granted, but Gold was a tough audience at the best of times. "This gets preachy" he scribbled, referring to a rather prescient remark on Charlie's part: "I foresee the day, in a future by no means remote, when the two or three cocktails for lunch, the several highballs in the evening, and the heavy weekend drinking that has become standard in much of our society, particularly among the professional class in their suburban homes, will be abandoned altogether by intelligent men and women, who want more out of life than hangovers."

much"); he bumped into an old acquaintance, Bette Davis, who remembered "that sweet little man on the couch" she'd met in Nantucket ten years before, and warmly introduced him to her well-mannered daughter, Barbara ("so polite").* But the pinnacle of that first superlative week was a performance of *Boris Godunov* at the Metropolitan Opera, which he attended with the Strauses and Ilse Bischoff, delighted by how well his friends took to each other. As for the show itself, it was "a glory beyond description," he wrote Rhoda; Dorothea, for her part, would always remember with deep tenderness the man who "could sit on the edge of his chair at a performance of *Boris Godunov* like a child with all the world's pageantry spread before him."

And why not? The world was his oyster! "The reception around town, in the advertising and TV offices, would surprise you, as it has surprised me," he wrote Anthonisen. "I get calls and offers by the dozens, merely because it is known in the profession that I at least *seem* to be on the beam again." CBS had made a "definite commitment" to hire Charlie to write a couple of radio scripts for *Suspense*, and possibly come up with a new soap opera too, while his old pal Max Wylie had put him in touch with Bill Moorwood, at *Medallion Theatre*, who wanted him to write a teleplay "at one thousand per throw"—this, all this, in addition to the "two [*sic*] scripts for Studio One," and "out of the blue" Carl Brandt had just called with the news that he'd sold one of Charlie's old stories, "A Midsummer Night," to a magazine called *Manhunt* for "one thousand bucks" (actually five hundred). And Charlie couldn't even remember what the story was about!

When his AA sponsor, Tom McGuire, admitted to being worried about him ("I hope you are not involved in any difficulty in New York"), Charlie was snappish: except for being damnably broke—for now—he was *fine*. Never better! Along with the many, many money-making opportunities flying at his head from every direction, he was diligently attending AA meetings with Max Wylie at the Lenox Hill chapter, where he spoke on the tenth anniversary of *The Lost Weekend*. His total rehabilitation as an artist and human being, in fact, had given Roger a marvelous idea for *What Happened*: "I absolutely and completely agreed with you that that novel couldn't be written until there was an end," he'd enthused back in December. "I may be off my rocker, but it seems to me . . . that

---

* The latter, as B. D. Hyman, would go on to write the scabrous memoir *My Mother's Keeper*.

really the end of [W]hat [H]appened could be the beginning of A. A." The final scene, as Roger saw it, would be that first-ever talk Charlie had given to the Barre AA in November, recounting his whole terrible ordeal from beginning to end, the tying together of "two ends of the string" to make a circle. . . .

Unfortunately Charlie was not sober, strictly speaking, nor had he been sober for the previous six months. On the contrary: now that he was no longer drinking, he was taking more pills than ever. As he'd later admit to AA (claiming he didn't realize, at the time, that it was verboten): "I couldn't meet a friend for lunch, I couldn't write a line, I couldn't attend an AA meeting, and most certainly I couldn't speak at an AA meeting, without the help of these drugs." Over the holidays he'd paid a visit to Charles and Phyllis (McGinley) Hayden, who'd introduced him to one of their Larchmont neighbors, Dr. Walter Modell, an eminent Cornell University Medical School professor and editor of the journal *Clinical Pharmacology and Therapeutics.* To this man Charlie eagerly confided his dependency on Seconal and the like, and afterward Modell wrote him a long commiserating letter about the difficulty (the *danger* even) of weaning oneself from such drugs. Seeing an opportunity—his furtive pill-taking had been "a load on [his] mind"—he showed the letter to Rhoda. "I only succeeded in sort of shifting the load from, say, the cerebellum to the medulla oblongata," Charlie wrote Modell of the terrible row that ensued. Rhoda had utterly refused to hear reason on the subject, and for a few days Charlie had furiously considered divorce (while hoping his "love for the children" would restrain him): "The more I thrive and the better I do," he fumed, "the less Rhoda will have to do with me."

McGuire had asked him to speak at a big AA banquet on February 13 at the Hotel du Pont in Wilmington, Delaware, and while Charlie professed to be very nervous about such large-scale exposure—especially given his recent laryngitis after reading "a good hundred pages" of *Farther and Wilder* aloud to the Haydens and Modells in Larchmont—he was nonetheless "looking forward to being able to do something, in a very small way, for [McGuire]." Truth be known, AA had been more fun than ever since Charlie had become one of its most sought-after speakers; indeed, the week of that Wilmington banquet, he'd given no fewer than six talks. Members responded so emotionally to the author of *The Lost Weekend*—such a kindly, courteous fellow in person!—that he had to take a lot of pills to get through it, and felt alternately exalted and guilty when people accosted him with fervid congratulations. In Wilmington, anyway, Charlie was a hit, though afterward he sheepishly revealed to Boom and their Malaga friend Barbara Peech—both were in the audience, along with the Strauses—that he had capsules in his pocket.

The next day he made the same confession to Dr. McGuire, a zealous Catholic and stolid purist when it came to both Church and AA doctrine. McGuire's response was, if anything, worse than Rhoda's. He said that he'd rather have seen Charlie "fall flat on [his] face" at the banquet than get through it on pills, and refused even to glance at Dr. Modell's letter about the difficulties of drug addiction. Charlie was deeply shaken by what seemed the end of a promising friendship, though on calmer reflection he realized that he and McGuire had little in common. "How are the mighty fallen and the something-something-something, or however the hell it goes," he wrote "Uncle Tom" a few days later, deploring the man's "closed-mind [*sic*] attitude" to the more tolerant, enlightened viewpoint embodied by Modell's letter: "You have your Church, your Virgin, your images and idols and such, which you accept without question (and quite rightly, for you) and which apparently give you something that I do not have at all. . . . But by the same token, you should not question *my* doubts in these matters." With a touch of seemly deprecation ("God help them"), he mentioned that his talk that night at the Lenox Hill chapter in New York would be attended by Marty Mann and her partner, Priscilla Peck, who'd visited him in Orford a few months back; next to Bill Wilson himself, Mann was easily the most illustrious figure in AA—the first woman to stay sober in the program, and founder of the National Council on Alcoholism. Another speaker that night was an old CBS colleague, Harry Frazee, and both would be introduced by their mutual friend Max Wylie.

The morning after his Lenox Hill appearance, Charlie woke up in the detox ward at Knickerbocker Hospital in Harlem (where, by an interesting coincidence, he'd paid an ambassadorial visit three weeks before). He'd had his first (alcoholic) slip as a member of AA. "I can never speak again!" he wanly declared to a new Lenox Hill friend, Dick Anderson, who'd come to sit at his bedside. "There's something about getting up in front of an audience that brings out the worst in me. I'm performing. I must never do it again!" "Charlie, you *must* do it," said Anderson, reassuring him with a folksy anecdote that Charlie would henceforth incorporate into his talks: A group of priests had a small AA chapter on the Hudson, and one priest was "on the circuit" like Charlie—much in demand as a speaker—until word got back to him that his celebrity was going to his head. "Father," he said to his superior, "do you think I should hide my light under a bushel?" "No, my son," the wise old priest replied, "but you shouldn't forget whose light it is!"

Once he got out of the hospital, Charlie phoned his friend Max and explained what had happened; he also mentioned the pills. To his bewilderment ("I am still confused by Max's reaction . . . "), Wylie denounced him for speaking at AA meetings under false pretenses, and moreover pointed out that his "first slip" was nothing of the kind, since essentially he'd been slipping the whole time. Poor Charlie was utterly deflated. Before leaving town he had lunch with Harry Frazee—who incidentally had been *far* more sympathetic than Max, Tom, or Rhoda—and admitted that his many alleged assignments from *Studio One*, *Medallion Theatre*, CBS, and so forth, had all come to naught: "Television, for some reason, intimidates the hell out of me," he wrote Frazee afterward; "I just can't deliver in that field; I am completed blocked when I try it." Indeed, the only thing he had to show for the whole six-week odyssey in New York was a bill from the Lotos Club for $345.69, which Roger regretfully submitted a week later, remarking that it almost entirely wiped out the $450 (after commission) Charlie had received from *Manhunt*.

RHODA'S ATTITUDE may be imagined. "But *why* did you drink at *all*?" she asked, during a somber chat at the kitchen table, once the children had gone to bed after giddily welcoming their father home and asking him a lot of questions about his trip (they "even asked about the hospital"). When Rhoda first learned that he'd leapt off the wagon again, she'd hastily written Baumgarten begging her *not* to give him any money: "I realize he'll be broke when he gets out of the hospital. But I'm broke too, with all the house bills to pay." And with this latest thirteenth chime of the clock echoing in her head, she also asked the agent to supply a complete list of checks that had been disbursed to Charlie that year. And now here the miscreant sat, all the more shaky and depressed for having taken only a couple of pills that night ("I've cut way down to almost nothing"). As for Rhoda's question about his slip, well, alcoholics have an impulse to drink—he replied, in effect—and he'd obeyed that impulse. At any rate she forgave him, and with typical punctilio dashed off a letter to Baumgarten calling off the audit ("I felt dishonest doing it behind Charlie's back . . . ").

A bleaker ordeal awaited Charlie the next night, when he attended his first closed meeting with the Barre AA since his lapse. "Wanted the pickup of a pill," he noted, "but somehow didn't take it." The reception was chilly. The "gang" made it immediately clear that Charlie would have to resign from the steering committee, and afterward, as transportation was being arranged for a meeting in Bethel, the mayor's wife ("our one 'lady' member, holier-than-thou") pointedly announced: "I volunteer my car—on one condition. And that is, no slippees riding with me!"

Charlie felt more isolated than ever, longing for his more worldly friends (people like Harry Frazee and Dick Anderson, that is, *not* the censorious Max Wylie) at Lenox Hill AA chapter. If only he could afford it, he'd hole up at a cheap hotel and attend meetings seven nights a week. Meanwhile his new chums tried to comfort him from afar: Anderson, himself a former pill user, wrote that he'd only begun to understand and respect himself once the "frights and fears" of addiction had ceased, and urged Charlie to keep fighting, while an affable adman at the Biow Company, Warren Ambrose, cheered him on with advice that might have seemed Rotarian once, but now was balm to his aching soul:

> Would I help more if I said, "For God's sake Charlie, stop kickin' the hell out of my 'fellow-man Jackson'! Let him up! Let him breathe and live and be happy! He's suffered enough! . . ."
> In other words, Charlie—*no* pills . . . *no* drinks . . . today!
> We *love* you, boy!

Life might have seemed pretty hopeless were it not for the fact that they'd finally, finally managed to sell the house in Orford. "It was like living on a sinking ship," Charlie wrote the Gershwins; with the proceeds, however, they were able to leave town with all bills paid, and Boom was delighted to put them up as long as they liked at his and Jim's houses in Malaga. They ended up staying the entire summer, during which Charlie was able to commute to New York, see his friends in Lenox Hill, and even pick up some nonimaginary TV work. As for Rhoda, she girded herself with the usual Zeno-like patience, while hoping against hope that the end of the Orford era just might prove a "turning point" of sorts: "Not that I'm girlish enough to think all troubles are over . . . But I do feel that I'm getting a little more independent in my reaction to them, and maybe I can tackle them a little less emotionally when they come up."

By the fall it seemed (not for the first time, to be sure) as though life were starting over. Through an AA friend they found a charming two-story house in Sandy Hook, Connecticut—a village in Newtown, about sixty miles from Manhattan—that had once belonged to Thurber. For $150 a month they got three bedrooms and an ideal writing studio for Charlie in the rear, with bunk beds, a fireplace, his own bathroom, and a picture window framing a pasture with grazing cows. As ever Charlie adorned the walls with his "Lar[e]s and Penates" (Garbo, Mann, Chaplin, Fitzgerald, et al.), and settled down into what he hoped would prove his productive middle years. Nor was he the bitter recluse he'd been in Orford. Not only was there a swell AA chapter at the local Trinity Episcopal Church, but the town was a veritable colony of suburban artists, including Charlie's old playwright friend from his Brattleboro days, Paul Osborn, and also the director "Gadge" Kazan, the actor "Freddy" March (Jackson's first choice, eight years before, to play Grandin in the abortive *Fall of Valor* movie), and Arthur Miller (later his neighbor at the Hotel Chelsea). Every Sunday there were hilarious softball games at the Bradley Smiths' (he a *Life* photographer, she a former Art Students Leaguer like Boom), and Charlie was even offered the second lead in a community theater production of *Bell, Book and Candle*.

Once the smoke had cleared, and the last glossy photo was hung, Charlie soberly assessed his future: all fiction writing, including *Farther and Wilder* (so he wrote friends), would simply have to wait until he'd gotten a few more TV assignments to ease the financial strain. That was in September. Then, suddenly, two months later, he sent a feverish five-page letter to the Strauses (and a carbon to Baumgarten) about a new acquaintance of his—called Reuben for the purpose of his letter as well as the story he proposed to write—who had recently "unburden[ed] himself" about his incredible, tragic past, a story "of almost stunning and legendary grandeur" whose implications Reuben himself "didn't begin even faintly to understand," but which had rocked Charlie to his core. Once his initial, extreme discomfiture had passed, though, he realized ("dog of a writer that I am") that he had "a powerful responsibility" to tell Reuben's story in the form of a novel—a great novel!—which must remain a secret, for now, between the four of them: "The reasons are two: in the first place, Rhoda would be plunged into despair at the very thought of my writing another novel (at a time like this, when we are so badly in need of money, and I should be earning a living in TV); and second, Rhoda knows 'Reuben' but knows nothing whatever of his story."

As for that story, it followed the "classic pattern" of "one of the great, universally-appealing Greek myths"—though Charlie was vague to the

point of coyness as to *which* (baldly obvious) myth—and would be titled
A Rain of Snares after one of the Psalms: "Upon the wicked He shall rain
snares, fire and brimstone, and an horrible tempest . . . "* Reuben grows
up in the home of a cruel father and stepmother, his natural mother
having run away when he was a toddler; soon Reuben himself flees and
joins the Navy, where he cultivates a curious predilection for "motherly
whores." In due course he returns home and "unwittingly kills his father"
(Charlie admitted he hadn't really "worked out" that part of the plot),
and then a few years later he meets an attractive older woman who proves
to be his own long-lost mother; so "overjoyed" are both that they cannot
restrain themselves from "a passionate, lost, headlong love-relationship"
that (Charlie hoped) would instill in even his most puritan readers a
sense "of the inexhaustible variety and mystery of a life which might, but
for God's grace, have been our own."

"In other words," he summed up, "I am finally beginning to feel alive
again, that I may still have a place or may yet regain one, and there is
much work ahead and good work to be done." *A Rain of Snares* was only
the beginning. He saw it as a short novel ("say 250 pages at the most")
that could easily be published by 1955, after which his books would
appear once a year, at least, as follows:

> . . . the collection of short stories called A MATTER OF LINES
> in 1956; A SECOND-HAND LIFE in 1957; the second collection
> BENEATH THE WAVE in 1958 (the title derives from Millay's "I
> do believe the most of me / Floats under water; and men see / Above
> the wave a jagged small / Mountain of ice, and that is all. / Only the
> depths of other peaks / May know my substance when it speaks, /
> And steadfast through the grinding jam / Remain aware of what I
> am. / Myself, I think, shall never know / How far beneath the wave I
> go . . . "). Then, at last (by which time I will know and understand it),
> in 1959, the big book WHAT HAPPENED, the first part of which
> you know, called FARTHER AND WILDER—and which, if you
> like can be published separately. . . .[†]

---

* As with his previous five books, Jackson also envisaged a Shakespeare quotation
for the title page—in this case, a couplet from *Measure for Measure:* "Well, heaven
forgive him! and forgive us all! / Some rise by sin, and some by virtue fall . . . " The
same quote would be used as the epigraph for *A Second-Hand Life,* suggesting a
similar concern with the ambiguity of certain received ideas about virtue and vice.
[†] *Beneath the Wave* was originally the title of the last volume (of three or four,

Only a few paragraphs survive of *A Rain of Snares*, and these are almost certainly the only ones Jackson wrote. The opening passage was rewritten at least ten times. "One no longer meets, in the modern age, a man who strikes one as a tragic hero," the simplest version begins.

> Our mediocre society, our classless culture, levels all men. There are no kings left; no more personages outstanding in a lonely nobility all the more pronounced, apparently, because of the fatal flaw that runs hand in hand with greatness . . . above all, no more great sinners who, it is said, are closer to God and the more beloved of God because of the blackness of their sins . . . all the blacker, the more dreadful and anomalous, because of their stature. Or, to put it another way, *only* black for very reason of that stature. . . .

The passage is retyped again and again, essentially unchanged except for a slight convolution of wording each time that makes it subtly *worse*, as if the author were taking a simple (too simple) idea and trying to torture it into something profound: "modern age" becomes "these standardized times"; "tragic hero" becomes "epic hero" becomes "hero in the epic sense," and so forth. Jackson also managed to write an ending of sorts—a few lines scribbled on tablet paper—which, he hoped, would make the reader realize, abruptly, by a kind of ironical sleight of hand, that the "wickedness" underlying the story has been thus perceived as a matter of *convention* merely, and may not "hold water at all" . . . so he told the Strauses. At any rate, it reads as follows:

> And so I left him there on the wide seabeach, under the revolving skies, a man condemned, like Dogberry's Borachio, to everlasting redemption.
>
> He was a man inexorably (?) chained to his destiny; struggle though he might and did—fall, rise, fall, to rise and struggle again—he was wedded forever.
>
> From now on the reader is on his own . . . but, whatever his reaction, to learn something, I hope, of the inexhaustible variety and mystery of a life which might, but for God's grace, have been one's own.

---

depending on whether Jackson was planning a trilogy or tetralogy at the moment) of *What Happened*, which in his notes he renamed *The Future Found*—this an inverted homage to Proust's final title, *The Past Recaptured* (*Le temps retrouvé*). The second volume of *What Happened* was usually titled *I, Too, Was There*.

These breathtakingly awful fragments were probably Jackson's last attempt at fiction for at least five years. A month after his frenzied pitch for *A Rain of Snares*, Baumgarten mildly inquired whether she might expect the rest of his "outline" as promised, but nothing materialized until almost a year later, on September 26, 1955, when Charlie suddenly announced (on J. Walter Thompson letterhead) that he had "Very Important Things to discuss—mostly a book," for which he hoped to get an advance and pay some of his more pressing bills.

Then, as a writer, he fell off the map for the rest of the decade.

Chapter Seventeen

A New Addiction

Jackson would always hate the idea of working in television ("It's a terrible medium"), though he was certainly grateful for the money. Once his first jobs began trickling in that summer (1954), he was finally able to repay long-standing personal loans to the Gershwins, Brackett, and his old playwright friend Howard Lindsay, and he even capitulated to his daughters' demand for a family TV, their first, a top-shelf model with a twenty-two-inch screen: "Monstrous in a nice house," he said. "And what do you get when you look?"

In the beginning he'd go to the city once a week and "make the rounds of the agencies," until his first teleplay was produced that October for *General Electric Theater,* "The High Green Wall," an adaptation of Evelyn Waugh's "The Man Who Liked Dickens." One can hardly imagine a more congenial assignment: Charlie adored Waugh so extravagantly that he'd reread *A Handful of Dust* (into which the "Dickens" story had been incorporated) four times in the summer of 1945 alone, when he was struggling with *The Fall of Valor* and hoping to pick up something of Waugh's genius for dialogue and narrative pace. "The High Green Wall" starred Joseph Cotten as the hapless Paul Henty—held captive in the Amazon by an illiterate lunatic who makes him read Dickens aloud—and the director of the twenty-six-minute teleplay was Nicholas Ray, no less, then at the height of his career, having just made *Johnny Guitar* (1954) and soon to make *Rebel Without a Cause* (1955). With such a promising pool of talent (and Ronald Reagan hosting!) one would expect a stellar result. George McCartney, a Waugh scholar, remembered enjoying "The High Green Wall" as a twelve-year-old in 1954, but when he revisited the show almost fifty years later (at a Museum of Modern Art retrospective), he found it "astonishingly dull": the "usually reliable" Cotten, he wrote, alternated "almost indistinguishably between two expressions: wounded nobility and weary bewilderment. To be fair, the role as written doesn't afford many opportunities to do much else."

Jackson also submitted a script for *Fork in the Road*, a new television series to be produced, at Marty Mann's behest, by the National Council on Alcoholism. Through the literary agent Audrey Wood, sample episodes were solicited from Jackson, William Inge, Tennessee Williams, and Gore Vidal. The last two apparently passed, but Inge submitted "Max" and Jackson adapted his short story about Grace Dana, "The Problem Child," which he thought Marty Mann would "respond to" and "perhaps even like": both she and Dana, after all, were from genteel backgrounds, and Mann had taken great pains to dispel the myth that alcoholism was primarily a male problem. As Jackson noted, his script was essentially a "one-woman show" and therefore required a highly skilled actress who could "indicate guile and duplicity throughout, and at the same time engage and hold our deepest sympathy and concern." Given that the teleplay's Grace Dana is, if anything, even more obnoxious than her counterpart in the story ("THROUGHOUT, THERE IS A HALF-SMILE ON HER PRETTY FACE, A SMILE OF SUPERIORITY WHICH SEEMS TO SAY: THESE PEOPLE SIMPLY DO NOT UNDERSTAND"), it would have taken an actress of Garbo-like subtlety to fill the bill, but in any case *Fork in the Road* was unable to find a sponsor.

Around this time, happily, Jackson was hired by the advertising agency J. Walter Thompson, producer of the live anthology drama, *Kraft Television Theatre*. As a script editor earning the princely wage of five hundred dollars a week, Jackson would no longer have to tax his dormant muse by writing for such an inimical genre ("I just can't deliver in that field"). Rather he'd be vetting scripts, written by others, that appealed to suburban viewers, mostly housewives, who not only watched *Kraft* for its family-oriented entertainment ("realism with a modest moral," as one JWT executive put it), but also for its practical advice about "gracious living," such as viewers found in the regular two-minute segments featuring a pair of disembodied hands preparing a simple but delicious meal using Kraft products. During its eleven-year run from 1947 to 1958, Kraft would broadcast 650 plays chosen from an estimated 18,845 scripts, and much of that winnowing was accomplished by Jackson and his boss, Ed Rice, a veteran radio writer who'd been with *Kraft* from the beginning and had had to learn on the job (and later impress on his assistants) the profound difference between an aural medium and a mostly visual one. Rice and Jackson were interviewed by an AP reporter in the summer of 1955, and for his part Charlie presented himself as a levelheaded professional who took his work very seriously indeed, emphasizing that a good TV program was absolutely dependent on a solid script: "One very obvious problem is that many good writers suffer from snobbishness about TV," he observed. "Perhaps that's because a show is over so quickly and they don't have the sense of tangible achievement that comes from a book. They forget that several million people will see their dramas—many more than will read their books."

It was hard to argue with that kind of mass-cult popularity, and the reporter was gratified to find "a first-rate American writer" such as Charles Jackson, author of *The Lost Weekend*, willing to labor "in the television vineyards." Charlie was also treated with some deference by his colleagues—because of his prestige as a writer, certainly, but also (perhaps) because his tenure coincided with a considerable uptick in the quality of JWT's programming. "The notion that an advertising agency must be a corporate dolt in TV theatrical matters is not standing up too well in one quarter," wrote the *New York Times* television critic, Jack Gould, on March 7, 1955. "The J. Walter Thompson Co., one of the largest agencies, is quietly walking off with some major honors for distinguished TV drama." So far that year, JWT had already produced a creditable abridgment of Eugene O'Neill's *Anna Christie*, while airing two live performances (first on January 12, followed by an unprecedented encore on February 9) of Rod Serling's "Patterns," a critique of corporate viciousness that's considered one of the greatest dramas of TV's Golden Age. Ironically, the story of an aging executive (Ed Begley) who is literally humiliated to death by his boss (Everett Sloane) gained much of its power from verisimilitude, as Serling reputedly based the cutthroat office politics of "Ramsey & Company" on J. Walter Thompson.

Be that as it may, *Kraft* continued for a while in this same ambitious vein, hoping to inspire its writers to greater heights by announcing a fifty-thousand-dollar award for best teleplay of the 1955–56 season, which included adaptations of John F. Kennedy's *Profiles in Courage* and Walter Lord's *Titanic* drama, *A Night to Remember*, as well as "one of the greatest of contemporary novels," *The Lost Weekend*. The last had been successfully adapted the previous year for *Robert Montgomery Presents*, but Jackson quietly declined to involve himself with *Kraft*'s version—he didn't want to seem proprietary about his own work (so he explained to the Newark *Courier*), and he might have also doubted that Montgomery's performance as Don Birnam could be matched by the workmanlike Joe Maross (*Kraft*'s last-minute replacement for Jack Lemmon, who'd recently won the Best Supporting Actor Oscar as Ensign Pulver in *Mister Roberts*). And then, just in general, Jackson kept a diffident distance from most of the "talent"—actors such as James Dean, Cloris Leachman, Paul Newman, Anthony Perkins, and many others who appeared in *Kraft* productions during the early stages of their careers—unless it was a question, say, of giving his daughters a thrill. On June 27, 1956, Kate and a friend came to NBC's Studio 8H and met Farley Granger and Joanne Woodward, appearing in an episode titled "Starfish" that Kate was allowed to watch from the control room. And Sarah accompanied her father to two of the annual banquets at the Waldorf, where well-known actors and directors were seated at individual tables representing their respective episodes that season.

The day before Kate's visit in 1956, Charlie wrote Sarah from New York as follows: "I'm so involved with a job that gets in the way of things I want to feel and think (my novel, to mention just one) that letters of mine, lately, seem to be just padding." Certainly he didn't write many letters anymore, or much else. His correspondence files at Brandt & Brandt, hitherto thick to bursting with his schmoozing, exuberant prose, fell suddenly silent, as it were, and would remain that way for the rest of his life (while his agents grumbled in memos about his unresponsiveness—how it took "a year and a day" to get in touch with him). His appointment diary for 1956 is pristinely free of a single entry, a single stroke of the pencil. "He was a forgotten, sad man when I knew him," said a friend from this time. "Nobody was talking about him anymore." That is to say, nobody was talking about him *except* as the (washed-up) author of *The Lost Weekend*, as if he hadn't published a word before or since. In 1958, when one of his daughters' friends (later Kate's husband) mentioned reading some of Jackson's stories for an English class at Goddard College, Charlie wrote

Sarah with a mixture of bitterness and pathetic pride: "John said 'Gosh, I didn't know he was *that* good!' And *I* say, a prophet is not only without honor in his own country but even in his own family."

The longer his silence as a writer persisted, the more he felt compelled to account for it by talking about the magnum opus he'd been working on these many, many years, *What Happened*—and the more he built it up, the more it hopelessly receded beyond his capabilities. It wasn't just a question of length, or exquisitely fine style, but also its sensational subject matter. At parties—especially gay parties—the euphoric, pill-popping Charlie would go on and on about how his novel would tell the *truth*, by God, and shock the world! "He was going to spill the beans about his life," the playwright Arthur Laurents recalled of one such spiel. "The implication was that he *didn't* 'tell all' in *The Lost Weekend*. He was very excited about [*What Happened*], and he was extremely persuasive: I remember thinking, 'I'm going to read that!' " And no wonder, given that Laurents himself was gay and Charlie left little doubt as to what the world would find so shocking. "But to be told 'honestly,' if there was such a thing, what would it not mean or cost?" Don muses in the "Preview" section of *Farther and Wilder*. "It would mean going down to the very bottom, exploring the past to discover the present. . . ." "Save till later," he scribbled in the margin, warning himself not to reveal *too* much at the outset about his adventures as "a kind of amorous animal-spirit, bodiless yet potent of body, charged with love yet ambiguous of sex, roaming the countryside like a Whitmanesque ghost . . ."

However: it was perhaps the worst time in American history, or at least the twentieth century, to be writing of such things. Gay soldiers had learned the strength of their numbers during the war, and when the Kinsey Reports advertised the matter to mainstream America, the backlash was fierce. Throughout the 1950s, Postmaster General Arthur Summerfield led a vigilant "antismut" campaign, prosecuting even the most benign forms of gay "pornography," while the State Department purged more than twice as many homosexuals as suspected communists from its ranks. The pressure to seem "regular" in corporate America was, needless to say, intense—and to this pressure, and any number of ineffable others, Jackson buckled.

At any rate he couldn't write, with or without pills, and was often crushingly miserable. Pat Hammond, walking to her train in Grand Central one night in 1955, spotted her old employer sitting alone in a club car. When she tapped on the glass, Jackson looked up but didn't seem to recognize her; he clawed the air with a weary "Go away" gesture, his face stricken. She never saw him again. One of the very few letters he wrote that year consisted mostly of a few lines copied from Gerard Manley Hopkins—one of the poet's last, "terrible" sonnets, about which Aldous Huxley had observed (as Charlie noted), "Never, I think, has the just man's complaint against the universe been put more forcibly":

> *THOU art indeed just, Lord, if I contend*
> *With thee; but, sir, so what I plead is just.*
> *Why do sinners' ways prosper? and why must*
> *Disappointment all I endeavor end?*
>
> *Wert thou my enemy, O thou my friend,*
> *How wouldst thou worse, I wonder, than thou dost*
> *Defeat, thwart me? . . .*
> *Mine, O thou lord of life, send my roots rain.*

•

THE HOPKINS PLAINT was for the benefit of Phyllis McGinley, one of the few old literary friends with whom he kept in touch—more than ever now that he was taking instruction in Catholicism, a move he'd been toying with throughout that wretched decade ("because I lack so much in my life"). His letters to Dorothea, meanwhile, had all but ceased; his heady artistic enthusiasms had curdled along with his writing, and he surely knew that Dorothea was bored stiff by his AA talk and bound to have even less truck with religious sentiment. McGinley, on the other hand, was an avid Catholic and moral traditionalist, declaring in *Good Housekeeping*, "Let Us Dare to Say It Out Loud—Unchastity Is a Sin." Her paeans to the quotidian pleasures of Larchmont, where she remained happily married to a phone company executive, would actually win her a Pulitzer Prize in 1961.* Charlie affected to admire the wit of her better work, while stopping well short of taking her altogether seriously; in an otherwise friendly review of a McGinley collection for the Sunday *Times* in 1954, he permitted himself the wish that she "would charm

---

* A more innocent time. In 1975, McGinley commemorated her seventieth birthday with a typical bit of verse: "Seventy is wormwood, / Seventy is gall. / But it's better to be seventy / Than not alive at all."

me less and disturb me more . . . let yourself go, honey!" And toward her Victorian social values he also endeavored to be indulgent: a few years later, after seeing *Who's Afraid of Virginia Woolf?*, he remarked to McGinley that he couldn't help thinking that such harrowing domestic scenes were being enacted all over America, to which she replied, "But not in Larchmont!"—their favorite catchphrase from then on.

That autumn of 1955 he gave her an account of his ever increasing spiritual fervor. Through his AA sponsor, Dr. McGuire—with whom he'd contritely reconciled for the time being—he'd been introduced to an idealistic young priest named Tom Reese, soon to become director of the Catholic Charities of Wilmington, which specialized in getting help for people with addictions to drugs and alcohol. Charlie was smitten with the whole scene. Much of his talk became at least obliquely religious ("Be sure to tell Mama to have fish on Friday!"), and his reading ditto. For McGinley he ticked off a list of recent titles, including *The Faith of Millions*, by Father John O'Brien; *The Everlasting Man*, by G. K. Chesterton; various works by Cardinal Newman ("rough-going"); and *Jesus and His Times*, by Daniel-Rops ("most thrilling of all"). And while he was not quite jaded enough to consider these on par with, say, *The Brothers Karamazov*, he found himself so "staggered" by the Gospel According to St. John that the likes of *Othello* and *Lear* seemed suddenly, after all, "only art."

The main point was to forget his misspent life, his terrible urges, his egoistic absorption in art for art's sake, whether it be his or others'—*to get outside of himself*, in short, a dilemma that love, psychiatry, and literature had all failed abysmally to solve. On this subject Charlie liked to quote Chesterton: "How much larger your life would be if your self could become smaller in it. . . . You would break out of this tiny and tawdry theatre in which your own little plot is always being played, and you would find yourself under a freer sky, in a street full of splendid strangers." How Charlie longed for such blessed oblivion! To stroll about wondering what these others, these splendidly various others, were thinking and feeling! Meanwhile, sitting in a pew of a late afternoon at St. Vincent Ferrer on the Upper East Side, he felt a kind of *gratitude* he never thought possible.

And so, on August 26, 1956, Charlie was baptized by Father Reese at the Church of St. Mary of the Immaculate Conception in Wilmington, a small ceremony witnessed by his daughter Kate and Dr. McGuire. More than five decades later, neither Kate nor Sarah was quite sure how long their father had continued attending Mass at St. Rose in Newtown and eating fish on Friday and sitting in placid reverie at St. Vin-cent Ferrer, though Charlie himself had put it at "three or four years," tops: "It was during a troubled period when I was living on drugs," he remembered in 1964, "and the whole 'conversion' was euphoria—one part drama and three-parts fake, as I was forced to conclude when I more or less 'came to.' "

NOW THAT he was working full-time in the city, Jackson only went home to Newtown on weekends, taking a one-room apartment on the top floor of the Dakota, at 72nd Street and Central Park West. As always, he made the most of his little space, transplanting an elegant old iron-ing board (for a coffee table) that he'd inherited from a great-aunt, his polar-bear rug, a nice sleeper sofa, and a number of choice pictures. At last only a small patch of bare wall remained by the door, which he was saving for what he hoped would be a framed quatrain—"A Prayer for the New Pied-à-terre"—written by his friend McGinley. She more than obliged him:

> *Lord, who blesses barn and barrow,*
> *Nest for wren and roof for sparrow,*
> *Castle, cottage, lighthouse, steeple,*
> *Attic for Artistic People,*
> *Walk-ups at important rents,*
> *Igloos, teepees, tenements,*
> *Villas where mimosa drowses,*
> *Maybe even ranch-type houses,—*
> *Bless, I beg, this building where*
> *Jackson has his pied-à-terre.*

> —PHYLLIS MCGINLEY /
> Larchmont (but of course), N.Y.

Charlie's social life in the city was a rather bifurcated affair. When he wasn't attending AA meetings, and chatting and playing cards with his more sedate AA acquaintances, he cultivated a diverse group of gay men (many, to be sure, in AA themselves). The dinner party where Arthur Laurents had heard all about *What Happened*, for instance, was an all-male gathering at the home of a TV director, Bill Corrigan, attended by older, somewhat well-heeled men and their younger charges; Charlie himself was excitedly flirting with Ken Boyer, the twenty-something boyfriend of pianist Arthur Whittemore. A more raffish milieu was a weekly "salon" held at a cold-water flat on First Avenue belonging to a man known as Sunshine. "Please do *not* throw cigarettes in the toilet," read the ornately lettered sign in Sunshine's bathroom. "They become soggy and hard to light." Jackson despised such silliness (at least among the less illustrious), and would have given the group a wide berth were it not for the fact that Sunshine's "was perhaps the only place, except an AA meeting"—according to Richard Lamparski, a young friend at the time—"where he could be certain that people would know who he was." It was a high price to pay for the odd ego boost. Usually the last to arrive ("explain[ing] that he had been the guest speaker at some AA chapter where the members simply wouldn't let him go"), Jackson would grow dour as the campiness waxed over the course of an evening. Their host was the most notorious perpetrator. One night, deadpan, he announced that Bill Inge's play *The Dark at the Top of the Stairs* had originally been about a black man living above a white family's flat; its then title, he said, was *The Darkie at the Top of the Stairs*. While the others held their laughter ("expecting the second shoe"), Jackson demanded to know where Sunshine had heard "such damn nonsense." The man suavely replied that his source had been none other than "an executive of the National Association for Making Advances Toward Colored People": "While the rest of us exploded," said Lamparski, Jackson "sputtered and left soon after."

One consolation was the charming protégés he encountered as a script editor for *Kraft*. From the Yale School of Drama came Ron Sproat and A. R. "Pete" Gurney, recipients of the J. Walter Thompson Fellowship in the summer of 1956.* As fellows, the two young men were allowed to observe *Kraft* productions from first rehearsal to final performance, and also to work as readers, choosing scripts and novels to send along to Charlie or one of the other editors. During the midmorning break they'd all chat around the coffee wagon, and soon Charlie began asking the young men to lunch; when Sproat mentioned he was looking for another apartment, Charlie promptly offered him a maid's room at the Dakota. (Sproat had to use a common bathroom in the hall, and was star-

---

* A. R. Gurney, of course, went on to become one of our most distinguished playwrights, while Sproat had an interesting career in television—mainly as creator of Barnabas Collins, the ambivalent vampire-protagonist of the horror soap *Dark Shadows*.

tled one night when he tried the door and was met by none other than *Boris Karloff*—then appearing in *The Lark* on Broadway—who, marking his astonishment, graciously explained that he sometimes used that toilet when he had guests.) Sproat was happy to be living at such a grand address, though soon he began to worry he'd have to move out. Nightly, almost, Charlie would invite him over for drinks (though he didn't drink himself) and importune him for sex; to be exact, he wanted to perform fellatio on the young man, who repeatedly protested that while he was very fond of Charlie (true), he was *straight*. Then one night they bumped into each other at a gay bar near the Dakota.

As it happened, Jackson wasn't the only one who'd been deceived on the subject of Sproat's homosexuality. "Pete Gurney was my closest friend," said Sproat, "and I was pretending to be straight because gay men weren't friends with straight men in those days." Jackson had "amazed" Gurney with frank talk about his own proclivities, and one day he blithely let drop that their mutual friend Ron was gay, too. Gurney was stunned ("I hate to think I was that intolerant then, but, as Ron said, those were different times"), and said as much to Sproat, who was almost traumatized with shame. Though Charlie might have assumed Gurney already knew, Sproat thought it far more likely his mentor had outed him by way of getting his own back for those rejections at the Dakota.*

Edward Pomerantz, another Yale student, had written a one-act play titled *The Garden* that Jackson professed to love (though he was unable to interest his colleagues), asking to meet the author. Pomerantz was "gaga" at the prospect: he'd seen *The Lost Weekend* as a movie-besotted eleven-year-old, and here was the novel's author! And he loved Eddie's play! One night the young man brought Jackson home to meet his parents for dinner in Washington Heights, and after a delightful time the

---

* Gurney would have learned the truth anyway: a few months later, he posted bail when Sproat was arrested for "disturbing the peace" in a car near the Yale campus, and—the implications notwithstanding ("In the fifties you could know and not know simultaneously")—he asked Sproat to be an usher at his wedding the following summer.

An interesting postscript to the Jackson-Sproat friendship: for his thesis at Yale, Sproat wrote a one-act adaptation of "Rachel's Summer," fleshing out the characters by basing them on people he knew. A production was staged at Yale, to which Charlie brought his family, though he disliked the play and said so ("That isn't my mother"). Later, when it was bought for TV's *United States Steel Hour*—starring Martha Scott as the mother and Patty ("Bad Seed") McCormack as Rachel—Jackson made a point of "charg[ing] a lot of money for the rights," as Sproat remembered.

two walked back to the Eighth Avenue subway, where Jackson said good night to the puzzled lad by patting him on the rump. "You know, Katharine Hepburn has sat in that chair," Charlie remarked during a subsequent evening at the Dakota. "Why don't you take your socks and shoes off? The rug is so soft . . . " At that point the penny dropped ("the pat on the ass!"), and Pomerantz politely declined to remove his shoes.

Jackson mentioned that Bill Inge lived downstairs and asked the young man if he'd like to meet him. As Pomerantz recalled, "I'm like, 'Oh my God: *Picnic! Bus Stop!* Wow, yeah, I'd *love* to . . .' " Because Inge was terrified of heights (one of his many phobias), he lived on the second floor over the Dakota's arched entrance, and when Charlie arrived with his guest, they found the playwright entertaining a "young toy boy," as Pomerantz put it (realizing, of course, that he was perceived the same way vis-à-vis Charlie). In the bathroom he found an eyelash curler on the sink. Meanwhile a blandish decorum prevailed: Jackson and Inge were nothing but chaste in their talk, mildly swapping AA and theater gossip. Though ten years younger and far more acclaimed at the time—*Picnic* had won the Pulitzer in 1953, and *The Dark at the Top of the Stairs* was about to begin a successful run on Broadway—Inge had a lot in common with Jackson: both were alcoholic pill-takers who wrote about the hypocrisy and thwarted longing of small-town life (Inge had grown up in Independence, Kansas), and both were gay and deeply unhappy about it. Indeed, Inge might have envied Jackson's relative good fortune in finding a woman as fine and understanding as Rhoda, given that Inge had lived alone for most of his adult life, pining the while (by all accounts) for a more conventional life. One day, when they were neighbors on Long Island, Arthur Laurents walked in on Inge wearing a corset; the latter, abashed, announced he was going to marry the actress Barbara Baxley—a wistful notion he considered for years, but never acted on.

For the most part Inge was a man without intimates, though Charlie was a friend insofar as he had any. Both were analyzed by Lawrence Kubie with roughly the same result, and when Inge was a mental patient at Austen Riggs in Stockbridge, Massachusetts, he made a nine-inch bronze statuette (a male nude with upraised arms) for Charlie in his expression therapy class. But the main connection, particularly during the Dakota years, was AA. The composer Ned Rorem noted in his diary that Jackson and Inge were the "star pupils" of their meetings, after which they'd adjourn en masse to Schrafft's or the Croydon for ice cream. (At least once, said Rorem, Charlie brought his "clear-faced and likable" daughter

Kate along.) The two older men, whatever their similarities otherwise, struck Rorem as a study in contrast: Charlie tended to be chattily animated in a group (no matter what his actual mood), whereas Inge was "somber and pessimistic, becoming more so with each new success."

Failure, however, did not lift his spirits. After winning an Oscar for *Splendor in the Grass* (1961), Inge went into a slow, grinding decline. "I'm feeling very good *now*, but the summer has been hellish," he wrote Charlie on August 26, 1963, explaining that he'd become suicidal during a recent trip to Kansas. Rather than kill himself, though, he'd invoked his faith in a "higher power" and attended some AA meetings: "[I was] determined to give up the sleeping pills (I'd been taking them every two or three nights, normal doses but enough to create an undermining kind of dependence and a compulsion to take one big dose that would be my last), and I began to catch hold. . . . And I feel that probably I'll be able to work well again. I haven't worked well now for a couple years." But his best work was all behind him, as he'd learn thoroughly in that final decade. The following year, he and Dick Berg—one of Charlie's old *Kraft* colleagues—wanted to option *The Fall of Valor* with their own money, hoping to get a studio deal once they'd attracted a big enough star. "*What* a break that would be," Charlie wrote his agent; "then no more time wasted on short-stories, full steam ahead to finish the novel . . ." The novel in question was *A Second-Hand Life*, but unfortunately no stars stepped forward to claim the part of Grandin, even with William Inge on board. "Whatever happens," Charlie wrote his demoralized friend, "you are the only one I would want to do the screen play, not only because of our old long friendship and your sympathy and understanding of the problem of the novel, but also because of your enviable skill and talent as a playright [*sic*]: I wish *I* had it."

Inge wished he still had it, too. After his play *Where's Daddy?* flopped in 1966, he declared himself fed up with "the frustrations, the anxieties, the pressures" of the "public arts," and moved to Los Angeles to live with his sister Helene. When a former assistant and friend, John Connolly, went out to visit him—phoning ahead to confirm date and hour—nobody answered the doorbell for a long time; finally Inge drifted out wearing a bathrobe, in an all but unreachable stupor ("Charlie was like that too," said Connolly, who'd known both men in New York; "he'd just quietly look at you"). On June 2, 1973, Inge was taken to UCLA Medical Center after a barbiturate overdose, but signed himself out the next day; a week later his sister found him dead in the garage, slumped over the steering wheel of his Mercedes. She told the *Times* that her brother had been depressed, though she didn't know why, and "did not believe he really knew either."

BY 1956 the popularity of anthology dramas such as *Kraft* had begun to wane in favor of sitcoms and other serials. JWT commissioned an outside study that recommended the agency "restimulate interest" by becoming more topical ("Newspapers and magazines will be watched to see what is being read and talked about"), which resulted in such episodes as "The Singing Idol," capitalizing on the Elvis Presley craze and even producing a hit single, "Teenage Crush." The overall trend, however, was downward in every way: wary of alienating more of their mainstream viewers, JWT saw to it that topical never meant *controversial*, killing a script by Allan Manings about the first black family to vote. Director Paul Bogart (later of *All in the Family* fame) remembered that an agency rep was on hand at all times to make sure a given show "didn't misstep," and the end product was perforce in keeping with a satirical "recipe for an average TV program" written by a disgruntled executive at the time, calling for a bland mixture of "Sponsor's Requirements" and "Staff Suggestions" ("However fresh and flavorful, they will curdle when combined with Agency Ideas, so they must be beaten until stiff").

And so Charlie's job, hardly a joy to begin with, became all the more hateful. An internal memo dated April 3, 1957, noted that a JWT employee named Chuck Spaulding had made a "most advantageous connection with a Canadian Oil Company" and hence was leaving *Kraft*; his duties would be assumed by Jackson, who (it was hoped) would "take advantage of his many contacts with publishers and writers." The precise nature of this fresh hell is hard to say, though it would seem Charlie didn't entirely satisfy in either his old or new capacity. Six weeks later an irascible producer at NBC wrote the agency a letter to the effect that the present *Kraft* editors and other personnel were "adequate (just) but not inspired," and that "a new slate may be required" to get the show back on its feet.

Perhaps it was not unrelated that Charlie suffered a bad overdose the following month, though something of the sort had been in the cards for a while. "I had arrived at the stage where I took twenty [Seconal] a day and could not get along unless," he later admitted in his AA talks. His daughters noticed that he often seemed "quite pale" and "shaky," and once, when Kate had arranged to meet him for a pre-matinee lunch at Sardi's, a stranger came instead and explained that her father was unwell and wouldn't be able to make it. In fact, he'd been hospitalized four times in a single year for overdoses, and his latest had landed him back in Bellevue. This time he "went off [his] head completely" and was taken in a straitjacket to the violent ward, where he raved for some three days until sensible enough to recognize a priest friend who paid him a visit. Just before his release two weeks later, a young psychologist summoned him to his office for a confidential chat. As Jackson would remember for AA:

> He said, "Look, you're an addict by nature and you always will be. . . . Just look at the record: twenty-two hospitalizations by now, and that's the way it will be. . . . I have only one word of advice for you, and that is: Ally yourself with a good, middle-aged, kindly psychiatrist. Not deep Freudian therapy, because you've had that. Just a sympathetic, kindly man to whom you can go two or three times a week as a confidant, and settle for the fact that you will be doing this probably for the rest of your life. And this may keep you out of trouble, but that's all I can suggest."

And yet Charlie managed again to steady himself. After a summer that can only be imagined, he entered an inpatient rehabilitation program at Columbia Presbyterian. Rhoda asked Kate and a friend to wait in the car while she visited him on August 6, and the girls were thrilled to spot Elizabeth Taylor and her husband Mike Todd leaving the hospital after the birth of their daughter, Liza. A week or so later, the incarcerated Charlie wrote Sarah that he was feeling "vastly improved" but "bored all to hell," and asked her to mention to Mama that there were twenty-two patients in the clinic and thus she should "bake [cookies] accordingly."

In truth Jackson was profoundly depressed, and with plenty of reason quite apart from the morbidities of withdrawal. For one thing he was hanging by a thread at J. Walter Thompson: they hadn't fired him outright, but clearly they weren't paying for his latest leave of absence either, given that his family was forced to move that autumn (1957) to a fifty-dollar-a-month rental on Main Street in Newtown ("floors sag, practically no closet space, in very bad shape"). Meanwhile, too, he and Rhoda were in the midst of a trial separation. "He feels completely homeless and alone just now," she wrote Boom in late September, "and it does make you feel sorry for him for he is. I know that he'll recover from it and bounce back (I almost fear that though—for if he bounces he'll get into trouble again) . . . " This last, nicely considered qualm conveys volumes of what the woman had been through over the years. As for Charlie, he was not only homeless in terms of his marital situation, but in actual fact, since he'd lost his little apartment at the Dakota amid the recent tumult. Wanly he wrote Kate that he hoped they could spare "some little nook or corner" on Main Street until he found a new place, and privately he wondered what his poor, retiring wife would do without him. Rhoda was less worried on that score: "My life may be dull by his standards," she wrote, "but it isn't empty. I don't have to be sustained by constant exposure to other people the way he does. He's a very lonely person."

"Kraft carried [my father] through the summer until January 1958," Sarah wrote in a college essay from around that time, and the word "carried" was used advisedly. He no longer had an office when he returned to the agency that fall, and the sense of doom was general. As a last desperate measure, the show was changing its name to the more "provocative" *Kraft Mystery Theater* ("Such titles as 'Climax' 'Suspense' 'Danger' connote to the viewer a type of story," NBC had recommended), and Talent Associates was replacing JWT as producer on March 26, 1958. A "production estimate" from the previous November indicated that most of the current staff would actually survive the regime change, but Charlie's departure was noted for December. *Kraft Mystery Theater* expired less than a year later, in September 1958.

Charlie was jobless, then, for much of that long year, and yet things might have been worse. He was back in his routine of spending weekdays in the city canvassing agencies—he'd managed to get his old room back at the Dakota (though he complained that he'd been unable to make it as "charming" as before)—and weekends he was again welcome at the little house on Main Street, as Rhoda had been somewhat persuaded that he was ready to make a lasting "readjustment, with the help of AA, after so many years of a different kind of life." Happily, too, Rhoda was able to find steady if low-paying employment in the research department of the Yale Center of Alcohol Studies, a position she would keep for the rest of her working life ("It's just a coincidence that we are both in this," Charlie quipped; along with Rhoda's eleven years at *Fortune*, though, it couldn't have hurt to be married to the author of *The Lost Weekend*).*

---

* The Center of Alcohol Studies evolved at Yale during the 1930s and 1940s, shortly before Jackson's novel was published, and both were influential in rousing the Amer-

Now that he wasn't writing fiction anymore, or even bothering (much) to pretend, Charlie's days at home had a way of passing slowly. "House lonely and cold today, really chilly," he wrote Sarah, who'd gone away to college that year. "Only smelly Juno"—their beloved boxer—"to keep me company (Mama in New Haven, Kate at school)." TV assignments were occasional at best: in October he wrote a sentimental adaptation of Fitzgerald's "Absolution" for a series titled *The Priesthood* ("devoted to an understanding of the human struggle of the Roman Catholic priest"), as well as a scenario for a single episode of *Naked City*, "The Other Face of Goodness," based on a subplot in *The Outer Edges* about a Raskolnikov-like college student who contemplates (and, in *Naked City*, actually commits) murder.

The year 1958 seemed to end on a high note when Jackson was hired as a script editor for Roy Winsor Productions. Winsor is best remembered as the creator (in 1951) of *Search for Tomorrow*, the first long-running TV soap, and he later served as producer of *Love of Life* and *The Secret Storm* before setting up his own company in 1955. Jackson found the man affable enough, and naturally was happy to "have a little money in [his] pocket, for a change," but otherwise it was dreary work. "Just came from watching the actors rehearse in the studio," he wrote Sarah, a few weeks into the job. "Not much fun after our big Kraft shows, and I don't expect to go to the studio again—that is, not until Kate comes down to visit me next month. I'll take her once, just for something to do."

By the following November he'd already parted with Winsor, and was scrambling for odd jobs again. Rhoda reported that he seemed "very edgy" about things: NBC had assigned him to write a pilot for a new series about alcoholism that didn't pan out, and meanwhile Rhoda advised Sarah to expect a lean Christmas ("Won't it be nice when we hit a year we don't have to say that?"), and leanness generally, at least until Papa was "well started on free lancing or else established in a job again." As it happened, though, the NBC pilot would be his last TV work of any kind, and by 1960 (according to his agent) he was "financially desperate."

MORE THAN EVER he was kept afloat by an obsessive devotion to AA—his "new addiction," as he liked to tell members all over the country, recount-

---

ican Medical Association to recognize alcoholism as a treatable illness—a policy officially adopted in the 1950s.

ing his latest conversion (circa June 1957) after the Bellevue psychologist had advised him to find a "kindly psychiatrist": "Certainly he was discounting AA entirely, and I thought: 'When I leave here, I must go back to AA and *really* see what it is, *really* give yourself up to it, *really* listen, stop talking, stop performing, stop patronizing the groups with your sympathy and see what it is that these people have."

As Richard Lamparski pointed out, Alcoholics *Anonymous* was definitely a "misnomer" in Jackson's case; attending a meeting with the author of *The Lost Weekend* was, he said, "like visiting a birth control clinic in the company of Margaret Sanger." When Lamparski went along for one of Charlie's talks, he recorded how the novelist was besieged by admirers who said that his book ("or seeing Ray Milland portray him [*sic*] on the screen") had saved their lives by sending them into the program. Nor did Charlie let any of it give him the big head. Like a combination of missionary and Fuller Brush salesman, he'd show off "the program" to whosoever expressed even the most fugitive curiosity, coaxing them one and all to meetings—coworkers at Winsor, the housekeeper at the Dakota (a Mrs. Young), various luminaries from stage and screen,* and his own fifteen-year-old daughter, Kate, who professed to love AA because "it [made her] like people," as she told her father after a meeting at Lenox Hill ("Which is really one of the great dividends of the Group," he wrote Sarah afterward, "and I'm glad she felt it"). Within a month of his being named chairman of that chapter in December 1958 (an honor, wrote Sarah, that "affected Papa and all of us greatly"), attendance had almost doubled, and his friend Max Wylie had more than forgiven Charlie his past lapses.

At AA's expense he flew all over the country to address "distant isolated groups," as he put it, though often his famous name packed ballrooms with hundreds of eager alcoholics who'd come to hear "our American De Quincey" tell his story—this illustrious writer who'd lectured at Dartmouth, Columbia, NYU, and "four or five different 57th Street saloons," as he was introduced to a big laugh. During a four-month interval in 1959 he spoke in Cleveland, Dallas ("1600 people," he jotted in his diary), Lewisburg, Worthington, Spirit Lake, and Sing Sing. Nor was he cowed by provincial squeamishness when it came to mentioning pills—a pio-

---

* Art Carney, for instance. The two became AA friends in the late 1950s, and in 1966 Charlie couldn't resist sharing the inside dope that Carney would be leaving the stage version of *The Odd Couple* because of an alcoholic relapse.

neer speaker in that respect ("some of you may object to having this kind of thing discussed . . . ")—a subject he was determined to broach after breaking his addiction in 1957. But then, his gratitude was vast, and he felt that nothing less than (almost) perfect candor would do; AA, after all, had succeeded where love, literature, psychiatry, and Catholicism had failed:

> In AA I realize that I have finally gotten outside of myself and belong with people. It's a marvelous reward. And I think now, with what I know about AA now, it's hard for me to understand how I could have resisted for so long. Even when I was in AA, on other props and crutches, like the pills, I wondered what was I afraid of? Why couldn't I let go of those things? I know what I was afraid of. I was afraid of facing myself, as I really was. Well, now I'm not afraid. How can I be, with two or three thousand friends who have been through this with me?

An aspect of facing himself meant facing his "own humdrum mediocrity," as he admitted to a bemused Dorothea, who under some duress had gone to the odd meeting and wondered what had become of the wistful, brilliant outsider she'd met a decade ago at Marlboro College: "I was forced to recognize a being I had not met before," she later wrote, "the small-towner at home on the back porch gossiping about the neighbors." Charlie was getting dull, all right, and knew it better than anybody—but the "rarefied heights" of great art were not for him. Rather he played bridge with the neighbors, a little annoyed by his wife's timid bidding, wishing his older daughter would come back from college so he could at least have a decent partner ("Don't expect to do anything when you're home," Rhoda alerted her, "but play fourth hand with him somewhere").

"They were years of a kind of grey, bleak, empty well-being," Jackson would reflect of this epoch: "apathy, spiritlessness, blank sobriety, and a vegetable health." At the time, though, he knew that a return to really ambitious writing—to any kind of ambition at all, apart from his great AA popularity—would mean a return to drink and drugs. Death, in short. And meanwhile his literary reputation, such as it was, had become little more than a tagline—"author of *The Lost Weekend*"—while his other books were reprinted, if at all, as a kind of genteel pornography: "Naked village . . . ," read the cover copy for *The Sisters* (alongside a garish painting of a clinching couple and a haggard, gray-haired deviant), as the 1958 Zenith Books paperback edition of *The Sunnier Side* had been retitled.

Nice simple home folks, you think. Pleasant, gentle upstate New Yorkers. Only one day you look around and everything is different.

You've seen the two girls sunning themselves on the dock before. But for the first time you notice whom they're watching. They're watching *you*. And there's a hunger in their eyes as they lie there, bare-legged in the sun . . .

There's a church in town, and a nimble-fingered deacon plays the organ there. Men and boys visit him. You've heard odd stories about these men and boys, and now your friend tries to make *you* one of them . . .

A part of Jackson the writer remained obstinately alive withal, and that part never entirely forgave AA for "flatten[ing] [him] out" in these years. The program, he wrote Kate in 1964, worked best "for the mindless": "the others, the gifted ones or the thinkers or the minds of a different quality, all of them, after a period of some years of sobriety, go peculiar—run off to monasterys [*sic*], get married or divorced when they shouldn't, turn queer or something, take to drugs . . ." Or (after a fashion) all of the above, though in 1964 this hadn't quite transpired yet; for the moment Jackson was just thinking out loud, for his daughter's benefit, wondering whether inebriation was perhaps "a necessary part" of certain people's lives: "How can we expect them to be 'normal' when such a strong influence or trait is taken away? I don't know, I'm merely asking rhetorically."

Chapter Eighteen

A Place in the Country

While keeping himself on such a tediously even keel, Jackson was sometimes reminded that he'd once made quite an impact on American culture. On March 3, 1959, his old acquaintance Glenway Wescott, then president of the National Institute of Arts and Letters, informed him that he would receive a $1,500 grant in literature at the award ceremonial in May, where his fellow honorees would include the likes of Truman Capote, Leon Edel, and Isaac Bashevis Singer. "I am overwhelmed—deeply moved, in fact," Jackson wrote Wescott, beseeching the Institute secretary to let him exceed the ten-person guest limit by two ("You can't think how much I am looking forward to receiving this honor"). Thus his wife, daughters, Boom, the Strauses, and various others were on hand to hear Charlie commended with a lofty citation written by his friend McGinley: "To Charles Jackson . . . whose muscular and masculine prose writing [has] extended the borders of artistic perception, and whose most celebrated novel, *The Lost Weekend*, is already a part of America's literary experience."

The following year Farrar, Straus and Cudahy acquired a paperback company, Noonday Press, whose inaugural line featured a new edition of *The Lost Weekend* with a panegyrical preface by John Farrar ("a masterpiece of fiction technique, of emotional power and, most important, of that particular variety of compassion for character and control of violent and special material that marked the great Russians and a few others"). And that wasn't all: sensing the possibility of a bona fide Jackson Revival—not to say some return on his considerable investment—Roger had arranged for Charlie to meet with Robert Giroux, editor-in-chief since 1955, to see if anything could be done about Jackson's work-in-progress, *A Second-Hand Life.* Stirred by the sudden interest, as well as the prospect of long-term unemployment, Charlie sent an outline of the novel to his old movie agent, Irving "Swifty" Lazar, in hope of getting "some advance loot from Hollywood" that would see him through completion; this failing, his devoted family rallied to keep him afloat. Not only was Rhoda working full-time at the Center of Alcohol Studies, but Sarah quit college that summer (1960) and took a job in New York (at Farrar, Straus and Cudahy), while Kate worked part-time too.

Not for nothing, though, had the novel languished these many years, and finally its author appealed to an old friend with a vaunted narrative gift, Charles Brackett. The problem, Jackson explained, was not his nymphomaniac heroine, Winifred, but rather the bland Harry Harrison, whose epiphany he envisaged as being similar to that of John Marcher in James's "The Beast in the Jungle"—that is, "his sudden awful realization that nothing ever *is* going to happen to him." But how to *dramatize* Harry's acedia? And how to account, plausibly, for his being a kind of emotional "eunuch" (as opposed to, say, a repressed homosexual)? "I could have him playing 'safe' by always going around with married women or with divorced Catholic women . . . " Brackett's response, if any, is unknown.

Meanwhile an old benefactor, Herb Mayes—the magazine editor who, ten years before, paid five thousand dollars for "The Sunnier Side"—had taken over as editorial director of *McCall's,* and the promise of such a lucrative market was the carrot Charlie needed to finish his first story in six years. "One o'Clock in the Morning" was based on an episode from the summer of 1954, when the family had stayed in Malaga with Boom; one night the fourteen-year-old Sarah had broken curfew to canoodle at the lake with an older boy, until her frantic father had interrupted the tryst with a knock on the car window.* In the story, the father's search

---

* Such was his consternation—though the two had only been kissing—that he arranged for Sarah to receive counseling from a priest friend in Philadelphia.

around the lake entails mortifying encounters with a state trooper as well as the father of his daughter's girlfriend, whom he wakes up to interrogate, and in the end he's forced to recognize that his daughter doesn't, after all, tell him *everything*. Mayes liked the basic idea, but asked for two more pages "to establish the fact that both characters are expecting too much of good nature, that they are both a little in the wrong," which Jackson obediently supplied. "The trouble with you, Daddy, is you're jealous," says the otherwise contrite daughter. "You just don't want me to grow up." The father manfully sees the truth in this, and henceforth vows to let go of the girl to some seemly degree.

Whatever satisfaction Jackson took in writing this trifle (which he'd originally submitted without a title) was dampened, perhaps, by the pandering involved; at any rate his creative impulse went promptly back into hibernation. "I now, like you, am convinced that you have a powerful and significant novel and one which will touch the hidden core of loneliness in many people," Carl Brandt, Jr. (the son of his former agent, who'd died of emphysema in 1957), had written him on October 24, 1960, after reading his client's outline for *A Second-Hand Life*. Then, three weeks later: "What's going on? How is the book coming, and when do we see you?" But Charlie didn't reply, and a few months later Rhoda mentioned a recent "overdose episode" in a letter to Sarah, who was now old enough (twenty-one) to know about such things.

ROGER STRAUS was legendary for his patience toward writers on his list, blithely letting deadlines pass as long as he felt reasonably certain that *someday* the wait would prove worthwhile. But even he had a limit, as the epic vagaries of Charles Jackson would eventually bear out. By 1960, as Roger noted, his friend had "red ink on the books to the tune of $9,398.94," which didn't include personal loans in the neighborhood of $2,700 ("or at least that is the total of the traceable sums in my file"), though almost to the end he continued to encourage Charlie and help him make ends meet. However, there simply wasn't as much to talk about now that Charlie only made "an occasional, embarrassed, dutiful allusion" to his stalled novel(s), as he would admit five years later in "The Sleeping Brain," where he nonetheless also claimed that his meetings with Roger had remained as frequent and affable as ever. His letters tell a different story: "Wanna take any bets on my lunch date with Roger tomorrow?" he wrote Sarah in 1961. "It's still on but momentarily I expect a cancellation."

Which should not have surprised him: during the hectic working day, at least, Roger was a man who liked to mix the "gossip, shop talk, good food and fun" that was all Charlie had to offer anymore with a little business; in any case the day came, at last, when there was a little business to discuss. By 1962—nine years after the author's first ecstatic inklings—*A Second-Hand Life* consisted of two completed parts (out of a planned five) and an outline, which Roger had read with grave misgiving, and over lunch one day at the Brussels he said as much, adding (so he recalled in 1978), "But you know, Charlie, I could be absolutely wrong, and there may well be a publisher who'll take it." Jackson would remember the moment—"the stunning crisis"—somewhat differently: "After an hour or so of the usual gay small-talk," he wrote in "The Sleeping Brain," "my publisher, my friend, suddenly said: 'You know? I don't believe in writer's blocks. I don't believe there is such a thing: it's a delusion or an excuse on the part of the writer who doesn't want to work.' " Whatever his exact words—and Straus was legendary for his candor, too—the gist of it, as far as Charlie was concerned, was *You're Through:* "It was a dreadful black hour and black day in my life. . . . I had to face the fact that my career, such as it was, was over . . . and I'd better forget it and do something else (at the age of 58)."

But Charlie endured. Soon he was back in the office of Brandt & Brandt, telling the whole sad story to his new agent, Carl Junior (Bernice Baumgarten had left the company after Carl Senior's death). "I think he feeling doomed," the younger Brandt recalled. "He thought the world was giving up on him . . . but [he was] fighting it all the way." After the two made an unsuccessful pitch for *A Second-Hand Life* to Putnam's (in part, no doubt, because the firm had recently published the first American edition of *Lolita*), Jackson and Brandt approached a new editor at Macmillan, Robert Markel, who happened to be the son of Frieda Lubelle, the treasurer at Brandt & Brandt for almost half a century and a great friend (and soft touch) to Charlie for many years. Markel was trying to build a list, and saw the chance to do something decent for a once-lauded author besides. Within a month of that bombshell at the Brussels, then, Charlie was back in business: Macmillan paid him $5,000 on signing, with another $2,500 due when (if) he delivered the manuscript.

But there was still, as Rhoda wrote Brandt, "the ramifications of the Straus situation": "I do get a little angry when I think that they're bleeding him for 50% of any money received until his advance from them is paid off." Or so she thought—Roger's actual terms were somewhat more flexible and forbearing. Charlie was allowed to keep his $5,000 Macmillan advance, in hopes that this would bestir him to finish, at long last, his novel, after which the entire balance of $2,500 would be remitted to Farrar, Straus and Cudahy along with any other earnings until his debt was satisfied. In the meantime, though, Roger wangled him another $2,500 advance, free and clear, arranging for the *Time* Reading Program to bring out a 1963 reprint of *The Lost Weekend;* that summer, too, Roger mailed (Special Delivery) two crisp ten-dollar bills in response to Charlie's phone call (collect) from a tuberculosis sanatorium in Saranac Lake, where he was badly in need of pocket money. "I wrote Roger a long chatty letter then, like the old days," Charlie reported to Kate, "and a similar, gayer one to Dorothea in Purchase in answer to a charming letter from her."

THE JACKSONS moved three times in three years after leaving the place on Main Street in 1959: first they rented a house on Boggs Hill Road in Newtown, then took an apartment above the barn on the same property, before spending a few months on Codfish Hill Road in Bethel, and finally (in the spring of 1962) settling in New Brunswick, New Jersey, because the Center of Alcohol Studies had moved to Rutgers. That September Charlie gave up his little apartment at the Dakota—a blow—and resigned himself to living seven days a week in the shadow of New Brunswick's Magyar Reformed Church on Somerset Street. "I *determined* to myself that I was going to like it if it killed me," he wrote Sarah, and to that end he appointed, exquisitely as ever, a room of his own at the back of their "cheap but absolutely charming" shotgun apartment on the second floor of a beige-brick house, whence he'd emerge most afternoons and walk a few blocks downtown to Newberry's five and dime, say, where he liked to buy pencils and playing cards and chat with folks as he'd done in Newark long ago. Thus, for a time, he was passably content.

But his body, which had weathered so much, began to betray him. Three years before, he'd developed a duodenal ulcer that was serious enough for his doctor to advise hospitalization (it would ultimately prove the immediate, merciful cause of his death). In the fall of 1962, though, his main complaint was a recurrence of tuberculosis in his collapsed right lung that threatened to spread to his "good" lung—namely the one that had done the work of assimilating three or four packs of cigarettes a day for the past thirty-five years. That October, at Middlesex Hospital, he underwent emergency surgery to remove the infected lower lobe as well as three (or four) ribs, after which walking became more difficult and lifting almost impossible. He also got hooked on Doriden, which at the time was considered a safe alternative to barbiturates but was in fact every bit as likely to lead to addiction and awful withdrawal symptoms, as Charlie learned when he tried quitting cold turkey in the spring of 1963. Taken to the Carrier Clinic—a psychiatric hospital in Belle Mead, New Jersey—he was heavily sedated in the hope of averting DTs and hence was wont to repeat himself, sweating and shaking, when his daughters visited, though he was competent enough to introduce them to various cronies on the ward, and was discharged in time to address (with Marty Mann) the annual AA banquet in Wilmington.

By June, alas, he was sicker than ever: "A constant fever," he wrote Kate, "*absolutely no sleep* (why I don't die of sheer exhaustion I'll never know . . . because the moment I lie down I can't breathe, my heart goes into a pounding panic, and I have to sit upright to calm down)." X-rays revealed the worst: what was left of his right lung was now destroyed and the infection had broken through the chest wall and attacked his "good" lung; without drastic surgery he would be dead in about six weeks. More cheerfully, it so happened that his medical expenses would be paid in full by the Will Rogers Memorial Fund, which ran a hospital in the Adirondacks that was free of charge to *anyone* in show business—old-time vaudevillians, burlesque dancers, TV script editors—who suffered from cardiopulmonary illness. Like every other patient at Will Rogers, Charlie would have a private room in a lovely Tudor mansion that looked like a luxury resort hotel, and yet was a leading research facility with a first-rate staff and state-of-the-art equipment.

"Long grueling drive to Saranac but we made it," Charlie scribbled in his appointment diary for July 17, 1963. "I was barely able to walk in. Rhoda did stupendous job of unpacking and settling me in while I was but *thoroughly* examined by Dr. Ayvazian. Lovely place, nice room and bath. Rhoda left—and it was a most difficult leave-taking for both of us." After sputum and urine and blood tests and "x-rays, x-rays, x-rays," doctors were still uncertain how to proceed, and so performed a bronchoscopy that Charlie described as "1 hour and 15 minutes of drowning"; three hours later, though, he was digesting dinner and watching *Judgment at Nuremberg*. A great sense of peace had begun to descend. "I needed to get away from home and my too dull environment there," he wrote his agent and editor, "even from my wife—all I needed was a change." For the time being, at least, he could do almost anything he liked: linger over breakfast ("with much *very good* coffee"), read every word of the newspaper, walk in the woods, sit on the lawn, and never once feel obliged to seem worthy of his wife's solicitude. And who needed it, given the "love, affection, and trust" between him and his chest surgeon, Warriner "Woody" Woodruff, as well as the medical director, Fred Ayvazian, a kindly Armenian who wrote mystery novels on the side (*Much Ado about Murder*, et al.). No wonder some patients were content to stay in Saranac Lake for years on end, though Charlie was determined not to become one of these "beachcombers": "I want to die, or get well quick and get *out* of here."

The dying part seemed more likely than not. After two weeks, Charlie "learned [his] fate": a complete pneumonectomy on the right side—a procedure that took a team of three surgeons almost five hours to perform, and left the patient's right arm, hand, and fingers frozen for weeks. That he was alive at all, indeed, was little short of a miracle; Dr. Woodruff informed him afterward that he, Charlie, was "the only one—yes, the only one—who had survived in his experience, this exact operation," or rather (as he alternatively related to Dorothea) the only one besides "a man of 42; and he died five days later." For his family's benefit he lovingly described the niceties: "Not only did they have to take out the right lung, but also a fistula, an empyema"—an accumulation of pus in the pleural cavity—"four ribs instead of the two that I had supposed, and (this surprised them most of all, though it meant nothing to me), the whole pleura and the lining of the whole chest wall."* As for that lining, Dr. Woodruff said it was "like cement" (the cutting of which was "less surgery than manual labor") because of scar tissue left over from years of pneumothorax punctures. "And think of it,—me sleeping soundly the while."

After a painful month of convalescence at the General Hospital, Charlie was moved to a "princely" room on the third floor of the sanatorium, and was soon able to resume little walks and write letters from his Adirondack chair on the lawn. Sometimes the sharp ends of his shorn ribs would give him agonizing tweaks—"those heavy horseshoes hanging inside my chest bang together once in a while or just move a little,

---

* Sometimes Charlie said it was four ribs removed, sometimes three, and the same vacillation applied to accounts of his surgery at Middlesex Hospital the year before; at any rate he was fairly consistent in claiming to be minus a *total* of seven ribs, so perhaps suffice to say it was three at one and four at the other (or vice versa).

and I hold my face still to keep from wincing and my mouth closed to suppress little helpless yips and yelps"—but Charlie was so glad to be alive, in such a gorgeous place, that he bore his misery with a kind of jaunty stoicism. "The movie tonight is 'Sodom and Gomorrah'—and do you think I'd miss that, after Steve Reeves and all?" he delightedly wrote Sarah, only a few days after his release from the hospital. "Then coming up is 'Diamond Head' (more sex we hope) and 'Dr. No' and then, after one postponement, 'Hud.'" Among patients and doctors alike, he was a beloved figure—a man for whom "there is no other word than charming," as a local columnist noted, especially regarding Charlie's tendency to be warm and "stupefyingly honest" with near-strangers. He made a point of attending Presbyterian services whenever Dr. Ayvazian's wife, Gloria ("Gloria Mundi" as he called her), sang a choir solo, and made no bones about his lavish admiration for her husband: "Yes, I knew Charles was gay," she laughed, many years later. "He had a crush on Fred! It was no secret. . . . He gave us a beautiful antique platter that I still have and that always reminds me of him." Among the ailing entertainers at Will Rogers, Charlie's gayness was rather less than shocking, and for his part he made a point of seeking out the more *outré* patients, such as Zita the stripper ("I've hardly ever met anyone more child-like . . . she's an absolute darling"), and Don the transvestite showgirl. As Charlie wrote Dr. Ayvazian after leaving Will Rogers:

> I asked Ruth Norman to give [Don] my record player, as I thought once the others got onto the nature of his career, which I had an inkling of very soon and nasty-minded Janet [another patient] got onto at once and made the most of it in dirty cracks to show her "sophistication"—I thought he would begin to feel isolated if not actually ostracised. . . . He is a remarkably intelligent and nice fellow, and I can only feel sorry for him from the depths of my heart. . . .
> A girl is what he wants to be more than anything else in the world.

By the time Charlie was able to leave—on November 21, 1963, after a four-month stay*—his feelings were profoundly mixed: on the one hand

---

* That is, the day before JFK's assassination in Dallas. Charlie adored the president even more than he'd once adored FDR, writing in one of his many abortive manuscripts from this time, "I came home to a blacker, more sorrowful and sorrowing weekend and weeks than any I had ever spent in the more than forty hospitals or sanatoria in which, for one reason or another—drink, drugs, phthisis [TB]—I had been obliged to 'serve time.' . . . "

he desperately missed his family and was eager to get on with his work, while on the other (as he'd presently remark in a promotional film starring Charles Jackson), "I felt now as though I were leaving home—I'd come to love the place so much." Physically he was much diminished. Within a few months he would begin to experience "drawing pains"—so called, by Charlie, to describe the sensation of being literally *drawn* to one side where most of his ribs were missing, their "bobbed" ends scraping against his right shoulder blade, which (he was told) might also have to be removed—though he was determined not to dwell on that. For now he was alive, and that was enough. "We refuse to let illness get us down," he proclaimed to a friend, "and as William Faulkner said in that by-now trite Nobel Prize Speech in Sweden: 'We shall prevail.' "

Charlie was so inspirational, and lovable, that the Will Rogers Fund implored him to write about his experience for *Reader's Digest*, though Charlie's own "aim" was *Life* ("I could even say, with all my ups and downs, that my aim has always been life"). On further consideration, though, it was decided that a mere magazine piece wasn't enough; Charlie himself, in all his plucky Chaplinesque glory, would be preserved for posterity in a nineteen-minute film shown all over the country at movie theaters and professional conferences. "Yes, I *am* the star," he proudly informed Dorothea, after an advance screening in New York, "and I speak the part, and I (or my voice) does the over-all narration, and it's *damned good* and I'm proud of it for doing so well a job I was utterly unused to and inexperienced in . . ." Trade journals agreed. *A Place in the Country* was "one of the best institutional films to date," and Charlie had quite acquitted himself as the protagonist/narrator: "If his voice is not professional, he more than makes up for it with the evident emotional influence on him made by his sojourn there."

Amid occasional speeches by Dr. Ayvazian and other doctors and patients, the film is almost wholly concerned with Jackson's progress as a kind of tubercular Everyman. "The years of pain finally leave your mind numb," he narrates, as we follow him in a station wagon to the hospital, which he warily enters wearing a gray suit and straw hat, presently exchanged for a lucky Japanese robe (a gift from Rhoda) prior to his examination by Dr. Ayvazian. "Tomorrow the medical staff decides my case," he later informs us, his pensive voice contrasted with a jolly gathering of patients in the rec room. "Downstairs a fire is going. People are chatting. Or singing around a piano ["I Left My Heart in San Francisco"]. . . . Here I am, wishing the hours away. And I don't know how much time I have left. . . . Charlie, it may be later than you think!"

But of course he survives—nay, he's reborn!—walking around the garden with a look of childlike wonder, cocking his head at birdsong and such. "To the people who gave me my second life," he concludes, "I thank you all. I was free: Free to live! Free to write again! . . . Now Rhoda—the children—my *other* home." And with that, he adjusts the brim of his hat and breezily relieves the driver of his (presumably empty) suitcase, tossing it into the backseat and embarking toward a future full of promise. It was touching because it was true. Charlie had been given another five years, and when they were over he would ask his mourners to remember him with donations to Will Rogers Memorial Hospital.

BACK IN SEPTEMBER 1962—shortly before he entered Middlesex Hospital for his lobectomy and, it turned out, a resumption of pill-taking—Charlie had again tried to write a story for *McCall's*, since he was "more than hanging on the ropes" financially, what with mounting medical bills and Kate now at Sarah Lawrence. As Charlie freely admitted to the latter, the story in question "[wasn't] worth telling, and one must *pretend* it is and work at keeping up the reader's interest at all cost." Whether he'd succeeded, according to the editors, was problematic, but such was their regard for the author that they were willing to pay an enormous sum (three thousand dollars) for a forty-page manuscript that they not only drastically shortened but "chewed to bits," said Rhoda, who intercepted the proofs while Charlie was withdrawing from Doriden at the Carrier Clinic: "I think letting his first MS in many years (and one written largely before this pill stuff started) get slaughtered would throw him way back," she protested to Brandt. As it happened, though, Charlie seriously objected to only *one* edit—but that a fatal one, as he saw it.

"The Loving Offenders"* is about an otherwise well-behaved girl in Arcadia, Bertha Schroeder, who murders her father, a cuckolded jeweler named Ernie. More than that, the story is an attenuated exercise in nostalgia—"worth telling," as Jackson would have it, only when he's evoking the incidental ambience of Main Street, such as Ernie Schroeder's shop: "On the walls around him were all those striking clocks, which, every hour on the hour and some at the half and quarter as well, would pull themselves together individually and in concert, with omi-

---

* From a favorite Shakespeare sonnet (42), and also the title (one may recall) of his never-completed play about a mother who loves her sons too much, with consequences that Freud and Krafft-Ebing might have foreseen.

nous, ratchety, interior wheezes for a second or two, and then let go."
When constrained to move the plot along, however, Jackson lapses into
cliché with an all but heedless abandon: Bertha's adulterous mother is
"pretty as a flower" but a "darn good scout," whereas Bertha herself is
"hard as nails," etc. Still, the author had been rather proud of his ambiguous ending (indeed the original title had been "Anybody's Guess"), when
the narrator asks Bertha *why* she shot her father: " 'Well,' Bertha said,
almost with a shrug, 'he was there, and the gun was there too, and—and
that's all.' " But such subtlety didn't wash with the fiction editor, Manon
Tingue, who insisted the heroine *expand* a bit on her motive, to wit:
" 'Well, sometimes I thought . . . that my poor father was a nothing. And
if only he had been a *something*, then maybe this wouldn't have . . . ' "
"I have always marveled at the curious ways of editors," Jackson wrote
Tingue afterward: "They buy a story because they like it—and then they
turn it into something else."

But once the check arrived—and Charlie was able to pay Kate's tuition
($1,200), dividing the rest between Middlesex Hospital, Bruno Motors,
and Boom—any remaining hard feelings vanished, and he began to rack
his brain for more story ideas ("I'm going to get out of debt if it kills
me"). That was the summer of 1963, a few weeks before he entered Will
Rogers, where his resolve was dissipated amid a leisurely convalescence.
"How are things?" his agent inquired that October. "Are you able to
work, or do [you] have any interest in working? Is there anything we
can do to help?" But Charlie didn't reply, except to slip into the offices
of Brandt & Brandt around Christmas, after which Frieda Lubelle was
obliged to circulate a memo to the effect that Charlie owed her, personally, thirty bucks, which should be paid to her directly out of the "first
amount of money" he managed to earn.

"So I was forced to ask myself the question, over and over," he wrote
in "The Sleeping Brain": "Did I want to prolong my life and keep my
health and remain that sad thing, a writer who did not write, one whose
reputation was all in the past; or should I say the hell with it and return
to my former indulgence in what Scott Fitzgerald called 'the subtler
poisons'?—and thus be released from my healthy prison, free once more
from fear, able to function as a writer again." An answer was suggested
in June 1964, when he returned to Will Rogers for minor "repairs"
(blunting the tips of his shorn ribs), and also to discuss the possibility of
removing, later, that bothersome right shoulder blade ("scapulectomy").
This time Charlie was given Darvon for pain and Librium for sleep,

but the latter (as usual) had the opposite effect: galvanized, he rented a typewriter and began writing through the night. As he described this breakthrough in *A Place in the Country**: "Now I *had* to write, and the ideas and words came tumbling out! All the words piling up behind my fear marched out across the keys of my typewriter—except for a regular interruption. In my life in hospitals, I've taken 100,000 pills . . . " Onscreen, a furiously typing Charlie absently waves off a nurse trying to get his attention, then his face lights up as he spies the pill cup in her hand; gulping down its contents with a smile, he resumes work while the camera lingers on the empty pill cup. "Oh, for so long I have had an inexplicable apathy about myself and my work, almost a despair, so that it seems often as if it couldn't matter *less* whether I ever finished the book or not," he wrote "Kate & everybody" in a six-page outpouring on June 10. "Now, mysteriously, I feel an upsurge, here, a renewal of a kind of confidence and belief in self that I have too long been without—and once again, life seems good, worthwhile, and the novel must be finished and find its place with the public."

Now he could see all the way through to the end—that balky Part Five, for instance, would consist of interior monologues alternating between Harry and Winifred ("a pure poem of despair"): brilliant!—and meanwhile, too, he'd come up with "a new story natural-born" for *McCall's*, "The Lady Julia." "I remembered a chamber-maid at home called Julia McIntyre, who worked at the Windsor Hotel (the Royal Hotel in that last McCalls story)," he wrote his family.[†]

A tall, handsome, very cultivated Danish chemist visited Newark, to start a new chemical factory, and stayed at the Windsor. Julia was

---

* Filmed in August 1964—two months after that second visit to Will Rogers—and released early the following year. As for his latest drug-fueled creative rebirth: surely he was given much the same medication during his previous visit in 1963, though there's little evidence of his wishing to write as a result. Probably he was too frail then even to consider any kind of sustained labor, whereas in 1964 he was in better physical shape and his medical treatment was less traumatic. In the second case, too, he was likely in the throes of a manic episode.

† The Windsor Hotel was the unsavory place where the pederastic organist, Bert Quance, washed up during his final days in Newark. In "The Loving Offenders," Quance's alter ego has a cameo at the "Royal Hotel": "Ray Verne had been an accomplished musician in his time; now he smelled all day long of Sneaky Pete. He was a character so far gone in what used to be known as moral turpitude that people at home no longer raised their eyebrows over Ray Verne, what he did, and the seedy company he kept."

cleaning his room one day (so the story goes) and said to him, wistfully: "Wouldn't it be a lovely day to go for a ride?" That did it. He
took her for a ride, fell truly in love with her, gave up his considerable
family back in Copenhagen (just like Gauguin, even to the very city),
installed her in an apartment, and then they lived together as man
and wife for years.

And that, indeed, was pretty much the story he proceeded to write—
another story "not worth telling," as he again confessed, though he labored for many weeks to make it otherwise, giving his heroine the kind of
twenty-four-karat heart of gold that couldn't fail to endear her to the average *McCall's* reader. Finishing "The Lady Julia" at 2:30 a.m. on July 23
(so noted in his diary), he left the manuscript on the kitchen table for
Rhoda and found her note the next day: "Charlie—the story is marvelous! . . . I've always felt your writing was going to grow—it wouldn't be
the brilliant breath-taking assault it used to be, but it would gain in depth
and compassion and understanding. . . . Julia is wonderful." As Charlie
promptly wrote his older daughter, he was now trembling with "fatigue
and emotion both," eager to reread his "marvelous" story but unable to
see the pages "for *tears* yet . . . "

It would take almost four months to produce a satisfactory version
for *McCall's*, and it would be hard to say which side found the process
more exhausting. "Treat my new baby kindlily," he'd entreated Manon
Tingue, who looked over the twelve-thousand-word typescript and
reached for her machete. When Charlie saw the first revision—just over
half his original length—he was plunged into "nearly suicidal" despair:
"What remains now is just a story of a whore's climb to a kind of position
of wealth and nothing more (no wonder the town hates her, now), with
all detail that showed kindness, heart, growth in stature, etc., taken out."
So he wrote Kate in a long, lachrymose letter evoking the veritable Cal-
vary he'd endured for her sake, since—on the very day he'd received his
eviscerated "baby"—Sarah Lawrence had demanded he pay his daughter's tuition, or else. "With this in mind," he wrote her, "I went up to
New York with no fight left in me at all, saw Manon and Carl and Herb
Mayes and said take it the way you want it, but pay me quick, and remove
my name from the story, for it is mine no longer. This they refused to do.
They wanted the name, and said mine was the only fiction writer's name
they ever featured on the cover, and that is true . . . "

The next day he wrote Kate again, this time in feverishly good fettle.

Her tuition was paid! As for "The Lady Julia," who cared what those hacks at *McCall's* made of it? "All can be restored and even re-written *my* way, when I re-publish it in my next collection of tales called ARCA-DIA RE-VISITED, as a companion volume to THE SUNNIER SIDE." Meanwhile Mayes was dangling an extra boodle for Charlie if he agreed to recast the story in a more redemptive mode. In Charlie's version, the Danish chemist kept Julia until he died in a factory explosion, whereupon she gave his fortune to the Church and disappeared, leaving a once-scandalized Arcadia to wonder if maybe they'd been hasty in judging her. But Mayes wanted Julia to exert herself in even *more* good works, wanted her and the chemist to be "quietly married" by a worldly priest, who in turn would preside over her subsequent death in child-birth, marveling at her goodness the while, which is finally celebrated by the whole town at "one of the largest [funerals] Arcadia had ever seen." And what did Charlie make of such wanton liberties? "I thank you with all my heart," he wrote Mayes, after considerable smoke had cleared. "I like the story 'The Lady Julia' . . . it is a story now, not just a long character-sketch; and I am grateful to you for your ideas as well as for the most generous and uncalled-for extra money."

But the long job had taken a toll—not least on Manon Tingue, who'd reacted badly to an addled charm offensive on Charlie's part. "Manon is under the impression that Charlie is anything but well," an anonymous Brandt & Brandt employee wrote in a memo, having been summoned by Tingue to discuss the matter over lunch. "Please, a note?" Charlie had written her on August 3, while awaiting further news of "The Lady Julia." "I pray for the results—*any* results—even if only money. My God how I need it. And how, too, I need you in my life—though you'll never believe me." When this failed to elicit a commensurate emotion, he tried phoning her at home and paving the way with a lot of friendly patter, and finally went over her head altogether and tried to deal exclusively with Mayes. "He can very soon wear out his welcome there," the memo writer concluded.

Chapter Nineteen

Homage to Mother Russia

More than Rhoda, more than Will Rogers, the love between Charlie and his daughters had kept him alive in recent years, though it chagrined him deeply that they regarded him as a doting papa first and a writer hardly at all. Back when he'd published five books, Sarah and Kate had been children, and the fact that their father was a "writer" meant little more (as he wrote in "The Sleeping Brain") "than if I had been a carpenter or a plumber or a postman." But all the while he'd looked forward to the day when he could share his work with them—even saving magazines for that purpose—and was crestfallen when, if anything, they seemed even more indifferent as young adults. (In fact they found the autobiographical element not only distressing but *distracting*—"Who was this person, who was that person?" Kate would wonder—and neither Sarah nor Kate finished *The Lost Weekend*, even, until after their father's death.) One of the high points of Charlie's life was the long-awaited night Sarah had phoned him from college to enthuse about "Rachel's Summer," though it left him in an awkward spot: If he could write so beautifully *then*, why wasn't he writing *now*?

And more than anything he hankered for Sarah's love and approval—because he already had them in such abundance, and so was all the more loath to lose them. "Papa loves me more than anything else in the world," she'd written in a college essay ("My Personality Shaped by Social Interaction / A Life History Paper").* "I love him too. Since we have always discussed everything, I feel no matter what happens I can go to my father and talk to him about it." This was true. Mikey Gilbert, her best friend at Connecticut College, remembered the way Sarah would sit on the floor of the dormitory phone booth at all hours chatting with her father. Such unconditional love brought out the best in both of them. When Sarah remarked in passing that she "loved [him] better" than Mama, he lost no time composing a gentle reprimand: "We may be closer, because we are more able to talk about things, but you deeply, deeply love your mother—I've always seen it and always known it, and it is right that you should. Your mother needs your love, and you must always make her feel it." But then, whatever else Rhoda was, she was not a demonstrative person. Sarah was startled, years later, when she reread her mother's letters and saw how confiding and affectionate they were—so removed, that is, from the reality of their everyday relationship. Rhoda rarely said "I love you," and was morally rigorous to a fault. "Work harder!" she'd admonish her daughter, a mediocre student in college, whereas Charlie would blame almost anyone *but* Sarah for bad grades ("such boring courses!"). And once, when the girl had taken someone else's English muffin from the communal fridge, and was threatened with possible suspension, Charlie was *outraged* ("You only took an English muffin!"), threatening to catch the next train to New London and give them all a piece of his mind. "But Sarah," said her mother, "that wasn't *your* English muffin!"

To Charlie, in short, she could do no wrong—and hadn't, arguably, for years. "My father is an alcoholic," she'd declared in her "Life History" paper. "Because of Papa's problem, I am more mature, I think, and understand our family and other people more thoroughly." As an honor student at Newtown High, Sarah had manifested her maturity in various ways: great popularity ("I made new friends easily"), a dazzling list of extracurricular accomplishments (Betty Crocker Homemaker of

---

* With the same bland frankness, she'd made the following comparison between herself and Kate: "Almost exact opposites, we have many differences in opinion and outlook. Enjoying good music and good art, she is a very interesting person and has an active and alive mind. I am just average." Sarah got an A− for this essay, which her father read with tears in his eyes: "You are the greatest pride and satisfaction in my life," he wrote her afterward.

Tomorrow Award, the Lions Club's George Trull Award, the D.A.R.'s Good Citizen Award, many offices in student government), stardom on the varsity softball and basketball teams, and a summer job as director of the local playground that entailed taking care of some fifty boys and girls ("Loving children, I enjoyed my work immensely"). For almost five years, too, she'd had a boyfriend who was also very mature and popular: Sam Curtis, scion of the Curtis Box family, one of the leading families in Newtown. Charlie adored Sam and vice versa (due in part to the former's enthusiastic influence, Sam majored in English and later moved out West to write poetry), though he forbade the young man to leave his car parked late at night outside their home on Main Street, lest the townsfolk get the wrong idea.

Expectations were naturally high when Sarah won a scholarship to Connecticut College—Rhoda's alma mater—though Charlie took pains to assure her that they only wanted her to do her best, "and if that isn't good enough, then we and you have to accept." As it turned out, alas, it *wasn't* good enough, and during her sophomore year, in February 1960, a sympathetic dean named Miss Babbott wrote her parents to that effect. Charlie replied immediately: "We did indeed know about Sarah's marks: one of the great things about Sarah is that she has always (and promptly) been honest with us . . . " He would come to New London right away, he wrote, to discuss the matter with her in person, and perhaps see if he could do a little in his own way to improve things. The visit, for Charlie, was a triumph. As he wrote Miss Babbott afterward, he'd had a *marvelous* time—meeting her, of course, was a great pleasure, while Sarah and her friends had treated him practically as one of the gang: they'd played a lot of bridge, gone to the movie *Brink of Life* ("where was certainly struck the 'grisly' note you warned me of"), and best of all had long, shoeless "bull-sessions" in the dorm, during which Charlie had frankly canvassed the other girls about his daughter's academic deficits (consensus: "she didn't allot her time properly")—which, however, he was determined to keep in perspective. "I consider myself so lucky to have a child like Sarah," he concluded for Miss Babbott's benefit, "whether she fails or succeeds, how can I not believe in God? By all the rules of my erratic past, Sarah should have turned out to be an unhappy mess."

In the end it was Sarah who decided to give up college as a bad job and learn secretarial work at Farrar, Straus and Cudahy, which would make it easier for the more intellectual Kate to attend college the following year. Sarah and her friend Mikey took an apartment on 20th Street, and a year later Sarah met her future husband, Alexander "Sandy" Piper III, a stockbroker at Paine, Webber, Jackson & Curtis. A twenty-six-year-old divorcé, Piper had dated Mikey a few times when she suggested he take Sarah instead to a basketball game: "They got along *much* better," she remembered, "and there was an attraction." Charlie noticed too, albeit from the bitter distance at which he was kept; in a poem he wrote Sarah on February 14, 1963, he expressed the rather skeptical hope that she accept him as her valentine:

> *. . . For today only, mind you—till some fine,*
> *Upright, downright, upstanding, downstanding son*
> *Of a you-know-what, some real cool cookie, one*
> *Who I hope knows good goods when he sees 'em*
> *Takes [you] away. . . .*

Doubtless it galled him that he'd yet to be introduced to the young man—a status quo that was still in place eight months later, though Sarah had thrown her father a bone or two that he (cooped up by then at Will Rogers) had energetically masticated. Since Sarah had mentioned, for instance, Sandy's reluctance to get married so soon after his divorce, it occurred to Charlie that perhaps the young man was in the midst of psychoanalysis "because of some emotional deficiency or lack"; but what could this be? Given that he didn't know Sandy yet (as he pointedly reminded Sarah) he could be mistaken, but:

I can't shake a peculiar nagging hunch I have, somewhere in the background, that Sandy's problem or *the* problem is a sexual one . . . and it has occurred to me, wildly (you know my lurid imagination) that Sandy may be impotent, or afraid of sex, or unable to function as he would like. Mind you, I most certainly don't mean homo, I mean a man who is basically afraid of elemental woman, and there are lots of them. . . .*

He'd persuaded Rhoda, too, that there was something a little shady about a guy who was divorced so young and determined to be hush-hush about it; what *could* it be, if not "un-virility"? "The adjustments of marriage are

---

* As Sarah has pointed out, her father's speculation about Sandy's alleged sexual "problem" was entirely unfounded.

difficult enough without a mal-adjustment of that order," wrote Rhoda (perhaps with a certain hard-won wisdom on that point) to her daughter. And meanwhile, along with his other "probing questions," Charlie wanted to know whether Sarah had ever, well, told Sandy about *him*?—that he was fun, lovable, easy to get along with ("I hope you have told him these things if, in your belief, they are true").

As he would painfully learn in the fullness of time, however, it hardly mattered whether she had or not. Sandy was a regular guy, all right, and certainly wanted to make things go with his new father-in-law, but he wasn't really interested in a deep relationship. He wasn't a reader, for one thing, and the fact that Sarah's father was the author of *The Lost Weekend* was mostly a source of embarrassment. As for Sandy's parents (the father also of Wall Street), they were very sweet and well-meaning and whatnot, but also *quite* uninterested in arty stuff and moreover apt to go on about "the Jews" and so forth. As Sarah would later explain, "All the reasons I married Sandy [were] all the reasons Papa didn't like him. I was not looking to repeat my father with my husband. I was looking for a stable life, I was looking for a steady income, and I thought I'd found that with this man and I thought I was in love with him."

Fair enough. At any rate she married him on Christmas Day, 1963, at a small service in the Kirkpatrick Chapel at Rutgers, with a reception afterward chez Jackson, where the host confided to the only two non-family guests (both named Mike) that he took a dim view of the bridegroom. The following Valentine's Day, indeed, his annual poem to his daughter was the most doleful yet:

> *Oh what to do about a Valentine that has gone astray*
> *Gone and got herself married and all that mushy stuff?*
> *Well you just try to keep on loving her any-way*
> *Chin up & all that, but I tell you, brother, it's rough.*
>
> *Rough because like when you've just said something witty,*
> *She smiles and looks back at you with a wide vague stare;*
> *And while she is charming as ever and just as pretty,*
> *You know who she's thinking of and you just aren't there. . . .*

But naturally he was determined to make the best of things—for Sarah's sake, of course, and because Sandy posed a special challenge: He was, after all, Tonio's "simple" and "average" writ large, and Charlie would never cease to pine for acceptance from such people (while perversely baiting them too). "I love that colored photograph on my dresser of smiling you and a smilinger Sandy," he wrote Sarah from Will Rogers in June 1964. "I look at it often with increasing pleasure and, yes, reassurance. That open, happy, frank, unselfconscious, and generous natural smile of Sandy's—well, anyone who looks like that can be only good.—Tell him this, unless you think it would embarrass him, but I mean it with my heart." But Sarah did *not* tell him, to her father's dismay, nor did he get any response from a book titled *Nymphomania* ("a subject he should know *all about*") that he'd left on Sandy's pillow after a stay in their apartment, and he might have wondered if his son-in-law had twigged to the implications of Nabokovian *poshlust* (philistine vulgarity), which Charlie had impishly discussed with him one night.

Things came to a head when Charlie returned from Will Rogers a week or so after writing about the "smilinger Sandy" portrait: soaring with renewed enthusiasm for his novel and life absolutely in general, he looked forward to heading straight to Sarah's place from his bus—"unless (wild thought) you'd like to drive up and get me?"—and having a lovely dinner with her and Sandy. "He was this charismatic, interested, interesting person who would just take over your life and it was wonderful," Sarah later remarked (with this occasion in mind) "—and then it just wasn't wonderful anymore. He didn't know boundaries." "Okay, Sarah," he wrote her from New Brunswick, "suppose you sit down now and write me or 'phone me or at least let me know in some way what the matter is." Having been given a not-so-subtle bum's rush after dinner that night, poor Charlie had stopped at a phone booth on his way out of town ("hot and streaming with sweat") to say goodbye, and had just assayed a little patter of bon mots when Sarah cut him short with, "Sorry, but we're playing bridge." Stunned, heartbroken ("my god, you don't *do* these things to people"), Charlie wondered if maybe he *bored* her nowadays, or was it his lack of money, or—or what? "Maybe I *am* an old poop . . . But I can do nothing unless I know."

Sarah, it bears repeating, was the love of his life, and he couldn't stand the thought of losing her. A month later he wrote a contrite letter admitting that he'd "resented Sandy because perhaps I was overfond of you," and vowed to do his utmost to remedy things. It was true he'd been bothered, in the past, by Sandy's tendency to leave her alone so much (weekends especially), but during a recent stay at their apartment he'd had a chat with the young man that helped shed some light. Waiting up until his son-in-law came home, around midnight, Charlie had remarked that he looked "like a million dollars," whereupon Sandy ("gay, pleasant, relaxed") mentioned a lively day on the golf course and said, "I *have* to be active"—explaining the sedentary rigors of Wall Street and so on. Charlie encouraged his daughter to pass this anecdote along to her husband—what with all it implied of fatherly acceptance and the like—but then caught himself, remembering (as Sarah was wont to point out) that Sandy just didn't care. "Well there, my friend, is a normal young man," he concluded. "I wish *I* didn't care what people thought of me." And still he worked harder than ever to woo the young man, calling him "Alexander the Great" and expressing a wish to be buried in the dressing gown Sandy had given him. And meantime, privately, he considered writing a new story titled, simply, "Loneliness": "A father trying to let go of his daughter trying not to call her—trying not to be like his own possessive mother who had driven him away."

In the same letter where he'd recounted that breezy midnight chat with his son-in-law, Charlie had written Sarah, "Funny, the mutations of life—and thank God for them! Kate, of all the people I know, has become, in effect, my alter ego: I am able to think with her, talk to her, write her as I write nobody else—on an objective, impersonal, almost disinterested level most unusual between a father and a daughter—not possessive, as I think I always used to be with you." Such effortless rapport had not come easily. "Kate *must* hurt someone, or she is not happy," he'd written Sarah six years before, when Kate was fifteen, "and her particular object of aggression since you went to college is me." During, say, a TV show that her father had scripted, Kate would make a point of reading throughout the broadcast, with maybe a bored glance or two at the screen, then leave without a word once it was over. Or if her overworked mother worried aloud that she'd be unable to attend the National Honor Society awards day—and Papa, of course, would be in New York—Kate would snap, "You went to Sarah's!" Suffice it to say, then, that her father's excessive doting on his firstborn had *not* gone unnoticed, and indeed Kate would struggle for years with a sense of being unloved—a problem she came by honestly. "And what about some mail sometime?" her needy father hectored her, typically, in 1962. "Are you just going to go on forever taking, and not giving?"

But then, too, they had their better traits in common, as Charlie discovered more and more now that Kate had gone off to college. "We must go see the Courbets—the great landscapes and thrilling awful seascapes," he wrote, one of his daily postcards to the girl during her freshman year at Sarah Lawrence ("Sadie Larry," said Charlie), usually featuring a favorite painting with some exuberant gloss on same. Kate was a true protégé: ripe for the sort of inspiration he could provide, and yet quite the captain of her own soul—her assertiveness becoming less an irritant as she got older ("you are liker Elizabeth [Bennet, in *Pride and Prejudice*] than any other female I ever knew"), at least in comparison with her sister's placid embrace of the bourgeois Pipers. The same year he wrote of Sarah's "downstanding son / Of a you-know-what" for Valentine's Day, he composed this bit of winsome doggerel for Kate:

> *Katie is the girl for me.*
> *She is my af-fin-i-ty.*
> *And I am hers—how else explain*
> *The fun, ideas, and sometimes pain*
> *That we upon each other shower?*
> *So be it. If it's in my power,*
> *No other dame would I prefer*
> *Excepting only, only her. . . .*

One of the highlights of 1963, for Charlie, had been Father's Day at "Sadie Larry" ("Be apprised that I have signed up for *ever*thing [*sic*]. . . . Looking forward—et comment!"), and a year later he promptly alerted Sarah when her little sister was elected president of the senior class. "You are my only perfect correspondent," he wrote the latter, though their correspondence was more than a trifle one-sided. Since, again, he hardly saw the point of diaries, and rarely wrote Dorothea anymore, Charlie's younger daughter had become, by default, the sounding board for his long ruminations on, say, the wrong-turnings of his career, his disenchantment with AA, various veiled and not-so-veiled hints about his sexuality ("I picked up The SYMPOSIUM and my god suddenly it was crystal-clear . . . "). The more he wrote her, though, the more he longed for her actual presence—the way they could "talk and talk forever" about *anything*, whereas Rhoda was "a non-discusser," and really what was there left to say?

The answer was very, very little. "We are seldom alone together, hardly ever talk," Charlie wrote Sarah, shortly after his return from Will Rogers in 1964. "Mama is home at 5, then there's news from 6:30 to 7:30 and often from 7:30 till 8 something else, so that I have to get in what

I have to say, if anything important, between commercials, then at 8:30 Mama is off to bed." In the early days they'd had the girls around to distract them, then for years Charlie had stayed in New York during the week, leaving his family to fend for themselves except for "that ratrace of meeting the train" on Friday, as Rhoda put it, "and getting dinner afterward," since Charlie could hardly boil an egg and was liable to starve if left unfed. Nowadays, à deux, both he and Rhoda were mindful of a certain fraught quality to their discourse; as he wrote in "Jim's Night Life" (a fragment inspired, he freely admitted, by his own marital plight), some of their dicier talking-points included "money, sex, the children, the past, the future," and hence conversation tended to proceed as follows:

> SHE: I saw Mrs. Meyer in the Supermarket.
> HE: Oh? . . .
> Or.
> SHE: We're having frankfurters and beans tonight. How many franks will you want?
> HE: Oh, two will be enough, thank you. . . .

Then an hour of TV and so to bed—their respective beds, rather: Charlie, for his part, "came alive" during these late hours, rehearsing all the bitter things he'd left unsaid while docilely eating his hot dogs ("He should have risen up a dozen times and pasted her one").

One of the reasons he "came alive" was because he was taking drugs again, and in the absence of much writing he felt a kind of thwarted gregariousness, when high, that fueled his anger toward his taciturn wife—anger that was already rampant, given her long-suffering opposition to "the subtler poisons," which of course was the *main* topic they elided lest a hideous row ensue. The three scribbled pages of "Jim's Night Life," not coincidentally, were dated "Feb. 21st 1963"—about a week before Charlie consented to the ordeal of withdrawing from Doriden at the Carrier Clinic—and now, in August 1964, he braced himself for a showdown of sorts at Boom's seaside cottage in Strathmere, where he and Rhoda were to spend ten days alone together. "Sounds awful to say," he wrote Kate a week before they left, "but it will be a kind of test for us both, a *good* test, for we need to get together without the disturbing distractions of The Rutgers Alcohol Studies thing, often my AA, *very* often my writing"—the last of which (at least since Will Rogers II) involved pill-taking. "Now my sole aim is to slide down these last ten years or so of our lives as gracefully as possible," he wrote Sarah a day later. "If we find a real communion together . . . then great: much will have been accomplished, to augur well for the fast diminishing future. If we don't, well, then we'll have to face that too." Meanwhile he was hedging his bets: his local doctor was out of town, so he fired a letter to Dr. Ayvazian ("Fritzalie") on August 4, asking him to expedite prescriptions for Darvon and Librium.

The Strathmere trip was a bust, needless to say, at least in terms of the marriage. Shortly after their return, on August 16, Charlie complained to Sarah about the "loneliness and silence of home," and two days later Rhoda gave him something else to be lonely about, returning to Malaga (and thence again to Strathmere, which Charlie dearly loved) for the Labor Day weekend. By herself. "My wife, I am sad to say, is a very sick woman," he wrote the next day to his Macmillan editor, Robert Markel, though on reflection he mailed the letter to *Boom* instead ("Knew you would be interested in this"), the better for his brother to grasp what kind of viper he was nourishing in his bosom.*

> I really only realized it this past week, how deeply disturbed and sick she is: and it gets worse the more I get better. . . . We have one car, I can't walk much more than two blocks, certainly can't carry things (I mean like bags of groceries, etc) and yesterday morning—Friday, Rhoda suddenly announced that she was taking off in the car and didn't know when she would be back. I asked, "Do you mean Tuesday, after Labor Day?" and she said she didn't know when she would be back. I stood there silent, determined to let her go without further question, because maybe she needs just that, and just before she left she said: "There's no coffee in the house, no bread, no milk, no Tab (that soft drink I drink) etc." I said, "That's all right, I can manage, I'll get them somehow," and she looked at me, there was a smile that still makes me shudder to think of because it wasn't malicious or sarcastic, it was horridly mirthful, and said, "Martyr"—and was gone. Well, I went out while it was still cool enough and though our neighborhood is somewhat up and down hill, I *did* manage—and came home to at least four days—and maybe more—of utter relief and peace.

---

* The letter—to "Dear Rob-bair" (Charlie's pet name for Markel)—was found among Boom's papers at Dartmouth, and also contains a lot of effusive assurances about the progress of *A Second-Hand Life* and various other projects. I read the letter over the phone to Markel, who assured me (with some regret) that he never received a copy.

Indeed he decided he could use a lot more "loneliness and silence," sweetly suggesting to Sarah that she invite her mother to New York for a few days ("Mama has lots of time coming to her").

WHATEVER THE UPS AND DOWNS of his marriage, Charlie was desperate for human contact. One day in August he'd gone to the Rutgers library and struck up a long chat with "one of the gals in the Info Department," who asked him what he did for a living. He told her ("the dreadful secret came out"), and the next day the woman's husband—Joseph Czapp, director of continuing education—gave him a call: Would Charlie be interested in teaching an evening extension class at the women's college? "I am enormously flattered at my age to receive such an offer," he promptly wrote a Sarah Lawrence professor he'd met during a recent visit, "because Kate, who loves me dearly, thinks at the same time (like all daughters) that her father doesn't know nothing." For the two-hour weekly lecture course, he would receive two hundred dollars a semester.

Charlie threw himself into the preparation, composing a syllabus that began with a long, cajoling "Note to the Students Intending to Enroll in *ENJOYMENT OF LITERATURE* Starting September 23rd and Taught by CHARLES JACKSON." Charlie had parsed his potential customers—wistful housewives and retirees—and was agonizingly chary of scaring them off with highbrow talk: "We want to read the books for their own sake and enjoy them because after all they were written in the first place *to be enjoyed* rather than studied . . ." And if you don't like a novel on the syllabus? Don't read it! Charlie had provided a list of alternative titles by the same author in every case but three: *Madame Bovary*, *Anna Karenina*, and *Portrait of a Lady*, because of their intense "reader-interest" and "identification values"; in fact he all but promised his prospective students that they wouldn't be able to put those novels down or their money back! "Far from being a cold, academic lecturer," he further assured them, "I am a frankly confessed and in some cases starry-eyed *fan* (there is no better word to describe it) . . ." To prove it, he would take a special approach to *Crime and Punishment* during their first session, regaling them with Raskolnikov's murder of the pawnbroker as told *in Charlie's own words*, as if from personal experience, followed by a reading of "The Sunnier Side" that would help them all reflect on why good literature often seems "truer" than real life. "I'm *always* curious about people," he concluded, "and I'm looking forward to meeting and knowing you."

Charlie had a wonderful time, attracting one of the biggest enrollments at the Extension Center. He loved revisiting old favorites like *Handful of Dust, Death in Venice, Dubliners*, et al., and preparing his lectures was a delightful pretext for avoiding work on his novel. He urged family and friends to attend his classes: Rhoda was coming for *Pride and Prejudice*, and he particularly wanted Sarah to bring Sandy for dinner on November 18, since they could all go to his class on *Anna Karenina* afterward (perhaps he was planning a few subtle hints about Sandy's resemblance to Karenin). During that first semester he appeared in New Jersey's *Star-Ledger* newspaper twice: one photograph showed him "in lively discussion" with two of his students, Mrs. Freda Sinnickson and Miss Suzanne Walker, while another—the *raffiné* author at his desk—accompanied a long feature article ("RUTGERS UNVEILS NOTED 'LOST' WRITER") by a rather tactless woman named Doris E. Brown. "Even most of his neighbors haven't known that the amiable, mild-mannered, little baldhead with the owlish spectacles . . . is the author of one of the most important books written in the past quarter century." Charlie was so thrilled by the publicity that he hardly minded the "little baldhead" crack, or even Miss Brown's reference to his "slightly prissy manner." ("You should have seen *her*!" he wrote Kate. "A dyke, yet. All butch and a yard wide.") Suddenly he was in demand: the Rotary Club invited him to appear at one of their lunches, and the celebrated poet John Ciardi shoved him in front of the crowd at an LBJ rally: "*Me* a political speaker!" Charlie marveled. "It wowed your mother."

Even his work was taking off again, after a long autumnal rut during which he'd often reflected on his own futility—especially in comparison with innovative young turks like Bruce Jay Friedman ("they've got us old-timers beat a mile"), whose paranoiac black humor he depressively admired. Why bother? Nowadays he was little better than a *McCall's* hack. Feeling especially sorry for himself one night, he quoted a pertinent aphorism from Logan Pearsall Smith: "The notion of making money by popular work, and then retiring to do good work on the proceeds, is the most familiar of all the devil's traps for the artist." "Artist!" Rhoda scoffed. "You've been using that excuse for 30 years!" All the keener a bodkin for being true.

The latest thunderbolt came from Pushkin, whose vast accomplishment despite an early death made Charlie even more ashamed of his lassitude. For years he'd put off reading *Eugene Onegin* because he didn't believe poetry could be translated, but finally he broke down and bought a paperback of Walter Arndt's rhyming translation, famously derided by

Nabokov, whose four-volume literal work was too expensive. Charlie was transported, despite Nabokov's taunts: "Oh heavens, give yourself the treat of your life," he wrote his fellow Russophile, Dorothea, praising Arndt and excitedly apprising his friend of the "World Masterpiece" he'd been inspired to write. On January 22, 1965, while he and Rhoda were on a bus to New York—en route to the preview of *A Place in the Country*—he was struck by "an idea out of the blue" and knew at once that his other projects ("the unfinished story Carl & Herb Mayes are palping for, so too for God knows how long the three-fourths done Second Hand Life") were "shot to hell." Instead he *had* to write a novel in Pushkin sonnets that would be a pastiche of *Onegin* and yet utterly different and *new* (as he scribbled in his notes, "The novel's a dead form, / They've all been written— / No place for it to go. / Well then let's go *backward*"). "It's a piece of work," he wrote Dorothea, "where style counts almost first, where words have to be exact, precise, unique, each one made for that spot or sense alone; where rhythm counts; and oh, wit (imagine me being witty—but there it is!); and with style and brilliance of les mots justes, if emotional content isn't there, or character insight, or evocative description, then all the rest is for naught."

For emotional content he relied, in part, on his adoration of his older daughter, whose aid he enlisted in suggesting a name for his eponymous hero ("I want it to be very American and plain, Whitman's idea of 'the divine average' "): Rufus "Bud" Boyd. And Sarah it was who served as the model for his Tatyana-like heroine, Mary—a naïf who grows up with Rufus in latter-day Fairfield, Connecticut, and one day declares her love in a letter posted by her devoted old nurse (based on Rhoda). Rufus, bound for the Ivy League, rejects her as a remnant of his provincial past. After traveling the world for some years, however, he comes to appreciate the prize he so blithely cast aside, and returns to find her a beautiful, fully blossomed young woman—married, alas, to a much older man. "In place of the valorous general" (in *Onegin*), Dorothea remembered of the latter, "there was substituted the mere suggestion of a human being. But in this blurred presentation, I was able to discern a familiar silhouette; short, plump, bald, Chaplinesque . . . "*

As for his repressed, "very *Yankee*" hero, Rufus, Charlie had a definite

---

* Writing several years later, Dorothea here recalls reading a part of *Rufus "Bud" Boyd* that almost certainly was never written, even in notes. No doubt Charlie related aspects of his story to her in person—including, perhaps, a plan to use himself as the model for his heroine's aged husband.

physical model in mind (though he denied any other similarity): Sarah's likable ex-boyfriend, Sam Curtis, whom he'd evidently found *very* handsome. Rufus was to appear first in his swimsuit, "like Adam on the primal day / . . . fresh from clay. / With breasts like flattened saddle bags / Muscled arms like twisted thick Byzantine columns"—etc. So fulsome was he on the subject that he took care to prepare a little apologia in his notes (later to be turned into verse): "For this is beauty, hardened reader, and you might as well get used to it, because there's going to be much more—it is *the thing* about Bud Boyd and about the only thing—so do not flinch from my description—the idea that a man would describe another man's beauty—why not? Where would we be without those Greeks who so loved the male human body that they gave us masterpiece upon masterpiece—each one . . . more dazzling and even 'upsetting' than the other . . ." Indeed, one of his aims, it seems, was to demystify homosexuality in the frankest terms yet, as Rufus faces the vagaries of his own nature amid the worldly temptations of Europe. "What does it matter how, as you young Americans say, you get your kicks, so long as you get them," a French lieutenant (in Jackson's notes) propositions the lad. "Two men old enough to know what they are doing, what they want . . . But you don't want; or don't know that you want or do.—So. Tant pis."

But considerations of theme, plot, and character are somewhat conjectural, since the only part of this "Ardent Salute to THE POET and Homage TO MOTHER RUSSIA" that survives in polished (and polished and polished) form is its eighteen-stanza "Dedication," for which Jackson followed the prosody of the single seventeen-line dedicatory stanza in *Onegin*, with its alternating masculine and feminine rhymes in iambic tetrameter. "Too mindful of our Russian treasure / Almost to pick up pen at all," he begins.

> *Only too grateful for the pleasure*
> *Ivan [Turgenev] and Lev [Tolstoy], Modeste [Mussorgsky] and Paul [?],*
> *Anton [Chekhov]—and I (O, don't exclude me!)—*
> *Have found, and cherished, in your [Pushkin's] verse;*
> *Yet dare I, though your gift elude me,*
> *Adopt your style, for bad or worse. . . .*

Perhaps the most amusing part, for Charlie, was mimicking the witty ("imagine me being witty"), intrusive Pushkinian narrator, the better to indulge in a lot of rueful humility:

Yet oft have I—(You too?)—been lost in
Old and new admiration of
Bob Lowell, Waugh, Proust, Keats, Jane Austen,
When suddenly my requited love
Turns to despair, sans provocation.
I cry within me: What's the use?
For us admirers, adoration
Can be a form of self-abuse.
Idolatry becomes castration
Of all our urges to create. . . .
So—some try drugs and some try slaking
Their thwarted aims with rye or beer;
Those who can do a little faking
Try parody; as I do here. . . .

So it went for the 306 lines of his "Dedication." Once he came to the main narrative, Jackson switched to the conventional fourteen-line Onegin stanza with its complex rhyme scheme (AbAbCCddEffEgg), and opened, quite in the spirit of Pushkin, with a gentle satire on mid-century exurbia:

The brash transistor now enlivens
The silent lovers' rustic lay;
For hundreds pastured in the drive-ins
The night is big with Doris Day.
Try "clover-leaf," that rural image:
It only means a traffic scrimmage. . . .

Four stanzas continue in this vein, until the flustered narrator reproaches himself for his incessant stalling and promises, at long last, to get on with the story proper:

Enough! Enough! You get the picture . . .
I've overdone it once again
With easy ridicule and stricture,
For which, forgive; and I'll explain:
I feel impelled to hurry! hurry!
I'm overcome with fret and worry
To set it down in any state
Before it is too late, too late . . .

Thus, while evoking the image of a dying writer rushing to realize, roughly, his final opus, Jackson was actually retyping over and over (with, occasionally, a word or two changed from the previous draft) his twenty-three or so finished stanzas—as if his main purpose, once inspiration had waned, was to give his wife the impression (not for the first time) that he was working on *something* behind his closed door. Many copies of these stanzas, and *only* these stanzas, survive.

Ultimately it was the story itself that stumped or at least scared Charlie, who wrote a monitory note on an index card and perhaps tacked it over his desk (along with the *Onegin* rhyme scheme): "I must remember that leaning on the Pushkin story, calling to mind its protagonists, using its forms . . . cannot do what the story itself fails to do. Must have its own life *first of all.*" And so he circled round and round that "Dedication"—with its easier theme of self-abasement—and even considered writing an *additional* prefatory verse about his "horror" of being a "bore" ("Dear reader, whose historic service / Is patience . . . "). At any rate, the actual tale of Rufus "Bud" Boyd seems never to have advanced (except in notes) beyond the following couplet: "Amid these scenes [Doris Day, etc.], with little talk, / Rufus and Mary walk and walk."

In another poem, written to Rhoda on their twenty-seventh anniversary (March 4, 1965), Charlie announced, " 'RUFUS (BUD) BOYD, / A Novel in Verse,' is put aside. / I've got to be busy or employed / With something that will bread provide." Which is not to say he didn't keep talking and talking about it, reading his witty "Dedication" aloud to guests, and possibly he never quite despaired of completing the other 235 stanzas of the story proper someday.*

AROUND THIS TIME, Charlie claimed to have kicked pills again—and therefore, again, to have lost the will to write. Not writing meant sitting idle in New Brunswick, though his Rutgers job had brought him in touch with the local literati, and that summer (1965) he was invited to teach at the Bread Loaf Writers' Conference in Middlebury, Vermont. The director was John Ciardi (founder of the Rutgers writing program), who

---

* Jackson had planned for the novel to be made up of six parts of forty stanzas each. In 1986 the Anglo-Indian novelist and poet Vikram Seth unwittingly picked up this fallen standard, producing his delightful novel *The Golden Gate*, written in 590 Onegin stanzas and somewhat inspired by the post-Arndt translation of Charles Johnston.

might have deemed Charlie to be just the ticket for the many women of a certain age who liked to attend the conference; they would know *The Lost Weekend*, of course, and feel inspired by the way its author, a charming contemporary, was still plugging away after a fashion.

But Charlie was at a very low ebb in his affairs, and on the bus to Vermont he felt "sick at heart"—a "fraud," a "has-been" who scarcely belonged among *real* writers and certainly had little to say to prospective students, all of whom would take a dim view of his imposture. Wanly unpacking his bag, Charlie was visited by "a kind fellow-author, a woman of national reputation," who noticed his discomfiture and asked whether he might like a few sleeping pills.* Seeing the poor man perk up, she gave him a dozen pills in a little white envelope, which she hoped would help "see [him] through for a few days." "Talk about the Windfall Department," Charlie recalled in "The Sleeping Brain."

> It saw me through, all right. . . . I found myself looking forward to the morning, to teaching, to talking about fiction and the novel, to meeting with the students. And to put it bluntly and, I hope, modestly (for actually I had little to do with it), the next morning I was better than good: my self-distaste gone, I enjoyed the occasion mightily, and felt in the stream of things again. It went on like that for the whole two weeks; I was renewed, and felt at the top of my form.

What Charlie was like "at the top of [his] form," to other eyes, is worth considering. Certainly it was memorable for those who attended the conference. Stephen Jones—one of that year's designated "scholars," whose novel Jackson critiqued—remembered being impressed and a little worried by the man's extreme animation: "Everybody looked at him like he's Don Birnam. 'You all right, Charlie?' Like he's a ticking time bomb." Faculty members were expected to give evening lectures, and Charlie was preceded by such eminences as Dudley Fitts and Richard Ellmann, to say nothing of the flamboyant William (*The Ugly American*) Lederer, stabbing the air with his corncob pipe ("talking about the time he taught Hemingway how to write for a case of brandy in China," as Jones characterized it). When it came time for Charlie to speak, Jones

---

* This "Angel of Mercy" (as Charlie described her) was almost certainly Nancy Hale (1908–88), a novelist who'd been a regular at Bread Loaf for many years. Ann Brower, whose husband, Brock, was also on the faculty in 1965, remembers Hale slipping her a valium after she'd received stressful news from home.

saw him drifting into a corner and downing a little airline-size bottle of liquor (his dozen pills long gone), before extolling the various books he loved and entreating his audience to read, read, read! "People at Middlebury [are] buying the Lost Weekend like mad," Rhoda reported to Kate "—bought out all Farrar Straus stock. And one student toured all the Vermont bookstores (a 150 mile trip) to come back with a copy of each of Papa's books for signatures."

And it wasn't just pills and liquor: Charlie was in love! "Things got a bit sticky between us," said John Weston, the other scholar assigned to Jackson. The two had first encountered each other at adjacent urinals. "I have two addictions," Charlie proclaimed, wild-eyed: "I am an alcoholic and a homosexual!" Weston got the distinct impression he was saying that to everyone ("as if he was trying to make a statement"), though it soon became clear that Weston was the particular object of Charlie's regard. A then-closeted (and married) high school teacher who'd published an apprentice novel, Weston never forgot the exquisite care Jackson took with the manuscript of his second novel, *The Telling*, which they discussed one night in Charlie's room until four in the morning. The latter lingered over every page, helpful if increasingly distrait, then abruptly lifted Weston's shirt and began kissing his chest. Rather like Ron Sproat before him, Weston tried to fend off his mentor ("a very nice man") as politely as possible, stressing the fact of his (Weston's) wife and quasi-straightness in general. But Charlie pleaded, and finally became petulant: All he wanted was to fellate the young man; was *that* so much to ask? ("I felt bad later," Weston reflected. "You know, I could have given that guy a little happiness for 15 minutes.") But apparently there were no hard feelings: "For John, a souvenir of that deeply rewarding time (for me) when we were friends and colleagues at Bread Loaf," Charlie inscribed *The Lost Weekend*, and for a year or so he wrote "melodic love letters" that Weston was at pains to hide from his wife in Tucson, though the marriage died a little later of natural causes.

Other attendees didn't receive quite the same passionate attention, though Jackson clearly endeavored to be frank but tactful. Miss Olive Schneider of Berea, Ohio—a soon-to-be-retired nurse—was so dismayed by her "one precious hour" with Jackson that she recounted it in narrative form and mailed him the result. Reminding him that she was one of six nurses sent to Bread Loaf because of a writing contest sponsored by the *American Journal of Nursing*, Miss Schneider described the way he seemed to rush through their conference, deploring her bad grammar ("You have split infinitives") and labored prose before allowing that her last story (of four) was perhaps the best. By then Schneider had tears in her eyes. As she recalled the scene:

> "I am very embarrassed," I said.
>
> "I had tears in my eyes yesterday," [said Jackson]. "One of the staff said something very unkind to me. It hurt me so terribly that I couldn't eat my lunch. We shouldn't quarrel like that."
>
> I was distressed that anyone would hurt this personable and kind man. "I think you do not know how much affection we all have for you," I said.
>
> "Thank you," he answered feelingly. "I'm very happy here, happier than I have been for three years. But when I called my wife and told her so, I hurt her feelings. . . . I spent eight hours with one man trying to help him with his novel. It was so good and so bad."
>
> I wonder if I felt envy for the chap who got eight hours of this busy man's time, and my manuscripts were discussed with finality in less than an hour. . . .

In the end Jackson asked to see her best story again, and the next day (the last of the conference) he pronounced it "excellent" and gave her pointers on how to get it published.

He returned to New Brunswick in triumph, lugging a suitcase full of books "inscribed with praise and gratitude," as Rhoda noted, "from about everyone there . . . " Writing a friend two weeks later, Charlie exulted, "If anybody got anything out of Breadloaf, it was *me*!" While chatting so much about craft, he'd realized anew how wise he was on the subject, suddenly *quite* sure (once again) what to do with *A Second-Hand Life*. And yes, on rereading his novel he saw what a marvel of "concentration, originality, and form" it was, a message he took to New York a few days later—*very* persuasively, it seems. "Macmillan expects it to be the big fall novel of 1966," he wrote Kate, "a foregone conclusion for Book of the month, etc., and a landslide success. . . . But I don't *want* that—not ever again. Don't want even to hear about it, as it does things to you. All I must do is think of the work itself and bring it off to *my* satisfaction—and not Liz Taylor's and M-G-M's." He had big, big plans. As soon as he polished off *A Second-Hand Life*, he'd return to *Rufus "Bud" Boyd*, then the long-fallow *Royalist* (about Bronson Winthrop), and finally he'd be ready to tackle his masterpiece again: *What Happened.*

Telling Rhoda as much when he got back from New York, he also mentioned the means (medicinal) by which this grand scheme would perforce be achieved. In that case—she replied, in effect—he would have to write his novel(s) elsewhere. At first Charlie balked: moving out would be too upsetting at the moment; he had to get on with his work, etc. But Rhoda was adamant ("You wanted it *then*," he reminded her afterward, "not only that very week but that very day"), and finally Charlie had to explain things to his agent and publisher.

And lo, it came to pass that Brandt & Brandt reserved Room 405 at the Hotel Chelsea ("on the same floor with Arthur Miller incidentally, and Tennessee just below"), while Macmillan agreed to subsidize him until February 1. Writing to inform Kate—who'd joined VISTA after graduation, and had just gone to Alabama for training—Charlie described the arrangement as a "temporary separation": "The whole thing has been discussed between us most amicably and without rancor, and it will only come to good. Mama wants to be alone, and she should be; I need the kind of moral support I get from my professional friends—I'll be seeing the Strauses, among others, and maybe twice a week my AA friends at Lenox Hill."

Charlie moved to the Chelsea on September 17, then a few days later returned to New Brunswick in Robert Markel's Volvo station wagon to spirit away his favorite books, photographs, and *objets*—this while Rhoda was absent: "For I am unsure of your present emotional state," he wrote her later that evening, "so apt to fluctuate." He was happy to report that his first few days in New York had been bliss, and conceded that a "permanent separation" might be in order after all. Still, he worried about how she would "get along alone," and meanwhile hoped they could at least be civil—indeed, he agreed with Sarah that they should "go right on 'as if everything were the same,' " visiting their daughters together, celebrating Christmas, and so on. The next day Rhoda wrote, with a kind of controlled heat, to disabuse Sarah of that idea and certain others:

> We've all been brain-washed. . . . Papa had convinced us all that I had nothing in my life that he didn't give me—that all interests, all activity, all relationships, stemmed from him and that without him I'd have nothing. That was true, in a way, because he so completely dominates everyone in his relationships. If you meet his interests and his varying enthusiasms all is well. And everything I might have had in my life was plowed under to conform to his interests, or even,

demands. As a result, over the years I have become more and more pallid as a person—anything that was me was scorned unless it fitted the area of his interests. This carried over into my relationships with other people—which put me forward in their eyes as a very poor shadow of this stronger personality.

You worry that I'll withdraw from life as a result of the separation. I've withdrawn for years—and now I feel free. I won't have this censure weighing down on me, burying me. . . .

Papa seems to feel that you plan to invite us together on occasion to dinner, or a party or Christmas or something. . . . Perhaps at some far future date it might be possible. But not now, or even soon. I suspect, I must say, that this idea is his—not yours.

At least she and Charlie agreed that everything had worked out for the best—indeed, it would be hard to say who was the more convincing on that point. "As for my morale and spirits," Charlie wrote a friend, "—terriff!"

Chapter Twenty

A Second-Hand Life

Charlie loved his little apartment at the Chelsea, and visitors always noticed the pride with which he showed it off. He had his own bath and kitchenette, and the sitting room was dominated by a gorgeous fireplace with a Carrara mantelpiece flanked by twisting Byzantine columns (rather like Rufus's muscled arms) and surmounted by a lovely, hazy mirror that went all the way up to a high ceiling. On subsequent trips to New Brunswick, he and the loyal Markel had lugged away the rest of his effects: an easy chair and ornate floor lamp (a gift from Ruby Schinasi); a typing table, chair, and file cabinet; his favorite records and music-room secretary; reproductions by Gauguin, Klee, Shahn, and some "charming odd water-color experiments" by Kate he'd recently had framed; and naturally his polar-bear rug, Staffordshire Shakespeare, and suckling Romulus and Remus that had figured so happily in *The Lost Weekend*—all of it, as ever, arranged just so: "neat as a pin," observed one journalist, "his books standing in serried ranks on the shelves, his paintings hung at precisely the right level, and not a speck of dust visible anywhere."

After years of quaint decline, the hotel was becoming hip again—"making the scene like a grandmother in a miniskirt," as the *Times* put it. Andy Warhol was even then shooting *Chelsea Girls*, and Charlie was somewhat in awe of it all. When the Strauses came for a visit, he giddily pointed out the doors of the more famous tenants: Tennessee and Arthur and Virgil (Thomson), of course, on whom he wouldn't *dream* of intruding, though he did visit the eccentric composer George Kleinsinger, and found himself ducking amongst trees and fluttering parakeets, fleeing altogether when he went to the bathroom and found a python in the tub! But mostly he was content to keep to himself. He was "living on a shoestring" until February, and besides he relished the maverick ethos. "CHARLES JACKSON: DO NOT DISTURB" read the sign on his door—incongruously enough, given the convivial fellow who resided therein. Typing in the wee hours, Charlie phoned the night clerk to inquire whether anyone had complained ("Lissen," the man replied, "this is the Chelsea"), and soon he was chatting up the staff in earnest. Stanley Bard, the manager, remembered how Charlie would often stop in his office just to say hello, and when the latter was ill or recovering from misadventures, Bard and others would make a point of checking on him. What Charlie appreciated best of all was a collective benignity on the subject of money: New York had declared the Chelsea a permanent landmark, and so the staff weren't quite as obliged to harass tenants—certainly not lovable artists like Charlie—over unpaid bills. "To the entire staff of New York's wonderful old Hotel Chelsea," he wrote in his "Card of Thanks" for *A Second-Hand Life*, "where this novel was largely written, while they put up with my self-indulgences, stalling, temperament, odd hours, and whistling in the dark."

Though Charlie was apt to pull the occasional all-nighter, most days followed an orderly pattern. Rising at six and putting on jacket and tie (he'd almost sooner be seen naked on the sidewalks than tieless), he'd stroll around the corner to the Riss Diner on Eighth Avenue, a noisy Greek place where the employees would cry out "Hello, Charlie!"—as would the newsie on 23rd Street where he stopped to buy his *Times*, as would various hookers slogging home after a long night. (Kate remembered eating at the Riss with her father and being introduced to one of his friends, a junky prostitute about her own age: "Salt of the earth; he loved her.") Back at the Chelsea he'd work until one, skip lunch (an economy), nap in the afternoon, then revise the day's output and return to the Riss for dinner.

This spartan routine seems to have taken shape over time. His appointment diary indicates an active social life during those first weeks, much of it AA-related, as he endeavored to reorient himself in the city. Around Thanksgiving (for want of other plans?) he consented to a busy AA junket in Detroit, addressing an audience of 1,200 and doing a fair amount of media too. "Funny, when you go out of town, you're treated like a movie star," he wrote Rhoda: "autographs, signing books, phone calls, and pictures all over the papers: like the old days, but quite meaningless." Be that as it may, the trip (probably his last for AA) exhausted him, and for weeks he was groggy with flu. When in better fettle, and desirous of company beyond the Riss and Chelsea, he'd travel some thirty blocks uptown to the Taft, where he'd had his "last drink" with Boom on Armistice Day, 1936. Nowadays he'd chat up strangers at the bar or mingle among the tables, hoping for a chance to reveal his identity; in most cases he'd either get a blank look or (if they'd seen the movie) "a derisive denial," as he told a friend. Returning late one night, he was struck by a little epiphany; as he scrawled on the back of an envelope (postmarked October 12, 1966) to an AA friend, Joe Besch: "A couple of weeks ago, as I came in at my usual hour of around 3 o'clock in the morning, I suddenly realized, with a start, something that had not occurred to me until then: that, for the past year, I had been living, and am still living, what can only be called a double life. Let me explain:"—but the note ended there.

What Jackson meant by a "double life" is an open question: there was his drug use in the midst of continued (but less and less frequent) AA activity, and of course there was his gay life, which was more pronounced than ever—bravely so: the Chelsea was its own world, to be sure, but Stonewall was still in the future. In 1966, *Time* concluded a feature story with what doubtless struck its editors as a handsome assertion: Homosexuality "deserves fairness, compassion, understanding and, when possible, treatment. But it deserves no encouragement, no glamorization, no rationalization, no fake status as a minority martyrdom, no sophistry about simple differences in taste—and, above all, no pretense that it is anything but a pernicious sickness." Less and less did Charlie seem to agree. Various friends spotted him, during the Chelsea era, milling about with obviously gay acquaintances, while seeming also, quite vividly, to lift the scrim on his own gay persona. When Weston's *The Telling* was published by David McKay in 1966, Charlie marched into the office of its editor, Eleanor Rawson, and insisted he be invited to the book party, where Weston was "on pins and needles" lest his flirtatious mentor say something indiscreet: "He was in love with me, and it blinded him to decorum."* It did not blind him, however, to what he considered the

---

* One hastens to remind the reader that Jackson hardly needed sexual attraction to take an interest in another writer's career. His other "scholar" at Bread Loaf,

novel's flaws, as he hooted at all the provocative "crotch-grabbing" that never comes to the point ("I don't like all this fancy dancing around the subject!"); similarly, his old AA friend Ned Rorem got the impression that Charlie had refused to give a blurb for his *Paris Diary* because he'd found the book "coy" in its revelations of gay life.

More than ever he seemed to prefer the company of gay men—the more open, the better. On January 27, 1966, he celebrated the twenty-second anniversary of *The Lost Weekend* by attending the ballet and having dinner with a young fashion designer, Stan Herman, and his partner, Gene Horowitz, a teacher who was about to publish his first novel, *Home Is Where You Start From*. Charlie had admired the book, phoning Francis Brown of the *Times* and getting permission to write a generous yet measured review ("Neither a strikingly original nor even a very 'modern' work . . . [but] a remarkable achievement on other and more lasting counts: it deals directly, successfully, objectively but full-heartedly with family life"). Charlie seemed to enjoy the couple's easy affection for each other, and reciprocated with a lot of bitchy, "hissing" humor (said Herman) that he might otherwise have taken pains to mitigate. And one wonders, too, how his meetings played out with a rough-hewn sailor named Peter Arthurs, who went on to write a notorious memoir of his friendship with the hard-drinking Irish author Brendan Behan. Arthur C. Clarke, of *Space Odyssey* fame, remembered how the sailor had introduced him to Jackson, Arthur Miller, and Norman Mailer, while incessantly telling stories about his homosexual romps with Behan ("I'd say that there bees some quare aul goings-on out there on them ships at sea," the latter purportedly remarked, just prior to a frenzied grab at Peter Arthurs's penis); finally Clarke urged his sailor friend to commit these chestnuts to paper, in the hope that it would help "keep Peter away from the gargle." Presumably Jackson made the same suggestion during his late-night meetings with Arthurs (noted in his diary), though he'd be long dead by the time his interest bore fruit, in 1981, when *With Brendan Behan* included an acknowledgment of Arthurs's "writing godfathers": Clarke, Mailer, Miller, and Jackson.

A little parade of unknown men marches through the pages of Charlie's final diaries, though individual names rarely appear more than once

---

Stephen Jones, was decidedly straight, and anyway Jackson made no advances; he did, however, press Jones's novel *Turpin* on Macmillan, which published it in 1968. "It was all because of Charlie, going extra steps when he didn't have to," said Jones. "God bless him."

or twice. On December 2, 1965, he received an "11 o'clock call from Mike (Room 621) who stayed several hrs. Very nice person!"; on March 5, 1966, "Nick" was expected "sometime during the day" ("*if* he doesn't forget"); and a man named Carlos scribbled (a childish cursive) into the space allotted for March 28, "I will be missing your's [*sic*] companiship [*sic*] for ever. Your: Carlos"—but the next day Jackson wrote (in his steadier hand), "Carlos called." Later that year and briefly into the next, he saw a lot of a "dear Norwegian friend" named Wintrup, for whose benefit he copied out and underlined a long passage from one of his favorite novels, Marguerite Yourcenar's *Memoirs of Hadrian*, in which the emperor writes about his young lover, Antinous, by way of reply to "the moralists" who consider "the pleasures of love among the enjoyments termed gross":

> But when these contacts persist and multiply about one unique being, to the point of embracing him entirely, when each fraction of a body becomes laden for us with meaning as overpowering as that of the face itself, when this one creature haunts us like music and torments us like a problem (instead of inspiring in us, at most, mere irritation, amusement, or boredom), when he passes from the periphery of our universe to its center, and finally becomes for us more indispensable than our own selves, then that astonishing [prodigy] takes place wherein I see much more an invasion of [the] flesh by the spirit than a simple play of the body alone.

•

AS FOR HIS PROGRESS on *A Second-Hand Life*, Charlie exuded confidence—for a while. Carl Brandt was spreading the word ("It's hard to believe, but . . . ") that his legendarily dilatory client had moved to New York and was, by God, finishing his novel at last. Robert Markel, for his part, was taking no chances. When Charlie complained that he couldn't find a couple of old short stories that he wanted to incorporate into the book, his editor was only too happy "to play hooky" and drive him back to New Brunswick so he could spend the afternoon scouring his files. When Charlie claimed to be delayed by the bodily pain of having to sit at his typewriter for hours on end, Markel invited him to talk into a recording device and send the tapes to Macmillan for typing. When the tapes arrived sporadically if at all, Markel sent his secretary to the Chelsea to take dictation. "To Alice Schwedock," Charlie wrote in his "Card of

Thanks," "who, after her own full day at her regular job, helped me sec-
retarily till many midnights." Schwedock was all of twenty-one, fresh
out of college, and didn't question the strange arrangement or the fact
that she wasn't getting paid for it; after walking on winter nights from
Macmillan at Fifth Avenue and 12th, she'd be greeted by a bathrobed
Charlie—"very kind and solicitous"—who would chat briefly and then
dictate while some Beethoven played on his old 78 records. There were
good nights and bad. Charlie knew he was being prodded, and was careful to have *some* kind of work ready for the young woman to type, though
he was often disappointed by the results (e.g., "a long dialogue scene,"
he wrote Rhoda, that was "just rambling"). Mindful, however, of Miss
Schwedock's wage slavery on his behalf, he gave her a framed Haitian
pastel at the end of their labors.

"I'm very proud of myself," he'd written Kate on November 30, "very
sure of the book, very certain that I have not only a totally original but
even a quite radical novel in the works. People may not like it, but god-
dammit they'll read it. And *I* like it, which is all that matters." He did
worry a little, though, about what the general reader would make of his
heroine's tireless pursuit of "the most beautiful thing in life, the human
penis." Surely they'd wonder how he *knew* of such things—in which case
they'd simply have to take his word for it that he'd "intuit[ed] them":
"God," he reassured his daughter, "if I had ever *experienced* some of the
things I've been writing about, I'd long since have been found dead—in
some alley, say, or sordid hall bedroom of a tenth-rate hotel." Nor was
he willing to compromise his vision by indulging in the kind of coyness he'd scorned in Rorem and Weston. When his editor—whose tastes
ran to the conservative—wanted to remove an especially lurid passage,
in fact the author's favorite, wherein Winifred peels away a policeman's
trousers to reveal "the tawny penis smooth and firm as a small column
of marble that had been warmed by the sun," Charlie was *outraged*, and
at length the passage was allowed to stand (as it were). But then, it was all
relative. Miss Schwedock wasn't at all shocked by Charlie's work—indeed
found the naughty parts "a bit dated," and perhaps that was a red flag of
sorts. Within five days, anyway, of that ebullient letter to Kate about his
"totally original" and "quite radical" novel, he wrote a far more tempered
assessment to his estranged wife: "A terrible life, this. One day, or three
days, I'm lifted up by the 'brilliance' of what I have done, and then I go
into a four or five day depression over what I *know* is its pedestrian mediocrity. . . . Much of the novel I simply despair of, because other parts are

so good, of such intense interest. But I don't think I've got it any more, and I mean it quite realistically. Now don't cheer me up: I *know* when it is bad, and a lot of it is that."

Whatever his mood on a given day, he had little alternative (other than death) to finishing the book. A month before his February deadline, he was almost out of Macmillan money, and Markel had taken a hard(ish) line against dispensing more. On January 7, Charlie wrote Rhoda of subsisting on graham crackers and milk, and two weeks later he scribbled a note (evidently unsent) in green marker on a piece of ragged brown paper: "*Dear* Mrs. Harvey [an AA friend?]: I have reached the bottom of the Macmillan money bags and need some more subsidy, for the final six or eight weeks. Thank you from my heart for letting me impose on you." And yet he seemed able to afford Seconal and/or Nembutal in rather large quantities. Stan Herman remembered a lot of "intoxicated" behavior on Charlie's part—either "very prissy and silly" or "morose"—and periodically he'd overdose and have to go to the emergency room. Markel sent his personal physician to check on Jackson at St. Vincent's Hospital that autumn, and it was Markel whom Charlie most inveigled into abetting his habit. "Nothing all day—sleep and awful depression," he'd noted in his diary on December 3 (the day before his despondent letter to Rhoda: "A terrible life, this"), and six days later he wrote: "To N[ew] B[runswick] with Bob. Prescription." Markel remembers the episode well. Once again Charlie had wanted to retrieve "something" from the house on Somerset, and when they started back to New York he casually asked the man to stop at a pharmacy near Rutgers. "I got the impression he'd failed to score in New York," said Markel, "and needed to go back to New Jersey to get [more pills]."*

By spring, his novel still unfinished, Charlie was living off handouts from Rhoda and Boom. At the beginning of April he mailed his brother a chunk of Xeroxed manuscript as proof of progress, and was (according to his diary) about to leave for an AA dinner in Washington, when he "unwittingly . . . stepped up the [drug] intake" and suffered an almost

---

* After her husband's death, Rhoda found pills stashed all over his apartment—behind books and records and the like. She considered reporting at least one doctor for overprescribing, though several were implicated, some of them mentioned by name in Charlie's "Card of Thanks" for *A Second-Hand Life.* The latter document—a long, effusive list of acknowledgments to sundry people ("Because, figuratively, it's been a long time between drinks")—was struck out by Macmillan as "unprofessional."

fatal overdose, coming to at Central Islip State Hospital on Long Island. A few days later Boom sent a calming note to Sarah, along with a check:

> You must have paid Charlie's hospital bill and if and when you go to the Chelsea you'll certainly be confronted by more. No reason for you to do it and this is to help. I'd send it to Charlie—as Rhoda and I have lately—but if he's not responsible and uses it for the Wrong thing it's best I send it to you—until he's able to take care of himself—which he should be soon. . . .
>
> If you have time get Charlie pyjamas or whatever. He'll be better off as soon as he gets back in his AA group.

But in fact he was almost through with AA. The Washington trip was among the last references in his diary, and it was Markel's impression that he'd stopped going to meetings.

Indeed, he hardly left the Chelsea for some four months after returning from Central Islip. Frightened by the mishap, he was determined to finish his novel sober—but found himself unable to write a word, or even approach the typewriter. "I did acrostics by the hour," he recalled in "The Sleeping Brain"; "I read Lolita and Hadrian's Memoirs and Tender Is the Night over and over again, though I knew them almost by heart. . . . I sat in a big chair and stared across my living room at the typewriter in the corner; and day after day I told myself: 'Now *look*, Charlie; all you've got to do is to get up out of this chair and go over and sit down at that typewriter.' But it had actually become, by now, a *physical* inability to make such a move." When he took up the matter with his friends, agent, and editor, he claimed that "their answers, even though they knew the hazards, were remarkably similar: 'No problem. You're a writer. It may be the price you have to pay. If you need pills to enable you to work, okay, take them. It's as simple as that.' "

His editor remembered it as a lot less simple. On the day ("one of the worst in my life") that Charlie mentioned his dilemma, Markel was angry at first ("he was terrifically manipulative like all drug users"), since essentially the matter had been laid in his lap, thus: If Markel told him *not* to take pills, well, he wouldn't—but neither would he finish the novel to which both men had committed so much time, effort, and (in Markel's case) money. What he needed was the man's *permission* to resume taking pills. "I didn't display the anger I felt," said Markel. "I tried to stay calm as possible because I didn't want to bruise him. . . . I was powerless to prevent it. He would have said it was my fault he wasn't writing. 'Charles,

you have to decide for yourself,' I said. 'It's your decision, not mine.' "
Jackson took that as a *yes*, and thereafter regarded Markel as all the more
complicit—a "literary obstetrician" (as Markel put it) whose partnership
he commended for posterity in a stanza meant for *Rufus "Bud" Boyd*:

> *The writer never works alone:*
> *His editor, if the truth were known . . .*
> *They share the joys, they share the ills,*
> *And quite agree on sleeping pills. . . .*
>   *Thus, to be fair to job and jobber,*
> *To even up the complex score*
> *(Through use of drugs you may deplore),*
> *It is the work of Sharl [Charles] and Robber [Robert]*
> *In sooth, we could not well unsnarl*
> *Which part was Robber, which was Sharl.*

But still Jackson hesitated: Was the novel worth risking his life for?
According to "The Sleeping Brain," he discussed the problem with a
doctor "very knowledgeable in this field" (Modell in Larchmont?), but
over the course of four hour-long sessions he "got nowhere"—in other
words, the doctor refused to tell him what he wanted to hear. "During
our final session," Jackson wrote, "I remember how coldly he said: 'Go
ahead, if you like; you're on your own. But I'll make you a bet. If you
return to barbiturates, you'll never finish the novel at all, Macmillan will
be stood up, and you'll be through. No other publisher will ever take
you on again.' " By then it was August, his novel was "reced[ing] further
and further," and Charlie had pretty much decided that "health was killing [him] as much as the pills ever would." Fate, as he perceived it, gave
him the final nudge. On August 20 ("a Black Day or a Red-Letter Day,
depending on one's viewpoint") he arrived at Boom's seaside cottage for a
weekend visit, and noticed that Jim Gates had left his medicine bag in the
guest room: "I didn't scruple or hesitate for a moment. I admit this quite
without self-blame; because it was, in a sense, not my doing at all—and
here was the answer." He filched a bottle of Nembutal and returned to
New York the next day. *A Second-Hand Life* was finished within a month.

JACKSON WAS ILL-ADVISED to rest on his laurels. As soon as word got out
that he'd delivered the manuscript, Farrar, Straus and Giroux pounced
with a "friendly 'alert,' " reminding Carl Brandt of his client's indebted-

ness to the firm. At first Jackson tried to interest "Karlkin" in pitching *Rufus "Bud" Boyd* as his next project: quoting "the rhapsodic Bob
Markel," he described his poem as a work of "Mozartian delight," and
insisted that the eighteen-stanza "Dedication" (enclosed) be sent forth-
with to *The New Yorker*, as Roger Straus had assured him the editors
would "publish it as a great coup" (despite their almost systematic rejection of Jackson's work over the previous twenty-one years). As for the
poem's main narrative, Charlie enclosed "only four stanzas" (i.e., all that
existed) just to give his agent "some idea of its tone," while promising to
regale him in person with the rest of the story ("you can't beat it"). Asked
forty-three years later what became of *Rufus "Bud" Boyd*, Brandt replied,
"I'm sure I did *something* simply because one would have to, under those
circumstances, and I also think I managed to blot it from my memory as
quickly as possible."

In time Charlie was forced to accept that his only marketable product
was his long-awaited "Birnam saga," *What Happened*, and so on March 16,
1967, he signed a Macmillan contract for its first volume, *Farther and
Wilder*, that provided a $2,500 advance up front, another $3,000 in six
monthly installments of $500 ("each to be paid on evidence of satisfac-
tory progress"), and a final $2,000 due on delivery in August. Charlie's
signature on the contract looks distinctly shaky, though he endeavored
to seem upbeat in the press: "Jackson has regained his old vitality as a
novelist," one journalist wrote, "and is far advanced into a long and ambitious novel which he believes to be the best he has ever written. . . . Four
hundred pages are done and the flow is gratifyingly steady." As a friend
recalled, the manuscript (somewhat less than four hundred pages) was
conspicuously stacked beside his portable typewriter, where it remained
in dusty, yellowing abeyance. Meanwhile Kate had taken a job in New
York that autumn (1966), and remembered her father as "very despondent" during her six months in town: she and Sarah took turns calling
him on alternate days ("just to see if he was alive or alert"), and both
made a point of regularly meeting him for lunch, during which he'd
often sit in mute, teary-eyed despair.

But at least he had the publication of *A Second-Hand Life* to look
forward to—his first novel in nineteen years! And so far he had reason to be optimistic: Boom, his most devoted fan, was unstinting in his
praise ("It's so moving," he wrote Sarah), and most of the people who'd
received advance copies—that is, practically everyone Charlie had ever
known, including childhood friends in Newark and even some of their

progeny—went out of their way to be as generous as possible. Dr. Fredric Wertham was almost as feverish in his praise as he'd been twenty years earlier with *The Fall of Valor*: "I have always regarded Charles Jackson as one of our most authentic writers," he wrote for Macmillan's publicity department. "*A Second-Hand Life* confirms this. . . . It is something new, a book one has to read if one wants to see some of the unfamiliar aspects of the temper of our times." Even some of the most formidable literary critics in America seemed eager to reassure Charlie, whose struggles over the years were well known. An old *Partisan Review* acquaintance, F. W. "Fred" Dupee, commended the author's "Awful Daring, as well as [his] patience and skill," mentioning that Truman Capote had also seemed to like the book. And Lionel Trilling—no less—had inferred from the little bit he'd found time to read ("Diana will follow") that Charlie had "lost none of that most important of the novelistic charms, a passionate concern with character and the intricate texture of life."

Those who didn't know the author personally, however, tended to be more circumspect. Mindful of Charlie's financial straits, Brandt had lost no time pressing the galleys on Hollywood agent H. N. Swanson, pointing out that a really game actress "could have a good deal of fun with this." But Swanson didn't see it: "I doubt very much if Charles Jackson's Second Hand Life will ever sell to pictures," he bluntly replied, noting the "grim" story and "unrelieved" heroine; indeed, he wondered if the novel was "good enough to spend money to have it copied," but agreed to put some feelers out. Brandt forged ahead: an executive at Paramount had told him that actress Patricia Neal might be up for a challenge, so he tracked her down to the Waldorf and rushed the galleys over ("Having spent seven years on it with the author I have no perspective, and consequently I am curious about your personal reaction beyond the purely professional"). For Charlie's part, he thought "a logical choice" to play Winifred was the young actress Elizabeth Hartman, whose debut performance as a blind girl in *A Patch of Blue* (1965), with Sidney Poitier, had earned her an Oscar nomination. Perhaps the fragile Hartman had struck him as a kindred spirit; in any case her career was already somewhat hindered by depression, and twenty years later she'd leap to her death from a fifth-floor window.

Whatever the prospects of *A Second-Hand Life* in Hollywood, Macmillan was making "a very big noise" about it (as Brandt wrote Swanson), confident that the comeback of a once-celebrated author, and never mind his piquant theme, would result in "A MACMILLAN money-maker," as a full-page ad touted in the April 17, 1967, issue of *Publishers Weekly*, featuring a sinister-looking Jackson on the cover. "Nineteen years is a very long time to wait for a new novel," blurbed Carl A. Kroch, president of Kroch's and Brentano's (and son of Adolph, Charlie's old employer), "but when that novel is as dazzling and—frankly—as daring as Charles Jackson's *A Second-Hand Life* the waiting is worth it. That one man should be able to expose and explore the compulsions of a male alcoholic and the appetites of a sex-obsessed woman, and do both with such power, is remarkable. This one will sell."

Two days before the publication date (August 10, 1967), Charlie was interviewed by Barbara Walters on the *Today* show,* for which he seems to have chatted guardedly about the nature of his heroine's pathology ("I think she *is* a nympho, Charlie, and I don't accept your definition of the word," William Inge wrote after the show, advising his friend that nymphomania was a matter of "gland disturbance"), and to have gotten bogged down in an explanation of his long silence as a writer, attributing it to lung problems. A more candid account was offered to Francis Brown, editor of the *Times Book Review*, for whom Charlie agreed to produce "a piece on Writer's Block . . . sometime close to publication": namely, "The Sleeping Brain." Reviewing *Selected Letters of Malcolm Lowry* in 1965, Jackson had rather primly deplored the myth of the "tormented" writer ("Are we really that tormented?") as little more than a pretext for self-destructive behavior. In the present piece, however, he not only reversed himself on that point, but repudiated for all time his longing to be one of Whitman's "divine average," to be accepted by what Mann had called "the happy, the blue-eyed, and the ordinary." Confessing that his work was almost wholly dependent on a "compulsive addiction to alcohol and/or drugs," Jackson wrote: "Perhaps it is tasteless on my part (but I most earnestly protest it is not a kind of special pleading, an asking for special favors or allowances) when I insist that writers *are* different, else they would not be writers in the first place, able to do what they cannot help doing and often don't even understand, no matter what the cost." His final verdict? *It was worth it.*

In due course, this apologia for substance abuse in the service of art—"an extraordinary personal statement," as Carl Brandt called it in

---

* The segment no longer exists in the NBC archives, though the gist of it can be cobbled together based on various letters in Jackson's papers and my interviews with his daughters.

his cover letter—would be rejected by *Playboy, Life, Harper's, Esquire,* and many others. As for the *Times Book Review*, Francis Brown had wondered if Jackson would be willing to "recast" the piece in light of his novel's critical reception, which perhaps resulted in Jackson's adding a single, unrepentant line: "Now, whether the new novel justifies all this is beside the point," he wrote: "I was alive again."

He was alive, though most critics agreed his novel was no crowning achievement, no vindication of his refusal to join "the growing glamorous company of Artists Who Died Young," as he'd written in regard to his legendary, irksomely prestigious contemporary and fellow alcoholic, Malcolm Lowry. " 'A Second-Hand Life' seems old and tired," Webster Schott observed in the Sunday *Times* on August 13, citing flaws that "gape like bottomless fissures"; the next day the newspaper published an even more scalding indictment by Thomas Lask, who called the book a "tasteless extravaganza in sexual promiscuity." And lest readers be enticed by what seemed, if nothing else, a pretty racy read, Lask was careful to disabuse them: Jackson "has made the whole subject [nymphomania] as tedious as the talk about the weather on a round-the-world cruise. Page after page is filled with dialogue obviously written to mark time, as heavy as lead and twice as inert." *Newsweek* agreed, finding an "oddly genteel clinicism" in even the most lyrically risqué passages, and reminding readers that *A Second-Hand Life* had been conceived, after all, in the midst of a more innocent decade ("poor, superserious Winnie seems like the slightly irrelevant older sister to the freewheeling females of our time"). All this and more—*much* more—during that first week of publication. "Charlie's morale is damn near non-existent," his agent noted on August 14, while still hoping for better press in the provinces. There was, in fact, something of this ("a searching study," said the Bergen *Record*), though hardly enough to cushion a sneering coup de grâce delivered two weeks later by (of course) *The New Yorker*, whose "Briefly Noted" critic took a dim view of Jackson's "obvious determination to see this thing through to the end at all costs. All the cost is to the reader."

To his credit, Jackson didn't take it altogether lying down. "Nobody can be 'wronger' than one's well-meaning friends," he'd cautioned twenty-four years earlier, referring to the almost universal praise from advance readers of *The Lost Weekend*—a notion he put aside after being pilloried for *A Second-Hand Life*. Marked in Charlie's hand as a possible "Adv[ertisement] for MacMillan," "CAN A WRITER TRUST HIS FRIENDS?" was a long list of blurbs compiled from all the kindly letters written by, say, eminent critics such as Irving Howe ("very venture-some"), his Bread Loaf protégé John Weston ("we knew you would do it"), and the wife of Rhoda's obstetrician, Midy McLane ("astonishing"). There was also Fred Dupee's letter, though Charlie saw fit to omit the man's observation that his two protagonists, Harry and Winifred, were not so much plausible characters as "agents of your inspired nostalgia and auto-eroticism," a point more decorously made by his old friend Marion "Bettina" Fabry, who described the two as "different aspects of the same person"—that is, Charlie himself.

Charlie, not incidentally, was bent on denying any such connection. Composing his own PR copy in the third person, he reiterated his line about "writ[ing] from intuition only"—*not* experience, and not clinical know-how either, as he was "untrained" in psychology and had no col-lege degree: "What [Jackson] produces comes out of his unconscious [last four words struck out: "off the top of his head" inserted] almost without premeditated thought." This from a writer who'd confessed, time and again, that almost every word of *The Lost Weekend* was true, who'd pre-pared the following personal statement for the Institute of Arts and Let-ters in 1959: "As a writer I have always had one hard and fast rule: Don't write about anything you don't know anything about. . . . Which is why I write so much about myself: what is true of me will be more or less true of the reader, for no one is unique." As Mary McCarthy had fore-seen in 1945, however—via her fictional portrait of Jackson (as "Herbert Harper" in *The Lost Week*)—he'd already "given himself away" to such an "improvident" degree in his first and (by far) best novel, that he had little left over, and what remained would have to be parceled in bits and pieces to various characters ("an assemblage of disjuncta [*sic*] membra poetae"). Previously he'd written an apprentice work of gay initiation, *Native Moment*, followed a decade later by *The Fall of Valor*—pioneering but dull, as he tried to write "objectively" and was loath to reveal too much of himself in the latently gay Grandin, given what he'd already hinted on that point in *The Lost Weekend*. And after that? As McCarthy predicted, he found himself with "very little left to say and very little interest in saying," though he'd always be powerfully nostalgic about his Arcadian childhood, and so a portion of good work remained.

He had written, then—and quite courageously for the times—about homosexuality, though he hadn't really examined the erotic aspects, the underside of his dapper, affable persona, the "compulsive excursions" into "the low and the lawless" to which he'd alluded in "An Afternoon with Boris," the "life coarse and rank" celebrated by his beloved Whitman. This, in part, was to be the burden of *What Happened*, and hence his agonies in bringing it off (aside from its impossibly ambitious scope); the prospect of writing about such matters with perfect frankness was, in the end, paralyzing, and so Jackson fell silent—as did a number of gay writers who, in effect, ran out of material, having gone as far as they could acceptably go: one thinks of E. M. Forster, whose last novel was finished forty-six years before his death in 1970, whereupon his only gay-themed work, *Maurice* (begun in 1913), was published at last; or Glenway Wescott, who petered out with *Apartment in Athens*, followed by a forty-two-year retirement; or even (a decidedly minor but telling instance) Walter Clemons, who published a well-received story collection in 1959 before giving up fiction entirely, lest (as he later admitted) he reveal too much and risk his career as an editor and book critic.* But of course there was another way—the way of Proust, Tennessee Williams, and Inge, to name a few, who dissembled their erotic longings in heterosexual form. No wonder Jackson was (periodically) so elated by the possibilities of *A Second-Hand Life*: not only could he finally "give free rein to his obsessive fantasies" (as a French critic, Georges-Michel Sarotte, surmised of the author) in the person of a nymphomaniac heroine, but also posit an existential opposite, Harry Harrison—the kind of "dull automaton" that Jackson had feared becoming if he "stifle[d]" his nature. As he'd written four decades before in "The Devil's Dialogue":

> "... *You're still young yet, and so far this repression*
> *Has had no serious damaging results;*
> *But give it time—a few years more!—and see*
> *The wreck of youth that you will have become ...*
> *Devoid of that ecstatic soul the gods*
> *Bestow alone upon their favorite children. ...*
> *I cannot bear to see you made a slave,*
> *Afraid to know or recognize yourself,*
> *Living in fear, your own dread Frankenstein!*"

Above all, perhaps, he could make the point that sexual proclivities have little to do with moral character one way or the other. Winifred's

---

* When John Cheever risked his far greater career by publishing the novel *Falconer* (1977), about a gay prison romance, Clemons ecstatically declared the book a "masterpiece" and campaigned successfully to put Cheever on the cover of *Newsweek*, alongside the caption "A Great American Novel: John Cheever's 'Falconer.' "

pursuit of "the human penis" is both a matter of appetite and an aspect of her "invincibly innocent" nature: though she wants nothing better than "to make one man happy," she refuses to indulge in the "hateful" hypocrisy of "play[ing] hard to get," even though it means forfeiting the love of her life, Jack Sanford, who exploits her sexually before marrying a more "respectable" woman. In a better world it would not be so, though Jackson seems typically ambivalent about things. On the one hand, Winifred is the "soul of courage—and yes, of honor; true honor," and her stoical acceptance of a bad reputation is understood to be so much noble self-sacrifice. Besides, Winifred knows better than most that "sex [has] nothing to do with love," having been deflowered by a local roué (not unlike her creator) at the tender age of eleven. On the other hand, wallowing in a "morass of compulsive meaningless sexuality" seems hardly desirable either. How compulsive and meaningless? Very: Winifred prefers summer to winter for the novel reason that it's easier to descry a man's penis through light fabric, and she becomes sad when she reads of a convict's execution because it means one less penis to be had ("if only once"). And what of the occupational hazards? At one point an aging Winifred is followed beyond the railroad tracks by a rough-looking stranger, who apparently knows of her infamy ("Hi, Winnie"): he puts his hands around her neck and considers strangling her, then merely rips off her blouse and ravishes her at length "in the cindery turfy grass." Later Winifred will reflect on the encounter with "a kind of fright" and realize it's time to mend her ways; in the moment, though, when most animals are *triste*, she lies in the man's arms and thinks: "This was the sort of experience that could and should happen all the time, whenever you felt like it, no questions asked, no accounting to anybody: you see somebody you know or want, and why shouldn't you have him or have each other?"

Perhaps; certainly it seems appealing when one considers the sad case of Harry Harrison, who on the outside, at least, is the author (bewigged) to a tee: dapper and "well-manicured," he affects a "cultivated and calculated outgoingness"—indeed, at age forty-five, is little more than persona, witty and pleasant but incapable of passion. A prosperous bachelor ("an architect of country houses"), Harry glides along the surface of life until his awful, Jamesian epiphany at the funeral of Jack Sanford, which he attends with his old friend Winifred:

> And then it dawned on him, with the force and shock of a physical blow, that nobody— nobody—would ever weep over him like that,

mourn his death, or remember him, in spite of everything, with love. For he had never loved anyone in his life, had never been able to give love and thus to receive it, and the ghastly emptiness of all his past years, his arid present, and his even more desolate future, swept over him like a flood.

Such is the life of a morbidly closeted homosexual, whose anxious, compulsory playacting the author knew well. But Harry is *not* homosexual, as he expressly and counterintuitively announces toward the end of the novel: "My God, one could say that the miserable tragedy of me is that I didn't even have enough drive to be a homosexual! No, it's just that I—I loathe myself, can't stand myself, can't, and could never, get outside of myself." Self-loathing, however, is not a cause but an effect, and Jackson fails to make any persuasive sense of it—having removed homosexuality from the picture, partly because it would suggest at least the ability to love, however repressed, and thus disrupt the novel's neat, dialectical scheme: "a woman . . . who has a tremendous, almost an abnormal capacity for love," as Jackson put it in 1953, "and a man who is unable to feel love at all." Things become especially muddled when Harry's formative years are recounted, as Jackson (having but one auto-biography to give away—often, here, in the form of old, cannibalized short stories) grafts his own artistic temperament on a character who'd hardly be apt to share it; note the parenthetical contortions that follow (my italics): "He wrote, *to his surprise*, little poems; painted pictures, picked out tunes on the piano, as if he might someday become (*which he knew in his heart of hearts he never would: he knew he just didn't have it*) an artist of sorts." If he knows, why bother? More convincing is Harry's memory of visiting a whorehouse with schoolmates at age seventeen—"a disastrous failure," as he's the only one who "fail[s] to rise to the occasion and go upstairs like a man": "Several years later, in college English, while reading *Measure for Measure*, he came upon a thought that described the thing for him perfectly, as far as he was concerned, and he understood it: 'Ever till now When men were fond, I smiled and wondered how.' " In the end Harry concludes that he must be "androgynous" (but not homosexual!)—whatever that's supposed to mean in his case.

More than anything Jackson published, *A Second-Hand Life* seems the work of a man under the influence of drugs—a man who could not soberly bear the fact that his best work was behind him: who could not, in short, imagine any life but that of a writer ("I was alive again"). Often, for the reader, it's like being buttonholed by a drunk who fancies himself the most interesting person in the room. Pages of dialogue or description ramble on, hypnotically, as when the author opens Part Three with a whimsical comparison of Geneva, New York, with Geneva, Switzerland, a digression that reads like a recitation from a seed catalogue ("acres and acres of roses, of delicate orchids, of vulnerable short-lived peonies, hairy poppies, hardier but quick-to-fade gladioli, exotic or domestic plants of every description . . . "), or when he recycles his 1944 letters written aboard the Super Chief bound for Hollywood, conferring on his heroine (similarly occupied) the curious "patriotism" he'd felt while in awe of the desert scenery—"a kind of chauvinism that reminded her, with shy pride, that this was her country, this was America, there was no place else like it on the whole face of the earth . . ." On it goes—page after maudlin page of atmosphere—until Winifred arrives in Palm Springs, whereupon it goes on some more: "This beauty of the night and the desert, this unknowing immense unregardful beauty, this impervious imperturbable majestic haunting mystical beauty . . . " As a pretext for lyricism, however, flowers and deserts can scarcely vie with "the most beautiful thing in life, the human penis"—or rather, the penis itself is a kind of "large exotic tropical flower opening gradually out and coming into bloom in slow motion—a sight that [Winifred] could have contemplated for hours . . . "

CARL KROCH WAS RIGHT: such a "daring" book (if properly advertised) was bound to sell, as connoisseurs of nymphomania weren't necessarily great readers of book reviews. *A Second-Hand Life* debuted at number 8 on the *Times* best-seller list for September 10, and lingered in the top ten for another two weeks. Far more momentous was the sale of paperback rights to New American Library for $110,000, half of which went to the author. Once the deal was assured in May 1967 (and one hopes this buffered the blows of August somewhat), Carl Brandt promptly sent a check to Stanley Bard at the Chelsea, who for months had been nothing but patient toward the indigent writer in Room 405: "May we add our thanks to those of Mr. Jackson and Macmillan for the courtesy, the kindness, and most of all the faith that you have brought to this situation?" Brandt wrote. "It is a splendid thing in these cynical days to have that kind of belief work out."

After years of debt, Charlie was free and clear—even rather rich!—and so, in one sense at least, his heroic perseverance had been rewarded.

And he knew exactly what he wanted to do with the money, though he couldn't do it alone. "One winter afternoon he called me," Dorothea Straus remembered.

His voice on the telephone was more husky than ever, interrupted at intervals by choking paroxysms of coughing. . . . Yet I could detect something of the old Charlie. "I've just sold a novel to a paper publishing house. . . . I know it's a potboiler but guess what I'm going to do with the money? I have decided to take a trip to Russia!" I was aware that his family should have profited from the proceeds, but the vision of Charlie in the St. Petersburg and Moscow of his dreams—sick and solitary, but joyous and awed—revived my feeling for him. "You come, too," he was continuing. "Let's go together." He never got there.

Chapter Twenty-One

Sailing Out to Die

The first mention in Charlie's diary ("Noon—Stanley") of his final companion, Stanley Zednik, appears on September 9, 1967, a day before the debut of *A Second-Hand Life* on the *Times* best-seller list. Stanley was a forty-year-old Czechoslovakian émigré, besides which little is known*; photographs show a blandly handsome man with a large head and wavy blond hair. He spoke English with a thick accent. According to Dorothea, "Charlie had picked him up in an all-night diner near the hotel"—doubtless the Riss—somewhat on the strength of his resurgent fame: "To [Stanley]," she wrote, "Charles Jackson was a dazzling celebrity and he the faithful servitor." We also know that Stanley worked at a factory of some sort ("Scotch tape," said Dorothea) in Brooklyn, where he lived on Nostrand Avenue near Brooklyn College before moving to the Chelsea.

Charlie had written Kate, in 1964, that homosexuality entailed "an acceptance of the facts and then a fitting of those facts into one's social world as best & intelligently as one can," and thus he endeavored to proceed where Stanley was concerned. Without going into detail, he divulged to friends that he'd "taken a companion," whom some were

---

* He died in 1998.

invited to meet; he was a little sheepish about the fact that Stanley was rough around the edges, though he seems to have been a decent fellow. As Boom sized up the situation for Sarah's benefit ("Weekend Chez Boom with Stanley," Charlie noted in his diary for September 16, 1967): "I rather believe Stanley is thoroughly honest and generous in trying to help Charlie. . . . Charlie is lucky to have such a devoted attendant and maybe we are too. I don't know if Stanley understands Charlie's two addictions thoroughly but I'm sure he doesn't encourage it. I think Stanley is very dumb (and for me dull) and Charlie is deceiving him. He'll crush him too." This, coming from Boom, was uncharacteristically harsh—it was written in January 1968, when Charlie was taking various turns for the worse—though accurate as far as it goes. Stanley's role, by all accounts, was mostly that of a loving caretaker,* as opposed to someone who could reciprocate Jackson's intellectual enthusiasms. Carl Brandt got the impression the two had little to say to each other—this borne out, perhaps, by several leftover pages divided into columns headed "S" and "C," suggesting they played a lot of rummy 500.

Whether or not Stanley was an ideal soulmate, he seems to have made Charlie happy much of the time; certainly the latter comported himself like a man who'd "taken a companion." Brock Brower's final glimpse of Jackson was during the intermission of a Broadway play in the spring of 1968. The writers had last met at Bread Loaf almost three years before, and already the change in Charlie was that of a chrysalis turned into a butterfly: He wore a long, royal blue coat with wide Edwardian lapels,† and (while Stanley hovered vaguely in the background) effusively congratulated Brower for his story "Rockabye" in a recent *Esquire*. "He was delighted with himself," said Brower, many years later. "I've never seen a closet case debouch from under the moths more flamboyantly for his grand finale." That night Brower pithily reported to his wife: "He's out!"

THE ADVENT of Stanley, for the other Jacksons, added a new strain to an already delicate situation. Everyone had been doing their best—Rhoda far from least. The worst of her pique toward Charlie soon passed after

---

* A couple of Stanley's household notes survive, both written in the same vein of affectionate reassurance. One reads: "Dear Charles, I left here at 10:35 a.m. and will be back soon I can [*sic*], / All my love, / Stanley." Evidently, though, he was not oblivious to his companion's shortcomings; after Jackson died, Stanley remarked to a mutual friend, "Charles was a very difficult person."
† Expressive, perhaps, of his late-life enthusiasm for the Beatles.

he moved to the Chelsea, and she called various friends in New York imploring them to keep an eye on him; also, despite earlier strictures, they did in fact spend Christmas together as a family. Indeed, she'd rather shamed Charlie with her generosity ("I was absolutely stunned by your presents," he wrote her afterward), giving him two Brooks shirts and a new book that named Jackson as an especially "outspoken and generous" proponent of the Fitzgerald Revival.* The following summer, too, as he struggled to finish his novel, Rhoda balked at her daughters' suggestion that she take a long-overdue trip to visit Kate in Arkansas—"I just feel Papa needs the money so badly it's not right"—but was finally persuaded to go.

Charlie's relationship with his Wall Street son-in-law, meanwhile, hadn't gotten any easier. Sandy's golf-playing neglect of his wife had always been hard for Charlie to swallow, and one night he was amazed to hear the young man blandly admit that, between marriages, he'd spent almost every night playing pinball in Times Square and "(get this)"—Charlie wrote Rhoda—"attending those appalling double-feature movies which, I'm told, are the sink of the city": "Frankly," he concluded, "I pray that they do not have a child." As for the kind of father Charlie expected such an "adolescent" to be—well, he'd spelled it out, more or less, in the subtle form of a "story idea" that he related to Sandy in a letter ("please show this to Sarah"):

> [It's] about one of those typical male American types who don't understand the female sex or indeed anybody else; who needs his wife only as a kind of buffer or shock absorber between him and the social world around him . . . that is, the amenities are left up to her, while he can go on living strictly for himself, etc. . . . you know the type, you've seen them—completely unimaginative etc etc. He is ten years married, has a child of eight years, then learns that his wife is pregnant again. [To condense a bit: the father does not *want* another child—can hardly stand the child he has—but finally figures that if one or the other kid dies, at least they'll have a "spare."] . . . The story comes to a dénouement when one day the first child is killed . . . and they *do* have one left—which he comes to detest with a passion, not because he misses the dead child at all or even feels bereaved, but

---

* *F. Scott Fitzgerald: A Critical Portrait*, by Henry Dan Piper, mentioned in Chapter Five.

because inwardly, unconsciously, without knowing it, he detests himself. The story is called . . . THE SPARE.

Whether Sandy was anything but mystified by such elliptical satire is unknown. He was not a communicative man. In any event, Charlie was the opposite of dismayed when his granddaughter, Alexandra (named after her father), was born on October 25, 1966. In a newspaper interview Charlie referred to the girl as his "pride and joy" ("The only thing of importance in my life is my family"), and composed the inevitable poem, "A Salute, A Blessing, and a Kind of Family Inventory for Alexandra," which lavished compliments on every member of the Jacksons and Pipers (*every* member: "What better Dad could any baby / Choose for a Pop: she picked a dandy")—except, of course, himself:

> *Which brings us up to Grandpa Jackson,*
> *Of whom the less that's said, the better.*
> *'Tis true the slob's an Anglo-Saxon,*
> *But he's not just all wet, he's wetter.*
> *Remember, though, while there's above you,*
> *A sky at all, he'll always love you.*

The last two lines were certainly true: as Sarah attests, he was "a doting grandfather" who loved playing with the toddler, however much her parents had begun to distance themselves.

Sarah was finding it harder and harder to reconcile her Piper life with that of her raffish father. The Chelsea was *not* her kind of milieu—even before Stanley (who "smelled" to boot) had entered the picture. As a child Sarah had scarcely considered her father a sexual being, and later was ill-prepared when he began dropping some pretty broad hints. "Well I guess I really am getting old"—he wrote her in 1964, while staying at her and Sandy's place on the Upper East Side—"to spend all of Saturday and all of Sunday sitting alone in your apartment, doing nothing . . . while all the city throbs with naughty joy without, I gladly accept the fact that my cruising days are over. No more the chase, thank God." That same summer he also let her know that *Memoirs of Hadrian* had become his "most

---

* Possibly the closest Jackson ever came to an anti-Semitic slur—this, no doubt, for the benefit of his in-laws, the kind of people who might well have consoled themselves with the fact that Charlie, at least, wasn't a Jew.

necessary book," and that he "absolutely identif[ied]" with the (gay) hero and "need[ed] him" in his life. As for Kate—whether or not she was quite willing or able, at the time, to process the information—Charlie seemed to take it for granted that she'd figured things out on some level, what with his casual remarks about "fitting" the fact of homosexuality into one's life, his ruminations about how "crystal-clear" Plato's message had finally become to him, and so forth. In the summer of 1963, while working for a family on Long Island, Kate had socialized with one of Edie Sedgwick's unhappy brothers—the gay, alcoholic Francis ("Minty")—whom Charlie had met in AA. When the young man hanged himself the following year, Charlie wrote a commiserating letter to Kate: "You speak of his problems. Besides alcoholism, I suspect he had sexual problems as well (my god who doesn't), though I never knew or heard anything definite."

Though everyone continued to do their best, it was Kate whom Charlie settled on—more and more definitely, and rather burdensomely—as a confidante. "Isn't he cute?" he remarked of Stanley ("as if he were a kind of curio") in her presence. As she recalled the episode, "It wasn't just affection, it was more like, 'This is my little indulgence . . . ' " Their rapport had become crucial to him. "*Great* week with Kate—a milestone," he'd scribbled in his diary two years before, in December 1965, when she'd come home for Christmas after four months with VISTA. The "milestone" had come about when Kate confided in him (*not* Rhoda) that she had a boyfriend in Arkansas, and the following Valentine's Day he wrote her an allusive poem:

> *Every guy has a gal he likes best;*
> *You alas, darling Kate, were mine.*
> *The "alas" is not spoken in jest:*
> *You can't be my Valentine.*
>
> *Another has taken your eye;*
> *I'm so mad I can hardly speak.*
> *You may call it love, but I—*
> *I can only call it damned cheek.*

—FORLORN

For the family especially, things began to fall apart in earnest after Charlie finished his novel. On Valentine's Day, 1967 (one year after the

"FORLORN" poem), Boom wrote Sarah: "Charlie phones often—in good form—hope he behaves himself for a while." But the next day Charlie overdosed again, and was taken to Freeport Hospital on Long Island. Sarah was the only one in New York at the time, and it was she who visited Freeport to make sure he was all right; she said nothing, however, to her sister—who'd just moved to Washington, D.C.—since for years she and Rhoda had conspired to "shield" Kate from the worst. "Relationships very strained," Charlie wrote in his diary on March 12, two weeks after his release from the hospital, when everyone (Boom too) had gathered in New Brunswick during a weekend visit from Kate, who (as Charlie also noted) was the one who volunteered to drive him back to New York that day.

Kate's growing solidarity with her father—embodied by her relative acceptance of the Stanley situation—flourished all the more, perhaps, because she *was* shielded from details that might have tested her sympathy far more than Stanley. "The check he sent out to Rhoda was ridiculous and I felt so sorry for her," Boom wrote Sarah (*his* confidante) in January 1968, not long after Charlie had received his windfall from the paperback sale of *A Second-Hand Life*. "I'll help her follow it up to collect a reasonable amount of what he owes her. Fortunately I had kept a clear account during the last two years—forgetting the big old ORFORD amount . . ." Toward the end, all sides were bruised. Charlie had any number of reasons (so he fancied) to feel sorry for himself, and was losing touch with reality in any case. After his death, Kate received a note in her father's handwriting (she thinks Stanley must have sent it) to the effect that Sarah and Rhoda were "terrible people," that only Kate and Stanley loved him (and vice versa). Horrified, she hid the note in her closet and didn't mention it for almost forty-two years.

A MOTIF in articles written about Jackson a year before his death, around the time of *A Second-Hand Life*, was that he "look[ed] much younger than his 64 years" (*Saturday Review*), despite his ghastly medical history and the fact that he smoked as much as ever (" 'They only took out one lung,' he quips, puffing on a cigarette"). On the inside, of course, he was a mess. The absence of so many ribs made him list ever more feebly to one side as he walked, and his remaining lung was "about gone," according to Rhoda (because of emphysema, she thought, not TB), until he could barely muster the steam to walk back and forth to the Riss for meals.

Somewhat forgivably, perhaps, he'd resumed drinking. "I always keep a few beers in the icebox," he told a startled guest. "I have two a day. No more, no less." For a while he might have stuck to that regime, but in due course he advanced to stingers and Tom Collinses, and by the end he was drinking them with breakfast. As for his Seconal habit, a mutual friend wrote that Stanley tried heroically to ration pills and hide the bottles, lest Charlie "eat them like candies until the bottle was empty or he was unconscious, whichever came first." On January 24, 1968, Boom wrote a despairing letter to Sarah:

> Charlie phoned yesterday—saying he was leaving in the afternoon for St. Croix. . . . He was all doped up and I even wondered whether he'd make the trip. I advised him going to a hospital instead and he didn't like it. Said he was sorry he called. Such complete distruction [*sic*] he's heading for himself and there's nothing any one can do about it. I told him his health was entirely in his hands. His health is being ruined and his brain damage is constantly more apparent. We know he's sick and suffers but he also likes the dope that puts him under and makes him WORSE.

Whether he made it to St. Croix is unknown, but doubtful; by mid-February he was in Regent Hospital on East 61st, recovering from another overdose. According to his diary, the doctor had "ordered Stan to be sick"—that is, to stay home from his job and help wean his friend off the pills, as he did for almost three weeks ("Stan returns to work," Charlie noted on March 14).

A crisis arose in May, when Stanley departed for a long-awaited trip to see his parents in Czechoslovakia for the first time in twenty years. Charlie affected to be happy for him and insisted he go, though in fact he was wretched: by then he could hardly care for himself, and was loath to impose on his exasperated family or, for that matter, whatever friends still lingered on the periphery of his life. Happily there was a third alternative—new friends, or admirers anyway, with whom he'd yet to wear out his welcome: a nice couple named Alex and Rae Lindsay from Englewood Cliffs, New Jersey. Alex was an adman who'd gotten a sudden, determined urge to reread *The Lost Weekend* after a two-martini lunch the previous August. He'd loaned and lost his only copy a few years back, and a number of bookstore clerks had assured him that it was long out of print. Recently, though, he'd read an article about the author, who was reported to be living (still!) at the Chelsea. Fortified with gin,

Lindsay called the hotel and told Jackson, in effect, that everyone kept saying *The Lost Weekend* was out of print. "Well," Jackson replied, coughing, "you can tell them that it's not only not out of print, but that it never *has* been out of print. It's in print in no less than 23 [14] languages!" He advised Lindsay to get in touch with Farrar, Straus and Giroux, then suddenly changed his mind: "If you come down here now," he said, "I'll give you a copy." Lindsay left work then and there. Like Don Birnam he was a frustrated writer whose drinking, over time, had worsened along with his frustration; at the Chelsea he admitted as much to Jackson, who signed one of his "dozen or so copies" as follows: "August 22, 1967. For Alex Lindsay—This old book of mine, with all the good luck in the world. In fact, good luck to us both! Faithfully yours, Charles Jackson." They shook hands, promising to meet again, though Lindsay thought it unlikely.

"You've never heard of them," Charlie wrote Rhoda almost ten months later, "but I have a couple of very good friends, a married pair, Alexander Lindsay (40 [41], born in Aberdeen!) and his wife Rae.

> He has a smallish adv. agency, she ghost-writes some woman's column (I forget the name). They leave [*sic*] in a lovely house (grounds, large pool), in Englewood Cliffs, just across the Geo. Washington Bridge, and have two children, Maria aged five, and Alex Jr. about a year old. I see them often and enjoy them, and they seem to enjoy me: Alex is a really rabid fan of mine, one of those rare birds who can cite verbatim passages from THE LOST WEEKEND, for instance, that I don't even remember. As an example, they call their cook "Holy Love," and when I said is that really her name, Alex said, "You're slipping, Jackson. That was the name of Helen's cleaning-woman in Lost Weekend."*

---

* "We never called Carole—our dear cleaning lady/baby sitter—'Holy Love,' so Alex was obviously joshing Charlie," Rae Lindsay e-mailed me in 2009. She also pointed out that Carole came once a week to clean or babysit, *not* cook: "Was Charlie trying to impress Rhoda with our 'grand' household?" she (astutely) conjectured. The column Rae ghosted (for Emily Wilkens) was "A New You," about health and beauty issues. "I'm just a hack," she remarked to Charlie, who hastened to reassure her: "No no no—you're *not* a hack. These are good. You write well, and clearly—don't ever think of yourself as a hack." Also, for what it's worth, Alex was born in Kilmarnock—not Aberdeen (where Rhoda's parents were born, hence the exclamation point)—and came to the States as a toddler.

Charlie wrote Rhoda that he was about to check himself into High Watch Farm (a Connecticut treatment center based on AA) for the duration of Stanley's absence, when the Lindsays phoned and invited him to stay at their house as long as he liked. ("Charlie called us a few days" after Stanley left, Alex Lindsay later wrote, "and it became clear how desperate he was, so we invited him to stay with us for an indefinite period.") "I accepted at once," said Charlie, adding poignantly (pointedly?): "it was nice to be wanted, and made me feel better just being there." Jackson had visited the Lindsays a couple of times before, and, as Rae recalled, had been dapper and somewhat vital then; during his final visit, though, he was plainly failing, and didn't bother to change out of a rather seedy bathrobe for five days. Still, he seemed in good spirits that first night, reading aloud from "Palm Sunday" and even refusing beer ("I just don't care about it"). "Well, Charlie," said Alex, around two in the morning, "I guess you can find your way to your room," indicating a study on the lower floor. As Alex remembered:

> Suddenly he sagged back on the couch and began to look at me with the most terrifying face I had ever seen: his eyes opened wide behind his glasses, his mouth turned down, lower teeth bared, and he began to breathe hard. "Charlie! What's wrong?!" I moved toward him and he continued to look at me helplessly, unable to speak. Finally he breathed, "Can't. Can't go down there. Help me."
>
> "What can I do? You want a glass of water?" I thought he was having a heart attack.
>
> "Can you give me something . . . some . . . pills . . . to help me?"

As it happened, Alex occasionally took Seconal to help him sleep when his psoriasis was acting up, and his wife gave two to Charlie; then they made up a bed for him on a couch near their bedroom. ("I felt no shame about this at all," Charlie wrote Rhoda. "It was a state I was in, and I had to accept it, and they did too.") The next day Alex found Charlie reading (and smoking) contentedly on a daybed in the downstairs study, where he betook himself each morning as soon as it began to turn light outside.

The highlight of that first night had been Charlie's discovery of the Beatles—whom he'd hitherto known only as "those maniacs who caused so much screaming on the Ed Sullivan show." Alex wanted to play their most recent album, *Sgt. Pepper's Lonely Hearts Club Band*, to which Charlie acquiesced at length, a good guest, while certain it would be "dreadful stuff." Instead he was "stunned," and eager as ever to share this final passion with his wife:

> The simple little song called She's Leaving Home shook me through and through with its compassion, its tragedy, its understanding and love: it is as perfect as *Madam[e] Bovary*, better than one of those good, English movie[s] about middle-class life whose protagonist is usually a starving spinster, and it all takes exactly two minutes. But *every one* of the songs on *Sgt. Pepper* album is perfect. Next we played *The Magical Mystery Tour*, and again I was astonished (I simply hadn't known they were like this), and finally *Revolver*. After that I didn't want to go further: it was all too rich and satisfactory to *need* more.

He excitedly phoned Kate in Washington to canvass her thoughts, and every evening when Alex came home from work, he'd find his guest "sitting at the diningroom table carefully reading an album cover while the Beatles pounded away."*

IN THAT long letter he wrote Rhoda about his stay at the Lindsays'—dated June 6, 1968, and perhaps the last substantial letter he ever wrote—he mentioned returning to the Chelsea after five days and ("Wonder of wonders") feeling so vastly improved that he sat right down and wrote a "highly saleable modern story, told mostly in dialogue, [illegible word] dramatic, about divorce—a natural for McCall's, though they haven't seen it yet." This is unlikely; at any rate, nothing of the sort survives. Probably his last attempt at formal composition was a review of some books about the Beatles, for which he managed a disorderly paragraph about the group's "stunning achievements" and "stupendous international fame" and "developing genius (for 'genius' is the word . . .)"—a spluttering wave of hyperbole that crashes thus:

> . . . what can one say about this prodigy of creativity without sounding like a gasping, seduced, incoherent teen-ager wetting his or her

---

* I am deeply indebted to Rae Lindsay for letting me see her husband's unpublished twenty-page memoir of his brief friendship with Jackson, which she found among some papers in her attic; as may be clear by now, much of this chapter is derived from that source. Sad to say, Alex Lindsay died of cirrhosis in 1974, only forty-seven years old.

pants (usually "her") prior to an agonized mass orgasm of helpless hero-worship in a throbbing, screaming second-balcony? The helplessness I readily admit to when the Beatles perform; at sixty-five I am, thank God, beyond the pants-wetting and at times the other [last five words struck out]. . . .

Where does it all come from? These books, good as they are, will not tell you, of course.

A parenthetical aside about the (similarly) ineffable greatness of Beethoven, Mozart, and Mussorgsky is scrawled at the bottom of the page; the rest is silence.

And what of *Farther and Wilder*? Attached to the typescript is a note in Jackson's hand that indicates its approximate status at the time of his death:

> Part I of novel / Called / "What Happened"
>   Opening section, part of which is here, runs to 204 pages.
>   Then: exactly 50 pages are finished of Second Section called "The Father" (so far) / But it will run to at least 200 or 300 more.
>   Then: A section (fraternity story) of Part 3 is finished and runs to 224 pages.

The "fraternity story" was almost certainly some version of *Native Moment*, whose surviving typescript is 242 pages long (surely Jackson was planning to revise this apprentice work, though it's possible he simply transposed the last two digits). According to a table of contents—assuming the novel's contents were meant to be essentially chronological—the "fraternity story," here titled "Primavera," was actually the seventh and last section of *Farther and Wilder*; "The Father" (about Thelma and Richard's death, and the father's subsequent departure) was indeed the second section (after "Preview"), followed by "Arcadia," "Emily Sparks" (about an influential schoolteacher who appears in various guises throughout Jackson's early work as well as the unpublished *Home for Good*), "Ray Verne" (a longer treatment of the molestation story told in "Palm Sunday"), and "Bettina" (about his friendship with Marion Fleck). Nothing of these four middle sections survives, or was likely ever written—rather, the material was recycled again and again in Jackson's "Arcadian Tales," published and unpublished, until he must have wondered at the alchemy required to make them shine anew in some other, more quintessential form. Assuming that each section was to be of comparable length—anywhere between 200 and 350 pages—this first volume alone would have run to between 1,500 and 2,000 pages or more. And then, of course, there were *other* planned volumes of *What Happened*, doubtless of equal heft, though each volume (as Jackson assured the reader in a prefatory note) would "be complete in itself and [could] be read as a single novel, without relation to its fellows."

"Without relation to its fellows"? Not exactly. Take the one section, "Preview," that Jackson had described so lovingly in a 1948 letter to "Stan, Bernice, and Company" (summarized at the beginning of Chapter Thirteen): this, again, was the only part of the book he seemed to envisage with perfect clarity, and indeed the only part he was able to complete, albeit some six years after that initial pitch. Add the fifty (rougher) pages of "The Father," and even a refurbished version of *Native Moment*, and *still* Jackson had hundreds and hundreds of pages to go on *Farther and Wilder* alone, never mind the entire colossus that was to be *What Happened*. Which is to say: as the preamble to a multivolume opus of Proustian magnitude, the 204-page "Preview" section might have served; as a discrete piece of writing, not so much. "The whole effect of this opening section is a rather lazy one," Jackson admitted in 1948, "a somewhat poetic evocation of middle class family life, which sets the mood for all that is to follow; but it also serves the practical purpose of setting down what the story is to be about. This opening section will be a long piece of 'fine writing,' with a strong accent on mood, feeling, atmosphere, et cetera . . . " All this is true, though the writing is finer in some places than others. As for the actual substance of "Preview"—a summer day in 1947, when Don Birnam hosts a long-awaited reunion of "his widely scattered family" at his fine New Hampshire home—various characters are introduced, themes are formulated and foreshadowed, but in terms of plot? "Nothing had come of the fabulous day," Don reflects on page 186. "Nothing had happened."

In other words, Jackson had signed a contract with Macmillan for a novel whose only viable section was essentially devoid of plot. And that was perhaps only the beginning of his worries. Rhoda, their daughters, and Rhoda's parents are all lovingly evoked in this fragment, but not so—*decidedly* not so—the rest of his family (the family that "he had not only long since grown away from but that he didn't even belong to any more"): namely, his brother Herb ("Gerald"), and Herb's wife, Bob ("Teddie"), small-minded clods whose idea of fun is to leave a plastic dog turd on the carpet; his mother, a melodramatic, self-pitying cow*; and even the long-suffering Boom ("Wick"), here traduced (wistfully) as "nothing more than a small-town queen." And what about the chief aesthetic advantage of the "Preview" section, as Jackson had articulated it twenty years before?—that is, to reassure readers that life had eventually worked out for Don Birnam (circa 1947), the knowledge of which would help them persevere, later, while following the younger Don along the "farther, wilder, more shattering" paths (per the Mann epigraph) that his life as a tormented artist would perforce take him . . . until this happy ending/beginning, where we find him a well-integrated paterfamilias living in that New Hampshire mansion. "In the purest sense of the words," Charlie had promised "Stan, Bernice, and Company," "it is a novel of affirmation and acceptance of life." So he might have thought (with certain qualms, to be sure) in 1948; but what about twenty years later? Was his life still a "success story" now that he was a decrepit addict at least somewhat estranged from his beloved family, living at the Chelsea with a barely literate factory worker?

Yes and no. At least it wasn't New Brunswick, and perhaps he'd actually come to accept (as he'd written in 1948) that "happiness as he [had] expected it to be [was] an illusion." Then, too, the essential fact remained: He'd managed to produce at least one classic novel and various works of lasting interest, against staggering odds, whatever the relative sterility of his later years.

That said, it wasn't a story he had time enough or energy to write.

IT WAS Alex Lindsay who noted the "200 pages" of *Farther and Wilder* resting forlornly on Jackson's desk ("untouched for God knows how long"), and many years later his wife, Rae, remembered that their guest hadn't bothered to write a word during his five-day stay, despite an office and typewriter and plenty of quiet. His terrible attacks of dread, she thought, were not so much fear of dying as fear of living—of being a lonely invalid without purpose.

His last published piece had been a poignant homage to the Chelsea for *Holiday* magazine. Written in the fall of 1967, it touches on certain romantic aspects of the hotel, as, for instance, its plaque in honor of Dylan Thomas, who was living at the Chelsea when he drank eighteen

---

* A portrait that would have squared awkwardly with the book's dedication: "To The Beloved Memory / Of My Mother / SARAH WILLIAMS JACKSON."

whiskies at the White Horse Tavern ("I think that's the record"), collapsed back at the hotel, and later expired at St. Vincent's Hospital—or, as the plaque more evocatively puts it, "from here sailed out to die": "The phrase is both madly unrealistic and poetically right," wrote Jackson, whose own end was presaged therein.

A few days after his return from the Lindsays', Jackson paid a final visit to Kate in Washington, where she worked for the Office of Economic Opportunity. Charlie had a "wonderful time," he wrote, though he might have worried a little about the hard-partying ethos of his daughter's Great Society colleagues, some of whom had marched on the Pentagon and were apt to smoke pot and whatnot at a party given in Charlie's honor. But at the time, again, he seemed to enjoy himself: one day he and Kate were taken on a speedboat ride along the Potomac, and Charlie also mentioned visiting, alone, the Iwo Jima Memorial (a well-known cruising spot, his daughter learned). Also, many years later, a friend told Kate that his ex-wife had received calls from Charlie after his trip, during which they mostly discussed suicide.

Returning to his empty apartment, Charlie was beside himself with lonely angst. "Pissed off / bad cold / tears" he scribbled among his notes for that last, long letter to Rhoda, who'd mildly rebuffed him when he called her to arrange a meeting on the pretext of being concerned about "Kate's friends." Before proceeding to more pleasant subjects (the Lindsays, the Beatles, his alleged story writing), he began this letter on a note of grievance:

> I would be less than honest if I didn't confess that I was really pissed off by your reaction to the proposition—or my wish, rather—that you come up to New York as soon as you could so that I could talk to you about something very pressing about our Kate (I used "our Kate" advisedly), because I thought, and still think that it was important. . . . You said, as casually as if it was nothing at all, "What is there to talk about?"—but the fact that I had called you should have told you it was urgent. . . . You wound up choosing a weekend that was two whole weeks away, as though Kate's problem, and my concern, were of no moment at all. Indifference of this kind I don't understand, in a parent who loves his or her offspring.

Quite apart from his usual personal concerns (which may or may not have included "Kate's friends"), he was especially distraught that day. Robert Kennedy had been shot. Because of this, and because of a bad cold, Charlie could hardly see his breakfast plate at the Riss, and vomited after returning to his room. When he learned that Kennedy had, in fact, died, Charlie phoned the Lindsays and became angry when Alex said he wouldn't be watching *all* the funeral proceedings (explaining that he'd been "wrung out" from the ordeal of JFK's assassination, though Jackson wasn't mollified). No doubt he also called Stanley that day; as the latter eventually told the Lindsays, Charlie had phoned him in Czechoslovakia at least three times, pleading for him to come home, until finally he agreed to cut his trip short by two weeks. "Stanya's return," Charlie noted in his diary for June 18.

A month or so later, perhaps, he paid his final visit to the Strauses, who invited him to their home in Purchase as a respite from the hot weather. Dorothea remembered the evening as a dreary one: "Charlie arrived looking shockingly old and shriveled. One shoulder was lower than the other and his body listed at an acute angle, as though fixed in a lopsided bow to death. Like a child with a new toy he showed me the oxygen unit he had to have with him at all times." The oxygen unit was indeed recent; he wouldn't need it for long. As a house present he offered Dorothea a copy of *Sgt. Pepper*, and they ended up chatting about their grandchildren: "It all had a hollow note." The next morning was cooler, and Charlie seemed somewhat revived. "Goodbye, Madame," he called jauntily from the bottom of the stairs, about to return to the city with Roger. "I love you!" She didn't reply. As she later explained, "I had rebuffed him because I was selfishly intent on the preservation of my own image of Charles Jackson, more important to me than the human being whose insistence at the moment was an intrusion." In time she would be surprised by the stubbornness of her grief.

Stanley, meanwhile, had been kept on his toes since his return. According to Alex Lindsay, Jackson overdosed at least three times in June and/or July: the first time Stanley got him quickly to Bellevue; the second time Charlie helped the Seconal along by drinking an entire quart of gin in fifteen minutes, but again his friend was too fast for him. By then Stanley might have wondered, though, whether he was doing Jackson any favors. "I have always felt," Charlie wrote Kate in 1964, "far from [suicide] being an act of weakness or cowardice, it might well be, under certain conditions, not only the most courageous thing a man could do but also, for him, the most intelligent"—and here he paraphrased a quote from Santayana that he'd first transcribed into his JAXON notebook some thirty years before: "Nothing is meaner than the anxiety to live on, to live on anyhow and in any shape; a spirit with any honor is not willing to live except in its own way; and a spirit with any wisdom is not over-eager to live at all."

One night Stanley returned from work and found Charlie sleeping in bed, a note written in red ink on the table beside him:

> Monday
> July 28th [29th], 1968

To Whom It May Concern,

If I have hurt anyone by this act (and I know I have: my beloved daughters, my dear friend Stanislaus) I beg forgiveness from my heart; but I can't help it. Life has become too physically painful for me to go on any longer, and I must bow out. <u>There is no other reason</u>.

> Charles Jackson*

"So this was the end," wrote Alex Lindsay. "But not as far as Stanley Zednik, now an expert in drug revival cases, was concerned. In minutes he had an ambulance at the door of the hotel; Charlie was placed in a stretcher and was shortly hospitalized."

This last attempt left Jackson more enfeebled than ever ("weak, ill and helpless"), and Stanley took a leave of absence from his job to care for him full-time.† One imagines that poor Charlie did his weary best to persuade his friend to let him go already, and perhaps he finally succeeded in this. According to the police report, Jackson took a fatal overdose of Seconal at 11:10 a.m. on Wednesday, September 18. Stanley told Alex Lindsay that he'd let Charlie out of his sight for all of ten minutes while he took a shower: "When he came out," Lindsay wrote, "he found Charlie sitting on a couch, his head back, mouth open, unconscious but breathing." An empty pill bottle lay at his feet; he'd hastily swallowed at least thirty Seconals—reminding one, somewhat, of Don's dream of deliverance in *The Lost Weekend*, when his ecstatic brother Wick gets to him before the blond-haired mob, pressing a pill box into his hand:

---

* This note—unmistakably in Jackson's hand—was found among Alex Lindsay's papers. Rhoda's and Boom's phone numbers are provided at the bottom of the page.
† "Charles, dear," read Stanley's other surviving note, "I went to pick-up my last check and will be back very soon. / All my love, / Stanley."

"Unable to bear the sight of Wick's relief, so soon to break into grief as passionate as his joy, . . . [he] slammed the pills into his mouth." Stanley, whose grief would be passionate too, may have performed (at least passively) a similar office: he seems to have told Lindsay that he summoned help immediately, as ever, but according to the hospital report he hadn't, in fact, called police until "45 min. after p[atien]t had taken unknown quantity of seconal tabs"; when questioned, apparently, he claimed he hadn't been in the apartment at the time.* In any case, Jackson didn't arrive at St. Vincent's until 12:08 p.m., and by then he'd stopped breathing and the brain damage was almost certainly irrevocable. He never regained consciousness.

His rosy, resilient body, however, refused to die for three days, and might have vegetated indefinitely were it not for a fortunate old wound. At St. Vincent's he'd begun breathing again on a respirator, and after the barbiturates had been filtered out of his system via hemodialysis—that is, catheters were inserted in his elbows and ankle, and the blood run through a dialysis machine—they flushed out his abdominal cavity, which ultimately detached a scab from the artery at the base of his duodenal ulcer. His blood pressure began to drop around 4:30 a.m. on September 21, and he was pronounced dead at 7:50.

It fell to his son-in-law, Sandy, to identify the remains. Rhoda was at an alcoholism conference in Washington, D.C., manning the Rutgers publications table; when she heard about Charlie's latest mishap—uncertain how serious it was—she called various people to check on him, and left as speedily as possible. But it was Sandy who happened to be available when Charlie suddenly bled to death. That afternoon he arrived at the hospital and confirmed that the deceased was indeed his father-in-law, whom he'd last seen "a month ago"; somewhat guardedly, perhaps, he allowed that Charlie had been "depressed, at certain times," but had "no previous history of mental disease" and had "lived a normal social life."

---

* Roger Straus was then at the Frankfurt Book Fair, and heard (from his wife?) that Stanley had been "working" when Charlie called to say his final goodbye ("He used to play teeter-totter Tessie with death," Roger remarked on another occasion. "I think it had to do with, do you really love me enough to keep me from dying?"): "This had happened so often before that his friend didn't quite believe it," said Roger in 1978, "and didn't get to him quite fast enough to have him pumped out . . ." This would seem to reflect the more or less received version of events.

Epilogue

Home for Good

Time's obituary was especially brusque: "Died. Charles Jackson, 65, melancholy novelist of guilt and frustration; in Manhattan. After striking it rich in 1944 with *The Lost Weekend*, the story of a classic binge, he had a long dry spell, writing mediocre books about homosexuality and paranoia. His last work was *A Second-Hand Life*, a novel of nymphomania published in 1967." Charlie's shade, one hopes, was consoled somewhat by the longer, more generous assessment in *The New York Times*, which included nice quotes from Carl Brandt ("[Jackson was] warm and straight . . . a dedicated amateur student of Shakespeare and Thomas Mann") and Robert Markel ("[he] felt life as deeply as anyone I've known, and this comes out in his work"), who implied that Jackson was hard at work on a new Don Birnam novel, *Farther and Wilder*, as long as "300 pages" at the time of his death. In his syndicated column, Mel Heimer described Jackson as "one of the nicest and gentlest souls I knew," a man who devoted himself to "yeoman work for Alcoholics Anonymous," while the *Times* of Geneva, New York—just a few miles from Newark—remembered the Finger Lakes author as "a child misunderstood by almost everyone . . . a boy searching for an answer which could only be found on the printed page."

Three days after Jackson's death, a memorial service was held at the Episcopal Church of the Resurrection on East 74th, down the block from Sarah's apartment. The proceedings reflected Rhoda's prudential if rather austere sensibility: there was no eulogy or reading from her husband's work; Charlie had been many things to many people, and very few of his friends could have done justice to so protean a figure. Roger Straus was still in Europe at the time, Dorothea was hardly one to speak at funerals, and Max Wylie—who'd known Charlie for three rather tumultuous decades—had only just that morning learned of his wife Lambie's death, after a long coma, at New York Hospital. He attended Charlie's memorial all the same. "There was nothing I could do for [Lambie] then, but there was a small bit I might do for Rhoda, Kate, and Sarah," he wrote in 1973—a kind of belated eulogy that, while touching, might have been a bit too candid for actual obsequies:

> [Charlie] stood up for all his friends, till (usually over a trifle) they "crossed" him. He could be pettish, girlish. He could also be manly. And enormously generous and understanding. He helped hundreds of people. He, to me, represented the classic paradox seen so often among gifted people: a steady dedication to his own work, often marred in his human relationships by spurts of the churlish, then as suddenly re-inspirited by adult returns to mature responses.

As for Dorothea, she dourly considered the "dusty red plush" of that "homely" Episcopal church and couldn't help reflecting how "inappropriate" it was for a romantic like Charlie, who "would have wanted it to be gorgeous and historic." Bemusing, too, was the sheer diversity of mourners—writers, editors, actors, AA people ("All were chapters in Charles Jackson's life: long or short, sad or comic, deep or trivial, linked together momentarily by the event of his death")—among whom the most visibly stricken, by far, was also the most anomalous: Stanley's "long, wavy blond hair," wrote Dorothea, "slicked down with water for the occasion, erupted here and there in unruly curls and his prominent cheekbones flamed, as though his shock and grief could not be tamed by the sanctimonious environment of the church. . . . The tears coursing down his face were as plentiful and unselfconscious as rain."

A few people gathered afterward at the Pipers' apartment. Finally, as the family was about to leave for the interment in Newark, Boom stopped on the sidewalk: "Oh my heavens! I forgot Charlie!" He recovered his brother's ashes from the mantelpiece, and off they went.

IN *The Lost Weekend*, Don Birnam loses himself in reveries of his Arcadian childhood, and longs desperately "to be home, home at last, home for good . . . Christ he was going *nuts* with sentimentality! Self-pity like this would drive him to suicide!" And so, at last, it had come to pass. On Wednesday, September 25, Charlie's ashes were buried in the East Newark Cemetery next to Thelma and Richard ("a lovely spot," he'd written in "Rachel's Summer," "grown up now with rose bushes and shrubbery"), on the other side of whom was their mother. The rector of St. Mark's Episcopal, where Charlie had been confirmed as a boy, officiated. Mildly conspicuous in his absence was Charlie's oldest brother, Herb, who'd also been omitted from the *Times* obituary. In recent years he and Bob had seemed less impressed than ever by the little fame Charlie had won in the world; to them he was an addict who'd written a few dirty books. As for his suicide, it was "his logical end"—an attitude Don Birnam had grasped only too well: "All were ready with the 'Too bad but he's much better off' or 'Only wonder is he didn't do it sooner.' " When Herb did get the news, he walked over to the house of their childhood friend Jack Burgess, who was sitting on the porch with his wife: "Well, Charlie's dead," Herb announced matter-of-factly. "Overdose." He knew they'd be interested, if not surprised, and so felt obliged to tell them; his manner was more pensive than callous. He hardly ever spoke of Charlie again. Shortly after his death, in 1979, his grandson Michael Kraham—who inherited the family home at 241 Prospect—had to widen a door in the backyard barn where Herb had spent so much of his adult life; between the partitions of an interior wall, he found hundreds of empty whiskey bottles.

Rhoda had received a sympathy card signed "With loveing affection / Your Friend / Stanley Zednik," and a few weeks after the funeral Carl Brandt urged her to get in touch so they could "have a talk about Stanley": "He has been on the phone to me, and he sent me a copy of his letter to you." The family was frankly worried that Stanley might blackmail them, or at least continue to surface in unpleasant ways ("I think there was the wish to bury Stanley with Papa," said Kate). Finally Rhoda and her daughters agreed to meet him at the Chelsea, where Stanley let it be known that all he wanted was a gold identification bracelet ("Charles Jackson / Six Chimney Farm / Orford, N.H.") that Charlie had always worn—a sentimental item, alas, much coveted by Kate and Sarah as well. But Rhoda readily agreed to give it to Stanley, and was startled by her daughters' "brokenhearted and furious" reactions afterward. As for

Stanley, he seemed more than appeased by the trinket; at any rate they never heard from him again.

After funeral expenses and various debts were paid, Charlie's net worth was assessed at $31,263, half of which went to Rhoda and the rest divided equally among Sarah, Kate, and Boom. Carl Brandt, meanwhile, was not sanguine about the literary estate's earning potential: Macmillan reported that sales of *A Second-Hand Life* had run their course, and at present there was little interest in reprinting Jackson's other books. A few months before his death, *The Fall of Valor* had been optioned to the movies for a paltry $1,500, and the option expired after two more payments of $1,000 apiece. Also, in 1969, Wychwood Productions in London paid a $3,500 option for *A Second-Hand Life*, which they proposed to rename *Winnie* and shoot on the cheap in Nova Scotia. But nothing came of that, either. "I can say with some certainty that over the next ten years the estate will earn somewhere between two and five thousand dollars," Brandt wrote the family's lawyer. "Whether it will earn anything more is really in the laps of the gods."

But the gods had ended their sport with Charles Jackson, at least for the time being. For a year or two after his death, Rhoda was emboldened to hope that her husband's unpublished and even unfinished work—various short stories, fragments of *Rufus "Bud" Boyd* and *Farther and Wilder*—might interest a publisher. "Charlie's work was too good to die out," she wrote Roger Straus, who thought it possible that Markel at Macmillan might be willing to take a chance, but no. Nor could Roger find a single paperback house interested in reprinting the other books, all but one of which (*The Outer Edges!*) were out of print as of 1970. Indeed, hardly a ripple of anything resembling a Jackson Revival appeared until five years after his death, when *The Serif* ("Quarterly of the Kent State University Libraries") published a handsome tribute issue with a portrait of the soigné author on its cover. Contents included "An Afternoon with Boris," memoirs by Dorothea Straus and Max Wylie, a bibliography by Shirley Leonard, and a critical essay by Louis Paskoff. Foremost among the happy few who noticed this issue was, of course, Rhoda, who wished above all that "Charlie could have seen it": "No-one would have re-read it more times than he would," she wrote the journal's editor, Alex Gildzen, "(although I may be a competitor, for it invokes so many emotions and memories that have slowly melted over the years). I hope the issue *will* serve to excite a new interest in Charlie's writing. It deserves it so."

To be sure, Jackson would have been crushed by his later obscurity. The fickleness of fame! Once, he'd had a special credit card at "21," hobnobbed with all sorts of celebrities (witness his Sardi's-like collection of fondly inscribed glossies); *The Lost Weekend* had been called a "masterpiece" in the *Times*, sold almost a million copies in the United States alone, added a phrase to the language, affected the perception of alcoholism the world over, and resulted in a classic movie that all but swept the Oscars . . . and yet: three months before his death (according to Alex Lindsay), Charlie could not find his name on a list of "300 American Authors," and now, forty-four years later, he still hasn't been included among the six-hundred-plus monographs in the exhaustive Twayne's United States Author Series.

Ah, but among other fiction writers—especially writers *who drink*—his achievement is well known. In 1988, Barry Hannah praised *The Lost Weekend* as "a miracle, handed down to Mr. Jackson by a higher power," and a decade later the novel was canonized by the supreme authority in such matters, Kingsley Amis: "Marvelous and horrifying . . . the best fictional account of alcoholism I have read." That same year, when the Modern Library announced its one hundred best English-language novels of the twentieth century, Howard Kupferberg suggested in *Parade* magazine that the jury would have done better to include *The Lost Weekend* ("a sensitive novel about a middle-class alcoholic that translates the whole problem of addiction into human terms").* And Jackson lays further claim to posterity as author of perhaps the first serious American novel whose foremost subject is homosexuality, *The Fall of Valor*, which may yet become a mainstay of academic "queer studies" programs. Jack Kisling, writing in the *Denver Post* about the 1986 Arbor House reprint, addressed the novel's more abiding aspects: "Although it is far less shocking today than it was initially, it raises questions about dead marriages and subtle emotional forces that are as devastating now as they were in the days when homosexuality was horrible and hush-hush." Fair enough, and one hopes that any rediscovery of *The Fall of Valor* will also lead readers to an even earlier (and better) treatment of the theme, "Palm Sunday," and thence to the singular collection in which that story appeared, *The Sunnier Side*.†

---

* And let us not forget that *The Lost Weekend* was briefly a title in the Modern Library—until, that is, a spurned Bennett Cerf removed it in favor of *Little Women* (see Chapter Seven). As for Jackson's 1998 *Parade* apologist, Howard Kupferberg, he'd first championed Jackson's novel ("by turns horrifying and curiously moving") fifty-four years earlier!—in the *New York Herald Tribune Book Review* on January 30, 1944.

† An edition of which was published in 1995 by Syracuse University Press. John

A remarkable life's work, all in all, even if only one book can arguably be called great—and not simply a great novel about addiction, but a great novel period, featuring one of the most fascinating characters in American literature, Don Birnam, who happens to be an alcoholic.

DURING HIS LIFE, Charlie never returned to Newark after his mother's death in January 1962; Boom, however, went as often as possible, taking a steady interest in his various nieces and nephews and godchildren, and even staying on civil terms with Herb and Bob. When he was diagnosed with liver cancer in the spring of 1971, he paid a last visit home before entering the hospital in Bridgeton, where Jim Gates had his practice. His old friend Barbara Peech was among the few people allowed to see him—she had to pretend to be a cousin—but Boom was "skeletal" by then and didn't want his friends to remember him that way in any case. He died on June 20 ("A brother, Herbert, survives," noted the *Times*), and his ashes were buried with Charlie and the others at East Newark Cemetery, where a headstone had long been waiting for him.

Rhoda retired from the Center of Alcohol Studies in 1972, and was determined to leave New Brunswick as soon as she got "Charlie's papers in shape," or so she wrote Carl Brandt.* A kind of prudent neutrality, however, prevented her from leaving until 1989, at the age of eighty-two, when she finally plumped for Washington, D.C., over Manhattan—where Sarah lived—because it was greener and quieter. Also, besides Kate, she

---

Crowley, the editor, saw fit to omit "The Sisters" and "In the Chair," while adding a later Arcadian Tale, "The Break." Though not set in Arcadia, "The Boy Who Ran Away" would also be a welcome addition to any future selection of Jackson's stories.
* Rhoda managed to collect and catalogue, after a fashion, most of her husband's papers, but never reached a final decision about what to do with them. For years there were two boxes of "Charles R. Jackson" papers at Dartmouth: one contained the working and final drafts of *The Lost Weekend*, which Charlie had long ago (1949) presented to the library in a handsome leather case embossed with a blue liquor bottle and the formula for alcohol ("$CH_3 * CH_2 * OH$"); the other box contained Charlie's and Rhoda's letters to Boom, which had been sold along with the latter's other papers by one Eleanor Bacon of Elmer, New Jersey (who was "very pleasantly surprised" by the sale price), in 1983. Finally, in 2002, Charlie's daughters sold to Dartmouth the remaining twenty boxes of his papers, which included copies of practically every letter he ever wrote as an adult. As he explained to Bubbles Schinasi in 1945, "Vain creature that I am (but not really vain: I only do it so I won't repeat myself in my next) I always keep carbons of my letters." One suspects, too, that he hoped a biographer would come along someday.

had a cousin in Washington, Alex Reid (the son of her mother's younger sister), with whom she was close. Together the two would pile into Reid's Porsche and go for long drives around the countryside, or else Rhoda would ride city buses all day, exploring. She had a nice tenth-floor apartment at 4000 Massachusetts Avenue—full of her husband's first editions and various *objets*—and was happy and vigorous until her death in 1993. In later years she forgave Charlie everything, and made a point of reminding others that his more difficult traits were subsidiary to a basic nobility. He hated self-pity, for instance, which had consumed his mother and irksomely persisted in himself—though he strove against it, *consciously*, as a matter of principle. "What he was really saying," Rhoda explained to Sarah, "was that it is for each of us to see our lives clearly, to realize that we have it in ourselves to make our lives. And that if, in self-pity, we start blaming others, or refuse to accept our own responsibilities for living, we destroy ourselves." Toward the end of Rhoda's life, Sarah asked her ("[our] only personal conversation") whether she had any regrets; far from citing her chaotic, improbable marriage as such, Rhoda insisted that Charlie had been—for her and Boom both—the best thing that ever happened to them. "[She said] how lucky they were to have known and loved this man—after all the hell they had gone through!" Sarah marveled many years later. "The hospitalizations, the books about family and themselves, the homosex—" She broke off. "Everything!" To which her sister added, "She always said nothing but things like, 'He was a good man. He had a lot of pain, but he was such a nice man.'"

Sarah and Sandy had another child together, Ross, before separating in 1977; they were finally divorced in 1981. Soon after her father's death Sarah became depressed, and began to see a psychiatrist, with whom she still checks in from time to time (when Boom died, for example); mostly, though, her later life has been serene. The qualities her father cherished in her—decency, modesty, conscientiousness—have stood her in good stead over the years. She was pleasantly surprised, at her fortieth high school reunion, when a number of people went out of their way to approach her and say how important her kindness, as a girl, had been to them. Such empathy has been part of her working life, too, as vice president of client services at a consulting firm in New York. "We all have our strengths," she said recently. "And I think probably I picked that up through Papa. I'm not a special person; I'm just nice, ordinary."

Kate's life has been (as her father so often predicted) more turbulent. "I take my duties rather seriously about Kate," said her godfather, Roger

Straus, in 1976—a time when the young woman was having, as he noted, "certain problems." Over the years she'd sometimes visit the house in Purchase ("She stayed in touch with the Strauses," said Sarah; "I was the 'boring' one"); Roger made a point of sending her FSG books he thought she might like, and Dorothea enjoyed reading Kate's letters, since they reminded her of Charlie. Indeed, so much of Kate's life, good and bad, seems a direct legacy of her father. She took his death very hard: around the time of his steep, final decline, she'd gone to Alaska (he'd given her five hundred dollars for the trip), and afterward she agonized over the possibility that he'd felt "abandoned" toward the end. But then, even before his death, she herself had been unhappy and drinking too much; at one point she called her father to ask "whether you could tell if you were going crazy or would you really just snap?" Very like her father, she felt all but hopelessly unloved ("Mr. Jackson, I don't think I've ever known anybody else in my life who needs love as badly as you do"). Once, she weepily confessed as much to her mother, who rushed into her bedroom and retrieved a photo of her holding Kate as a baby: "Kate, *look* at this," she said: "Is this not love?" "Mama," Kate replied, "I'm twenty-nine! This was when I was six months!"

By then Kate was "wretched" in "every category" of life: unemployed, broke, depressed, in bad health. Finally Rhoda insisted she come home with her to New Brunswick, where she tried rationing her daughter to two drinks before dinner. After two whopping gin and tonics, Kate would anxiously wait and wait for her mother to retire for the night—but Rhoda would *not* retire, and thus Kate finally realized she needed help. One morning she phoned one of Charlie's old AA friends, who advised her to go to High Watch Farm in Connecticut. She ended up staying three months; her last drink was on May 13, 1972. And since? For the most part Kate has attained a kind of steady contentment that eluded her father. In 1993 she reconnected with a childhood friend from her Newtown days, John Hallock, and the two eventually married. A piquant coincidence: John's father was a graphic designer whose work included—a few years before any Hallocks had met any Jacksons—the original jacket art for *The Outer Edges*, a Miro-esque arrangement of interconnecting lines.

It might have served better as the jacket art for *What Happened*, given the author's thematic concern with the curious serendipity of life amid seeming chaos—chaos that might be revealed as crystalline order, if seen from a great height . . . though it's our common lot to stay grounded and hope for the best. "This is a note in case anything goes wrong," Charlie

had written Rhoda, Sarah, and Kate on September 29, 1962, just prior to
his lobectomy and rib resection at Middlesex Hospital.

> I want you all to know, and remember, that not only have I always
> loved you, but that I always will love you, wherever I am or you
> are. . . .
>
> In many ways my life has been a failure. I never husbanded my
> luck, I didn't guard and protect my talent, I let things slide, I hadn't
> the least thought ever of discipline or self-preservation; but that was
> because I was ill in another way, alcoholically, and so many years
> not myself. But in one way, and I think the only important way, I
> have been *anything but* a failure, and that is in you two children, my
> dear Sarah and Kate. There is no man I know luckier than I am in
> my children, and believe me, this is a great thing to have got out of
> life, and I guess, really, the only worthwhile thing, the only thing
> that counts. My gratitude to you both for this, and to your Mother,
> and all my love, always and always.
>
> Papa

Acknowledgments

I came to this book in a rather crabwise fashion. For several years my life was consumed with work on two big literary biographies—Richard Yates and John Cheever—and I'd hoped to write something a little quirkier this time. My first thought was a book along the lines of Strachey's *Portraits in Miniature:* in my case, a collection of profiles about promising but forgotten writers. I was piqued by examples of these (Calvin Kentfield, Nathan Asch, Flannery Lewis, to name a few) that I'd encountered in the course of my research on Yates and Cheever, and thought it might be fun to examine why it is, sometimes, that talent is not enough. Some writers burn out, some have bigger demons, and sometimes life just goes ineffably awry. But what, in each case, is the *process* whereby a good and even prolific writer achieves all but total oblivion?

I considered Charles Jackson for my roster of literary losers, but he didn't quite fit: after all, he'd been rather famous for a time, and *The Lost Weekend* would always be famous as a classic movie based on a vastly (and unfairly) lesser-known novel—a novel I happened to love. Ever since college I'd had a much-thumbed copy of the *Time* Reading Program edition, and while considering my latest project I took a moment to reread that heartening "Editors' Preface" about how Jackson had become, as of 1963, chairman of the New Brunswick AA. This, I thought, had the makings of a nice redemptive fable. Then I did a Google search and discovered that Jackson had killed himself at the Hotel Chelsea—a mere five years after that vaunted chairmanship!

Until three or four years ago, the online finding aid for the Charles R. Jackson Papers at Dartmouth indicated only two boxes: one containing drafts of *The Lost Weekend*, the other some three hundred pages of letters from Charlie and Rhoda to Boom. I ordered copies of the latter, which certainly attested to the autobiographical nature of *The Lost Weekend*. Given that Boom (like the solicitous Wick in the novel) was forever cleaning up after his brother's messes, their relationship seemed to have become strained in later years, and the letters taper off in the late 1950s—right around the time

Jackson stopped drinking *and* writing fiction. What, I wondered, happened next? How did he go from being a celebrated AA spokesman (a recording of his 1959 talk to the Cleveland AA is available online) to an uncloseted, pill-popping suicide at the Chelsea?

I got in touch with Jackson's daughters, who remembered very little of their father's dark side. "People are always saying, 'Oh my God, your father was *Charles Jackson?*' " Sarah told me. " 'Do *you* have a story!' Well, in fact, Papa had a story, but he did his best to shield us from his demons and just be a loving father." Willing to cooperate (albeit not without qualms at first) in a venture that might help restore their father's literary reputation, both Sarah and Kate submitted to interviews and also sent me every pertinent document they could find, including letters their father had written them during their college years in the late '50s and early '60s. And here indeed was a different side of Charles Jackson—the man described by Dorothea Straus as a "warm, proud father [and] companionable husband"—and of course I was more intrigued than ever. Again: what had led this admirable man to the Chelsea and Stanley Zednik (not to mention the 1967 best-seller lists)? When I gave some hint of my puzzlement, Kate Jackson asked if I'd seen her father's papers at Dartmouth, and I mentioned the one box of letters to Boom. "Oh no," she said, "there are at least twenty boxes!"—that is, the *bulk* of her father's papers, which she and Sarah hadn't actually relinquished until 2002.

I got in touch with Eric Esau, the superb Dartmouth librarian who'd once alerted me to a crucial, undiscovered cache of letters from the young John Cheever to Reuel Denney. Eric promptly disinterred the twenty boxes of uncatalogued Jackson papers from the library basement—where they might have languished forever—and presently I received a rough inventory of their contents from Kate. Awaiting my perusal, it seemed, were parts of Jackson's vast unfinished "Birnam saga," *Farther and Wilder*, piles of other unpublished manuscripts, diaries, photographs, and hundreds of letters between Jackson and his family, friends, fellow writers, and various movie stars. Given the prospect of mining this mother lode, I tabled my little book of literary profiles and decided to propose a full-length biography of Jackson.

It's been a delightful project from beginning to end, and for that I have many people to thank—above all (obviously) Jackson's daughters, Sarah and Kate. No matter how grinding or unseemly my curiosity, they responded with the same judicious courtesy, and often went beyond what even I consider the call of duty. After I'd almost despaired of the Kafkaesque process of prying sixty-year-old medical records out of the former Mary Hitchcock Hospital in Hanover—Charles Jackson's "favorite little hospital" for drying out—Sarah persevered, until the amazing day when she mailed me the whole fat packet. As for Kate, her early trip to the Rauner library on behalf of this project was indicative: for many months, when I most needed help, she sent me a steady stream of e-mails—stray memories, people to contact, helpful details, and leads of every conceivable kind. And both women fed me lavishly in their homes—Sarah's on the Upper East Side, Kate's in western Connecticut—even while I badgered them with my incessant questions. Throughout I was deeply moved, and remain so, by how tenderly they remember their father; he was right to consider himself *"anything but* a failure" in that particular respect.

I spent a very fruitful afternoon in the front parlor of Herb Jackson's old house at 241 Prospect Street, Newark, where his grandson Michael Kraham now lives with his family. Michael could hardly have been more friendly and forthcoming—a repository of family lore, as was the house itself: one of Boom's braided rugs is on the floor, one of his cut-paper lambs (such as Charlie gave Judy Garland for Christmas in 1944) is over the fireplace, and of course in the backyard is the barn where Michael's grandfather spent much of his adult life as a boozy recluse. I also had a number of delightful conversations with Herb's oldest daughter, Sally Wilson, who shed priceless light on the peculiar Arcadian ethos that her uncle Charlie evoked in his fiction.

My research would have taken twice as long, and been half as enjoyable, without the help of Eric Esau at Dartmouth. Without going into tedious detail, suffice it to say that most people would have charged a retainer for what he did out of the goodness of his heart. Best of all he became a friend, and the sweetness of his company was the highlight of my trips to New Hampshire—the time we visited Six Chimney Farm, for instance, and were graciously entertained by the present owners, Allen and Bonnie Reid Martin, whom I hope to see again soon. I also owe a special debt of gratitude to Professor John W. Crowley at the University of Alabama, one of the most gracious academics I've ever had the pleasure to know: not only did he present me (as a permanent gift!) with his collection of Jackson first editions and paperbacks, but he also wrote me a number of long, helpful e-mails and shared his excellent scholarship (both published and non-) on Jackson's work. And without the help of Rae Lindsay I could scarcely have written the last chapter of this book, key portions of which are based on an unpublished memoir by her late husband, Alex, which she managed to find in a cobwebby pocket of her attic. Many thanks, too, to Carol Rosenthal of the Newark Public Library, who sent me as much Jacksoniana as she could lay her hands on (her son had portrayed the novelist in the local Cemetery Walk). Carol also arranged for me to be given a guided tour of Newark by the amiable Mary Elizabeth Smith, of the Newark-Arcadia Historical Society, whose knowledge of certain rumors about the Jackson family reminded me yet again that, as Charlie liked to say, "In a small town it's practically impossible not to know practically everything about practically everybody else." Julia Fifield—the grande dame of Orford, age 106 and still voting (Republican) as of this writing—would certainly agree, and I thank her for chatting with me and letting me see the marvelous diaries of her stepfather, Ned Warren, who took such a keen interest in the everyday lives of his neighbors ("Jacksons lighted up tonight").

The following people sent letters, photographs, and/or other helpful material, and in some cases also submitted to interviews: Steven M. L. Aronson, Gloria Ayvazian, Pepa Ferrer Devan, Thillman Fabry, Gregory George, Pat Hammond, Haidee Becker Kenedy, Richard Lamparski, Harold and Elsie Quance, Alexandra Piper Seed, Alice Schwedock Small, Laura Straus, and Principal Kevin Whitaker of Newark High School.

A number of others also granted interviews or else provided written reminiscences: Michael Baden, M.D., David Bain, Stanley Bard, A. Scott Berg, Andrew Besch, Alexandra Mayes Birnbaum, Nancy Bloomer, Robert S. Bloomer, Tom Bloomer, Kerry Boeye, Paul Bogart, Bruce Bohrmann, Ben Bradlee, Carl Brandt, Jr., Philip Brickner, M.D., Bill Brock, John Brock, Ann Montgomery Brower, Brock Brower, Gilbert Burgess, Joseph Caldwell, David Chanler, Gerald Clarke, John Connolly, Norman Corwin, Ann Davis, Seymour Epstein, Gene Farley, Mikey Gilbert, William A. Graham, Ann Green, A. R. Gurney, Geoffrey Hendricks, Stan Herman, Roberta Richmond Jenkins, Stephen Jones, Jeannie McLane Jones, Arthur Laurents, Richard Mallary, Robert Markel, Edward Pomerantz, Elizabeth Reid, Hilda Richmond, Robert Richmond, Ned Rorem, Edwin Safford, Diane Rowand Simons, Ron Sproat, Roger W. Straus III, Barbara Peech Streeter, Grace Streeter, William Toomey, John Weston, Alexandra Whitelock, and Margot Wilkie.

Many librarians and other nice people helped with my research, and I'm afraid this is a very incomplete list: Kathy Kienholz (American Academy of Arts and Letters); Charis Emily Shafer (Butler Library, Columbia); Erika Gorder (Douglass College, Rutgers); Lynn Eaton (Duke University); Rebecca Fawcett (Hood Museum, Dartmouth); Marcel LaFlamme (Independence Community College); Craig S. Simpson (Kent State University); Lia Apodaca (Library of Congress); Mark Genszler and Sally Andrews (Marlboro College); Laura Ruttum (New York Public Library); Laura Dodson and Mary Anne Vandivort (Norfolk Public Library); Sandra Stelts (Penn State Libraries); Charles E. Greene and AnnaLee Pauls (Princeton University Library); Jean Cannon (Harry Ransom Humanities Research Center); Nicolette A. Dobrowolski, Kyle C. Harris, and Mary O'Brien (Syracuse University Library); Todd Vradenburg (Will Rogers Institute); Karen Miller and Nancy Wagner (Wilmette Public Library); Nelson Aldrich, Nick Anthonisen, Jerry Rosco, and Ralph Voss.

That a great publisher is still willing to subsidize books about obscure but deserving authors is reassuring to say the least, and my editor at Knopf, Deborah Garrison, is the embodiment of this spirit. Again, too, I thank Deb's wonderful assistant, Caroline Zancan, who always returns my e-mails with cheerful efficiency. And I would be lost *and* broke without the services of my lovable, enterprising agent, David McCormick. This book is dedicated to my best friend, Michael Ruhlman, without whom it probably wouldn't have been written for any number of reasons too complicated to go into; I owe *much* to this good man, period. And finally, as ever, my usual tearful gratitude to my wife, Mary, and our sweet daughter, Amelia.

Notes

Most of Jackson's letters and manuscripts are at the Rauner Special Collections Library, Dartmouth; unless otherwise noted, his unpublished work may be found in this collection. To the extent that an obsessive person is capable, I've tried to curtail citational clutter. Interview subjects are cited initially, and thereafter only when needed for the sake of clarity; when a source (of any kind) is explicitly given in the text, or glaringly obvious, I omit further citation below. Letters are cited in almost every case, unless three aspects of provenance are sufficiently established in the text: *who* was writing to *whom*, and *when* (the last is trickiest, of course—how much temporal context is enough: a week? a month? a season?). Jackson's published fiction is only cited when its contents are quoted for their biographical (as opposed to critical) interest.

The following abbreviations appear in these notes:

Academy	American Academy of Arts and Letters
BB	Bernice Baumgarten (CJ's agent)
BW	Bronson Winthrop
CBJ	Cecilia Bolles "Bob" Jackson (CJ's sister-in-law)
CJ	Charles Jackson
CJ/AA-59	CJ's address to Cleveland AA, circa May 1959; posted at http://www.xa-speakers.org/pafiledb.php?action=file&id=1797
CUCOHC	Columbia University Center for Oral History Collection
D-HH	Dartmouth-Hitchcock Hospital (formerly Mary Hitchcock)
DS	Dorothea Straus
DS-*Paper*	Straus, Dorothea. *Paper Trail: A Recollection of Writers.* Wakefield, RI: Moyer Bell, 1997.
DS-*Show*	Straus, Dorothea. *Showcases.* Boston: Houghton Mifflin Company, 1974.
Duke	David M. Rubenstein Rare Book and Manuscript Library, Duke University
EC	*Earthly Creatures.* New York: Farrar, Straus & Young, 1953.

FSJ   Frederick Storrier Jackson (CJ's younger brother)
FV   *The Fall of Valor.* New York: Rinehart & Company, 1946.
F&W   *Farther and Wilder,* unpublished ms., Rauner.
HFG   *Home for Good,* unpublished ms., Rauner.
HJ   Herb Jackson (CJ's older brother)
JFC   Jackson Family Collection
KFC   Kraham Family Collection
KSU   Kent State University Library
KWJ   Kate Winthrop Jackson (CJ's younger daughter)
LN   Barnett, Lincoln. *The Lost Novelist.* New York: Rinehart & Company, 1948. Unpaginated promotional brochure.
LW   *The Lost Weekend.* New York: Farrar & Rinehart, 1944.
OE   *The Outer Edges.* New York: Rinehart & Company, 1948.
Princeton   Princeton University Library Manuscripts Division
PSU   Penn State University Libraries
Ransom   Harry Ransom Humanities Research Center, University of Texas
Rauner   Rauner Special Collections Library, Dartmouth College
RBJ   Rhoda Booth Jackson (CJ's wife)
RS   Roger W. Straus, Jr.
SHL   *A Second-Hand Life.* New York: The Macmillan Company, 1967.
SJP   Sarah Jackson Piper (CJ's older daughter)
SS   *The Sunnier Side: Twelve Arcadian Tales.* New York: Farrar, Straus & Company, 1950.
SWJ   Sarah Williams Jackson (CJ's mother)
Syracuse   Syracuse University Library
Vassar   Archives and Special Collections Library, Vassar College

Prologue

3   "Charles Jackson has made": Philip Wylie, "Wingding," *New York Times Book Review,* Jan. 30, 1944, 7.

4   "Not only did I know": "Production Notes," Turner Classic Movies DVD edition of *The Lost Weekend.*

4   "a bright, erratic problem child": Ray Milland, *Wide-Eyed in Babylon* (New York: William Morrow & Co., 1974), 218.

4   "Jackson was eyed somewhat in the manner": *LN.*

4   "One third of the history": "Editors' Preface," Time Reading Program Special Edition of *The Lost Weekend* (New York: Time Inc., 1963), x.

4   "I have become so used to having people say": *SS,* 37.

5   "exerted a profound influence on the field": Selden D. Bacon, "Introduction," Time Reading Program Special Edition of *The Lost Weekend* (New York: Time Inc., 1963), xv.

5   "If he does not find escape or evasion": "Editors' Preface," ibid., xiii.

5   "like a sandpiper's beak": DS-*Show,* 77.

5   "His prim appearance contradicted": DS-*Paper,* 95.

5   "a massive Don Birnam saga": *LN.*

6   "Malcolm Lowry as novelist was fortunate": CJ, "We Were Led to Hope for More," *New York Times Book Review,* Dec. 12, 1965, 20.

Chapter One • ET IN ARCADIA EGO

7 Malbie had "probably" suffered fatal injuries: "Two High School Pupils Killed," *New York Times*, Nov. 13, 1916.

7 "one of the most beautiful young ladies": "Three Killed in Fatal Automobile Accident," *Newark Union-Gazette*, Nov. 18, 1916, 1.

9 "Where the globe stops": CJ to Samuel Taylor, May 23, 1952, Rauner.

9 "A minister's son": "The Dreamer," *Newark Courier*, Nov. 15, 1923, 4.

9 "the car was completely smashed": *F&W*.

9 "No, no, there's nothing *wrong*—": Ibid.

10 "a good ten thousand at least": Ibid.

10 "trivial, vain man": *EC*, 108.

10 "nostrils distended": *F&W*.

10 "You even blow your nose like your father!": Ibid.

10 "Papa was proud": Ibid.

11 "At school Jackson stood invariably": *LN*.

11 "THE STORY OF STRONGHEART": *SS*, 88.

12 "My uncle is an Indian": CJ to Howard and Dorothy Lindsay, April 17, 1944, Rauner.

12 "He pretended not to recognize": CJ to FSJ, April 17, 1944, Rauner.

12 "These, then, were the things which occupied": *SS*, 89.

12 "I'm just a fan": *HFG*.

12 "Can you do this sort of thing": *Information, Please!*, Jan. 7, 1946, broadcast, JFC.

13 "whoever it was . . . 'Acres of Diamonds' ": CJ to Mary McCarthy, July 22, 1945, Rauner.

13 "a band of gypsies": *EC*, 89.

14 "Must have been a shotgun wedding": FSJ to CBJ, Feb. 23, 1968, KFC.

14 "Your grandfather Herbert Williams [Jr.]": "B. W. F." to CBJ, Feb. 14, 1967, KFC.

14 "a big sweaty man": *F&W*.

14 "very religious, frugal people": Quoted in a family genealogy written by CBJ, JFC.

14 "Next to the mahogany music cabinet": CJ, *Three Flowers*, unpublished ms., Rauner.

15 "That American Girl!": CBJ's genealogy, JFC.

16 "the glow of many cigars": CJ to Samuel Taylor, May 23, 1952, Rauner.

17 "Don't tell *me* . . . no social distinctions": CJ to Carl Brandt and Robert Markel, June 22, 1964, Rauner.

17 "the very middle of the middle class": CJ to Samuel Taylor, May 23, 1952, Rauner.

18 "I nearly always managed": *SS*, 146.

19 "He was a dear little boy, Rhoda": Kate H. Bloomer to RJ and CJ, May 20, 1940, JFC.

18 scouts "would marvel at his courage": *LW*, 200.

18 "Tonio! spiritual brother!": Ibid., 19.

18 "how did you happen . . . *writer?*": CJ, "The Sleeping Brain," unpublished ms., Rauner.

19 "He was always viewed . . . flaky": Author int. Tom Bloomer, May 15, 2009.

19 "This afternoon I went up": CJ to Walter Hallagan, Dec. 17, 1918, JFC.

19 "The tragedy of homosexuals": Richard Lamparski, unpublished ms., courtesy of the author.

19 "he constantly creates with this local area": Don Casilio, "Author of Lost Weekend Works on 3-Volume Novel," *Newark Courier-Gazette*, April 12, 1956, C1.

20 well-advised not to "pursue identifications": author int. Kerry Boeye, March 4, 2009.

20 "I am sure people still": Kerry Boeye, "Charles R. Jackson" (essay written for the Hoffman Foundation Wayne County History Scholarship), Newark-Arcadia Historical Society.

20 "In a small town it's practically impossible": *SS*, 56.

20 "It is a real pleasure": Luceine Heniore to CJ, June 25, 1949, Rauner.

20 "I did, indeed, thank my lucky stars": Luceine Heniore to CJ, March 26, 1950, Rauner.

20 "the first family of Newark": Carole Nary and John Zornow, "Newark's 1928 Murder Mystery," *Newark Courier-Gazette*, March 28, 2003.

22 "I'm *not* Thelma": Author int. Sally Jackson Wilson, June 29, 2009.

23 "Dad was there all the time": CJ to Walter Hallagan, Dec. 17, 1918, JFC.

23 "the mistake of her life": CBJ's genealogy, JFC.

23 "Well, you see, I never knew my father": CJ to Mary McCarthy, July 31, 1952, Vassar.

24 "I wouldn't have dreamed": CJ to FSJ, Aug. 22, 1952, Rauner.

24 "a disease of emotional immaturity": Quoted in Jim Bishop, *The Glass Crutch: The Biographical Novel of William Wynne Wister* (Garden City, NY: Doubleday, Doran & Co., Inc., 1945), 229.

24 "It is my belief that alcoholism": CJ, "What's So Funny about a Drunk?," *Cosmopolitan*, May 1946, 136.

24 "a creature of sighs and bewilderment": CJ, *Simple Simon: A Play in Three Acts*, unpublished ms., Rauner.

24 "an Ibsenesque study": CJ to Howard and Dorothy Lindsay, April 17, 1944, Rauner.

25 "Do you remember the Presbyterian Church": J. R. Elliott to CJ, April 2, 1950, Rauner.

25 "Also something about Homo Sexual": SWJ to CJ, Oct. 15, 1942, Rauner.

26 "To succeed you've got to get out": "Newark's Child Prodigy of Yester Year Remembers Triumph as Church Organist" (newspaper article, c. 1937, hand-transcribed for author by Elsie Quance, wife of Herbert Quance's grand-nephew, Harold).

26 "I never heard the term [pedophile]": Author int. Harold Quance, Dec. 29, 2009.

26 " 'Pretend it isn't so' ": *SS*, 30.

27 "I had been writing all my life": CJ to DS, June 6, 1951, Rauner.

Chapter Two • SIMPLE SIMON

29 three-story, redbrick "firetrap": CJ to Samuel Taylor, May 23, 1952, Rauner.

29 "You are just the way I was": CJ to KWJ, Feb. 5, 1954, JFC.

30 a "dreadful fiasco": CJ to Samuel Taylor, May 30, 1952, Rauner.
30 "honor and credit" to the school: CJ, "The Last Time," unpublished ms., Rauner.
30 "to general hilarity": *F&W.*
30 "When I'd finish a poem": Harvey Breit, "Talk with Charles Jackson," *New York Times Book Review*, April 30, 1950, 19.
31 "first thing tomorrow morning": *LN.*
31 "She was a natural actress": Author int. Gene Farley, Dec. 1, 2009.
31 "A God, a God their severance ruled!": Marion Fleck to CJ (c. July 1953), Rauner.
32 "anathema to social life in Arcadia": CJ ms. fragment (probably *Simple Simon*, the novel), Rauner.
32 "She was the companion": CJ, "A Red-Letter Day" (published in slightly different form as "An Innocent Love Affair" in *Today's Woman*, March 1951), Rauner.
33 "A couple of large mattresses": CJ, "School Notes," *Newark Courier*, Oct. 16, 1919.
33 a "second home" even: *SS*, 246.
34 "The six-ten trolley speaks the close": CJ, "Elegy Written in Newark Churchyard," *Newark Courier*, July 27, 1922, 1.
34 "high-brow": *SS*, 252.
34 "I was always very fond of Allyn": CJ to "Adelaide," June 19, 1947, Rauner.
34 the figure of Justice's "big buzooms": CJ, "Don't Call Me Sonny," *Esquire*, July 1953, 42.
34 exhorted graduates "to keep themselves clean": "Newark HS Graduates Twenty-Five—Hon. Charles G. Jordan Principal Speaker," *Newark Courier*, June 13, 1921, 1.
35 Firemen's Picnic a "Howling Success": Ibid., Aug. 18, 1921, 1.
35 "The girl, reformed, wins the hand": Ibid., Nov. 15, 1923, 5.
36 "with just a shade of swaggering": CJ, *Simple Simon: A Play in Three Acts*, unpublished ms., Rauner.
36 "Where have I been today?": CJ, "The Wind," *The Phoenix*, Nov. 1922, 32, Syracuse.
37 "The Rubaiyat of Why-I-Am": Ibid., Jan. 1923, 15.
37 "the vogue for masculine nick-names": Ibid., Feb. 1923, 7.
37 "A Book of Curses": Ibid., April 1923, 13.
37 "And here he is . . . Can you beat it?!!?!!?!!?!!": CJ to Marion Fleck (c. early Dec. 1922), Rauner.
38 "Gee, I'm thrilled to tears!": Marion Fleck to Betty Colclough (c. Dec. 1922), Rauner.
38 "continually rested, with keen enjoyment": *Native Moment*, unpublished ms., Rauner.
41 "shocks, humiliations, accidents, failures": Richard R. Peabody, *The Common Sense of Drinking* (Boston: Little, Brown & Co., 1931), 62.
42 "busted out of Syracuse": Author int. Michael Kraham, March 13, 2010.
42 "is to the local theatregoer": *Newark Courier*, Sept. 27, 1923, 1.
42 "She is never to escape": CJ, *Simple Simon: A Play in Three Acts*, unpublished ms., Rauner.
43 "as leading a very gay and glamorous life": Marion Fabry to CJ (c. Summer 1938), Rauner.

44 "I like [the wife] so much better": Marion Fabry to CJ (c. March 1939), Rauner.
44 "It's a wonderful picture": Marion Fabry to CJ (c. late Oct. 1944), Rauner.
44 "how beautifully you write": CJ to Marion Fabry, Nov. 3, 1944, Rauner.
44 "Look, your paintings": Author int. Gene Farley, Dec. 1, 2009.
44 passing into "abler hands": *Newark Courier*, May 1, 1924, 1.
45 "The time has come, the walrus said": Quoted in *Newark Courier*, May 8, 1924, 1.
47 "Horrific (and lousy)": CJ, "JAXON" notebook, Rauner.
48 share this "little-known book": CJ, "Callow Comments," *Newark Courier*, Dec. 4, 1924, 4.
48 getting "into serious trouble thereby": CJ to DS, July 14, 1953, Rauner.
49 "Hey! What do you think": CJ to FSJ, Oct. 16, 1940, Rauner.

Chapter Three • SOME SECRET SORROW

50 "everybody knew him and had always known him": *LW*, 49.
50 "perfectly wonderful" birthday: SWJ to FSJ, April 1, 1925, Rauner.
50 "in charge of the French department": CJ to T. S. Matthews, June 21, 1940, Rauner.
50 "the initial source of his great knowledge": RBJ to Shirley Hood, June 21, 1969, Rauner.
50 "he's a crotchety old bastard": CJ to Ted Amussen, July 17, 1945, Rauner.
51 "sampling such Bohemian diversions": *LN*.
51 fallen in with a group of "fairies": Author int. Kerry Boeye, March 4, 2009.
52 "Don't be afraid to be happy": CJ to DS, Nov. 24, 1953, Rauner.
52 "The slogan to solicit subscriptions": CJ to Maurice Friedman, Aug. 5, 1964, Rauner.
53 "compulsive excursions": CJ, "An Afternoon with Boris," *Serif* 10, no. 3 (1973), 8.
55 "[Thor] feels very sad": BW to CJ, Nov. 20, 1930, Rauner.
55 Jackson "crashed her table": CJ to Norma Chambers, Oct. 30, 1944, Rauner.
55 "wrapt up in . . . the Bohemian life": CJ, *The Royalist*, unpublished ms., Rauner.
56 Stimson referred to his friend . . . Exquisite: Godfrey Hodgson, *The Colonel: The Life and Wars of Henry Stimson* (New York: Alfred A. Knopf, 1990), 54.
57 an expert on "the scandals and mysteries": Quoted in David McCullough, *Mornings on Horseback* (New York: Simon & Schuster, 1982), 69.
57 "easily entangled in worldly trifles": Edith Wharton, *A Backward Glance* (New York and London: D. Appleton-Century Co., 1934), 96.
57 "Was Lady Macbeth a mother?": CJ, *Uncle Mr. Kember* (alternative version of *The Royalist*), unpublished ms., Rauner.
58 "All through the Twenty's Mr. Winthrop": CJ to KWJ, June 30, 1964, JFC.
58 "It is pretty grand in its simplicity": BW to CJ, Dec. 15, 1930, Rauner.
58 "fairly throttled [him]": BW to CJ, n.d. (c. early 1931?), Rauner.
58 "truly magical charm": *F&W*.
59 "very artistic bars" in the Village: CJ, *The Royalist*, Rauner.
59 "There's nobody in the entire US": CJ to FSJ, Sept. 15, 1949, Rauner.
60 "So far as I remember": RBJ to Shirley Hood, June 21, 1969, Rauner.

61 "rais[ing] three mouthfuls of blood": Dr. John J. Lloyd, "Resume of History of Mr. Charles Jackson," June 24, 1938, Rauner.
61 "in the heart of the White Deer Mountains": CJ, *The Royalist*, Rauner.
61 "Remember the night the three of us": Harry P. Bodley to CJ, Jan. 2 [1944], Rauner.
62 "I didn't tell her this last part": CJ to RBJ, May 22, 1944, Rauner.
62 "She was an ideal researcher": Bernard A. Drabeck and Helen E. Ellis, ed., *Archibald MacLeish: Reflections* (Amherst: University of Massachusetts Press, 1986), 80.
62 "a remarkably interesting woman": CJ to Bennett Cerf, Jan. 19, 1946, Rauner.
62 they seemed "totally unrelated": DS-*Show*, 78.
62 "their children often spoke of a gray-and-white number": *F&W*.
62 "the finest woman [he] ever knew": Max Wylie, "Charles Reginald Jackson," *Serif* 10, no. 3 (1973), 30.
63 showering the two with "fantastic gifts": CJ, *The Royalist*, Rauner.
63 "Come for him in the night": CJ, "JAXON" notebook, Rauner.
64 "I kept a notebook on it": Rochelle Girson, "TB Made a Writer of Jackson," *Tucson Daily Citizen*, Oct. 18, 1953, 26.
64 deemed "highbrow" in a bad way: CJ, "Strictly Personal," in *The Stature of Thomas Mann*, ed. Charles Neider (New York: New Directions, 1947), 45.
64 "You read *Der Zauberberg*": Ibid., 46. The second part of this quote ("so *krankhaft*, so *morbide*") appears in CJ's unpublished story/memoir, "Arrival," Rauner.
64 characterized as "a kind friend": CBJ's genealogy, JFC.
64 an old reprobate had "taken a shine": Author int. Michael Kraham, March 13, 2010.

Chapter Four • MAGIC MOUNTAIN

65 "for emergencies or spending money": CJ, *Uncle Mr. Kember*, unpublished ms., Rauner.
66 "Davos was a world to itself": CJ, "Arrival," unpublished ms., Rauner.
67 "You and Dorothy": CJ to Marion ("Tom") Holzapfel Faughner Wilson, Aug. 10, 1945, Rauner.
67 "characteristic assumption" around Davos: CJ, "Arrival," Rauner.
68 "TO MY VALENTINE": CJ, "JAXON" notebook, Rauner.
68 "like a child at a party": CJ, *Loving Offenders*, unpublished ms., Rauner.
69 "doubtless she had learned": CJ, "Ping-Pong," unpublished ms., Rauner.
69 "ardent supporters of Hitler": CJ to Marion ("Tom") Holzapfel Faughner Wilson, Aug. 10, 1945, Rauner.
70 "Walt Whitman's Orchestra": CJ, "Cousin Edith," unpublished ms., Rauner.
70 "fell on each other's necks": CJ to RBJ, July 18, 1944, Rauner.
70 "I can't *look* at another drink!": Author int. Barbara Peech Streeter, June 21, 2009.
70 " 'Why do you only come to bed": *LW*, 186.
71 "You are like a plant of slow growth": CJ to KWJ, June 30, 1964, JFC. Also quoted in *LW*, 203.

71 his condition was "excellent": Dr. John J. Lloyd, "Resume of History of Mr. Charles Jackson," June 24, 1938, Rauner.

71 urged him to be "sensible just once": BW to CJ, Dec. 15, 1930, Rauner.

71 "Tired and ill" by the time: CJ to DS (c. July 1951), Rauner.

71 "It is most distressing": BW to CJ, Dec. 15, 1930, Rauner.

71 "it was his nature": CJ, *Uncle Mr. Kember,* unpublished ms., Rauner.

72 Jackson described him as "rugged, athletic": CJ to KWJ, June 30, 1964, JFC.

72 "A thrilling afternoon": CJ, "JAXON" notebook, Rauner.

72 "blended into one prodigious note": *EC,* 146.

73 "Alcohol had a place": Forrest Glen Robinson, *Love's Story Told: A Life of Henry A. Murray* (Cambridge, MA: Harvard University Press, 1992), 192.

73 "there was a barrier of ignorance": CJ to KWJ, June 30, 1964, JFC.

73 "My life as a pedagogue is ended": Transcribed in CJ's "JAXON" notebook, Rauner.

73 "I should think that life in Russia": BW to CJ (c. Feb. 1931), Rauner.

74 "I am afraid that what you have often": BW to CJ, March 23, 1931, Rauner.

74 "Everything has been worth while": BW to CJ (c. May 1931), Rauner.

75 Rhoda would later . . . "feverishly": RBJ to Shirley Hood, June 21, 1969, Rauner.

76 took a job as a feeder in a jigsaw factory: Anne Rothe, ed., *Current Biography 1944* (New York: H. W. Wilson, 1945), 325.

76 "Just when Eaton needed a tight rein": Claire Douglas, *Translate This Darkness: The Life of Christiana Morgan, the Veiled Woman in Jung's Circle* (New York: Simon & Schuster, 1993), 209.

77 "It is our misfortune that frequently": "Ralph Monroe Eaton," *Harvard Crimson,* April 16, 1932.

77 "This seems to me—this kind of thing": CJ to FSJ, July 1, 1953, Rauner.

77 "From the hot hell of life": Transcribed in CJ's "JAXON" notebook, Rauner.

Chapter Five • A DISEASE OF THE NIGHT

78 Charlie "liked the whole *idea*": Reminiscences of Roger W. Straus, Jr., Jan. 11, 1978, on page 596, CUCOHC.

79 "Confirmed drunk—(myself)": CJ, "JAXON" notebook, Rauner.

79 "an egomaniac with an inferiority complex": John W. Crowley, *Drunkard's Rigadoon: A Study of Charles Jackson,* unpublished ms., courtesy of author.

80 Alcoholics "are self-important": CJ, "The More Social Disease," unpublished ms., Rauner.

80 "the only paradise . . . never thrown out": CJ, *Arcadia USA,* unpublished screen treatment, Rauner.

81 "I do not for a second . . . 'excuse' Fitzgerald": CJ to family, June 10, 1964, JFC.

82 "deliberately prophetic": CJ to RBJ, Jan. 7, 1966, Rauner.

82 "How much will you sell the plates": Matthew J. Bruccoli, ed., *F. Scott Fitzgerald: A Life in Letters* (New York: Scribner, 1994), 474.

82 Jackson found the manuscript "truly wonderful": CJ to BB, Nov. 16, 1949, Rauner.

82 "Well, we met—": CJ to Charles Brackett, July 12, 1945, Rauner.

83 "[Jackson and I] talked of Scott": Sheilah Graham, *The Rest of the Story* (New York: Coward-McCann, 1964), 215.

83 He "lacked prudence": Quoted in CJ, "The Critics and Fitzgerald," *New York Times Book Review*, April 29, 1951, 3.

83 "nightmare weeks": CJ to Harry Kemp, Oct. 19, 1945, Rauner.

84 "Remember . . . the applejack closet?": CJ to Thorborg Ellison, Sept. 17, 1943, Rauner.

85 "was absolute perfection in every detail": CJ to Henry Ginsberg, Jan. 21, 1946, Rauner.

86 "Send me some money at once": CJ to FSJ, April 23, 1936, Rauner.

86 "my favorite joint": CJ to Ross Evans, June 23, 1944, Rauner.

86 a scene "written directly . . . experience": CJ to RBJ, Jan. 7, 1966, Rauner.

86 "thoroughly competent cast": Quoted in Frank Rich, "Tomorrow's Monday," *New York Times*, Oct. 21, 1985.

87 "I thought they were all gay": Author int. Margot Wilkie, Jan. 16, 2010.

87 "I began as leading man": John Becker to Jerome Hill, May 17, 1935, Minnesota Historical Society Library.

88 "At considerable expense I went": CJ, "The More Social Disease," Rauner.

89 "He could almost gauge the length": *LW*, 53.

89 "fancy psycho-analytical labels": CJ to William W. Wister, Dec. 19, 1936, Rauner.

90 "Childish he was, but not that childish": *LW*, 55.

90 "Dear [Paul]—Look what I found": CJ to ["Paul Spofford"], Oct. 3, 1937, Rauner.

91 "Homosexuality is assuredly no advantage": Quoted in Laura Z. Hobson, *Laura Z.—A Life: Years of Fulfillment* (New York: Donald I. Fine, 1986), 285.

92 "By my lack of generosity": CJ to John Becker, Jan. 22, 1944, Rauner.

93 "I could write a book . . . fraternity": CJ to BB, June 23, 1943, Rauner.

94 "so wise, so witty, so good-humoured": CJ to FSJ (c. Feb. 1936), Rauner.

95 "[*Native Moment*] has received more than the usual attention": Alan C. Collins to CJ, Dec. 23, 1936, Rauner.

96 "if not the week and the month": CJ, "The More Social Disease," Rauner.

96 he'd been there "twice as a patient": CJ to James van Tour, Nov. 9, 1942, Rauner.

96 "like butter rum Life Savers": Author int. SJP and KWJ, Sept. 10, 2008.

96 responded with "perfect lucidity": *LN*.

96 "Did you know that Nancy": CJ to SWJ, April 22 (1936), Rauner.

97 his days as an "incurable inebriate": Quoted in CJ to Stanley Rinehart and BB, Dec. 3, 1945, Rauner.

98 "absolutely untrue in every aspect": Irving Hoffman, "Tales of Hoffman," *Hollywood Reporter*, Jan. 28, 1946, 3.

98 "I have found it hard to write": Lewis Titterton to CJ, May 6, 1936, Rauner.

98 "It was the week of the Gideon [*sic*]": Leonard Lyons, "The Lyons Den" (syndicated column), Sept. 25, 1968.

98 "For years Charlie was here": RBJ to FSJ (c. April 27, 1936), Rauner.

99 "I would sing you a clever song": CJ, "JAXON" notebook, Rauner.

99 "they lost everything in Scotland": RBJ to FSJ (c. late Jan. 1953), Rauner.

99 "in a perverse and childish way": CJ, "The More Social Disease," Rauner.

100 "prevented by his habit": Richard Peabody, *The Common Sense of Drinking* (Boston: Little, Brown & Co., 1931), 67.

101 "Gary Cooper . . . Jean Arthur so much": CJ to FSJ, April 30 (1936), Rauner.

101 "I didn't want to live this way": CJ/AA-59.

101 "That's the last drink I'll ever take": *LN*.

Chapter Six • SWEET RIVER

102 "Philadelphia Main Line Wisters": Jim Bishop, *A Bishop's Confession* (Boston, Toronto: Little, Brown & Co., 1981), 185.

103 "one hundred per cent licked": Jim Bishop, *The Glass Crutch: The Biographical Novel of William Wynne Wister* (Garden City, NY: Doubleday, Doran & Co., Inc., 1945), 215.

103 appropriated by Bill Wilson: Mel Barger, *New Wine* (Center City, MN: Hazelden, 1991), 118.

103 "A fairly exhaustive inquiry": Richard Peabody, *The Common Sense of Drinking* (Boston: Little, Brown & Co., 1931), 82.

104 "He never mentioned the moral aspects": Bishop, *The Glass Crutch*, 222–23.

104 he "attended all large fires": "Richard R. Peabody; Psychologist and Writer Made Study of Drinking Habits," *New York Times*, April 27, 1936.

105 "A truly great man had left the scene": Bishop, *The Glass Crutch*, 241.

105 "Dr. Peabody . . . first authority to state": Katherine McCarthy, "The Emmanuel Movement and Richard Peabody," *Journal of Studies on Alcohol* 45, no. 1 (1984); posted at http://www.aabibliography.com/historyofaa/reco1.htm.

105 "We regard each other as two average": CJ to Wister, Dec. 19, 1936, Rauner.

106 "I consider that you are cured": Wister to CJ, Sept. 16, 1937, Rauner.

106 a "big slug psychiatrist" threatened: Wister to CJ, April 23, 1943, Rauner.

106 "neither nurse nor servant": Bishop, *The Glass Crutch*, 292.

107 "Oh well, I guess I've outgrown Bill Wister": CJ to Stephen H. Sherman, Oct. 4, 1943, Rauner.

107 "[It] was simply . . . comprehension": CJ to Wister, Jan. 29, 1945, Rauner.

107 "Mr. Jackson's unusual ability": Wister to Stanley Rinehart, n.d., Rauner.

107 "The smiler turned out to be strange": Bishop, *A Bishop's Confession*, 184.

107 "the man who cured Charles Jackson": Nila Mack to CJ, n.d., Rauner.

108 "I thought your letter": CJ to Wister, Jan. 29, 1945, Rauner.

108 "a lay witch-doctor": Wolcott Gibbs, "The Rover Boys on a Bender," *New York Times Book Review*, Nov. 18, 1945, 4.

108 "By the way," he wrote: CJ to Isabel Leighton, Feb. 14, 1946, Rauner.

108 "Alone and lonely": Jim Bishop, "Jim Bishop: Reporter" (syndicated column), Jan. 12, 1975.

109 "after a brief illness": "William Wynne Wister," *New York Times*, Jan. 5, 1947, 53.

109 "the skepticism I meet on all sides": CJ to Wister, Dec. 19, 1936, Rauner.

109 "trembling like a whippet": CJ to Max Wylie, May 11, 1945, Rauner.

109 "No, but I should have been published": Max Wylie, "Charles Reginald Jackson," *Serif* 10, no. 3 (1973), 29–30.

109 "Where have *you* been!": *LN*.

110 "Without any doubt Charles Jackson": Quoted in CJ to Wister, Sept. 28, 1941, Rauner.

111 "He had inspired that work": Author int. Norman Corwin, June 9, 2009.

111 "Do I know Norman Corwin indeed!": CJ to Leonora Schinasi, April 7, 1945, Rauner.

111 "a rare and superior person": Howard Lindsay to CJ (c. late Jan. 1953), Rauner.

111 "To this day": Nila Mack to CJ, n.d., Rauner.

111 "three-sheets to the wind": CJ to DS, March 22, 1951, Rauner.

112 "In the early years we": CJ to SJP, Aug. 2, 1964, JFC.

112 "she is one of FORTUNE magazine's": CJ to Franklin D. Roosevelt, Oct. 22, 1942, Rauner.

112 "A mother's prayers . . . answered": SWJ to CJ, Oct. 15, 1942, Rauner.

112 "it's the same excitement . . . addiction": RBJ to FSJ, July 3 (1947), Rauner.

112 "If you should write the story": CJ to "Stan [Rinehart], Bernice [BB], and Company," Feb. 27, 1948, Rauner.

113 "The irony of it!": Charles P. Weston to FSJ, April 4, 1953, Rauner.

113 "more than [she] could handle": Quoted in Eva LeRoy to FSJ, April 20, 1953, Rauner.

113 "I knew on my birthday": "Flew" to FSJ, Jan. 15, 1953, Rauner.

113 "the perversity of the Fates": CJ to SJP, Aug. 2, 1964, JFC.

113 "MY WIFE IS A GOOD WOMAN": CJ, "JAXON" notebook, Rauner.

113 "Since Charlie was gay": Author int. Ron Sproat, March 25, 2009.

113 "with sixteen tenant houses": CJ to SWJ, April 22 (1936), Rauner.

114 "My god, you can't *say* that!": CJ, "The Sleeping Brain," unpublished ms., Rauner.

114 "He saw himself . . . everyman": Mary McCarthy, *The Lost Week, or The Caged Lion*, unpublished ms., Vassar.

114 "We like your story, 'Palm Sunday' ": Dwight Macdonald to CJ, May 8, 1939, Rauner.

114 "You probably think I'm crazy": CJ to Macdonald, July 11, 1939, Rauner.

114 "Today the whole city is agog": Philip Rahv to CJ, Aug. 22, 1939, Rauner.

115 "If PALM SUNDAY by any chance": CJ to Macdonald, July 11, 1939, Rauner.

115 "If I had it then, why . . . got it now?": CJ to DS, (c. July 1951), Rauner.

115 "a deliberate troublemaker": CJ/AA-59.

115 "Used it all," he'd declare: Mary Morris, "Mary Morris Goes to See the Author of 'The Lost Weekend,' " *PM*, undated clipping (c. early 1944), Rauner.

116 "I knew," he said, "I could pick it up": Trudi McCullough, "Novel About a Drunkard Makes Alcoholics Wince," *Milwaukee Journal*, March 29, 1944, 33.

116 "rather on the dull side": CJ to Lewis Titterton, Oct. 16, 1941, Rauner.

116 "in a purely impersonal": CJ to BW, Oct. 15, 1940, Rauner.

116 "a happy moment for me": CJ to "Miss Nelson," Oct. 2, 1945, Rauner.

117 "growing reluctance to bring a child": *EC*, 77.

117 they "drove through lights": Nila Mack to CJ, May 11 (1945?), Rauner.

117 "O, then my anxious prayer": CJ, "A Sestina for Sarah," *The Conning Tower* (column by F.P.A.), *New York Post*, May 12, 1941.

117 "It was as perfect as a seashell": DS-*Show*, 79.

117 "indescribably charming to him": *F&W*.

117 "like a love-sick fool": CJ, "A Salute, A Blessing, and a Kind of Family Inventory for Alexandra," unpublished ms., JFC.

118 "[I] was sorry when the final session came": CJ to "Paul," Sept. 7, 1941, Rauner.

118 "Herman Land is a discovery": CJ to Davidson Taylor, Aug. 4, 1941, Rauner.

118 "amusing family situation": CJ to Phillips H. Lord, May 19, 1941, Rauner.

118 "Incidentally, doesn't that strike you": CJ to Sam Slate, Aug. 25, 1941, Rauner.

118 "In the history of soap opera": James Thurber, "Soapland," *The New Yorker*, June 12, 1948, 51.

119 "I kept two people on a raft": Alex Lindsay, "Charles Jackson's Long, Lost Weekend: A Personal Memoir," unpublished ms., courtesy of Rae Lindsay.

119 "the bright spot of his life": CJ to Jim and Liz Hart, July 25, 1942, Rauner.

120 "I'm getting fonder of 'Sweet River' ": CJ to Alan Wallace, Aug. 2, 1942, Rauner.

120 "I am sick unto death": CJ to Liz Hart, Aug. 25, 1942, Rauner.

120 "and drinking too much on the side": Ibid.

120 Only then—"drunk with excitement": CJ to Jim and Liz Hart, July 25, 1942, Rauner.

120 "When you know why the scripts": Wylie, "Charles Reginald Jackson," 30.

120 "We both think": Lambie Wylie to CJ, July 19, 1942, Rauner.

120 "like the spoiled child I am": CJ to Jim and Liz Hart, July 25, 1942, Rauner.

121 "[This] is understood by the author": Quoted in CJ to F. W. Dupee, July 18, 1942, Rauner.

121 "The terror is there all right": Quoted in CJ to Jim and Liz Hart, July 25, 1942, Rauner.

121 "I can see every reviewer": Ibid.

121 "a completely narcissistic character": CJ to Stephen H. Sherman, Aug. 4, 1942, Rauner.

121 "extraordinarily revealing study": Sherman to CJ, Aug. 8, 1942, Rauner.

122 "I ate it up too, read it 20 times": CJ to James Gould Cozzens, Aug. 10, 1942, Rauner.

122 "I don't see anything so wonderful": Quoted in CJ to FSJ (c. 1946?), Rauner.

122 "You said I wouldn't like . . . written" SWJ to CJ, Oct. 15, 1942, Rauner.

122 "In the long run, of course": CJ to Mary McCarthy, July 13, 1945, Vassar.

Chapter Seven • THE LOST WEEKEND

123 "Only yesterday . . . playpen": CJ to KWJ (c. Aug. 1957), JFC.

123 "probably the most talked-about": CJ to James van Tour, Nov. 9, 1942, Rauner.

123 "The only doubt in our minds": Tour to CJ, Nov. 27, 1942, Rauner.

124 "No, don't tell me anything": Quoted in CJ to BB, July 12, 1950, Rauner.

124 her verdict ("a fine job"): BB to CJ, June 22, 1943, Rauner.

124 "wouldn't mind at all the passages": CJ to BB, June 23, 1943, Rauner.

124 "I finished the manuscript": Stanley M. Rinehart to BB, Aug. 2, 1943, Rauner.

124 "*Every*body came in to meet me": CJ to RBJ, Aug. 4, 1943, Rauner.

124 "the only logical title": CJ to Rinehart, Aug. 28, 1943, Rauner.

125 "without throwing the book": Ibid.

125 "I am doing so well . . . shameful": CJ to Thorborg Ellison, Sept. 17, 1943, Rauner.

125 "Who's that sweet little man": CJ to FSJ, April 17, 1944, Rauner.

126 "on account of the reputation": CJ to Marvin Harms, Aug. 3, 1943, Rauner.

126 "and I think it *still* stinks": CJ to FSJ, Nov. 28, 1943, Rauner.

126 "scare the average reader": CJ to Rinehart, Sept. 17, 1943, Rauner.

126 "I can think of few documents": Stephen H. Sherman to Farrar & Rinehart, Sept. 21, 1943, Rauner.

126 "launch[ing] the book on a flood": CJ to Rinehart, Sept. 22, 1943, Rauner.

126 thought it a "humdinger": Rinehart to CJ, Sept. 24, 1943, Rauner.

127 "the very soul of the dipsomaniac": Morris Fishbein to Rinehart, Dec. 28, 1943, Rauner.

127 "expert and wonderful": Quoted in Anne Rothe, ed., *Current Biography 1944* (New York: H. W. Wilson, 1945), 326.

127 "continuous subtle pleading": Haven Emerson to Rinehart, Jan. 5, 1944, Rauner.

127 "the only unflinching story": Lewis's blurb appears on the jacket of the third hardback edition of *LW.*

127 "Here's my honest reaction": William Seabrook to Rinehart, Jan. 19, 1944, Rauner.

128 "Willie Tells All [in *Asylum*]": CJ to James van Tour, Nov. 9, 1942, Rauner.

128 "another drastic attempt": Jay A. Graybeal, "William Buehler Seabrook," *Carroll County Times*, Oct. 28, 2001; posted at http://hscc.carr.org/research/yesteryears/cct2001/011028.htm.

128 "After reading the book": Harvey Breit and Marjorie Bonner Lowry, eds., *Selected Letters of Malcolm Lowry* (New York and Philadelphia: J. B. Lippincott Co., 1965), 63.

128 he'd "beaten him to it": CJ, "We Were Led to Hope for More," *New York Times Book Review*, Dec. 12, 1965, 4.

128 "The mescal-inspired phantasmagoria": Quoted in Breit and Lowry, eds., *Selected Letters of Malcolm Lowry*, 61.

129 "There they are . . . lumped": Edna Ferber to Rinehart (c. early Jan. 1944), Rauner.

129 "I resent and protest . . . bitterly": CJ to Ferber, Jan. 6, 1944, Rauner.

130 "most interested in Charles Jackson": Quoted in CJ to Charles Brackett, Feb. 12, 1945, Rauner.

130 "I have seen many small allusions": CJ to Ferber, Feb. 1, 1945, Rauner.

130 good friend and "severest critic": so CJ noted for Rinehart's benefit at the bottom of a letter from Elling Aannestad to CJ, Dec. 19, 1943, Rauner.

130 cautioned Jackson . . . "simple style": Aannestad to CJ, n.d., Rauner.

130 "most prized single letter": CJ to Ted Robinson, July 12, 1945, Rauner.

130 "one of the most brilliant performances": Robinson to CJ, Jan. 1, 1944, PSU.

130 "Five days out of a man's life": Quoted in Mark Connelly, *Deadly Closets: The Fiction of Charles Jackson* (Lanham, MD: University Press of America, 2001), 1.

131 "Gobs of celebs": CJ to FSJ, Jan. 18, 1944, Rauner.

131 "Isn't it wonderful it is the party": SWJ to CJ (c. late Jan. 1944), Rauner.

131 "that special Wylie excitement": CJ to Rinehart, Sept. 22, 1943, Rauner.

131 by means of "expert advice": Philip Wylie, "Philip Wylie Jabs a Little Needle into Complacency," *AA Grapevine*, Sept. 1944; posted at http://silkworth.net/grapevine/wylie_jabs.html.

131 Reviews of *The Lost Weekend*: Philip Wylie, in *New York Times Book Review*, Jan. 30, 1944, 7; John Chamberlain, in *New York Times*, Jan. 29, 1944, 11; Herbert Kupferberg, in *New York Herald Tribune Weekly Book Review*, Jan. 30, 1944, 4; Harrison Smith, in *Saturday Review of Literature*, Jan. 29, 1944, 5; "Damnation," *Time*, Feb. 28, 1944, 102; Edmund Wilson, in *The New Yorker*, Feb. 5, 1944, 78; Robert Gorham Davis, in *Partisan Review*, Spring 1944, 199.

132 "The irrational newspaper reviews": CJ to Aannestad, July 12, 1945, Rauner.

133 "the book conveys . . . isolation": Philip Rahv to CJ, Feb. 1, 1944, Rauner.

133 "Jackson's purpose is to describe": Granville Hicks's reader's report on *LW*, Syracuse.

134 "I have never once resorted": CJ to Bennett Cerf, Jan. 26, 1946, Rauner.

137 "Oh, I'm not as broke": "Trade Winds," *Saturday Review*, Sept. 2, 1967, 7.

137 "I lead off and am No. 1": CJ to RBJ, July 3, 1944, Rauner.

137 "a fine photograph of me": CJ to FSJ and SWJ, March 6, 1945, Rauner.

137 "the nearest American equivalent": CJ to Rinehart, June 28, 1945, Rauner.

137 "Cerf and I know each other": CJ to Maurice Friedman, Aug. 5, 1964, Rauner.

138 Charlie "is pretty well disturbed": Carl Brandt to BB, Sept. 8, 1950, Rauner.

138 "It was a character study": *EC*, xi.

138 "It was absolutely honest": CJ to Warren Ambrose, March 1, 1954, Rauner.

138 "writing in the dark": CJ, "The Sleeping Brain," unpublished ms., Rauner.

138 "Not a single telegram": CJ to family, July 24, 1963, JFC.

138 "The important thing is your work": Mary Morris, "Mary Morris Goes to See the Author of 'The Lost Weekend,' " *PM*, undated clipping (c. early 1944), Rauner.

139 he'd been "greatly concerned": "Newark Author of Best Seller Gets Script Job in Hollywood," *Newark Courier-Gazette*, March 23, 1944.

139 "of all the old gang": Katherine Saverhill Beales to CJ, n.d., Rauner.

139 Miss Munson "looked the book over": R.A.S. Bloomer to CJ, Dec. 28, 1943, Rauner.

139 "We are very flattered": Louise E. Van Duser to CJ, April 23, 1944, Rauner.

139 "That's what appealed to me": CBJ to CJ, Jan. 15, 1944, Rauner.

139 "Certainly you—or Don": HJ to CJ, Jan. 6, 1944, Rauner.

140 "She seemed pleased to be telling me": CJ to FSJ, Jan. 18, 1944, Rauner.

140 "Oh that *terrible* book": CJ's notes for *The Royalist*, dated March 17, 1950, Rauner.

140 "You've staged such a wonderful come back": BW to CJ, Aug. 24 (1943), Rauner.

140 "the happiest evening of my life": CJ to "Miss Nelson," Oct. 2, 1945, Rauner.

140 "I hate to think it's finished": CJ to RBJ, July 17, 1944, Rauner.

141 "oddly significant, no?": CJ to Alan Wallace, June 22, 1944, Rauner.

Chapter Eight · THE MGM LION

142 "the *Uncle Tom's Cabin*" of alcoholism: "Charles Jackson, Famous Author of 'Lost Weekend,' Is Opposed to Prohibition in Every Form," *The Beverage Times*, Oct. 30, 1944, 1.

142 "Almost everybody has somebody": Mary Morris, "Mary Morris Goes to See the Author of 'The Lost Weekend,' " *PM*, undated clipping (c. early 1944), Rauner.

142 "Since the publication": Francis Sill Wickware, "Liquor: Current studies in medicine and psychiatry are bringing enlightenment to the 30,000-year-old problem of drinking," *Life*, May 27, 1946.

142 "turned completely upside down": CJ, "The More Social Disease," unpublished ms., Rauner.

143 "It was Don Birnam!" he'd retort: *LN*.

143 one third "pure invention": "Editors' Preface," *Time* Reading Program Special Edition of *The Lost Weekend* (New York: Time Inc., 1963), x.

143 "I wish . . . that you'd say": "Lost Weekend's author loves the movie," *PM's Sunday Picture News*, Nov. 25, 1945, 3.

143 "I have yet to receive a fan letter": CJ to CBJ, Jan. 13, 1954, Rauner.

143 "I do not see how you can go on": CJ to Rohanna Lee, Jan. 29, 1945, Rauner.

143 "I'm one of the 'Helens' . . . ": Lee to CJ, May 21, 1944, Rauner.

143 "in black and white": Mrs. G. F. Lyle to CJ, Feb. 14, 1944, Rauner.

143 his "great sense of responsibility": CJ to Charles Brackett, Jan. 2, 1945, Rauner.

143 "It was a dirty trick to play": CJ to Lyle, Jan. 31, 1945, Rauner.

144 "Others shouldn't be deprived": "Charles Jackson . . . Opposed to Prohibition in Every Form," 1.

144 "I'm a novelist, not a public speaker": CJ to Russel Holman, Sept. 25, 1945, Rauner.

144 "simple souls" and "weaklings": Joseph Kessel, *The Road Back: A Report on Alcoholics Anonymous* (New York: Alfred A. Knopf, 1962), 150; CJ is referred to as "N" in the book.

144 "a curious combination of organizing propaganda": Sally and David R. Brown, *A Biography of Mrs. Marty Mann: The First Lady of Alcoholics Anonymous* (Center City, MN: Hazelden, 2001), 118.

144 "Every member should read": Carlton Hoste to CJ, Feb. 15, 1944, Rauner.

145 failed to offer "any real substitute": CJ to Carl Brandt, Jan. 26, 1946, Rauner.

145 "I am a writer first of all": CJ to "Mr. Tyler," Oct. 30, 1944, Rauner.

145 "Just a word now about Charles Jackson": Marion May R., "CJ Speaks at Hartford AA," *AA Grapevine*, Jan. 1945.

145 "Strike me dead if this sounds corny": CJ to Dorothy Parker, Dec. 5, 1944, Rauner.

145 "I'm awfully tired of all this": "In Our Midst," *Where*, Dec. 7–15, 1945, 5.

146 "Dr. Gorrell and—and that fellow": CJ to Anton J. Carson, July 12, 1945, Rauner.

146 "I wanted to stand up": CJ, "What's So Funny about a Drunk?," *Cosmopolitan*, May 1946, 134.

146 "I'm god damned sick of the subject": CJ to Carl Brandt, Jan. 26, 1946, Rauner.

147 "a bloody bore": CJ/AA-59.

147 "Will I have the courage": CJ to FSJ and SWJ, Dec. 16, 1943, Rauner.

147 "One best seller did it": Hedda Hopper, "Screen News Here and in H-wood," *New York Times*, March 22, 1944, Amusements 17.

147 "modest in spite of his mushrooming": "Newark Author of Best Seller Gets Script Job in Hollywood," *Newark Courier-Gazette*, March 23, 1944.

148 "Shower baths, barber shop, super-de-luxe": CJ to SWJ, April 16, 1944, Rauner.

148 "I hope she connects the author": CJ to FSJ, April 17, 1944, Rauner.

148 her "Lost-Weekend number": CJ to RBJ, June 9, 1944, Rauner.

148 "I think you're a great writer": CJ to RBJ, April 26, 1944, Rauner.

148 "as though the friendship": Mary McCarthy, *The Lost Week, or The Caged Lion*, unpublished ms., Vassar.

148 "Why I am wanted by these people": CJ to RBJ, Aug. 3, 1944, Rauner.

149 Tracy "hounded [him] for days": CJ to McCarthy, July 13, 1945, Vassar.

149 "hung onto [Jackson] for dear life": CJ to Marion Fabry, Nov. 3, 1944, Rauner.

149 "Well, it's all fun": CJ to FSJ, May 6, 1944, Rauner.

149 "This fantastic town!": CJ to RBJ, July 2, 1944, Rauner.

149 "I still can't get over it": CJ to Max and Lambie Wylie, June 13, 1944, Rauner.

149 "They tell the story about": CJ to FSJ, April 20, 1944, Rauner.

149 "Arsur is hard to work with": CJ to RBJ, July 11, 1944, Rauner.

150 "Story by Harry Ruskin": CJ to RBJ, May 2, 1944, Rauner.

150 "Already ballyhooed": "Virtually All M-G-M Players In 'Nor All Your Tears,' " *Box Office*, June 3, 1944, 51.

150 "absorb some of the atmosphere": CJ to FSJ, May 3, 1944, Rauner.

150 "paved [his] way with social": CJ to RBJ, May 29, 1944, Rauner.

150 "You must remember bad Bick": CJ to Whitfield Cook, Nov. 21, 1944, Rauner.

150 "We have many many laughs": CJ to RBJ, May 4, 1944, Rauner.

150 a "sharp letter" from his mother: CJ to RBJ, July 3, 1944, Rauner.

151 keep them "as a kind of diary": CJ to RBJ, May 11, 1944, Rauner.

151 "we never know what to say": CJ to RBJ, May 12, 1944, Rauner.

151 "Lately I have longed for you": CJ to RBJ, June 12, 1944, Rauner.

151 still "a so-called 'celeb' ": CJ to RBJ, June 13, 1944, Rauner.

151 "it's the 20th Century neurosis": CJ to RBJ, June 22, 1944, Rauner.

151 "prestige and independence": Lincoln Barnett, "The Happiest Couple in Hollywood," *Life*, Dec. 11, 1944, 101.

152 "a triumph, nothing less": CJ to FSJ, May 6, 1944, Rauner.

152 "more sense of horror": "Editors' Preface," *Time* Reading Program Edition of *LW*, xii.

152 "Next picture coming up": CJ to RBJ, May 10, 1944, Rauner.

152 "luckiest guy in the world": CJ to RBJ, July 11, 1944, Rauner.

152 "Yesterday I read that four": CJ to Philip Wylie, May 24, 1944, Rauner.

152 "and certainly for not less": CJ to RBJ, May 24, 1944, Rauner.

152 "I feel, and will always feel": CJ to Carl Brandt, July 15, 1946, Rauner.

152 "I wish this did me some good": CJ to Thomas Mann, Jan. 26, 1946, Rauner.

153 "a pretty penny—up in six figures": Louella Parsons, " 'Lost Weekend,' Psychological Story of a Drunk, to Be Filmed," unpaginated clipping (source unknown) dated June 2, 1944, Rauner.

153 "DO NOT DISTURB": CJ to Alma Pritchard, June 13, 1944, Rauner.

153 "If they bring it off": Barnett, "The Happiest Couple in Hollywood," 103.

153 "the easiest script we wrote": Bernard F. Dick, *Billy Wilder* (Cambridge, MA: Da Capo Press, 1996), 68.

153 "Simply won't permit such a thing": CJ to RBJ, June 3, 1944, Rauner.

153 "original & effective": CJ to RBJ, June 27, 1944, Rauner.

153 "knowledge of 'psychopathia' ": CJ to Leonard Shannon, March 26, 1945, Rauner.

153 "careful delineation": "Radio: The Week in Review," *Time*, Feb. 21, 1955.

153 "remember her? the lovely girl": CJ to RBJ, June 9, 1944, Rauner.

154 "Romance, hell": CJ to RBJ, May 18, 1944, Rauner.

154 "like a ton of bricks": CJ to Mrs. John Retzer, Feb. 14, 1945, Rauner.

154 "I all but fell in love": CJ to RBJ, June 3, 1944, Rauner.

154 "like the girl and boy next door": Charles Kaiser, *The Gay Metropolis: 1940–1996* (Boston and New York: Houghton Mifflin Co., 1997), 192.

154 seemed "all but lifeless": CJ to Judy Garland, April 18, 1945, Rauner.

154 ". . . Once, within a wood": CJ to RBJ, June 10, 1944, Rauner.

155 "no man in his right mind": CJ to RBJ, June 14, 1944, Rauner.

155 akin to a "Nazi demonstration": CJ to RBJ, June 20, 1944, Rauner.

155 "the slightest twinge of jealousy": CJ to RBJ, June 29, 1944, Rauner.

155 "Alas, how are the mighty fallen": CJ to Pritchard, June 26, 1944, Rauner.

156 a bad case of "stage-fright": CJ to RBJ, June 15, 1944, Rauner.

156 "Then you must talk with him": CJ, "Strictly Personal," in *The Stature of Thomas Mann*, ed. Charles Neider (New York: New Directions, 1947), 49.

157 "I know of no book": CJ to DS, Aug. 17, 1953, Rauner.

157 "I was really delighted": Mann to CJ, Aug. 18, 1945, Rauner.

157 "generous and gratifying impulse": Mann to CJ, Nov. 4, 1948, Rauner.
157 "the most entertainingly articulate": Barnett, "The Happiest Couple in Hollywood," 112.
157 "It's genuinely tragic": CJ to RBJ, July 17, 1944, Rauner.
158 His "nicest day in Hollywood": CJ to RBJ, July 3, 1944, Rauner.
158 "out of all the people": CJ to Charles Brackett, Aug. 6, 1960, Rauner.
158 he was "hot and bothered": CJ to P. Wylie, June 12, 1944, Rauner.
158 "Damn it to hell": CJ to RBJ, May 23, 1944, Rauner.
158 "the unhappiest man alive": CJ to RBJ, June 12, 1944, Rauner.
159 "the other writers say": CJ to RBJ, June 8, 1944, Rauner.
159 "I proposed that my fall option": CJ to Brandt, July 18, 1944, Rauner.
159 "I have been taken in and how": CJ to RBJ, July 10, 1944, Rauner.
159 "I think he remembered": CJ to Lily Messinger, Nov. 22, 1944, Rauner.

Chapter Nine • SIX CHIMNEY FARM

161 "the most beautiful town in America": Quoted in CJ, "Noted Author Delivers Some Caustic Comments on His Wealthy Neighbors," *Manchester Union Leader,* Aug. 1, 1946.
161 "absolute peak of fulfillment": CJ to RBJ, May 14, 1944, Rauner.
161 "When I'm rich . . . mine!": DS-*Show,* 79.
161 "one of the most beautiful houses": Quoted in CJ to Alan Wallace, June 22, 1944, Rauner.
161 "He also did the Capitol": CJ to FSJ, Nov. 28, 1943, Rauner.
162 "paid for twice over": CJ to Nila Mack, July 10, 1944, Rauner.
162 "but won't it be wonderful": CJ to RBJ, June 10, 1944, Rauner.
162 "study-and-retreat-and-bedroom": CJ to RBJ, June 7, 1944, Rauner.
163 "the colors more beautiful": CJ to Mrs. John Retzer, Feb. 14, 1945, Rauner.
163 "ne'er-do-well husband": *F&W* (in which Fred Brock appears as "George Marr").
163 "To Kittuh, written in the poet's Heart's Blood": CJ, "JAXON" notebook, Rauner.
164 "at whatever rental or cost": CJ to RBJ, June 13, 1944, Rauner.
164 "I read your manuscript": Isabelle Booth to CJ (c. early Aug. 1943), JFC.
165 "Boom, you can't realize": CJ to FSJ, Dec. 5, 1944, Rauner.
165 "That Dreadful Book": CJ to Stanley M. Rinehart, March 8, 1945, Rauner.
165 "I know you write": Leonard Lyons, "The Lyons Den" (syndicated column), Sept. 26, 1968.
166 "Why do you suppose Mr. Jackson": CJ, "What's So Funny about a Drunk?," *Cosmopolitan,* May 1946, 135.
166 "Ned loved everybody": Author int. Ann Davis, July 18, 2009.
166 "Mr. Jackson to Hanover": My deepest gratitude to Julia Fifield (age 104 in 2009) for letting me see her stepfather's hilarious diary.
166 "defensive before this impulsiveness": Daniel Doan, "Random Thoughts in Memory of Charles Jackson," unpublished ms., Rauner.
167 "Those kids aren't worth educating": Author int. Robert Richmond, Aug. 7, 2009.
167 "to encourage [Sarah and Kate]": CJ to Buck Lilienthal, Feb. 28, 1945, Rauner.

167 "I've never seen Rhoda": CJ to Jesse Lilienthal, April 16, 1945, Rauner.

167 "He was in a dark suit": Author int. Julia Fifield, July 18, 2009.

167 "Anti-Semitism . . . awful here": CJ to Mrs. John Retzer, Feb. 14, 1945, Rauner.

168 "white girl" had married a Jew: Author int. KWJ, June 10, 2009.

168 "You've got to write not one": Mary Morris, "Mary Morris Goes to See the Author of 'The Lost Weekend,' " *PM*, undated clipping (c. early 1944), Rauner.

168 "merely a chapter, so to speak": CJ to Rinehart, Sept. 17, 1943, Rauner.

168 "how you [*sic*] got out of it": John J. Lloyd to CJ, Jan. 17, 1944, Rauner.

168 "to solve psychiatric problems": Marion May R., "CJ Speaks at Hartford AA," *AA Grapevine*, Jan. 1945.

168 "in a more leisurely and novelistic style": "Newark Author of Best Seller Gets Script Job in Hollywood," *Newark Courier-Gazette*, March 23, 1944.

168 "It will be a story about the reaction": CJ to RBJ, May 3, 1944, Rauner.

169 "Well, the Ulrichs poem": CJ to RBJ, May 11, 1944, Rauner.

169 "The stars have not dealt me": A. E. Housman, *Additional Poems*, XVII; posted at http://www.chiark.greenend.org.uk/~martinh/poems/complete_housman.html.

169 "there is nothing so important": BB to CJ, May 18, 1944, Rauner.

170 "the two parts of [his] famous novel": Philip Wylie to CJ, May 18, 1944, Rauner.

170 "I feel confident": CJ to RBJ, May 23, 1944, Rauner.

170 "a kind of half-hearted finger-exercise": CJ to P. Wylie (et al.), May 24, 1944, Rauner.

170 "I am very sorry but I never discuss": CJ to James Neill Northe, March 27, 1945, Rauner.

170 "The story will be heavy": CJ to P. Wylie (et al.), May 24, 1944, Rauner.

171 "is your first responsibility": P. Wylie to CJ, July 25, 1944, Rauner.

171 "them's my sentiments also": Ted Amussen to CJ, May 29, 1944, Rauner.

171 "decadence and death": CJ to Rinehart, June 2, 1944, Rauner.

171 "There are a great many things": BB to CJ, June 6, 1944, Rauner.

172 "I am a little tired of writing": CJ to F. W. Dupee, Jan. 8, 1945, Rauner.

172 "if examined properly": CJ to Rinehart, June 2, 1944, Rauner.

172 "We talked solid from 7 pm to 1 am": CJ to RBJ, June 14, 1944, Rauner.

172 "account of a war neurosis": CJ to George Davis, June 22, 1944, Rauner.

172 "the domination of the uniform": CJ to Anton J. Carlson, July 12, 1945, Rauner.

172 "trying to steer a safe and sane": CJ to Jim and Liz Hart, Nov. 21, 1944, Rauner.

172 "POSSIBLE COPY FOR CATALOGUE": CJ to Helen Rinehart, March 19, 1945, Rauner.

173 "So you are a shipyard worker": CJ to Fritz Requardt, Feb. 15, 1945, Rauner.

173 "a delusion and a snore": CJ to Robert Nathan, July 15, 1945, Rauner.

173 "to [his] eternal credit": CJ to RBJ, Aug. 7, 1944, Rauner.

173 "Remember how we used to read him": CJ to Marion Fabry, Nov. 3, 1944, Rauner.

173 "You have left a good many friends": Gregory Peck to CJ, Oct. 21, 1944, Rauner.

173 "I like to show off": CJ to Peck, Oct. 30, 1944, Rauner.

173 "I subscribe to 'em all": CJ to Judy Garland, April 18, 1945, Rauner.

173 "What will people think?": Quoted in CJ to FSJ, Sept. 12, 1944, Rauner.

173 a "stunning picture" of Garland: CJ to Nathan, Oct. 13, 1944, Rauner.

173 "Like the adorer I was": CJ to Nathan, Feb. 19, 1945, Rauner.

174 "For Judy, who is one": CJ to FSJ, Dec. 5, 1944, Rauner.

174 "CHARLIE DEAR, DUE TO CHANGES": Quoted in CJ to FSJ, April 19, 1945, Rauner.

174 "all tingly in the legs": CJ to Garland, April 18, 1945, Rauner.

174 "The sins of MGM were never": CJ to Katharine Hepburn, Nov. 22, 1944, Rauner.

174 "faint qualms" about the union: CJ to Minnellis, June 29, 1945, Rauner.

174 Jackson blamed such "violent rumors": CJ to Mrs. John Retzer, Feb. 14, 1945, Rauner.

174 "Wait till Orford hears of our guests": CJ to Fabry, Nov. 3, 1944, Rauner.

174 "almost an anxiety to see me": CJ to RBJ, Aug. 7, 1944, Rauner.

174 "How nice, how very nice": CJ to Hepburn, Dec. 4, 1944, Rauner.

175 "too busy a gal": CJ to Hepburn, June 28, 1945, Rauner.

175 "I don't know who I am": Robert Benchley to CJ, Oct. 12, 1944, Rauner.

175 she'd "gone 'off' again": CJ to Benchley, Oct. 16, 1944, Rauner.

175 "wonderful talk all day": CJ to Fabry, Nov. 3, 1944, Rauner.

175 "She still keeps on the wagon": CJ to Benchley, March 9, 1945, Rauner.

175 "I'm going to need you in my life": CJ to Dorothy Parker, Dec. 5, 1944, Rauner.

176 bringing in "badly needed cash": CJ to Stanley M. Rinehart, Aug. 27, 1945, Rauner.

176 "Sweet Kate, bonnie Kate": CJ to Hepburn, Aug. 30, 1945, Rauner.

176 "free, modernized, American": CJ, *The Seagull*, unpublished film treatment, Rauner.

176 "You ask about Garbo": CJ to BB, Nov. 20, 1944, Rauner.

177 "truly dramatic action": CJ to Hume Cronyn and Jessica Tandy, Dec. 6, 1944, Rauner.

177 "somewhat hastily," he confessed: CJ, *The Seagull*, Rauner.

177 "I know you will simply fall in love": CJ to Leland Hayward, July 15, 1945, Rauner.

178 insisted it "belong[ed] to her": CJ to RBJ, May 19, 1944, Rauner.

178 "I've never been in on such a brilliant": CJ to RBJ, July 24, 1944, Rauner.

178 "Such wonderful company": CJ to Nathan, Oct. 13, 1944, Rauner.

178 "The New Yorker has just bought five": CJ to Fabry, Nov. 3, 1944, Rauner.

178 "thought lovingly of Horace": CJ, "Funny Dream," *The New Yorker*, March 17, 1945, 62.

178 "I think Sally [Benson]": William Maxwell to CJ, n.d., Rauner.

179 " 'Dreams Are Funny' sounds to me": CJ to Maxwell, Jan. 31, 1945, Rauner.

179 "I want to send one to Judy": CJ to Maxwell, March 23, 1945, Rauner.

179 "I won't begin to tell you": CJ to Amussen, Jan. 2, 1945, Rauner.

179 "Their main reaction": Maxwell to CJ, April 23, 1945, Rauner.

179 "I was frankly log-rolling": CJ to Liz Hart, June 6, 1945, Rauner.

180 "nobody cares about them": Maxwell to Carl Brandt, Sept. 20, 1950, Rauner.

180 "to hell with The New Yorker": CJ to BB, July 18, 1951, Rauner.

180 "are artful, full of evasions": CJ to DS, June 6, 1951, Rauner.

180 "it's one story for a change": CJ to BB, Jan. 28, 1952, Rauner.

180 a little too patly "clinical": Maxwell to BB, Feb. 11, 1952, Rauner.

180 "I could punch him in the nose": CJ to BB, Aug. 22, 1952, Rauner.

Chapter Ten • WILL AND ERROR

181 "I took it to bed with me that night": Ray Milland, *Wide-Eyed in Babylon* (New York: William Morrow & Co., 1974), 211.

182   "I just want to tell you": Oliver Jensen, " 'Lost Weekend' Hangover: Milland is haunted by alcoholic he portrayed," *Life*, March 11, 1946, 23.

182   "the Hitchcock signature": CJ to Robert Nathan, Oct. 13, 1944, Rauner.

182   "Hello, Charlie," he muttered: Alton Cook, "Movies: Author of 'Lost Weekend' Is Sick of Alcohol Topic"; undated clipping (source unknown), Rauner.

182   "FOR COMMENT SEE CELIA'S SPEECH": Quoted in *LN*.

182   "far better than they were": CJ to Charles Brackett, Nov. 22, 1944, Rauner.

182   "To please the Hays office": Louella Parsons, " 'Lost Weekend,' Psychological Story of a Drunk, to Be Filmed," unpaginated clipping (source unknown) dated June 2, 1944, Rauner.

182   "trusting to luck": CJ to Nathan, Feb. 19, 1945, Rauner.

183   "Now, naturally I resent": CJ to Brackett and Billy Wilder, Jan. 2, 1945, Rauner.

183   "Since the night I first read": CJ to Brackett and Wilder, Jan. 8, 1945, Rauner.

183   "I am beginning to loathe": CJ to Nathan, Feburary 19, 1945, Rauner.

184   "Charlie, I've got a fine present": Quoted in CJ to Philip Rahv, March 5, 1945, Rauner.

184   he was "flattered enormously": CJ to FSJ and SWJ, March 6, 1945, Rauner.

184   "Words, words, words": CJ's rewritten ending of *LW* movie included with his letter to Brackett, March 27, 1945, Rauner.

185   "derive a small (but very small)": CJ to Brackett, Aug. 21, 1945, Rauner.

185   ". . . there are wanderers in the middle mist": Quoted in CJ to FSJ, Sept. 9, 1944, Rauner.

185   that kind of "lavender taint": CJ to Sam Hershfeld, Dec. 6, 1944, Rauner.

185   "You'd be surprised what a difference": CJ to Ted Amussen, Nov. 21, 1944, Rauner.

185   "I read it over and think, 'my god' ": CJ to Hume Cronyn, Nov. 22, 1944, Rauner.

185   "when the story begins": CJ to Rahv, Jan. 12, 1944 (actually 1945), Rauner.

186   "every single syllable": CJ to Stanley M. Rinehart, Jan. 29, 1945, Rauner.

186   "Elling was simply unable": CJ to BB, Feb. 12, 1945, Rauner.

186   seemed "mightily impressed": CJ to Elling Aannestad, Feb. 13, 1945, Rauner.

186   "one of the most interesting" CJ to Rinehart, March 8, 1945, Rauner.

187   pruning "all the passages": CJ to Arthur Kober, Feb. 12, 1945, Rauner.

187   "homosexual to start with": CJ to Jesse Lilienthal, Feb. 13, 1945, Rauner.

187   "[Anyone] who dares to write": CJ to Rinehart, April 25, 1945, Rauner.

187   "the 'fatigue' of marriage": CJ to Amussen, March 27, 1945, Rauner.

187   "The books of Dreiser": "Lost Weekend Author Speaks to English Classes," *The Dartmouth*, May 10, 1946.

188   "agents, publishers, Metro": CJ to FSJ, Dec. 6, 1944, Rauner.

188   "He pretty much knew": Author int. Pat Hammond, July 18, 2009.

188   "working harder and harder": CJ to Hume Cronyn, Dec. 6, 1944, Rauner.

188   "I don't sleep at all": CJ to Cronyns, Nov. 22, 1944, Rauner.

188   "This drug [Seconal]": Patient Notes, March 10, 1945, D-HH.

189   "man-eating public or publisher": *HFG*.

189   "He can't deny that he has done": RBJ to FSJ (c. early 1951), Rauner.

189   "favorite little hospital": CJ/AA-59.

189   because of "overwork": CJ to HJ, March 23, 1945, Rauner.

189   "On a scale of one to ten": G. F. Cahill, Jr., "Memorial: Sven Martin Gundersen 1904–1998"; posted at http://www.ncbi.nlm.nih.gov/pmc/articlesPMC 2194408/.

190   "I haven't a nickle [*sic*]": CJ to Brackett, Nov. 22, 1944, Rauner.

190 "Charlie was a very high liver": Columbia University oral history interview (c. 1976) with RS.

190 "the coal bill has been": CJ to FSJ and SWJ, March 6, 1945, Rauner.

190 "dies a thousand deaths": CJ to William L'Engle, July 17, 1945, Rauner.

190 "God knows *I'm* not doing it": CJ to BB, Aug. 27, 1945, Rauner.

191 "a little on the gloomy side": CJ to RBJ, June 10, 1944, Rauner.

191 "I love Bob dearly": CJ to Rinehart, July 12, 1945, Rauner.

191 "for the really interesting people": Mary McCarthy, *The Lost Week, or The Caged Lion*, unpublished ms., Vassar.

191 "Mr. Jackson does not like to meet": Quoted in Reuel K. Wilson, *To the Life of the Silver Harbor: Edmund Wilson and Mary McCarthy on Cape Cod* (Lebanon, NH: University Press of New England, 2008), 117.

191 "quite a whirl": CJ to Rinehart, July 12, 1945, Rauner.

191 "a kind of lotus-land": CJ to Amussen, July 11, 1945, Rauner.

192 "Bob will only be happiest": CJ to Brackett, July 12, 1945, Rauner.

192 "I seem, to myself, a very old man": Nathan to CJ (c. mid-July 1945), Rauner.

192 "a warm human something": CJ to BB, Oct. 11, 1950, Rauner.

193 "high point of the week": CJ to BB, July 11, 1945, Rauner.

193 "Mary and Clem all but tore me to shreds": CJ to Rahv, July 12, 1945, Rauner.

193 "I liked you so much": CJ to McCarthy (c. July 9, 1945), Vassar.

193 "A satire, it was to be": Mary McCarthy, "The Novels That Got Away," *New York Times Book Review*, Nov. 25, 1979, 3.

193 "You and your visit here" McCarthy to CJ (c. July 11, 1945), Rauner.

193 "wouldn't leave [him] a shred": CJ to BB, July 10, 1952, Rauner.

193 "My life is in your hands": CJ to McCarthy, July 13, 1945, Vassar.

195 "Dear Minx": CJ to McCarthy, Aug. 8, 1945, Vassar.

195 "very very John Marquand": Quoted in Reuel K. Wilson, *To the Life of the Silver Harbor*, 118.

196 "touch so much as a comma": CJ to Liz Hart, June 6, 1945, Rauner.

196 "Does the war cause the deterioration": Quoted in CJ to Amussen, June 25, 1945, Rauner.

197 "So help me God I finally know": CJ to Amussen (et al.), June 25, 1945, Rauner.

197 "because Farrar & Rinehart wouldn't": CJ to KWJ, Aug. 1, 1964, JFC.

197 "She thinks that I only get confused": CJ to Rahv, July 12, 1945, Rauner.

197 "100% in favor": Amussen to CJ, July 8, 1945, Rauner.

198 "so far superior to The Lost Weekend": CJ to BB, July 11, 1945, Rauner.

198 "I am, as you know": Philip Wylie to CJ, June 8, 1944, Rauner.

198 "penchant for using difficult words": CJ to P. Wylie, Sept. 4, 1944, Princeton.

198 "Nuts to you": P. Wylie to CJ, Sept. 13, 1944, Princeton.

198 his "literary conscience": CJ to P. Wylie, Feb. 12, 1945, Rauner.

198 "Dear Charlie, old kid": P. Wylie to CJ, July 16, 1945, Princeton.

201 "the gist of which was": CJ to Russel Crouse, Jan. 26, 1946, Rauner.

201 "much in need": CJ to SJP, Sept. 23, 1958, JFC.

201 Barr expressed his "very serious concern": Kevin Lally, *Wilder Times: The Life of Billy Wilder* (New York: Henry Holt and Co., 1996), 144.

202 "She was so thrilled": CJ to Brackett, March 27, 1945, Rauner.

202 "If they would have given *me*": Lally, *Wilder Times*, 150.

202 "positively limp" by the end: CJ to BB, Feb. 12, 1945, Rauner.

202 "Paramount has succeeded": Quoted in "Production Notes," Turner Classic Movies DVD edition of *The Lost Weekend*.

202 "I can't sleep nights": CJ to Leland Hayward, July 15, 1945, Rauner.

202 "ah, there!" he noted of the last: CJ to Brackett, Aug. 21, 1945, Rauner.

202 "I believe it's the only movie": CJ to Henry Ginsberg, Jan. 21, 1946, Rauner.

203 accosted him "for a good two hours": CJ to Brackett and Wilder, May 7, 1946, Rauner.

203 agreed to a "drastically altered" version: Sam Boal, "Britain Censors 'Lost Weekend,' " *Paris Post*, Sept. 11, 1945, 1.

204 "a praise binge for *The Lost Weekend*": Lally, *Wilder Times*, 160.

204 According to a 1936 study: Norman Jolliffe, "The Alcoholic Admissions to Bellevue Hospital," *Science*, March 27, 1936, 306–9.

204 "the best and most disturbing": Bosley Crowther, "A Study in Dipsomania," *New York Times*, Dec. 3, 1945.

204 "pretty consistently gratified": James Agee, "The Lost Weekend," *The Nation*, Jan. 22, 1946.

205 "credit to their smallest bit-player": CJ to Rinehart, Jan. 27, 1946, Rauner.

205 "for the reason of your omission": Brackett to CJ, March 11, 1946, Rauner.

205 "quiver[ing] with pleasure": DS-*Show*, 85.

Chapter Eleven • THE FALL OF VALOR

206 "I remember your telling me": CJ to Elling Aannestad, July 12, 1945, Rauner.

206 "Well that sort of thing": CJ to RBJ, April 21, 1944, Rauner.

207 "perverted sense of values": RBJ to FSJ, April 10 (1946), Rauner.

207 "You're the guy who knocks drinking": Leonard Lyons, "The Lyons Den" (syndicated column), July 15, 1946.

207 "Though I never did see much": CJ to Leonora Schinasi, Feb. 28, 1945, Rauner.

207 "chic beyond Vogue's wildest dreams": CJ to RBJ, July 18, 1944, Rauner.

207 "My story MONEY did not sell": CJ to FSJ, April 11 (1952), Rauner.

207 Hillyard, "in desperate need": *EC*, 95.

207 "I've many times seen you raise": CJ to Nila Mack, April 24, 1945, Rauner.

208 "bundle of nerves": Bennett Cerf, "Trade Winds," *Saturday Review*, Feb. 2, 1946, 18.

208 "spout quotes by the yard" CJ to Katharine Hepburn, Jan. 18, 1946, Rauner.

208 " 'The counterfeit presentment' ": Jackson's daughter Kate kindly provided me with old 78 recordings of his *Information, Please!* appearances.

208 "I got sixty eight letters": CJ to HJ, Jan. 18, 1946, Rauner.

208 "authors . . . less than dirt": CJ to Stark Young, Jan. 19, 1946, Rauner.

208 a writer "should never be called on": CJ to Victor Wolfson, Oct. 9, 1945, Rauner.

209 "after the talk has got started": CJ to Ingrid Hallen, Aug. 7, 1946, Rauner.

209 "one of the most distinguished books": Quoted in *LN*.

209 reminiscent of "WAR AND PEACE": CJ to Carl Brandt, Jan. 26, 1946, Rauner.

209 "in plain English": CJ to Mary McCarthy, July 16 (1945), Vassar.

209 "the best novel published in America": CJ to FSJ, Oct. 8, 1945, Rauner.

209 "To hell with The Lost Weekend": CJ to Klaus Perls, Nov. 5, 1945, Rauner.

209 "Greek in it's [*sic*] bigness": CJ to Stark Young, Jan. 19, 1946, Rauner.

209 "Brother, you don't know": CJ to Brandt, Jan. 26, 1946, Rauner.

209 "If you think I'm worth any dough": CJ to Perls, Jan. 20, 1946, Rauner.

210 "in view of [his] unusually fine": Henry Ginsberg to CJ, Feb. 19, 1946, Rauner.

210 "If you are still interested": CJ to Billy Wilder, May 7, 1946, Rauner.

210 "All I want to do now": CJ to FSJ, March 10, 1946, Rauner.

211 "the will to survive in a hostile world": "Psychiatry in Harlem," *Time*, Dec. 1, 1947.

211 "I take a rather serious view": Frederic Wertham to Sven M. Gundersen, Feb. 9, 1946, D-HH.

211 "Patient admitted in a greatly fatigued": Patient Notes, March 13, 1946, D-HH.

211 "practically in a state of collapse": CJ to Lee and Ira Gershwin, March 11, 1946, Rauner.

211 "Nobody ever perpetrated": CJ to Brackett and Wilder, March 13, 1946, Rauner.

212 "Anybody else in these United States": CJ to Brackett and Wilder, May 7, 1946, Rauner.

213 "Who packed the bags": RBJ to FSJ, April 10 (1946), Rauner.

214 "optimistic about the whole situation": Wertham to CJ, May 16, 1946, Rauner.

214 "out, impossible, verboten": CJ to Wertham, May 17, 1946, Rauner.

214 "This is neither Munich": Quoted in CJ, "Noted Author Delivers Some Caustic Comments on His Wealthy Neighbors," *Manchester Union Leader*, Aug. 1, 1946.

214 "I pray that God Almighty": Quoted in *LN*.

215 Jackson "moved back to the city": "City vs. Country," *Life*, March 17, 1947, 95.

215 "what time [his] light went out": "Would You Rather Live in a Small Town or a Big City?" *Town Meeting: Bulletin of America's Town Meeting of the Air*, Dec. 26, 1946, 21.

216 "After a week or two": Ibid., 9.

216 Warren himself felt "proud again": John Pillsbury, "Orford May Hold Forum, Invite Jackson to Speak," *Manchester Union Leader*, Aug. 3, 1946, 3

216 "test the validity": "Charles Jackson Sees Bigotry and Intolerance in Neighboring Orford," *The Dartmouth*, Sept. 9, 1946, 1.

217 "but the third novel is about syphilis": CJ to McCarthy, July 13, 1945, Vassar.

217 "novel of marriage": CJ to Roy Myers, Aug. 10, 1946, Rauner.

217 "cause as much tongue-wagging": Bennett Cerf, "Trade Winds," *Saturday Review*, undated clipping (c. summer 1946), Rauner.

217 "Empty ninety percent of this year's novels": Wertham, "The Tragedy of Deviation from the Norm," unpublished review of *FV*, Rauner.

217 "I'm afraid this letter": CJ to FSJ, Sept. 10, 1946, Rauner.

217 Reviews of *The Fall of Valor*: R. E. Kingery, in *Library Journal*, Sept. 15, 1946, 1207; Charles Poore, in *New York Times*, Oct. 3, 1946, 25; Clifton Fadiman, in *New York Herald Tribune Weekly Book Review*, Oct. 4, 1946, 7; A. C. Spectorsky, in *Chicago Sun Book Week*, Oct. 6, 1946, 3; Harrison Smith, in *Saturday Review*, Oct. 5, 1946, 12; Edmund Wilson, in *The New Yorker*, Oct. 5, 1946, 118; Robert Gorham Davis, *New York Times Book Review*, Oct. 6, 1946, 8.

218 envisaged "another sensational hit": Thomas Mann to CJ, Oct. 5, 1946, Rauner.

223 "In your Lost Weekend style": P. Wylie to CJ, July 16, 1945, Princeton.

223 "a dull story, about dull people": Edward Weeks, "The Atlantic Bookshelf," *The Atlantic*, Dec. 1946, 150.

224 "the style and spirit": Quoted in Patience Ross to BB, Febuary 18, 1947, Rauner.

224 Jackson, "outraged," changed publishers: BB to Ross, March 5, 1947, Rauner.

224 "a slow tumid emotion": Quoted in Ross to BB, April 9, 1947, Rauner.

224 "I have become awfully hard boiled": CJ to Isabel Leighton, Feb. 14, 1946, Rauner.

224 "$150,000 just to have them": Irving Lazar to CJ, Feb. 16, 1946, Rauner.

224 "GABLE'S BACK": Quoted in CJ to Roy Myers, Aug. 10, 1946, Rauner.

224 "downright lunacy": W. R. Wilkerson, "Trade Views," *Hollywood Reporter*, Aug. 13, 1946, 1.

224 The "homosexual angle": Thomas R. Pryor, "Jerry Wald, the Big Idea Man," *New York Times*, Jan. 19, 1947, X5.

225 "It is difficult to exaggerate": Quoted in CJ to Rinehart, April 1, 1948, Rauner.

225 "the problem of homosexuality": CJ to KWJ, Aug. 1, 1964, JFC.

225 "a place of utmost honor": Richard Amory, "Charles Jackson's 'The Fall of Valor,' " *Vector*, April 1972; posted at http://home.earthlink.net/~richardamory .com/id3.html.

226 "If you see a photograph": Harrison Kinney, ed., *The Thurber Letters: The Wit, Wisdom and Surprising Life of James Thurber* (New York: Simon & Schuster, 2002), 405.

226 "I longed for some ice-cold beer": Joseph Kessel, *The Road Back: A Report on Alcoholics Anonymous* (New York: Alfred A. Knopf, 1962), 151.

226 "What do you know, I'm drinking again": CJ/AA-59.

226 "It took him five years": Richard R. Peabody, *The Common Sense of Drinking* (Boston: Little, Brown & Co., 1931), 123–24.

226 "brilliant actress who finds it easy": Marjory Adams, "Charles Jackson Amazed by Legends Now Surrounding Him," *Boston Daily Globe*, June 20, 1945, Amusements 14.

Intermezzo • BOOM IN MALAGA

228 "[Flew will] be dreadfully": R. Hamlet to FSJ, n.d., Rauner.

228 "It is enchanting to be back": Monroe Wheeler to FSJ, March 31, 1947, Rauner.

229 "You can be sure Reggie": CJ to FSJ, Sept. 7 (1941), Rauner.

229 "just crazy about Boomer": Author int. Barbara Peech Streeter, June 28, 2009.

229 "you may expect [as a gift]": CJ to SJP, Sept. 18, 1958, JFC.

231 "Boom was Mrs. Tiggy-Winkle": Author int. Pepa Ferrer Devan, April 10, 2009.

231 "But how terrible, the language": FSJ to SJP, Aug. 4, 1966, JFC.

232 whinging about "sick headaches": *F&W.*

232 "given [her] a home": CBJ's genealogy, JFC.

232 "rub her eyes in the most corny": CJ to FSJ, Oct. 8, 1945, Rauner.

232 "I have gotten where I am afraid": SWJ to FSJ, Sept. 28, 1945, Rauner.

232 "I often think that Sal": CJ to CBJ, Jan. 13, 1954, Rauner.

233 "I don't know when I have felt": SWJ to FSJ, Oct. 25, 1949, Rauner.

233 "My Gosh, Fred," Bob wrote: CBJ to FSJ, Aug. 12, 1956, Rauner.

234 "Well, Boom was off somewhere": Author int. Barbara Peech Streeter, June 21, 2009.

234 "Foolish woman or not": *EC*, 112.

235 "I don't seem to enjoy anyone but you": James M. Gates to FSJ, July 31, 1946, Rauner.

235 "Jim is still out of control": RBJ to SJP, March 22, 1972, JFC.

Chapter Twelve • THE OUTER EDGES

236 "It's about time I stopped dishing": CJ to Ted Amussen, May 13, 1946, Rauner.

237 "As the outline stands": BB to CJ, Feb. 20, 1947, Rauner.

237 "which ain't hay, even by Texas standards": CJ to Adelaide Getty, June 19, 1947, Rauner.

237 "The novel is a horrible headache": CJ to Herb F. West, Aug. 26, 1947, Rauner.

238 "It wasn't the same old Lazar": CJ to Lee and Ira Gershwin, June 19, 1947, Rauner.

238 "Nothing could make me": *LN.*

238 "a book I know you always deplored": CJ to RBJ, June 6, 1968, Rauner.

238 "He's a terrible addict": RBJ to FSJ, July 3 (1947), Rauner.

239 "On May 28, 1947, you filled": Gundersen to Caswell-Massey Co., July 9, 1947, D-HH.

239 "Only when his speech thickens": RBJ to FSJ, Oct. 18 (1947), Rauner.

240 "he was what was called": e-mail from Arthur Laurents to author, Nov. 23, 2009.

240 "Persons habitually or occasionally": Quoted in Michael Paller, "The Couch and Tennessee," *Tennessee Williams Annual Review* no. 3 (2000); posted at http://www.tennesseewilliamsstudies.org/archives/2000/3paller.htm.

240 "I respect the book completely": Lawrence S. Kubie to Laura Z. Hobson, Sept. 17, 1946, Rauner.

241 "I said, 'Larry, how come'": Reminiscences of Roger W. Straus, Jr., Jan. 11, 1978, on page 363 in CUCOHC.

242 "A choice of a partner": Quoted in Georges-Michel Sarotte, *Like a Brother, Like a Lover: Male Homosexuality in the American Novel and Theater from Herman Melville to James Baldwin* (Garden City, NY: Anchor Press/Doubleday, 1978), xi.

242 "as either normal or neurotic": Quoted in Kenneth Lewes, *The Psychoanalytic Theory of Homosexuality* (New York: Simon & Schuster, 1988), 130.

242 "unraveled the Kinsey report": "Dr. Kinsey's Misremembers," *Time*, June 14, 1948.

242 "That I had a deep psychological aversion": CJ, "The More Social Disease," unpublished ms., Rauner.

242 *"The only effective way of fighting"*: Edmund Bergler, *Homosexuality: Disease or Way of Life?* (New York: Hill & Wang, 1956), 302.

243 the psychoanalyst "must be merciless": Quoted in Paller, "The Couch and Tennessee."

243 "I never knew if he were": CJ to DS, March 29, 1951, Rauner.

243 "give Kubie a wide berth": CJ to Strauses, Nov. 14, 1953, Rauner.

243 "This is the kind of thing": Quoted in CJ to Alice Morris, June 12, 1952, Rauner.

243 he was "over-drugged": CJ to KWJ, Aug. 1, 1964, JFC.

243 *"Crime and Punishment, Junior"*: Quoted in Bennett Cerf, "Trade Winds," *Saturday Review*, Nov. 29, 1947.

243 "I think you listened to too many": Charles Brackett to CJ, Aug. 12, 1946, Rauner.

244 "self-portraiture at its best": Brackett to CJ, May 10, 1948, Rauner.

244 "How does it feel to be famous?": "Authors' Ordeal: Five writers get a full dose of lionizing from Richmond booklovers," *Life*, May 17, 1948, 157.

244 "It was an interesting idea": The MGM reader's report, dated Jan. 2, 1948, is among CJ's papers at Rauner.

244 "very much interested": A. H. Weiler, "Random Notes about Pictures . . . ," *New York Times*, June 27, 1948, X3.

245 "I couldn't be happier about it": CJ to BB, Aug. 15, 1949, Rauner.

245 Reviews for *The Outer Edges*: Alice Hackett, in *Publishers Weekly*, May 15, 1948; Nash K. Burger, in *New York Times Book Review*, May 27, 1948, 23; William DuBois, in *New York Times*, May 30, 1948, 5; Lee Rogow, *Saturday Review*, May 29, 1948, 16; Sterling North, *New York Post*, May 27, 1948; Lewis Gannett, *New York Herald Tribune*, June 4, 1948; J. M. Lalley, *The New Yorker*, June 5, 1948, 101; John Woodburn, *New Republic*, June 7, 1948, 25; "The Lost Effort," *Time*, June 21, 1948, 108.

245 "very bad book year": BB to RBJ, Aug. 3, 1948, Rauner.

249 "upon the sad, sophisticated": Angus Wilson, "New Novels," *The Listener*, April 6, 1950.

249 "[holding] an audience of about ten": CJ to RBJ, Aug. 13, 1948, Rauner.

249 "Only after a long time": CJ to RBJ, July 14, 1944, Rauner.

250 His "poems, which I love": CJ to DS, Jan. 27, 1965, JFC.

251 "Cured, I am frizzled, stale": Robert Lowell, "Home after Three Months Away"; posted at http://www.poets.org/viewmedia.php/prmMID/15285.

251 only "great originals": CJ to Brackett, Sept. 14, 1954, Rauner.

252 fell over "dead of shock": CJ to RBJ, Sept. 13, 1948, Rauner.

252 "to eat strange foods": CJ to RBJ, Aug. 20, 1948, Rauner.

252 "all childish stormy ego": CJ to RBJ, Aug. 24, 1948, Rauner.

252 "nothing less than a pig": CJ to RBJ, Sept. 14, 1948, Rauner.

252 A copy of Jackson's script: Found among CJ's papers at Rauner.

253 "which will earn me (I truly know)": CJ to Roy Myers, Aug. 20, 1946, Rauner.

253 "When I meet the guy I'll know": Quoted in CJ to Fanny Brice, Oct. 13, 1948, Rauner.

254 "Jackson was about to start": Leonard Lyons, "The Lyons Den" (syndicated column), Nov. 30, 1948.

254 "We would retrench in every way": CJ to Gershwins, Dec. 2, 1948, Rauner.

255 "I felt really sorry for him": Interview with Norman Katkov; posted at http://www.classictvhistory.com/OralHistories/norman_katkov.html.

Chapter Thirteen • WHAT HAPPENED

256 tempted to "chuck everything": CJ to BB, March 23, 1945, Rauner.

256 "a character sketch merely": CJ to "Stan [Rinehart], Bernice, and Company," Feb. 27, 1948, Rauner.

256 "ultimate wordage" . . . Tolstoy: *LN*.

256 "If a man could ever set down": CJ, *A Letter from Home*, radio script, Rauner.

257 "True Confessions": CJ to DS, Feb. 2, 1951, Rauner.

257 "Who was Charles Jackson?": DS-*Show*, 76.

259 "not long-term debt at all": RBJ to BB, Nov. 20, 1948, Rauner.

259 "spending so riotously": CJ to Gershwins, Dec. 2, 1948, Rauner.

259 "My errors of three and two years ago": CJ to BB, July 11, 1949, Rauner.

259 "to keep him bucked up": *LN.*

259 "I'm quite sore about their silence": CJ to Leonora Schinasi, June 20, 1947, Rauner.

260 "In all my experience": CJ memo to Rinehart & Co. (c. Feb. 1948), Rauner.

260 "just allowed [*The Outer Edges*]": RBJ to BB, July 29 [1948], Rauner.

260 "There is more advertising to come": BB to CJ, July 8, 1948, Rauner.

260 "The very thought of Rinehart": CJ to Walter Pisole, Aug. 5, 1948, Rauner.

260 "battled for [*The Lost Weekend*]": John Farrar to CJ, March 1, 1946, Rauner.

261 "the practically unheard-of royalty": CJ to Gershwins, Dec. 2, 1948, Rauner.

261 "By Saturday noon I thought": CJ to BB, April 4, 1949, Rauner.

261 "In spite of his meticulous grooming": DS-*Show,* 77.

262 "a proper, important, medium-sized": Ian Parker, "Showboat" (profile of RS), *The New Yorker,* April 8, 2002, 58.

262 "members ex-officio of his family": DS-*Show,* 78.

262 "I'd be so happy": CJ to DS, Dec. 28, 1949, Rauner.

262 "puckish, penetrating, opinionated": Max Wylie, "Charles Reginald Jackson," *Serif* 10, no. 3 (1973), 31.

262 "unshaven, wild-eyed" appearance: DS-*Show,* 81.

263 "I'm willing to share a bath": CJ to RS, Dec. 24, 1953, Rauner.

263 "Truly, darling Dolly": CJ to DS, Jan. 2, 1951, Rauner.

263 "Levin so often just misses": CJ to DS, Nov. 19, 1951, Rauner.

263 "I am embarked on a world Masterpiece": CJ to DS, Jan. 27, 1965, JFC.

263 "I do not know what literary rank": DS-*Show,* 83.

264 "an excuse to describe everything": CJ to BB, Dec. 11, 1948, Rauner.

264 "she thought it tedious, verbose": CJ to BB, Dec. 15, Rauner.

265 "Nobody who reads the magazine": BB to CJ, May 4, 1949, Rauner.

266 deplored the "namby pamby": Margaret Cousins to BB, April 15, 1949, Rauner.

266 "Really it seems as though": CJ to BB, July 20, 1949, Rauner.

266 "I am of the era of Ethel Nicholoy": Luceine Heniore to CJ, June 25, 1949, Rauner.

268 "the elementary mistake": Review of *The Sunnier Side, Times Literary Supplement,* Nov. 10, 1950.

268 "a *won*derful short story": CJ to BB, Aug. 15, 1949, Rauner.

268 abidingly "astonished": *New York Herald Tribune Book Review,* unpaginated clipping dated March 5, 1950, Rauner.

268 "The Sunnier Side" "says so much": Cousins to BB, Nov. 2, 1949, Rauner.

268 "I do not know whether": Cousins to CJ, Nov. 15, 1949, Rauner.

269 "a distinguished job": Carl Brandt to CJ, March 6, 1950, Rauner.

270 "At last report": *Hartford Courant,* unpaginated clipping dated May 7, 1950, Rauner.

270 "Only five reviewers out of fifty-seven": "In and Out of Books," *New York Times Book Review,* May 28, 1950, 8.

270 Reviews for *The Sunnier Side:* Charles Poore, in *New York Times,* April 13, 1950, 27; Alice Morris, in *New York Times Book Review,* April 16, 1950, 5; Frederic Morton, in *New York Herald Tribune Book Review,* April 16, 1950, 7.

272 "the one [he was] fondest of": as CJ noted in his inscription of *SS,* dated Nov. 11, 1950, to some New Hampshire friends, DeWitt and Gertrude Mallary.

272 "There seems to be little plot": Sybil Walters, " 'Lost Weekend' Author writes Another Book," *Newark Courier,* March 23, 1950, 1.

272 autumn "while [he still could]": CJ to Strauses, Oct. 25 (1949), Rauner.
272 he'd "unconsciously" used the name: CJ to BB, Jan. 10, 1949, Rauner.
272 "Look, Charlie": Author int. Michael Kraham, March 13, 2010.
272 "For my sake if not your own": *F&W.*
273 "He was the kind of guy": Author int. Gilbert Burgess, March 2, 2010.

Chapter Fourteen • THE OUTLANDER

275 "highbrow, therefore balls": CJ to "Paul," May 13, 1946, Rauner.
276 "Creative," he explained: Quoted in memo dated Sept. 27, 1950, from Marlboro president, Walter Hendricks, *re* CJ's "Practical Writing" course, Rauner.
276 "inspiration" rather than . . . "impulse": Rochelle Girson, "TB Made a Writer of Jackson," *Tucson Daily Citizen,* Oct. 18, 1953, 26.
277 "I'm glad you find teaching": BB to CJ, Oct. 26, 1950, Rauner.
277 finish his "new long novel": David Dempsey, "In and Out of Books," *New York Times Book Review,* Dec. 31, 1950, 5.
277 "I'm shooting the works": Harvey Breit, "Talk with Charles Jackson," *New York Times Book Review,* April 30, 1950, 19.
277 "The best novel I've found in years": Roger Bourne Linscott, New York *Herald Tribune Weekly Book Review,* Nov. 3, 1946.
277 American "cult of success": Marlboro College press release, Aug. 22, 1949, Rauner.
278 "the best writing": CJ, "The Sleeping Brain," unpublished ms., Rauner.
278 "in a writing lull": RBJ to FSJ, Feb. 14 (1949), Rauner.
278 "It had not burned down": CJ, "The Sleeping Brain," Rauner.
278 "My God I'm even incapable": CJ to BB, July 20, 1949, Rauner.
279 he'd written "about 800 pages": Timothy S. Reed, "Jackson Ruthless with Own Novels and Dialogue," *The Dartmouth,* Dec. 11, 1950, 1.
279 composed of "the same material": CJ to BB, Dec. 15, 1948, Rauner.
279 "the peculiar fish that a writer is": CJ to BB, Sept. 17, 1949, Rauner.
279 "I was talked out of it": CJ to Mary McCarthy, Nov. 24, 1953, Vassar.
280 But after an "excellent beginning": CJ to BB, June 5, 1950, Rauner.
280 "a kind of block or protest": CJ to BB, July 12, 1950, Rauner.
280 "my fondest dream at the moment": CJ to BB, Feb. 13, 1951, Rauner.
280 "In spite of fine moments": William Maxwell to BB, March 12, 1951, Rauner.
281 "desperately in debt": CJ to BB, Feb. 2, 1951, Rauner.
281 "No one, of course, has approached": William Maxwell, Feb. 20, 1951, Rauner.
282 her morale was "persistently low": RBJ to FSJ, Oct. 25 (1950), Rauner.
282 their guest's "endless talking": DS-*Show,* 86–88.
283 "We're in a drying out phase": RBJ to FSJ (c. late Jan. 1951), Rauner.
284 "he looks like the Seven Dwarfs": CJ to DS, March 29, 1951, Rauner.
284 "represents Shakespeare's most important": Niels L. Anthonisen, "The Ghost in Hamlet," *American Imago* 22, no. 4 (1965), 232.
284 "I'm not exactly Dostoyevsky!": CJ to KWJ, Aug. 1, 1964, JFC.
284 "in my usual self-interested fashion": CJ to SJP, Aug. 2, 1964, JFC.
284 "Jesus, what a cruel community!": CJ to DS, March 22, 1951, Rauner.
285 "Papa doesn't feel well": Author int. KWJ, March 14, 2010.

285 "Your father drinks whis-kee": CJ to Gershwins, Dec. 2, 1948, Rauner.

285 "a pain in the ass to live with": CJ to CBJ, Jan. 13, 1954, Rauner.

285 "The secret inner mirror": *F&W.*

286 "Make Katie stop teasing me": CJ to DS, March 22, 1951, Rauner.

286 "Africa, Rome, Barcelona, Paris": CJ to Strauses, Oct. 25 (1949?), Rauner.

286 "unconsciously would like to be rid": CJ to Alice Morris, June 9, 1952, Rauner.

287 "And I find it increasingly hard": CJ to BB, May 7, 1951, Rauner.

287 "ever invented out of whole cloth": CJ to BB and Carl Brandt, May 30, 1951, Rauner.

287 "I should be giving that energy" CJ to Strauses, June 1, 1951, Rauner.

287 didn't "feel up to it intellectually": CJ to McCarthy, July 13, 1945, Vassar.

288 "The now-dead protagonist": CJ to "Mrs. Harvey," Jan. 21, 1966, Rauner.

290 declaring it a "masterpiece": Quoted in CJ to SWJ, June 26, 1951, Rauner.

291 read it with "profound interest": Margaret Cousins to Carl Brandt, July 20, 1951, Rauner.

291 "utterly disgusted" and "depressed": CJ to BB and Brandt, Sept. 5, 1951, Rauner.

291 "I wish Mr. Jackson would get back": Kathryn Bourne to Brandt, Aug. 8, 1951, Rauner.

291 "Whee! No!": Lilian Kastendike to Brandt, Aug. 30, 1951, Rauner.

292 pressure was "unbearable": RBJ to FSJ (c. Sept. 1951), Rauner.

292 "Sounds corny but it's ghastly": CJ to BB and Brandt, Oct. 10, 1951, Rauner.

292 "the nosiest of women": CJ to BB, Sept. 20, 1950, Rauner.

292 "no nice children's parties": CJ to DS, Nov. 1, 1951, Rauner.

293 "*Pa*-pa, why don't you go to a job": CJ to DS, Nov. 18, 1953, Rauner.

293 help "tide [Charlie] over": CJ to DS, Dec. 15, 1953, Rauner.

Chapter Fifteen • THE BOY WHO RAN AWAY

299 "a grueling task": Quoted in CJ to Alice Morris, June 9, 1952, Rauner.

299 "God knows who reads the Bazaar": CJ to Carl Brandt, Oct. 14, 1952, Rauner.

300 "a little too agonized": CJ to Mary McCarthy, Sept. 7, 1953, Vassar.

300 "tremendous burst of productivity": CJ to Phyllis McGinley, July 28, 1952, Syracuse.

300 "a kind of American *Madame Bovary*": CJ to DS, July 9, 1952, Rauner.

302 "sound[ing] cool, experienced": DS-*Show*, 88–89.

302 the "indescribable" terror: CJ, "The More Social Disease," unpublished ms., Rauner.

303 her "first concern" should be: RBJ to FSJ, Jan. 16 (1953), Rauner.

303 It was "demoralizing": RBJ to FSJ (c. Jan. 30, 1953), Rauner.

304 Roger thought . . . "quickie": RBJ to FSJ, April 8 [1953], Rauner.

304 his usual springtime "re-birth": CJ to McGinley, June 9 (1953), Syracuse.

306 "Do try to do a story that's a little": Brandt to CJ, June 11, 1953, Rauner.

306 started "careening around": Author int. KSJ, June 10, 2009.

306 the results were "grim": CJ to BB, July 23, 1953, Rauner.

306 "LIEBESTOD shook me up": Bob Pinkerton to Brandt, Aug. 7, 1953, Rauner.

307 "For the first time, I had had enough": DS-*Show*, 82.

307 "I'm leaving today": CJ/AA-59.
308 "I am neither a 'foolish' nor wise": C. Dudley Saul to CJ, Feb. 28, 1944, Rauner.

Chapter Sixteen • A RAIN OF SNARES

312 "Of course the town has had": RBJ to FSJ, Aug. 13, 1953, Rauner.
312 "I was the whole cheese!": CJ/AA-59.
312 "flabbergasted," Jackson asked why: RBJ to FSJ (c. Aug. 28, 1953), Rauner.
313 "In my loneliness": CJ, "The More Social Disease," unpublished ms., Rauner.
313 "having the time of [his] life": CJ to H. T. "Tom" McGuire, Nov. 27, 1953, Rauner.
313 "with the elegant name": CJ to DS, Nov. 24, 1953, Rauner.
314 drown her ("for your own sake"): CJ to KWJ, Jan. 28, 1954, Rauner.
314 "one of his alcoholic pipe-dreams": RBJ to FSJ, Aug. 13, 1953, Rauner.
314 Reviews of *Earthly Creatures:* Budd Schulberg, in *New York Times Book Review,* Sept. 13, 1953, 4; William Peden, in *Saturday Review,* Oct. 10, 1953, 17; "Briefly Noted," *The New Yorker,* Sept. 19, 1953, 119–20.
315 "We have never seen Mr. Jackson better": Harvey Breit, "In and Out of Books," *New York Times Book Review,* Oct. 4, 1953, 8.
315 "between-the-linesier": CJ to Leland Hayward, Oct. 1, 1953, Rauner.
316 "Very nice, but after all": Elliott W. Schryver to Carl Brandt, Oct. 9, 1953, Rauner.
316 "marvelous, almost Dostoyevskean idea": CJ to BB, May 15, 1953, Rauner.
317 "I think I covered a little": CJ to DS, Oct. 7, 1953, Rauner.
317 "much too cerebral for selling": CJ to Strauses, Sept. 3, 1953, Rauner.
317 "in [his] callower drunkener": CJ to DS, Oct. 19, 1953, Rauner.
317 "the psychology of writers": William Maxwell to BB, Nov. 12, 1953, Rauner.
317 "extremely well-written tale": Frank DeBlois to Carl Brandt Jr., June 6, 1962, Rauner.
318 "It has dignity, humor, calm": CJ to RS, Dec. 30, 1953, Rauner.
319 "well, everything to do": CJ to Walter and Merriman Modell, Jan. 9, 1954, Rauner.
319 "watched [him] like a hawk": CJ to DS, Oct. 19, 1953, Rauner.
320 "shake the complacency": CJ to CBJ, Jan. 13, 1954, Rauner.
321 "I never did finish it": CJ to Elling Aannestad, Sept. 14, 1954, Rauner.
321 "three *not quite so definite*": CJ to Dorothy Stickney, Dec. 15, 1953, Rauner.
321 "blind as a bat but marvelous": CJ to Niels Anthonisen, Jan. 28, 1954, Rauner.
321 "I like him so much": CJ to RBJ, Jan. 28, 1954, Rauner.
322 the man who "could sit on the edge": DS-*Show,* 90.
322 "at one thousand per throw": CJ to Strauses, Jan. 12, 1954, Rauner.
322 "I hope you are not involved": Quoted in CJ to McGuire, Jan. 29, 1954, Rauner.
322 "I absolutely and completely agreed": RS to CJ, Dec. 2, 1953, Rauner.
323 "a load on [his] mind": CJ to Walter Modell, Dec. 23, 1953, Rauner.
323 "love for the children": CJ to McGuire family, Dec. 24, 1953, Rauner.
323 reading "a good hundred pages": CJ to McGuire, Feb. 5, 1954, Rauner.
323 "looking forward to being able": CJ to McGuire, Jan. 20, 1954, Rauner.
324 "fall flat on [his] face": Quoted in CJ to McGuire, Feb. 18, 1954, Rauner.
324 "I can never speak again!": CJ/AA-59.

325 "I am still confused by Max's": CJ to Warren Ambrose, March 1, 1954, Rauner.

326 "Wanted the pickup of a pill": CJ to Dick Anderson, March 3, 1954, Rauner.

326 "It was like living": CJ to Ira and Lee Gershwin, Sept. 14, 1954, Rauner.

326 "Not that I'm girlish enough": RBJ to FSJ, April 16 (1954), Rauner.

327 "Lar[e]s and Penates": CJ to FSJ, Sept. 25, 1954, Rauner.

Chapter Seventeen • A NEW ADDICTION

331 "It's a terrible medium": CJ to KWJ, Feb. 5, 1954, JFC.

331 "Monstrous in a nice house": CJ to FSJ, Sept. 25, 1954, Rauner.

331 "make the rounds of the agencies": CJ to Howard Lindsay and Dorothy Stickney, Sept. 14, 1954, Rauner.

332 he found it "astonishingly dull": George McCartney, "Waugh on Television," *Evelyn Waugh Newsletter and Studies* 34, no. 3 (2004); posted at http://www.lhup .edu/jwilson3/newsletter_34.3.htm.

332 Marty Mann would "respond to": Quoted in John W. Crowley "A Charles Jackson Diptych," *Syracuse University Library Associates Courier* 32 (1997), 45.

332 "realism with a modest moral": Michael Mashon, "Kraft Television Theatre"; posted at http://www.museum.tv/eotvsection.php?entrycode=krafttelevis.

333 "One very obvious problem": Charles Mercer, "Radio's Popularity Increasing Despite Inroads of Television," *Kokomo Tribune* (A.P.), July 21, 1955, 12.

334 "one of the greatest of contemporary": John McLaughlin to Kraft executive personnel, Feb. 20, 1956, Duke.

334 "I'm so involved with a job": CJ to SJP (c. June 26, 1956), JFC.

334 "He was a forgotten, sad man": Author int. Edward Pomerantz, March 7, 2009.

335 "John said 'Gosh, I didn't know' ": CJ to SJP, Sept. 23, 1958, JFC.

335 "The implication was that he *didn't*": Author int. Arthur Laurents, April 8, 2009.

336 "Never, I think, has the just": CJ to Phyllis McGinley (c. 1955), Syracuse.

336 "because I lack so much": CJ to McGinley, Aug. 1, 1952, Syracuse.

336 "Let Us Dare to Say It Out Loud": Quoted in Herbert R. Mayes, *The Magazine Maze* (Garden City, NY: Doubleday & Co., 1980), 53.

336 "would charm me less": CJ, "To the Heart of the Times," *New York Times Book Review*, Sept. 19, 1954, 4.

337 "But not in Larchmont!": Author int. Robert Markel, Aug. 20, 2008.

337 "Be sure to tell Mama": DS-*Show*, 89.

337 "How much larger your life": Quoted in CJ to William Inge, Feb. 1, 1956, Rauner.

338 "It was during a troubled period": CJ to Maurice Friedman, Aug. 5, 1964, Rauner.

339 "Please do *not* throw cigarettes": Richard Lamparski, unpublished ms., courtesy of the author.

340 "Pete Gurney was my closest friend": Author int. Ron Sproat, March 25, 2009.

340 "I hate to think I was": E-mail from A. R. Gurney to author, Feb. 15, 2010.

340 "In the fifties you could know": Author int. Gurney, April 8, 2009.

341 the "star pupils" of their meetings: Ned Rorem, *The New York Diary of Ned Rorem* (New York: George Braziller, 1967), 145.

341 "clear-faced and likable" daughter: Rorem to John W. Crowley, July 15, 1996, courtesy of John W. Crowley.

342 *"What* a break that would be": CJ to Carl Brandt, Jr., July 4, 1964, Rauner.

342 "Whatever happens": CJ to Inge, Dec. 5, 1964, Rauner.

342 "the frustrations, the anxieties": Quoted in "William Inge, Playwright, Is Dead," *New York Times*, June 11, 1973, 38.

342 "Charlie was like that too": Author int. John Connolly, July 6, 2009.

343 "restimulate interest": John F. Devine to Arthur C. Farlow, et al., Feb. 8, 1956, Duke.

343 a given show "didn't misstep": Author int. Paul Bogart, Dec. 8, 2009.

343 "recipe for an average TV program": "Early 'Recipe' Reveals TV's Darker Side," *60 Years of Advertising on TV;* posted at http://www.tvweek.com/2008/04/23/TVAdSpread3.pdf.

343 "most advantageous connection": Memo from Maury Holland to Ed Rice, et al., April 3, 1957, Rauner.

343 "adequate (just) but not inspired": George McGarrett to Dan Seymour, May 16, 1957, Duke.

344 "floors sag, practically no closet space": RBJ to FSJ, Sept. 26 (1957), Rauner.

345 "Kraft carried [my father]": SJP, "My Personality Shaped by Social Interaction / A Life History Paper," paper written for sociology class at Connecticut College, dated Dec. 17, 1958, Rauner.

345 "Such titles as 'Climax' ": McGarrett to Seymour, May 16, 1957, Duke.

345 "readjustment, with the help of AA": RBJ to SJP, Dec. 10, 1958, JFC.

345 "It's just a coincidence that we are both": Doris E. Brown, "Rutgers Unveils Noted 'Lost' Writer," *The Star-Ledger*, Oct. 4, 1964, 14.

346 "House lonely and cold today": CJ to SJP, Sept. 18, 1958, JFC.

346 "devoted to an understanding": TV listings, *Bridgeport Post*, Oct. 2, 1958, 39.

346 happy to "have a little money": CJ to SJP, Jan. 23 (1959), JFC.

346 he seemed "very edgy": RBJ to SJP, Nov. 17, 1959, JFC.

346 he was "financially desperate": Carol Brandt to Ben Benjamin, Sept. 26, 1960, Rauner.

347 "it [made her] like people": CJ to SJP, Sept. 21, 1958, JFC.

347 "affected Papa and all of us": SJP, "My Personality Shaped by Social Interaction," Rauner.

347 "distant isolated groups": Joseph Kessel, *The Road Back: A Report on Alcoholics Anonymous* (New York: Alfred A. Knopf, 1962), 152.

347 "our American De Quincey": CJ/AA-59.

348 his "own humdrum mediocrity": CJ to DS, Jan.13, 1954, Rauner.

348 "I was forced to recognize": DS-*Show*, 90.

348 "Don't expect to do anything": RBJ to SJP, March 5, 1959, JFC.

348 "They were years of a kind of grey": CJ, "The Sleeping Brain," unpublished ms., Rauner.

349 worked best "for the mindless": CJ to KWJ, June 26, 1964, JFC.

Chapter Eighteen • A PLACE IN THE COUNTRY

350 "You can't think how much": CJ to Felicia Geffen, April 2, 1959, Academy.

351 "some advance loot from Hollywood": CJ to Charles Brackett, Aug. 6, 1960, Rauner.

352 two more pages "to establish": Quoted in Margaret Cousins to Carl Brandt, Jr., Sept. 20, 1960, Rauner.

352 "The trouble with you, Daddy": CJ, "One o'Clock in the Morning," *McCall's*, April 1961, 179.

352 "red ink on the books": RS to Carol Brandt, Jan. 13, 1960, Rauner.

353 "gossip, shop talk, good food": CJ, "The Sleeping Brain," unpublished ms., Rauner.

353 "But you know, Charlie": Reminiscences of Roger W. Straus, Jr., Jan. 11, 1978, on page 365 of CUCOHC.

353 "I think he was feeling doomed": Author int. Carl Brandt, Jr., March 11, 2010.

353 "the ramifications of the Straus situation": RBJ to Brandt, March 1, 1963, Rauner.

354 "I wrote Roger a long chatty letter": CJ to KWJ, July 2, 1963, JFC.

354 "I *determined* to myself": CJ to SJP, Aug. 2, 1964, JFC.

355 "1 hour and 15 minutes of drowning": CJ to KWJ, "July 1963," JFC.

355 "I needed to get away": CJ to Brandt and Robert Markel, June 22, 1964, Rauner.

356 "love, affection, and trust": CJ to KWJ, July 2 (28?), 1963, JFC.

356 "I want to die, or get well": CJ to SJP, July 28, 1963, JFC.

356 Charlie "learned [his] fate": CJ, pocket diary 1963, JFC.

356 Charlie, was "the only one": CJ to KWJ "& everybody," June 10, 1964, JFC.

356 only one besides "a man of 42": CJ to DS, Jan. 27, 1965, JFC.

356 moved to a "princely" room: CJ to SJP, Sept. 23, 1963, JFC.

356 "those heavy horseshoes": CJ to SJP, Oct. 1, 1963, JFC.

357 "there is no other word": Arthur Slattery, "Adirondacks Personalities," unpaginated clipping (source unknown) dated July 29, 1963, Rauner.

357 "Yes, I knew Charles was gay": Author int. Gloria Ayvazian, Feb. 27, 2010.

357 "I asked Ruth Norman": CJ to Fred and Gloria Ayvazian, Aug. 4, 1964, Rauner.

357 "I came home to a blacker": CJ, "In Remembrance of Him," unpublished ms., Rauner.

358 "I felt now as though": *A Place in the Country*, promotional film for Will Rogers Hospital (1965), courtesy of the Will Rogers Institute.

358 "drawing pains": CJ to KWJ, April 8, 1964, JFC.

358 "We refuse to let illness": CJ to Bob Whitehead, Dec. 5, 1964, Rauner.

358 "I could even say, with all": CJ to Brandt and Markel, June 22, 1964, Rauner.

358 "Yes, I *am* the star": CJ to DS, Jan. 27, 1965, JFC.

358 "one of the best institutional films": "Will Rogers Short: 'A Place in the Country,' " unidentified clipping, JFC.

359 "more than hanging on the ropes": RBJ to Brandt, March 1, 1963, Rauner.

359 "[wasn't] worth telling": CJ to KWJ, Oct. 1, 1962, JFC.

359 "On the walls around him": CJ, "The Loving Offenders," *McCall's*, July 1963, 139.

360 "I have always marveled": CJ to Manon Tingue, July 4, 1964, Rauner.

360 "I'm going to get out of debt": CJ to SJP, May 30, 1963, JFC.

361 "a pure poem of despair": CJ to Brandt and Markel, June 22, 1964, Rauner.

362 "Treat my new baby kindlily": CJ to Tingue, July 4, 1964, Rauner.

362 "What remains now is just a story": CJ to KWJ, July 31, 1964, JFC.

363 "one of the largest [funerals]: CJ, "The Lady Julia," *McCall's*, April 1965, 166.

363 "Manon is under the impression": Anonymous internal Brandt & Brandt memo to Frieda Lubelle and "DB" (Carl "Denny" Brandt?), Aug. 24, 1964, Rauner.

Chapter Nineteen • HOMAGE TO MOTHER RUSSIA

365 "You are the greatest pride": CJ to SJP, Feb. 6, 1959, JFC.
365 "Work harder!" she'd admonish: Author int. SJP, Jan. 25, 2009.
366 "We did indeed . . . Sarah's marks": CJ to "Miss Babbott," March 14, 1960, JFC.
367 "They got along *much* better": Author int. Mikey Gilbert, April 22, 2009.
367 "because of some emotional deficiency": CJ to SJP, Oct. 21, 1963, JFC.
369 "a subject he should know": CJ to SJP (c. early July 1964), JFC.
370 calling him "Alexander the Great": CJ to Alexander Piper, March 22, 1965, JFC.
370 "Kate *must* hurt someone": CJ to SJP, Oct. 4, 1958, JFC.
370 "You went to Sarah's!": Quoted in RBJ to SJP, June 1, 1960, JFC.
370 "And what about some mail sometime?": CJ to KWJ, Oct. 15, 1962, JFC.
370 "We must go see the Courbets": CJ to KWJ, Oct. 5, 1962, JFC.
371 "you are liker Elizabeth": CJ to KWJ, June 30, 1964, JFC.
371 "Be apprised that I have signed up": CJ to KWJ, May 7, 1963, JFC.
371 "talk and talk forever": CJ to Maurice Friedman, Aug. 5, 1964, Rauner.
372 "that ratrace of meeting the train": RBJ to SJP, Feb. 5, 1959, JFC.
374 "the dreadful secret came out": CJ to Friedman, Aug. 5, 1964, Rauner.
375 "Even most of his neighbors": Doris E. Brown, "Rutgers Unveils Noted 'Lost' Writer," *The Star-Ledger*, Oct. 4, 1964, 14.
375 "*Me* a political speaker!": CJ to KWJ, Oct. 5, 1964, JFC.
375 "they've got us old-timers beat": CJ to SJP (c. early July 1964), JFC.
375 "The notion of making money": Quoted in CJ to SJP, Sept. 2, 1964, JFC.
376 "I want it to be very American": CJ to SJP, Jan. 27, 1965, JFC.
376 "In place of the valorous general": DS-*Paper*, 103.
380 he felt "sick at heart"—a "fraud": CJ, "The Sleeping Brain, unpublished ms. Rauner."
380 "Everybody looked at him": Author int. Stephen Jones, May 18, 2009.
381 "Things got a bit sticky": E-mail from John Weston to author, March 25, 2009.
382 "You have split infinitives": Olive Schneider to CJ, Sept. 6, 1965, Rauner.
382 "inscribed with praise and gratitude": RBJ to KWJ, Sept. 3, 1965, JFC.
382 "If anybody got . . . Breadloaf": CJ to Margaret Cousins, Sept. 16, 1965, Ransom.
382 "concentration, originality, and form": CJ to KWJ, Sept. 15, 1965, JFC.
383 "You wanted it *then*": CJ to RBJ, Sept. 23, 1965, Rauner.
384 "As for my morale and spirits": CJ to Cousins, Sept. 16, 1965, Ransom.

Chapter Twenty • A SECOND-HAND LIFE

385 "charming odd water-color": CJ to KWJ, Sept. 15, 1965, JFC.
385 "neat as a pin": John Barkham, "Among Books and Authors," typescript perhaps intended for *Bergen Record*, c. July 1967, Rauner.
385 "making the scene like a grandmother": Richard R. Lingeman, "Where Home Is Where It Is," *New York Times Book Review*, Dec. 24, 1967, 153.

386 "living on a shoestring": CJ to Margaret Cousins, Sept. 16, 1965, Ransom.

386 "CHARLES JACKSON: DO NOT DISTURB": Alex Lindsay, "Charles Jackson's Long, Lost Weekend: A Personal Memoir," unpublished ms., courtesy of Rae Lindsay.

386 "Lissen," the man replied: CJ, "The Chelsea Hotel," *Holiday*, Feb. 1968, 109.

386 cry out "Hello, Charlie!": Joe O'Sullivan, "And Like That . . . ," typescript written for UPI, perhaps unpublished, dated July 1, 1967, Rauner.

387 "Funny, when you go out of town": CJ to RBJ, Dec. 4, 1965, Rauner.

387 "a derisive denial": Lindsay, "Charles Jackson's Long, Lost Weekend."

387 Homosexuality "deserves fairness": Quoted in Charles Kaiser, *The Gay Metropolis: 1940—1996* (Boston and New York: Houghton Mifflin Co., 1997), 168–69.

387 Weston was "on pins and needles": Author int. John Weston, March 25, 2009.

388 provocative "crotch-grabbing": Author int. Stephen Jones, May 18, 2009.

388 he'd found the book "coy": Ned Rorem to Alex Gildzen, Dec. 27, 1973, KSU.

388 "Neither a strikingly original": CJ, "Into Another Intensity," *New York Times Book Review*, Jan. 30, 1966, 17.

388 a lot of bitchy, "hissing" humor: Author int. Stan Herman, April 11, 2009.

388 "I'd say that there bees some quare": Peter Arthurs, *With Brendan Behan* (New York: St. Martin's Press, 1981), 24.

389 "the pleasures of love": Quoted in CJ to Al Wintrup, Dec. 27, 1966, Rauner.

389 "It's hard to believe": Carl Brandt Jr. to Robert Brown, Oct. 18, 1965, Rauner.

389 "to play hooky": CJ to RBJ, Dec. 4, 1965, Rauner.

390 "very kind and solicitous": Author int. Alice Schwedock Small, Oct. 27, 2009.

390 "a long dialogue scene": CJ to RBJ, Jan. 7, 1966, Rauner.

390 "the most beautiful thing": *SHL*, 60.

391 "I got the impression he'd failed": Author int. Robert Markel, Sept. 9, 2008.

391 "unwittingly . . . stepped up": CJ, "The Sleeping Brain," unpublished ms., Rauner.

393 pounced with a "friendly 'alert' ": Margaret Nicholson to Brandt, Aug. 31, 1966, Rauner.

394 "the rhapsodic Bob Markel": CJ to Brandt, Oct. 23, 1966, Rauner.

394 "Jackson has regained": John Barkham, "Among Books and Authors."

394 "It's so moving": FSJ to SJP, Sept. 22, 1966, JFC.

395 the author's "Awful Daring": F. W. Dupee to CJ, July 7, 1967, Rauner.

395 "Diana will follow": Lionel Trilling to CJ, Oct. 24, 1967, Rauner.

395 "could have a good deal of fun": Brandt to H. N. Swanson, Feb. 10, 1967, Rauner.

395 "Having spent seven years": Brandt to Patricia Neal, March 13, 1967, Rauner.

395 "a logical choice" to play Winifred: Quoted in Brandt to Swanson, April 13, 1967, Rauner.

396 "a piece on Writer's Block": Brandt to Swanson, April 13, 1967, Rauner.

396 "Are we really that tormented?": CJ, "We Were Led to Hope for More," *New York Times Book Review*, Dec. 12, 1965, 4.

396 Reviews of *A Second-Hand Life:* Webster Schott, in *New York Times Book Review*, Aug. 13, 1967, 14; Thomas Lask, in *New York Times*, Aug. 14, 1967, 29; "Body Worship," *Newsweek*, Aug. 14, 1967, 88; John Barkham, in Bergen *Evening Record*, Aug. 19, 1967, 9; "Briefly Noted," *The New Yorker*, Aug. 26, 1967, 98.

397 "Charlie's morale is damn near": Brandt to Swanson, Aug. 14, 1967, Rauner.

397 "Nobody can be 'wronger' ": CJ to Stanley Rinehart, Sept. 17, 1943, Rauner.

398 "agents of your inspired nostalgia": Dupee to CJ, July 7, 1967, Rauner.

399 "give free rein to": Georges-Michel Sarotte, *Like a Brother, Like a Lover: Male*

Homosexuality in the American Novel and Theater from Herman Melville to James Baldwin (Garden City, NY: Anchor Press/Doubleday, 1978), 109.

403 "One winter afternoon he called me": DS-*Show*, 91.

Chapter Twenty-One · SAILING OUT TO DIE

404 "Charlie had picked him up": DS-*Show*, 92.

404 "taken a companion": Author int. Robert Markel, Aug. 20, 2008.

405 "Charles was a very difficult": Alex Lindsay, "Charles Jackson's Long, Lost Weekend: A Personal Memoir," unpublished ms., courtesy of Rae Lindsay.

405 "I've never seen a closet case": E-mail from Brock Brower to author, April 20, 2009.

406 "I just feel Papa needs the money": RBJ to SJP, May 24, 1966, JFC.

406 "attending those appalling double-feature": CJ to RBJ, Jan. 7, 1966, Rauner.

406 "please show this to Sarah": CJ to Alexander Piper, March 22, 1965, Rauner.

407 "The only thing of importance": Joe O'Sullivan, "And Like That . . . ," typescript written for UPI, perhaps unpublished, dated July 1, 1967, Rauner.

407 "Well I guess I really am getting old": CJ to SJP (c. early July 1964), JFC.

407 his "most necessary book": CJ to SJP, Aug. 2, 1964, JFC.

408 "You speak of his problems": CJ to KWJ, June 26, 1964, JFC.

408 "Isn't he cute?": Author int. KWJ, March 14, 2010.

409 "look[ed] much younger": "Trade Winds," *Saturday Review*, Sept. 2, 1967, 7.

409 remaining lung was "about gone": RBJ to Shirley Hood, July 1, 1969, Rauner.

409 "I always keep a few beers": Alex Lindsay, "Charles Jackson's Long, Lost Weekend."

411 "We never called Carole": E-mail from Rae Lindsay to author, Sept. 7, 2009.

417 "The phrase is both madly unrealistic": CJ, "The Chelsea Hotel," *Holiday*, Feb. 1968, 104.

417 Charlie had a "wonderful time": CJ to RBJ, June 6, 1968, Rauner.

418 "Charlie arrived looking shockingly old": DS-*Show*, 92.

418 "I have always felt": CJ to KWJ, June 26, 1964, JFC.

420 "depressed, at certain times": "Identification of Body," St. Vincent Hospital records.

420 "He used to play teeter-totter Tessie": Doreen Carvajal, "A Publisher's Trademark: Low Advances and High Prestige," *New York Times*, Sept. 23, 1996.

420 "This had happened so often": Reminiscences of Roger W. Straus, Jr., Jan. 11, 1978, on page 362 of CUCOHC.

Epilogue · HOME FOR GOOD

421 "Died. Charles Jackson, 65": "Milestones," *Time*, Sept. 27, 1968.

421 "warm and straight": "Charles Jackson, Author of 'Lost Weekend,' Dies," *New York Times*, Sept. 22, 1968, 88.

421 "one of the nicest and gentlest": Mel Heimer, "My New York" (syndicated column), October 21, 1968.

421 "a child misunderstood": "Author Charles Jackson dies," *Geneva Times,* Sept. 23, 1968, unpaginated clipping, Newark (N.Y.) Public Library.

422 "There was nothing I could do": Max Wylie, "Charles Reginald Jackson," *Serif* 10, no. 3 (1973), 31.

422 "dusty red plush": DS-*Show,* 75.

422 "Oh my heavens! I forgot Charlie!": E-mail from SJP to author, Feb. 6, 2010.

423 "Well, Charlie's dead": Author int. Gilbert Burgess, March 2, 2010.

423 "have a talk about Stanley": Carl Brandt, Jr., to RBJ, Oct, 11, 1968, Rauner.

424 "I can say with some certainty": Brandt to George F. Coleman, Oct. 1, 1968, JFC.

424 "Charlie's work was too good": RBJ to RS, June 15, 1970, Rauner.

424 "No-one would have re-read": RBJ to Alex Gildzen, May 5, 1973, KSU.

425 "a miracle, handed down to Mr. Jackson": David Madden and Peggy Bach, eds., *Rediscoveries II* (New York: Carroll & Graf Publishers, 1988), 131.

425 "Marvelous and horrifying": Kingley Amis's blurb appears on a 1998 reprint of *LW* published by Black Spring Press (London).

425 "a sensitive novel": Herbert Kupferberg, "What's Up This Week: Now, About That List of the '100 Best Novels of the 20th Century' . . . ," *Parade,* Oct. 11, 1998, 18.

425 "Although . . . less shocking": Jack Kisling, "The Bookbag," *Denver Post,* Sept. 28, 1986.

426 "A brother, Herbert, survives": "Frederick S. Jackson," *New York Times,* June 21, 1971, 32.

426 "Charlie's papers in shape": RBJ to Brandt, March 19, 1973, Rauner.

426 "Vain creature that I am": CJ to Leonora Schinasi, Feb. 28, 1945, Rauner.

427 "What he was really saying": RBJ to SJP, Feb. 22, 1971, JFC.

427 "I take my duties rather seriously": Reminiscences of Roger W. Straus, Jr., Jan. 11, 1978, on page 362 of CUCOHC.

428 "whether you could tell if you were": Author int. KWJ, March 14, 2010.

Index

PERMISSIONS ACKNOWLEDGMENTS

Grateful acknowledgment is made to the following for permission to reprint previously published and unpublished material:

Columbia University: Excerpts from "Reminiscences of Roger W. Straus, Jr., 1981" from oral history interviews at Columbia University. Reprinted by permission of Columbia University Center for Oral History.

Harold Matson Co., Inc.: Excerpt of unpublished letter by Margaret Cousins to Charles Jackson, copyright by Margaret Cousins. Reprinted by permission of Harold Matson Co., Inc. All rights reserved.

Harold Ober Associates, Inc.: Excerpt of unpublished letter by Philip Wylie to Charles Jackson. Reprinted by permission of Harold Ober Associates, Inc. on behalf of Karen Wylie Pryor.

Nathaniel R. Benchley: Robert Benchley quote courtesy of the Estate of Robert Benchley as administered by Nat Benchley, Executor.

Simon & Schuster, Inc.: Excerpts from *A Second-Hand Life* by Charles Jackson. Copyright © 1967 by Charles Jackson. Reprinted by permission of Scribner, a division of Simon & Schuster, Inc. All rights reserved.

Vassar College Libraries: Excerpt of unpublished manuscript "The Lost Week or The Caged Lion" by Mary McCarthy. Reprinted by permission of Special Collections at Vassar College Libraries.

Printed in the United States
by Baker & Taylor Publisher Services